D0066536

PHP PROGRAMMING WITH MYSQL

SECOND EDITION

PHP PROGRAMMING WITH MYSQL

DON GOSSELIN, DIANA KOKOSKA,

ROBERT EASTERBROOKS

COURSE TECHNOLOGY
CENGAGE Learning

Australia • Brazil • Japan • Korea • Mexico • Singapore • Spain • United Kingdom • United States

COURSE TECHNOLOGY
CENGAGE Learning

PHP Programming with MySQL, Second Edition

Don Gosselin, Diana Kokoska, Robert Easterbrooks

Executive Editor: Marie Lee

Acquisitions Editor: Amy Jollymore

Managing Editor: Tricia Coia

Senior Product Manager: Alyssa Pratt

Developmental Editor: Dan Seiter

Content Project Manager: Jennifer Feltri

Editorial Assistant: Zina Kresin

Art Director: Marissa Falco

Text Designer: Shawn Girsberger

Cover Designer: Cabbage Design Company

Cover Image: © CSA Images

Print Buyer: Julio Esperas

Copy Editor: Camille Kiolbasa

Proofreader: Andrea Schein

Indexer: Alexandra Nickerson

Compositor: Integra

© 2011 Course Technology, Cengage Learning

ALL RIGHTS RESERVED. No part of this work covered by the copyright herein may be reproduced, transmitted, stored or used in any form or by any means—graphic, electronic, or mechanical, including but not limited to photocopying, recording, scanning, digitizing, taping, Web distribution, information networks, or information storage and retrieval systems, except as permitted under Section 107 or 108 of the 1976 United States Copyright Act—without the prior written permission of the publisher.

For product information and technology assistance, contact us at
Cengage Learning Customer & Sales Support, 1-800-354-9706

For permission to use material from this text or product, submit all requests online at **www.cengage.com/permissions**
Further permissions questions can be e-mailed to
permissionrequest@cengage.com

Library of Congress Control Number: 2009940005

ISBN-13: 978-0-5387-4584-0
ISBN-10: 0-5387-4584-3

Course Technology
20 Channel Center Street
Boston, MA 02210
USA

Cengage Learning is a leading provider of customized learning solutions with office locations around the globe, including Singapore, the United Kingdom, Australia, Mexico, Brazil, and Japan. Locate your local office at: **www.cengage.com/global**

Cengage Learning products are represented in Canada by Nelson Education, Ltd.

To learn more about Course Technology, visit
www.cengage.com/coursetechnology

Purchase any of our products at your local college store or at our preferred online store **www.ichapters.com**

Some of the product names and company names used in this book have been used for identification purposes only and may be trademarks or registered trademarks of their respective manufacturers and sellers.

Course Technology, a part of Cengage Learning, reserves the right to revise this publication and make changes from time to time in its content without notice.

Printed in the United States of America
2 3 4 5 6 7 13 12 11 10

Brief Contents

Contents

CHAPTER 2 Functions and Control Structures **74**

CHAPTER 3 Manipulating Strings. **124**

CHAPTER 4 Handling User Input **188**

x

xiii

Preface

PHP: Hypertext Preprocessor, or PHP, is an open source programming language that is used for developing interactive Web sites. More specifically, PHP is a scripting language that is executed from a Web server. Created in 1995, PHP is one of the fastest-growing programming languages today. The TIOBE Programming Community Index[1] ranked PHP as the third most popular programming language in the world.

One of the primary reasons for PHP's popularity is its simplicity. The language is relatively easy to learn, allowing new programmers to quickly incorporate PHP functionality into a Web site. MySQL is an open source relational database that is often used with PHP. Together, PHP and MySQL are becoming one of the most popular technology combinations for Web site development.

PHP is a dynamic, growing language with new functionality added on a regular basis. PHP is supported by a community of developers and users who add features and contribute updates that expand the functionality of the code. The **PHP Group** coordinates the development efforts of more than 400 user groups in more than 80 countries. Although the PHP Group does not impose formal specifications, it does issue recommendations for how PHP should and should not be used. Complete documentation for all versions of the PHP language is available at *www.php.net*. You should bookmark this site, because it will become your primary point of reference as you progress through this book.

Appendix A provides a refresher on scripting in XHTML, validating XHTML code (including an explanation of the Strict DTD), and formatting with Cascading Style Sheets (CSS).

PHP Programming with MySQL teaches Web development with PHP and MySQL for students with little programming or database experience, although knowledge of XHTML and Web page design is helpful. This book covers the basics of PHP and MySQL along with introductions to advanced topics, including object-oriented programming and how to build Web sites that incorporate authentication and security. After you complete this course, you will be able to use PHP and MySQL to build professional-quality, database-driven Web sites.

[1] The TIOBE Programming Community Index at *http://www.tiobe.com/index.php/content/paperinfo/tpci/index.html* for September 2009.

The Approach

This book introduces a variety of techniques, focusing on what you need to know to start writing PHP scripts. In each chapter, you build and create PHP scripts using the new concepts introduced in the chapter. Each chapter ends with a chapter summary, review questions, Reinforcement Exercises, and Discovery Projects that highlight major concepts and let you apply the concepts you have learned. The Reinforcement Exercises include both guided and free-form exercises that reinforce the skills you learn in the chapter and provide additional ways to apply your knowledge in new situations. At the end of each chapter, you will also complete Discovery Projects to apply the skills you learned in the chapter and expand the functionality of an ongoing comprehensive Web site project.

Overview of This Book

The examples and exercises in this book will help you achieve the following objectives:

- Learn how to use PHP with well-formed Web pages

- Understand PHP variables and data types and the operations that can be performed on them

- Add functions and control structures to your PHP scripts

- Use PHP to manipulate strings

- Use PHP with Web forms

- Access files and directories with PHP

- Use PHP to manipulate data in arrays

- Work with databases and MySQL

- Manipulate MySQL databases with PHP

- Save state information using hidden form fields, query strings, cookies, and sessions

- Include object-oriented programming techniques in your PHP scripts

PHP Programming with MySQL presents 10 chapters that cover specific aspects of PHP and MySQL Web development. Chapter 1 introduces the basic structure and syntax of PHP and discusses variables, data types, expressions, and operators. This early introduction of key PHP concepts gives students a framework for better understanding more advanced concepts and techniques later in this book, and allows them to work on more comprehensive projects from the start. Chapter 2 covers functions and introduces structured logic using control structures and statements. Chapter 3 discusses techniques for manipulating strings. Chapter 4 introduces dynamic hyperlinks, processing form data, and handling user input with PHP. Chapter 5 explains how to read and store data in text files on a local computer. Chapter 6 covers advanced techniques for working with indexed and associative arrays. Chapter 7 introduces how to work with MySQL databases, while Chapter 8 discusses techniques for working with MySQL databases with PHP. Chapter 9 explains how to save state information using hidden form fields, query strings, cookies, and sessions. Chapter 10 presents basic object-oriented programming techniques that you can use in your PHP scripts.

New to This Edition!

This edition includes several enhancements:

- The previous edition of this book included chapters on Web scripting and configuring a Web server. To allow this book to introduce PHP scripting in the first chapter, these two topics have been moved to Appendix A and Appendix B.

- Facts, Carefuls, and Pointers appear in the margin for easier identification.

- Examples have been enhanced, and exercises and projects have been updated. A comprehensive Web development project that applies chapter concepts begins in Chapter 1 and continues through Chapter 10, resulting in a PHP code demonstration site.

- The chapter on manipulating strings (now Chapter 3) has been expanded to include Perl Compatible Regular Expressions (PCRE).

- A new chapter, Handling User Input (Chapter 4), contains separate, expanded coverage of Web forms and Web templates.

- The chapter on files and directories (now Chapter 5) has a new topic that discusses uploading and downloading files.

- The chapter on manipulating arrays (Chapter 6) now includes coverage of square bracket notation to process form input.

- Debugging techniques are introduced in the database chapters as they naturally occur in the scripts. Advanced topics are covered in the appendix.

- Two appendices have been added. Appendix E addresses error handling and debugging, and Appendix F discusses connecting to SQL Server and Oracle databases.

- Supplemental materials have been expanded with the addition of a midterm exam, final exam, and comprehensive guided project.

Features

PHP Programming with MySQL is a superior textbook because it includes the following features:

CHAPTER OBJECTIVES. Each chapter in this book begins with a list of the important concepts to be mastered within the chapter. This list provides you with a quick reference to the contents of the chapter as well as a useful study guide.

ILLUSTRATIONS AND TABLES. Illustrations help you visualize common components and relationships. Tables list conceptual items and examples in a visual and readable format.

 POINTERS. These helpful asides provide you with practical advice and proven strategies related to the concept being discussed.

 FACTS. These notes provide additional helpful information on specific techniques and concepts.

 CAREFUL. These short warnings point out troublesome issues that you need to watch for when writing PHP scripts.

SHORT QUIZZES. Quick comprehension checks at the end of each major topic assess understanding of the section material.

SUMMING UP. These brief overviews of chapter content provide a helpful way to recap and revisit the ideas covered in each chapter.

COMPREHENSION CHECK. This set of 20 review questions reinforces the main ideas introduced in each chapter. These questions will help you determine how well you understand the concepts covered in the chapter.

 REINFORCEMENT EXERCISES. Although it is important to understand the concepts behind PHP programming, no amount of theory can improve on applied knowledge. To this end, along with conceptual explanations, each chapter provides Reinforcement Exercises for each major topic to give you practical experience. Because the Reinforcement Exercises require different solutions from the exercises in the chapter, they provide you with a wider variety of situations to practice implementing PHP.

DISCOVERY PROJECTS. The Discovery Projects at the end of each chapter are designed to help you apply what you have learned to a single, comprehensive Web site. The Web site will become more diverse and functional as you progress through the chapters. In addition, many of the Discovery Projects can be translated or modified into real-world Web applications.

Instructor Resources

The following supplemental materials are available when this book is used in a classroom setting. All of the resources available with this book are provided to the instructor on a CD.

- **Electronic Instructor's Manual**. The Instructor's Manual that accompanies this textbook includes additional instructional material to assist in class preparation, including items such as Sample Syllabi, Chapter Outlines, Technical Notes, Lecture Notes, Quick Quizzes, Teaching Tips, Discussion Topics, and Sample Midterm and Final Projects.

- **ExamView®**. This textbook is accompanied by ExamView, a powerful testing software package that allows instructors to create and administer printed, computer (LAN-based), and Internet exams. ExamView includes hundreds of questions that correspond to the topics covered in this text, enabling students to generate detailed study guides that include page references for further review. The computer-based and Internet testing components allow students to take exams at their computers, and save the instructor time by grading each exam automatically.

- **PowerPoint Presentations**. This book comes with Microsoft PowerPoint slides for each chapter. These are included as a teaching aid for classroom presentation and can be made available to students on the network for chapter review or printed for classroom distribution. Instructors can add their own slides for additional topics they introduce to the class.

- **Data Files**. Files that contain all of the data necessary for completing the Reinforcement Exercises and Discovery Projects are provided through the Course Technology Web site at *www.cengage. com/coursetechnology*, and are also available on the Instructor's Resource CD.

- **Solution Files**. Solutions to end-of-chapter review questions, Reinforcement Exercises, and Discovery Projects are provided on the Teaching Tools CD and the Course Technology Web site at *www.cengage.com/coursetechnology*. The solutions are password protected.

- **Distance Learning**. Course Technology is proud to present online test banks in WebCT and Blackboard, to provide the most complete and dynamic learning experience possible. Instructors are encouraged to make the most of the course, both online and offline. For more information on how to access your online test bank, contact your local Course Technology sales representative.

Acknowledgements

A text such as this represents the hard work of many people, not just the authors. We would like to thank all the people who helped make this book a reality. First and foremost, we thank Dan Seiter, Development Editor; Tricia Coia, Managing Editor; Alyssa Pratt, Senior Product Manager and Amy Jollymore, Acquisitions Editor, for helping us get the job done. We also thank Jennifer Feltri and Tintu Thomas, Content Project Managers.

Many, many thanks to the reviewers who provided plenty of comments and positive direction during the development of this book: Mathew Cantore, Hudson Valley Community College; Kathleen Harmeyer, University of Baltimore; Michael McLaughlin, Brigham Young University – Idaho; and Zizhong Wang, Virginia Wesleyan College.

We also thank our families and friends for their support during this process. We would especially like to thank our spouses, John and Linda, for putting up with our odd schedules and long hours. Diana would like to recognize her students at the University of Maine at Augusta, who make teaching such an enjoyable experience. Bob's children, Teresa and Phillip, provided plenty of enthusiastic support and encouragement as well.

Read This Before You Begin

The following information will help you as you prepare to use this textbook.

To the User of the Data Files

To complete the steps and projects in this book, you will need data files that have been created specifically for this book. You can obtain the files electronically from the Course Technology Web site by connecting to *www.cengage.com/coursetechnology* and then searching for this book title.

Using Your Own Computer

You can use a computer in your school lab or your own computer to complete the chapters, Reinforcement Exercises, and Discovery Projects in this book. To use your own computer, you will need the following:

- **A Web browser**, such as Microsoft Internet Explorer 7 or later or Mozilla Firefox 3 or later.

- **A code-based HTML editor** or a text editor, such as Notepad++. A word-processing program will not work, as it inserts formatting information into the document that will cause your scripts to fail.

- **An FTP client** that will allow you to upload your completed files to a remote Web server.

If you choose to install your own PHP Web server, but not use one of the *x*AMP packages as explained in Appendix B, you will need the following:

Appendix B contains detailed instructions on how to use *x*AMP to install an Apache Web server, PHP, and MySQL.

- **A Web server**, such as Apache HTTP Server or Microsoft Internet Information Services.

- **PHP 5 or later**. PHP is a server-side scripting language developed by the PHP Group (*http://www.php.net/*).

- **MySQL 4.1 or later**. MySQL is an open source database developed by MySQL AB (*http://www.mysql.com/*).

To the Instructor

To complete all the exercises and chapters in this book, your students must work with a set of data files. You can obtain the data files through the Course Technology Web site at *www.cengage.com/coursetechnology*.

Course Technology Data Files

You are granted a license to copy the data files to any computer or computer network used by people who have purchased this book.

Visit Our World Wide Web Site

Additional materials designed especially for this book might be available for your course. Periodically search *www.cengage.com/coursetechnology* for more information and materials to accompany this text.

CHAPTER 1

Getting Started with PHP

In this chapter you will:

◎ Create basic PHP scripts

◎ Create PHP code blocks

◎ Work with variables and constants

◎ Study data types

◎ Use expressions and operators

PHP: Hypertext Preprocessor, or PHP, is an open-source, server-side programming language. PHP is specifically designed to fill the gap between static HTML pages and fully dynamic pages, such as those generated through CGI code. PHP is embedded directly in the XHTML source code; throughout the book you will apply the W3C standard syntax and structure for XHTML documents and integrate CSS to format the document for browser display. You will explore the basic syntax and structure of the PHP scripting language and learn to upload files to a remote server.

As you progress through the book, functional examples and comprehensive, hands-on learning activities will reinforce the concepts presented and demonstrate how PHP and MySQL work together to provide the Web developer with a set of tools that build content-rich Web applications with database connectivity.

You will write your PHP scripts in a basic text editor. An editor designed to work with XHTML, with features such as built-in syntax highlighting and indentation, is helpful but not necessary. To run the PHP script, you will need an FTP client to upload the PHP source code files to a Web server and have access to a browser to view the Web pages on the Internet. In this chapter, you will study the basics of how to create PHP scripts.

Creating Basic PHP Scripts

JavaScript and PHP are both referred to as **embedded languages** because code for both languages is embedded within a Web page (either an HTML or XHTML document). You type this code directly into a Web page as a separate section. Although JavaScript code can be added to standard Web page documents that have an extension of .html, a Web page document containing PHP code must have an extension of .php. Whenever a request is made for a document with an extension of .php, the Web server sends the file to the scripting engine for processing. The scripting engine then processes any PHP code it encounters. Although PHP files use an extension of .php, they can contain the same HTML or XHTML elements you would find in a static Web page. The scripting engine ignores any non-PHP code and only processes the PHP code it finds within PHP code blocks (which you study next). The Web server then returns the results of the PHP script and any HTML or XHTML elements found in the PHP file to the client, where the file is rendered by the client's Web browser. In most cases, the results returned from a PHP script, such as database records, are formatted with HTML or XHTML elements. This means that PHP code is never sent to a client's Web browser; only the resulting Web page that is generated from the PHP code and HTML or

XHTML elements found within the PHP file are returned to the client. Later in this chapter, you will see an example of a Web page that is returned to a client from a PHP file that contains both PHP code and XHTML elements. First, you need to learn about PHP code blocks.

Short Quiz

1. Define the term "embedded language" as it applies to PHP.

2. Why should you avoid using the .php extension if the document contains only XHTML code?

3. Explain why you do not see any PHP code when you view the source code of a PHP page in the browser.

It is possible to create a PHP file that does not need to contain any PHP code. However, if the file contains no PHP code, you should name the file with an extension of .html to avoid having the file processed by the scripting engine unnecessarily.

You can use any valid extension you want for your PHP scripts, provided that your Web server is configured to process the extensions you use with the scripting engine. However, .php is the default extension that most Web servers use to process PHP scripts. For this reason, the files you create with this book that contain PHP code will have an extension of .php.

Creating PHP Code Blocks

You write PHP scripts within **code declaration blocks**, which are separate sections on a Web page that are interpreted by the scripting engine. You can include as many code declaration blocks as you want within a document. This section discusses the following four types of code declaration blocks you can use to write PHP:

- Standard PHP script delimiters

- The `<script>` element

- Short PHP script delimiters

- ASP-style script delimiters

Standard PHP Script Delimiters

The standard method of writing PHP code declaration blocks is to use the `<?php` and `?>` script delimiters. A **delimiter** is a character or sequence of characters used to mark the beginning and end of a code segment. When the scripting engine encounters the `<?php` and `?>` script delimiters, it processes any code between the delimiters as PHP. The individual lines of code that make up a PHP script are called **statements**. You need to use the following syntax in a document to tell the Web server that the statements that follow must be interpreted by the scripting engine:

```
<?php
statements;
?>
```

The following script contains a single statement that writes the text "Explore Africa!" to a Web browser window using an echo statement, as you will study shortly:

```php
<?php
echo "Explore Africa!";
?>
```

Notice that the preceding statement ends in a semicolon. PHP, along with other programming languages, including C++ and Java, requires you to end all statements with a semicolon. Note that the primary purpose of a semicolon is to identify the end of a statement, not the end of a line. Just as Web browsers ignore white space in an HTML or XHTML document, the scripting engine ignores white space within code blocks. For this reason, semicolons are critical to identify the end of a statement. This also means that you do not need to place each statement on its own line. For example, the following script contains two echo statements on the same line, with each statement ending in a semicolon:

```php
<?php
echo "Explore "; echo "Africa!";
?>
```

Further, statements can be placed on the same line with the <?php and ?> script delimiters, as follows:

```php
<?php echo "Explore "; echo "Africa!"; ?>
```

Although the preceding syntax is legal, for better readability you should typically use separate lines for the <?php and ?> script delimiters and for each statement within a code block. However, many of the examples in this book show delimiters and statements on the same line to conserve space.

The PHP Group officially recommends that you use standard PHP script delimiters to write PHP code declaration blocks. One reason is that standard PHP script delimiters are guaranteed to be available on any Web server that supports PHP. (As you will learn shortly, both short PHP script delimiters and ASP-style script delimiters can be disabled.) However, the primary reason for using standard PHP script delimiters is that they are the only method that is completely compliant with XML. (The Web page examples and exercises in this book are written in XHTML, which is based on XML.) XML is preferred for Web development not only because it is the basis of XHTML documents, but because it has become the standard for exchanging data on the Internet. For this reason, you should always ensure that any Web pages or scripts you create are compliant with XML.

Even though the PHP Group officially recommends that you use standard PHP script delimiters to write PHP, some Web developers prefer the other types of code declaration blocks, so you should be able to recognize the other delimiters when you see them.

To create a PHP script that contains standard PHP script delimiters:

1. Create a new document in your text editor.

2. Type the <!DOCTYPE> declaration, <html> element, header information, and <body> element. Use the strict DTD and "PHP Code Blocks" as the content of the <title> element. Your document should appear as follows:

```
<!DOCTYPE html PUBLIC "-//W3C//DTD XHTML 1.0
Strict//EN"
"http://www.w3.org/TR/xhtml1/DTD/xhtml1-strict.dtd">
<html xmlns="http://www.w3.org/1999/xhtml">
<head>
<title>PHP Code Blocks</title>
<meta http-equiv="content-type"
      content="text/html; charset=iso-8859-1" />
</head>
<body>
</body>
</html>
```

3. Add the following paragraph element and standard PHP script delimiters to the document body. Be sure to nest the script delimiters within the paragraph element. The paragraph element forces the output from the script delimiters to render on a separate line.

```
<p>
<?php
?>
</p>
```

4. Add the following echo statement (shown in bold) between the script delimiters:

```
<p>
<?php
echo "This text is displayed using standard PHP
script delimiters. ";
?>
</p>
```

5. Save the document as **PHPCodeBlocks.php** in the Chapter directory for Chapter 1. Be sure to use an extension of .php, which is required for your Web server to recognize the file as a PHP script.

6. Use FTP to upload the PHPCodeBlocks.php file to the Web server. Once you have successfully uploaded the document, validate it with the W3C XHTML Validator at *http://validator.w3.org/*. (Instructions for validating XHTML documents are included in Appendix A.)

7. Open the PHPCodeBlocks.php file in your Web browser by entering the following URL: *http://<yourserver>/PHP_Projects/Chapter.01/Chapter/PHPCodeBlocks.php* (replacing *<yourserver>* with the name of the Web server provided by your instructor). You should see the Web page shown in Figure 1-1.

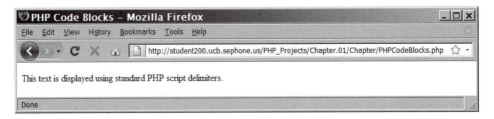

Figure 1-1   Output of a PHP script with standard PHP script delimiters

8. Close your Web browser window.

The `<script>` Element

A second option for creating PHP code blocks is to use the XHTML **`<script>` element**. When the `<script>` element is used with PHP, you must assign a value of "php" to the `language` attribute of the `<script>` element to identify the code block as PHP. When the PHP scripting engine encounters a `<script>` element with "php" assigned to its `language` attribute, it processes any code within the element as PHP on the server before returning the Web page. The syntax for using PHP with the `<script>` element is as follows:

```
<script language="php">
statements;
</script>
```

The following example contains the same `echo` statement you saw with the standard PHP script delimiters, but this time the statement is contained within a PHP `<script>` element:

```
<script language="php">
echo "Explore Africa!";
</script>
```

Like the standard PHP script delimiters, the <script> element is always available on any Web server that supports PHP. Unfortunately, the <script> element's language attribute is deprecated in XHTML. Further, the scripting engine ignores <script> elements that include the type attribute, which is required for compatibility with both the strict and transitional DTDs. For this reason, you cannot validate documents that include PHP <script> elements.

To add a PHP <script> element to the PHPCodeBlocks.php document:

1. Return to the **PHPCodeBlocks.php** document in your text editor.

2. Add the following paragraph element and <script> element to the end of the document body:

```
<p>
<script language="php">
</script>
</p>
```

3. Add the following echo statement (shown in bold) between the script delimiters:

```
<p>
<script language="php">
echo "This text is displayed using a PHP script
section.";
</script>
</p>
```

4. Save the PHPCodeBlocks.php document, upload it to the Web server, and then open it from your Web server. Your Web browser should appear similar to Figure 1-2.

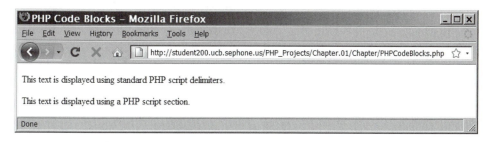

Figure 1-2 Output of a PHP script after adding a PHP script section

5. Close your Web browser window.

Short PHP Script Delimiters

A simplified method of writing PHP code declaration blocks is to use the short <? and ?> script delimiters. Short PHP script delimiters are similar to standard PHP script delimiters, except they do not include 'php' in the opening delimiter. The syntax for short PHP script delimiters is as follows:

```
<? statements; ?>
```

The following example shows how to use short delimiters with the echo statement you saw earlier:

```
<? echo "Explore Africa!"; ?>
```

Unlike the <?php and ?> script delimiters and the <script> element, which are always available on any Web server that supports PHP, the short <? and ?> delimiters can be disabled in a Web server's php.ini configuration file. Because a Web server on which your PHP script will run might not always be under your control, the PHP Group discourages the use of short delimiters, especially when developing scripts that will be redistributed and used by other Web developers. Although you can use short PHP script delimiters if you prefer, your PHP scripts will not work if your Web site is hosted by an ISP that does not support short PHP script delimiters. Another reason to avoid the short <? and ?> delimiters is that you cannot use them in XML documents, although you can use them in XHTML documents, including documents that conform to the strict DTD. With XML documents, you must use the <?php and ?> script delimiters.

To add short PHP script delimiters to the PHPCodeBlocks.php document:

1. Return to the **PHPCodeBlocks.php** document in your text editor.

2. Add the following paragraph element and short PHP script delimiters to the end of the document body:

    ```
    <p>
    <?
    ?>
    </p>
    ```

3. Add the following echo statement (highlighted in bold) between the script delimiters:

    ```
    <p>
    <?
    echo "This text is displayed using short PHP
    script delimiters.";
    ?>
    </p>
    ```

4. Save the PHPCodeBlocks.php document, upload it, and open it from your Web server. Your Web browser should appear similar to Figure 1-3.

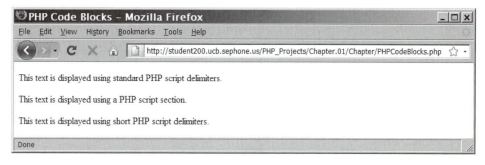

PHP Code Blocks – Mozilla Firefox

File   Edit   View   History   Bookmarks   Tools   Help

http://student200.ucb.sephone.us/PHP_Projects/Chapter.01/Chapter/PHPCodeBlocks.php

This text is displayed using standard PHP script delimiters.

This text is displayed using a PHP script section.

This text is displayed using short PHP script delimiters.

Done

Figure 1-3   Output of a PHP script after adding short PHP script delimiters

5. Close your Web browser window.

ASP-Style Script Delimiters

Some Web developers prefer to use the ASP-style script delimiters of <% and %> to develop PHP scripts. The syntax for ASP-style script delimiters is similar to that of short PHP script delimiters, as follows:

```
<% statements; %>
```

The following example shows how to use ASP-style script delimiters with the echo statement you saw earlier:

```
<% echo "Explore Africa!"; %>
```

Like short PHP script delimiters, ASP-style script delimiters are compliant with XHTML, including the strict DTD, but not with XML. ASP-style script delimiters can also be enabled or disabled in the php.ini configuration file, so you should not use them unless you are sure they are enabled on any Web servers on which your PHP scripts will run. Unless you are a hard-core ASP developer who only uses PHP occasionally, or if you are using an HTML editor that does not support PHP script delimiters, there is little reason to use ASP-style script delimiters.

To add ASP-style script delimiters to the PHPCodeBlocks.php document:

1. Return to the **PHPCodeBlocks.php** document in your text editor.

2. Add the following paragraph element and ASP-style script delimiters to the end of the document body:

```
<p>
<%
%>
</p>
```

3. Add the following echo statement (shown in bold) between the script delimiters:

```
<p>
<%
echo "This text is displayed using ASP-style
script delimiters.";
%>
</p>
```

4. Save the PHPCodeBlocks.php document, upload it, and open it from your Web server. Your Web browser should appear similar to Figure 1-4.

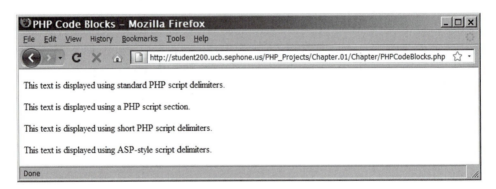

Figure 1-4   Output of a PHP script after adding ASP-style script delimiters

5. Close your Web browser window.

Understanding Functions

Before you start writing PHP scripts, you need to understand the basics of functions. The term **function** refers to a subroutine (or individual statements grouped into a logical unit) that performs a specific task. PHP includes numerous built-in functions that perform various types of tasks. You will work with many built-in PHP functions throughout this book. To execute a function, you must invoke, or **call**, it from somewhere in your script. The statement that calls a function is referred to as a **function call** and consists of the function name followed by any data that the function needs. The data (which you place in parentheses following the function name) are called

arguments or **actual parameters**. Sending data to a called function is called **passing arguments**. Many functions generate, or return, some sort of a value that you can use in your script. For example, PHP includes a round() function that rounds a decimal value to the nearest whole number. You pass a number as an argument to the round() function, which calculates and returns the nearest whole number. The following statement calls the round() function and passes to it a value of 3.556. The round() function calculates and returns a value of 4, which is then displayed with an echo statement.

```php
<?php echo round(3.556); ?>
```

Many functions can accept multiple arguments, which you separate with commas. For example, the second argument you pass to the round() function determines the number of digits after the decimal point that it should use to round the number. The following statement calls the round() function and then passes to it a first argument of 3.556 and a second argument of 2. The round() function calculates and returns a value of 3.56 (rounded to two decimal places), which is then displayed with an echo statement.

You learn more about functions, including how to create your own, in Chapter 2.

```php
<?php echo round(3.556, 2); ?>
```

To create a PHP script that uses the phpinfo() function to create a Web page that lists diagnostic information for the current PHP configuration on the Web server:

1. Create a new document in your text editor.

2. Type the <!DOCTYPE> declaration, <html> element, header information, and <body> element. Use the strict DTD and "PHP Diagnostic Information" as the content of the <title> element.

3. Add the following standard PHP script delimiters and phpinfo() function to the document body. Be certain to include the parentheses and semicolon in the statement containing the phpinfo() function.

    ```php
    <?php
    phpinfo();
    ?>
    ```

4. Save the document as **PHPTest.php** in the Chapter directory for Chapter 1 and upload the document to the Web server. You will not be able to validate this page with the W3C XHTML Validator because the phpinfo() function inserts a second set of HTML headers.

5. Open the PHPTest.php file in your Web browser by entering the following URL: *http://<yourserver>/PHP_Projects/Chapter.01/Chapter/PHPTest.php*. You should see a Web page

similar to the one shown in Figure 1-5, which lists diagnostic information for PHP.

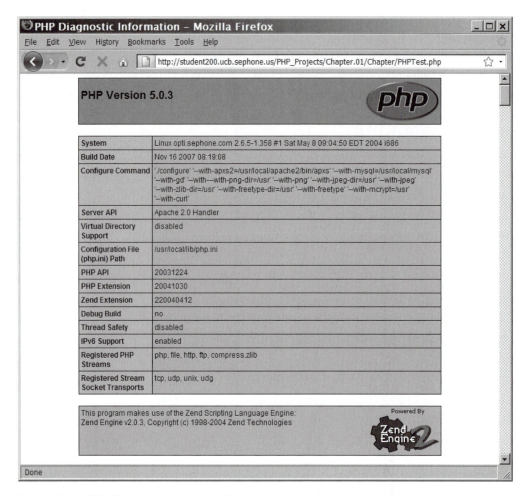

Figure 1-5   PHP Diagnostic Information Web page

6. Close your Web browser window.

Displaying Script Results

When you write a PHP script, you will often want to display the results of the script in the Web page that is returned as a response to a client. For example, you might want the Web page to display database records that the client requested or the result of a calculation that was processed by the PHP script. Recall that the scripting engine ignores any non-PHP code and only processes the PHP code it finds within PHP code blocks. The Web server then returns the results of the PHP script and any HTML or XHTML elements found in the PHP file to the client, where it is rendered by the client's Web browser. To return these script results to the client, you must use an echo statement, which you've already seen, or the print statement. The **echo** and **print statements** create new text on a Web page that is returned as a response to a client.

You might be thinking that the echo and print statements are functions. Actually, they are not functions, but language constructs of the PHP programming language. A **programming language construct** refers to a built-in feature of a programming language. The echo and print statements are nearly identical, but they have some differences. For example, the print statement returns a value of 1 if it is successful or a value of 0 if it is not successful, while the echo statement does not return a value. You need to learn a little more about functions before you can understand why the print statement returns a value. However, keep in mind that you can use the exact same syntax with the print statement that you use with the echo statement.

To modify the PHPCodeBlocks.php document so it uses print statements instead of echo statements:

1. Return to the **PHPCodeBlocks.php** document in your text editor.

2. Replace each of the echo statements with a print statement. For example, the statement within the standard PHP script delimiters should read as follows:

```php
<?php
print "This text is displayed using standard PHP
script delimiters.";
?>
```

3. Save the PHPCodeBlocks.php document, upload it, and then open it from your Web server. The document should render the same as it did with the echo statements.

4. Close your Web browser window.

You should understand that the only reason to use the echo and print statements is to include the results of a PHP script within a Web page that is returned to a client. For example, you might want to return a new Web page based on information a user enters into a form for an online transaction and submits to a Web server. You can use a PHP script to process the submitted information and return a new Web page to the client that displays the sales total, order confirmation, and so on. If you simply want to display text in a Web page that is returned to the client, there is no need to use anything but standard XHTML elements. The procedures for submitting and processing data are a little too complicated for this introductory chapter. In this chapter, you use the echo and print statements to return the results of a script to a client in order to learn the basics of PHP.

For both the echo and print statements, you need to include a text string that contains the text that will appear in the Web browser. A **literal string** is text that is contained within double or single quotation marks. As you saw earlier, the following echo statement uses double quotation marks to display the text "Explore Africa!" in the Web browser window:

```php
<?php echo "Explore Africa!"; ?>
```

You can also use single quotation marks with the preceding echo statement, as follows:

```php
<?php echo 'Explore Africa!'; ?>
```

The echo and print statements support multiple arguments. If you want to pass multiple arguments to the echo and print statements, separate them with commas, just as with arguments passed to a function. In the following example, three text string arguments are passed to the echo statement:

```php
<?php echo "Explore Africa, ", "South America, ",
        " and Australia!"; ?>
```

To create a script that passes multiple arguments to an echo statement:

1. Create a new document in your text editor.

2. Type the <!DOCTYPE> declaration, <html> element, header information, and <body> element. Use the strict DTD and "How to Talk Like a Pirate" as the content of the <title> element.

3. Add the following heading element to the document body:

    ```html
    <h1>How to Talk Like a Pirate</h1>
    ```

4. Next, add paragraph tags and a standard PHP script delimiter to the end of the document body:

    ```php
    <?php
    ?>
    ```

5. Now add the following echo statement to the PHP code block:

    ```php
    echo "Avast me hearties! ",
        "Return handsomely with some fine swag, ye
        scurvy dogs! ",
        "Else, we be keelhaulin' ye' next morn...";
    ```

6. Save the document as **PirateTalk.php** in the Chapter directory for Chapter 1, and upload the document to the Web server. After you upload the document, attempt to validate it with the W3C XHTML Validator. You will get a "text is not allowed here" error, which you will fix in a later exercise.

7. Open the PirateTalk.php file from your Web server by entering the following URL: *http://<yourserver>/PHP_Projects/ Chapter.01/Chapter/PirateTalk.php*. Your Web browser should appear similar to Figure 1-6.

Figure 1-6 "How to Talk Like a Pirate" Web page

8. Close your Web browser window.

You can also use parentheses with the `echo` and `print` statements in the same manner that you use them with functions, as follows:

```php
<?php echo("Explore Africa, ", "South America, ",
    " and Australia!"); ?>
```

You will not use parentheses with most of the `echo` and `print` statements you write in this book. However, you should be able to recognize the parenthesized version as just another form of the `echo` and `print` statements, not a separate type of function.

So far, the arguments you have seen and used with the `echo` statements have consisted of plain text that is rendered in the Web browser's default font. To format the output of text that is displayed with `echo` and `print` statements, you can use any XHTML formatting elements you want as part of the text string arguments. The following code shows a modified version of the previous script, but this time the `echo` statement includes several XHTML elements to format the appearance of the text string in a Web browser. Figure 1-7 shows how the script is rendered in a Web browser.

```php
<?php echo "<p>Explore <strong>Africa</strong>, <br />",
    "<strong>South America</strong>, <br />",
    " and <strong>Australia</strong>!</p>"; ?>
```

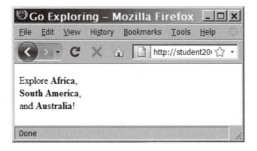

Figure 1-7 Output of an `echo` statement with XHTML elements

To modify the PirateTalk.php script so the `echo` statement includes XHTML elements:

1. Return to the **PirateTalk.php** script in your text editor.

2. Modify the values passed to the `echo` statement so they include paragraph and line break elements, as follows:

```
echo "<p>Avast me hearties!<br />",
        "Return handsomely with some fine swag,<br />ye
        scurvy dogs!<br />",
        "Else, we be keelhaulin' ye' next morn...</p>";
```

You study additional techniques for working with text strings in Chapter 3.

3. Save the PirateTalk.php file and upload it to the Web server. Validate the document with the W3C XHTML Validator (the error should be gone now), and then open the document from your Web server. The document should appear similar to Figure 1-8.

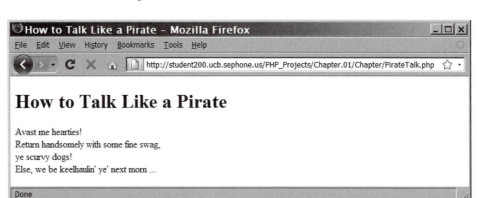

Figure 1-8 "How to Talk Like a Pirate" Web page after adding XHTML elements to the `echo` statement

4. Close your Web browser window.

Creating Multiple Code Declaration Blocks

You can include as many PHP script sections as you want within a document. However, when you include multiple script sections in a document, you must include a separate code declaration block for each section. The following document includes two separate script sections. The script sections create the information that is displayed beneath the <h2> heading elements.

```
. . .
</head>
<body>
<h1>Multiple Script Sections</h1>
<h2>First Script Section</h2>
<?php echo "<p>Output from the first script
section.</p>"; ?>
<h2>Second Script Section</h2>
<?php echo "<p>Output from the second script
section.</p>"; ?>
</body>
</html>
```

Remember that PHP code declaration blocks execute on a Web server before a Web page is sent to a client. If users were to view the source document after they received the PHP document, they would not see any PHP code declaration blocks. Instead, the users would only see the results returned from the PHP code. The following example shows how the source code for the preceding document appears after a user receives it. Notice that the PHP code declaration blocks have been converted to elements and text. Figure 1-9 shows how the text and elements appear in a Web browser.

```
. . .
</head>
<body>
<h1>Multiple Script Sections</h1>
<h2>First Script Section</h2>
<p>Output from the first script section.</p>
<h2>Second Script Section</h2>
<p>Output from the second script section.</p>
</body>
</html>
```

Figure 1-9 Output of a document with two PHP script sections

Even though many people may enjoy talking like a pirate, the PirateTalk.php document is of limited use in demonstrating how to write PHP scripts. Therefore, in the next exercise, you will write a PHP script that displays the results of several built-in PHP functions using multiple script sections. You will use the phpversion(), zend_version(), and ini_get() functions. The **phpversion()** function returns the version of PHP that processed the current page. The **zend_version()** function returns the version number of the Zend Engine, which is PHP's scripting engine. The **ini_get()** function returns the value assigned to a directive in the php.ini configuration file. You need to pass the name of a directive to the ini_get() function, surrounded by quotation marks.

To create a script with multiple script sections:

1. Create a new document in your text editor.

2. Type the <!DOCTYPE> declaration, <html> element, header information, and <body> element. Use the strict DTD and "PHP Environment Info" as the content of the <title> element.

3. Add the following heading element to the document body:

   ```
   <h1>PHP Environment Info</h1>
   ```

4. Add the following elements, text, and PHP code block to the document body. The code block displays the PHP version number using the `phpversion()` function.

```
<p>This page was rendered with PHP version
<?php
echo phpversion();
?>.
</p>
```

5. Add the following elements, text, and PHP code block to the end of the document body. The code block displays the Zend Engine version number using the `zend_version()` function.

```
<p>The PHP code was rendered with Zend Engine
version
<?php
echo zend_version();
?>.
</p>
```

6. Finally, add the following elements, text, and PHP code blocks to the end of the document body. The code blocks use the `ini_get()` function to display PHP's default MIME type and the maximum amount of time that a PHP script is allowed to execute.

```
<p>PHP's default MIME type is
<?php
echo ini_get("default_mimetype");
?>.
</p>
<p>The maximum allowed execution time of a PHP
script is
<?php
echo ini_get("max_execution_time");
?>
seconds.</p>
```

7. Save the document as **MultipleScripts.php** in the Chapter directory for Chapter 1. After you save and upload the document, validate it with the W3C XHTML Validator.

8. Open the MultipleScripts.php file from your Web server by entering the following URL: *http://<yourserver>/PHP_Projects/Chapter.01/Chapter/MultipleScripts.php*. Your Web browser should appear similar to Figure 1-10.

Figure 1-10 Web page with multiple PHP scripts

9. Close your Web browser window.

Case Sensitivity in PHP

Unlike XHTML and JavaScript, programming language constructs in PHP are mostly case insensitive, although there are some exceptions. This means that you can use any of the following versions of the echo statement without receiving an error message:

Exceptions to PHP's case insensi-tivity include variable and constant names, which are case sensitive. You will study variables and constants later in this chapter.

```php
<?php
echo "<p>Explore <strong>Africa</strong>, <br />";
Echo "<strong>South America</strong>, <br />";
ECHO " and <strong>Australia</strong>!</p>";
?>
```

Even though you can use whatever case you want, be certain to use the letter cases presented in this book for consistency and to make it easier to locate any problems in your scripts.

Adding Comments to a PHP Script

When you write a script, whether in PHP or any other programming language, it is considered good programming practice to add com-ments to your code. **Comments** are lines you place in your code that do not get executed, but provide helpful information. Comments include the name of the script, your name and the date you created the program, notes to yourself, or instructions to future programmers who might need to modify your work. When you are working with long scripts, comments make it easier to understand how a program is structured.

PHP supports two kinds of comments: line comments and block comments. A **line comment** automatically terminates at the end of the line in which it is inserted. To create a line comment, add either two forward slashes (//) or the pound symbol (#) before the text you want to use as a comment. (You do not need to include both.) The // or # characters instruct the scripting engine to ignore all text immediately following the characters to the end of the line. You can place a line comment either at the end of a line of code or on its own line.

Block comments allow multiple lines of comment text to be added. You create a block comment by adding a forward slash and an asterisk (/*) before the start of the text that you want included in the block, and adding an asterisk and a forward slash (*/) after the last character in the block. Any text or lines between the opening /* characters and the closing */ characters are ignored by the PHP engine. The following code shows a PHP code block containing line and block comments. If a client requests a Web page containing the following script in a Web browser, the scripting engine ignores the text marked with comments.

```php
<?php
/*
This line is part of the block comment.
This line is also part of the block comment.
*/
echo "<h1>Comments Example</h1>"; // Line comment
// This line comment takes up an entire line.
# This is another way of creating a line comment.
/* This is another way of creating
a block comment. */
?>
```

Block comments cannot be nested inside other block comments. A block comment stops at the first */, regardless of how many /* characters precede it.

To add comments to the PHP Environment Info Web page:

1. Return to the **MultipleScripts.php** document in your text editor.

2. Add the following block comment immediately after the first opening PHP script delimiter:

```php
/*
PHP code for Chapter 1.
The purpose of this code is to demonstrate how to
add multiple PHP code blocks to a Web page.
*/
```

Comments created with two slashes (//) or the /* and */ characters are also used in C++, Java, and JavaScript. Comments created with the pound symbol (#) are used in Perl and shell script programming.

3. Next, add the following line comments immediately after the block comment, taking care to replace *your name* with your first and last name and *today's date* with the current date:

```php
// your name
# today's date
```

4. Save the MultipleScripts.php document, upload it to the Web server, and validate the document with the W3C XHTML Validator. Open the document from your Web server to ensure that the comments are not displayed.

5. Close your Web browser window.

Short Quiz

1. How many code declaration blocks can be inserted in a PHP document?

2. Why does the PHP Group recommend that you use standard PHP script delimiters to write PHP code declaration blocks?

3. What character or characters are used as delimiters to separate multiple arguments (parameters) in a function declaration or function call?

4. Describe the type of information that the phpinfo() function generates.

5. Identify the two types of comments available in PHP and indicate when each would be used.

Using Variables and Constants

One of the most important aspects of programming is the ability to store values in computer memory and to manipulate those values. These stored values are called variables. The values, or data, contained in variables are classified into categories known as data types. In this section, you will learn about PHP variables and data types, and the operations that can be performed on them.

The values a program stores in computer memory are commonly called **variables**. Technically speaking, though, a variable is actually a specific location in the computer's memory. Data stored in a specific variable often changes. You can think of a variable as similar to a storage locker—a program can put any value into it, and then retrieve the value later for use in calculations. To use a variable in a program, you first have to write a statement that creates the variable and assigns it a name. For example, you can have a program that creates a variable to store the current time. Each time the program runs, the current time is different, so the value varies.

Programmers often talk about "assigning a value to a variable," which is the same as storing a value in a variable. For example, a shopping cart program might include variables that store the current customer's name and purchase total. Each variable will contain different values at different times, depending on the name of the customer and the items the customer is purchasing.

Naming Variables

The name you assign to a variable is called an **identifier**. You must observe the following rules and conventions when naming a variable:

- Identifiers must begin with a dollar sign ($).

- Identifiers may contain uppercase and lowercase letters, numbers, or underscores (_). The first character after the dollar sign must be a letter.

- Identifiers cannot contain spaces.

- Identifiers are case sensitive.

One common practice is to use an underscore character to separate individual words within a variable name, as in `$my_variable_name`. Another option is to use initial capital letters for each word in a variable name, as in `$MyVariableName`.

Unlike other types of PHP code, variable names are case sensitive. Therefore, the variable named `$MyVariable` is completely different from one named `$Myvariable`, `$myVariable`, or `$MYVARIABLE`. If you receive an error when running a script, be sure that you are using the correct case when referring to any variables in your code.

Declaring and Initializing Variables

Before you can use a variable in your code, you have to create it. The process of specifying and creating a variable name is called **declaring** the variable. The process of assigning a first value to a variable is called **initializing** the variable. Some programming languages allow you to first declare a variable without initializing it. However, in PHP, you must declare and initialize a variable in the same statement, using the following syntax:

```
$variable_name = value;
```

The equal sign in the preceding statement assigns an initial value to (or initializes) the variable you created (or declared) with the name *$variable_name*.

If you attempt to declare a variable without initializing it, you will receive an error.

The value you assign to a variable can be a literal string, a numeric value, or a Boolean value. For example, the following statement assigns the literal string "Don" to the variable $MyName:

```
$MyName = "Don";
```

When you assign a literal string value to a variable, you must enclose the text in single or double quotation marks, as shown in the preceding statement. However, when you assign a numeric or Boolean value to a variable, do not enclose the value in quotation marks or PHP will treat the value as a string instead of a number. The following statement assigns the numeric value 59 to the variable $RetirementAge:

```
$RetirementAge = 59;
```

In addition to assigning literal strings, numeric values, and Boolean values to a variable, you can assign the value of one variable to another. For instance, in the following code, the first statement declares a variable named $SalesTotal and assigns it an initial value of 0. (Remember that in PHP you must initialize a variable when you first declare it.) The second statement creates another variable named $CurOrder and assigns it a numeric value of 40. The third statement then assigns the value of the $CurOrder variable (40) to the $SalesTotal variable.

```
$SalesTotal = 0;
$CurOrder = 40;
$SalesTotal = $CurOrder;
```

Displaying Variables

To display a variable with the echo statement, you simply pass the variable name to the echo statement, but without enclosing it in quotation marks, as follows:

```
$VotingAge = 18;
echo $VotingAge;
```

If you want to display text strings and variables in the same statement, you can pass them to the echo statement as individual arguments, separated by commas. For example, the following code displays the text shown in Figure 1-11. Notice that the text and elements are contained within quotation marks, but the $VotingAge variable is not.

```
echo "<p>The legal voting age is ", $VotingAge, ".</p>";
```

Figure 1-11 Output from an `echo` statement that is passed text and a variable

You can also include variable names inside a text string, although the results you see on the screen depend on whether you use double or single quotation marks around the text string that includes the variable name. If you use double quotation marks, the value assigned to the variable will appear. For example, the following statement displays the same output that is shown in Figure 1-11:

```
echo "<p>The legal voting age is $VotingAge.</p>";
```

By contrast, if you use a variable name in a text string enclosed by single quotation marks, the name of the variable will appear. For example, the following statement displays the output shown in Figure 1-12:

```
echo '<p>The legal voting age is $VotingAge.</p>';
```

Figure 1-12 Output of an `echo` statement that includes text and a variable surrounded by single quotation marks

Modifying Variables

You can modify the variable's value at any point in a script. The following code declares a variable named `$SalesTotal`, assigns it an initial value of 40, and displays it using an `echo` statement. The third statement changes the value of the `$SalesTotal` variable and the fourth statement displays the new value. Figure 1-13 shows the output in a Web browser.

The two adjacent dollar signs are not special syntax. The first dollar sign, because it is not immediately followed by a variable name, is treated as a literal dollar sign character and displayed on the page. The second dollar sign and the variable name that follows it are treated as an identifier, and the value of the identifier is displayed on the page.

```
$SalesTotal = 40;
echo "<p>Your sales total is $$SalesTotal</p>";
$SalesTotal = 50;
echo "<p>Your new sales total is $$SalesTotal</p>";
```

Figure 1-13 Results of a script that includes a changing variable

It's an old tradition among programmers to practice a new language by writing a script that prints or displays the text "Hello World!". If you are an experienced programmer, you have undoubtedly created "Hello World" programs in the past. If you are new to programming, you will probably create "Hello World" programs as you learn programming languages. Next, you will create your own "Hello World" program in PHP. You will create a simple script that displays the text "Hello World!", says "Hello" to the sun and the moon, and displays a line of scientific information about each celestial body. You will use variables to store and display each piece of information.

To create the "Hello World" program:

1. Create a new document in your text editor.

2. Type the <!DOCTYPE> declaration, <html> element, header information, and <body> element. Use the strict DTD and "Hello World" as the content of the <title> element. Your document should appear as follows:

   ```
   <!DOCTYPE html PUBLIC "-//W3C//DTD XHTML 1.0
   Strict//EN"
   "http://www.w3.org/TR/xhtml1/DTD/xhtml1-strict.dtd">
   <html>
   <head>
   <title>Hello World</title>
   </head>
   <body>
   </body>
   </html>
   ```

3. Add the following standard PHP script delimiters to the document body:

   ```
   <?php
   ?>
   ```

4. In the code block, type the following statements to declare the variables containing the names of each celestial body, along with variables containing scientific information about each celestial body:

```
$WorldVar = "World";
$SunVar = "Sun";
$MoonVar = "Moon";
$WorldInfo = 92897000;
$SunInfo = 72000000;
$MoonInfo = 3456;
```

5. Add the following statements to the end of the script section to display the values stored in each of the variables you declared and initialized in the last step:

```
echo "<p>Hello $WorldVar!<br />";
echo "The $WorldVar is $WorldInfo miles from the
     $SunVar.<br />";
echo "Hello ", $SunVar, "!<br />";
echo "The $SunVar's core temperature is
     approximately $SunInfo
     degrees Fahrenheit.<br />";
echo "Hello ", $MoonVar, "!<br />";
echo "The $MoonVar is $MoonInfo miles in
     diameter.</p>";
```

6. Save the document as **HelloWorld.php** in the Chapter directory for Chapter 1. After you save and upload the document, validate it with the W3C XHTML Validator.

7. Open the HelloWorld.php file in your Web browser by entering the following URL: *http://<yourserver>/PHP_Projects/Chapter.01/Chapter/HelloWorld.php*. You should see the Web page in Figure 1-14.

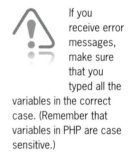

If you receive error messages, make sure that you typed all the variables in the correct case. (Remember that variables in PHP are case sensitive.)

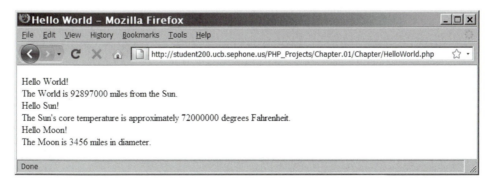

Figure 1-14 Output of HelloWorld.php

8. Close your Web browser window.

Defining Constants

A **constant** contains information that does not change during the course of program execution. You can think of a constant as a variable with a static value. A common example of a constant is the value of pi (π), which represents the ratio of the circumference of a circle to its diameter. The value of pi never changes from a constant value of approximately 3.141592.

Unlike variable names, constant names do not begin with a dollar sign ($). In addition, it is common practice to use all uppercase letters for constant names. When you create a constant, you do not declare and initialize it the way you declare a variable. Instead, you use the **define() function** to create a constant. The syntax for the define() function is as follows:

```
define("CONSTANT_NAME", value);
```

The value you pass to the define() function can be a text string, number, or Boolean value. In the following example, the first constant definition passes a text string to the define() function while the second constant definition passes a number:

```
define("DEFAULT_LANGUAGE", "Navajo");
define("VOTING_AGE", 18);
```

Remember that you cannot change the value of a constant after you define it in your program. If you attempt to use the **define()** function to change the value of an existing constant, you will receive an error.

By default, constant names are case sensitive, as are variables. However, you can make constant names case insensitive by passing a Boolean value of TRUE as a third argument to the define() function, as follows:

```
define("DEFAULT_LANGUAGE", "Navajo", TRUE);
```

With the preceding statement, you can refer to the DEFAULT_LANGUAGE constant using any letter case, including default_language or Default_Language. However, standard programming convention is to use all uppercase letters for constant names, so you should avoid making your constant names case insensitive.

When you refer to a constant in code, remember *not* to include a dollar sign, as you would with variable names. You can pass a constant name to the echo statement in the same manner as you pass a variable name (but without the dollar sign), as follows:

```
echo "<p>The legal voting age is ", VOTING_AGE, ".</p>";
```

The preceding statement displays the text "The legal voting age is 18." in the Web browser. Unlike variables, you cannot include the constant name within the quotation marks that surround a text string. If you do, PHP treats the constant name as ordinary text that is part of the string. For example, consider the following statement, which includes the constant name within the quotation marks that surround the text string:

```
echo "<p>The legal voting age is VOTING_AGE.</p>";
```

Instead of displaying the value of the constant (18), the preceding statement displays "The legal voting age is VOTING_AGE." in the Web browser.

PHP includes numerous predefined constants that you can use in your scripts.

To replace the $WorldInfo, $SunInfo, and $MoonInfo variables in the HelloWorld.php script with constants:

1. Return to the **HelloWorld.php** document in your text editor.

2. Replace the $WorldInfo, $SunInfo, and $MoonInfo variable declarations with the following constant definitions:

```
define("WORLD_INFO", 92897000);
define("SUN_INFO", 72000000);
define("MOON_INFO", 3456);
```

3. Replace the $WorldInfo, $SunInfo, and $MoonInfo variable references in the echo statements with the new constants. The modified echo statements should appear as follows:

```
echo "<p>Hello ", $WorldVar, "!<br />";
echo "The $WorldVar is ", WORLD_INFO,
     " miles from the $SunVar.<br />";
echo "Hello ", $SunVar, "!<br />";
echo "The $SunVar's core temperature is
     approximately ",
     SUN_INFO, " degrees Fahrenheit.<br />";
echo "Hello ", $MoonVar, "!<br />";
echo "The $MoonVar is ", MOON_INFO, " miles in
     diameter.</p>";
```

4. Save and upload the HelloWorld.php document and then validate it with the W3C XHTML Validator.

5. Open the HelloWorld.php document from your Web server. The Web page should look the same as it did before you added the constant declarations.

6. Close your Web browser window.

Short Quiz

1. Describe the two-step process of making a variable available for use in the PHP script.

2. Explain the syntax for displaying a variable or variables in the PHP script using the echo or print statements.

3. How do you make a constant name case insensitive?

30

Working with Data Types

PHP also supports a "resource" data type, which is a special variable that holds a reference to an external resource, such as a database or XML file.

Variables can contain many different kinds of values—for example, the time of day, a dollar amount, or a person's name. A **data type** is the specific category of information that a variable contains. The concept of data types is often difficult for beginning programmers to grasp because in real life you don't often distinguish among different types of information. If someone asks you for your name, your age, or the current time, you don't usually stop to consider that your name is a text string and that your age and the current time are numbers. However, a variable's specific data type is very important in programming because the data type helps determine the manner in which the value is stored and how much memory the computer allocates for the data stored in the variable. The data type also governs the kinds of operations that can be performed on a variable.

The term NULL refers to a data type as well as a value that can be assigned to a variable. Assigning the value NULL to a variable indicates that the variable does not contain a usable value. A variable with a value of NULL has a value assigned to it—null is really the value "no value." You assign the NULL value to a variable when you want to ensure that the variable does not contain any data. For instance, with the $SalesTotal variable you saw earlier, you may want to ensure that the variable does not contain any data before you use it to create another purchase order.

Data types that can be assigned only a single value are called **primitive types**. PHP supports the five primitive data types described in Table 1-1.

Data Type	Description
Integer numbers	The set of all positive and negative numbers and zero, with no decimal places
Floating-point numbers	Positive or negative numbers with decimal places or numbers written using exponential notation
Boolean	A logical value of "true" or "false"
String	Text such as "Hello World"
NULL	An empty value, also referred to as a NULL value

Table 1-1 Primitive PHP data types

The PHP language also supports **reference**, or **composite**, data types, which can contain multiple values or complex types of information, as opposed to the single values stored in primitive data types. The two reference data types supported by the PHP language are arrays and objects. In this chapter, you will study basic array techniques. You will learn about advanced arrays and objects in later chapters.

Many programming languages require that you declare the type of data that a variable contains. Such programming languages are called **strongly typed programming languages**. Strong typing is also known as **static typing** because the data type for a variable will not change after it has been declared. Programming languages that do not require you to declare the data types of variables are called **loosely typed programming languages**. Loose typing is also known as **dynamic typing** because the data type for a variable can change after it has been declared. PHP is a loosely typed programming language. In PHP, you are not required to declare the data type of variables, and, in fact, you are not allowed to do so. Instead, the PHP scripting engine automatically determines what type of data is stored in a variable and assigns the variable's data type accordingly. The following code demonstrates how a variable's data type changes automatically each time the variable is assigned a new literal value.

```
$ChangingVariable = "Hello World";  // String
$ChangingVariable = 8;              // Integer number
$ChangingVariable = 5.367;          // Floating-point
                                    // number
$ChangingVariable = TRUE;           // Boolean
$ChangingVariable = NULL;           // NULL
```

The next two sections focus on two commonly used data types: numeric and Boolean.

Numeric Data Types

Numeric data types are an important part of any programming language and are particularly useful for arithmetic calculations. PHP supports two numeric data types: integers and floating-point numbers. **Integers** are positive and negative numbers and zero, with no decimal places. The numbers –250, –13, 0, 2, 6, 10, 100, and 10,000 are examples of integers. The numbers –6.16, –4.4, 3.17, .52, 10.5, and 2.7541 are not integers; they are floating-point numbers. A **floating-point number** contains decimal places or is written in exponential notation. **Exponential notation**, or **scientific notation**, is a shortened format for writing very large numbers or numbers with many decimal places. Numbers written in exponential notation are represented by a value between –10 and 10 that is multiplied by 10 raised to some power. The notation for "times ten raised to the power" is an uppercase or lowercase *E*. For example, the number 200,000,000,000 can be written in exponential notation as 2.0e11, which means "two times ten to the power eleven."

Although you cannot declare a data type when you first create a variable, you can force a variable to be converted to a specific type. You learn how to force a variable to be a specific type at the end of this section.

Strictly speaking, there are differences between the terms "strong typing" and "static typing," and between "loose typing" and "dynamic typing." The specifics of these differences are beyond the scope of this book. The terms "strongly typed" and "loosely typed" are used here in the generic sense, not in the technical sense.

To create a script that assigns integers and exponential numbers to variables and displays the values:

1. Create a new document in your text editor.

2. Type the `<!DOCTYPE>` declaration, `<html>` element, header information, and `<body>` element. Use the strict DTD and "Display Numbers" as the content of the `<title>` element.

3. Add the following standard PHP script delimiters to the document body:

```
<?php
?>
```

4. Add the following lines to the script section; they declare an integer variable and a floating-point variable:

```
$IntegerVar = 150;
$FloatingPointVar = 3.0e7; // floating-point
                           // number 30000000
```

5. Finally, to display the values of the variables, add the following statements to the end of the script section:

```
echo "<p>Integer variable: $IntegerVar<br />";
echo "Floating-point variable: $FloatingPointVar</p>";
```

6. Save the document as **DisplayNumbers.php** in the Chapter directory for Chapter 1, upload the document to the Web server, and validate the document with the W3C XHTML Validator.

7. Open the DisplayNumbers.php file in your Web browser by entering the following URL: *http://<yourserver>/ PHP_Projects/Chapter.01/Chapter/DisplayNumbers.php*. The integer 150 and the number 30000000 (for the exponential expression 3.0e7) should appear in your Web browser window, as shown in Figure 1-15.

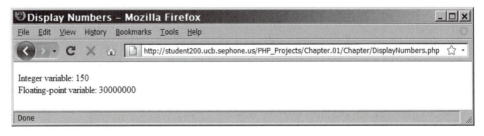

Figure 1-15   Output of DisplayNumbers.php

8. Close your Web browser window.

Boolean Values

A **Boolean value** is a value of "true" or "false". (You can also think of a Boolean value as either "yes" or "no", or "on" or "off".) Boolean values are most often used for deciding which parts of a program should execute and for comparing data. In programming languages other than PHP, you can use the integer value 1 to indicate a Boolean value of TRUE and 0 to indicate a Boolean value of FALSE. In PHP programming, however, you can only use the words TRUE or FALSE to indicate Boolean values. PHP then converts the values TRUE and FALSE to the integers 1 and 0. For example, when you attempt to use a Boolean variable of TRUE in a mathematical operation, PHP converts the variable to an integer value of 1. The following shows a simple example of a variable that is assigned the Boolean value of TRUE. Figure 1-16 shows this output in a Web browser. Notice that the Boolean value of TRUE is displayed as the integer 1.

```
$RepeatCustomer = TRUE;
echo "<p>Repeat customer: $RepeatCustomer</p>";
```

Figure 1-16 Output of a Boolean value

Arrays

An **array** is a set of data represented by a single variable name. You can think of an array as a collection of variables contained within a single variable. You use arrays when you want to store groups or lists of related information in a single, easily managed location. Lists of names, courses, test scores, and prices are typically stored in arrays. Figure 1-17 conceptually shows how you can store the names of the Canadian provinces using a single array named $Provinces[]. Array names are often referred to with the array operators ([and]) at the end of the name to clearly define them as arrays. You can use the array to refer to each province without having to retype the names and possibly introduce syntax errors through misspellings.

The identifiers you use for an array name must follow the same rules as identifiers for variables: Array names must begin with a dollar sign, can include uppercase and lowercase letters, can include numbers or underscores (but not as the first character after the dollar sign), cannot include spaces, and are case sensitive.

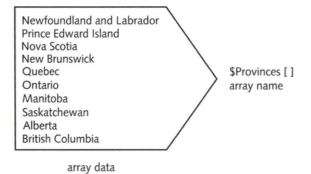

Newfoundland and Labrador
Prince Edward Island
Nova Scotia
New Brunswick
Quebec
Ontario
Manitoba
Saskatchewan
Alberta
British Columbia

$Provinces [ ]
array name

array data

Figure 1-17 Conceptual example of an array

Declaring and Initializing Indexed Arrays

In PHP, you can create numerically indexed arrays and associative arrays. In this chapter, you will study numerically indexed arrays. You will learn how to use associative arrays in Chapter 6.

An **element** refers to a single piece of data that is stored within an array. By default, the numbering of elements within a PHP array starts with an index number of zero (0). (This numbering scheme can be very confusing for beginners.) An **index** is an element's numeric position within the array. You refer to a specific element by enclosing its index in brackets at the end of the array name. For example, the first element in the $Provinces[] array is $Provinces[0], the second element is $Provinces[1], the third element is $Provinces[2], and so on. This also means that if you have an array consisting of 10 elements, the 10th element in the array has an index of 9.

You create an array using the array() construct or by using the array name and brackets. The array() construct uses the following syntax:

```
$array_name = array(values);
```

The following code uses the array() construct to create the $Provinces[] array:

```
$Provinces = array("Newfoundland and Labrador", "Prince
Edward Island", "Nova Scotia", "New Brunswick", "Quebec",
"Ontario", "Manitoba", "Saskatchewan", "Alberta", "British
Columbia");
```

The following code shows another example of the preceding array declaration, but this time with line breaks to make it more readable:

```
$Provinces = array(
    "Newfoundland and Labrador",
    "Prince Edward Island",
    "Nova Scotia",
```

```
"New Brunswick",
"Quebec",
"Ontario",
"Manitoba",
"Saskatchewan",
"Alberta",
"British Columbia"
);
```

 Note that the final element in the array does not have a comma following the value. Inserting a comma after the final element will cause a syntax error.

To create a script that declares and initializes an array using the array() construct:

1. Create a new document in your text editor.

2. Type the <!DOCTYPE> declaration, <html> element, header information, and <body> element. Use the strict DTD and "Central Valley Civic Center" as the content of the <title> element.

3. Add the following elements, text, and standard PHP script delimiters to the document body:

```
<h1>Central Valley Civic Center</h1>
<h2>Summer Concert Season</h2>
<?php
?>
```

4. Add the following lines to the script section to declare and initialize an array named $Concerts[]:

```
$Concerts = array("Jimmy Buffett", "Chris Isaak",
"Bonnie Raitt", "James Taylor", "Alicia Keys");
```

5. Save the document as **Concerts.php** in the Chapter directory for Chapter 1.

You can also use the following syntax to assign values to an array by using the array name and brackets:

```
$Provinces[] = "Newfoundland and Labrador";
$Provinces[] = "Prince Edward Island";
$Provinces[] = "Nova Scotia";
$Provinces[] = "New Brunswick";
$Provinces[] = "Quebec";
$Provinces[] = "Ontario";
$Provinces[] = "Manitoba";
$Provinces[] = "Saskatchewan";
$Provinces[] = "Alberta";
$Provinces[] = "British Columbia";
```

Unlike in variables, the preceding statements in arrays do not overwrite the existing values. Instead, each value is assigned to the $Provinces[] array as a new element using the next consecutive index number.

To add more elements to an array using statements that include the array name and brackets:

1. Return to the **Concerts.php** document in your text editor.

2. Add the following statements immediately after the statement containing the `array()` construct:

```
$Concerts[] = "Bob Dylan";
$Concerts[] = "Ryan Cabrera";
```

3. Save the Concerts.php document.

Most programming languages require that all elements in an array be of the exact same data type. However, in PHP, the values assigned to different elements of the same array can be of different data types. For example, the following code uses the `array()` construct to create an array named `$HotelReservation`, which stores values with different data types in the array elements:

```
$HotelReservation = array(
      "Don Gosselin", // guest name (string)
      2,              // # of nights (integer)
      89.95,          // price per night (floating-point)
      true);          // nonsmoking room (Boolean)
```

Accessing Element Information

You access an element's value the same way you access the value of any variable, except you include brackets and the element index. For example, the following code displays the value of the second element ("Prince Edward Island") and fifth element ("Quebec") in the `$Provinces[]` array. Figure 1-18 shows the output.

```
echo "<p>Canada's smallest province is
      $Provinces[1].<br />";
echo "Canada's largest province is $Provinces[4].</p>";
```

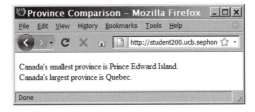

Figure 1-18 Output of elements in the `$Provinces[]` array

To find the total number of elements in an array, use the `count()` function. You pass to the `count()` function the name of the array whose elements you want to count. The following code uses the `count()` function to display the number of elements in the `$Provinces[]` array and the `$Territories[]` array. Figure 1-19 shows the output.

```
$Provinces = array("Newfoundland and Labrador", "Prince
Edward Island", "Nova Scotia", "New Brunswick", "Quebec",
"Ontario", "Manitoba", "Saskatchewan", "Alberta", "British
Columbia");
$Territories = array("Nunavut", "Northwest Territories",
"YukonTerritory");
echo "<p>Canada has ", count($Provinces), " provinces and ",
     count($Territories), " territories.</p>";
```

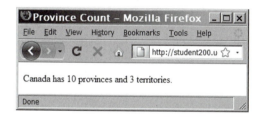

Figure 1-19 Output of the `count()` function

To add statements that use the `count()` function to display the number of scheduled concerts and the names of each performer:

1. Return to the **Concerts.php** document in your text editor.

2. Add the following output statements to the end of the code block, but above the closing ?> delimiter:

```
echo "<p>The following ", count($Concerts),
     " concerts are scheduled:</p><p>";
echo "$Concerts[0]<br />";
echo "$Concerts[1]<br />";
echo "$Concerts[2]<br />";
echo "$Concerts[3]<br />";
echo "$Concerts[4]<br />";
echo "$Concerts[5]<br />";
echo "$Concerts[6]</p>";
```

3. Save and upload the Concerts.php document and then validate it with the W3C XHTML Validator.

4. Open the Concerts.php file in your Web browser by entering the following URL: *http://<yourserver>/PHP_Projects/ Chapter.01/Chapter/Concerts.php*. Your Web browser should appear similar to Figure 1-20.

38

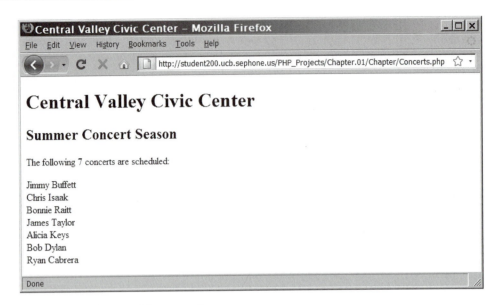

Figure 1-20 Output of Concerts.php

A looping statement provides a more efficient method for displaying all the elements of an array. You will learn about looping statements in Chapter 2.

5. Close your Web browser window.

PHP includes the `print_r()`, `var_export()`, and `var_dump()` functions, which you can use to display or return information about variables. These functions are most useful with arrays because they display the index and value of each element. You pass to each function the name of an array (or other type of variable). The following `print_r()` function displays the index and values of each element in the `$Provinces[]` array. Figure 1-21 shows the output. Notice in the figure that the 10 Canadian provinces are assigned to elements 0 through 9 in the `$Provinces[]` array.

```
print_r($Provinces);
```

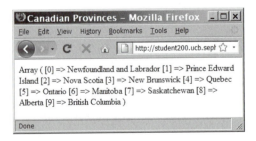

Figure 1-21 Output of the `$Provinces[]` array with the `print_r()` function

The print_r() function does not include any XHTML formatting tags, so the array elements are displayed as a continuous string of text. To display the array elements on individual lines instead, place the print_r() function between echo statements for opening and closing XHTML <pre> tags.

```
echo "<pre>";
print_r($Provinces);
echo "</pre>";
```

Modifying Elements

You modify values in existing array elements in the same fashion as you modify values in a standard variable, except that you include the index for an individual element of the array. The following code assigns values to the first three elements in an array named $HospitalDepts[]:

```
$HospitalDepts = array(
    "Anesthesia",        // first element (0)
    "Molecular Biology", // second element (1)
    "Neurology");        // third element (2)
```

After you have assigned a value to an array element, you can change it later, just as you can change other variables in a script. To change the first array element in the $HospitalDepts[] array from "Anesthesia" to "Anesthesiology," you use the following statement:

```
$HospitalDepts[0] = "Anesthesiology";
```

To modify the second and third elements in the $Concerts[] array from Bonnie Raitt and James Taylor to Joe Cocker and Van Morrison:

1. Return to the **Concerts.php** document in your text editor.

2. Add the following statements above the first echo statement:

```
$Concerts[2] = "Joe Cocker";
$Concerts[3] = "Van Morrison";
```

3. Save and upload the Concerts.php document and then validate it with the W3C XHTML Validator.

4. Open the Concerts.php file in your Web browser by entering the following URL: *http://<yourserver>/PHP_Projects/Chapter.01/Chapter/Concerts.php*. The concert list should include Joe Cocker and Van Morrison instead of Bonnie Raitt and James Taylor.

5. Close your Web browser window.

Avoiding Assignment Notation Pitfalls

In this section, you have learned three different assignment syntaxes. Each does something completely different, and it is easy to get them confused.

This statement assigns the string "Hello" to a variable named `$list`.

```
$list = "Hello";
```

This statement assigns the string "Hello" to a new element appended to the end of the `$list` array.

```
$list[] = "Hello";
```

This statement replaces the value stored in the first element (index 0) of the `$list` array with the string "Hello".

```
$list[0] = "Hello";
```

Short Quiz

1. Explain why you do not need to assign a specific data type to a variable when it is declared.

2. Positive and negative numbers and 0 with no decimal places belong to which data type?

3. Explain how you access the value of the second element in an array named `$signs`.

4. What function can be used to determine the total number of elements in an array?

5. Illustrate the value of using the `print_r()` function to return information about an array variable.

Building Expressions

Variables and data become most useful when you use them in an expression. An **expression** is a literal value or variable (or a combination of literal values, variables, operators, and other expressions) that can be evaluated by the PHP scripting engine to produce a result. You use operands and operators to create expressions in PHP. **Operands** are variables and literals contained in an expression. A **literal** is a static value such as a string or a number. **Operators** are symbols,

40

such as the addition operator (+) and multiplication operator (*), which are used in expressions to manipulate operands. You have worked with several simple expressions so far that combine operators and operands. Consider the following statement:

```
$MyNumber = 100;
```

This statement is an expression that results in the literal value 100 being assigned to $MyNumber. The operands in the expression are the $MyNumber variable name and the integer value 100. The operator is the equal sign (=). The equal sign is a special kind of operator, called an assignment operator, because it assigns the value 100 on the right side of the expression to the variable ($MyNumber) on the left side of the expression. Table 1-2 lists the main types of PHP operators. You will learn more about specific operators in the following sections.

This is not a comprehensive list of all supported PHP operator types. Several complex operator types are beyond the scope of this book and are not included in this list.

Type	Description
Array	Performs operations on arrays
Arithmetic	Performs mathematical calculations
Assignment	Assigns values to variables
Comparison	Compares operands and returns a Boolean value
Logical	Performs Boolean operations on Boolean operands
Special	Performs various tasks; these operators do not fit within other operator categories
String	Performs operations on strings

Table 1-2   PHP operator types

You study string operators in Chapter 3 and arrays in Chapter 6.

PHP operators are binary or unary. A **binary operator** requires an operand before and after the operator. The equal sign in the statement $MyNumber = 100; is an example of a binary operator. A **unary operator** requires a single operand either before or after the operator. For example, the increment operator (++), an arithmetic operator, is used for increasing an operand by a value of 1. The statement $MyNumber++; changes the value of the preceding $MyNumber variable to 101.

The operand to the left of an operator is known as the left operand, and the operand to the right of an operator is known as the right operand.

Next, you will learn more about the different types of PHP operators.

Arithmetic Operators

Arithmetic operators are used in PHP to perform mathematical calculations, such as addition, subtraction, multiplication, and division. You can also use an arithmetic operator to return the modulus of a calculation, which is the remainder left when you divide one number by another number.

Arithmetic Binary Operators

Table 1-3 lists the PHP binary arithmetic operators and their descriptions.

Symbol	Operation	Description
+	Addition	Adds two operands
−	Subtraction	Subtracts the right operand from the left operand
*	Multiplication	Multiplies two operands
/	Division	Divides the left operand by the right operand
%	Modulus	Divides the left operand by the right operand and returns the remainder

Table 1-3   PHP arithmetic binary operators

The following code shows examples of expressions that include arithmetic binary operators. Figure 1-22 shows how the expressions appear in a Web browser.

```
// ADDITION
$x = 100;
$y = 200;
$ReturnValue = $x + $y; // $ReturnValue is assigned the
                                 value 300
echo '<p>$ReturnValue after addition expression: ',
     $ReturnValue, "</p>";
// SUBTRACTION
$x = 10;
$y = 7;
$ReturnValue = $x - $y; // $ReturnValue changes to 3
echo '<p>$ReturnValue after subtraction expression: ',
     $ReturnValue, "</p>";
// MULTIPLICATION
$x = 2;
$y = 6;
$ReturnValue = $x * $y; // $ReturnValue changes to 12
echo '<p>$ReturnValue after multiplication expression: ',
     $ReturnValue, "</p>";
// DIVISION
$x = 24;
$y = 3;
$ReturnValue = $x / $y; // $ReturnValue changes to 8
echo '<p>$ReturnValue after division expression: ',
     $ReturnValue, "</p>";
// MODULUS
$x = 3;
$y = 2;
$ReturnValue = $x % $y; // $ReturnValue changes to 1
echo '<p>$ReturnValue after modulus expression: ',
     $ReturnValue, "</p>";
```

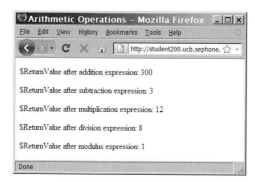

Figure 1-22   Results of arithmetic expressions

Notice in the preceding code that when PHP performs an arithmetic calculation, it performs the operation on the right side of the
assignment operator and then assigns the value to a variable on the
left side of the assignment operator. For example, in the statement
`$ReturnValue = $x + $y;`, the operands $x and $y are added, and
then the result is assigned to the `$ReturnValue` variable on the left
side of the assignment operator.

You might be confused by the difference between the division (/)
operator and the modulus (%) operator. The division operator performs a standard mathematical division operation. In comparison,
the modulus operator returns the remainder left from the division of
two integers. The following code, for instance, uses the division and
modulus operators to return the result of dividing 15 by 6. The result
is a value of 2.5, because 6 goes into 15 exactly 2.5 times. But if you
express this in whole numbers, 6 goes into 15 only 2 times, with a
remainder of 3. Thus, the modulus of 15 divided by 6 is 3 because 3 is
the remainder after the integer division. Figure 1-23 shows the output.

```
$DivisionResult = 15 / 6;
$ModulusResult = 15 % 6;
echo "<p>15 divided by 6 is
     $DivisionResult.</p>"; // displays '2.5'
echo "The whole number 6 goes into 15 twice, with a
     remainder of $ModulusResult.</p>"; // displays '3'
```

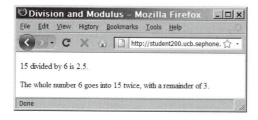

Figure 1-23   Division and modulus expressions

You can include a combination of variables and literal values on the right side of an assignment statement. For example, any of the following addition statements are correct:

```
$ReturnValue = 100 + $y;
$ReturnValue = $x + 200;
$ReturnValue = 100 + 200;
```

However, you cannot include a literal value as the left operand of an assignment operator because the PHP scripting engine must have a variable to which to assign the returned value. Therefore, the statement 100 = $x + $y; causes an error.

When performing arithmetic operations on string values, the PHP scripting engine attempts to convert the string values to numbers. The variables in the following example are assigned as string values instead of numbers because they are contained within quotation marks. Nevertheless, the PHP scripting engine correctly performs the multiplication operation and returns a value of 6.

```
$x = "2";
$y = "3";
$ReturnValue = $x * $y; // the value of $ReturnValue is 6
```

Arithmetic Unary Operators

Arithmetic operations can also be performed on a single variable using unary operators. Table 1-4 lists the unary arithmetic operators available in PHP.

Symbol	Operation	Description
++	Increment	Increases an operand by a value of 1
--	Decrement	Decreases an operand by a value of 1

Table 1-4   PHP arithmetic unary operators

The increment (++) and decrement (--) unary operators can be used as prefix or postfix operators. A **prefix operator** is placed before a variable. A **postfix operator** is placed after a variable. The statements ++$MyVariable; and $MyVariable++; both increase $MyVariable by 1. However, the two statements return different values. When you use the increment operator as a prefix operator, the value of the operand is increased by a value of 1 before it is returned. When you use the increment operator as a postfix operator, the value of the operand is increased by a value of 1 after it is returned. Similarly, when you use the decrement operator as a prefix operator, the value of the operand is decreased by a value of 1 before it is returned, and when you use the decrement operator as a postfix operator, the value of the operand is decreased by a value of 1 after it is returned. If you intend to assign the incremented or decremented value to another variable, it makes a difference whether you use the prefix or postfix operator.

You use arithmetic unary operators in any situation in which you prefer a simplified expression for increasing or decreasing a value by 1. For example, the statement $Count = $Count + 1; is identical to the statement ++$Count;. As you can see, if your goal is only to increase the value of a variable by 1, it is easier to use the unary increment operator.

For an example of when you would use the prefix operator or the postfix operator, consider an integer variable named $StudentID that is used for assigning student IDs in a class registration script. One way of creating a new student ID number is to store the last assigned student ID in the $StudentID variable. When it's time to assign a new student ID, the script could retrieve the last value stored in the $StudentID variable and then increase its value by 1. In other words, the last value stored in the $StudentID variable will be the next number used for a student ID number. In this case, you would use the postfix operator to increment the value of the expression *after* it is returned by using a statement similar to $CurStudentID = $StudentID++;. If you are storing the last assigned student ID in the $CurStudentID variable, you would want to increment the value by 1 and use the result as the next student ID. In this scenario, you would use the prefix operator, which increments the value of the expression *before* it is returned using a statement similar to $CurStudentID = ++$StudentID;.

Figure 1-24 shows a simple script that uses the prefix increment operator to assign three student IDs to a variable named $CurStudentID. The initial student ID is stored in the $StudentID variable and initialized to a starting value of 100. Figure 1-25 shows the output.

```
$StudentID = 100;
$CurStudentID = ++$StudentID; // assigns '101'
echo "<p>The first student ID is ",
    $CurStudentID, "</p>";                     ⎯ prefix increment operator
$CurStudentID = ++$StudentID; // assigns '102'
echo "<p>The second student ID is ",
    $CurStudentID, "</p>";
$CurStudentID = ++$StudentID; // assigns '103'
echo "<p>The third student ID is ",
    $CurStudentID, "</p>";
```

Figure 1-24   Script that uses the prefix increment operator

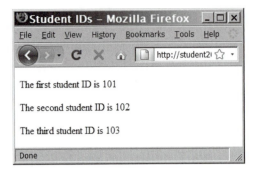

Figure 1-25 Output of the prefix version of the student ID script

The script in Figure 1-26 performs the same tasks, but uses a postfix increment operator. Notice that the output in Figure 1-27 differs from the output in Figure 1-25. Because the first example of the script uses the prefix increment operator, which increments the $StudentID variable *before* it is assigned to $CurStudentID, the script does not use the starting value of 100. Rather, it first increments the $StudentID variable and uses 101 as the first student ID. In comparison, the second example of the script does use the initial value of 100 because the postfix increment operator increments the $StudentID variable *after* it is assigned to the $CurStudentID variable.

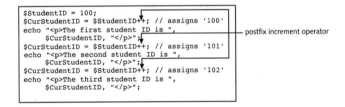

```
$StudentID = 100;
$CurStudentID = $StudentID++; // assigns '100'
echo "<p>The first student ID is ",
    $CurStudentID, "</p>";
$CurStudentID = $StudentID++; // assigns '101'
echo "<p>The second student ID is ",
    $CurStudentID, "</p>";
$CurStudentID = $StudentID++; // assigns '102'
echo "<p>The third student ID is ",
    $CurStudentID, "</p>";
```
postfix increment operator

Figure 1-26 Script that uses the postfix increment operator

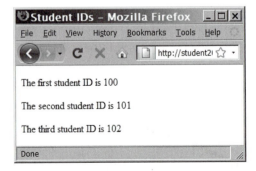

Figure 1-27 Output of the postfix version of the student ID script

To create a script that performs arithmetic calculations:

1. Create a new document in your text editor.

2. Type the `<!DOCTYPE>` declaration, `<html>` element, header information, and `<body>` element. Use the strict DTD and "Arithmetic Examples" as the content of the `<title>` element.

3. Add the following standard PHP script delimiters to the document body:

```
<?php
?>
```

4. Add the following statements to the script section to declare two variables. These statements include a `$Number` variable to contain a number, which you will use in several arithmetic operations, and a `$Result` variable to contain the value of each arithmetic operation.

```
$Number = 100;
$Result = 0;
```

5. Now add the following statements that perform addition, subtraction, multiplication, and division operations on the `$Number` variable and assign each value to the `$Result` variable. The `$Result` variable is displayed after each assignment statement.

```
$Result = $Number + 50;
echo '<p>$Result after addition = ', $Result, "<br />";
$Result = $Number / 4;
echo '$Result after division = ', $Result, "<br />";
$Result = $Number - 25;
echo '$Result after subtraction = ', $Result, "<br />";
$Result = $Number * 2;
echo '$Result after multiplication = ', $Result,
"<br />";
```

6. Next, add the following two statements. The first statement uses the increment operator to increase the value of the `$Number` variable by 1 and assigns the new value to the `$Result` variable. The second statement displays the `$Result` variable. Notice that the increment operator is used as a prefix operator, so the new value is assigned to the `$Result` variable. If you had used the postfix increment operator, the `$Number` variable would have been incremented by 1 after the old value of the `$Number` variable was assigned to the `$Result` variable.

```
$Result = ++$Number;
echo '$Result after increment = ', $Result, "</p>";
```

7. Save the document as **ArithmeticExamples.php** in the Chapter directory for Chapter 1, upload the document to the Web server, and then validate the document with the W3C XHTML Validator.

8. Open the ArithmeticExamples.php file in your Web browser by entering the following URL: *http://<yourserver>/PHP_Projects/Chapter.01/Chapter/ArithmeticExamples.php*. Figure 1-28 shows the output.

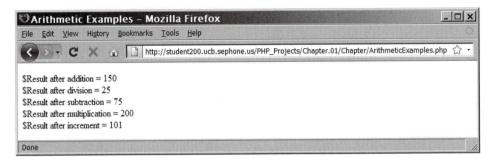

Figure 1-28 Output of ArithmeticExamples.php

9. Close your Web browser window.

Assignment Operators

Assignment operators are used for assigning a value to a variable. You have already used the most common assignment operator, the equal sign (=), to assign values to the variables that you declared. The equal sign assigns an initial value to a new variable or assigns a new value to an existing variable. For example, the following code creates a variable named $MyFavoriteSuperHero, uses the equal sign to assign it an initial value, and then uses the equal sign again to assign it a new value:

```
$MyFavoriteSuperHero = "Superman";
$MyFavoriteSuperHero = "Batman";
```

PHP includes other assignment operators in addition to the equal sign. These additional operators, called **compound assignment operators**, perform mathematical calculations on variables and literal values in an expression and then assign a new value to the left operand. Table 1-5 displays a list of the common PHP assignment operators.

Symbol	Operation	Description
=	Assignment	Assigns the value of the right operand to the left operand
+=	Compound addition assignment	Adds the value of the right operand to the value of the left operand and assigns the new value to the left operand
-=	Compound subtraction assignment	Subtracts the value of the right operand from the value of the left operand and assigns the new value to the left operand
*=	Compound multiplication assignment	Multiplies the value of the right operand by the value of the left operand and assigns the new value to the left operand
/=	Compound division assignment	Divides the value of the left operand by the value of the right operand and assigns the new value to the left operand
%=	Compound modulus assignment	Divides the value of the left operand by the value of the right operand and assigns the remainder (modulus) to the left operand

Table 1-5   Common PHP assignment operators

The following code shows examples of the different assignment operators. Figure 1-29 shows the output.

```
echo "<p>";
$x = 100;
$y = 200;
$x += $y; // $x changes to 300
echo $x, "<br />";
$x = 10;
$y = 7;
$x -= $y; // $x changes to 3
echo $x, "<br />";
$x = 2;
$y = 6;
$x *= $y; // $x changes to 12
echo $x, "<br />";
$x = 24;
$y = 3;
$x /= $y; // $x changes to 8
echo $x, "<br />";
$x = 3;
$y = 2;
$x %= $y; // $x changes to 1
echo $x, "<br />";
$x = "100";
$y = 5;
$x *= $y; // $x changes to 500
echo $x, "</p>";
```

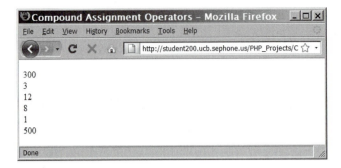

Figure 1-29 Assignment operators

To create a script that uses assignment operators:

1. Create a new document in your text editor.

2. Type the <!DOCTYPE> declaration, <html> element, header information, and <body> element. Use the strict DTD and "Assignment Examples" as the content of the <title> element.

3. Add the following standard PHP script delimiters to the document body:

    ```
    <?php
    ?>
    ```

4. Type the following statements in the script section. These statements perform several compound assignment operations on a variable named $ChangingVar. After each assignment operation, the result is displayed.

    ```
    $ChangingVar = 100;
    $ChangingVar += 50;
    echo "<p>";
    echo "Variable after addition assignment =
    $ChangingVar<br />";
    $ChangingVar -= 30;
    echo "Variable after subtraction assignment =
    $ChangingVar<br />";
    $ChangingVar /= 3;
    echo "Variable after division assignment =
    $ChangingVar<br />";
    $ChangingVar *= 8;
    echo "Variable after multiplication assignment =
    $ChangingVar<br />";
    $ChangingVar %= 300;
    echo "Variable after modulus assignment =
    $ChangingVar</p>";
    ```

5. Save the document as **AssignmentExamples.php** in the Chapter directory for Chapter 1, upload the document to the Web server, and then validate the document with the W3C XHTML Validator.

6. Open the AssignmentExamples.php file in your Web browser by entering the following URL: *http://<yourserver>/PHP_Projects/Chapter.01/Chapter/AssignmentExamples.php*. Figure 1-30 shows the output.

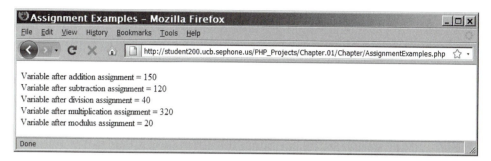

Figure 1-30 Output of AssignmentExamples.php

7. Close the Web browser window.

Comparison and Conditional Operators

Comparison operators are used to determine how one operand compares to another. A Boolean value of TRUE or FALSE is returned after two operands are compared. For example, the statement 5 < 3 returns a Boolean value of FALSE because 5 is not less than 3. Table 1-6 lists the PHP comparison operators.

Symbol	Operation	Description
==	Equal	Returns TRUE if the operands are equal
===	Strict equal	Returns TRUE if the operands are equal and of the same data type
!= or <>	Not equal	Returns TRUE if the operands are not equal
!==	Strict not equal	Returns TRUE if the operands are not equal or not of the same data type
>	Greater than	Returns TRUE if the left operand is greater than the right operand
<	Less than	Returns TRUE if the left operand is less than the right operand
>=	Greater than or equal to	Returns TRUE if the left operand is greater than or equal to the right operand
<=	Less than or equal to	Returns TRUE if the left operand is less than or equal to the right operand

Table 1-6 PHP comparison operators

The comparison operator == consists of two equal signs and performs a different function from the one performed by the assignment operator, which consists of a single equal sign (=). The comparison operator compares values, whereas the assignment operator assigns values.

Comparison operators are often used with two kinds of special statements: conditional statements and looping statements. You will learn how to use comparison operators in such statements in Chapter 2.

You can use number or string values as operands with comparison operators. When two numeric values are used as operands, the PHP scripting engine compares them numerically. For example, the statement $ReturnValue = 5 > 4; results in TRUE because the number 5 is numerically greater than the number 4. When two non-numeric values are used as operands, the PHP scripting engine compares them in alphabetical order. The statement $ReturnValue = "b" > "a"; returns TRUE because the letter *b* is alphabetically greater than the letter *a*. When one operand is a number and the other is a string, the PHP scripting engine attempts to convert the string value to a number. If the string value cannot be converted to a number, a value of FALSE is returned. For example, the statement $ReturnValue = 10 == "ten"; returns a value of FALSE because the PHP scripting engine cannot convert the string "ten" to a number. However, the statement $ReturnValue = 10 == "10"; returns a value of TRUE because the PHP scripting engine can convert the string "10" to a number.

The comparison operator is often used with another kind of operator, the conditional operator. The **conditional operator** executes one of two expressions, based on the results of a conditional expression. The syntax for the conditional operator is conditional_expression ? expression1 : expression2;. If conditional_expression evaluates to TRUE, expression1 executes. If conditional_expression evaluates to FALSE, expression2 executes.

The following code shows an example of the conditional operator:

```
$BlackjackPlayer1 = 20;
  ($BlackjackPlayer1 <= 21) ? $Result =
      "Player 1 is still in the game." : $Result =
      "Player 1 is out of the action.";
echo "<p>", $Result, "</p>";
```

In the example, the conditional expression checks to see if the $BlackjackPlayer1 variable is less than or equal to 21. If $BlackjackPlayer1 is less than or equal to 21, the text "Player 1 is still in the game" is assigned to the $Result variable. If $BlackjackPlayer1 is greater than 21, the text "Player 1 is out of the action" is assigned to the $Result variable. Because $BlackjackPlayer1 is equal to 20, the conditional statement returns a value of TRUE, the first expression executes, and "Player 1 is still in the game" appears on the screen. Figure 1-31 shows the output.

Figure 1-31 Output of a script with a conditional operator

To create a script that uses comparison and conditional operators:

1. Create a new document in your text editor.

2. Type the `<!DOCTYPE>` declaration, `<html>` element, header information, and `<body>` element. Use the strict DTD and "Comparison Examples" as the content of the `<title>` element.

3. Add the following standard PHP script delimiters to the document body:

   ```php
   <?php
   ?>
   ```

4. Add the following statements to the script section to perform various comparison operations on two variables. Notice that the comparison statements use the conditional operator to assign a text value of TRUE or FALSE to the $ReturnValue variable.

   ```php
   $Value1 = "first text string";
   $Value2 = "second text string";
   $ReturnValue = ($Value1 == $Value2 ? "true" :
   "false");
   echo '<p>$Value1 equal to $Value2: ', $ReturnValue,
   "<br />";
   $Value1 = 50;
   $Value2 = 75;
   $ReturnValue = ($Value1 == $Value2 ? "true" :
   "false");
   echo '$Value1 equal to $Value2: ', $ReturnValue,
   "<br />";
   $ReturnValue = ($Value1 != $Value2 ? "true" :
   "false");
   echo '$Value1 not equal to $Value2: ', $ReturnValue,
   "<br />";
   $ReturnValue = ($Value1 <> $Value2 ? "true" :
   "false");
   echo '$Value1 not equal to $Value2: ', $ReturnValue,
   "<br />";
   $ReturnValue = ($Value1 > $Value2 ? "true" :
   "false");
   ```

54

```
echo '$Value1 greater than $Value2: ', $ReturnValue,
"<br />";
$ReturnValue = ($Value1 < $Value2 ? "true" :
"false");
echo '$Value1 less than $Value2: ', $ReturnValue,
"<br />";
$ReturnValue = ($Value1 >= $Value2 ? "true" :
"false");
echo '$Value1 greater than or equal to $Value2: ',
$ReturnValue, "<br />";
$ReturnValue = ($Value1 <= $Value2 ? "true" :
"false");
echo '$Value1 less than or equal to $Value2 : ',
$ReturnValue, "<br />";
$Value1 = 25;
$Value2 = 25;
$ReturnValue = ($Value1 === $Value2 ? "true" :
"false");
echo '$Value1 equal to $Value2 AND the same data
type: ',
$ReturnValue, "<br />";
$ReturnValue = ($Value1 !== $Value2 ? "true" :
"false");
echo '$Value1 not equal to $Value2 AND not the same
data type: ',
$ReturnValue, "</p>";
```

5. Save the document as **ComparisonExamples.php** in the Chapter directory for Chapter 1, upload the document to the Web server, and then validate the document with the W3C XHTML Validator.

6. Open the ComparisonExamples.php file in your Web browser by entering the following URL: *http://<yourserver>/ PHP_Projects/Chapter.01/Chapter/ComparisonExamples.php*. Figure 1-32 shows the output.

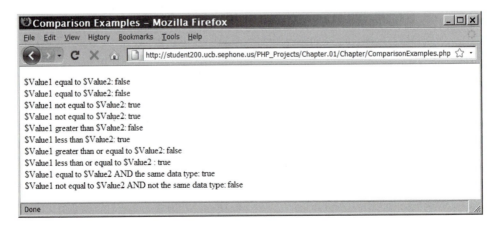

Figure 1-32 Output of ComparisonExamples.php

7. Close your Web browser window.

Logical Operators

Logical operators are used for comparing two Boolean operands for equality. **Boolean operands** are operands that are limited to the values TRUE or FALSE. For example, a script for an automobile insurance company might need to determine whether a customer is male *and* under 21 to determine the correct insurance quote. As with comparison operators, a Boolean value of TRUE or FALSE is returned after two operands are compared. Table 1-7 lists the PHP logical operators.

Symbol	Operation	Description
&& or AND	Logical And	Returns TRUE if both the left operand and right operand return a value of TRUE; otherwise, it returns a value of FALSE
|| or OR	Logical Or	Returns TRUE if either the left operand or right operand returns a value of TRUE; otherwise (neither operand returns a value of TRUE), it returns a value of FALSE
XOR	Logical Exclusive Or	Returns TRUE if only one of the left operand or right operand returns a value of TRUE; otherwise (neither operand returns a value of TRUE or both operands return a value of TRUE), it returns a value of FALSE
!	Logical Not	Returns TRUE if an expression is FALSE and returns FALSE if an expression is TRUE

Table 1-7 PHP logical operators

For the logical Or operator, you can use either || or OR. For the logical And operator, you can use either && or AND. The logical Or, logical Exclusive Or, and the logical And operators are binary operators (requiring two operands), whereas the logical Not (!) operator is a unary operator (requiring a single operand). Logical operators are often used with comparison operators to evaluate expressions, allowing you to combine the results of several expressions into a single statement. For example, the logical And operator is used to determine whether two operands return an equivalent value. The operands themselves are often expressions. The following code uses the logical And (&&) operator to compare two separate expressions:

```
$Gender = "male";
$Age = 17;
$RiskFactor =
    $Gender=="male" && $Age<=21; // returns TRUE
```

In the preceding example, the $Gender variable expression evaluates to TRUE because it is equal to "male" and the $Age variable expression evaluates to TRUE because its value is less than or equal to 21. Because both expressions are TRUE, $RiskFactor is assigned a value of TRUE. The statement containing the logical And operator (&&) essentially says, "If variable $Gender is equal to 'male' *and* variable $Age is less than or equal to 21, then assign a value of TRUE to $RiskFactor. Otherwise, assign a value of FALSE to $RiskFactor." In the following code, however, $RiskFactor is assigned a value of FALSE because the $Age variable expression does not evaluate to TRUE. Notice that the following code uses the AND version of the logical And operator.

```
$Gender = "male";
$Age = 28;
$RiskFactor =
        $Gender=="male" AND $Age<=21; // returns FALSE
```

The logical Or operator checks to see if either expression evaluates to TRUE. For example, the statement containing the logical Or operator (||) in the following code says, "If variable $SpeedingTicket is greater than 0 *or* variable $Age is less than or equal to 21, then assign a value of TRUE to $RiskFactor. Otherwise, assign a value of FALSE to $RiskFactor."

```
$SpeedingTicket = 2;
$Age = 28;
$RiskFactor =
        $SpeedingTicket > 0 || $Age <= 21; // returns TRUE
```

The $RiskFactor variable in the preceding example is assigned a value of TRUE because the $SpeedingTicket variable expression evaluates to TRUE, even though the $Age variable expression evaluates to FALSE. This result occurs because the logical Or operator returns TRUE if *either* the left *or* right operand evaluates to TRUE. The following example shows another version of the preceding code, but this time using the OR version of the logical Or operator:

```
$SpeedingTicket = 2;
$Age = 28;
$RiskFactor =
        $SpeedingTicket > 0 OR $Age <= 21; // returns TRUE
```

The following code is an example of the logical Not (!) operator, which returns TRUE if an operand evaluates to FALSE and returns FALSE if an operand evaluates to TRUE. Notice that because the logical Not (!) operator is unary, it requires only a single operand.

```
$TrafficViolations = true;
$SafeDriverDiscount =
        !$TrafficViolations; // returns FALSE
```

The following code is an example of the logical Exclusive Or (XOR) operator, which returns TRUE if only one of the operands is TRUE, but not both.

```
$RightSideSteering = true;
$Country = "England";
$IncorrectSteering =
    $RightSideSteering == true
    XOR $Country == "England"; // returns FALSE
```

To create a script that uses logical operators:

 Logical operators are often used within conditional and looping statements such as the if...else, for, and while statements. You will learn about conditional and looping statements in Chapter 2.

1. Create a new document in your text editor.

2. Type the <!DOCTYPE> declaration, <html> element, header information, and <body> element. Use the strict DTD and "Logical Examples" as the content of the <title> element.

3. Add the following standard PHP script delimiters to the document body:

   ```
   <?php
   ?>
   ```

4. Add the following statements to the script section that use logical operators on two variables. The conditional expressions evaluate the logical expressions and then assign a text value of TRUE or FALSE to the $ReturnValue variable.

   ```
   $TrueValue = true;
   $FalseValue = false;
   $ReturnValue = ($TrueValue ? "true" : "false");
   echo "<p>$ReturnValue<br />";
   $ReturnValue = ($FalseValue ? "true" : "false");
   echo "$ReturnValue<br />";
   $ReturnValue = ($TrueValue || $FalseValue ? "true" :
   "false");
   echo "$ReturnValue<br />";
   $ReturnValue = ($TrueValue && $FalseValue ? "true" :
   "false");
   echo "$ReturnValue<br />";
   echo "</p>";
   ```

5. Save the document as **LogicalExamples.php** in the Chapter directory for Chapter 1, upload the document to the Web server, and then validate the document with the W3C XHTML Validator.

6. Open the LogicalExamples.php file from your Web server by entering the following URL: *http://<yourserver>/PHP_Projects/Chapter.01/Chapter/LogicalExamples.php*. Figure 1-33 shows the output.

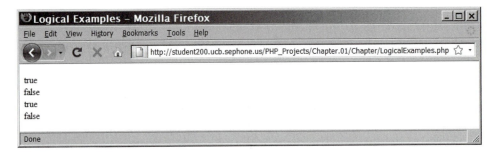

Figure 1-33   Output of LogicalExamples.php

7. Close the Web browser window.

Special Operators

PHP also includes the special operators that are listed in Table 1-8. These operators are used for various purposes and do not fit within any other category.

Symbol	Operation
[and]	Accesses an element of an array
=>	Specifies the index or key of an array element
,	Separates arguments in a list
? and :	Executes one of two expressions based on the results of a conditional expression
instanceof	Returns TRUE if an object is of a specified object type
@	Suppresses any errors that might be generated by an expression to which it is prepended (or placed before)
(int), (integer), (bool), (boolean), (double), (string), (array), (object)	Casts (or transforms) a variable of one data type into a variable of another data type

Table 1-8   PHP special operators

You will be introduced to the special PHP operators as necessary throughout this book, beginning with the casting operators in the next section.

Type Casting

Even though PHP automatically assigns the data type of a variable, sometimes you want to ensure that a variable is of the data type expected by your script. One way to ensure this is through **casting**, or **type casting**, which copies the value contained in a variable of one data type into a variable of another data type. The PHP syntax for casting variables is $NewVariable = (new_type) $OldVariable;. The (new_type) portion of the syntax is the type-casting operator representing the type to which you want to cast the variable. Note that casting does not change the data type of the original variable. Rather, casting copies the data from the old variable, converts it to the data type specified by the type-casting operator, and then assigns the value to the new variable.

Type-casting operators are useful because the data type of variables can change during the course of program execution. This can cause problems if you attempt to perform an arithmetic operation on a variable that happens to contain a string or the NULL value. For example, the first statement in the following code assigns a string value of "55 mph" to a variable named $SpeedLimitMiles. The second statement then multiplies the $SpeedLimitMiles variable by 1.6 to convert the value to kilometers. Notice that the second statement also includes the (int) operator, which converts the string value in the $SpeedLimitMiles variable to an integer.

```
$SpeedLimitMiles = "55 mph";
$SpeedLimitKilometers = (int) $SpeedLimitMiles * 1.6;
echo "$SpeedLimitMiles is equal to
    $SpeedLimitKilometers kph";
```

The third statement in the preceding code displays the text "55 mph is equal to 88 kph" to the Web browser. The (int) operator converted the string value of "55 mph" to an integer value of 55, which was multiplied by 1.6 to calculate the kilometers. To be honest, the PHP scripting engine would have performed the type cast automatically, without the (int) operator. However, it doesn't hurt to use type casting to ensure that your variables are of the expected data type. This is especially true if you need to perform operations on data that is entered by users. As you will learn in Chapter 4, one of the most common uses of PHP is to process form data that is submitted from a client. You cannot be sure that a user will enter form data correctly, so it's a good idea for you to ensure that the data entered is of the type expected by your script.

PHP can convert a string to a numeric value if the string starts with a numeric value. Any subsequent non-numeric characters are ignored.

You can also perform a type cast with the settype() function.

Instead of just guessing data types, you can view a variable's type by using the gettype() function, which returns one of the following strings, depending on the data type:

- Boolean

- Integer

- Double

- String

- Array

- Object

- Resource

- NULL

- Unknown type

You pass the name of a variable to the gettype() function as a parameter using the syntax gettype($variable_name);. For example, the first statement in the following code declares a double variable named $MortgageRate (a **double** is a PHP floating-point number). The second statement passes the name of the $MortgageRate variable to the gettype() function. The value returned from the gettype() function is then displayed by an echo statement. The following code displays the text string "double" to the screen.

```
$MortgageRate = .0575;
echo gettype($MortgageRate);
```

Although you can use the gettype() function to view a variable's data type, there are easier ways within PHP to determine if a variable is of a specific data type. The best way is to use one of the 15 is_*() functions that test for various kinds of data types. Each function returns a Boolean value to indicate whether the variable is of a given data type. For instance, the is_numeric() function tests whether a variable contains a numeric data type, whereas the is_string() function tests whether a variable contains a string data type. There are also more specific is_*() functions, such as the is_int() function, which tests whether a variable is an integer data type, and the is_double() function, which tests whether a variable is a double data type. To use an is_*() function, you pass a variable name as an argument to the function you want to use. The following example uses the is_double() function along with the conditional operator to test the data type of the $MortgageRate variable. The conditional expression passes the $MortgageRate variable to the is_double() function, and then determines whether the returned result is TRUE. Because the $MortgageRate variable is a double data type, a value of TRUE is returned with the text "The variable contains a decimal number."

```
$MortgageRate = .0575;
$Result = ((is_double($MortgageRate)) ?
    "The variable contains a decimal number." :
    "The variable does not contain a decimal number.");
echo $Result;
```

The following example contains a modified version of the miles-to-kilometers script. This time, a conditional operator uses the is_int() function to determine whether the $SpeedLimitMiles variable is an integer. If the variable is an integer, its value is simply multiplied by 1.6 and assigned to the $SpeedLimitKilometers variable. However, if the variable is not an integer (in this case, it's not), its value is cast to an integer data type before being multiplied by 1.6 and assigned to the $SpeedLimitKilometers variable.

```
$SpeedLimitMiles = "55 mph";
$SpeedLimitKilometers = ((is_int($SpeedLimitMiles)) ?
    $SpeedLimitMiles * 1.6 :
    (int) $SpeedLimitMiles * 1.6);
echo "$SpeedLimitMiles is equal to
    $SpeedLimitKilometers kph";
```

Understanding Operator Precedence

When using operators to create expressions in PHP, you need to be aware of the precedence of an operator. The term **operator precedence** refers to the order in which operations in an expression are evaluated. Table 1-9 shows the order of precedence for PHP operators. Operators in the same grouping in Table 1-9 have the same order of precedence. When performing operations with operators in the same precedence group, the order of precedence is determined by the operators' **associativity**—that is, the order in which operators of equal precedence execute. Associativity is evaluated on a left-to-right or a right-to-left basis.

Symbol	Operator	Associativity
new clone	New object—highest precedence	None
[]	Array elements	Right to left
++ --	Increment/Decrement	Right to left
(int) (double) (string) (array) (object)	Cast	Right to left
@	Suppress errors	Right to left

Table 1-9   Operator precedence in PHP *(continues)*

(continued)

Symbol	Operator	Associativity
`instanceof`	Types	None
`!`	Logical Not	Right to left
`* / %`	Multiplication/division/modulus	Left to right
`+ - .`	Addition/subtraction/string concatenation	Left to right
`< <= > >= <>`	Comparison	None
`== != === !==`	Equality	None
`&&`	Logical And	Left to right
`||`	Logical Or	Left to right
`?:`	Conditional	Left to right
`= += -= *= /= %= .=`	Assignment	Right to left
`AND`	Logical And	Left to right
`XOR`	Logical Exclusive Or	Left to right
`OR`	Logical Or	Left to right
`,`	List separator—lowest precedence	Left to right

Table 1-9 Operator precedence in PHP

The preceding list in Table 1-9 does not include bitwise operators.

Operators in a higher grouping have precedence over operators in a lower grouping. For example, the multiplication operator (*) has a higher precedence than the addition operator (+). Therefore, the statement 5 + 2 * 8 evaluates as follows: The numbers 2 and 8 are multiplied first for a total of 16, and then the number 5 is added, resulting in a total of 21. If the addition operator had a higher precedence than the multiplication operator, the statement would evaluate to 56 because 5 would be added to 2 for a total of 7, which would then be multiplied by 8.

As an example of how associativity is evaluated, consider the multiplication and division operators, which have an associativity of left to right. This means that the statement 30 / 5 * 2 results in a value of 12—although the multiplication and division operators have equal precedence, the division operation executes first due to the left-to-right associativity of both operators. If the operators had right-to-left associativity, the statement 30 / 5 * 2 would result in a value of 3 because the multiplication operation (5 * 2) would execute first. By comparison, the assignment operator and compound assignment operators, such as the compound multiplication assignment operator (*=), have an associativity of right to left. Therefore, in the following code, the assignment operations take place from right to left. The variable $x is incremented by 1 *before* it is assigned to the $y variable using the compound multiplication assignment operator (*=). Then, the value of variable $y is assigned to variable $x. The result assigned to both the $x and $y variables is 8.

```
$x = 3;
$y = 2;
$x = $y *= ++$x;
```

You can use parentheses with expressions to change the associativity with which individual operations in an expression are evaluated. For example, the statement 5 + 2 * 8, which evaluates to 21, can be rewritten to (5 + 2) * 8, which evaluates to 56. The parentheses tell the PHP scripting engine to add the numbers 5 and 2 before multiplying by the number 8. Using parentheses forces the statement to evaluate to 56 instead of 21.

Short Quiz

1. What symbol is used to divide the left operand by the right operand and return the remainder?

2. Explain the difference between an assignment operator and a compound assignment operator.

3. Explain the difference between a prefix operator and a postfix operator.

4. Define the term "associativity" as it applies to the order of precedence.

Summing Up

- JavaScript and PHP are both referred to as embedded languages because code for both languages is embedded within a Web page (either an HTML or XHTML document).

- You write PHP scripts within code declaration blocks, which are separate sections within a Web page that are interpreted by the scripting engine.

- The individual lines of code that make up a PHP script are called statements.

- The term "function" refers to a subroutine (or individual statements grouped into a logical unit) that performs a specific task.

- Comments are nonexecuting lines that you place in code to contain various types of remarks, including the name of the script, your name and the date you created the program, notes to yourself, or instructions to future programmers who might need to modify your work. Comments do not appear in output or change the functionality of the script.

- The values a program stores in computer memory are commonly called variables.

- The name you assign to a variable is called an identifier.

- A constant contains information that cannot change during the course of program execution.

- A data type is the specific category of information that a variable contains.

- PHP is a loosely typed programming language.

- An integer is a positive or negative number or zero, with no decimal places.

- A floating-point number contains decimal places or is written in exponential notation.

- A Boolean value is a logical value of "true" or "false".

- An array contains a set of data represented by a single variable name.

- An expression is a single literal value or variable, or a combination of literal values, variables, operators, and other expressions, that can be evaluated by the PHP scripting engine to produce a result.

- Operands are variables and literals contained in an expression. A literal is a value such as a string or a number.

- Operators are symbols, such as the addition operator (+) and multiplication operator (*), used in expressions to manipulate operands.

- A binary operator requires an operand before and after the operator.

- A unary operator requires a single operand either before or after the operator.

- Arithmetic operators are used in the PHP scripting engine to perform mathematical calculations, such as addition, subtraction, multiplication, and division.

- Assignment operators are used for assigning a value to a variable.

- Comparison operators are used to determine how one operand compares with another.

- The conditional operator executes one of two expressions, based on the results of a conditional expression.

- Logical operators are used to perform operations on Boolean operands.

- Casting or type casting creates an equivalent value in a specific data type for a given value.

- Operator precedence is the order in which operations in an expression are evaluated.

Comprehension Check

1. What is the default extension that most Web servers use to process PHP scripts?

    a. .php

    b. .html

    c. .xhtml

    d. .ini

2. What do you use to separate multiple arguments that are passed to a function?

    a. a period (.)

    b. a comma (,)

    c. a forward slash (/)

    d. a backward slash (\)

3. You create line comments in PHP code by adding _____ to a line you want to use as a comment. (Choose all that apply.)

    a. ||

    b. **

    c. #

    d. //

4. Block comments begin with /* and end with _____.

   a. */

   b. /*

   c. //

   d. **

5. Which of the following is a valid variable name?

   a. SalesOrder

   b. salesOrder

   c. $SalesOrder

   d. $1SalesOrder

6. You are not required to initialize a variable when you first declare it in PHP. True or False?

7. Which is the correct syntax for declaring a variable and assigning it a string?

   a. $MyVariable = "Hello";

   b. $MyVariable = "Hello"

   c. "Hello" = $MyVariable;

   d. $MyVariable = Hello;

8. Explain the concept of data types.

9. Explain the purpose of the NULL data type.

10. A loosely typed programming language _____.

    a. does not require data types of variables to be declared

    b. requires data types of variables to be declared

    c. does not have different data types

    d. does not have variables

11. How many decimal places does an integer store?

    a. zero

    b. one

    c. two

    d. as many as necessary

12. Which of the following values can be assigned to a Boolean variable? (Choose all that apply.)

    a. TRUE

    b. FALSE

    c. 1

    d. YES

13. Which of the following refers to the first element in an indexed array named `$Employees[]`?

    a. `$Employees[0]`

    b. `$Employees[1]`

    c. `$Employees[first]`

    d. `$Employees[a]`

14. The modulus operator (%) _____.

    a. converts an operand to base 16 (hexadecimal) format

    b. returns the absolute value of an operand

    c. calculates the percentage of one operand compared to another

    d. divides two operands and returns the remainder

15. What value is assigned to the `$ReturnValue` variable in the statement `$ReturnValue = 100 != 200;`?

    a. TRUE

    b. FALSE

    c. 100

    d. 200

16. Which arithmetic operators can be used as both prefix and postfix operators? (Choose all that apply.)

    a. ++

    b. --

    c. +

    d. -

17. The logical And (&&) operator returns TRUE if _____.

    a. the left operand returns a value of TRUE

    b. the right operand returns a value of TRUE

    c. the left operand and right operand both return a value of TRUE

    d. the left operand and right operand both return a value of FALSE

18. What value is assigned to the $ReturnValue variable in the statement $ReturnValue = !$x;, assuming that $x has a value of TRUE?

    a. TRUE

    b. FALSE

    c. NULL

    d. undefined

19. The order of priority in which operations in an expression are evaluated is known as _____.

    a. prerogative precedence

    b. operator precedence

    c. expression evaluation

    d. priority evaluation

20. What is the value of the expression 4 * (2 + 3)?

    a. 11

    b. -11

    c. 20

    d. 14

Reinforcement Exercises

 Exercise 1-1

In this project, you will create and modify a script that stores interest rates in an array.

1. Create a new document in your text editor.

2. Type the `<!DOCTYPE>` declaration, `<html>` element, header information, and `<body>` element. Use the strict DTD and "Interest Array" as the content of the `<title>` element.

3. Add the following standard PHP script delimiters to the document body:

```
<?php
?>
```

4. Add the following statements to the script section:

```
$InterestRate1 = .0725;
$InterestRate2 = .0750;
$InterestRate3 = .0775;
$InterestRate4 = .0800;
$InterestRate5 = .0825;
$InterestRate6 = .0850;
$InterestRate7 = .0875;
```

5. Using the `array()` construct, modify the statements you added in the preceding step so the variables are saved in an array named `$RatesArray`. Also, add statements to the program that display the contents of each array element.

6. Save the document as **InterestArray.php** in the Projects directory for Chapter 1, upload the document to the server, and then validate it with the W3C XHTML Validator. After the document is valid, open it in your Web browser to see how it renders.

7. Close your Web browser window.

 ## Exercise 1-2

What value is assigned to `$ReturnValue` for each of the following expressions?

1. `$ReturnValue = 2 == 3;`

2. `$ReturnValue = "2" + "3";`

3. `$ReturnValue = 2 >= 3;`

4. `$ReturnValue = 2 <= 3;`

5. `$ReturnValue = 2 + 3;`

6. `$ReturnValue = (2 >= 3) && (2 > 3);`

7. `$ReturnValue = (2 >= 3) || (2 > 3);`

Exercise 1-3

You use the number_format() function when you want to format the appearance of a number. The number_format() function adds commas that separate thousands and determines the number of decimal places to display. You can pass two arguments to the number_format() function: The first argument represents the literal number or variable you want to format, and the second argument determines the number of decimal places to display. If you exclude the second argument, the number is formatted without decimal places.

In this project, you will create a script that demonstrates how to use the number_format() function.

1. Create a new document in your text editor.

2. Type the <!DOCTYPE> declaration, <html> element, header information, and <body> element. Use the strict DTD and "Single Family Home" as the content of the <title> element.

3. Add the following standard PHP script delimiters to the document body:

```
<?php
?>
```

4. Add the following statements to the script section. The first statement assigns an integer value to a variable named $SingleFamilyHome. The second statement then formats the value in the $SingleFamilyHome variable and assigns the formatted number to the $SingleFamilyHome_Print variable. The number in the $SingleFamilyHome_Print variable will include a comma that separates the thousands and will include two decimal places. The final statement displays the formatted number on the screen.

```
$SingleFamilyHome = 399500;
$SingleFamilyHome_Display =
    number_format($SingleFamilyHome, 2);
echo "<p>The current median price of a single family
    home in Pleasanton, CA is
    $$SingleFamilyHome_Display.</p>";
```

5. Save the document as **SingleFamilyHome.php** in the Projects folder for Chapter 1, upload the document to the server, and then validate it with the W3C XHTML Validator. After the document is valid, close it in your text editor, and then open it in your Web browser to see how it renders. You should see the text "The current median price of a single family home in Pleasanton, CA is $399,500.00." displayed on the screen.

6. Close your Web browser window.

 ## Exercise 1-4

Write a script that assigns the days of the week to an array named $Days[]. Use output statements to display "The days of the week in English are: " along with the values in the $Days[] array. Following the output statements, reassign the values in the $Days[] array with the days of the week in French. Sunday is *Dimanche*, Monday is *Lundi*, Tuesday is *Mardi*, Wednesday is *Mercredi*, Thursday is *Jeudi*, Friday is *Vendredi*, and Saturday is *Samedi*. Then use output statements to display "The days of the week in French are: " along with the French values in the $Days[] array. Save the document as **DaysArray.php**.

 ## Exercise 1-5

You can use the round(), ceil(), and floor() functions to round a fraction up or down to the nearest whole number. The round() function rounds a fraction to the nearest whole number, the ceil() function rounds a fraction up to the nearest whole number, and the floor() function rounds a fraction down to the nearest whole number. Write a script that demonstrates the use of these functions. Save the document as **RoundedValues.php**.

 ## Exercise 1-6

Write a script that uses a conditional operator to determine whether a variable contains a number and whether the number is even. You need to use the is_numeric() function and the conditional operator. For floating-point numbers, you need to use the round() function to convert the value to the nearest whole number. Save the document as **IsEven.php**.

Discovery Projects

At the end of each chapter, you will apply the concepts you have learned to a single, ongoing project. When completed, this project will be a comprehensive Web site that demonstrates application of many of the PHP concepts covered in the textbook. The Chinese zodiac theme was selected because it lends itself well to many of the PHP constructs you will learn in future chapters. All files for the Chinese Zodiac site will be saved in a folder named ChineseZodiac in the root Web folder on the server.

The following Discovery Projects will prepare you for the design and development of your site:

Discovery Project 1-1

You will need to select a color scheme and design or find free Chinese zodiac graphic elements. You can search on the Web for free theme sets or image sets that contain banners, borders, background images, buttons, icons, lines, and bullets designed around a specific theme.

If your site layout is designed to have buttons at the top and a text navigation bar on the left, you will want a banner that is approximately 392×72 pixels. If you plan to have both the button navigation and text navigation at the top, you will want a banner that is approximately 468×60 pixels.

Create a Web banner image with a title of "The Chinese Zodiac" and a subtitle of "A Code Demonstration for PHP".

Save the banner image as ChineseZodiacBanner with an appropriate graphic extension *(.jpg, .gif, or .png)* in an Images folder within the ChineseZodiac folder and upload the document to the server.

Open the ChineseZodiacBanner image in both Internet Explorer and Mozilla Firefox to determine if it displays well on the Web.

Discovery Project 1-2

Create nine buttons (approximately 150×30 pixels) with the following face texts and filenames: "Home Page" = HomePage.*img*, "Site Layout" = SiteLayout.*img*, "Control Structures" = ControlStructures.*img*, "String Functions" = StringFunctions.*img*, "Web Forms" = WebForms.*img*, "Midterm Assessment" = MidtermAssessment.*img*, "State Information" = StateInformation.*img*, "User Templates" = UserTemplates.*img*, and "Final Project" = FinalProject.*img*. Replace *.img* with the appropriate extension for the image file type, such as .jpg, .gif, or .png. Save the buttons in the Images folder within the ChineseZodiac folder and upload the buttons to the server.

Discovery Project 1-3

Research the Chinese zodiac and write a few paragraphs about it in your text editor to acquaint your audience with the concept of the Chinese horoscope and its origin. Cite your sources. Save the document as **ChineseZodiac.txt** in the ChineseZodiac folder and upload the document to the server.

Discovery Project 1-4

Search for free images (in any size) for each of the 12 signs of the Chinese zodiac. You will use these images in later projects. Try to find images that are similar in size, style, and form. Try to keep the height of the image between 50 and 100 pixels, and the width of the image between 50 and 150 pixels. Use the name of the sign as the name of the image file (as in Rooster.jpg or Pig.gif). Save each of the images with an appropriate extension in the Images folder within the ChineseZodiac folder, and upload the images to the server.

Functions and Control Structures

In this chapter, you will:

◎ Study how to use functions to organize your PHP code

◎ Learn about variable scope

◎ Make decisions using `if`, `if...else`, and `switch` statements

◎ Repeatedly execute code using `while`, `do...while`, `for`, and `foreach` statements

◎ Learn about `include` and `require` statements

So far, the code you have written has consisted of simple statements placed within script sections. However, almost all programming languages, including PHP, allow you to group programming statements into logical units. In PHP, groups of statements that you can execute as a single unit are called **functions**. You will learn how to create your own custom functions in this chapter. The code you have written so far has also been linear in nature. In other words, your programs start at the beginning and end when the last statement in the program executes. Decision-making and looping statements allow you to determine the order in which other statements execute in a program. Controlling the flow of code and making decisions during program execution are two of the most fundamental skills required in programming. In this chapter, you will learn about decision-making statements and flow-control statements.

Working with Functions

In Chapter 1, you learned that PHP includes numerous built-in functions that you can use in your scripts. Functions are useful because they make it possible to treat a related group of PHP statements as a single unit. In this section, you will learn how to write custom functions. Then, you will learn how to use these functions in your scripts.

Defining Functions

Before you can use a function in a PHP program, you must first create, or define, it. The lines of code that make up a function are called the **function definition**. The syntax for defining a function is as follows:

```php
<?php
function name_of_function(parameters) {
    statement(s);
}
?>
```

Parameters are placed within the parentheses that follow the function name. A **formal parameter**, or simply a **parameter**, is a variable that is passed to a function when it is called. To declare a parameter, you only need to place the parameter name within the parentheses of a function definition. In other words, you do not need to explicitly declare and initialize a parameter as you do a regular variable. For example, suppose you want to write a function named `calculateSalesTotal()` that calculates the sales total of a number contained in a parameter named `$Subtotal` for an online transaction. The function name would be written as

As shown in the preceding example, functions must be contained within `<?php ... ?>` tags, like all PHP code.

Functions do not have to contain parameters. Many functions only perform a task and do not require external data. For example, you might create a function that displays the same message each time a user visits your Web site; this type of function only needs to be executed and does not require any other information.

76

calculateSalesTotal($Subtotal). In this case, the function declaration is declaring a new formal parameter (which is a variable) named $Subtotal. Functions can contain multiple parameters separated by commas. To declare three separate number parameters in the calculateSalesTotal() function, you might write the function name as calculateSalesTotal($Subtotal, $SalesTax, $Shipping). Note that parameters such as $Subtotal, $SalesTax, and $Shipping receive their values when you call the function from elsewhere in your program. You can also assign default values to a parameter as follows:

```
function sampleFunction($Num1="100", $Num2="200",
$Num3="300") {
     echo ("<p>$Num1</p>");
     echo ("<p>$Num2</p>");
     echo ("<p>$Num3</p>");
}
```

Following the parentheses that contain the function parameters is a set of curly braces (called function braces) that contain the function statements. Function statements do the actual work of the function (such as calculating the sales total), and must be contained within the function braces. The following example of a function displays the names of multiple companies:

```
function displayCompanyName($Company1, $Company2,
$Company3) {
     echo "<p>$Company1</p>";
     echo "<p>$Company2</p>";
     echo "<p>$Company3</p>";
}
```

Notice how the preceding function is structured. The opening curly brace is on the same line as the function name, and the closing curly brace is on its own line following the function statements. Each statement between the curly braces is indented five character spaces. This structure is one standard format used by PHP programmers. However, other formats are used; many originated with other programming languages and were carried forward to use with PHP. Remember that tabs, spaces, and line breaks are included to help the programmer and are ignored by the PHP scripting engine. For simple functions, it is often easier to include the function name, curly braces, and statements on the same line. For example, the following simplified version of the displayCompanyName() function is declared on a single line:

```
function displayCompanyName($Company) {
     echo "<p>$Company</p>"; }
```

Calling Functions

A function definition does not execute automatically. Creating a function definition only names the function, specifies its parameters, and organizes the statements it will execute. As you learned in Chapter 1, you must use a function call to execute a function from elsewhere in your program. When you pass arguments to a function, the value of each argument is assigned to the value of the corresponding formal parameter in the function definition. (Again, remember that formal parameters are simply variables that are declared within a function definition.)

In PHP 3 and earlier, it was necessary to put a function definition above any calling statements to ensure that the function was created before it was actually called. If you did not follow this convention, you received an error. This convention is no longer necessary in PHP 4 and later versions, but you should continue to place your function definitions above any calling statements to comply with good programming practices. The following code shows a script that displays the name of a company. Figure 2-1 shows the output. Notice that the function is defined above the calling statement.

```php
function displayCompanyName($CompanyName) {
    echo "<p>$CompanyName</p>";
}
displayCompanyName("Course Technology");
```

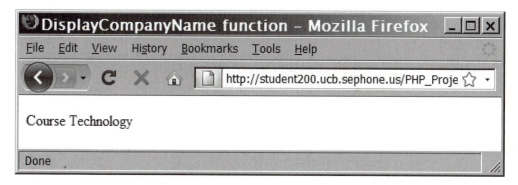

Figure 2-1   Output of a call to a custom function

The script that generates the output shown in Figure 2-1 contains a statement that calls the function and passes the literal string "Course Technology" to the function. When the displayCompanyName() function receives the literal string, it assigns the string to the $CompanyName variable.

Unlike variables, function names are case insensitive, which means you can call the displayCompanyName() function with any of the following statements:

```
displayCompanyName("Course Technology");
DisplayCompanyName("Course Technology");
DISPLAYCOMPANYNAME("Course Technology");
```

However, it is good practice to always call a function using the same case that was used to define the function name.

Returning Values

In many instances, you might want your program to receive the results from a called function and then use those results in other code. For instance, consider a function that calculates the average of a series of numbers that are passed to it as arguments. Such a function is useless if your program cannot display or use the result elsewhere. As another example, suppose you have created a function that simply displays the name of a company. Suppose also that you want to alter the program so it uses the company name in another section of code. You can return a value from a function to a calling statement by assigning the calling statement to a variable. The following statement calls a function named averageNumbers() and assigns the return value to a variable named $ReturnValue. The statement also passes three literal values to the function.

```
$ReturnValue = averageNumbers(1, 2, 3);
```

To actually return a value to a $ReturnValue variable, the code must include a return statement within the averageNumbers() function. A **return statement** returns a value to the statement that called the function. The following script contains the averageNumbers() function, which calculates the average of three numbers. The script also includes a return statement that returns the value (contained in the $Result variable) to the calling statement.

In PHP, a function does not necessarily have to return a value.

```
function averageNumbers($a, $b, $c) {
    $SumOfNumbers = $a + $b + $c;
    $Result = $SumOfNumbers / 3;
    return $Result;
}
```

In the next steps, you will create a script that contains two functions. The first function displays a message when it is called, and the second function returns a value that is displayed after the calling statement.

To create a script that contains two functions:

1. Create a new document in your text editor. Type the `<!DOCTYPE>` declaration, `<html>` element, header information, and `<body>` element. Use the strict DTD and "Two Functions" as the content of the `<title>` element.

2. Add the following script section to the document body:

```php
<?php
?>
```

3. Add the first function to the script section as follows. This function writes a message to the screen using an argument that will be passed to it from the calling statement.

```php
function displayMessage($FirstMessage) {
    echo "<p>$FirstMessage</p>";
}
```

4. Add the second function, which displays a second message, to the end of the script section. In this case, the message ("This message was returned from a function.") is defined within the function itself. The only purpose of this function is to return the literal string to the calling statement.

```php
function returnMessage() {
    return "<p>This message was returned from a
            function.</p>";
}
```

5. Add the following three statements to the end of the script section. The first statement displays the text string "This message was displayed from a function." in the Web browser. This statement does not receive a return value. The second statement assigns the function call to a variable named `$ReturnValue`, but does not send any arguments to the function. The third statement writes the value of the `$ReturnValue` variable to the screen.

```php
displayMessage("This message was displayed from a
function.");
$ReturnValue = returnMessage();
echo $ReturnValue;
```

6. Save the document as **TwoFunctions.php** in the Chapter directory for Chapter 2, and then upload the document to the Web server.

7. Open the TwoFunctions.php file in your Web browser by entering the following URL: *http://<yourserver>/PHP_Projects/Chapter.02/Chapter/TwoFunctions.php*. You should see the Web page shown in Figure 2-2.

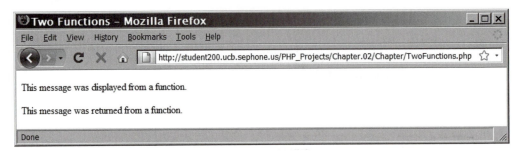

Figure 2-2 Output of TwoFunctions.php

>   **8.** Close your Web browser window.

Passing Parameters by Reference

Normally, the value of a variable is passed as the parameter of a function. PHP passes the parameter **by value**, which means that a local copy of the variable is created to be used by the function. Any changes made to the parameter's value within the function are lost when control is passed from the function back to the program.

Sometimes you would like the function to change the value of the parameter. If so, you can pass the parameter **by reference**—instead of a local copy, the actual variable is used within the function. Any changes to that variable made by the function will remain after the function completes.

Using an ampersand when calling the function will generate a warning message.

To pass by reference, you insert an ampersand (&) before the dollar sign of the parameter name in the function declaration. You call the function using the same syntax as before, and do not add an ampersand before the name of the variable being passed as a parameter.

The following example includes two functions. The first, `IncrementByValue()`, accepts the parameter by value. The second, `IncrementByReference()`, accepts the parameter by reference. Figure 2-3 shows the output.

```php
<?php
function IncrementByValue($CountByValue) {
    ++$CountByValue;
    echo "<p>IncrementByValue() value is
        $CountByValue.</p>";
};

function IncrementByReference(&$CountByReference) {
    ++$CountByReference;
    echo "<p>IncrementByReference() value is
        $CountByReference.</p>";
};
```

```
$Count = 1;
echo "<p>Main program starting value is $Count.</p>";
IncrementByValue($Count);
echo "<p>Main program between value is $Count.</p>";
IncrementByReference($Count);
echo "<p>Main program ending value is $Count.</p>";
?>
```

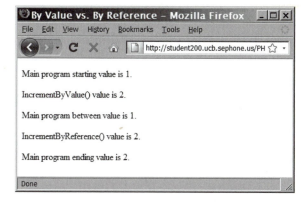

Figure 2-3 Function declarations by value and by reference

As you can see in Figure 2-3, both functions increment the parameter. However, when control returns to the main program, the value of $Count is only changed after calling IncrementByReference().

In scripts that include functions, where and how you declare variables is very important. In the following section, you will study variable scope, a topic that will help you understand how to use variables in scripts that include functions.

 When passing a parameter by reference, the calling function must pass a variable. Passing a constant, a static value, or an expression will cause the PHP script to fail.

Short Quiz

1. Explain the two-step process of creating user-defined functions in a PHP script.

2. Describe the purpose of the return statement in a function.

3. Explain why some functions do not need parameters.

4. Explain why some functions do not have a return statement.

5. Explain the difference between passing a parameter to a function by value versus by reference.

Understanding Variable Scope

When you use a variable in a PHP program, particularly a complex program, you need to be aware of the **variable's scope**—that is, you need to think about where in your program a declared variable can be used. A variable's scope can be either global or local. A **global variable** is declared outside a function and is available to all parts of your program. A **local variable** is declared inside a function and is only available within that function. Local variables cease to exist when the function ends. If you attempt to use a local variable outside the function in which it is declared, you will receive an error message.

The following script includes a function that contains a local variable. When the function is called, the local variable displays successfully within the function. However, when the script tries to display the local variable from outside the function definition, an error message is generated because the local variable ceases to exist when the function ends.

```php
<?php
$GlobalVariable = "Global variable";
function scopeExample() {
    $LocalVariable = "<p>Local variable</p>";
    echo "<p>$LocalVariable</p>"; // displays
                                  // successfully
}
scopeExample();
echo "<p>$GlobalVariable</p>";
echo "<p>$LocalVariable</p>"; // error message
?>
```

The `global` Keyword

With many programming languages, global variables are automatically available to all parts of your program, including functions. However, this is not the case in PHP. As an example, the output statement in the following script generates an error because `$GlobalVariable` is not recognized within the scope of the `scopeExample()` function:

```php
<?php
$GlobalVariable = "Global variable";
function scopeExample() {
    echo "<p>$GlobalVariable</p>"; // error message
}
scopeExample();
?>
```

In PHP, you must declare a global variable with the `global` keyword inside a function definition to make the variable available within

The formal parameters within the parentheses of a function declaration are local variables.

the scope of that function. When you declare a global variable with the `global` keyword, you do not need to assign the variable a value, as you do when you declare a standard variable. Instead, your declaration statement only needs to include the `global` keyword along with the name of the variable. The correct syntax is `global $variable_name;`. The following code shows a modified version of the preceding script. This time, the code declares the global variable within the function, which allows the output message to be displayed successfully.

```php
<?php
$GlobalVariable = "Global variable";
function scopeExample() {
    global $GlobalVariable;
    echo "<p>$GlobalVariable</p>";
}
scopeExample();
?>
```

 It is considered good programming practice to pass a global variable to a function as a parameter by reference rather than use the `global` keyword. Whenever possible, you should pass the variable to the function. Using the `global` keyword when passing the variable by reference is not possible.

Short Quiz

1. Define the term *variable scope*.

2. Explain the difference between a local variable and a global variable.

3. A variable declared outside of a function must be declared to be available within the function by using which keyword?

Making Decisions

When you write a computer program, regardless of the programming language, you often need to execute different sets of statements depending on some predetermined criteria. For example, you might create a program that needs to execute one set of code in the morning and another set of code at night. Or, you might create a program that depends on user input to determine exactly what code to run. For instance, suppose you create a Web page through which users place online orders. If a user clicks an Add to Shopping Cart button, a set of statements must execute to build the list of items to be purchased. However, if the user clicks a Checkout button, an entirely different set of statements must execute to complete the transaction. The process of determining the order in which statements execute in a program is called **decision making** or **flow control**. The most common type of decision-making statement is the if statement, which you study in the following section.

if Statements

The **if statement** is used to execute specific programming code if the evaluation of a conditional expression returns a value of TRUE. The syntax for a simple if statement is as follows:

```
if (conditional expression)
     statement;
```

The if statement contains three parts: the keyword if, a conditional expression enclosed within parentheses, and the executable statements. Note that the conditional expression must be enclosed within parentheses.

The statement immediately following the if statement in this example can be written on the same line as the if statement itself. However, using a line break and indentation makes the code easier for the programmer to read.

If the condition being evaluated returns a value of TRUE, the statement immediately following the conditional expression executes. After the if statement executes, any subsequent code executes normally. Consider the following code. The if statement uses the equal (==) comparison operator to determine whether the variable $ExampleVar is equal to 5. (You learned about operators in Chapter 1.) Because the condition returns a value of TRUE, two echo statements execute. The first echo statement is generated by the if statement when the condition returns a value of TRUE, and the second echo statement executes after the if statement is completed.

```
$ExampleVar = 5;
if ($ExampleVar == 5) // Condition evaluates to 'TRUE'
     echo "<p>The variable is equal to $ExampleVar.</p>";
echo "<p>This text is generated after the 'if'
statement.</p>";
```

In contrast, the following code displays only the second echo statement. The condition evaluates to FALSE because $ExampleVar is assigned the value 4 instead of 5.

```
$ExampleVar = 4;
if ($ExampleVar == 5) // Condition evaluates to 'FALSE'
    echo "<p> This text will not appear.</p>";
echo "<p> This is the only text that appears.</p>";
```

You can use a command block to construct a decision-making structure for performing multiple statements with a single if statement. A **command block** is a group of statements contained within a set of braces, similar to the way function statements are contained within a set of braces. Each command block must have an opening brace ({) and a closing brace (}). If a command block is missing either brace, an error occurs. The following code shows a script that runs a command block if the conditional expression within the if statement evaluates to TRUE:

```
$ExampleVar = 5;
if ($ExampleVar == 5) { // Condition evaluates to 'TRUE'
    echo "<p>The condition evaluates to true.</p>";
    echo '<p>$ExampleVar is equal to ', "$ExampleVar.</p>";
    echo "<p>Each of these lines will be displayed.</p>";
}
echo "<p>This statement always executes after the 'if'
statement.</p>";
```

When an if statement contains a command block, the statements in the command block execute when the if statement condition evaluates to TRUE. After the command block executes, the code that follows executes normally. When the condition evaluates to FALSE, the command block is skipped, and the statements that follow execute. If the conditional expression within the if statement in the preceding code evaluates to FALSE, only the echo statement following the command block executes.

In the next steps, you will create a script to roll a pair of dice and evaluate the outcome. For this exercise, you will use the function rand(1,6), which generates a random integer from 1 to 6.

To create the dice script:

1. Create a new document in your text editor. Type the <!DOCTYPE> declaration, <html> element, header information, and <body> element. Use the strict DTD and "Dice Roll" as the content of the <title> element.

2. Add the following script section to the document body:

   ```
   <?php
   ?>
   ```

3. Add the following code to the beginning of the script section. This will create the $FaceNamesSingular and $FaceNamesPlural arrays and populate them with text.

   ```
   $FaceNamesSingular = array("one", "two", "three",
   "four", "five", "six");
   $FaceNamesPlural = array("ones", "twos", "threes",
   "fours", "fives", "sixes");
   ```

4. Now create the CheckForDoubles function. It takes two parameters, $Die1 and $Die2, and uses echo statements and the global $FaceNamesSingular and $FaceNamesPlural arrays to display one of two different messages, depending on whether $Die1 equals $Die2 (doubles were rolled).

```
function CheckForDoubles($Die1, $Die2) {
    global $FaceNamesSingular;
    global $FaceNamesPlural;
    if ($Die1 == $Die2) // Doubles
        echo "The roll was double ",
            $FaceNamesPlural[$Die1-1], ".<br />";
    if ($Die1 != $Die2) // Not Doubles
        echo "The roll was a ",
            $FaceNamesSingular[$Die1-1],
            " and a ", $FaceNamesSingular[$Die2-1],
            ".<br />";
}
```

5. Now create the DisplayScoreText() function. This function takes one parameter, $Score, and displays a string that shows the special name for that score. At this point, the DisplayScoreText() function only displays a message for a select few scores and displays nothing for the others.

```
function DisplayScoreText($Score) {
    if ($Score == 2)
        echo "You rolled snake eyes!<br />";
    if ($Score == 3)
        echo "You rolled a loose deuce!<br />";
    if ($Score == 5)
        echo "You rolled a fever five!<br />";
    if ($Score == 7)
        echo "You rolled a natural!<br />";
    if ($Score == 9)
        echo "You rolled a nina!<br />";
    if ($Score == 11)
        echo "You rolled a yo!<br />";
    if ($Score == 12)
        echo "You rolled boxcars!<br />";
}
```

6. Now define the $Dice[] array, using the rand(1,6) function to generate the random values for the first two elements of the array. Add the two values together and store the results in the $Score variable. Then display a message showing the total score.

```
$Dice = array();
$Dice[0] = rand(1,6);
$Dice[1] = rand(1,6);
$Score = $Dice[0] + $Dice[1];
echo "<p>";
echo "The total score for the roll was
$Score.<br />";
```

7. Finally, call the CheckForDoubles() function using the two elements of the $Dice[] array as the parameters, and call the

DisplayScoreText() function using the $Score variable as the parameter.

```
CheckForDoubles($Dice[0],$Dice[1]);
DisplayScoreText($Score);
echo "</p>";
```

8. Save the document as **DiceRoll.php** in the Chapter directory for Chapter 2, and then upload the document to the Web server.

9. Open the DiceRoll.php file in your Web browser by entering the following URL: *http://<yourserver>/PHP_Projects/ Chapter.02/Chapter/DiceRoll.php*. You should see a Web page similar to the one shown in Figure 2-4. Each time you refresh the page, the rand(1,6) function will generate two new values, one for each of the dice, and the page will change to display the information for the new roll values.

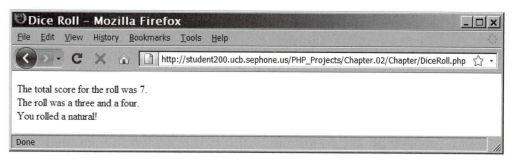

Figure 2-4 Output of DiceRoll.php

10. Close your Web browser window.

if...else Statements

So far, you've learned how to use an if statement to execute a statement (or statements) if a condition evaluates to TRUE. In some situations, however, you might want to execute one set of statements when the condition evaluates to FALSE, and another set of statements when the condition evaluates to TRUE. In these cases, you need to add an else clause to your if statement. For instance, suppose you create a form that includes a check box that users click to indicate whether they want to invest in the stock market. When the user submits the form to a PHP script, an if statement in the script might contain a conditional expression that evaluates the user's input. If the condition evaluates to TRUE (the user clicked the check box), the if statement displays a Web page on recommended stocks. If the condition evaluates to FALSE (the user did not click the check box), the statements in an `else` clause display a Web page on other types of investment opportunities.

An `if` statement that includes an `else` clause is called an **if . . . else statement**. You can think of an `else` clause as a backup plan that is implemented when the condition returns a value of FALSE. The syntax for an `if . . . else` statement is as follows:

```
if (conditional expression)
     statement;
else
     statement;
```

An `if` statement can be constructed without the `else` clause. However, the `else` clause can only be used with an `if` statement.

You can use command blocks to construct an `if . . . else` statement as follows:

```
if (conditional expression) {
     statements;
}
else {
     statements;
}
```

The following code shows an example of an `if . . . else` statement:

```
$Today = "Tuesday";
if ($Today == "Monday")
     echo "<p>Today is Monday</p>";
else
     echo "<p>Today is not Monday</p>";
```

In the preceding code, the `$Today` variable is assigned a value of "Tuesday." If the condition (`$Today == "Monday"`) evaluates to FALSE, control of the program passes to the `else` clause, the statement `echo "<p>Today is not Monday</p>";` executes, and the string "Today is not Monday" is displayed. If the `$Today` variable had been assigned a value of "Monday," the condition (`$Today == "Monday"`) would have evaluated to TRUE, and the statement `echo "<p>Today is Monday</p>";` would have executed. Only one statement or command block executes: either the statement or command block following the `if` statement or the statement or command block following the `else` clause. Regardless of which statement or command block executes, any code following the `if . . . else` statements executes normally.

The PHP code for the DiceRoll.php document you created earlier uses multiple `if` statements to evaluate whether the dice roll resulted in doubles. Although the multiple `if` statements function properly, they can be simplified using an `if . . . else` statement.

To simplify the DiceRoll.php script by replacing two if statements with one if . . . else statement:

1. Return to the **DiceRoll.php** document in your text editor.

2. Because you only need the if statement to test for doubles, you can display the message for rolls that are not doubles in the else clause. Modify the CheckForDoubles() function so that the two if statements are replaced with a single if . . . else statement. The following code shows how the statements for the CheckForDoubles() function should look:

```
if ($Die1 == $Die2) // Doubles
    echo "The roll was double ",
        $FaceNamesPlural[$Die1-1], ".<br />";
else // Not Doubles
    echo "The roll was a ",
        $FaceNamesSingular[$Die1-1],
        " and a ", $FaceNamesSingular[$Die2-1],
        ".<br />";
```

3. Save and upload the DiceRoll.php document.

4. Open the DiceRoll.php file in your Web browser by entering the following URL: *http://<yourserver>/PHP_Projects/ Chapter.02/Chapter/DiceRoll.php*. You should still see a Web page similar to the one shown in Figure 2-4. Use the refresh button to verify that both doubles and nondoubles are displayed correctly.

5. Close your Web browser window.

Nested if and if . . . else Statements

As you have seen, you can use a control structure such as an if or if . . . else statement to allow a program to make decisions about what statements to execute. In some cases, however, you might want the statements executed by the control structure to make other decisions. For instance, you might have a program that uses an if statement to ask users if they like sports. If users answer "yes", you might want to run another if statement that asks users whether they like team sports or individual sports. You can include any code you want within the code block for an if or if . . . else statement; these statements can include other if or if . . . else statements.

When one decision-making statement is contained within another decision-making statement, they are referred to as **nested decision-making structures**. An if statement contained within an if statement or within an if . . . else statement is called a nested if statement. Similarly, an if . . . else statement contained within an if or if . . . else statement is called a nested if . . . else statement.

You use nested if and if...else statements to perform conditional evaluations that must be executed after the original conditional evaluation. For example, the following code evaluates two conditional expressions before the echo statement executes:

```
if ($SalesTotal >= 50)
    if ($SalesTotal <= 100)
        echo "<p>The sales total is between 50 and 100,
            inclusive.</p>";
```

The echo statement in the preceding example only executes if the conditional expressions in both if statements evaluate to TRUE.

The PHP code in the DisplayScoreText() function of the DiceRoll.php document is somewhat inefficient because it contains an extended series of if statements, all of which need to be processed. A more efficient method of performing the same task is to divide the scores into groups. For example, by checking if doubles were rolled, we could divide the list into two groups: one for score names that are for doubles only, and another for score names that do not apply to doubles. If doubles were rolled, the if portion of the statement executes the code that selects the text to display from one set of if statements. However, if doubles were not rolled, the else portion of the statement will select the text to display from the second group of if statements.

To modify the DiceRoll.php program so it uses nested if...else statements to display the score text:

1. Return to the **DiceRoll.php** document in your text editor.

2. Modify the CheckForDoubles() function to return a Boolean value indicating whether doubles were rolled by adding the text shown in bold.

Braces were added to both the if and else portions of the if...else statement so that each section could contain two statements: the original echo statement and the new statement that assigns the appropriate value (TRUE or FALSE) to the $ReturnValue variable.

```
function CheckForDoubles($Die1, $Die2) {
    global $FaceNamesSingular;
    global $FaceNamesPlural;
    $ReturnValue = false;

    if ($Die1 == $Die2) { // Doubles
        echo "The roll was double ",
            $FaceNamesPlural[$Die1-1], ".<br />";
        $ReturnValue = true;
    }
    else { // Not Doubles
        echo "The roll was a ",
            $FaceNamesSingular[$Die1-1],
            " and a ",
            $FaceNamesSingular[$Die2-1], ".<br />";
        $ReturnValue = false;
    }

    return $ReturnValue;
}
```

3. Modify the `DisplayScoreText()` function to accept a second parameter, which is a Boolean value that is TRUE if doubles were rolled and FALSE otherwise. Add the text shown in bold to the function declaration:

```
function DisplayScoreText($Score, $Doubles) {
```

4. Modify the `DisplayScoreText()` function body to use nested `if...else` statements. Use the new $Doubles Boolean parameter to determine if doubles were rolled or not. Check for the two scores that can only occur if doubles were rolled within the command block for the `if` portion of the statement, and check for the remainder in the command block for the `else` portion of the statement. When finished, your code should appear as follows:

```
function DisplayScoreText($Score, $Doubles) {
    if ($Doubles) { // Doubles were rolled
        if ($Score == 2) // Double ones
            echo "You rolled snake eyes!<br />";
        if ($Score == 12) // Double sixes
            echo "You rolled boxcars!<br />";
    }
    else { // Doubles were not rolled
        if ($Score == 3)
            echo "You rolled a loose deuce!<br />";
        if ($Score == 5)
            echo "You rolled a fever five!<br />";
        if ($Score == 7)
            echo "You rolled a natural!<br />";
        if ($Score == 9)
            echo "You rolled a nina!<br />";
        if ($Score == 11)
            echo "You rolled a yo!<br />";
    }
}
```

5. Modify the call to the `CheckForDoubles()` function to store the return value in a variable called $Doubles. Pass this new value as the second parameter to the `DisplayScoreText()` function. The code should appear as follows, with the new code in bold:

```
$Doubles = CheckForDoubles($Dice[0],$Dice[1]);
DisplayScoreText($Score, $Doubles);
```

6. Save the DiceRoll.php document and upload the document to the Web server.

7. Open the DiceRoll.php file in your Web browser by entering the following URL: *http://<yourserver>/PHP_Projects/Chapter.02/Chapter/DiceRoll.php*. You should still see a Web page similar to the one shown in Figure 2-4.

8. Close your Web browser window.

switch Statements

Another PHP statement that is used for controlling program flow is the switch statement. The **switch statement** controls program flow by executing a specific set of statements depending on the value of an expression. The switch statement compares the value of an expression to a value contained within a special statement called a case label. A **case label** represents a specific value and contains one or more statements that execute if the value of the case label matches the value of the switch statement's expression. For example, your script for an insurance company might include a variable named $CustomerAgeGroup. A switch statement can evaluate the variable and compare it to a case label within the switch construct. The switch statement might contain several case labels for different age groups that calculate insurance rates based on a customer's age. If the $CustomerAgeGroup variable is equal to 25, the statements that are part of the "25" case label execute and calculate insurance rates for customers who are 25 or older. Although you could accomplish the same task using if or if . . . else statements, using a switch statement makes it easier to organize the different branches of code that can be executed.

A switch statement consists of the following components: the keyword switch, an expression, an opening brace, one or more case statements, a default label, and a closing brace. A case statement consists of a case label, the executable statements, and the keyword break. The syntax for the switch statement is as follows:

```
switch (expression) {
    case label:
        statement(s);
        break;
    case label:
        statement(s);
        break;
    . . .
    default:
        statement(s);
        break;
}
```

A `case` label consists of the keyword `case`, followed by a literal value or variable name, followed by a colon. PHP compares the value returned from the `switch` statement expression to the literal value or value of the variable named following the `case` keyword. If a match is found, the statements following the `case` label statements execute. For example, the `case` label `case 3.17:` represents a floating-point integer value of 3.17. If the value of a `switch` statement expression equals 3.17, the `case 3.17:` label statements execute. You can use a variety of data types as `case` labels within the same `switch` statement. The following code shows examples of four `case` labels:

```
case $ExampleVar:    // variable name
     statement(s);
     break;
case "text string": // string literal
     statement(s);
     break;
case 75:             // integer literal
     statement(s);
     break;
case -273.4:         // floating-point literal
     statement(s);
     break;
```

Another type of label used within `switch` statements is the `default` label. The **default label** contains statements that execute when the value returned by the `switch` statement expression does not match any `case` label. A `default` label consists of the keyword `default` followed by a colon.

When a `switch` statement executes, the value returned by the expression is compared to each `case` label in the order in which it is encountered. After a matching label is found, its statements execute. Unlike the `if...else` statement, execution of a `switch` statement does not automatically stop after the particular `case` label statements execute. Instead, the `switch` statement executes all its statements until it ends. A `switch` statement ends automatically after the PHP interpreter encounters its closing brace (`}`). You can, however, use a special kind of statement, called a `break` statement, to exit a `switch` statement after it has performed its required task. **A break statement** is used to exit control structures.

The following code shows a `switch` statement contained within a function. When the function is called, it is passed an argument named `$AmericanCity`. The `switch` statement compares the contents of the `$AmericanCity` argument to the `case` labels. If a match is found, the city's state is returned and a `break` statement ends the `switch` statement. If a match is not found, the value "United States" is returned from the `default` label.

A `case` label can be followed by a single statement or multiple statements. However, unlike with `if` statements, multiple statements for a `case` label do not need to be enclosed within a command block in PHP.

Other programming languages, such as Java and C++, require all `case` labels within a `switch` statement to be of the same data type.

A `break` statement is also used to exit other types of control statements, such as the `while`, `do...while`, and `for` looping statements. You will learn about these statements later in this chapter.

```
function city_location($AmericanCity) {
    switch ($AmericanCity) {
        case "Boston":
            return "Massachusetts";
            break;
        case "Chicago":
            return "Illinois";
            break;
        case "Los Angeles":
            return "California";
            break;
        case "Miami":
            return "Florida";
            break;
        case "New York":
            return "New York";
            break;
        default:
            return "United States";
            break;
    }
}
echo "<p>", city_location("Boston"), "</p>";
```

94

You do not have to include a break statement after the statements for the final case or default statement, but it is normally included as a good programming practice.

To modify the DiceRoll.php script to use a switch statement for the score text:

1. Return to the **DiceRoll.php** document in your text editor.

2. Replace the nested if . . . else statements with the following switch statement in the DisplayScoreText() function. Note the use of the nested if . . . else statement in the default case that allows the DisplayScoreText() function to display a message for all of the possible rolls:

```
switch ($Score) {
    case 2:
        echo "You rolled snake eyes!<br />";
        break;
    case 3:
        echo "You rolled a loose deuce!<br />";
        break;
    case 5:
        echo "You rolled a fever five!<br />";
        break;
    case 7:
        echo "You rolled a natural!<br />";
        break;
    case 9:
        echo "You rolled a nina!<br />";
        break;
```

```
        case 11:
            echo "You rolled a yo!<br />";
            break;
        case 12:
            echo "You rolled boxcars!<br />";
            break;
        default:
            if ($Score % 2 == 0) { /* An even
                                number */
                if ($Doubles) {
                    echo "You rolled a hard
                            $Score!<br />";
                }
                else { /* Not doubles */
                    echo "You rolled an easy
                            $Score!<br />";
                }
            }
            break;
    }
```

3. Save and upload the DiceRoll.php document.

4. Open the DiceRoll.php file in your Web browser by entering the following URL: *http://<yourserver>/PHP_Projects/ Chapter.02/Chapter/DiceRoll.php*. The program should function just as it did in the previous three examples with the addition of the new messages for easy and hard even scores.

5. Close your Web browser window.

Short Quiz

1. What are the three required components of an if statement?

2. Describe how the use of command blocks makes an if . . . else control structure more efficient.

3. Explain the purpose of the default label in a switch statement.

Repeating Code

The statements you have worked with so far execute one after the other in a linear fashion. The if, if . . . else, and switch statements select only a single branch of code to execute, then continue to the statement that follows. But what if you want to repeat the same statement, function, or code section 5 times, 10 times, or 100 times? For example, you might want to perform the same calculation until a specific number is found. In this case, you need to use a **loop statement**, a control structure that repeatedly executes a statement or a series of statements while a specific condition is TRUE or until a specific condition becomes TRUE. In this chapter, you will learn about four types of loop statements: while, do...while, for, and foreach statements.

while Statements

One of the simplest types of loop statements is the **while statement**, which repeats a statement or series of statements as long as a given conditional expression evaluates to TRUE. The syntax for the while statement is as follows:

```
while (conditional expression) {
     statement(s);
}
```

Many programmers often name counter variables $Count, $Counter, or something similar. The letters i, j, k, l, x, y, and z are also commonly used as counter names. Using a name such as count, or the letter i (for increment) helps you to remember (and lets other programmers know) that the variable is being used as a counter.

The conditional expression in the while statement is enclosed within parentheses following the keyword while. As long as the conditional expression evaluates to TRUE, the statement or command block that follows executes repeatedly. Each repetition of a looping statement is called an **iteration**. When the conditional expression evaluates to FALSE, the loop ends and the next statement following the while statement executes.

A while statement keeps repeating until its conditional expression evaluates to FALSE. To ensure that the while statement ends after performing the desired tasks, you must include code that tracks the progress of the loop and changes the value produced by the conditional expression. You can track the progress of a while statement, or any other loop, with a counter. A **counter** is a variable that increments or decrements with each iteration of a loop statement.

The following code shows a simple script that includes a while statement. The script declares a variable named $Count and assigns it an initial value of 1. The $Count variable is then used in the while statement conditional expression ($Count <= 5). As long as the $Count variable is less than or equal to 5, the while statement loops. Within the body of the while statement, the echo statement displays the value of the $Count variable, then the $Count variable increments by a value of 1. The while statement loops until the $Count variable increments to a value of 6.

```
$Count = 1;
while ($Count <= 5) {
    echo "$Count<br />";
    ++$Count;
}
echo "<p>You have displayed 5 numbers.</p>";
```

The preceding code displays the numbers 1 to 5, with each number representing one iteration of the loop. When the counter reaches 6, the message "You have displayed 5 numbers." appears, thus demonstrating that the loop has ended. Figure 2-5 shows the output of this simple script.

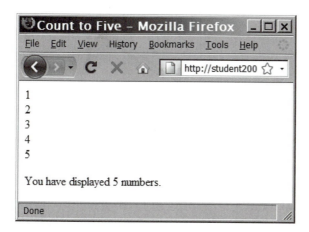

Figure 2-5 Output of a `while` statement using an increment operator

You can also control the repetitions in a `while` loop by decrementing (decreasing the value of) counter variables. Consider the following script:

```
$Count = 10;
while ($Count > 0) {
    echo "$Count<br />";
    --$Count;
}
echo "<p>We have liftoff.</p>";
```

In this example, the initial value of the $Count variable is 10, and the decrement operator (--) is used to decrease the value of the $Count variable by 1. When the $Count variable is greater than zero, the statement within the `while` loop displays the value of the $Count variable. When the value of $Count is equal to zero, the `while` loop ends, and the statement immediately following it displays. Figure 2-6 shows the script output.

Figure 2-6   Output of a `while` statement using a decrement operator

There are many ways to change the value of a counter variable and to use a counter variable to control the repetitions of a `while` loop. The following example uses the `*=` assignment operator to multiply the value of the `$Count` variable by 2. When the `$Count` variable reaches a value of 128 (the first multiple of 2 greater than 100), the `while` statement ends. Figure 2-7 shows the script output.

```
$Count = 1;
while ($Count <= 100) {
     echo "$Count<br />";
     $Count *= 2;
}
```

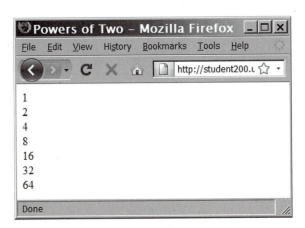

Figure 2-7   Output of a `while` statement using the assignment operator `*=`

To ensure that the `while` statement will eventually end, you must include code within the body of the `while` statement that changes the value of the conditional expression. For example, you may have a `while` statement that displays even numbers between 0 and 100. You need to include code within the body of the `while` statement that ends the loop after the last even number (100) displays. If you do not include code that changes the value used by the conditional expression, your program will be caught in an infinite loop. In an **infinite loop**, a loop statement never ends because its conditional expression is never FALSE. Consider the following `while` statement:

```
$Count = 1;
while ($Count <= 10) {
     echo "The number is $Count";
}
```

Although the `while` statement in the preceding example includes a conditional expression that checks the value of a `$Count` variable, there is no code within the `while` statement body that changes the `$Count` variable value. The `$Count` variable will continue to have a value of 1 through each iteration of the loop. This means that the text string "The number is 1" will be displayed repeatedly until the user closes the Web browser window.

You can use the `continue` statement to halt a looping statement and restart the loop with a new iteration.

To modify the DiceRoll.php script to evaluate five rolls using a `while` statement:

1. Return to the **DiceRoll.php** document in your text editor.

2. Immediately after the declaration of the `$Dice` array, declare and initialize two new variables: `$DoublesCount` and `$RollNumber`.

   ```
   $DoublesCount = 0;
   $RollNumber = 1;
   ```

3. After the new variable declarations, create a `while` loop by adding the code shown in bold. Also, revise the echo statement by making the change shown in bold.

   ```
   while ($RollNumber <= 5) {
        $Dice[0] = rand(1,6);
        $Dice[1] = rand(1,6);
        $Score = $Dice[0] + $Dice[1];
        echo "<p>";
        echo "The total score for roll $RollNumber was
             $Score.<br />";
        $Doubles = CheckForDoubles($Dice[0],$Dice[1]);
        DisplayScoreText($Score, $Doubles);
        echo "</p>";
        if ($Doubles)
             ++$DoublesCount;
        ++$RollNumber;
   } // End of the while loop
   ```

4. Add the following line after the `while` loop to display the number of times doubles were rolled:

```
echo "<p>Doubles occurred on $DoublesCount of the
five rolls.</p>";
```

5. Save and upload the DiceRoll.php document.

6. Open the DiceRoll.php file in your Web browser by entering the following URL: *http://<yourserver>/PHP_Projects/ Chapter.02/Chapter/DiceRoll.php*. Figure 2-8 shows how the program appears in a Web browser.

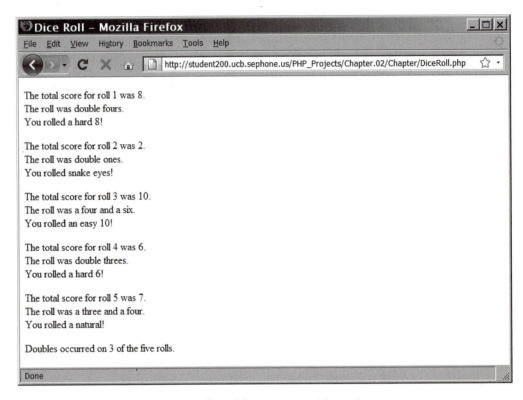

Figure 2-8 Output of DiceRoll.php after adding a `while` statement

7. Close your Web browser window.

do...while Statements

Another PHP looping statement, similar to the `while` statement, is the do...while statement. The **do...while statement** executes a statement or statements once, then repeats the execution as long as a given conditional expression evaluates to TRUE. The syntax for the do...while statement is as follows:

```
do {
    statement(s);
} while (conditional expression);
```

As you can see in the syntax description, the statements execute before a conditional expression is evaluated. Unlike the simpler while statement, the statements in a do . . . while statement always execute once before a conditional expression is evaluated.

The following do . . . while statement executes once before the conditional expression evaluates the count variable. Therefore, a single line that reads "The count is equal to 2" appears. After the conditional expression ($Count < 2) executes, the $Count variable is equal to 2. This causes the conditional expression to return a value of FALSE, and the do . . . while statement ends.

```
$Count = 2;
do {
    echo "<p>The count is equal to $Count</p>";
    ++$Count;
} while ($Count < 2);
```

Note that the preceding example includes a counter within the body of the do . . . while statement. As with the while statement, you need to include code that changes the conditional expression to prevent an infinite loop.

In the following example, the while statement never executes because the count variable does not fall within the range of the conditional expression:

```
$Count = 2;
while ($Count < 2) {
    echo "<p>The count is equal to $Count</p>";
    ++$Count;
}
```

The following script shows an example of a do . . . while statement that displays the days of the week, using an array:

```
$DaysOfWeek = array("Monday", "Tuesday", "Wednesday",
"Thursday", "Friday", "Saturday", "Sunday");
$Count = 0;
do {
    echo $DaysOfWeek[$Count], "<br />";
    ++$Count;
} while ($Count < 7);
```

In the preceding example, an array is created containing the days of the week. A variable named $Count is declared and initialized to zero. (Remember, the first subscript or index in an array is zero.) Therefore, in the example, the statement $DaysOfWeek[0]; refers to Monday. The first iteration of the do . . . while statement displays "Monday" and then increments the `count` variable by 1. The conditional expression in the `while` statement then checks to determine when the last element of the array has been displayed. As long as the count is less than seven (which is one number higher than the index of the largest element in the `$DaysOfWeek[]` array), the loop continues. Figure 2-9 shows the output of the script in a Web browser.

Figure 2-9   Output of days of week script in a Web browser

Next, you will replace the `while` statement in the DiceRoll.php script with a do . . . while statement. Because the two types of statements are so similar, there is little benefit in replacing the `while` statement. You will add a do . . . while statement to the script for practice.

To use a do . . . while statement:

1. Return to the **DiceRoll.php** document in your text editor.

2. Change the `while` statement to a do . . . while statement, as follows:

```
do {
     $Dice[0] = rand(1,6);
     $Dice[1] = rand(1,6);
     $Score = $Dice[0] + $Dice[1];
     echo "<p>";
     echo "The total score for roll $RollNumber was
          $Score.<br />";
     $Doubles = CheckForDoubles($Dice[0],$Dice[1]);
     DisplayScoreText($Score, $Doubles);
     echo "</p>";
     if ($Doubles)
          ++$DoublesCount;
     ++$RollNumber;
} while ($RollNumber <= 5); /* End of the do . . .
                              while loop */
```

3. Save and upload the DiceRoll.php document.

4. Open the DiceRoll.php file in your Web browser by entering the following URL: *http://<yourserver>/PHP_Projects/
   Chapter.02/Chapter/DiceRoll.php*. The output should still
   appear as shown in Figure 2-8.

5. Close your Web browser window.

for Statements

So far, you have learned how to use the while and the do . . . while
statements to repeat, or loop through, code. You can also use the
for statement to loop through code. Specifically, the **for statement**
is used for repeating a statement or series of statements as long as a
given conditional expression evaluates to TRUE. The for statement
performs essentially the same function as the while statement: if a
conditional expression within the for statement evaluates to TRUE,
the for statement executes and continues to execute repeatedly until
the conditional expression evaluates to FALSE.

A primary difference between while and for statements is that,
in addition to a conditional expression, the for statement can also
include code that initializes a counter and changes its value with each
iteration. This is useful because it provides a specific place for you to
declare and initialize a counter, and to update its value, which helps
prevent infinite loops. The syntax of the for statement is as follows:

```
for (counter declaration and initialization; condition;
      update statement) {
      statement(s);
}
```

When the PHP interpreter encounters a for loop, the following steps
occur:

1. The counter variable is declared and initialized. For example,
   if the initialization expression in a for loop is $Count = 1;,
   a variable named $Count is declared and assigned an initial
   value of 1. The initialization expression is only started once,
   when the for loop is first encountered.

2. The for loop condition is evaluated.

3. If the condition evaluation in Step 2 returns a value of TRUE,
   the for loop statements execute, Step 4 occurs, and the process starts over again with Step 2. If the condition evaluation
   in Step 2 returns a value of FALSE, the for statement ends and
   the next statement following the for statement executes.

You can omit any of the three parts of the for statement, but you must include the semicolons that separate each section. If you omit a section, be sure you include code within the body that will end the for statement, or your program might get caught in an infinite loop.

104

4. The update statement in the for statement is executed. For example, the $Count variable may increment by 1.

The following script shows a for statement that displays the contents of an array:

```php
$FastFoods = array("pizza", "burgers", "french fries",
"tacos", "fried chicken");
for ($Count = 0; $Count < 5; ++$Count) {
    echo $FastFoods[$Count], "<br />";
}
```

As you can see in this example, the counter is initialized, evaluated, and incremented within the parentheses. You do not need to include a declaration for the $Count variable before the for statement, nor do you need to increment the $Count variable within the body of the for statement. Figure 2-10 shows the output of the fast foods script.

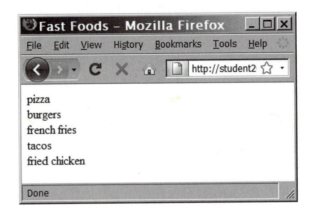

Figure 2-10 Output of the fast foods script

Using a for statement is more efficient because you do not need as many lines of code. Consider the following while statement:

```php
$Count = 1;
while ($Count <= 5) {
    echo "$Count<br />";
    ++$Count;
}
```

You could achieve the same flow control more efficiently by using a for statement as follows:

```php
for ($Count = 1; $Count <= 5; ++$Count) {
    echo "$Count<br />";
}
```

The following code shows an example of the "days of the week" script you saw earlier. This time, however, the script includes a for statement instead of a do . . . while statement. Notice that the declaration of the $Count variable, the conditional expression, and the statement that increments the $Count variable are now all contained within the for statement. Using a for statement instead of a do . . . while statement simplifies the script somewhat because you do not need as many lines of code.

```
$DaysOfWeek = array("Monday", "Tuesday", "Wednesday",
"Thursday", "Friday", "Saturday", "Sunday");
for ($Count = 0; $Count < 7; ++$Count) {
    echo $DaysOfWeek[$Count], "<br />";
}
```

To replace the do . . . while statement in DiceRoll.php with a for statement:

1. Return to the **DiceRoll.php** document in your text editor.

2. Change the do . . . while statement to a for statement, as follows:

```
for ($RollNumber = 1; $RollNumber <= 5;
++$RollNumber) {
        $Dice[0] = rand(1,6);
        $Dice[1] = rand(1,6);
        $Score = $Dice[0] + $Dice[1];
        echo "<p>";
        echo "The total score for roll $RollNumber was
            $Score.<br />";
        $Doubles = CheckForDoubles($Dice[0],$Dice[1]);
        DisplayScoreText($Score, $Doubles);
        echo "</p>";
        if ($Doubles)
            ++$DoublesCount;
} // End of the for loop
```

3. Save and upload the DiceRoll.php document.

4. Open the DiceRoll.php file in your Web browser by entering the following URL: *http://<yourserver>/PHP_Projects/Chapter.02/Chapter/DiceRoll.php*. The output should still appear as shown in Figure 2-8.

5. Close your Web browser window.

foreach Statements

The **foreach statement** is used to iterate or loop through the elements in an array. With each loop, a foreach statement moves to the next element in an array. Unlike other types of looping statements, you do not need to include any sort of counter within a foreach statement. Instead, you specify an array expression within a set of parentheses following the `foreach` keyword. The basic syntax for the `foreach` statement is as follows:

```
foreach ($array_name as $variable_name) {
statement(s);
}
```

During each iteration, a `foreach` statement assigns the value of the current array element to the *$variable_name* argument specified in the array expression. You use the *$variable_name* argument to access the value of the element that is available in an iteration. For example, the following code declares the same $DaysOfWeek[] array you've seen a few times in this chapter. During each iteration, the expression in the `foreach` statement assigns the value of each array element to the $Day variable. An echo statement within the `foreach` statement's braces displays the value of the current element.

You will receive an error if you attempt to use a `foreach` statement with any variable types other than arrays.

```
$DaysOfWeek = array("Monday", "Tuesday", "Wednesday",
"Thursday", "Friday", "Saturday", "Sunday");
foreach ($DaysOfWeek as $Day) {
    echo "<p>$Day</p>";
}
```

The `foreach` statement in the preceding code simply displays the days of the week to the Web browser.

The more advanced form of the `foreach` statement allows you to retrieve both the index (or key) and the value of each array element.

```
foreach ($array_name as $index_name => $variable_name) {
statement(s);
}
```

This form of the `foreach` statement works almost exactly the same as the basic form. The only difference is that the index of the current array element is stored in the *$index_name* variable. For example, the following code declares the $DaysOfWeek[] array again. During each iteration, the expression in the `foreach` statement assigns the index value of each array element to the $DayNumber variable and the value of each array element to the $Day variable. An echo statement within the `foreach` statement's braces displays the index and value of the current element. Figure 2-11 shows the output of this version.

```
$DaysOfWeek = array("Monday", "Tuesday", "Wednesday",
"Thursday", "Friday", "Saturday", "Sunday");
foreach ($DaysOfWeek as $DayNumber => $Day) {
    echo "<p>Day $DayNumber is $Day</p>";
}
```

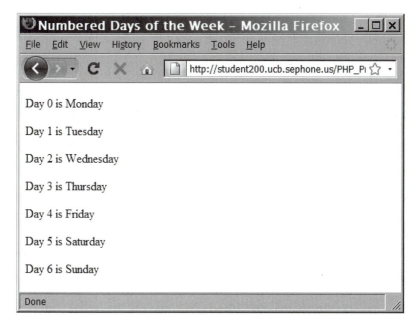

Figure 2-11 Output of the `foreach` script with index values

To create a final version of DiceRoll.php that displays all possible outcomes of rolling two dice:

1. Return to the **DiceRoll.php** document in your text editor.

2. Immediately after the declaration of the `$FaceNamesSingular` and `$FaceNamesPlural` arrays, declare a new array named `$FaceValues`, as follows:

   ```
   $FaceValues = array( 1, 2, 3, 4, 5, 6);
   ```

3. Delete the declaration of the `$Dice` array and add a new declaration for a variable named `$RollCount`, as follows:

   ```
   $RollCount = 0;
   ```

4. Create a new array called `$ScoreCount` and initialize it using the following `for` loop:

   ```
   $ScoreCount = array();
   for ($PossibleRolls = 2; $PossibleRolls <= 12;
   ++$PossibleRolls) {
        $ScoreCount[$PossibleRolls] = 0;
   }
   ```

5. Replace the `for` statement with the following two nested `foreach` statements:

```
foreach ($FaceValues as $Die1) {
        foreach ($FaceValues as $Die2) {
```

6. Delete the two calls to `rand(1,6)` and the `$Score` variable assignment, and insert the following lines in their place:

```
++$RollCount;
$Score = $Die1 + $Die2;
++$ScoreCount[$Score];
```

7. Modify the call to the `CheckForDoubles()` function to use `$Die1` and `$Die2` instead of `$Die[0]` and `$Die[1]`.

```
$Doubles = CheckForDoubles($Die1,$Die2);
```

8. Replace the single closing brace for the `for` loop with two closing braces for the two `foreach` loops:

```
} // End of the foreach loop for $Die2
} // End of the foreach loop for $Die1
```

9. Modify the `echo` statement that displays the doubles count with an `echo` statement that displays the doubles count and the roll count.

```
echo "<p>Doubles occurred on $DoublesCount of the
$RollCount rolls.</p>";
```

10. Finally, add a `foreach` loop to display the number of times each score occurred. Use the second form of the `foreach` statement to get the array index, which is the score.

```
foreach ($ScoreCount as $ScoreValue => $ScoreCount) {
        echo "<p>A combined value of $ScoreValue
                occurred $ScoreCount of $RollCount
                times.</p>";
}
```

11. Save and upload the DiceRoll.php document.

12. Open the DiceRoll.php file in your Web browser by entering the following URL: *http://<yourserver>/PHP_Projects/ Chapter.02/Chapter/DiceRoll.php*. The output should appear as shown in Figure 2-12.

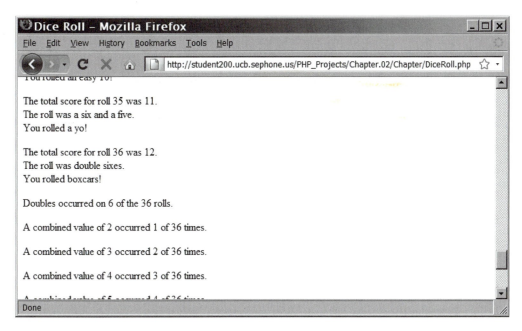

Figure 2-12 Output of DiceRoll.php with `foreach` statements

13. Close your Web browser window.

Short Quiz

1. All loops require what feature to ensure that the looping will eventually end and not result in an infinite loop?

2. What four looping structures are used in PHP?

3. Explain the purpose of a "counter" variable when executing a loop.

4. Which type of looping structure is used to iterate through elements of an array?

Including Files

The `include`, `require`, `include_once`, and `require_once` statements, much like the `echo` statement, are not considered actual functions, but rather language constructs that are built into PHP. The primary use of the `include` and `require` statements is to reuse content on multiple Web pages by allowing you to insert the content of an external file, called an include file, in your PHP scripts.

The difference between the two statements is that the `include` statement only generates a warning if the include file cannot be found, whereas the `require` statement halts the processing of the Web page and displays an error message if the include file cannot be found. The `include_once` and `require_once` statements are similar to the `include` and `require` statements, except they assure that the external file is added to the script only once, which helps to avoid conflicts with variable values or function names that might occur if the file was included multiple times.

The PHP scripting engine starts fresh for each include file. This means that if you use PHP code in the include file, it must be contained within a PHP script section. If the calling PHP file already contains the four basic XHTML tags (`<html>`, `<head>`, `<title>`, and `<body>`), the include file requires only that XHTML formatting tags be used with XHTML content. The include file is typically saved with a prefix of inc_ to identify it as an include file, as opposed to a complete .php file. An extension of .php is still used so that the file will be processed by the PHP scripting engine. However, different servers use different configurations, so you need to verify the appropriate file extension to use with your ISP.

One common use of the `include` and `require` statements is to display common header and footer content at the top and bottom of every page of your Web site. Instead of copying and pasting the header and footer code into each individual page, you can simply put your header content in one include file and your footer content in another include file. Then, on each page that you want the header and footer to appear, you can simply refer to the include file with either an `include` or `require` statement.

Another common use of include files is to store sensitive information that the program needs, but that should not be available to Web site visitors. Because the path of the filename passed to the `include` and `require` statements is based on the server's file system, not the Web-accessible file structure, you can store include files outside of the file structure available to Web browsers. For example, assume that your server is configured so that the public_html folder in your user home directory is available for Web site visitors. For the user dgosselin, any file stored in /home/users/dgosselin/public_html/ or its subdirectories would be browsable. However, if dgosselin created the folder /home/users/dgosselin/php_include/, that folder would not be browsable. Any files stored in /home/users/dgosselin/php_include/ will be processed by the PHP scripting engine if the files are included using one of the `include` family of statements.

 The `include` family of statements supports relative and absolute path notation. That means you can include a file from the parent folder by using the "`../`" notation, as in `include("../inc_CommonHeader.php");`. Similarly, if you were to place the included files in a folder named Includes, you could use the notation `include("Includes/inc_CommonHeader.php");` to access the files in the Includes subdirectory.

Short Quiz

1. Describe the purpose of the group of `include`, `require`, `include_once`, and `require_once` statements.

2. When might you want to use the `require` statement instead of the `include` statement?

3. Why is it important that you add PHP script delimiters to each PHP block in the include file?

4. Explain why one might want to save all include files in a separate folder and how this folder can be accessed.

Summing Up

- The lines of code that make up a function are called the function definition.

- A function parameter that is passed by a value is a local copy of the variable.

- A function parameter that is passed by a reference is a reference to the original variable.

- A global variable is declared outside a function and is available to all parts of your program.

- A local variable is declared inside a function and is only available within that function.

- The process of determining the order in which statements execute in a program is called decision making or flow control.

- The `if` statement is used to execute specific programming code if the evaluation of a conditional expression returns a value of TRUE.

- An `if` statement that includes an `else` clause is called an `if...else` statement. An `else` clause executes when the condition in an `if...else` statement evaluates to FALSE.

- When one decision-making statement is contained within another decision-making statement, they are referred to as nested decision-making structures.

- The `switch` statement controls program flow by executing a specific set of statements depending on the value of an expression.

- A loop statement is a control structure that repeatedly executes a statement or a series of statements while a specific condition is TRUE or until a specific condition becomes TRUE.

- A `while` statement tests a condition prior to executing a series of statements at each iteration of the loop.

- The `do...while` statement tests a condition after executing a series of statements.

- The `for` statement combines the initialization, conditional evaluation, and update portions of a loop into a single statement.

- The `foreach` statement is used to iterate or loop through the elements in an array.

- The `include`, `require`, `include_once`, and `require_once` statements insert the contents of an external file at the location of the statement.

Comprehension Check

1. A(n) _____ allows you to treat a related group of PHP commands as a single unit.

   a. statement

   b. variable

   c. function

   d. event

2. Functions must contain parameters. True or False?

3. Explain how to use a `return` statement to return a value to a statement that calls a function.

4. A variable that is declared outside a function is called
   a _____ variable.

   a. local

   b. class

   c. program

   d. global

5. A local variable must be declared _____.

   a. before a function

   b. after a function

   c. within the braces of a function definition

   d. with the local keyword

6. Explain the difference between passing a parameter to a function by value versus by reference.

7. Which of the following is the correct syntax for an if statement?

   a. `if ($MyVariable == 10);`

      `echo "Your variable is equal to 10.";`

   b. `if $MyVariable == 10`

      `echo "Your variable is equal to 10.";`

   c. `if ($MyVariable == 10)`

      `echo "Your variable is equal to 10.";`

   d. `if ($MyVariable == 10),`

      `echo "Your variable is equal to 10.";`

8. An if statement can include multiple statements provided that they _____.

   a. execute after the if statement's closing semicolon

   b. are not contained within a command block

   c. do not include other if statements

   d. are contained within a command block

9. Which is the correct syntax for an `else` clause?

   a. `else (echo "Displayed from an else clause.";`

   b. `else echo "Displayed from an else clause.";`

   c. `else "echo 'Displayed from an else clause.'";`

   d. `else; echo "Displayed from an else clause.";`

10. The `switch` statement controls program flow by executing a specific set of statements, depending on _____.

    a. the result of an `if...else` statement

    b. the version of PHP being executed

    c. whether an `if` statement executes within a function

    d. the value returned by a conditional expression

11. Decision-making structures cannot be nested. True or False?

12. When the value returned by a `switch` statement expression does not match a `case` label, the statements within the _____ label execute.

    a. `exception`

    b. `else`

    c. `error`

    d. `default`

13. You can exit a `switch` statement using a(n) _____ statement.

    a. `break`

    b. `end`

    c. `quit`

    d. `complete`

14. Each repetition of a looping statement is called a(n) _____.

    a. recurrence

    b. iteration

    c. duplication

    d. reexecution

15. Which of the following is the correct syntax for a `while` statement?

   a. `while ($i <= 5, ++$i) {`

          `$echo "<p>$i</p>";`
       `}`

   b. `while ($i <= 5) {`

           `$echo "<p>$i</p>";`
           `++$i;`
       `}`

   c. `while ($i <= 5);`

           `$echo "<p>$i</p>";`
           `++$i;`

   d. `while ($i <= 5; $echo "<p>$i</p>") {`

           `++$i;`
       `}`

16. Counter variables _____. (Choose all that apply.)

   a. can only be incremented

   b. can only be decremented

   c. can be incremented or decremented

   d. do not change

17. Explain how an infinite loop is caused.

18. Which of the following is the correct syntax for a `for` statement?

   a. `for ($i = 0; $i < 10; ++$i)`

          `echo "Displayed from a for statement.";`

   b. `for ($i = 0, $i < 10, ++$i)`

          `echo "Displayed from a for statement.";`

   c. `for {`

          `echo "Displayed from a for statement.";`
       `} while ($i = 0; $i < 10; ++$i)`

   d. `for ($i = 0; $i < 10);`

          `echo "Displayed from a for statement.";`
          `++$i;`

19. When is a `for` statement initialization expression executed?

    a. when the `for` statement begins executing

    b. with each repetition of the `for` statement

    c. when the counter variable increments

    d. when the `for` statement ends

20. The `foreach` statement can only be used with arrays. True or False?

Reinforcement Exercises

 Exercise 2-1

In this project, you will create a simple document that contains a conditional operator you will rewrite into an `if...else` statement.

1. Create a new document in your text editor.

2. Type the `<!DOCTYPE>` declaration, `<html>` element, document head, and `<body>` element. Use the strict DTD and "Conditional Script" as the content of the `<title>` element.

3. Create a script section in the document body that includes the following code, but replace the conditional expression statement with an `if...else` statement. Note that the strings are enclosed in single quotation marks so that the name of the variable will be displayed, not the value.

```php
<?php
$IntVariable = 75;
($IntVariable > 100) ? $Result = '$IntVariable is
greater than 100'
    : $Result = '$IntVariable is less than or equal
    to 100';
echo "<p>$Result</p>";
?>
```

4. Save the document as **ConditionalScript.php** in the Projects directory for Chapter 2, and then upload the document to the server.

5. Open the ConditionalScript.php file in your Web browser by entering the following URL: *http://<yourserver>/PHP_Projects/Chapter.02/Projects/ConditionalScript.php*.

6. Close your Web browser window.

Exercise 2-2

In this project, you will write a `while` statement that displays all odd numbers between 1 and 100 on the screen.

1. Create a new document in your text editor.

2. Type the `<!DOCTYPE>` declaration, `<html>` element, document head, and `<body>` element. Use the strict DTD and "Odd Numbers" as the content of the `<title>` element.

3. Create a script section in the document body with a `while` statement that displays all odd numbers between 1 and 100 on the screen.

4. Save the document as **OddNumbers.php** in the Projects directory for Chapter 2, and then upload the document to the server.

5. Open the OddNumbers.php file in your Web browser by entering the following URL: *http://<yourserver>/PHP_Projects/Chapter.02/Projects/OddNumbers.php*.

6. Close your Web browser window.

Exercise 2-3

In this project, you will identify and correct the logic flaws in a `while` statement.

1. Create a new document in your text editor.

2. Type the `<!DOCTYPE>` declaration, `<html>` element, document head, and `<body>` element. Use the strict DTD and "While Logic" as the content of the `<title>` element.

3. Create a script section in the document body that includes the following code:

```php
<?php
$Count = 0;
while ($Count > 100) {
        $Numbers[] = $Count;
        ++$Count;
foreach ($Count as $CurNum)
        echo "<p>$CurNum</p>";
}
?>
```

4. The code you typed in the preceding step should fill the array with the numbers 1 through 100 and then display them on the screen. However, the code contains several logic flaws that prevent it from running correctly. Identify and correct the logic flaws.

5. Save the document as **WhileLogic.php** in the Projects directory for Chapter 2, and then upload the document to the server.

6. Open the WhileLogic.php file in your Web browser by entering the following URL: *http://<yourserver>/PHP_Projects/ Chapter.02/Projects/WhileLogic.php*.

7. Close your Web browser window.

 Exercise 2-4

In this project, you will modify a nested if statement so it instead uses a compound conditional expression. You will use logical operators such as || (or) and && (and) to execute a conditional or looping statement based on multiple criteria.

1. Create a new document in your text editor.

2. Type the <!DOCTYPE> declaration, <html> element, document head, and <body> element. Use the strict DTD and "Gas Prices" as the content of the <title> element.

3. Create a script section in the document body that includes the following variable declaration and nested if statement:

```php
<?php
$GasPrice = 2.57;
if ($GasPrice >= 2) {
    if ($GasPrice <=3)
        echo "<p>Gas prices are between
            $2.00 and $3.00.</p>";
}
?>
```

4. Modify the nested if statement you created in the previous step so it uses a single if statement with a compound conditional expression. You need to use the && (and) logical operator.

5. Add an else clause to the if statement that displays "Gas prices are not between $2.00 and $3.00" if the compound conditional expression returns FALSE.

6. Save the document as **GasPrices.php** in the Projects directory for Chapter 2 and upload the document to the server.

7. Open the GasPrices.php file in your Web browser by entering the following URL: *http://<yourserver>/PHP_Projects/ Chapter.02/Projects/GasPrices.php*.

8. Close your Web browser window.

 ## Exercise 2-5

In this project, you will create header and footer pages that you will add to a Web page with the include statement.

1. Create a new document in your text editor and type the <!DOCTYPE> declaration, <html> element, document head, and <body> element. Use the strict DTD and "Coast City Computers" as the content of the <title> element.

2. Add the following text and elements to the document body:

```
<h2>Memorial Day Sale</h2>
<ul>
<li>Compaq Presario m2007us Notebook:
<strong>$799.99</strong></li>
<li>Epson Stylus CX6600 Color All-In-One Printer,
Print/Copy/Scan: <strong>$699.99</strong></li>
<li>Proview Technology Inc. KDS K715s 17-inch LCD
Monitor,
Silver/Black: <strong>$199.99</strong></li>
<li>Hawking Technology Hi-Speed Wireless-G Cardbus
Card:
<strong>$9.99</strong></li>
</ul>
```

3. Add the following PHP code section and `include` statement to the beginning of the document body. This statement includes an external file named inc_header.php at the start of the Web page.

```
<?php include("inc_header.php"); ?>
```

4. Add the following PHP code section and `include` statement to the end of the document body. This statement includes an external file named inc_footer.php at the end of the Web page.

```
<?php include("inc_footer.php"); ?>
```

5. Save the document as **CoastCityComputers.php** in the Projects directory for Chapter 2.

6. Create a new document in your text editor and add the following text and elements:

```
<table width="100%" style="border: 0">
<tr><td><h1>Coast City Computers</h1></td>
<td style="text-align: right"><strong>Buy Online or
Call 1-800-555-1212</strong></td></tr></table><hr />
```

7. Save the document as **inc_header.php** in the Projects directory for Chapter 2.

8. Create a new document in your text editor and add the following text and elements:

```
<hr />
<table width="100%" style="border: 0">
<tr><td><strong>Updated</strong> 06 January,
2010</td>
<td style="text-align: right">&copy; 2003 by Coast
City Computers.</td>
</tr>
<tr><td>
    <a href="http://validator.w3.org/check/
    referer"><img
        src="http://www.w3.org/Icons/valid-xhtml10"
        alt="Valid XHTML 1.0!" height="31"
        width="88" /></a>
</td>
<td style="text-align: right; vertical-align:
top">All Rights Reserved.</td></tr>
</table>
```

9. Save the document as **inc_footer.php** in the Projects directory for Chapter 2.

10. Upload the CoastCityComputers.php, inc_header.php, and inc_footer.php files to the server.

11. Open the CoastCityComputers.php file in your Web browser by entering the following URL: *http://<yourserver>/PHP_Projects/Chapter.02/Projects/CoastCityComputers.php*. The contents of the header and footer documents should appear on the Web page.

12. Close your Web browser window and text editor.

 ## Exercise 2-6

You will use an appropriate looping statement to write a script that displays a list of the Celsius equivalents of zero degrees Fahrenheit through 100 degrees Fahrenheit. To convert Fahrenheit to Celsius, subtract 32 from the Fahrenheit temperature, and then multiply the remainder by (5/9). To convert Celsius to Fahrenheit, multiply the Celsius temperature by (9/5), and then add 32. Use the round() function you learned in Chapter 1 to display the Celsius temperature to one place after the decimal point. Save the document as **TempConversion.php**.

The index page is the default page that a Web server displays in the browser if a specific filename is not part of the requested URL. If you enter *http://<yourserver>/ChineseZodiac/* in the browser, by default the Web server will search the ChineseZodiac Web folder for an index page using a list of filenames defined in the server configuration. A standard list of filenames would likely include the following: index.html, index. php, index.shtml, and index.htm. The first filename from the list that the server encounters (from left to right) will be opened in the browser.

Discovery Projects

The Chinese zodiac site is a comprehensive project that will be updated in the Discovery Projects section at the end of each chapter. All files for the site will be saved in a directory named ChineseZodiac in the base Web folder on the server.

Discovery Project 2-1

In your text editor, use XHTML scripting to develop the Chinese zodiac template page, which will include five sections: Header, Footer, Text Navigation, Button Navigation, and Dynamic Content. These sections will be populated with five include files. Use a table layout with CSS formatting or lay out the entire site with CSS. For this initial layout page, insert a placeholder in each section (i.e., [This is the header placeholder]) to identify the content that will be included later. Save the file as **index.php**, upload it to the ChineseZodiac folder, and view the file in the Web browser to verify that it displays as intended.

Discovery Project 2-2

For each of the template sections in the index.php page, create an include file. Remember that an include file requires only the XHTML tags to format the content, not the entire XHTML skeleton tags (<html>, <head>, <title>, and <body>).

Include Filenames	Description
inc_header.php	Inserts the banner image created in Discovery Project 1-1.
inc_button_nav.php	Inserts the nine buttons created in Discovery Project 1-2. Code to submit the buttons will be inserted in a later project.
inc_text_links.php	Inserts the code for a text links bar. Code to turn the text links into hyperlinks will be inserted in a later project.
inc_footer.php	Inserts a copyright symbol and the current year.
inc_home.php	Inserts a placeholder [Insert home page content here].

Table 2-1 Include files for the Chinese zodiac Web site

Create an Includes folder within the ChineseZodiac folder. Save each of the include files (with the names listed in Table 2-1) and upload the files to the Includes folder in the ChineseZodiac folder in the root Web directory on the server.

Because directory precedence is set in the server configuration file, it is important to test your server's order of precedence.

Discovery Project 2-3

In index.php, replace the [Placeholders] with `include` statements to include the five include files created in Discovery Project 2-2, passing the name of the respective include file to the `include` statement. Save the index.php file and upload the document to the ChineseZodiac folder on the server. View index.php in the browser to verify that each of the template sections displays the correct include file.

Discovery Project 2-4

Write a `for` loop that displays a table with the 12 Chinese zodiac signs as column headers, and with the years displayed below the appropriate column heading. Begin the table with the year 1912 and end with the current year. You may want to use the modulus operator to determine the number of columns in each row of the table.

Use an array to store and display a picture of the appropriate sign below the text header in each column. Use the pictures that you found and uploaded in Discovery Project 1-4.

Save the script as **Chinese_Zodiac_for_loop.php** in the ChineseZodiac folder and upload the document to the Web server.

Discovery Project 2-5

Modify the previous script to display the same table using a `while` loop. Save the script as **Chinese_Zodiac_while_loop.php** in the ChineseZodiac folder and upload the document to the Web server.

CHAPTER 3

Manipulating Strings

In this chapter you will:

- ◎ Construct text strings
- ◎ Work with single strings
- ◎ Work with multiple strings and parse strings
- ◎ Compare strings
- ◎ Use regular expressions

PHP is most commonly used for producing valid XHTML code and for processing form data submitted by users. Because all XHTML code and form data are strings, a good PHP programmer must be adept at dealing with strings. This chapter discusses techniques for manipulating strings.

Constructing Text Strings

As you learned in Chapter 1, a text string contains zero or more characters surrounded by double or single quotation marks. You can use text strings as literal values or assign them to a variable. For example, the first statement in the following code displays a literal text string, whereas the second statement assigns a text string to a variable. The third statement then uses the echo statement to display the text string assigned to the variable. Figure 3-1 shows the output of this code.

```
echo "<p>PHP literal text string</p>";
$StringVariable = "<p>PHP string variable</p>";
echo $StringVariable;
```

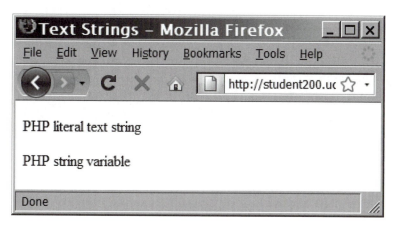

Figure 3-1   Different ways of displaying text strings

You can also surround a text string with single quotation marks. Regardless of the method you use, a string must begin and end with the same type of quotation mark. For example, echo "<p>This is a text string.</p>"; is valid because it starts and ends with double quotation marks. Likewise, echo '<p>This is a text string.</p>'; is valid because it begins and ends with single quotation marks. By contrast, the statement echo "<p>This is a text string.</p>'; is invalid because it starts with a double quotation mark and ends with a single quotation mark. In this case, the string would display incorrectly because the PHP scripting engine cannot tell where the literal string begins and ends.

125

When you want to include single quotes within a literal string, the easiest method is to surround the literal string with double quotation marks. Likewise, to include double quotes within a literal string, you can surround the string with single quotation marks. For example, the following statement assigns a text string surrounded by double quotation marks to the $LatinQuote variable. Figure 3-2 shows the output of the echo statement.

```
$LatinQuote = '<p>"Et tu, Brute!"</p>';
echo $LatinQuote;
```

Figure 3-2 Displaying a string that contains double quotation marks

Later in this chapter, you will learn other methods to include quotation marks and other special characters in text strings.

Working with String Operators

Up to this point, you have displayed values from multiple literal strings and variables by passing them to the echo and print statements as multiple arguments separated by commas. For example, the following code passes two literal strings and a variable to the echo statement:

```
$Speaker = "Julius Caesar";
echo '<p>"Et tu, Brute!", exclaimed ', $Speaker, ".</p>";
```

In PHP, you can also use two operators to combine strings. The first of these operators is the **concatenation operator** (.). The following code uses the concatenation operator to combine several string variables and literal strings, and assigns the new value to another variable:

```
$City = "Paris";
$Country = "France";
$Destination = "<p>" . $City . " is in "
    . $Country . ".</p>";
echo $Destination;
```

The combined value of the $City and $Country variables and the literal strings that are assigned to the $Destination variable is <p>Paris is in France.</p>.

You can also combine strings using the **concatenation assignment operator** (.=). The following code combines two text strings, but without using the $City or $Country variables:

```
$Destination = "<p>Paris";
$Destination .= " is in France.</p>";
echo $Destination;
```

Again, the value of the $Destination variable is "<p>Paris is in France.</p>".

To build a string using the concatenation assignment operator:

1.   Create a new document in your text editor.

2.   Type the <!DOCTYPE> declaration, <html> element, document head, and <body> element. Use the strict DTD and "Musical Scale" as the content of the <title> element.

3.   Add the following script section to the document body:

```
<?php
?>
```

4.   Insert the following array in the script section:

```
$MusicalScale = array("do", "re", "mi", "fa", "so",
"la", "ti");
```

5.   Build an output string using a foreach loop with the $MusicalNotes array, as follows:

```
$OutputString="The notes of the musical scale are: ";
foreach ($MusicalScale as $CurrentNote)
     $OutputString .= " " . $CurrentNote;
```

6.   Add the following statements to display the results in your browser window.

```
echo "<p>$OutputString</p>";
```

7.   Save the file as **MusicalScale.php**, upload it to the Chapter folder for Chapter 3, and then open the file in your Web browser by entering the following URL: *http://<yourserver>/PHP_Projects/Chapter.03/Chapter/ MusicalScale.php*. Figure 3-3 shows the output.

127

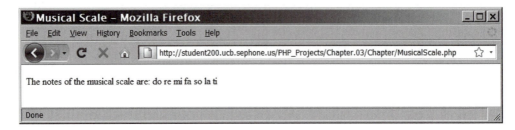

Figure 3-3 Output of MusicalScale.php

8. Close your Web browser window.

Adding Escape Characters and Sequences

You need to take extra care when using single quotation marks with possessives and contractions in strings surrounded by single quotation marks because the PHP scripting engine always looks for the first closing single quotation mark to match an opening single quotation mark. For example, consider the following statement:

```
echo '<p>This code's not going to work.</p>';
```

This statement displays incorrectly because the PHP scripting engine assumes that the literal string ends with the apostrophe following "code." To get around this problem, you should include an escape character before the apostrophe in "code's". An **escape character** tells the compiler or interpreter that the character that follows it has a special purpose. In PHP, the escape character is the backslash (\). Placing a backslash in front of an apostrophe tells the PHP scripting engine to treat the apostrophe as a regular keyboard character, such as "a," "b," "1," or "2," and not as part of a single quotation mark pair that encloses a text string. The backslash in the following statement tells the PHP scripting engine to display the apostrophe following the word "code" as an apostrophe:

```
echo '<p>This code\'s going to work.</p>';
```

There's no need for a backslash before an apostrophe if you surround the text string with double quotation marks, as follows:

```
echo "<p>This code's going to work.</p>";
```

Although the apostrophe in the preceding statement displays correctly, other characters require an escape character within a string surrounded by double quotation marks. The escape character combined with one or more other characters is called an **escape sequence**. The backslash followed by an apostrophe (\') is an example of an escape sequence. Most escape sequences carry out special functions; for example, the escape sequence \t inserts a tab into a string. Table 3-1 describes the escape sequences that can be added to a double-quoted string in PHP.

Escape Sequence	Description
\\	Inserts a backslash
\$	Inserts a dollar sign
\r	Inserts a carriage return
\f	Inserts a form feed
\"	Inserts a double quotation mark
\t	Inserts a horizontal tab
\v	Inserts a vertical tab
\n	Inserts a new line
\x*h*	Inserts a character whose hexadecimal value is *h*, where *h* is one or two hexadecimal digits (0-9, A-F), case insensitive
\o	Inserts a character whose octal value is *o*, where *o* is one, two, or three octal digits (0-7)

Table 3-1   PHP escape sequences within double quotation marks

Within a literal string surrounded by double quotation marks, the backslash will be displayed if you place it before any character other than those listed in Table 3-1.

129

As a good programming practice, you should include an \n escape sequence at the end of an echo statement output string as needed to properly format the XHTML source code generated by the PHP script. Although this normally has no effect on the Web browser display, it makes the XHTML source code easier to read and debug. The print statement automatically appends a "new line" character to the string it returns.

Notice that the backslash is one of the characters inserted into a string by an escape sequence. Because the escape character itself is a backslash, you must use the escape sequence \\ to include a backslash as a character in a string. For example, to include the path "C:\Course Technology\1687-5\" in a string, you must include a backslash escape character before every literal backslash you want to appear in the string, making each single backslash into a pair of backslashes:

```
echo "<p>My PHP files are located in
C:\\Course Technology\\1687-5\\.</p>";
```

The following code shows another example of an escape character, this time with the double quotation escape sequence (\"). Figure 3-4 shows the output.

```
$Speaker = "Julius Caesar";
echo "<p>\"Et tu, Brute!\" exclaimed $Speaker.</p>";
```

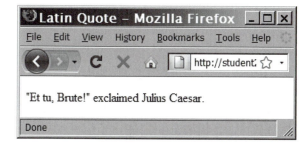

Figure 3-4   Using escape sequences for double quotes

Because the string in the previous example contained a variable, the string would not display as intended if you used single quotes around it, as discussed previously. Remember from Chapter 1 that variables are not expanded when the string is enclosed in single quotes. Similarly, the escape sequences listed in Table 3-1 will be treated as literal text if the string is enclosed in single quotes.

An alternative to using the double quotation mark escape sequence is to use single quotation marks for the starting text portion of the literal string and then combine the $Speaker variable with the concatenation operator, as follows:

```php
$Speaker = "Julius Caesar";
echo '<p>"Et tu, Brute!" exclaimed '
    . $Speaker . ".</p>";
```

To use escape sequences to format text:

1. Create a new document in your text editor.

2. Type the <!DOCTYPE> declaration, <html> element, document head, and <body> element. Use the strict DTD and "Formatted Text" as the content of the <title> element.

3. Add the following script section to the document body:

```php
<?php
?>
```

4. Declare and initialize a variable called $DisplayValue, as follows:

```php
$DisplayValue=9.876;
```

5. Add the following PHP code to display some unformatted text. Be sure to include the code for the opening and closing XHTML <pre> tags. Normally, the Web browser will treat all new lines, carriage returns, and tabs as spaces. Using the <pre> tag tells the Web browser not to convert those characters to spaces.

```php
echo "<pre>\n";
echo "Unformatted text line 1. ";
echo "Unformatted text line 2. ";
echo "$DisplayValue = $DisplayValue";
echo "</pre>\n";
```

6. Add the following PHP code to display some formatted text:

```php
echo "<pre>\n";
echo "Formatted text line 1. \r\n";
echo "\tFormatted text line 2. \r\n";
echo "\$DisplayValue = $DisplayValue";
echo "</pre>\n";
```

7. Save the file as **FormattedText.php**, upload it to the server, and then open the file in your Web browser by entering the following URL: *http://<yourserver>/PHP_Projects/Chapter.03/Chapter/ FormattedText.php*. Figure 3-5 shows the output. Notice that the unformatted lines run together but the formatted lines do not. The second formatted line is indented, and the value of $DisplayValue (9.876) appears at the beginning of the third line of the unformatted section. However, the text "$DisplayValue" appears at the beginning of the third line of the formatted section.

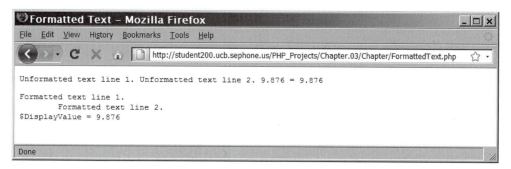

Figure 3-5 Output of FormattedText.php

8. Close your Web browser window.

Simple and Complex String Syntax

Values and variables can be combined in a literal string using simple or complex syntax. **Simple string syntax** allows you to use the value of a variable within a string by including the variable name inside a text string enclosed by double quotation marks (not single quotation marks). For example, the following code displays the text "Do you have any broccoli?" in the Web browser:

```
$Vegetable = "broccoli";
echo "<p>Do you have any $Vegetable?</p>";
```

When the PHP scripting engine encounters a dollar sign within a text string, it attempts to evaluate any characters that follow the dollar sign as part of the variable name until it comes to a character that is not allowed in an identifier, such as a space. With the preceding example, the $Vegetable variable is interpreted correctly because the question mark is not a legal character for an identifier. However, consider the following version of the preceding code:

```
$Vegetable = "tomato";
echo "<p>Do you have any $Vegetables?</p>";
```

Because an 's' is appended to the $Vegetable variable name, the preceding echo statement displays incorrectly. The PHP scripting engine is attempting to locate a variable named $Vegetables (plural), which has not been declared, so no text is displayed in place of the variable name. To make the preceding code work, you need to surround the variable name with curly braces ({}), as shown in the following example. This type of structure, in which variables are placed within curly braces inside a string, is called **complex string syntax**.

```php
$Vegetable = "carrot";
echo "<p>Do you have any {$Vegetable}s?</p>";
```

The preceding echo statement displays the text string "Do you have any carrots?" Complex string syntax is only recognized if the opening brace is immediately before or after a variable's dollar sign. The following version of the preceding code also displays correctly:

```php
$Vegetable = "carrot";
echo "<p>Do you have any ${Vegetable}s?</p>";
```

However, if you place any characters between the opening brace and the dollar sign, the contents of the string are interpreted as literal values. For example, because the following code includes a space between the opening brace and the dollar sign, the echo statement displays the text string "Do you have any { carrot}s?":

```php
$Vegetable = "carrot";
echo "<p>Do you have any { $Vegetable}s?</p>";
```

To display a list of authors and their works:

1. Create a new document in your text editor.

2. Type the <!DOCTYPE> declaration, <html> element, document head, and <body> element. Use the strict DTD and "Books and Authors" as the content of the <title> element.

3. Add the following script section to the document body:

   ```php
   <?php
   ?>
   ```

4. Declare and initialize an array called $Books, as follows:

   ```php
   $Books = array("The Adventures of Huckleberry Finn",
       "Nineteen Eighty-Four",
       "Alice's Adventures in Wonderland",
       "The Cat in the Hat");
   ```

5. Declare and initialize an array called $Authors, as follows:

   ```php
   $Authors = array("Mark Twain",
       "George Orwell",
       "Lewis Carroll",
       "Dr. Seuss");
   ```

6. Declare and initialize an array called `$RealNames`, as follows:

```
$RealNames = array("Samuel Clemens",
     "Eric Blair",
     "Charles Dodson",
     "Theodor Geisel");
```

7. Create a `for` loop to display a string that combines the values from the three arrays, as follows. Note the use of complex string syntax to ensure that the PHP scripting engine handles the array elements correctly.

```
for ($i = 0; $i < count($Books); ++$i)
     echo "<p>The real name of {$Authors[$i]}, ".
          "the author of \"{$Books[$i]}\", ".
          "is {$RealNames[$i]}.</p>";
```

8. Save the file as **BooksAndAuthors.php**, upload it to the server, and then open the file in your Web browser by entering the following URL: *http://<yourserver>/PHP_Projects/Chapter.03/Chapter/BooksAndAuthors.php*. Figure 3-6 shows the output in your Web browser window.

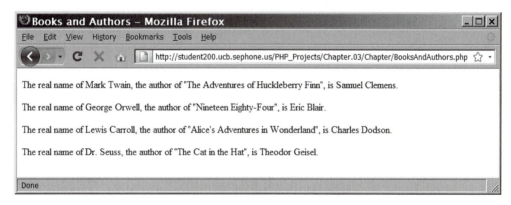

Figure 3-6 Output of the Books and Authors script

9. Close your Web browser window.

Short Quiz

1. Explain the difference between a concatenation operator and a concatenation assignment operator.

2. Describe two ways to display double quotation marks within a literal string.

3. Describe the use of curly braces in complex string syntax.

Working with a Single String

PHP provides a large number of functions for analyzing, altering, and parsing text strings. In this section, you will study basic techniques for manipulating an individual string, including how to count characters and words. You will also learn how to transpose, convert, and change the case of text within a string.

Counting Characters and Words in a String

You will often find it necessary to count characters and words in strings. For example, you might need to count characters in a password to ensure that a user selects a password with a minimum number of characters. Or, you might have a Web page that allows users to submit classified ads that cannot exceed a maximum number of words.

The most commonly used string-counting function is the `strlen()` function, which returns the total number of characters in a string. You pass to the `strlen()` function a literal string or the name of a string variable whose characters you want to count. For example, the following code uses the `strlen()` function to count the number of characters in a variable named `$BookTitle`. The `echo` statement displays "The book title contains 23 characters."

The `strlen()` function counts escape sequences such as \n as one character.

```
$BookTitle = "The Cask of Amontillado";
echo "<p>The book title contains " . strlen($BookTitle)
    . " characters.</p>";
```

Another commonly used string-counting function is the `str_word_count()` function, which returns the number of words in a string. You pass to the `str_word_count()` function a literal string or the name of a string variable whose words you want to count. The following example shows a modified version of the preceding code, but this time with the `str_word_count()` function. The `echo` statement displays "The book title contains 4 words."

```
$BookTitle = "The Cask of Amontillado";
echo "<p>The book title contains " .
    str_word_count($BookTitle)
    . " words.</p>";
```

To show the length and word count of some book titles:

1. Return to the **BooksAndAuthors.php** script in your text editor.

2. Change the content of the `<title>` element to "Title Information."

3. Delete the $Authors and $RealNames arrays.

4. Modify the for loop to display the information about the book titles, as follows:

```
for ($i = 0; $i < count($Books); ++$i)
echo "<p>The title \"{$Books[$i]}\" contains " .
    strlen($Books[$i]) . " characters and " .
    str_word_count($Books[$i]) . " words.</p>";
```

5. Save the file as **TitleInfo.php**, upload it to the server, and then open the file in your Web browser by entering the following URL:
http://<yourserver>/PHP_Projects/Chapter.03/Chapter/ TitleInfo.php. Figure 3-7 shows the output in your Web browser window.

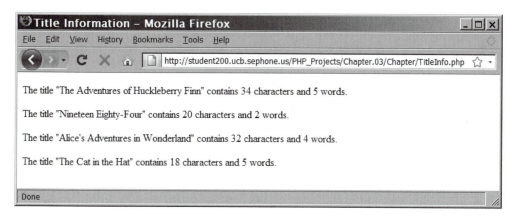

Title Information – Mozilla Firefox

File   Edit   View   History   Bookmarks   Tools   Help

http://student200.ucb.sephone.us/PHP_Projects/Chapter.03/Chapter/TitleInfo.php

The title "The Adventures of Huckleberry Finn" contains 34 characters and 5 words.

The title "Nineteen Eighty-Four" contains 20 characters and 2 words.

The title "Alice's Adventures in Wonderland" contains 32 characters and 4 words.

The title "The Cat in the Hat" contains 18 characters and 5 words.

Done

Figure 3-7   Output of the Title Information script

6. Close your Web browser window.

Modifying the Case of a String

When working with strings, you often cannot guarantee that they will be in the correct case. This is especially true when dealing with strings from external sources, such as database queries or user form input. PHP provides several functions for manipulating the case of a string.

For many types of codes, whether within the computer world or not, text strings are expected to appear only in uppercase letters. For example, U.S. state and Canadian province postal abbreviations should always be uppercase. The strtoupper() function converts all of the letters in a string to uppercase. Similarly, the strtolower() function converts all of the letters in a string to lowercase. For

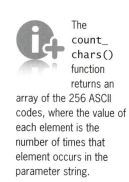

The count_chars() function returns an array of the 256 ASCII codes, where the value of each element is the number of times that element occurs in the parameter string.

The ucfirst() and lcfirst() functions only change the first character of a string. The ucwords() function only changes the first character of each word. These functions do not change the case of any other character in a string. To ensure that the remaining characters in a string are lowercase when using the ucfirst() and ucwords()functions, you need to use the strtolower() function on the string first. To ensure that the remaining characters are uppercase when using the lcfirst() function, you need to use the strtoupper() function on the string first.

example, this function is useful when converting a document from HTML to XHTML, because the XHTML standard specifies that all element and attribute tags must be lowercase.

When working with natural languages, more complex conversions are needed. Sentences in English start with an uppercase letter. The ucfirst() function ensures that the first character of a string is uppercase. If you need the reverse of ucfirst(), the lcfirst() function converts the first character of a string to lowercase. Titles of books, songs, poems, and articles usually have the first letter of each word capitalized. The ucwords() function converts the first character of each word in a string to uppercase.

Consider the following example and the output shown in Figure 3-8:

```
$ConfusingText = "tHIS seNTEnCE iS HArD to rEAD.";
echo "<h1>Confusing Text</h1>\n";
echo "ucfirst: " . ucfirst($ConfusingText) . "<br />\n";
echo "lcfirst: " . lcfirst($ConfusingText) . "<br />\n";
echo "ucwords: " . ucwords($ConfusingText) . "<br />\n";
$LowercaseText = strtolower($ConfusingText);
echo "<h1>Lowercase Text</h1>\n";
echo "ucfirst: " . ucfirst($LowercaseText) . "<br />\n";
echo "lcfirst: " . lcfirst($LowercaseText) . "<br />\n";
echo "ucwords: " . ucwords($LowercaseText) . "<br />\n";
```

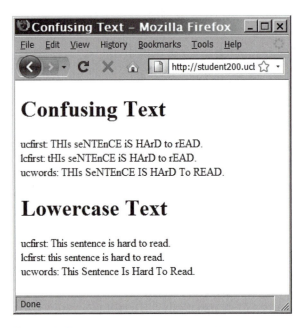

Figure 3-8 Using the ucfirst(), lcfirst(), and ucwords() functions

In the three lines under the "Confusing Text" title, it is still very difficult to read the text, because the strings are a mix of uppercase and lowercase letters. In addition, it is hard to see what changed in the three lines. The three lines under the "Lowercase Text" title are much clearer to read and it is easier to see what changed, because all of the text started in lowercase.

To manipulate the case of a string:

1. Create a new document in your text editor.

2. Type the `<!DOCTYPE>` declaration, `<html>` element, document head, and `<body>` element. Use the strict DTD and "Word Play" as the content of the `<title>` element.

3. Add the following script section to the document body:

```php
<?php
?>
```

4. Declare and initialize a string called `$StartingText`, as follows:

```php
$StartingText = "mAdAm, i'M aDaM.";
```

5. Add the following four lines of code to convert and display the string in uppercase and lowercase:

```php
$UppercaseText = strtoupper($StartingText);
$LowercaseText = strtolower($StartingText);
echo "<p>$UppercaseText</p>\n";
echo "<p>$LowercaseText</p>\n";
```

6. Add the following four lines to display the text with different mixes of uppercase and lowercase letters:

```php
echo "<p>" . ucfirst($LowercaseText) . "</p>\n";
echo "<p>" . lcfirst($UppercaseText) . "</p>\n";
$WorkingText = ucwords($LowercaseText);
echo "<p>$WorkingText</p>\n";
```

7. Save the file as **WordPlay.php**, upload it to the server, and then open the file in your Web browser by entering the following URL:
http://<yourserver>/PHP_Projects/Chapter.03/Chapter/ WordPlay.php. Figure 3-9 shows the output in your Web browser window.

The `ucfirst()` and `ucwords()` functions do not always capitalize a proper name correctly, such as in strings that require more than one capital letter. Consider trying to convert the strings "des moines", "mary-elizabeth", and "dimaggio" to the proper names "Des Moines", "Mary-Elizabeth", and "DiMaggio". The `ucfirst()` function will convert the strings to "Des moines", "Mary-elizabeth", and "Dimaggio", respectively. The `ucwords()` function will properly convert "des moines" to "Des Moines", but its conversions of the other two strings will match those of the `ucfirst()` function.

138

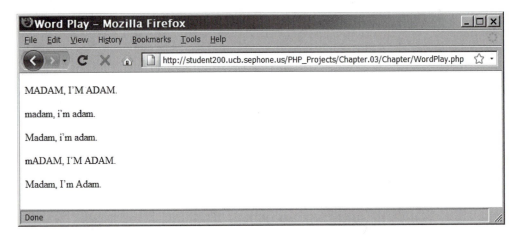

MADAM, I'M ADAM.

madam, i'm adam.

Madam, i'm adam.

mADAM, I'M ADAM.

Madam, I'm Adam.

Figure 3-9   Output of WordPlay.php

8.   Close your Web browser window.

Encoding and Decoding a String

Turning on the PHP configuration setting "ENT_NOQUOTES" disables the conversion of the double quotation mark. Turning on the PHP configuration setting "ENT_QUOTES" enables the conversion of the single quotation mark.

Because of the close relationship between XHTML, the Internet, and PHP, several functions are built into PHP for dealing with Web pages. The `htmlspecialchars()` and `htmlspecialchars_decode()` functions in XHTML are only useful for processing strings. XHTML has five reserved characters: the ampersand (&), double quotation mark ("), single quotation mark ('), left angle bracket or "less than" symbol (<), and right angle bracket or "greater than" symbol (>). To display these characters as text on an XHTML page, they should be encoded using HTML character entities. The `htmlspecialchars()` function converts any occurrence of these five characters to their equivalent HTML character entity. Specifically, '&' becomes '&', '"' becomes '"', ''' becomes ''', '<' becomes '<', and '>' becomes '>'. The `htmlspecialchars_decode()` function performs the reverse operation, converting the HTML character entities into their equivalent characters.

Passwords are required for secure access to a Web site. Storing passwords as plain text strings creates security and privacy issues. The `md5()` function is a way to avoid storing passwords as plain text. The `md5()` function uses a strong encryption algorithm (called the Message-Digest Algorithm) to create a one-way hash of the entered string. A **one-way hash** is a fixed-length string based on the entered text, from which it is nearly impossible to determine the original text.

Because it is a one-way hash, there is no equivalent decode function for the `md5()` function. In theory, a one-way hash makes it impossible to convert the stored hash value back to the original password to compare against an entered password. Instead, the entered password is passed to the md5() function, and the resulting hash value is compared against the stored hash value. If the two are the same, the entered password is considered to be valid.

Other Ways to Manipulate a String

If a string has leading or trailing spaces, the trim() function will remove them. To remove only the leading spaces, use the ltrim() (left trim) function. To remove only the trailing spaces, use the rtrim() (right trim) function.

To return only a portion of a string, use the substr() function. This function takes the input string as the first parameter, the starting position as the second parameter, and the length of the string to return as an optional third parameter. For numbers that are zero or positive, the starting position is calculated from the start of the string, with zero being the first character. For negative numbers, the starting position is calculated from the end of the string, with –1 being the last character. If the length is omitted or is greater than the remaining length of the string, the entire remainder of the string is returned. Figure 3-10 shows the output of the following example:

```
$ExampleString = "woodworking project";
echo substr($ExampleString,4) . "<br />\n";
echo substr($ExampleString,4,7) . "<br />\n";
echo substr($ExampleString,0,8) . "<br />\n";
echo substr($ExampleString,-7) . "<br />\n";
echo substr($ExampleString,-12,4) . "<br />\n";
```

PHP provides a number of functions for encrypting strings using different algorithms.

Although converting a one-way hash value back to the original value is supposedly impossible, hackers have managed to "crack" many one-way hash algorithms, including the md5() algorithm. Encryption algorithms, like physical locks, will not stop someone who is determined to defeat them.

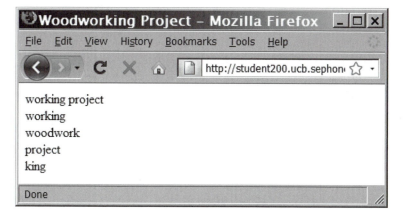

Figure 3-10   Some examples using the substr() function

Many more functions are available in PHP to manipulate the characters in a string. Although they will not all be discussed in this section, two deserve special mention. The `strrev()` function reverses the order of the characters in a string, and the `str_shuffle()` function randomly scrambles the order.

To add the `md5()`, `substr()`, `strrev()`, and `str_shuffle()` functions to the Word Play example:

1. Return to the **WordPlay.php** script in your text editor.

2. Add the following five lines before the end of the PHP block:

```
echo "<p>" . md5($WorkingText) . "</p>\n";
echo "<p>" . substr($WorkingText,0,6) . "</p>\n";
echo "<p>" . substr($WorkingText,7) . "</p>\n";
echo "<p>" . strrev($WorkingText) . "</p>\n";
echo "<p>" . str_shuffle($WorkingText) . "</p>\n";
```

3. Save the WordPlay.php file, upload it to the server, and then open the file in your Web browser by entering the following URL: *http://<yourserver>/PHP_Projects/Chapter.03/Chapter/WordPlay.php*. Figure 3-11 shows the new Web page.

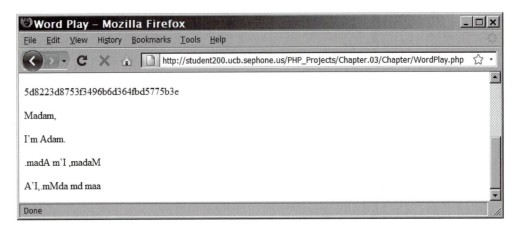

Figure 3-11   Output of the Word Play script

4. Close your Web browser window.

Short Quiz

1. What string function would you use to determine the number of characters in a password that a user has entered?

2. What string function would you use to determine if an essay keyed in a `<textarea>` form input field exceeds the maximum number of words allowed?

3. What two string functions could be used to convert the case of text strings to all uppercase or all lowercase letters?

Working with Multiple Strings

PHP provides many functions for splitting a string into substrings, merging multiple strings, and changing one string based on another. In this section, you will study basic techniques for working with more than one string.

Finding and Extracting Characters and Substrings

When applied to text strings, the term **parsing** refers to the act of dividing a string into logical component substrings or tokens. This is essentially the same process as the parsing (rendering) that occurs in a Web browser when it extracts the necessary formatting information from a Web page before displaying it on the screen. In the case of a Web page, the document itself is one large text string from which formatting and other information needs to be extracted. However, at a programming level, parsing usually refers to the extraction of information from string literals and variables.

In some situations, you will need to find and extract characters and substrings from a string. For example, if your script receives an e-mail address, you may need to extract the name portion of the e-mail address or domain name. Several functions in PHP allow you to find and extract characters and substrings from a string.

There are two types of string search and extraction functions: functions that return a numeric position in a text string and those that return a character or substring. Both functions return a value of FALSE if the search string is not found. To use functions that return the numeric position in a text string, you need to understand that the position of characters in a text string begins with a value of 0, the same as with indexed array elements. For example, the `strpos()` function performs a case-sensitive search and returns the position of the first occurrence of a substring within a string. You pass two arguments to the `strpos()` function: The first argument is the string you want to search, and the second argument contains the substring for which you want to search. If the search substring is not found, the `strpos()` function returns a Boolean value of FALSE. The following code uses the `strpos()` function to determine whether the `$Email` variable contains an @ character. Because the position of text strings begins with 0, the echo statement returns a value of 9, even though the @ character is the 10th character in the string.

```
$Email = "president@whitehouse.gov";
echo strpos($Email, '@'); // returns 9
```

If you simply want to determine whether a character exists in a string, you need to keep in mind that PHP converts the Boolean values TRUE and FALSE to 1 and 0, respectively. However, these values are character positions within a string. For example, the following statement returns a value of 0 because "p" is the first character in the string:

```
$Email = "president@whitehouse.gov";
echo strpos($Email, 'p'); // returns 0
```

To determine whether the `strpos()` function (and other string functions) actually returns a Boolean FALSE value and not a 0 representing the first character in a string, you must use the strict equal operator (`===`) or the strict not equal operator (`!==`). The following example uses the `strpos()` function and the strict not equal operator to determine whether the `$Email` variable contains an @ character:

You first encountered the strict not equal operator in Chapter 1.

```
$Email = "president@whitehouse.gov";
if (strpos($Email, '@') !== FALSE)
    echo "<p>The e-mail address contains an @ character.</p>";
else
    echo "<p>The e-mail address does not contain an @
        character.</p>";
```

To return the last portion of a string, starting with a specified character, you use `strchr()` or `strrchr()`. You pass to both functions the string and the character for which you want to search. Both functions return a substring from the specified characters to the end of the string. The only difference between the two functions is that the `strchr()` function starts searching at the beginning of a string, whereas the `strrchr()` function starts searching at the end of a string. The following code uses the `strrchr()` function to return the top-level domain (TLD) of the e-mail address in the `$Email` variable:

Because the e-mail address in the `$Email` variable in this example only contains a single period, you can use either the `strchr()` or `strrchr()` function.

```
$Email = "president@whitehouse.gov";
echo "<p>The top-level domain of the e-mail address is "
    . strrchr($Email, ".") . ".</p>";
```

To use the `strpos()` function to check whether e-mail addresses contain ampersands and a period to separate the domain name from the top-level domain:

1. Create a new document in your text editor.

2. Type the `<!DOCTYPE>` declaration, `<html>` element, document head, and `<body>` element. Use the strict DTD and "E-Mail Validator" as the content of the `<title>` element.

3. Add the following script section to the document body:

```php
<?php
?>
```

4. Declare an array called `$EmailAddresses`. Populate the list with several valid and invalid e-mail addresses. The following code provides a good starting point, but you may add more addresses.

```php
$EmailAddresses = array(
    "john.smith@php.test",
    "mary.smith.mail.php.example",
    "john.jones@php.invalid",
    "alan.smithee@test",
    "jsmith456@example.com",
    "jsmith456@test",
    "mjones@example",
    "mjones@example.net",
    "jane.a.doe@example.org");
```

The three top-level domains `.test`, `.example`, and `.invalid`, as well as the three domains `example.com`, `example.net`, and `example.org`, are special names that will never connect to a real server.

5. Add the following function to the beginning of the script section, immediately after the declaration statement for the `$EmailAddresses` array. The function uses two `strpos()` functions to determine whether the string passed to it contains an ampersand and a period. If the string contains both characters, a value of TRUE is returned. If not, a value of FALSE is returned.

```php
function validateAddress($Address) {
    if (strpos($Address, '@') !== FALSE &&
        strpos($Address,
        '.') !== FALSE)
            return TRUE;
    else
            return FALSE;
}
```

6. Add the following `foreach` statement immediately after the `validateAddress` function declaration. The `if` conditional expression passes the `$Address` variable to the `validateAddress()` function. If the function returns a value of `FALSE`, the `echo` statement executes.

```
foreach ($EmailAddresses as $Address) {
    if (validateAddress($Address) == FALSE)
        echo "<p>The e-mail address <em>$Address</em>
            does not appear to be valid.</p>\n";
}
```

7. Save the file as **PHPEmail.php**, upload it to the server, and then open the file in your Web browser by entering the following URL: *http://<yourserver>/PHP_Projects/Chapter.03/Chapter/PHPEmail.php*. The output for the preceding addresses is shown in Figure 3-12.

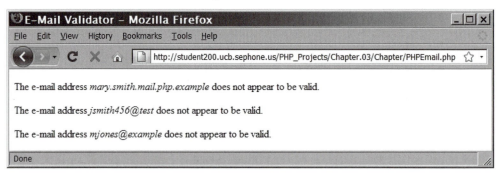

Figure 3-12 Output of the E-Mail Validator script

8. Close your Web browser window.

Replacing Characters and Substrings

In addition to finding and extracting characters in a string, you might need to replace them. PHP provides a number of functions to replace text within a string, including `str_replace()`, `str_ireplace()`, and `substr_replace()`.

The `str_replace()` and `str_ireplace()` functions both accept three arguments: the string you want to search for, a replacement string, and the string in which you want to replace characters. The replacement functions do not modify the contents of an existing string. Instead, they return a new string, which you can assign to a variable, use in an `echo` statement, or use in your script in some other way. The following example demonstrates how to use the `str_replace()` function to replace "president" in the $Email variable with "vice.president".

```
$Email = "president@whitehouse.gov";
$NewEmail = str_replace("president", "vice.president",
$Email);
echo $NewEmail;
        // displays 'vice.president@whitehouse.gov'
```

Instead of replacing all occurrences of characters within a string, the `substr_replace()` function allows you to replace characters within a specified portion of a string. You pass to the `substr_replace()` function the string you want to search, the replacement text, and the starting and ending positions of the characters you want to replace. If you do not include the last argument, the `substr_replace()` function replaces all the characters from the starting position to the end of the string. For example, the following code uses the `strpos()` and `substr_replace()` functions to replace "president" in the $Email variable with "vice.president."

```
$Email = "president@whitehouse.gov";
$NameEnd = strpos($Email, "@");
$NewEmail = substr_replace($Email, "vice.president", 0,
    $NameEnd);
echo $NewEmail;
        // displays 'vice.president@whitehouse.gov'
```

The following code demonstrates how to use the `substr_replace()` function to replace text from one string when storing the value in a new variable. The code uses the `strpos()` and `strrpos()` functions to locate the starting and ending positions of the word "Medical" in "American Medical Association". The `substr_replace()` function then replaces the word "Medical" with the word "Heart", changing the name to "American Heart Association" when storing the value in the new location. Figure 3-13 shows the results.

```
$FirstStudyPublisher = "American Medical Association";
$MiddleTermStart = strpos($FirstStudyPublisher, " ") + 1;
$MiddleTermEnd = strrpos($FirstStudyPublisher, " ") -
$MiddleTermStart;
$SecondStudyPublisher = substr_
replace($FirstStudyPublisher, "Heart",
    $MiddleTermStart, $MiddleTermEnd);
echo "<p>The first study was published by the
    $FirstStudyPublisher.</p>\n";
echo "<p> The second study was published by the
    $SecondStudyPublisher.</p>\n";
```

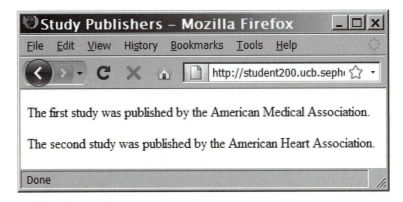

Figure 3-13   Output of the Study Publisher script

To use the `str_replace()` function to display a list of American presidents and their terms in office:

1. Create a new document in your text editor.

2. Type the `<!DOCTYPE>` declaration, `<html>` element, document head, and `<body>` element. Use the strict DTD and "Presidential Terms" as the content of the `<title>` element.

3. Add the following script section to the document body:

```php
<?php
?>
```

4. Declare an array called `$Presidents`. Populate the list with the names of the first five presidents, as follows:

```php
$Presidents = array(
    "George Washington",
    "John Adams",
    "Thomas Jefferson",
    "James Madison",
    "James Monroe");
```

5. Declare an array called `$YearsInOffice`. Populate the list with the terms of the first five presidents, as follows:

```php
$YearsInOffice = array(
    "1789 to 1797",
    "1797 to 1801",
    "1801 to 1809",
    "1809 to 1817",
    "1817 to 1825");
```

6. Declare a template string for the output as follows:

```php
$OutputTemplate = "<p>President [NAME] served from
[TERM]</p>\n";
```

7. Add the following `foreach` loop to retrieve each president and create an output string from the template string:

```
foreach ($Presidents as $Sequence => $Name) {
    $TempString = str_replace("[NAME]", $Name,
        $OutputTemplate);
    $OutputString = str_replace("[TERM]",
        $YearsInOffice[$Sequence],
        $TempString);
    echo $OutputString;
}
```

8. Save the file as **Presidents.php**, upload it to the server, and then open the file in your Web browser by entering the following URL:
http://<yourserver>/PHP_Projects/Chapter.03/Chapter/Presidents.php. Figure 3-14 shows the output.

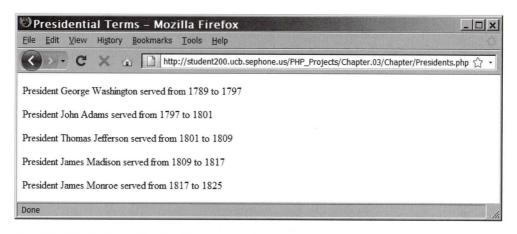

Figure 3-14 Output of the Presidents.php script

9. Close your Web browser window.

Dividing Strings into Smaller Pieces

If you receive a text string that contains multiple data elements separated by a common delimiter, you will probably want to split the string into its individual elements. A **delimiter** is a character or string that is used to separate components in a list. The delimiter is usually not found in any of the elements. For example, you may receive a list of names, separated by commas. Although you could use some of the string functions you've seen so far to manually parse such a string into smaller pieces, you can save yourself a lot of work by using the `strtok()` function to break a string into smaller strings, called **tokens**. When it is first called, the syntax for the `strtok()` function

If you specify an empty string as the second argument of the strtok() function, or if the string does not contain any of the separators you specify, the strtok() function returns the entire string.

is $variable = strtok(*string*, *separators*);. The strtok() function assigns to $variable the token (substring) from the beginning of the string to the first separator. To assign the next token to $variable, you call the strtok() function again, but only pass to it a single argument containing the separator. The PHP scripting engine keeps track of the current token and assigns the next token to $variable, starting at the first character after the separator, each time the strtok() function is called and until the end of the string is reached. If there are no characters between two separators, between the start of the string and the first separator, or between the last separator and the end of the string, strtok() returns an empty string.

The first statement in the following code assigns the names of the first five American presidents to the $Presidents variable, separated by semicolons. The first strtok() function assigns the first token (George Washington) to the $President variable. The while statement then displays the token and assigns the next token to the $President variable. The while loop iterates through the tokens until the $President variable is equal to NULL. Figure 3-15 shows the output.

```php
$Presidents = "George Washington;John Adams;Thomas
Jefferson;James Madison;James Monroe";
$President = strtok($Presidents, ";");
while ($President != NULL) {
    echo "$President<br />";
    $President = strtok(";");
}
```

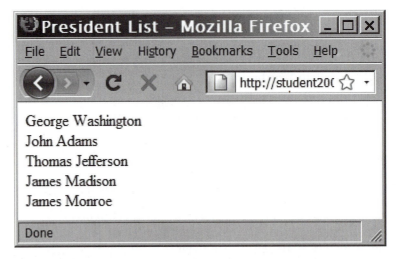

Figure 3-15   Using strtok() to divide a list using semicolons

The strtok() function does not divide a string into tokens by using a substring that is passed as its second argument. Instead, it divides a string into tokens using any of the characters that are passed in the second argument. For example, if you include a semicolon and a space ("; ") in the second argument for the strtok() function, the string is split into tokens at each semicolon or space in the string. The following example contains a modified version of the preceding code. In this version, the *separators* arguments passed to the strtok() functions contain a semicolon and a space. For this reason, the string is split into tokens at each semicolon and individual space in the $Presidents variable, as shown in Figure 3-16.

```
$Presidents = "George Washington;John Adams;Thomas
Jefferson;James Madison;James Monroe";
$President = strtok($Presidents, "; ");
while ($President != NULL) {
    echo "$President<br />";
    $President = strtok("; ");
}
```

Figure 3-16 Using strtok() to divide a list using semicolons and spaces

To look for empty fields in a UNIX password file record using the strtok() function:

1. Create a new document in your text editor.

2. Type the <!DOCTYPE> declaration, <html> element, document head, and <body> element. Use the strict DTD and "Password Fields" as the content of the <title> element.

3. Add the following script section to the document body:

```php
<?php
?>
```

4. Declare and initialize a string called $Record, as follows:

```php
$Record = "jdoe:8W4dS03a39Yk2:1463:24:John
Doe:/home/jdoe:/bin/bash";
```

5. Declare an array called $PasswordFields, as follows:

```php
$PasswordFields = array(
    "login name",
    "optional encrypted password",
    "numerical user ID",
    "numerical group ID",
    "user name or comment field",
    "user home directory",
    "optional user command interpreter");
```

6. Enter the following code to tokenize the string and display a message for each missing field:

```php
$FieldIndex = 0;
$ExtraFields = 0;
$CurrField = strtok($Record, ":");
while ($CurrField != NULL) {
    if ($FieldIndex < count($PasswordFields))
        echo "<p>The
            {$PasswordFields[$FieldIndex]} is
            <em>$CurrField</em></p>\n";
    else {
        ++$ExtraFields;
        echo "<p>Extra field # $ExtraFields is
            <em>$CurrField</em></p>\n";
    }
    $CurrField = strtok(":");
    ++$FieldIndex;
}
```

7. Save the file as **PasswordFields.php**, upload it to the server, and then open the file in your Web browser by entering the following URL:
http://<yourserver>/PHP_Projects/Chapter.03/Chapter/ PasswordFields.php. Figure 3-17 shows the output.

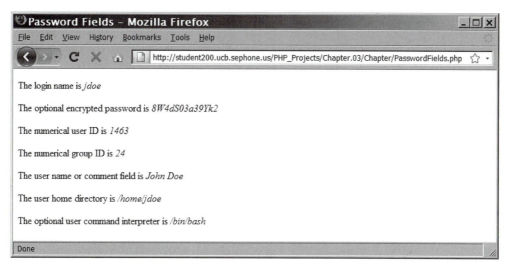

Figure 3-17 Using `strtok()` to parse a password record

8. Close your Web browser window.

Converting between Strings and Arrays

In addition to splitting a string into tokens, you can split a string into an array, in which each array element contains a portion of the string. In most cases, you will probably find it more useful to split a string into an array instead of tokens because you have more control over each array element. With strings that are split with the `strtok()` function, you can only work with a substring if it is the current token. Although tokenizing a string is useful if you want to quickly display or iterate through the tokens in a string, you need to assign the tokens to another variable or array if you want to modify the tokens in any way. By contrast, when you split a string into an array, portions of the string are automatically assigned to elements.

You use the `str_split()` or `explode()` function to split a string into an indexed array. The `str_split()` function splits each character in a string into an array element, using the syntax `$array = str_split(string[, length]);`. The *length* argument represents the number of characters you want assigned to each array element. The `explode()` function splits a string into an indexed array at a specified separator. The syntax for the `explode()` function is `$array = explode(separator, string);`. Be sure to notice that the order of the arguments for the `explode()` function is the reverse of the arguments for the `strtok()` function. The following code demonstrates how to split the `$Presidents` string into an array named `$PresidentArray`:

```
$Presidents = "George Washington;John Adams;Thomas
Jefferson;James Madison;James Monroe";
$PresidentArray = explode(";", $Presidents);
foreach ($PresidentArray as $President) {
    echo "$President<br />";
}
```

If the string does not contain the specified separator, the entire string is assigned to the first element of the array. Also, unlike the `strtok()` function, the `explode()` function does not separate a string at any character that is included in the *separator* argument. Instead, the `explode()` function evaluates the characters in the *separator* argument as a substring. For example, a semicolon and a space separate each president's name in the following code. Therefore, you pass "; " as the *separator* argument of the `explode()` function.

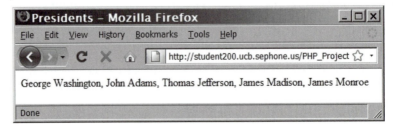

If you pass to the `explode()` function an empty string as the *separator* argument, the function returns a Boolean value of FALSE.

```
$Presidents = "George Washington; John Adams; Thomas
Jefferson; James Madison; James Monroe";
$PresidentArray = explode("; ", $Presidents);
foreach ($PresidentArray as $President) {
    echo "$President<br />";
}
```

The opposite of the `explode()` function is the `implode()` function, which combines an array's elements into a single string, separated by specified characters. The syntax for the `implode()` function is `$variable = implode(separator, array);`. The following example first creates an array named `$PresidentsArray`, then uses the `implode()` function to combine the array elements into the `$Presidents` variable, separated by a comma and a space. Figure 3-18 shows the output.

```
$PresidentsArray = array("George Washington", "John
Adams", "Thomas Jefferson", "James Madison", "James
Monroe");
$Presidents = implode(", ", $PresidentsArray);
echo $Presidents;
```

Figure 3-18 Using `implode()` to build a string from an array

To modify PasswordFields.php so the record is split into an array instead of tokens:

1. Return to the **PasswordFields.php** script in your text editor.

2. Replace the declaration and initialization of $CurrField with the following statement:

```
$Fields = explode(":",$Record);
```

3. Replace the while loop with a foreach loop as follows:

```
foreach ($Fields as $FieldIndex => $FieldValue) {
    if ($FieldIndex < count($PasswordFields))
        echo "<p>The
            {$PasswordFields[$FieldIndex]} is
            <em>$FieldValue</em></p>\n";
    else {
        ++$ExtraFields;
        echo "<p>Extra field # $ExtraFields is
            <em>$FieldValue</em></p>\n";
    }
}
```

4. Save the PasswordFields.php file, upload it to the server, and then open the file in your Web browser by entering the following URL: *http://<yourserver>/PHP_Projects/Chapter.03/ Chapter/ PasswordFields.php*. The output should still look like Figure 3-17.

5. Close your Web browser window.

Short Quiz

1. What function can be used to determine if a specific character exists in a string?

2. What is the difference between the str_replace() function and the str_ireplace() function?

3. What functions are used to split a string into an indexed array?

Comparing Strings

In Chapter 1, you studied various operators that you can use with PHP, including comparison operators. Although comparison operators are most often used with numbers, they can also be used with strings. The following statement uses the comparison operator (==) to compare two variables containing text strings:

```
$Florida = "Miami is in Florida.";
$Cuba = "Havana is in Cuba.";
if ($Florida == $Cuba)
     echo "<p>Same location.</p>";
else
     echo "<p>Different location.</p>";
```

Because the text strings are not the same, the `else` clause displays the text "Different location." You can also use comparison operators to determine whether one letter occurs later in the alphabet than another letter. In the following code, the first `echo` statement executes because the letter "B" occurs later in the alphabet than the letter "A":

```
$FirstLetter = "A";
$SecondLetter = "B";
if ($SecondLetter > $FirstLetter)
     echo "<p>The second letter occurs later in the alphabet
          than the first letter.</p>";
else
     echo "<p>The second letter occurs earlier in the alphabet
          than the first letter.</p>";
```

You use the `ord()` function to return the ASCII value of a character, and the `chr()` function to return the character for an ASCII value.

The comparison operators actually compare individual characters according to their position in **American Standard Code for Information Interchange**, or **ASCII**, which are numeric representations of English characters. ASCII values range from 0 to 255. Lowercase letters are represented by the values 97 ("a") to 122 ("z"). Uppercase letters are represented by the values 65 ("A") to 90 ("Z"). Because lowercase letters have higher ASCII values than uppercase letters, the lowercase letters are evaluated as being "greater" than the uppercase letters. For example, an uppercase letter "A" is represented by ASCII value 65, whereas a lowercase letter "a" is represented by ASCII value 97. For this reason, the statement `"a" > "A"` returns a value of `TRUE` because the uppercase letter "A" has a lower ASCII value than the lowercase letter "a."

To sort a list of e-mail addresses:

1. Reopen the **PHPEmail.php** script in your text editor.

2. Add the following function immediately after the validateAddress() function. The function uses a nested for loop to order the elements in the $EmailAddresses[] array. The conditional expression in the if statement uses the comparison operator to compare each array element.

```
function sortAddresses($Addresses) {
    $SortedAddresses = array();
    $iLimit = count($Addresses)-1; /* Set the upper
        limit for the outer loop */
    $jLimit = count($Addresses); /* Set the upper
        limit for the inner loop */
    for ($i = 0; $i<$iLimit; ++$i) {
        $CurrentAddress = $Addresses[$i];
        for ($j = $i+1; $j<$jLimit; ++$j) {
            if ($CurrentAddress > $Addresses[$j]) {
                $TempVal = $Addresses[$j];
                $Addresses[$j] = $CurrentAddress;
                $CurrentAddress = $TempVal;
            }
        }
        $SortedAddresses[] = $CurrentAddress;
    }
    return($SortedAddresses);
}
```

3. Add the following code immediately after the declaration of the sortAddresses function. This code sorts the list and displays the sorted results as a string.

```
$SortedAddresses = sortAddresses($EmailAddresses);
$SortedAddressList = implode(", ", $SortedAddresses);
echo "<p>Sorted Addresses: $SortedAddressList</p>\n";
```

4. Change the foreach statement to use $SortedAddresses instead of $EmailAddresses. The foreach statement should appear as follows:

```
foreach ($SortedAddresses as $Address) {
```

5. Save the PHPEmail.php file, upload the file to the browser, and then open the file in your Web browser by entering the following URL:
http://<yourserver>/PHP_Projects/Chapter.03/Chapter/ PHPEmail.php. Figure 3-19 shows the output.

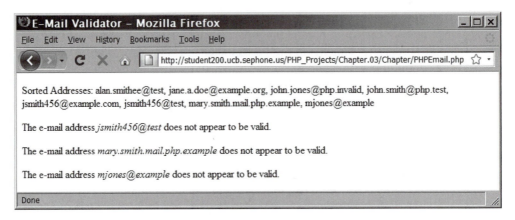

Figure 3-19 A sorted list of e-mail addresses

6. Close your Web browser window.

In the next few sections, you will study additional functions that you can use to compare strings in PHP.

String Comparison Functions

PHP provides many string comparison functions to determine a wide variety of relationships between strings. Many are designed for special purposes, but several are useful in a number of different situations.

The comparison functions you will probably use most often are strcasecmp() and strcmp(). The only difference between the two is that the strcasecmp() function performs a case-insensitive comparison of strings, whereas the strcmp() function performs a case-sensitive comparison. Both functions accept two arguments representing the strings you want to compare. It's important to understand that most string comparison functions base their comparisons on the ASCII values at the first position where the characters in the two strings differ. Once this first differing character position is found, the ASCII value of the character in the first string argument is compared with the ASCII value of the corresponding character in the second string argument. If the ASCII value in the first string argument is less than that of the second, the functions return a value less than 0, usually −1. However, if the ASCII value of the character in the second string argument is greater than the ASCII value of the corresponding character in the first string argument, the functions return a value greater than 0, usually 1. For example, consider the following strcmp() function, which compares the strings "Dan" and "Don". Because the "a" in "Dan" has a lower ASCII value than the "o" in "Don", the function returns a value less than 0.

```
strcmp("Dan", "Don"); // returns a value < 0
```

In comparison, the following statement, which switches the "Dan" and "Don" arguments, returns a value greater than 0:

```
strcmp("Don", "Dan"); // returns a value > 0
```

If both string values are equal, the strcmp() function returns a value of 0, as in the following example:

```
strcmp("Don", "Don"); // returns 0
```

Keep in mind that the strcmp() function performs a case-sensitive comparison of two strings. The following statement returns a value less than 0 because the uppercase "D" in the first string has a lower ASCII value than the lowercase "d" in the second string:

```
strcmp("Don", "don"); // returns a value < 0
```

In the special case in which all the corresponding characters in the two strings are the same, but one string argument is shorter than the other, the shorter string argument is considered to be less than the longer one. The following statement returns a value greater than 0 because "Donald" is longer than "Don":

```
strcmp("Donald", "Don"); // returns a value > 0
```

To perform a case-insensitive comparison of two strings, use the strcasecmp() function, which converts the text in both strings to lowercase before they are compared. The following statement returns a value of 0 because it uses the case-insensitive strcasecmp() function:

```
strcasecmp("Don", "don"); // returns 0
```

The strncmp() and strncasecmp() functions are very similar to the strcmp() and strcasecmp() functions, except that you need to pass a third integer argument representing the number of characters you want to compare in the strings. The following code uses the strncmp() function to compare the first three letters in two text strings:

```
$FirstCity = "San Diego";
$SecondCity = "San Jose";
if (strncmp($FirstCity, $SecondCity, 3) == 0)
    echo "<p>Both cities begin with 'San'.</p>";
```

To modify the sortAddresses() function so it uses the strcasecmp() function instead of comparison operators to sort the e-mail addresses in the e-mail script:

1. Return to the **PHPEmail.php** script in your text editor.

2. Modify the conditional expression in the `if` statement within the `sortAddresses()` function so it uses the `strcasecmp()` function instead of the comparison operator, as follows:

```
if (strcasecmp($CurrentAddress,$Addresses[$j]) > 0) {
```

3. Save the PHPEmail.php file, upload it to the server, and then open the file in your Web browser by entering the following URL: *http://<yourserver>/PHP_Projects/Chapter.03/Chapter/ PHPEmail.php*. The results should still appear as shown in Figure 3-19.

4. Close your Web browser window.

Determining the Similarity of Two Strings

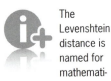

The Levenshtein distance is named for mathematician Vladimir Levenshtein, who developed the algorithm in 1965.

The `similar_text()` and `levenshtein()` functions are used to determine the similarity between two strings (known as the **Levenshtein distance**). The `similar_text()` function returns the number of characters that two strings have in common, whereas the `levenshtein()` function returns the number of characters you need to change for two strings to be the same. Both functions accept two string arguments representing the values you want to compare.

The following code demonstrates how to use the two functions with the names "Don" and "Dan". Figure 3-20 shows the output.

```
$FirstName = "Don";
$SecondName = "Dan";
echo "<p>The names \"$FirstName\" and \"$SecondName\
" have " . similar_text($FirstName, $SecondName) .
" characters in common.</p>";
echo "<p>You must change " . levenshtein($FirstName,
$SecondName). " character(s) to make the names
\"$FirstName\" and \"$SecondName\" the same.</p>";
```

Figure 3-20 Checking the similarity of two names

Determining if Words Are Pronounced Similarly

You can use the soundex() and metaphone() functions to determine whether two strings are pronounced similarly. Both functions return a value representing how words sound. The soundex() function returns a value representing a name's phonetic equivalent, whereas the metaphone() function returns a code representing an English word's approximate sound. For example, consider the last name of the author of this book, Gosselin. The soundex() function returns a value of "G245" for this string, whereas the metaphone() function returns a value of "KSLN." The following code uses the metaphone() function to compare the name with an alternative spelling, "Gauselin":

```
$FirstName = "Gosselin";
$SecondName = "Gauselin";
$FirstNameSoundsLike = metaphone($FirstName);
$SecondNameSoundsLike = metaphone($SecondName);
if ($FirstNameSoundsLike == $SecondNameSoundsLike)
    echo "<p>The names are pronounced the same.</p>";
else
    echo "<p>The names are not pronounced the same.</p>";
```

Because both versions of the name are pronounced the same way, the preceding code displays "The names are pronounced the same."

Although they perform the same type of function, the soundex() and metaphone() functions cannot be used with each other because they represent words with different kinds of values. To compare the name "Gosselin" with the alternative spelling of "Gauselin," you must compare the values returned from two soundex() functions, as follows:

```
$FirstName = "Gosselin";
$SecondName = "Gauselin";
$FirstNameSoundsLike = soundex($FirstName);
$SecondNameSoundsLike = soundex($SecondName);
if ($FirstNameSoundsLike == $SecondNameSoundsLike)
    echo "<p>The names are pronounced the same.</p>";
else
    echo "<p>The names are not pronounced the same.</p>";
```

Short Quiz

1. What is the difference between the strcasecmp() function and the strcmp() function?

2. Why is the lowercase "a" considered to occur later in the alphabet than the uppercase "A"?

3. Explain the difference between the similar_text() function and the levenshtein() function.

Working with Regular Expressions

One of the more accurate ways of parsing strings involves **regular expressions**, which are patterns that are used for matching and manipulating strings according to specified rules. With scripting languages such as PHP, regular expressions are most commonly used for validating submitted form data. For example, you can use a regular expression to ensure that a user enters a date in a specific format, such as *mm/dd/yyyy*, or a telephone number in the format (###) ###-####.

Most scripting languages support some form of regular expressions. PHP supports Perl Compatible Regular Expressions (PCRE). Table 3-2 lists some of the PCRE functions available in PHP.

Function	Description
preg_match(*pattern, string*)	Performs a search for a matching pattern
preg_match_all(*pattern, string*)	Performs a search for a matching pattern, returns the number of matches found
preg_replace(*pattern, replacement, string[, limit]*)	Performs a replacement of a matching pattern
preg_split(*pattern, string [, limit]*)	Divides an input string into an array of strings that are separated by a specified matching pattern
preg_grep(*pattern, array*)	Filters an input array and returns an array of those elements that match the specified pattern
preg_quote(*string*)	Returns a string that is the input string with any character that has special meaning for a PCRE preceded by the escape character (\)

Table 3-2 PCRE functions

The most commonly used PCRE function is preg_match(). You pass to the function a regular expression pattern as the first argument and a string containing the text you want to search as the second argument. The function returns a value of 1 if a specified pattern is matched or a value of 0 if it's not. The following code demonstrates how to determine whether the $String variable contains the text "course technology," with lowercase letters. The code uses a case-sensitive pattern by default, so the if statement displays "No match" because the value in the $String variable includes uppercase initials.

```
$String = "Course Technology";
if (preg_match("/course technology/", $String))
```

```
    echo "<p>Match found</p>";
else
    echo "<p>No match</p>";
```

In comparison, the following code displays "Match found" because it uses a case-insensitive pattern modifier after the pattern:

```
$String = "Course Technology";
if (preg_match("/course technology/i", $String))
    echo "<p>Match found</p>";
else
    echo "<p>No match</p>";
```

The preceding examples were a simple demonstration of how to use the `preg_match()` function. There is no point in using regular expression functions with the preceding examples because you can more easily determine whether the two strings match by using the comparison operator (==) or a string comparison function. The real power of regular expressions comes from the patterns you write.

Writing Regular Expression Patterns

A regular expression pattern is a symbolic representation of the rules that are used for matching and manipulating strings. As an example of a common regular expression, consider the following code:

```
if (preg_match("/^[_a-z0-9-]+(\.[_a-z0-9-]+)*@[a-z0-9-]+
(\.[a-z0-9-]+)*(\.[a-z]{2,3})$/i", $Email) ==0)
    echo "<p>The e-mail address is not in a valid
            format.</p>";
```

The preceding code uses the `preg_match()` function to determine whether the $Email variable is in a valid format for an e-mail address. If the `preg_match()` function returns a value of 0, an echo statement displays an appropriate message. As you can see, the logic is straightforward: If the e-mail address doesn't match the regular expression, the message is displayed. The complex part of the code is the pattern passed as the first argument to the `preg_match()` function.

You can find many types of prewritten regular expressions on the Regular Expression Library Web page at *http://www.regexlib.com/*.

Regular expression patterns are enclosed in **delimiters**. The first character in the pattern string is considered the **opening delimiter**. All characters after the opening delimiter are considered part of the pattern until the next occurrence of the opening delimiter character, called the **closing delimiter**. Any characters after the closing delimiter are considered to be pattern modifiers.

Although you can use any character except a letter, number, or the backslash as a delimiter character, the most common character is the forward slash (/). If a forward slash is part of the search pattern, you can either use the escape character before the forward slash (\/) or choose another valid character that is not part of the pattern.

Regular expression patterns consist of literal characters and **metacharacters**, which are special characters that define the pattern matching rules in a regular expression. Table 3-3 lists the metacharacters that you can use with PCRE.

Metacharacter	Description
.	Matches any single character
\	Identifies the next character as a literal value
^	Anchors characters to the beginning of a string
$	Anchors characters to the end of a string
()	Specifies required characters to include in a pattern match
[]	Specifies alternate characters allowed in a pattern match
[^]	Specifies characters to exclude in a pattern match
–	Identifies a possible range of characters to match
|	Specifies alternate sets of characters to include in a pattern match

Table 3-3　PCRE metacharacters

Matching Any Character

You use a period (.) to match any single character in a pattern. A period in a regular expression pattern specifies that the pattern must contain a value where the period is located. For example, the following code specifies that the $ZIP variable must contain five characters. Because the variable only contains three characters, the preg_match() function returns a value of 0.

```
$ZIP = "015";
preg_match("/...../", $ZIP); // returns 0
```

In comparison, the following preg_match() function returns a value of 1 because the $ZIP variable contains five characters:

```
$ZIP = "01562";
preg_match("/...../", $ZIP); // returns 1
```

Because the period only specifies that a character must be included in the designated location within the pattern, you can include additional characters within the pattern. The following preg_match() function returns a value of 1 because the $ZIP variable contains the required five characters along with the ZIP+4 characters.

```
$ZIP = "01562-2607";
preg_match("/...../", $ZIP); // returns 1
```

Matching Characters at the Beginning or End of a String

The ^ metacharacter anchors characters to the beginning of a string, and the $ metacharacter anchors characters to the end of a string. An **anchor** specifies that the pattern must appear at a particular position in the string. To specify an anchor at the beginning of a line, the pattern must begin with the ^ metacharacter. The following example specifies that the $URL variable begin with http. Because the variable does begin with "http", the preg_match() function returns 1.

```
$URL = "http://www.dongosselin.com";
preg_match("/^http/", $URL); // returns 1
```

All literal characters following the ^ metacharacter in a pattern compose the anchor. This means that the following example returns 0 because the $URL variable does not begin with "https" (only "http" without the s), as is specified by the anchor in the pattern:

```
$URL = "http://www.dongosselin.com";
preg_match("/^https/", $URL); // returns 0
```

To specify an anchor at the end of a line, the pattern must end with the $ metacharacter. The following demonstrates how to specify that a URL end with com:

```
$Identifier = "http://www.dongosselin.com";
preg_match("/com$/", $Identifier); // returns 1
```

The preceding code returns 1 because the URL assigned to the $Identifier variable ends with com. However, the following code returns 0 because the URL assigned to the $Identifier variable does not end with gov:

```
$Identifier = "http://www.dongosselin.com";
preg_match("/gov$/", $Identifier); // returns 0
```

Matching Special Characters

To match any metacharacters as literal values in a regular expression, escape the character with a backslash. For example, a period (.) metacharacter matches any single character in a pattern. If you want to ensure that a string contains an actual period and not the metacharacter, you need to escape the period with a backslash. The top-level domain in the following code is appended to the domain name with a comma instead of a period. However, the regular expression returns 1 because the period in the expression is not escaped.

```
$Identifier = "http://www.dongosselin,com";
echo preg_match("/.com$/", $Identifier); // returns 1
```

To correct the problem, you must escape the period in the pattern as follows:

```
$Identifier = "http://www.dongosselin,com";
echo preg_match("/\.com$/", $Identifier); // returns 0
```

Escaping a dollar sign requires a little more work. Because the dollar sign is used to indicate a variable name in PHP, it needs to be preceded by a backslash for PHP to interpret it as a literal $ character. Therefore, when using double quotation marks around the pattern string, you need to enter two backslashes (\\) to insert the literal backslash, followed by a backslash and a dollar sign (\$) to include the literal dollar sign. Altogether, this becomes three backslashes followed by a dollar sign (\\\$). Another option is to use single quotes around the pattern string, and to use a single backslash before the dollar sign (\$). The following code demonstrates how to use both techniques:

```
$Currency="$123.45";
echo preg_match('/^\$/', $Currency); // returns 1
echo preg_match("/^\\\$/", $Currency); // returns 1
```

Specifying Quantity

Metacharacters that specify the quantity of a match are called **quantifiers**. Table 3-4 lists the quantifiers that you can use with PCRE.

Quantifier	Description
?	Specifies that the preceding character is optional
+	Specifies that one or more of the preceding characters must match
*	Specifies that zero or more of the preceding characters can match
{n}	Specifies that the preceding character repeat exactly n times
{n,}	Specifies that the preceding character repeat at least n times
{,n}	Specifies that the preceding character repeat up to n times
{$n1$, $n2$}	Specifies that the preceding character repeat at least $n1$ times but no more than $n2$ times

Table 3-4 PCRE quantifiers

The question mark quantifier specifies that the preceding character in the pattern is optional. The following code demonstrates how to use the question mark quantifier to specify that the protocol assigned to the beginning of the $URL variable can be either http or https.

```
$URL = "http://www.dongosselin.com";
preg_match("/^https?/", $URL); // returns 1
```

The addition quantifier (+) specifies that one or more sequential occurrences of the preceding characters match, whereas the asterisk quantifier (*) specifies that zero or more sequential occurrences of the preceding characters match. As a simple example, the following code demonstrates how to ensure that data has been entered in a required field.

```
$Name = "Don";
preg_match("/.+/", $Name); // returns 1
```

Similarly, because a numeric string might contain leading zeroes, the following code demonstrates how to check whether the $NumberString variable contains zero or more leading zeroes:

```
$NumberString = "00125";
preg_match("/^0*/", $NumberString); // returns 1
```

The { } quantifiers allow you to more precisely specify the number of times that a character must repeat sequentially. The following code shows a simple example of how to use the { } quantifiers to ensure that a ZIP code consists of at least five characters:

```
preg_match("/ZIP: .{5}$/", " ZIP: 01562"); // returns 1
```

You can validate a ZIP code much more efficiently with character classes, which are covered later in this chapter.

The preceding code uses the period metacharacter and the { } quantifiers to ensure that the $ZIP variable contains a minimum of five characters. The following code specifies that the $ZIP variable must consist of at least five characters but a maximum of 10 characters, in case the ZIP code contains the dash and four additional numbers that are found in a ZIP+4 number:

```
preg_match("/(ZIP: .{5,10})$/", "ZIP: 01562-2607");
    // returns 1
```

Specifying Subexpressions

As you learned earlier, regular expression patterns can include literal values; any strings you validate against a regular expression must contain exact matches for the literal values contained in the pattern. You can also use parentheses metacharacters ((and)) to specify the characters required in a pattern match. Characters contained in a set of parentheses within a regular expression are referred to as a **subexpression** or **subpattern**. Subexpressions allow you to determine the format and quantities of the enclosed characters as a group. As

Notice that the telephone number regular expression pattern includes the ∧ and $ metacharacters to anchor both the beginning and end of the pattern. This ensures that a string exactly matches the pattern in a regular expression.

an example, consider the following pattern, which defines a regular expression for a telephone number:

```
"/^(1 )?(\(.{3}\) )?(.{3})(\-.{4})$/"
```

The first and second groups in the preceding pattern include the ? quantifier. This allows a string to optionally include a 1 and the area code. If the string does include these groups, they must be in the exact format of "1 " for the first pattern and "(*nnn*) " for the second pattern, including the space following the area code. Similarly, the telephone number itself includes two groups that require the number to be in the format of "*nnn*" and "-*nnnn*." Because the "1 " and the area code pattern are optional, all of the following statements return a value of 1:

```
preg_match("/^(1 )?(\(.{3}\) )?(.{3})(\-.{4})$/", "555-
1234");
preg_match("/^(1 )?(\(.{3}\) )?(.{3})(\-.{4})$/", "(707)
555-1234");
preg_match("/^(1 )?(\(.{3}\) )?(.{3})(\-.{4})$/", "1 (707)
555-1234");
```

Defining Character Classes

As with the string comparisons earlier, the ranges are based on the ASCII values of the characters. Ranges must be specified from smallest to largest value.

You use **character classes** in regular expressions to treat multiple characters as a single item. You create a character class by enclosing the characters that make up the class with bracket ([]) metacharacters. Any characters included in a character class represent alternate characters that are allowed in a pattern match. As an example of a simple character class, consider the word "analyze," which the British spell as "analyse." Both of the following statements return 1 because the character class allows either spelling of the word:

```
preg_match("/analy[sz]e/", "analyse"); // returns 1
preg_match("/analy[sz]e/", "analyze"); // returns 1
```

In comparison, the following regular expression returns 0 because "analyce" is not an accepted spelling of the word:

```
preg_match("/analy[sz]e/", "analyce"); // returns 0
```

You cannot use the range [A-z] or the range [a-Z] to match all letters. The range [A-z] contains all of the characters with ASCII values of 65 ('A') through 122 ('z'), which includes nonalphabetic characters such as '[' and '∧'. The range [a-Z] means a range from 97 to 90, which is not in order from smallest to largest value.

You use a hyphen metacharacter (-) to specify a range of values in a character class. You can include alphabetical or numerical ranges. You specify all lowercase letters as [a-z], all uppercase letters as [A-Z], and all letters as [A-Za-z]. You specify all numeric characters as [0-9].

The following statements demonstrate how to ensure that only the values A, B, C, D, or F are assigned to the $LetterGrade variable. The character class in the regular expression specifies a range of A-D or the character "F" as valid values in the variable. Because the variable is assigned a value of "B", the preg_match() function returns 1.

```
$LetterGrade = "B";
echo preg_match("/[A-DF]/", $LetterGrade); // returns 1
```

In comparison, the following preg_match() function returns 0 because E is not a valid value in the character class:

```
$LetterGrade = "E";
echo preg_match("/[A-DF]/", $LetterGrade); // returns 0
```

To specify optional characters to exclude in a pattern match, include the ∧ metacharacter immediately after the opening bracket of a character class. The following examples demonstrate how to exclude the letters E and G-Z from an acceptable pattern in the $LetterGrade variable. Any ASCII character not listed as being excluded will match the pattern. The first preg_match() function returns a value of 1 because the letter A is not excluded from the pattern match, whereas the second preg_match() function returns a value of 0 because the letter E is excluded from the pattern match.

```
$LetterGrade = "A";
echo preg_match("/[∧EG-Z]/", $LetterGrade); // returns 1
$LetterGrade = "E";
echo preg_match("/[∧EG-Z]/", $LetterGrade); // returns 0
```

The following statements demonstrate how to include or exclude numeric characters from a pattern match. The first statement returns 1 because it allows any numeric character, whereas the second statement returns 0 because it excludes any numeric character.

```
echo preg_match("/[0-9]/", "5"); // returns 1
echo preg_match("/[∧0-9]/", "5"); // returns 0
```

Note that you can combine ranges in a character class. The first statement demonstrates how to include all alphanumeric characters and the second statement demonstrates how to exclude all lowercase and uppercase letters:

```
echo preg_match("/[0-9a-zA-Z]/", "7"); // returns 1
echo preg_match("/[∧a-zA-Z]/", "Q"); // returns 0
```

The following statement demonstrates how to use character classes to create a phone number regular expression pattern:

```
preg_match("/∧(1 )?(\([0-9]{3}\) )?([0-9]{3})(\-[0-9]{4})$/",
"1 (707) 555-1234"); // returns 1
```

As a more complex example of a character class, examine the following e-mail validation regular expression that you saw earlier in this chapter. At this point, you should recognize how the regular expression pattern is constructed. The statement uses a case-insensitive pattern modifier, so letter case is ignored. The anchor at the beginning of the pattern specifies that the first part of the e-mail address must include one or more of the characters A-Z (uppercase or lowercase), 0-9, an underscore (_), or a hyphen (-). The second portion of the pattern specifies that the e-mail address can include a dot separator, as in "don.

gosselin." The pattern also requires the @ character. Following the literal @ character, the regular expression uses patterns like those in the name portion of the e-mail address to specify the required structure of the domain name. The last portion of the pattern specifies that the top-level domain must consist of at least two, but not more than three, alphabetic characters.

```
preg_match("/^[_a-z0-9-]+(\.[_a-z0-9-]+)*@[_a-z0-9-]
+(\.[_a-z0-9-]+)*(\.[a-z]{2,3})$/i", $Email);
```

If you include any of the three special characters -, ^, or] anywhere else in the character class, you will not get the desired results.

The backslash character is not an escape character within a character class. To include a literal hyphen (-) in a character class, it must be the final character before the closing bracket. Otherwise, it is interpreted as a range indicator. To include a literal circumflex (^), it must be the final character before the closing bracket or the literal hyphen. To include a literal closing bracket (]), it must be the first character after the opening bracket or negation symbol.

PCRE includes special character types that you can use to represent different types of data. For example, the \w expression can be used instead of the "_0-9a-zA-Z" pattern to allow any alphanumeric characters and the underscore character. Table 3-5 lists the PCRE character types.

Escape Sequence	Description
\a	alarm (hex 07)
\cx	"control-x", where x is any character
\d	any decimal digit
\D	any character not in \d
\e	escape (hex 1B)
\f	formfeed (hex 0C)
\h	any horizontal whitespace character
\H	any character not in \h
\n	newline (hex 0A)
\r	carriage return (hex 0D)
\s	any whitespace character
\S	any character not in \s
\t	tab (hex 09)
\v	any vertical whitespace character
\V	any character not in \v
\w	any letter, number, or underscore character
\W	any character not in \w

Table 3-5　PCRE character types

The following statements demonstrate how to include and exclude numeric characters from a pattern match using the \d (digit) and \D (not a digit) character types:

```
preg_match("/\d/", "5"); // returns 1
preg_match("/\d/", "A"); // returns 0
preg_match("/\D/", "5"); // returns 0
preg_match("/\D/", "A"); // returns 1
```

As a more complex example, the following statement demonstrates how to compose the e-mail validation regular expression with class expressions:

```
preg_match("/^[\w-]+(\.[\w-]+)*@[\w-
]+(\.[\w-]+)*(\.[a-zA-Z]{2,})$/", $Email);
```

Matching Multiple Pattern Choices

To allow a string to contain an alternate set of patterns, you separate the strings in a regular expression pattern with the | metacharacter. This is essentially the same as using the Or operator (||) to perform multiple evaluations in a conditional expression. For example, to allow a string to contain either "vegetarian" or "vegan," you include the pattern vegetarian | vegan.

The following code demonstrates how to check whether a top-level domain at the end of a string contains a required value of either .com, .org, or .net. The first statement returns a value of 0 because the URL contains a top-level domain of .gov, whereas the second statement returns a value of 1 because the top-level domain contains a valid value of .com.

```
echo preg_match("/\.(com|org|net)$/i",
    "http://www.dongosselin.gov"); // returns 0
echo preg_match("/\.(com|org|net)$/i",
    "http://www.dongosselin.com"); // returns 1
```

Pattern Modifiers

PCRE patterns may be followed by optional pattern modifiers. **Pattern modifiers** are letters placed after the closing delimiter that change the default rules for interpreting matches. The most common pattern modifier is i, which indicates that the case of a letter does not matter when searching. Some other pattern modifiers change how newline characters affect searches. For example, newline characters typically divide an input string into search strings. The m pattern modifier allows searches across newline characters. Also, the s pattern modifier changes how the . (period) metacharacter works. Normally, the . metacharacter does not match the newline character, but it will with the s modifier.

To modify the validateAddress() function so that it uses regular expressions instead of the strpos() function to check the format of the e-mail addresses in the e-mail script:

1. Return to the **PHPEmail.php** script in your text editor.

2. Modify the conditional expression in the if statement within the validateAddress() function so it uses the preg_match() function instead of the strpos() function, as follows:

```
if (preg_match("/^[\w-]+(\.[\w-]+)*@" .
        "[\w-]+(\.[\w-]+)*(\.[[A-Za-z]{2,})$/i",
        $Address)==1)
```

3. Save the PHPEmail.php file, upload it to the server, and then open the file in your Web browser by entering the following URL: *http://<yourserver>/PHP_Projects/Chapter.03/Chapter/ PHPEmail.php*. As shown in Figure 3-21, more invalid messages were found using regular expressions.

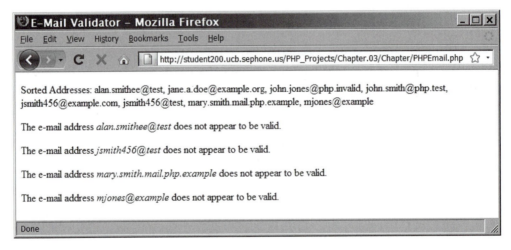

Figure 3-21 Output of PHPEmail.php using regular expressions

4. Close your Web browser window.

Short Quiz

1. What character is used to match any single character in a pattern?

2. How do you specify that you want to ensure that a string contains an actual period and not just any character?

3. Describe the purpose of quantifiers in determining if a string matches a pattern.

4. How are subexpressions or subpatterns used in a regular expression?

5. Describe the purpose of the | metacharacter.

Summing Up

- The concatenation operator (.) and the concatenation assignment operator (.=) can be used to combine two strings.

- An escape character tells the compiler or interpreter that the character following the escape character has a special purpose. An escape character combined with one or more other characters is called an escape sequence.

- Simple string syntax allows you to use the value of a variable within a string by including the variable name inside a text string with double quotation marks.

- The type of structure in which variables are placed within curly braces inside a string is called complex string syntax.

- The most commonly used string-counting function is the `strlen()` function, which returns the total number of characters in a string.

- The `str_word_count()` function returns the number of words in a string.

- The `strtoupper()`, `strtolower()`, `ucfirst()`, `lcfirst()`, and `ucwords()` functions all change the case of characters in the string.

- The `substr()` function returns the specified portion of a string.

- When applied to text strings, the term "parsing" refers to the act of dividing a string into logical component substrings or tokens.

- There are two types of string search and extraction functions: functions that return a numeric position in a text string and those that return a character or substring.

- You use the `str_replace()`, `str_ireplace()`, and `substr_replace()` functions to replace text in strings.

- The strtok() function breaks a string into smaller strings, called tokens.

- You use the str_split() or explode() function to split a string into an indexed array, in which each character in the string becomes a separate element in the array.

- The implode() function combines an array's elements into a single string, separated by specified characters.

- The strcasecmp() function performs a case-insensitive comparison of strings, whereas the strcmp() function performs a case-sensitive comparison of strings.

- The similar_text() and levenshtein() functions are used to determine the similarity of two strings.

- You can use the soundex() and metaphone() functions to determine whether two strings are pronounced similarly.

- Regular expressions are a pattern of specially formatted strings that can be used to validate the structure of a string.

- Regular expressions are made up of both literal characters and special characters, called metacharacters, which define the pattern-matching rules.

- In a regular expression, a backslash character is used to match metacharacters as literal values.

- Quantifiers are metacharacters that specify the number of times a particular match may occur.

- Subexpressions are characters contained in parentheses within a regular expression. The format and quantity of the characters in the subexpression can be defined as a group.

- A character class is a set of multiple characters enclosed in square brackets ([]) that are treated as a single unit.

- The | metacharacter allows a string to be composed of an alternate set of substrings. The | metacharacter performs essentially the same function as the Or (||) operator in conditional expressions.

Comprehension Check

1. Which of the following echo statements is invalid?

   a. echo "<p>Welcome to the *combat zone*!</p>";

   b. echo '<p>Welcome to the "combat zone"!</p>';

c. `echo "<p>Welcome to the 'combat zone'!</p>";`

d. `echo '<p>Welcome to the 'combat zone'!</p>';`

2. Which of the following operators can be used with strings? (Choose all that apply.)

    a. `.`

    b. `==`

    c. `.=`

    d. `+=`

3. Explain why you need to use escape characters in strings.

4. What is the escape sequence for a single quotation mark?

    a. `\\`

    b. `\'`

    c. `\~`

    d. There is no escape sequence for a single quotation mark.

5. Which of the following character sets do you use for complex string syntax?

    a. `{}`

    b. `[]`

    c. `()`

    d. `// //`

6. Explain why you need to use complex string syntax. Be sure to include an example.

7. If you include an array within a text string, you need to use complex string syntax. True or False?

8. Which of the following functions returns the length of a string?

    a. `strlen()`

    b. `strspn()`

    c. `substr_count()`

    d. `strcspn()`

9. Which of the following functions performs a case-sensitive search for specified characters in a string and returns a substring from the last occurrence of the specified characters to the end of the string?

   a. substr()

   b. strstr()

   c. strrchr()

   d. strpos()

10. Explain the difference between the two types of extraction functions.

11. Explain how to determine whether the strpos() function (and other string functions) actually returns a Boolean value of FALSE and not a 0 representing the first character in a string.

12. Which of the following functions allows you to replace characters within a specified portion of a string?

   a. str_ireplace()

   b. str_replace()

   c. substr_replace()

   d. strstr()

13. Explain how to use the strtok() function to break a string into tokens and then navigate through each token.

14. If you specify an empty string as the second argument of the strtok() function, or if the string does not contain any of the separators you specify, the strtok() function returns a value of FALSE. True or False?

15. Which of the following functions splits each character in a string into an array element?

   a. str_split()

   b. split()

   c. explode()

   d. implode()

16. String comparison operators and most string comparison functions compare individual characters according to their ASCII value. True or False?

17. Which of the following functions returns the number of characters you need to change for two strings to be the same?

    a. `similar_text()`

    b. `levenshtein()`

    c. `soundex()`

    d. `metaphone()`

18. Which of the following quantifiers can be used to specify the quantity of a match in a regular expression? (Choose all that apply.)

    a. question mark (?)

    b. minus sign (-)

    c. asterisk (*)

    d. plus sign (+)

19. A \. is used to match any single character in a pattern. True or False?

20. Which of the following character pairs match characters at the beginning and end of a string in a regular expression?

    a. * and *\

    b. || and ||

    c. ^ and $

    d. # and #

Reinforcement Exercises

Exercise 3-1

In this project, you will create a script that validates whether a credit card number contains only integers. The script will remove dashes and spaces from the string. After the dashes and spaces are removed, the script should reject the credit card number if it contains any other non-numeric characters.

1. Create a new document in your text editor.

2. Type the <!DOCTYPE> declaration, <html> element, document head, and <body> element. Use the strict DTD and "Validate Credit Card" as the content of the <title> element.

3. Add the following text and elements to the document body:

```
<h1>Validate Credit Card</h1><hr />
```

4. Add the following script section to the document body:

```
<?php
?>
```

5. Declare a $CreditCard array that contains three values: an empty string, a valid credit card number with numbers and dashes, and a credit card number with four initial uppercase letter Os.

```
$CreditCard = array(
    "",
    "8910-1234-5678-6543",
    "OOOO-9123-4567-0123");
```

6. Add the following statements to iterate through each of the elements in the $CreditCard array to determine if the element contains a value.

```
foreach ($CreditCard as $CardNumber) {
    if (empty($CardNumber))
        echo "<p>This Credit Card Number is
            invalid because it contains an empty
            string.</p>";
```

7. Add the following else clause to validate the credit card number. The code uses str_replace() functions to remove any dashes and spaces in the number. Then, a nested if...else statement checks whether the new value is numeric. If the number is not numeric, a warning is displayed. If the number is numeric, the modified credit card number is displayed in the Web browser.

```
else {
    $CreditCardNumber = $CardNumber;
    $CreditCardNumber = str_replace("-", "",
        $CreditCardNumber);
    $CreditCardNumber = str_replace(" ", "",
        $CreditCardNumber);
    if (!is_numeric($CreditCardNumber))
    echo "<p>Credit Card Number " .
        $CreditCardNumber . " is not a valid
        Credit Card number because it contains
        a non-numeric character. </p>";
```

```
        else
            echo "<p>Credit Card Number " .
                $CreditCardNumber . " is a valid
                Credit Card number.</p>";
    }
}
```

8. Save the document as **ValidateCreditCard.php** in the Projects directory for Chapter 3 and upload the file to the server.

9. Open ValidateCreditCard.php in your Web browser by entering the following URL: *http://<yourserver>/PHP_Projects/Chapter.03/Projects/ ValidateCreditCard.php*. Test the script to see if it displays a message for an empty string, strips dashes and spaces from the credit card numbers, and identifies which credit card numbers are valid.

10. Close your Web browser window.

Exercise 3-2

In this project, you will create a script that uses comparison operators and functions to compare two strings to see if they are the same.

1. Create a new document in your text editor.

2. Type the <!DOCTYPE> declaration, <html> element, document head, and <body> element. Use the strict DTD and "Compare Strings" as the content of the <title> element.

3. Add the following text and elements to the document body:
   ```
   <h1>Compare Strings</h1><hr />
   ```

4. Add the following script section to the document body:
   ```
   <?php
   ?>
   ```

5. In the script section, declare and initialize two string variables:
   ```
   $firstString = "Geek2Geek";
   $secondString = "Geezer2Geek"
   ```

6. Add the following if statement to the script section. If both the $firstString and $secondString contain a value, the statements in the if statement execute. The nested if statement uses the comparison operator (==) to determine if both strings are the same. If the strings are not the same, the else clause uses the similar_text() and levenshtein() functions to compare the strings.

```
if ( !empty($firstString) && !empty($secondString)) {
    if ($firstString == $secondString)
        echo "<p>Both strings are the same.</p>";
    else {
        echo "<p>Both strings have "
            . similar_text($firstString,
            $secondString)
            . " character(s) in common.<br />";
        echo "<p>You must change " .
            levenshtein($firstString,
            $secondString) . " character(s) to
            make the strings the same.<br />";
    }
}
```

7. At the end of the script section, add the following else clause, which executes if either the $firstString or the $secondString contains an empty value.

```
else
    echo "<p>Either the \$firstString variable or
        the \$secondString variable does not
        contain a value so the two strings cannot
        be compared.
        </p>";
```

8. Save the document as **CompareStrings.php** in the Projects directory for Chapter 3 and upload the file to the server.

9. Open CompareStrings.php in your Web browser by entering the following URL:
http://<yourserver>/PHP_Projects/Chapter.03/Projects/CompareStrings.php.

10. Close your Web browser window.

 Exercise 3-3

In this project, you will create a script that uses regular expressions to validate that an e-mail address is valid for delivery to a user at example.org. For an e-mail address to be in the correct format, only *username* or *first.last* may appear before the @ symbol, and only *example.org* or *mail.example.org* may appear after the @ symbol.

1. Create a new document in your text editor.

2. Type the `<!DOCTYPE>` declaration, `<html>` element, document head, and `<body>` element. Use the strict DTD and "Validate Local Address" as the content of the `<title>` element.

3. Add the following text and elements to the document body:

```
<h1>Validate Local Address</h1><hr />
```

4. Add the following script section to the document body:

```
<?php
?>
```

5. In the script section, declare an `$email` array that contains five e-mail addresses:

```
$email = array(
    "jsmith123@example.org",
    "john.smith.mail@example.org",
    "john.smith@example.org",
    "john.smith@example",
    "jsmith123@mail.example.org");
```

6. Add the following statements to iterate through each of the elements in the `$email` array to determine if it is in the correct format:

```
foreach ($email as $emailAddress){
    echo "The email address &ldquo;" . $emailAddress .
        "&rdquo; ";
    if (preg_match("/^(([A-Za-z]+\d+)|" .
        "([A-Za-z]+\.[A-Za-z]+))" .
        "@((mail\.)?)example\.org$/i",
        $emailAddress)==1)
        echo " is a valid e-mail address.";
    else
        echo " is not a valid e-mail address.";
}
```

7. Save the document as **ValidateLocalAddress.php** in the Projects directory for Chapter 3 and upload the file to the server.

8. Open ValidateLocalAddress.php in your Web browser by entering the following URL: *http://<yourserver>/PHP_Projects/Chapter.03/Projects/ ValidateLocalAddress.php*. Test the script to see if it specifies

which e-mail addresses are valid and which are not. The second and fourth e-mail addresses should be invalid.

9. Close your Web browser window.

 Exercise 3-4

A palindrome is a word or phrase that is identical forward or backward, such as the word "racecar." A standard palindrome is similar to a perfect palindrome, except that spaces and punctuation are ignored in a standard palindrome. For example, "Madam, I'm Adam" is a standard palindrome because the characters are identical forward or backward, provided you remove the spaces and punctuation marks. Write a script that checks words or phrases stored in two separate string variables to determine if they are a perfect palindrome. If you feel ambitious, see if you can modify the program to check for standard palindromes. Save the perfect palindrome script as **PerfectPalindrome.php** and the standard palindrome script as **StandardPalindrome.php**.

 Exercise 3-5

Write a PHP program that checks the elements of a string array named $Passwords. Use regular expressions to test whether each element is a strong password.

For this exercise, a strong password must have at least one number, one lowercase letter, one uppercase letter, no spaces, and at least one character that is not a letter or number. (*Hint:* Use the [^0-9A-Za-z] character class.) The string should also be between 8 and 16 characters long.

The $Passwords array should contain at least 10 elements, and at least six of the elements should fail. Ensure that one entry fails each of the five regular expression tests and that at least one fails because of the length. Display whether each password in the $Passwords array was strong enough, and display the test or tests that a password failed if it is not strong enough. Save the script as **PasswordStrength.php**.

Discovery Projects

The Chinese zodiac site is a comprehensive project that will be updated in the Discovery Projects section at the end of each chapter. All files for the site will be saved in a folder named ChineseZodiac in the root Web folder on the server.

Discovery Project 3-1

Create a new text document in your text editor and include **home_links_bar.inc** at the top of the file. Remember that you will need to insert a PHP script section to insert the include file.

Insert the text from the ChineseZodiac.txt file that you researched in Discovery Project 1-3. Format the text using XHTML formatting tags or style it with CSS style definitions. Save the file as **inc_chinese_zodiac.php** and upload it to the Includes folder in the ChineseZodiac folder on the server. A link to this file will be added in Discovery Project 4-5.

Discovery Project 3-2

Create a new text document in your text editor and include **home_links_bar.inc** at the top of the file. Remember that you will need to insert a PHP script section to insert the include file.

Insert content describing the role of PHP in Web development and why it has become the highest-rated tool in the Web developer's toolkit. Format the text using XHTML formatting tags or style it with CSS style definitions.

Save the file as **inc_php_info.php** and upload the file to the Includes folder in the ChineseZodiac folder on the server. A link to this file will be added in Discovery Project 4-5.

Discovery Project 3-3

In your text editor, use XHTML scripting to create a text links bar with two text links: PHP and Chinese Zodiac. Format the text using XHTML formatting tags or style it with CSS style definitions. These links will be enabled in Discovery Project 4-5. Save the file as **inc_home_links_bar.php** and upload the file to the Includes folder in the ChineseZodiac folder on the server. A link to this file will be added in the Discovery Projects in Chapter 4.

Discovery Project 3-4

The `levenshtein()` function and the `similar_text()` function both calculate the difference between two strings. Because they use different algorithms, they can come up with different answers. In this project, you create a script that illustrates the differences by finding the most similar Chinese zodiac sign names using the two functions.

1. Create a new document in your text editor.

2. Type the `<!DOCTYPE>` declaration, `<html>` element, document head, and `<body>` element. Use the strict DTD and "Similar Names" as the content of the `<title>` element.

3. Add the following text, elements, and PHP script section to the document body:

```
<h1>Similar Names</h1><hr />
<?php
?>
```

4. In the script section, declare the `$SignNames` array and variables to track the smallest value from the `levenshtein()` function and the largest value from the `similar_text()` function. Note that the `levenshtein()` function returns the number of differences, so a small return value indicates that the two strings are similar, while a large return value indicates that the two strings are different. In contrast, the `similar_text()` function returns the number of matching characters, so a small return value indicates that the two strings are different, while a large return value indicates that the two strings are similar.

 When searching for the largest value, you initialize your test variable to a number below the smallest number you could possibly find (usually 0). When searching for the smallest value, you initialize your test variable to a number above the highest number you could possibly find.

```
$SignNames = array(
          "Rat",
          "Ox",
          "Tiger",
          "Rabbit",
          "Dragon",
          "Snake",
          "Horse",
          "Goat",
          "Monkey",
          "Rooster",
          "Dog",
          "Pig");
$LevenshteinSmallest = 999999;
$SimilarTextLargest = 0;
```

5. Add the following nested `for` loops to the end of the script section. The initial value and conditional of each `for` loop are designed so that each element of the array will be compared once to every other element of the array. Within the inner `for` loop, you retrieve the value from the `levenshtein()` function for each pair of names and compare the returned value to the smallest value found so far. If the returned value is smaller, this pair of names is closer, so you store the returned value as the smallest

value found so far and save the pair of names associated with that value. You then do the same thing with the similar_text() function, except that you test for the largest value.

```
for ($i=0; $i<11; ++$i) {
    for ($j=$i+1; $j<12; ++$j) {
        $LevenshteinValue =
            levenshtein($SignNames[$i],
                $SignNames[$j]);
        if ($LevenshteinValue <
            $LevenshteinSmallest) {
            $LevenshteinSmallest =
                $LevenshteinValue;
            $LevenshteinWord1 =
                $SignNames[$i];
            $LevenshteinWord2 =
                $SignNames[$j];
        }
        $SimilarTextValue =
            similar_text($SignNames[$i],
                $SignNames[$j]);
        if ($SimilarTextValue >
            $SimilarTextLargest) {
            $SimilarTextLargest =
                $SimilarTextValue;
            $SimilarTextWord1 =
                $SignNames[$i];
            $SimilarTextWord2 =
                $SignNames[$j];
        }
    }
}
```

6. Add the following code to the end of the script section to display the pairs of words that the functions determined are the most similar.

```
echo "<p>The levenshtein() function has determined that
    &quot;$LevenshteinWord1&quot; and
    &quot;$LevenshteinWord2&quot; are the most
    similar names.</p>\n";
echo "<p>The similar_text() function has determined that
    &quot;$SimilarTextWord1&quot;
    and &quot;$SimilarTextWord2&quot; are the most
    similar names.</p>\n";
```

7. Save the document as **SimilarNames.php** in the ChineseZodiac directory and upload the file to the server.

8. Open SimilarNames.php in your Web browser by entering the following URL:
http://<yourserver>/ChineseZodiac/SimilarNames.php.
Figure 3-22 shows the output.

183

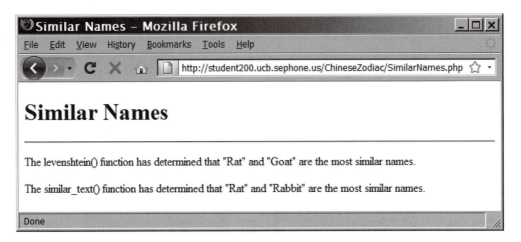

The levenshtein() function has determined that "Rat" and "Goat" are the most similar names.

The similar_text() function has determined that "Rat" and "Rabbit" are the most similar names.

Figure 3-22   Output of SimilarNames.php

9.   Close your Web browser window.

Discovery Project 3-5

In this project, you will create a script that determines which of the 12 Chinese zodiac sign names can be made using the letters in each of a set of phrases.

1.   Create a new document in your text editor.

2.   Type the <!DOCTYPE> declaration, <html> element, document head, and <body> element. Use the strict DTD and "Embedded Words" as the content of the <title> element.

3.   Add the following text, elements, and PHP script section to the document body:

```
<h1>Embedded Words</h1><hr />
<?php
?>
```

4.   In the script section, declare the $Phrases and $SignNames arrays as follows:

```
$Phrases = array(
        "Your Chinese zodiac sign tells a lot about
        your personality.",
        "Embed PHP scripts within an XHTML
        document.");
    $SignNames = array(
        "Rat",
        "Ox",
        "Tiger",
        "Rabbit",
        "Dragon",
```

```
        "Snake",
        "Horse",
        "Goat",
        "Monkey",
        "Rooster",
        "Dog",
        "Pig");
```

5. Add a function named `BuildLetterCounts()`. The first statement converts all of the letters in the string to uppercase. The second statement uses the `count_chars()` function to create an array of the counts of the 256 ASCII characters. The final statement returns the newly created array.

```php
function BuildLetterCounts($text) {
    $text = strtoupper($text);
    $letter_counts = count_chars($text);
    return $letter_counts;
}
```

6. Add a function named `AContainsB()`. The function takes two arrays created by the `BuildLetterCounts()` function from Step 5. First, a default return value (TRUE) is set, then the `ord()` function is used to get the ASCII values of the first and last capital letters ('A' and 'Z'). These values define the range of characters that need to be tested. Finally, you use a `for` loop to check the counts for each uppercase letter. At any iteration, if the count for the current character from array `$A` is less than the count for the current character from array `$B`, the word cannot be made from the letters in the phrase, so the return value is set to FALSE.

```php
function AContainsB($A, $B) {
    $retval = TRUE;
    $first_letter_index = ord('A');
    $last_letter_index = ord('Z');
    for ($letter_index = $first_letter_index;
            $letter_index <= $last_letter_index;
            ++$letter_index) {
        if ($A[$letter_index] < $B[$letter_index]) {
            $retval = FALSE;
        }
    }

    return $retval;
}
```

7. Create a `foreach` loop to step through each of the phrases. Use the `BuildLetterCounts()` function to create an array of the counts of the ASCII characters in the phrase. Initialize a list of the words that can be made as the `$GoodWords` array,

and a list of the words that cannot be made as the $BadWords array.

```
foreach ($Phrases as $Phrase) {
    $PhraseArray = BuildLetterCounts($Phrase);
    $GoodWords = array();
    $BadWords = array();
}
```

8. Immediately after initializing the $BadWords array, create an inner foreach loop to step through each of the sign names. Use the BuildLetterCounts() function to create an array of the counts of the ASCII characters in the sign name. Use the AContainsB() function to determine if the sign name (B) can be made with the letters in the phrase (A). If the AContainsB() function returns TRUE, add the sign name to the $GoodWords array. If the AContainsB() function returns FALSE, add the sign name to the $BadWords array.

```
foreach ($SignNames as $Word) {
    $WordArray = BuildLetterCounts($Word);
    if (AContainsB($PhraseArray, $WordArray))
        $GoodWords[] = $Word;
    else
        $BadWords[] = $Word;
}
```

9. After the inner foreach loop, add the following code to display the list of words that can and cannot be made from the phrase.

```
echo "<p>The following words can be made from
    the letters in the phrase
    &quot;$Phrase&quot;:";
foreach ($GoodWords as $Word)
    echo " $Word";
echo "</p>\n";
echo "<p>The following words can not
    be made from the letters in the phrase
    &quot;$Phrase&quot;:";
foreach ($BadWords as $Word)
    echo " $Word";
echo "</p>\n";
echo "<hr />\n";
```

10. Save the document as **EmbeddedWords.php** in the ChineseZodiac directory and upload the file to the server.

11. Open EmbeddedWords.php in your Web browser by entering the following URL:
http://<yourserver>/ChineseZodiac/EmbeddedWords.php.
Figure 3-23 shows the output.

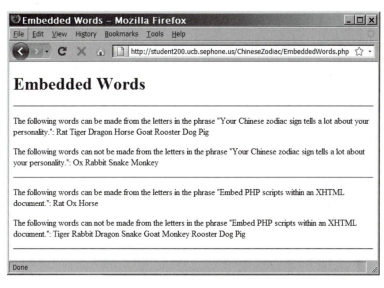

Figure 3-23 Output of EmbeddedWords.php

12. Close your Web browser window.

Links to Similar Names.php and Embedded Words.php will be added in Discovery Project 5-3.

CHAPTER 4

Handling User Input

In this chapter, you will:

◎ Learn about autoglobal variables

◎ Build XHTML Web forms

◎ Process form data

◎ Handle submitted form data

◎ Create an All-in-One form

◎ Display dynamic data based on a URL token

Two of the most common ways that PHP interfaces with the user are by accessing values from fill-in forms that are submitted to a PHP script and by handling events, such as dynamically displaying pages when the user clicks a hyperlink. The data needed to process these interactions is stored in PHP autoglobals.

Using Autoglobals

PHP includes various predefined global arrays, called **autoglobals** or **superglobals**, which contain client, server, and environment information that you can use in your scripts. Table 4-1 lists the PHP autoglobals.

Array	Description
$_COOKIE	An array of values passed to the current script as HTTP cookies
$_ENV	An array of environment information
$_FILES	An array of information about uploaded files
$_GET	An array of values from a form submitted with the "get" method
$_POST	An array of values from a form submitted with the "post" method
$_REQUEST	An array of all the elements in the $_COOKIE, $_GET, and $_POST arrays
$_SERVER	An array of information about the Web server that served the current script
$_SESSION	An array of session variables that are available to the current script
$GLOBALS	An array of references to all variables that are defined with global scope

Table 4-1   PHP autoglobals

Autoglobals are **associative arrays**, which are arrays whose elements are referred to with an alphanumeric key instead of an index number. An example of an associative array is a list of a company's payroll information that uses each employee's last name instead of an index number to refer to elements in the array. To refer to an element in an associative array, you place an element's key in single or double quotation marks inside the array brackets. For example, the following statements display three elements of the $_SERVER autoglobal. The $_SERVER["SCRIPT_NAME"] element displays the path and name of the current script, the $_SERVER["SERVER_SOFTWARE"] element displays the name of the server software that executed the script, and the $_SERVER["SERVER_PROTOCOL"] element displays the server protocol that was used to request the script. Figure 4-1 shows the output.

You will work with most of the autoglobals in later chapters.

```
echo "<p>The name of the current script is ",
$_SERVER["SCRIPT_NAME"], "<br />";
echo "This script was executed with the following server
     software: ", $_SERVER["SERVER_SOFTWARE"], "<br />";
echo "This script was requested with the following server
     protocol: ", $_SERVER["SERVER_PROTOCOL"], "</p>";
```

You will learn how to create associative arrays in Chapter 6.

190

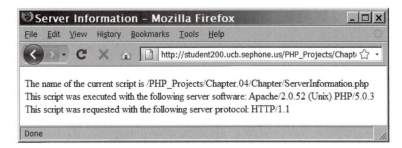

Figure 4-1   Output of a script that references the $_SERVER autoglobal

You can use the getenv() function to retrieve the value of an element in the $_ENV array.

As shown in the previous example, the $_SERVER autoglobal contains information about the Web server and the PHP scripting engine, as well as detailed information about the current Web page request. The elements that are available with the $_SERVER autoglobal depend on the Web server that executes the PHP script.

The phpinfo() function displays the elements of the $_ENV array and their values in the "Additional Modules" section, under the "Environment" heading. You can revisit the PHPTest.php script you created in Chapter 1 to see the output of the phpinfo() function by opening http://<yourserver>/ PHP_Projects/Chapter.01/ Chapter/PHPTest.php in your Web browser.

You can use the $_SERVER["SCRIPT_NAME"] element to include the full URL path and script name of the current script. This is useful when creating a link back to the current page, either as the action attribute of an All-in-One Web form or as a link to a different view of a Web page template. Both options are discussed later in this chapter. Use of the similar $_SERVER["PHP_SELF"] element should be avoided because it includes any additional path information appended to the URL. Attackers can take advantage of this additional path information to insert dangerous XHTML code into your Web page. The $_SERVER["SCRIPT_NAME"] element does not include additional path information, so hackers cannot use this method to attack your Web site.

The $_ENV autoglobal contains the environmental variables set for the operating system on the machine that hosts the Web server. **Environmental variables** are variables that programs use to interact with the system. Unlike the $_SERVER autoglobal, which contains a predefined list of elements, the $_ENV elements change depending on the operating system and the machine's configuration.

Most $_SERVER and $_ENV element values should not be displayed on a public Web page because they contain important information that a hacker could use to identify weaknesses of the server.

As mentioned in Chapter 2, you must use the global keyword to reference a global variable within the scope of a function. You can also use the $GLOBALS autoglobal array to refer to the global version of a variable from inside a function. To refer to a global variable with the $GLOBALS autoglobal, you use the variable's name as the key in single or double quotation marks inside the array brackets. The following example shows a modified version of the script containing the scopeExample() function you saw in Chapter 2. In this example, the script references $GlobalVariable using the $GLOBALS autoglobal instead of the global keyword.

```php
<?php
$GlobalVariable = "Global variable";
function scopeExample() {
    echo "<p>" . $GLOBALS["GlobalVariable"] . "</p>";
}
scopeExample();
?>
```

The $_GET, $_POST, and $_REQUEST autoglobals contain data entered in Web forms and URL tokens. All of these are discussed in greater detail later in this chapter. The $_FILES autoglobal contains data about files uploaded to the server using Web forms, as you will learn in Chapter 5. The $_COOKIE and $_SESSION autoglobals contain different types of state information, which are explained in Chapter 9.

For more information on any of the autoglobals, see the online PHP documentation at *http://www.php.net/docs.php*.

When using the variable name as an index for the $GLOBALS array, you omit the leading dollar sign ($) from the name.

191

Short Quiz

1. Which element of the $_SERVER autoglobal is used to refer to the current script?

2. What keyword is used to reference a global variable within the scope of a function?

3. Autoglobals are considered associative arrays. True or False?

Building XHTML Web Forms

Web forms are Web pages with interactive controls that allow users to enter data in text input boxes, select an option from a drop-down list, or choose a response from a check box or radio button control. Web forms also provide a method for electronically submitting the form data entered by the user to a program on the server that processes the user's input.

Web forms are used whenever the server requires information from the user. For e-commerce sites, order processing and billing are accomplished via Web forms. Web forms allow visitors to subscribe to a mailing list or newsletter. Search engine sites use Web forms to allow visitors to enter search keywords.

A Web form is a standard XHTML page. The only difference is that a Web form requires a <form> section that contains XHTML markup, controls (text input boxes, radio buttons, check boxes, selection lists, text area boxes), and a submit button to send the form values to the server for processing. A reset button to clear the form data is optional.

Adding an `action` Attribute

The `<form>` opening tag requires an `action` attribute. The value of the `action` attribute identifies the program on the Web server that will process the form data when the form is submitted. A PHP script is often used to process form data.

`<form action="http://www.example.com/HandleFormInput.php">`

Adding a `method` Attribute

The opening `<form>` tag must also contain a `method` attribute, which defines how the form data is submitted to the server. The value of the `method` attribute will be either "post" or "get." When form data is submitted using the "post" method, the form data is embedded in the request message. When form data is submitted using the "get" method, the form data is appended to the URL specified in the form's `action` attribute.

Earlier in this chapter, you were introduced to two autoglobals, $_POST and $_GET, which allow you to access the values that are submitted to a PHP script from a Web form. When a Web form is submitted, PHP automatically creates and populates two global arrays: the $_POST array, which contains values of forms that are submitted using the post method, and the $_GET array, which contains values from forms that are submitted using the get method.

When you click a form's Submit button, each field on the form is sent to the Web server as a name/value pair. When the post method is used, the name portion of the name/value pair becomes the key, or index, of an element in the $_POST autoglobal array and the value portion is assigned as the value of the array element. The get method is used in the same way, except that the name portion of the name/value pair becomes the key of an element in the $_GET autoglobal array.

When you use the get method to submit form data to the processing script, the form data is appended to the URL specified by the `action` attribute. Name/value pairs appended to the end of a URL are called **URL tokens**. The form data is separated from the URL by a question mark (?), the individual elements are separated by an ampersand (&), and the element name is separated from the value by an equal sign (=). Spaces in the *name* and *value* fields are encoded as plus signs (+), and all other characters except letters, numbers, hyphens (-), underscores (_), and periods (.) are encoded using a percent sign (%) followed by the two-digit hexadecimal representation of the character's ASCII value. For example:

```
http://www.example.net/process_Scholarship.php?fName=
John&lName=Smith&Submit=Send+Form
```

In the preceding example, three form elements were submitted to the process_Scholarship.php script as URL tokens: fName, which is set to "John"; lName, which is set to "Smith"; and "Submit" (the name of the submit button), which is set to "Send Form", the value assigned to the submit button.

The get method is useful as a debugging technique because it allows you to see the names and values that are being sent to the Web server. The get method is also useful for creating static links to a dynamic server process, as you will learn later in this chapter.

Because many forms request confidential information, such as Social Security numbers and passwords, or may contain a field that requires the user to enter more than 100 characters, examples will use the post method to submit form data for the remainder of this book.

To create an XHTML form that contains two text input boxes for users to enter their first and last names and two buttons to clear or submit the form data:

1. Create a new document in your text editor. Type the !DOCTYPE declaration, <html> element, header information, and <body> element. Use the strict DTD and "Scholarship Form" as the content of the <title> element.

2. Add the following XHTML content to the document body:

    ```
    <h2 style="text-align:center">Scholarship Form</h2>
    <form name="scholarship" action=
        "process_Scholarship.php"
        method="post">
    <p>First Name: <input type="text" name="fName" /></p>
    <p>Last Name: <input type="text" name="lName" /></p>
    <p><input type="reset" value="Clear Form" /> 
     <input type="submit" name="Submit" value=
    "Send Form" />
    </form>
    ```

3. Save the document as **Scholarship.html** in the Chapter directory for Chapter 4. Because Scholarship.html contains only XHTML markup, you can view this document in the browser locally. You should see the Web page shown in Figure 4-2.

The get method restricts the number of characters that can be appended to a single variable to 100.

An HTTP request with URL tokens is not secure. It is stored in plain text in log files on any machine between the client and server computers, as well as on the client and server computers themselves. Because the get method encodes the data in the URL, it would not be practical to use the get method to submit sensitive information, such as Social Security numbers or passwords.

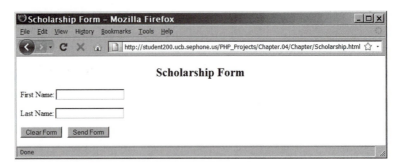

Figure 4-2 The scholarship form

4. Close your Web browser window.

Short Quiz

1. Explain the function of the `action` and `method` attributes in the opening `<form>` tag.

2. Explain the difference(s) in how form data is submitted using the post and get methods.

3. Describe the limitations of using the get method to submit form data.

Processing Form Data

The second half of the procedure for using Web forms is processing the form data once it is submitted. This is done in a **form handler**—a program or script that processes the information submitted from a Web form. A form handler includes code for verifying that the user entered the minimum amount of data needed to process the form, validating entered data to ensure that it is appropriate for the field, performing any tasks needed for the data submitted, and returning appropriate output as a Web page.

Retrieving Submitted Data

After the user fills out the fields in the Scholarship.html Web form and clicks the submit button using the post method, the names (`fName`, `lName`, and `Submit`) that were assigned to the controls in the Scholarship form automatically become keys in the `$_POST` autoglobal array. Also, the values the user enters in the First Name and Last Name input boxes ("John" and "Smith" in the following example) and the value assigned to the submit button ("Send Form") become the values in the $_POST array that can be accessed by the processing script.

To create a form handler for the Scholarship.html form:

1. Create a new document in your text editor. Type the !DOCTYPE declaration, <html> element, header information, and <body> element. Use the strict DTD and "Scholarship Form" as the content of the <title> element.

2. Add the opening and closing tags for the PHP script section in the body of the document:

```
<?php
?>
```

3. Add the following code to retrieve and display the data entered on the form:

```
$firstName = $_POST['fName'];
$lastName = $_POST['lName'];
echo "Thank you for filling out the scholarship form,
     ".$firstName." ".$lastName . ".";
```

4. Save the document as **process_Scholarship.php** in the Chapter directory for Chapter 4.

5. Upload both Scholarship.html and process_Scholarship.php to the server and then open Scholarship.html in the Web browser by entering the following URL: *http://<yourserver>/ PHP_Projects/Chapter.04/Chapter/Scholarship.html*.

6. Enter a first name and last name in the appropriate fields and submit the form to the process_Scholarship.php form handler. Figure 4-3 shows sample output in a Web browser window.

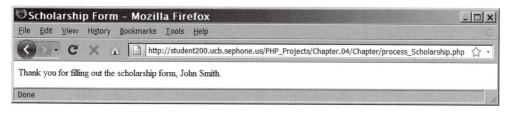

Figure 4-3 Output of the scholarship form handler

7. Close your Web browser window.

Handling Special Characters

The previous example displays correctly unless the user enters an apostrophe in the First Name or Last Name text box on the Web form. Recall from Chapter 3 that you should use escape sequences for special characters in text strings, especially single or double quotes, because they may cause problems when the PHP scripting engine attempts to identify the end of a string. Because the data a user submits to a PHP script may contain single or double quotes, you should use escape sequences for any user data your script receives, especially before you write it to a data source, such as a text file or database. Older versions of PHP include a feature called **magic quotes**, which automatically adds a backslash (\) to any single quote ('), double quote ("), or NULL character contained in form data that a user submits to a PHP script. For example, if you enter a last name with an apostrophe (such as "O'Hara") in the Last Name text box in the scholarship form and then submit the form to a PHP script, magic quotes automatically escape the single quote, and the output appears as shown in Figure 4-4.

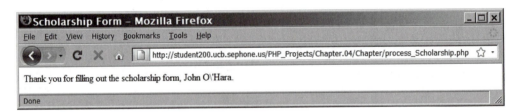

Figure 4-4 The entered string from the Web form with magic quotes

Remember that you can check whether any of the magic quote directives are enabled by running the phpinfo() function that you used in Chapter 1. When you revisit the PHPTest.php script you created in Chapter 1, you will see the magic_quotes_gpc, magic_quotes_runtime, and magic_quotes_sybase directives listed under the PHP Core section.

Magic quotes are enabled within your php.ini configuration file with the directives listed in Table 4-2.

Directive	Description
magic_quotes_gpc	Applies magic quotes to any user-submitted data
magic_quotes_runtime	Applies magic quotes to runtime-generated data, such as data received from a database
magic_quotes_sybase	Applies Sybase-style magic quotes, which escape special characters with a single quote (') instead of a backslash (\)

Table 4-2 Magic quote directives

By default, magic_quotes_gpc is the only magic quote directive enabled in the php.ini configuration file.

196

Magic quotes are unpopular with programmers because it's easy to forget whether they are enabled or disabled in PHP on a particular server. Many PHP programmers have spent hours trying to determine why backslashes were being added to data their scripts received, only to discover that the culprit was a magic quote directive in the php.ini configuration file. You should ask your ISP to disable magic quotes in the php.ini configuration file.

 See Appendix D for an explanation of security issues associated with magic quotes.

Fortunately, PHP provides an alternate method to escape strings, even if magic quotes are disabled. The `addslashes()` function accepts a single argument representing the text string you want to escape and returns a string containing the escaped string. For example, assume that a visitor to the scholarship form page enters the last name "O'Hara". If magic quotes are enabled, the `$_POST['lName']` autoglobal element contains the value "O\'Hara". The following code escapes the single quote in the last name O'Hara in the same manner; the output will be the same as shown in Figure 4-4:

```php
$firstName = addslashes($_POST['fName']);
$lastName = addslashes($_POST['lName']);
echo "Thank you for filling out the scholarship form, " .
    $firstName . " " . $lastName . ".";
```

The existence of the `addslashes()` function is actually another reason why magic quotes are unpopular. If you execute the `addslashes()` function on user-submitted data when magic quotes are turned on, you will get unexpected results. First, magic quotes will add a slash before the apostrophe (O\'Hara). Then the `addslashes()` function will add a slash before both the slash and the apostrophe (O\\\'Hara). The result is that three slashes are added when you only want one. For example, if you execute the preceding code when magic quotes are enabled, the text string appears as shown in Figure 4-5.

 Because of the problems they can cause, you should ask your ISP to turn off magic quotes on the server and rely on the `addslashes()` function to escape user-submitted text strings.

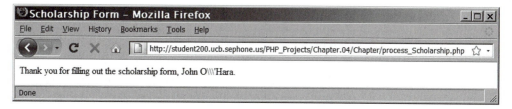

Figure 4-5 The form string after magic quotes and `addslashes()`

PHP also provides a function to reverse the changes made by magic quotes or the `addslashes()` function. The `stripslashes()` function removes any slashes that occur before a single quote ('), double quote ("), or NULL character. All other slashes are ignored.

 As of version 5.3, magic quotes are deprecated in PHP. As of version 6.0, they have been removed.

To handle magic quotes in the process_Scholarship.php script:

1. Reopen the **process_Scholarship.php** script in your editor.

2. Modify the assignment of the $firstName and $lastName variables to use the stripslashes() function by adding the code shown in bold:

```php
<?php
$firstName = stripslashes($_POST['fName']);
$lastName = stripslashes($_POST['lName']);
echo "Thank you for filling out the scholarship form,
    ".$firstName." ".$lastName . ".";
?>
```

3. Save the process_Scholarship.php script, upload it to the server, and then open Scholarship.html in the Web browser by entering the following URL: *http://<yourserver>/ PHP_Projects/Chapter.04/Chapter/Scholarship.html.*

4. Enter a first name or last name that contains an apostrophe to test if the stripslashes() removed the backslashes inserted by magic quotes. Figure 4-6 shows the output for the name "John O'Hara".

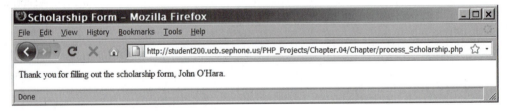

Figure 4-6 The scholarship form after magic quotes are removed

5. Close the browser window.

Short Quiz

1. Describe how an autoglobal $_POST array is populated when the post method is used to submit form data.

2. Describe the role of magic quotes in working with string data.

3. What function is used to remove the backslashes added by magic quotes or the addslashes() function?

Handling Submitted Form Data

Once the data from a Web form is submitted, it needs to be processed by the form handler in several steps. First, the form handler needs to verify that the entered information is complete, valid, and safe. If the information is not complete or valid, the form handler needs to provide feedback to the visitor. Next, the form handler needs to prepare the submitted data for use. Finally, the form handler needs to use the submitted data.

Determining if Form Variables Contain Values

The first step in validating form data is to determine if fields have data entered in them. When form data is posted using the post or get method, all controls except unchecked radio buttons and check boxes get sent to the server, whether they contain data or not. Because of this, simply checking to see if there is an element in the $_POST or $_GET array is not sufficient to determine if a value was entered. The empty() function can be used to determine if a variable contains values. The empty() function returns a value of FALSE if the variable being checked has a nonempty and nonzero value, and a value of TRUE if the variable has an empty or zero value.

 The empty() function returns a value of FALSE for a numeric value of 0. If you are validating a numeric field for which 0 is a valid entry, you must check for a value of 0 separately.

Validating Entered Data

Often, determining that a value has been entered for a form field is not sufficient. Some fields require a specific type of data, such as an integer or a decimal value, or data in a specific format, such as a date or an e-mail address. Different techniques will help verify that the value entered in a field is appropriate for the type of data that should have been entered.

The best way to ensure valid form data is to build the Web form with controls (such as check boxes, radio buttons, and selection lists) that only allow the user to select acceptable responses. This method only works if the user is confined to a predefined set of responses. However, information such as a user name, password, or e-mail address is unique for each user. This data needs to be validated to ensure that the entered values are usable for the type of data required.

 Any data passed to a form handler needs to be validated to protect against form-based hacking attempts. Appendix E contains details on protecting your site against these attacks.

Validating Numeric Data

All data entered in a form is actually string data. PHP automatically converts string data to numeric data if the string is in numeric format. The is_*() family of functions can be used to ensure that the user enters numeric values where necessary. Comparison functions ensure that values are within a required range. Finally, the round() function can be used to ensure that numbers have the appropriate number of digits after the decimal point, if any. All of these functions were introduced in Chapter 1.

For example, the following function ensures that the entered field, passed as the $data parameter, is a four-digit year between 1900 and 2100:

```php
function validateYear($data, $fieldName) {
    global $errorCount;
    if (empty($data)) {
        echo "<p>The field $fieldName is
            required.</p>\n";
        ++$errorCount;
        $retval = "";
    } else { // Only clean up the input if it isn't empty
        $data = trim($data);
        $data = stripslashes($data);
        if (is_numeric($data)) {
            $data = round($data);
            if (($data >= 1900) &&
                ($data <= 2100)) {
                $retval = $data;
            } else {
                echo "<p>The field $fieldName must be
                    between 1900 and 2100.</p>\n";
                ++$errorCount;
                $retval = "";
            }
        } else {
            echo "<p>The field $fieldName must be a
                number between 1900 and 2100.</p>\n";
            ++$errorCount;
            $retval = "";
        }
    }
    return($retval);
}
```

Validating String Data

Many of the string functions covered in Chapter 3 can be used to produce strings with consistent formatting. Regular expression functions are some of the best tools for verifying that string data meets the strict formatting required for e-mail addresses, Web page URLs, or date values. In Chapter 3, you used regular expressions in successive examples to continually refine the requirements of an e-mail address and to isolate strings that were not in the correct format.

Strings are often not formatted as expected. The user may enter spaces before or after a text entry, or magic quotes may add escape characters before a single or double quotation mark. In this chapter and the previous one, you have been introduced to two functions that will assist in cleaning up posted data: the stripslashes() function, which removes the leading slashes for escape sequences in strings; and the trim() function, which removes any leading or trailing white space from a string.

For example, the following function ensures that the entered field, passed as the $data parameter, is a telephone number in the form ###-###-####:

```
function validatePhoneNumber($data, $fieldName) {
    global $errorCount;
    if (empty($data)) {
        echo "<p>The field $fieldName is
            required.</p>\n";
        ++$errorCount;
        $retval = "";
    } else { // Only clean up the input if it isn't empty
        $data = trim($data);
        $data = stripslashes($data);
        $pattern = "/\d{3}-\d{3}-\d{4}/";
        if (preg_match($pattern, $data)) {
            $retval = $data;
        } else {
            echo "<p>The field $fieldName must be a
                telephone number in the form
                ###-###-####.</p>\n";
            ++$errorCount;
            $retval = "";
        }
    }
    return($retval);
}
```

Handling Multiple Errors

A common but poor programming practice is to stop processing a form when an error is found and display the error to the user. The user corrects the error, only to find that another field in the form is also filled out incorrectly. For a large and complex form, this can result in multiple attempts before a form is processed successfully.

A better practice is to record the error, usually in an array, and continue processing the form. This allows the script to display a complete list of all the errors found. Users can then go back and correct all of the errors at one time.

To validate the input of the Scholarship.html form:

1. Return to the **process_Scholarship.php** document in your text editor.

2. Add a new function, displayRequired(). This function accepts one argument, $fieldName, which is the name of the field as it appears on the Web form. This function displays an error message.

```php
function displayRequired($fieldName) {
    echo "The field \"$fieldName\" is required.<br />n";
}
```

3. Add a second new function called validateInput() below the displayRequired() function. This function takes two parameters. The first parameter, $data, is a string to be vali-. dated. The second parameter, $fieldName, is the name of the form field. The function returns the $data parameter after it has been cleaned up. Notice that the function uses the global variable $errorCount.

```php
function validateInput($data, $fieldName) {
    global $errorCount;
    if (empty($data)) {
        displayRequired($fieldName);
        ++$errorCount;
        $retval = "";
    } else { // Only clean up the input if it isn't
             // empty
        $retval = trim($data);
        $retval = stripslashes($retval);
    }
    return($retval);
}
```

4. Immediately after the validateInput() function, declare and initialize a new variable called $errorCount as follows:

```php
$errorCount = 0;
```

5. Modify the assignment statements for the $firstName and $lastName variables to receive the output of the validateInput() function:

```php
$firstName = validateInput($_POST['fName'],
"First name");
$lastName = validateInput($_POST['lName'],
"Last name");
```

6. Add a conditional statement immediately after the value of $lastName has been assigned. This statement will either display the total number of errors or a "Thank you" message if there were no errors.

```
if ($errorCount>0)
     echo "Please use the \"Back\" button to
          re-enter the data.<br />\n";
else
     echo "Thank you for filling out the scholarship
          form, " . $firstName . " " . $lastName . ".";
```

7. Save the document and upload it to the Web server.

8. Open the Scholarship.html page in the Web browser by entering the following URL: *http://<yourserver>/PHP_Projects/ Chapter.04/Chapter/Scholarship.html.*

9. Attempt to submit the form to the process_Scholarship.php form handler without entering any data for the first or last name fields. You should see the result shown in Figure 4-7, with two error messages.

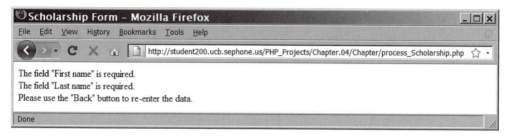

Figure 4-7   Empty input with form validation

10. Close the Web browser window.

Redisplaying the Web Form

In the previous example, error messages were displayed after you validated the data input on the form. However, when you went back to the form, you needed to rekey the information in the form controls. A better option would be to redisplay the form with the controls set to the values that the user entered the last time the form was submitted. As a result, the user only has to enter data for fields that were left empty or did not contain a valid response. The user does not have to retype data that was entered correctly the first time. This type of form is often called a **sticky form**.

To redisplay the Web form, you need to add the XHTML form elements to the output of the PHP script. Because the Web form only needs to be redisplayed if there was an error in the Web form validation, the code to output the Web form should be part of the error-handling section of the script. The code to redisplay the Web form can go into a function for convenience in isolating that part of the code from the remainder of the script.

204

The most convenient way to embed large portions of XHTML code within a PHP script is to use **advanced escaping from XHTML.** When you insert a PHP script section, you are escaping from XHTML. With advanced escaping, you close one PHP script section, insert some XHTML elements, and then open another PHP script section to continue the script. Any XHTML code between the two script sections is considered output, as it would have been using an echo or print statement. You have already seen some simple examples of advanced escaping in Chapter 1, where multiple PHP script sections appeared in a single PHP script.

If the closing tag for the first PHP script section is within a function or the control block for a conditional structure, the XHTML code will only be displayed when the function is called or the conditional control block is executed. If the closing tag for the first PHP script section is within the control block of a looping structure, the XHTML code will be displayed with each iteration of the loop.

The following code declares a function named ShowHomePageLink(). The function displays an image and a message, both of which are hyperlinks to index.php. This function could have been coded as a series of echo or print statements, but it is much easier to read using advanced escaping.

When you close the PHP script section within a control block or function declaration, the PHP script will continue from within the control block or function declaration when the next PHP script section begins.

```
function ShowHomePageLink() {
     ?>
<p>
<a href="index.php"><img src="images/homelink.gif" /></a>
<br />
<a href="index.php">Home Page</a>
</p>
     <?php
}
```

The following exercise illustrates how to redisplay the Web form. Advanced escaping from XHTML will be used to display the Web form. Additionally, the Web form will be a sticky form, keeping the values of the fields that were entered correctly.

To redisplay the Web form within the process_Scholarship.php script:

1. Reopen the **process_Scholarship.php** script in your editor.

2. Add the following function to redisplay the Web form:

```
function redisplayForm($firstName, $lastName) {
?>
<h2 style = "text-align:center">Scholarship Form</h2>
<form name="scholarship" action="process_
Scholarship.php"
     method="post">
```

```
<p>First Name: <input type="text" name="fName"
value="<?php echo $firstName; ?>" /></p>
<p>Last Name: <input type="text" name="lName"
value="<?php echo $lastName; ?>" /></p>
<p><input type="reset" value="Clear Form" /> 
 <input type="submit" name="Submit" value="Send
Form" />
</form>
<?php
}
```

This code is nearly identical to the code in Scholarship. html and could be copied from there. The only difference is the addition of a "value" attribute to each of the input controls, which is used to make a sticky form.

205

3. Modify the if clause of the final if...else statement to call the redisplayForm() function if there were errors. Add the text shown in bold below:

```
if ($errorCount>0) {
    echo "Please re-enter the information below.<br />\n";
    redisplayForm($firstName, $lastName);
}
else
```

4. Save the document and upload it to the Web server.

5. Open the Scholarship.html page in the Web browser by entering the following URL: *http://<yourserver>/PHP_Projects/Chapter.04/Chapter/Scholarship.html*.

6. Attempt to submit the form without entering any data for one of the two fields. You should see a result similar to that shown in Figure 4-8, with one error message and the Web form with the value you entered automatically reinserted into the same field. Enter data for the empty field and resubmit the form to see the "Thank you" message.

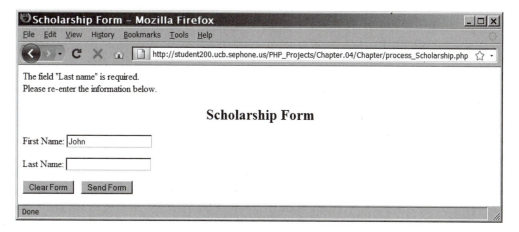

Figure 4-8 The error message with the redisplayed sticky form

7. Close your Web browser window.

The mail() function may not be available on your server (or your local machine, if you are running a local PHP server). In addition to properly configuring PHP to send mail, you need to have an e-mail program available on the server or the local machine. If the mail() function is not available on your system, you will not be able to perform the exercise in this section.

Using the Submitted Data

Once the data entered into the Web form is validated, it needs to be used. Exactly how the data is used varies depending on the purpose of the form. In some cases, information can be written to or queried from a database. In other cases, a file can be downloaded to the user. In this section, the data from the Web form will be used to generate an e-mail message and display a confirmation message for the user.

E-mailing the Web Form

In PHP, an e-mail message is sent using the mail() function. The basic syntax for this function is mail(recipient(s), subject, message).

The value you assign to the recipient(s) argument is a string of one or more e-mail addresses in the standard format for an "Address Specifier", as defined by the Internet Message Format documentation. The two simplest forms of address specifiers are the plain e-mail address, as in jdoe@example.net, and the recipient's name followed by the e-mail address in angle brackets, as in Mary Smith <mary.smith@example.com>.

The subject field is a text string that will appear as the subject field of the e-mail message. The subject string should be plain text with no XHTML tags or character entities. The message field is a text string that will appear as the body of the message. Unless special syntax (called MIME format) is used, the message field should also be plain text with no XHTML tags or character entities.

A fourth optional additional_headers argument can include additional headers that are typically found in e-mail messages, such as From, Cc, Bcc, and Date headers. For the From, Cc, and Bcc headers, the same address specifier syntax is used as in the recipient(s) field. The additional_headers argument needs to be formatted to conform to the syntax of headers in the Internet Message Format documentation. Each header needs to be on its own line. The line must start with the header name, followed by a colon, a space, and the value of the header element. For example:

```
Date: Fri, 03 Apr 2009 16:05:50 -0400
From: Linda M. Jones <linda@jones.example.com>
CC: Mary R. Jones <mary@jones.example.com>
```

Any valid e-mail header may be added using the additional_headers argument. However, depending on the configuration of PHP and the mail program on the Web server, some headers may be excluded and others may be overwritten with values defined by the server.

The mail() function returns a value of TRUE if a message was sent successfully or FALSE if it was not. The return value comes in handy when displaying a status message for the user, which will be discussed next. The following example demonstrates how to send the results of the scholarship form as a simple e-mail message:

```
$To = "webmaster@example.edu";
$Subject = "Message from the Web Form";
$Message = $formMessage;
$Headers="From: $fname $lName <$emailAddress>";
mail ($To, $Subject, $Message, $Headers);
```

Displaying a Status Message for the User

Once all required fields on the form have been filled in and validated, and any action such as sending an e-mail message has been completed, the user should receive a status message in the browser. A standard practice as part of the status message is to thank the user for completing the form. You can also display the results of any actions initiated while processing the form data. For example, the status message could display "Your message has been sent" if the mail() function returned TRUE, or "Your message could not be sent at this time" if the mail() function returned FALSE.

To send e-mail from the scholarship form:

1. Reopen the **process_Scholarship.php** script in your text editor.

2. Replace the else portion of the final if...else statement with the following code block:

```
{ // Send an e-mail
// replace the "recipient@example.edu" with your
// e-mail address
$To = "recipient@mail.edu";
$Subject = "Scholarship Form Results";
$Message = "Student Name: " . $firstName. " " .
        $lastName;
$result = mail($To, $Subject, $Message);
if ($result)
    $resultMsg = "Your message was
            successfully sent.";
else
    $resultMsg = "There was a problem sending
            your message.";
}
```

3. Add the following code immediately before the end of the final code block of the PHP script section. Using advanced escaping and coding the message in XHTML rather than in

Electronic mail is not encrypted, and any information contained in an e-mail message should be considered insecure. You should not e-mail personal or financial information entered through a Web form. Unless the Web form is a simple "Contact Us" page, you should consider storing the information in a file or database, and using the mail() function only as a notification tool.

207

the PHP script section allows you to more easily format the data using CSS.

```php
?>
<h2 style = "text-align:center">Scholarship
Form</h2>
<p style = "line-height:200%">Thank you for filling
out the scholarship form<?php
        if (!empty($firstName))
            echo ", $firstName"
    ?>. <?php echo $resultMsg; ?>
<?php
```

4. Save the file and upload it the server.

5. Open the Scholarship.html page in the Web browser by entering the following URL: *http://<yourserver>/PHP_Projects/Chapter.04/Chapter/Scholarship.html*. Figure 4-9 shows the status message displayed in the browser window after the form has been successfully submitted.

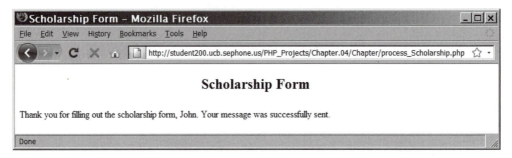

Figure 4-9   Sending e-mail for the scholarship form

6. Close your Web browser window.

Short Quiz

1. Under which conditions does the `empty()` function return TRUE?

2. Explain the process of efficiently handling multiple errors.

3. Define the term "advanced escaping from XHTML".

4. What are the three required arguments of the `mail()` function?

Creating an All-in-One Form

If you have a large form with many fields, or if your form requires intensive processing, it would be more efficient to use separate documents for the Web form and the form handler, as you have done so far in this chapter with the XHTML Web form (Scholarship.html) and the PHP script that processed the form (process_Scholarship.php). This is known as a **two-part form**, because you have one page that displays the form and one page that processes the form data. However, for simple forms that require only minimal processing, it's often easier to use an **All-in-One form**—a single script used to display a Web form and process its data. When the user clicks the submit button, the script submits the form data to the current script. You then use validation code to determine if data exists when the page is first displayed, and to ensure that the user has completed all the required form fields and has entered valid responses.

The PHP script for an All-in-One form can be organized using two conditionals. The first conditional determines if the data has been submitted and needs to be validated. The second conditional determines if the form needs to be redisplayed, either because of a validation error or because the user is opening the page for the first time, or if the form data should be processed.

Validating an All-in-One Form

The All-in-One form uses an `if` conditional to determine if data has been submitted from the Web form or if the Web page is being viewed for the first time. The **isset() function** can be used to determine if the $_POST['Submit'] variable has been set (in other words, if the Submit button has been pressed). The argument that is passed to the isset() function is the value that was assigned to the control's name attribute (name='Submit') in the Web form. The isset() function is not the inverse of the empty() function, in that a variable can be set to an "empty" value, such as the empty string (""), 0, NULL, or FALSE. All of these values will cause the empty() function to return TRUE, because the variable is set to an empty value, and will also cause the isset() function to return TRUE, because the variable has been initialized.

The only way that an initialized variable can become uninitialized, causing the isset() function to return FALSE, is to call the unset() function with the variable name as the parameter.

If the $_POST['Submit'] variable is set (declared and initialized), the script will check to see if all required fields are completed and all responses are valid. If the $_POST['Submit'] variable has not been declared and initialized, the Web form will be displayed.

```
if (isset($_POST['Submit'])) {
    // Validate the data
}
```

Processing the Web Form

Once the data submitted by the user has been validated, the second conditional checks to see if the submitted data passed the validation process. If all of the validation checks succeeded for the submitted data (all required data has been entered and in the correct format), then the data is processed and the user receives a status message.

Redisplaying the Web Form

If the submitted data did not pass all of the validation checks, or if the data has not yet been entered, the All-in-One form will display the Web form, allowing the user to enter data for the first time or re-enter data that did not pass validation. As with the two-part form, you should make the redisplayed form a sticky form, using the `else` clause of the second conditional.

```
if (isset ($_POST['Submit'])) {
     // Process the data
}
else {
     // Display the Web form
}
```

To create a simple All-in-One form:

1. Create a new document in your text editor. Type the !DOCTYPE declaration, `<html>` element, header information, and `<body>` element. Use the strict DTD and "Number Form" as the content of the `<title>` element.

2. Add the opening and closing tags for the PHP script section in the body of the document:

   ```
   <?php
   ?>
   ```

3. Create and initialize a Boolean variable called `$DisplayForm`, which will be used to determine if the Web form should be redisplayed, and a string variable called `$Number`:

   ```
   $DisplayForm = TRUE;
   $Number = "";
   ```

4. Add the following code to check whether the form data has been entered. If it has, the data will be validated:

   ```
   if (isset($_POST['Submit'])) {
        $Number = $_POST['Number'];
        if (is_numeric($Number)) {
             $DisplayForm = FALSE;
        } else {
   ```

```
        echo "<p>You need to enter a numeric
            value.</p>\n";
        $DisplayForm = TRUE;
    }
}
```

5. Add the following code to display the form, including the entered value for the number field. Note the use of advanced embedding of XHTML.

```
if ($DisplayForm) {
?>
<form name="NumberForm" action="NumberForm.php"
    method="post">
<p>Enter a number: <input type="text" name="Number"
value="<?php echo $Number; ?>" /></p>
<p><input type="reset" value="Clear Form" /> 
 <input type="submit" name="Submit" value="Send
Form" /></p>
</form>
<?php
}
```

You could also use action= "<?php echo $_SERVER ["SCRIPT_NAME"]; ?>" in the preceding <form> tag. The $_SERVER["SCRIPT_ NAME"] element contains the name of the current script.

6. Add an else clause to use the form data once it is entered correctly, as follows:

```
else {
    echo "<p>Thank you for entering a number.</p>\n";
    echo "<p>Your number, $Number, squared is " .
        ($Number*$Number) . ".</p>\n ";
    echo "<p><a href=\"NumberForm.php\">Try
        again?</a></p>\n";
}
```

7. Save the document as **NumberForm.php** in the Chapter directory for Chapter 4 and upload the document to the server.

8. Open the Number Form page in the Web browser by entering the following URL: *http://<yourserver>/PHP_Projects/ Chapter.04/Chapter/NumberForm.php*. You should see the form shown in Figure 4-10.

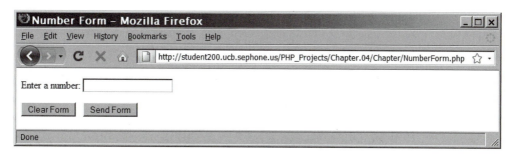

Figure 4-10 The NumberForm.php form when first opened

9. Enter a non-numeric value and click the submit button. The form should reopen with an error message and the value you entered in the text control. When you try again with a numeric value, you should see the "Thank you" message.

10. Close your Web browser window.

Short Quiz

1. Describe the structure of an All-in-One form.

2. How would a form handler determine if the Submit button has been pressed?

3. What family of functions can check whether a user entered a number in a field on a Web form?

Displaying Dynamic Content Based on a URL Token

Unlike the post method, which is ideal for working with forms, the get method is ideal for embedding options in a hyperlink. By passing URL tokens to a PHP script, many different types of information can be displayed from the same script. By using a Web page template with static sections and a dynamic content section, a single PHP script can produce the same content as multiple static XHTML pages. Web page templates have an additional advantage of giving all of the pages a consistent user interface.

Using a Web Page Template

The structure of a PHP-powered Web site is often developed using a template—a single Web page that is divided into sections. As an example, Figure 4-11 shows the layout of a Web page template with the following sections: Header, Button Navigation, Dynamic Content, and Footer.

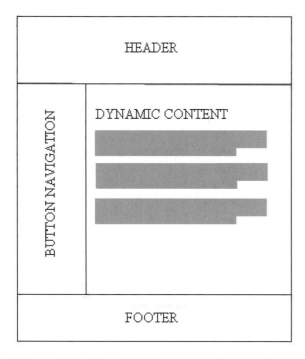

Figure 4-11 A sample Web page template page layout

You learned in Chapter 2 that when you insert the contents of an include file in a PHP script, the content of the XHTML document is displayed in the browser. The following code would insert the contents of the inc_header.php file in the header section:

```php
<?php include("inc_header.php") ?>
```

If you had 50 individual pages in your Web site and the same header, button navigation, and footer on each page, and you needed to add another e-mail address to the header content on each page, you would have to make the addition on all 50 pages. Using a Web page template, you could make the change only once—in the inc_header.php file for the previous example. The header, button navigation, and footer sections are static because the content does not change unless you modify the include file. When a user navigates within a Web site that uses static XHTML pages, a new page with a new header, footer, and button navigation is opened each time. With Web page templates, the content of the dynamic section will change but the content and layout of the static sections will not.

Navigating within a Web Page Template

You can navigate within a Web page template using hyperlinks and buttons, just as you can within the pages of a static XHTML Web site. There are some minor differences, which are explained in this section.

Using Text Hyperlinks for Navigation

When using text hyperlinks to navigate within a Web page template, the values that specify which dynamic content to show must be appended to the filename in the "href" attribute of the anchor tag. You use the notation for the get method discussed earlier in this chapter, with a question mark between the URL and the name/value pairs, an ampersand between name/value pairs, and an equal sign between the name and the value.

The following XHTML code creates a text hyperlink that replaces the current include file that displays in the dynamic data section. In this example, only one name/value pair is being passed, so there is no need for the ampersand. The name being passed in the example is "page", and the value of "page" is "home_page". The index.php script will check the value of the $_GET['page'] array element to determine which page to show in the dynamic data section.

```
<a href="index.php?page=home_page">Home</a>
```

Using Form Image Buttons for Navigation

The following XHTML code is inserted between an opening and closing `<form>` tag in the section in which you want the buttons to display. Each button requires a unique value for the name attribute.

```
<input type="image" src="home.jpg" name="home"
    style="border:0" alt="Home" />
```

In the preceding example, the $_GET or $_POST array would have two elements for this button: "home_x" and "home_y".

Displaying the Dynamic Content

Code inserted in the dynamic data section of the index.php file determines which include file to display in the dynamic data section when a user clicks a button or activates a hyperlink. Throughout this chapter, you have used the $_GET and $_POST autoglobals, which store the submitted form values in an array. The $_REQUEST autoglobal can be used to access the result from form data sent with either the get or post methods. The following code, keyed in the dynamic data section of the index.php file, processes the information submitted with either method:

```
$displayContents = $_REQUEST["page"];
```

Form image buttons do not pass a value. Instead, the x- and y-coordinates are sent in the form "*Button.x*" and "*Button.y*", where "Button" is the value of the name attribute. In PHP, the periods are replaced by underscores (_) for the $_GET and $_POST array indexes. For example, the corresponding array index for Button.x is Button_x in the $_GET or $_POST arrays, and the corresponding array index for Button.y is Button_y.

There are security risks to using the $_REQUEST autoglobal. It includes the contents of the $_COOKIE autoglobal as well as the $_GET and $_POST autoglobals, so hackers could use cookies to pass invalid and potentially harmful content to a form handler. Because of the risk, you should avoid using the $_REQUEST autoglobal whenever possible. Appendix E covers this topic and other security risks.

214

To create a simple Web page template:

1. Create a new file in your editor as follows and save it as **inc_header.html** in the Chapter directory for Chapter 4:

```
<h1 style="text-align: center">Sample Web Template</h1>
```

2. Create a new file in your editor as follows and save it as **inc_footer.php** in the Chapter directory for Chapter 4:

```
<p>Today's Date: <?php echo date('r'); ?></p>
```

3. Create a new file in your editor as follows and save it as **inc_home.html** in the Chapter directory for Chapter 4:

```
<h2>Home Page</h2>
<p>This is the default home page that displays
whenever a new visitor comes to the site</p>
```

4. Create a new file in your editor as follows and save it as **inc_about.html** in the Chapter directory for Chapter 4:

```
<h2>About Me</h2>
<p>This is the page that tells about me and my Web
site.</p>
```

5. Create a new file in your editor as follows and save it as **inc_contact.html** in the Chapter directory for Chapter 4:

```
<h2>Contact Me</h2>
<p>This is the page where people can use a Web form
to send me an e-mail.</p>
```

6. Create a new file in your editor as follows and save it as **inc_buttonnav.html** in the Chapter directory for Chapter 4:

```
<form action="WebTemplate.php" method="get">
<input type="submit" name="content" value="Home" /><br />
<input type="submit" name="content" value="About Me"
/><br />
<input type="submit" name="content" value="Contact
Me" /><br />
</form>
```

7. Create a new document in your text editor. Type the !DOCTYPE declaration, <html> element, header information, and <body> element. Use the strict DTD and "Web Template" as the content of the <title> element.

8. Add the following code to the body of the document:

```php
<?php include ("inc_header.html"); ?>
<div style = "width:20%; text-align:center; float:left">
<?php include ("inc_buttonnav.html"); ?>
</div>
<!-- Start of Dynamic Content section -->
<?php
?>
<!-- End of Dynamic Content section -->
<?php include ("inc_footer.php"); ?>
```

9. Locate the PHP script section within the "Dynamic Content" section, which is where the button input will be processed to determine which content page to display. Add the following PHP code within the block:

```php
if (isset($_GET['content'])) {
    switch ($_GET['content']) {
        case 'About Me':
            include('inc_about.html');
            break;
        case 'Contact Me':
            include('inc_contact.html');
            break;
        case 'Home': // A value of 'Home' means to
                     // display the default page
        default:
            include('inc_home.html');
            break;
    }
}
else // No button has been selected
    include('inc_home.html');
```

10. Save the file as **WebTemplate.php** in the Chapter folder for Chapter 4 and upload the file to the Web server.

11. Open WebTemplate.php in a Web browser by entering the following URL: *http://<yourserver>/PHP_Projects/ Chapter.04/Chapter/WebTemplate.php*. It should appear as shown in Figure 4-12.

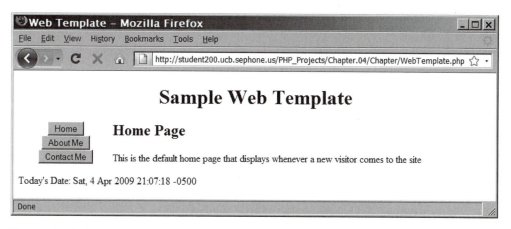

Figure 4-12 The Web page template script output

12. Click the buttons in the button navigation bar. The content in the dynamic content section changes to reflect the selected button.

13. Close your Web browser window.

In the preceding example, the buttons were all named "content". If text hyperlinks are added, the same name can be used as the name in the name/value pair, and the same code can process both. If you need more buttons or text hyperlinks, simply use the name "content" and a different value, and add that value as a case in the switch statement.

```
<a href="WebTemplate.php?content=Home">Home Page</a>
```

Short Quiz

1. Explain the purpose of using a Web page template for Web site development.

2. Describe the notation for the get method used with a text hyperlink to target dynamic content to a section of a Web page template.

3. What autoglobal can be used to access the values of both the get and the post methods?

Summing Up

- PHP includes various predefined global arrays, called autoglobals or superglobals, which contain client, server, and environment information that you can use in your scripts.

- Web forms are standard XHTML Web pages with interactive controls that allow users to enter data.

- The <form> tag requires an action attribute to identify the script that will process the submitted data and a method attribute to identify whether the data will be sent using the get or post method.

- The $_POST autoglobal contains data submitted from a form using the post method; the $_GET autoglobal contains data submitted from a form using the get method or through a hyperlink.

- Web forms may have two components: the data entry form page and the data processing script.

- Magic quotes may be enabled for a PHP server. If enabled, the PHP scripting engine inserts an escape character before a single quotation mark, double quotation mark, or NULL character in any submitted form data.

- The addslashes() function inserts an escape character before a single quotation mark, double quotation mark, or NULL character in a string. The stripslashes() function removes the escape character before a single quotation mark, double quotation mark, or NULL character in a string.

- The first step in processing form data is to validate the input.

- The empty() function determines if the entered value has an empty or zero value.

- The is_*() family of functions determines if the entered value is of the required data type.

- Regular expressions determine if an entered string value is formatted correctly for the required type of entry.

- The user should be notified at the same time of all errors in the values entered into the form.

- Sticky forms are forms that are redisplayed if any errors are found during the validation process. The fields in a sticky form are populated with the values the user entered previously.

- Advanced escaping from XHTML is a convenient way to display XHTML code within a PHP script section.

- The mail() function is used to send mail from PHP; it can be used to send form data via e-mail when the form has been successfully completed and validated.

- All-in-One Web forms combine the data entry form page and the data processing script into a single script.

- The isset() function determines if the entered value has been initialized (or set).

- URL tokens use the get method and additional data appended to the URL to submit information to a PHP script.

- Web page templates combine static elements and a dynamic content section within a Web page.

- Web page templates can use the include() function within a conditional or switch statement to display dynamic content from different include files within the same section of the template.

Comprehension Check

1. Which of the following autoglobals can you use to access submitted form values? (Choose all that apply.)

   a. $_GET

   b. $_POST

   c. $_SERVER

   d. $_REQUEST

2. Which of the following separates the URL from the form data in a get request?

   a. ?

   b. &

   c. =

   d. +

3. Which of the following separates multiple name/value pairs from each other in a get request?

   a. ?

   b. &

   c. =

   d. +

4. What is the maximum length of a value in a get request?

5. Describe the difference in how data is sent to the Web server for the get and post methods.

6. Contrast the two-part Web form with the All-in-One Web form.

7. What are magic quotes and why are they used?

8. Which function removes the slashes that are added by magic quotes?

9. The empty() function is used to do which of the following? (Select all that apply.)

   a. Clear the value of a variable.

   b. Check if the length of a string variable is 0.

   c. Check to see if the value of a variable is NULL.

   d. Check to see if the value of a numeric variable is 0.

10. The is_*() family of functions can be used to verify that the user entered the correct data type in a form field. True or False?

11. A user should fix each data entry error before being notified of the next one. True or False?

12. A(n) _____ form redisplays a form with the previously entered values already filled in.

   a. error

   b. sticky

   c. prefilled

   d. Web

13. Explain the purpose of advanced escaping from XHTML.

14. Explain why the isset() function is not an inverse of the empty() function.

15. The _____ function can be used to determine if data has been submitted to an All-in-One form.

    a. `is_posted()`

    b. `submitted()`

    c. `isset()`

    d. `data_found()`

16. URL tokens use the post method. True or False?

17. Web page templates are made of _____ and _____ sections.

    a. form, script

    b. image, text

    c. static, dynamic

    d. content, template

18. With Web page templates, every page needs to be modified to change an image in the header section. True or False?

19. Describe two methods used to navigate within a Web page template.

20. The _____ autoglobal contains all of the elements of both the `$_GET` and `$_POST` autoglobals.

    a. `$_REQUEST`

    b. `$_RESPONSE`

    c. `$_FORM`

    d. `$_SESSION`

Reinforcement Exercises

 Exercise 4-1

Create a Web form to help in creating "Jumble" puzzles. Create a form that has four input fields named Word1, Word2, Word3, and Word4, as well as "Reset" and "Submit" buttons. Create a form processing script that verifies that all four words are entered, that all of them contain only letters, and that all four are between 4 and 7 characters long. Once all of the words have been verified as correct, use the `strtoupper()` and `str_shuffle()` functions to produce four jumbled sets of letters.

To create the Jumble Maker form:

1. Create a new document in your text editor. Type the `!DOCTYPE` declaration, `<html>` element, header information, and `<body>` element. Use the strict DTD and "Jumble Maker" as the content of the `<title>` element.

2. Add the following XHTML form tags in the body of the document:

```
<form action=
      "process_JumbleMaker.php" method="post">
Word 1: <input type="text" name="Word1" /><br />
Word 2: <input type="text" name="Word2" /><br />
Word 3: <input type="text" name="Word3" /><br />
Word 4: <input type="text" name="Word4" /><br />
<input type="reset" value="Clear Form" /> 
 <input type="submit" name="Submit" value="Send
Form" />
</form>
```

3. Save the document as **JumbleMaker.html** in the Projects directory for Chapter 4.

4. Create a new document in your text editor. Type the `!DOCTYPE` declaration, `<html>` element, header information, and `<body>` element. Use the strict DTD and "Jumble Maker" as the content of the `<title>` element.

5. Add the opening and closing tags for the PHP script section in the body of the document:

```
<?php
?>
```

6. Add the `displayError()` function to the script section. This function displays the error message, and takes two parameters: `$fieldName`, which is the name of the field as it appears on the Web form; and `$errorMsg`, which describes the error for the user. There is no return value for this function.

```
function displayError($fieldName, $errorMsg) {
    global $errorCount;
    echo "Error for \"$fieldName\": $errorMsg<br />\n";
    ++$errorCount;
}
```

7. Create a second function called validateWord() below the displayError() function. This function takes two parameters. The first parameter, $data, is a string to be validated. The second parameter, $fieldName, is the name of the form field. The function returns the $data parameter after it has been cleaned up. Notice that the function uses the global variable $errorCount.

```php
function validateWord($data, $fieldName) {
    global $errorCount;
    if (empty($data)) {
        displayError($fieldName,"This field is
        required");
        $retval = "";
    } else { // Only clean up the input if it isn't
            // empty
        $retval = trim($data);
        $retval = stripslashes($retval);
        if ((strlen($retval)<4) ||
           (strlen($retval)>7)) {
            displayError($fieldName,"Words must be
                        at least four and at most
                        seven letters long");
        }
        if (preg_match("/^[a-z]+$/i",$retval)==0) {
            displayError($fieldName,"Words must be
                        only letters");
        }
    }
    $retval = strtoupper($retval);
    $retval = str_shuffle($retval);
    return($retval);
}
```

8. Immediately after the validateWord() function, declare and initialize a new variable called $errorCount and a new array called $words[] as follows:

```php
$errorCount = 0;
$words = array();
```

9. Add assignment statements for the $words array variable to receive the output of the validateWord() function for each form field:

```php
$words[] = validateWord($_POST['Word1'], "Word 1");
$words[] = validateWord($_POST['Word2'], "Word 2");
$words[] = validateWord($_POST['Word3'], "Word 3");
$words[] = validateWord($_POST['Word4'], "Word 4");
```

10. Add a conditional statement immediately after the values of $words have been assigned. This statement will display the total number of errors found or the shuffled words if there were no errors.

```
if ($errorCount>0)
    echo "Please use the \"Back\" button to
        re-enter the data.<br />\n";
else {
    $wordnum = 0;
    foreach ($words as $word)
        echo "Word ".++$wordnum.": $word<br />\n";
}
```

11. Save the document as **process_JumbleMaker.php** in the Projects directory for Chapter 4.

12. Upload JumbleMaker.html and process_JumbleMaker.php to the Web server.

13. Open the JumbleMaker.html page in the Web browser by entering the following URL: *http://<yourserver>/ PHP_Projects/Chapter.04/Projects/JumbleMaker.html.*

14. Test the form. It should only show the jumbled results if all four words were entered correctly.

15. Close your Web browser window.

 ## Exercise 4-2

In this exercise, you will create an All-in-One form that is a working "Contact Me" page. This page will have inputs for the subject, the sender's name, the sender's e-mail address, and the message. The form will also send a copy of the message to the sender.

1. Create a new document in your text editor. Type the !DOCTYPE declaration, <html> element, header information, and <body> element. Use the strict DTD and "Contact Me" as the content of the <title> element.

2. Add the opening and closing tags for the PHP script section in the body of the document:

```
<?php
?>
```

3. Add a function called `validateInput()`. This function takes two parameters. The first parameter, `$data`, is a string to be validated. The second parameter, `$fieldName`, is the name of the form field. The function returns the `$data` parameter after it has been cleaned up. Notice that the function uses the global variable `$errorCount`.

```php
function validateInput($data, $fieldName) {
    global $errorCount;
    if (empty($data)) {
        echo "\"$fieldName\" is a required field.<br
            />\n";
        ++$errorCount;
        $retval = "";
    } else { // Only clean up the input if it isn't
            // empty
        $retval = trim($data);
        $retval = stripslashes($retval);
    }
    return($retval);
}
```

4. Add a function called `validateEmail()` immediately after the `validateInput()` function. This function is almost exactly like the `validateInput()` function, but it adds a regular expression test to validate that the entered e-mail address is in the correct format. Note that the regular expression used is the same one introduced in Chapter 3.

```php
function validateEmail($data, $fieldName) {
    global $errorCount;
    if (empty($data)) {
        echo "\"$fieldName\" is a required
            field.<br />\n";
        ++$errorCount;
        $retval = "";
    } else { // Only clean up the input if it isn't
            // empty
        $retval = trim($data);
        $retval = stripslashes($retval);
        $pattern = "/^[\w-]+(\.[\w-]+)*@" .
            "[\w-]+(\.[\w-]+)*" .
            "(\.[[a-z]]{2,})$/i";
        if (preg_match($pattern, $retval)==0) {
        echo "\"$fieldName\" is not a valid e-mail
                address.<br />\n";
            ++$errorCount;
        }
    }
    return($retval);
}
```

5. Add a function called `displayForm()` immediately after the `validateEmail()` function. This function takes one parameter for each form field, and displays the form. It uses the parameters for sticky form functionality.

```php
function displayForm($Sender, $Email, $Subject,
$Message) {
?>
<h2 style = "text-align:center">Contact Me</h2>
<form name="contact" action="ContactForm.php"
    method="post">
<p>Your Name: <input type="text" name="Sender"
value="<?php
    echo $Sender; ?>" /></p>
<p>Your E-mail: <input type="text" name="Email"
    value="<?php echo $Email; ?>" /></p>
<p>Subject: <input type="text" name="Subject"
value="<?php
    echo $Subject; ?>" /></p>
<p>Message:<br />
<textarea name="Message"><?php echo $Message;
    ?></textarea></p>
<p><input type="reset" value="Clear Form" /> 
     <input type="submit" name="Submit"
    value="Send Form" /></p>
</form>
<?php
}
```

6. Immediately after the `displayForm()` function, declare and initialize a set of variables as follows:

```php
$ShowForm = TRUE;
$errorCount = 0;
$Sender = "";
$Email = "";
$Subject = "";
$Message = "";
```

7. Next, add the following code to check for and validate the input. Note that `$_POST['Email']` is checked with the `validateEmail()` function instead of the `validateInput()` function.

```php
if (isset($_POST['Submit'])) {
    $Sender =
        validateInput($_POST['Sender'],"Your Name");
    $Email =
        validateEmail($_POST['Email'],"Your E-mail");
    $Subject =
        validateInput($_POST['Subject'],"Subject");
    $Message =
        validateInput($_POST['Message'],"Message");
```

```
            if ($errorCount==0)
                $ShowForm = FALSE;
            else
                $ShowForm = TRUE;
    }
```

8. Next, add a conditional statement that checks the value of $ShowForm. If $ShowForm is TRUE, the form is displayed. Otherwise, an e-mail message is sent and a status message is displayed. Note that a copy is sent to the sender.

```
if ($ShowForm == TRUE) {
    if ($errorCount>0) // if there were errors
        echo "<p>Please re-enter the form
            information below.</p>\n";
    displayForm($Sender, $Email, $Subject,
            $Message);
}
else {
    $SenderAddress = "$Sender <$Email>";
    $Headers = "From: $SenderAddress\nCC:
            $SenderAddress\n";
    // Substitute your own email address for
    // recipient@example.com
    $result = mail("recipient@example.com",
            $Subject, $Message, $Headers);
    if ($result)
        echo "<p>Your message has been sent. Thank you, "
            . $Sender . ".</p>\n";
    else
        echo "<p>There was an error sending your
            message, " .
            $Sender . ".</p>\n";
}
```

9. Save the document as **ContactForm.php** in the Projects directory for Chapter 4 and upload the document to the Web server.

10. Open ContactForm.php by entering the following URL: *http://<yourserver>/PHP_Projects/Chapter.04/Projects/ContactForm.php*. Verify that the form validates the input fields correctly, redisplays the sticky form when there are errors, and sends the e-mail message when there are no errors.

11. Close your Web browser window.

228

The strip-slashes() function was introduced earlier in this chapter. The htmlentities() function was discussed in Chapter 3.

Exercise 4-3

Create an include file to assist with debugging Web forms. The include file should create a table to display the contents of the $_REQUEST autoglobal. The table will have two columns showing each name/value pair. Use the advanced foreach statement syntax to retrieve the index and value of each element of the $_REQUEST array. Be sure to use the stripslashes() and htmlentities() functions before displaying the text in the Web page. Save the document as **inc_requestDump.php**. Create a second document to test the include file. Save the second document as **RequestDump.php**.

Exercise 4-4

Create a two-part form that calculates an employee's weekly gross salary, based on the number of hours worked and an hourly wage that you choose. Use an HTML document named **Paycheck.html** as a Web form with two text boxes—one for the number of hours worked and one for the hourly wage. Use a PHP document named **Paycheck.php** as the form handler. Compute any hours over 40 as time-and-a-half. Be sure to verify and validate the submitted form data and provide appropriate error messages for invalid values.

Exercise 4-5

Create an All-in-One sticky form to solve the common "two trains are moving toward each other" word problem. The form should have three inputs, all numbers greater than 0: the speed of Train A ($SpeedA), the speed of Train B ($SpeedB), and the distance between the two trains ($Distance). For this problem, you will need the following equations:

```
$DistanceA = (($SpeedA / $SpeedB) * $Distance) /
    (1 + ($SpeedA / $SpeedB));
$DistanceB = $Distance - $DistanceA;
$TimeA = $DistanceA / $SpeedA;
$TimeB = $DistanceB / $SpeedB;
```

In the preceding equations, $DistanceA and $DistanceB are the distances traveled by Trains A and B, respectively; $TimeA and $TimeB are how long Trains A and B traveled, respectively ($TimeA should equal $TimeB). If $SpeedA or $SpeedB is allowed to be 0, PHP will display a "division by zero not allowed" error. Save the document as **TwoTrains.php** in the Projects directory for Chapter 4.

Discovery Projects

In the following projects, you will continue to design and develop the Chinese Zodiac site that you began in Chapter 1. All files for the Chinese Zodiac site will be saved in a directory named ChineseZodiac in the base Web folder on the server.

The following projects will add interactivity to the Chinese Zodiac Web page template by displaying alternative content in the dynamic content section of the index.php file when the user clicks a button or activates a hyperlink.

Discovery Project 4-1

In your text editor, create new include files with a placeholder for page content for each of the pages identified by the buttons and text links. (The inc_home_page.php file has already been created.) The contents of the pages will be populated in later projects.

Target Page	Include Filenames	Page Content
site_layout	inc_site_layout.php	[Insert site layout content here]
control_structures	inc_control_structures.php	[Insert control structure content here]
string_functions	inc_string_functions.php	[Insert string function content here]
web_forms	inc_web_forms.php	[Insert Web forms content here]
midterm_assessment	inc_midterm_assessment.php	[Insert midterm assessment content here]
state_information	inc_state_information.php	[Insert state information content here]
user_templates	inc_user_templates.php	[Insert user template content here]
final_project	inc_final_project.php	[Insert final project content here]

Table 4-3   Pages for Discovery Project 4-1

Save the files and upload them to the Includes folder in the ChineseZodiac folder on the server.

Discovery Project 4-2

1.   Reopen the **inc_button_nav.php** file created in Discovery Project 2-2. The file is in the Includes folder in the ChineseZodiac folder. Insert the code to convert the first of eight button images to hyperlinks that display the destination

file in the dynamic data section of the Chinese Zodiac Web page template (index.php).

```
<a href = "index.php?page=home_page">
<img class="btn" src="Images/ButtonHomePage.gif"
alt="[Home Page]" title="Home Page"style =
     "border:0" /></a><br />
```

2. Continue to add code for the other seven button images targeting the content to the dynamic data section. Use the appropriate "Target Page" value from Table 4-3 as the value of each **page** parameter.

3. Save the file and upload it to the Web server.

Discovery Project 4-3

1. Reopen the **inc_text_links.php** file created in Discovery Project 2-2 in your text editor. The file is stored in the Includes folder in the ChineseZodiac folder. Modify the first text hyperlink to display the destination file in the dynamic data section of the Chinese Zodiac Web page template (index.php), as shown in the following code:

```
<a href = "index.php?page=home_page">Home Page</a>
```

2. Continue including additional code for the other seven hyperlinks in the text links bar, targeting the content to the dynamic data section. Use the appropriate "Target Page" value from Table 4-3 as the value of each **page** parameter.

3. Save the file and upload it to the Web server.

Discovery Project 4-4

1. Reopen the **index.php** file created in Discovery Project 2-2 in your text editor. The file is in the ChineseZodiac folder. Replace the script section for the dynamic content section of the Web page template.

```
if (isset($_GET['page'])) {
    switch ($_GET['page']) {
        case 'site_layout':
            include('Includes/inc_site_layout.php');
            break;
        case 'control_structures':
            include('Includes/' .
                'inc_control_structures.php');
            break;
```

```
            case 'string_functions':
                include('Includes/' .
                    'inc_string_functions.php');
                break;
            case 'web_forms':
                include('Includes/inc_web_forms.php');
                break;
            case 'midterm_assessment':
                include('Includes/' .
                    'inc_midterm_assessment.php');
                break;
            case 'state_information':
                include('Includes/' .
                    'inc_state_information.php');
                break;
            case 'user_templates':
                include('Includes/' .
                    'inc_user_templates.php');
                break;
            case 'final_project':
                include('Includes/' .
                    'inc_final_project.php');
                break;
            case 'home_page': // A value of
                              // 'home_page' means
                              // to display the
                              // default page
            default:
                include('Includes/inc_home.php');
                break;
        }
    }
    else // If no button has been selected, then display
         // the default page
        include('Includes/inc_home.php');
```

2. Save the file and upload it to the ChineseZodiac folder on the Web server.

3. Open the index.php page in the Web browser by entering the following URL: *http://<yourserver>/ChineseZodiac/index.php*.

4. Verify that the content of the dynamic content section changes each time you click a button or activate a text hyperlink.

5. Close your Web browser window.

Discovery Project 4-5

Reopen **inc_home_links_bar.php** (created in Discovery Project 3-3) in your text editor and enclose the two labels in <a> tags. The value for the href attribute of both <a> tags will be index.php, but each page will have different URL tokens to specify the information that should be displayed. You will continue to use the page URL token to specify the home page by using the value home_page. Additionally, you will use the section URL token with different values to determine which of the two versions of the home page to display: either the one with the PHP information (section=php) or the one with the Chinese zodiac information (section=zodiac). For the PHP text link, the href value of the <a> tag should be index.php?page=home_page&section=php. For the Chinese zodiac text link, the href value of the <a> tag should be index.php?page=home_page&section=zodiac. Save inc_home_links_bar.php and upload the file to the Includes folder in the ChineseZodiac folder on the server.

In your text editor, reopen the **inc_home.php** document that you created in Discovery Project 2-2. Replace the placeholder [Insert home page content here] with a PHP code section that includes inc_home_links_bar.php at the top of the file.

At the end of the PHP code section, add the following code:

```
if (isset($_GET['section'])) {
    switch ($_GET['section']) {
        case 'zodiac':
            include('Includes/inc_chinese_zodiac.php');
            break;
        case 'php': // A value of 'php' means
                    // to display the default page
        default:
            include('Includes/inc_php_info.php');
            break;
    }
}
else // If no section has been selected, then display the
     // default page
    include('Includes/inc_php_info.php');
```

Save the file as inc_home.php and upload it to the Includes folder in the ChineseZodiac folder on the server.

Open *http://<yourserver>/ChineseZodiac/index.php* in the browser and test each button and text hyperlink to verify that the content of the dynamic data section changes when a button or text link is clicked.

Working with Files and Directories

In this chapter, you will:

◎ Understand file types and permissions

◎ Work with directories

◎ Upload and download files

◎ Write data to files

◎ Read data from files

◎ Open and close a file stream

◎ Manage files and directories

Many programming tasks for a Web site require some form of data storage. User files need to be uploaded and downloaded. Form data needs to be saved and retrieved. Online calendars and blogs need to be updated. One method of performing all of these tasks is through files stored on the Web server. In this chapter, you will study how to read, write, and manipulate files.

Understanding File Types and Permissions

You need to understand two important file concepts before you can work with files in PHP. The first concept is file types, which affect how information is stored in files and retrieved from them. The second concept is file permissions, which determine the actions that a specific user can and cannot perform on a file.

Understanding File Types

In PHP, you can specify a file as one of two types: *binary* or *text*. A **binary file** is a series of characters or bytes for which PHP attaches no special meaning. Any structure to the data is determined by the application that reads from or writes to the file. A **text file**, in contrast, is assumed to have only printable characters and a small set of control or formatting characters. The formatting characters are the binary equivalents of the escape sequences you learned in Chapter 3, and are listed in Table 5-1.

Escape Sequence	Meaning	Byte Value		
		Decimal	**Octal**	**Hexadecimal**
\t	Horizontal tab	9	011	09
\r	Line feed	10	012	0A
\v	Vertical tab	11	013	0B
\f	Form feed	12	014	0C
\n	Carriage return	13	015	0D

Table 5-1 Control characters in a text file

Different operating systems use different escape sequences to identify the end of a line. UNIX/Linux platforms use the \n carriage return escape sequence, Macintosh applications usually use the \r line feed escape sequence, and Windows operating systems use the \n carriage return escape sequence followed by the \r line feed escape sequence. The following code shows examples from all three operating systems:

```
This is how you end a line on UNIX/Linux platforms.\n
This is how you end a line on Windows operating systems.\n\r
This is how you end a line on Macintosh operating
    systems.\r
```

If you do not use the correct end-of-line escape sequence, you may have problems when working with text files on different platforms. For example, each name in the following list ends with the \n carriage return escape sequence, as required for UNIX/Linux operating systems:

```
Blair, Dennis\n
Hernandez, Louis\n
Miller, Erica\n
Morinaga, Scott\n
Picard, Raymond\n
```

If you open a text file that contains the preceding lines in the Notepad text editor on a Windows operating system, the \n characters are not recognized as end-of-line markers. Instead, all of the separate strings are displayed as one continuous string, and the font's "nondisplayable character" symbol (in this case, a rectangle) is displayed in place of the \n characters, as shown in Figure 5-1.

Prior to OS X, all Macintosh applications and the Macintosh operating system used the \r line feed escape sequence to identify the end of a line. Starting with OS X, the Macintosh operating system is built on a Linux core. So, although most Macintosh applications still use the \r escape sequence as the end-of-line marker, most command-line and operating system programs use the UNIX/Linux \n carriage return escape sequence.

235

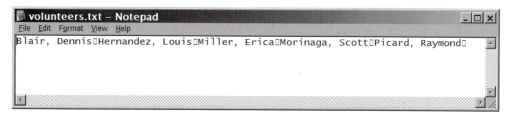

Figure 5-1 Displaying a UNIX/Linux text file using Notepad in Windows

For the lines to display correctly in Windows, they must end with the \n\r escape sequence pair, as follows:

```
Blair, Dennis\n\r
Hernandez, Louis\n\r
Miller, Erica\n\r
Morinaga, Scott\n\r
Picard, Raymond\n\r
```

The PHP file functions that you study in this chapter can usually accommodate any of these escape sequences and end lines in a text file appropriately, regardless of the operating system. Although the examples in this book use the \n carriage return escape sequence that is supported by UNIX/Linux operating systems, the PHP scripts you write will function correctly on any platform. However, keep in mind that if you attempt to open a text file that does not contain the required characters for the current operating system, the line breaks may not appear correctly in your text editor. As a general rule, you should choose the appropriate end-of-line escape sequence for your Web server.

Working with File Permissions

As you work through this chapter, keep in mind that your ability to access files on a local computer or network depends on the security permissions that have been granted to the files and to the directories where they are stored. The owner of a resource, such as a file or directory, can usually grant permission to access the resource. The owner is typically the person who created the resource. Otherwise, the network administrator is in charge of granting permissions to resources.

Typical permissions include the abilities to read, write, modify, and execute. For example, you might have permission to read a file, but not to write to it. The procedures for manually granting permissions to resources depend on the server's operating system.

Changing Permissions

PHP provides the chmod() function for changing the permissions of a file within PHP. The name "chmod" is a contraction of "change mode"; mode is another word for permissions. The syntax for the chmod() function is chmod(*filename*, *mode*), where *filename* is the name of the file to change, and *mode* is an integer specifying the permissions for the file. The value of *mode* defines three types of permission (read, write, and execute) for three levels of access (the file's owner or user, users in the group associated with the file, and all other users).

The easiest way to ensure that the proper permissions are set is to always use a four-digit octal (base 8) value when assigning permissions—octal values encode three bits per digit, which matches the three permission bits per level of access. When PHP parses a numeric value that contains a leading zero, the number is assumed to be in octal format, so the leftmost digit should be 0. The remaining digits are assigned a value, as indicated in Table 5-2. To assign more than one permission for an access level, add the values for the permissions together.

> See your operating system's documentation for information on how to manually set permissions for resources such as files and directories.

> PHP modeled the chmod() function after the UNIX chmod utility, so values for the *mode* parameter of the chmod() function match those in the chmod utility. For other operating systems, the chmod() function converts the *mode* flags into the equivalent permissions for the underlying operating system.

Permissions	First Digit (Leftmost) Always 0	Second Digit User (u)	Third Digit Group (g)	Fourth Digit (Rightmost) Other (o)
Read (r)	0	4	4	4
Write (w)	0	2	2	2
Execute (x)	0	1	1	1

Table 5-2   Octal values for the *mode* parameter of the chmod() function

For example, the following code assigns read, write, and execute permissions to the user, read and execute permissions to the group, and no permissions for others for the file example.exe:

```
chmod("example.exe", 0750);
```

The following example assigns read permissions to all users, but only gives the user permission to write to the index.html file:

```
chmod("index.html", 0644);
```

The same permission bits apply to directories as well as files, but the interpretation of the permissions is slightly different. "Read" permission for a directory means that the user can list the files in a directory. "Write" permission means that the user can add new files to the directory. "Execute" permission means that the user can access the files in the directory (assuming that the user has permissions for the file itself).

Checking Permissions

For reading the permissions associated with a particular file, PHP provides the fileperms() function. This function takes a filename as the only parameter, and returns an integer bitmap of the permissions associated with the file. As with the chmod() function, the results will be more meaningful when displayed in octal rather than decimal. You can use PHP's decoct() function to convert a decimal value to an octal value. Also, because the fileperms() function contains more information than just the file permissions, the permissions can be extracted by using the arithmetic modulus operator (%) with an octal value of 01000. (Remember that the leading 0 indicates to PHP that the value is in octal.)

```
$perms = fileperms($testfile);
$perms = decoct($perms % 01000);
echo "file permissions for $testfile: 0" . $perms . "<br />\n";
```

Write permission normally implies delete permission as well.

As implied in this discussion, if users do not have "read" permission on a directory but have "read" permission on a file within the directory, they can open the file as long as they know the name of the file. The users will not be able to see the file in a directory listing, though.

Short Quiz

1. Explain the difference between a binary file and a text file.

2. What are the different end-of-line markers for Windows, Macintosh, and UNIX/Linux?

3. What functions are used to change and retrieve the permissions of a file?

4.   What are the three typical permissions for files and directories?

5.   What are the three levels of access for files and directories?

Working with Directories

Before you learn more about working with files in PHP, you should become familiar with how PHP works with directories. By knowing how to create, read, and move between directories, you can examine the changes that you make to files. PHP includes functions for reading the contents of a directory and for creating new directories.

Reading Directories

With PHP, you can read the names of files and directories that exist within any specified directory for which you have the appropriate permissions. To read the contents of a directory, you use the PHP functions listed in Table 5-3.

Function	Description
chdir(*directory*)	Changes to the specified directory
chroot(*directory*)	Changes the root directory of the current process to the specified directory
closedir(*handle*)	Closes a directory handle
getcwd()	Gets the current working directory
opendir(*directory*)	Opens a handle to the specified directory
readdir(*handle*)	Reads a file or directory name from the specified directory handle
rewinddir(*handle*)	Resets the directory pointer to the beginning of the directory
scandir(*directory*[, *sort*])	Returns an indexed array containing the names of files and directories in the specified directory

Table 5-3   PHP directory functions

To iterate through the entries in a directory, you open a handle to the directory with the opendir() function. A **handle** is a special type of variable that PHP uses to represent a resource such as a file or directory. You can then use the readdir() function to return the file and directory names from the open directory. Each time you call the readdir() function, it moves a directory pointer to the next entry in the directory. A **directory pointer** is a special type of variable that refers to the currently selected record in a directory listing. When you first open the directory using the opendir() function, the directory pointer is reset to the start of the directory listing. The directory pointer is a way of keeping track of where you are in a directory. After the directory pointer reaches the end of the directory, the readdir() function returns a value of FALSE. The following code demonstrates how to use the readdir() function to display the names of the files in the PHP program directory. Notice that the readdir() function is included as the conditional expression for the while statement. As long as the readdir() function does not return a value of FALSE, the while loop continues displaying the names of the directory entries. Also notice at the end of the code that the directory handle is closed with the closedir() function.

When the PHP scripting engine reads a directory, entries are returned for the directory navigation shortcuts: "." for the current directory and ".." for the parent directory (the directory above the current directory).

```php
$Dir = "/var/html/uploads";
$DirOpen = opendir($Dir);
while ($CurFile = readdir($DirOpen)) {
    echo $CurFile . "<br />\n";
}
closedir($DirOpen);
```

To create a new Web page that displays the contents of the "files" subdirectory:

1. Create a new document in your text editor.

2. Type the <!DOCTYPE> declaration, <html> element, header information, and <body> element. Use the strict DTD and "View Files" as the content of the <title> element.

3. Add the following script section to the document body:

```php
<?php
?>
```

4. Add the following code to the script section to read the files in the "files" subdirectory. Notice that the while statement uses the strcmp() function to exclude the "." and ".." entries.

```php
$Dir = "files";
$DirOpen = opendir($Dir);
while ($CurFile = readdir($DirOpen)) {
    if ((strcmp($CurFile, '.') != 0) &&
        (strcmp($CurFile, '..') != 0))
    echo "<a href=\"files/" . $CurFile . "\">" .
        $CurFile . "</a><br />\n";
}
closedir($DirOpen);
```

5. Save the document as **ViewFiles.php** in the Chapter directory for Chapter 5 and upload the file to the server.

6. Create a subdirectory named **files** under the Chapter directory for Chapter 5. Upload three files of your choosing to the files subdirectory.

7. Open the ViewFiles.php file in your Web browser by entering the following URL: *http://<yourserver>/PHP_Projects/ Chapter.05/Chapter/ViewFiles.php*. Figure 5-2 shows the output for three files named kitten.jpg, polarbear.gif, and gorilla.gif.

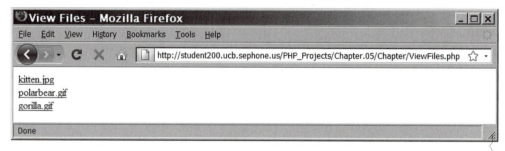

Figure 5-2   Listing of the "files" subdirectory using the opendir(), readdir(), and closedir() functions

8. Close your Web browser window.

Starting with PHP 5.0, you can use the scandir() function, which returns an indexed array containing the names of files and directories in the specified directory, instead of using the opendir(), readdir(), and closedir() functions. The following code shows how to display the names of the files and directories in the PHP program directory. Notice that this version does not use the opendir() or closedir() functions. Instead, it just uses the scandir() function to return the names of the entries in the PHP program directory to an array named $DirEntries, which are then displayed with a foreach loop.

```
$Dir = "/var/html/uploads";
$DirEntries = scandir($Dir);
foreach ($DirEntries as $Entry) {
    echo $Entry . "<br />\n";
}
```

When you use the readdir() function to return the entries in a directory, the entries are not sorted, but instead are returned in the order in which they are stored by your operating system. One benefit of using the scandir() function instead of the readdir() function is that the scandir() function sorts the returned entries in ascending alphabetical order. If you pass a value of 1 as a second argument

to the scandir() function, as shown in the following example, the
entries are sorted in descending alphabetical order:

```
$Dir = "/var/html/uploads";
$DirEntries = scandir($Dir, 1);
foreach ($DirEntries as $Entry) {
    echo $Entry . "<br />\n";
}
```

To modify the ViewFiles.php script so it uses the scandir() function:

1. Return to the **ViewFiles.php** file in your text editor.

2. Replace the existing statements in the script section with the
   following statements that use the scandir() function:

   ```
   $Dir = "files";
   $DirEntries = scandir($Dir);
   foreach ($DirEntries as $Entry) {
       if ((strcmp($Entry, '.') != 0) &&
               (strcmp($Entry, '..') != 0))
           echo "<a href=\"files/" . $Entry . "\">" .
               $Entry .
               "</a><br />\n";
   }
   ```

3. Save the ViewFiles.php file and upload it to the server.

4. Open the ViewFiles.php file in your Web browser by entering the following URL: *http://<yourserver>/PHP_Projects/
   Chapter.05/Chapter/ViewFiles.php*. Figure 5-3 shows the new
   sorted list of files.

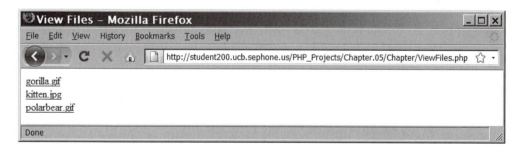

Figure 5-3 Listing of the "files" subdirectory using the scandir() function

5. Close your Web browser window.

Creating Directories

You can use the mkdir() function to create a new directory. To create a new directory within the current directory, simply pass the
name of the directory you want to create to the mkdir() function.

The following statement creates a new directory named "volunteers" within the current directory:

```
mkdir("volunteers");
```

To create a new directory in a location other than the current directory, you can use a relative or absolute path. For example, the first statement in the following code uses a relative path to create a new directory named "event" at the same level as the current directory by using the "`..`" notation to refer to the parent directory. The second statement uses an absolute path to create a new directory named "utilities" in the PHP program directory.

```
mkdir("../event");
mkdir("/bin/PHP/utilities");
```

If you attempt to create a directory that already exists, you will receive an error like the one shown in Figure 5-4.

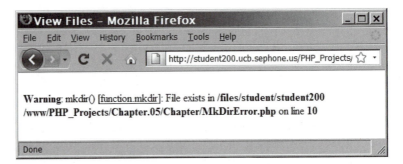

Figure 5-4 Warning that a directory already exists

You will also receive a warning if you attempt to create a new directory within a directory that doesn't exist. In the next section, you will learn how to check whether a directory exists before attempting to access it or create a new directory within it.

Obtaining File and Directory Information

To successfully work with files and directories, you need to be able to obtain information about them. Some of the most important information about the file system includes whether the files and directories exist and whether you have the necessary permissions to work with them. Table 5-4 lists the common PHP file and directory status functions.

Function	Description
file_exists(filename)	Determines whether a file or directory exists
is_dir(filename)	Determines whether a filename specifies a directory
is_executable(filename)	Determines whether a file is executable
is_file(filename)	Determines whether a filename specifies a regular file
is_link(filename)	Determines whether a filename specifies a symbolic link
is_readable(filename)	Determines whether a file is readable
is_writable(filename) or is_writeable(filename)	Determines whether a file is writable

Table 5-4   PHP file and directory status functions

The is_readable(), is_writable() (or is_writeable()), and is_executable() functions check the permissions of a file or directory to determine whether the PHP scripting engine has read, write, or execute permissions, respectively. The is_dir(), is_file(), and is_link() functions are used to differentiate among the three most common entries in a directory listing. A **symbolic link**, which is identified with the is_link() function, is a reference to another file elsewhere on the system, not a file itself. Because each of these functions return FALSE if a file does not exist, the file_exists() function does not need to be used in conjunction with the other functions. By using these functions before attempting to manipulate a file or directory, you will ensure that the script runs correctly and does not produce errors.

You can use the is_dir() function to check whether a specified filename is a directory before attempting to access it. The following example demonstrates how to use the is_dir() function before using the scandir() function:

```php
$Dir = "/var/html/uploads";
if (is_dir($Dir)) {
    $DirEntries = scandir($Dir, 1);
    foreach ($DirEntries as $Entry) {
        echo $Entry . "<br />\n";
    }
}
else
    echo "<p>The directory " . htmlentities($Dir) .
        " does not exist.</p>\n";
```

PHP includes other types of functions that return additional information about files and directories. Table 5-5 lists common file and directory information functions.

Function	Description
fileatime(filename)	Returns the last time the file was accessed
filectime(filename)	Returns the last time the file information was modified
filemtime(filename)	Returns the last time the data in a file was modified
fileowner(filename)	Returns the name of the file's owner
filesize(filename)	Returns the size of the file in bytes
filetype(filename)	Returns the file type

Table 5-5 Common file and directory information functions

The file type returned by the filetype() function is a text string that contains one of the following values: "fifo", "char", "dir", "block", "link", "file", "socket", or "unknown". Most of these refer to special resource types that you will not encounter. All of the examples in this chapter return either "dir" for a directory or "file" for a file.

The following code demonstrates how to use two of the functions listed in Table 5-5: filesize() and filetype(). The script builds a table that contains the filename, file size, and file type. Figure 5-5 shows the output.

```
$Dir = "/var/html/uploads";
if (is_dir($Dir)) {
    echo "<table border='1' width='100%'>\n";
    echo "<tr><th>Filename</th><th>File Size</th>
        <th>File Type</th></tr>\n";
    $DirEntries = scandir($Dir);
    foreach ($DirEntries as $Entry) {
        $EntryFullName = $Dir . "/" . $Entry;
        echo "<tr><td>" . htmlentities($Entry) .
            "</td><td>" .
        filesize($EntryFullName) . "</td><td>" .
        filetype($EntryFullName) . "</td></tr>\n";
    }
    echo "</table>\n";
}
else
    echo "<p>The directory " . htmlentities($Dir) .
        " does not exist.</p>\n";
```

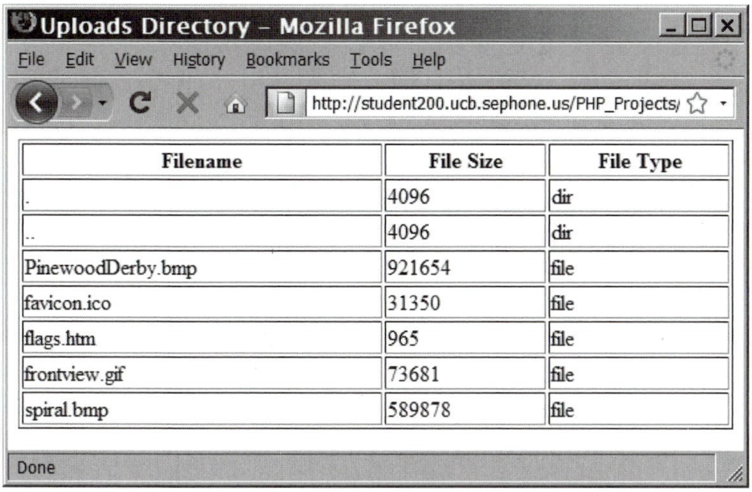

Figure 5-5 Output of a script with file and directory information functions

To create a more detailed directory listing:

1. Return to the **ViewFiles.php** file in your text editor.

2. Replace the existing statements in the script section with the following statements that use the scandir() function:

```php
$Dir = "files";
$DirEntries = scandir($Dir);
echo "<table border='1' width='100%' >\n";
echo "<tr><th colspan='4'>Directory listing for
<strong>" . htmlentities($Dir) . "</strong></th>
</tr>\n";
echo "<tr>";
echo "<th><strong><em>Name</em></strong></th>";
echo "<th><strong><em>Owner ID</em></strong></th>";
echo "<th><strong><em>Permissions</em></strong>
</th>";
echo "<th><strong><em>Size</em></strong></th>";
echo "</tr>\n";
foreach ($DirEntries as $Entry) {
    if ((strcmp($Entry, '.') != 0) &&
            (strcmp($Entry, '..') != 0)) {
        $FullEntryName=$Dir . "/" . $Entry;
        echo "<tr><td>";
        if (is_file($FullEntryName))
            echo "<a href=\"$FullEntryName\">" .
                htmlentities($Entry). "</a>";
        else
            echo htmlentities($Entry);
        echo "</td><td align='center'>" .
            fileowner($FullEntryName);
        if (is_file($FullEntryName)) {
            $perms = fileperms($FullEntryName);
```

```
                          $perms = decoct($perms % 01000);
                          echo "</td><td align='center'>
                                  0$perms";
                            echo "</td><td align='right'>" .
                                  number_format(filesize($Full
                                  EntryName), 0) .
                                  " bytes";
                 }
                 else
                       echo "</td><td colspan='2'
                                  align='center'>&lt;DIR&gt;";
                       echo "</td></tr>\n";
           }
     }
     echo "</table>\n";
```

3. Save the ViewFiles.php file and upload it to the server.

4. Open the ViewFiles.php file in your Web browser by entering the following URL: *http://<yourserver>/PHP_Projects/ Chapter.05/Chapter/ViewFiles.php*. Figure 5-6 shows the expanded list of files.

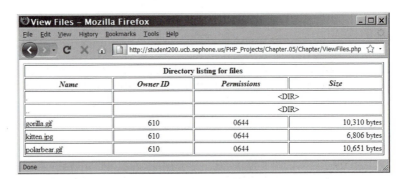

Figure 5-6 A detailed listing of the "files" subdirectory

5. Close your Web browser window.

Short Quiz

1. What three functions are used to iterate through files and directories in a specific directory?

2. What function returns an indexed array containing the names of files and directories in the specified directory?

3. What is one benefit of using the scandir() function versus the readdir() function?

4. What function is used to create a directory?

5. What two functions are used to determine if a directory entry is a file or a directory?

Uploading and Downloading Files

Sometimes, a Web application allows visitors to upload files from their local computer, referred to as the **client**, to the Web server. More often, a Web site or application allows visitors to download files from the Web server to their client. Depending on the specific Web application, the files may be simple text files or they may be more complex file types, such as images, documents, or spreadsheets. This section describes how to upload and download files.

Uploading Files

Visitors using a Web application often want to customize pages with custom graphics. For example, a registered member of a social networking Web site may want to post pictures on a profile page. Other users may want to upload documents to be used for online collaboration and review. PHP provides a method for transferring files from a user's client machine to the Web server.

Selecting the File

Files are uploaded in PHP through forms. The form's `method` attribute must be "POST" for a file to be uploaded. An additional attribute, named `enctype`, must be added to the opening `<form>` tag, and must be set to "multipart/form-data". This instructs the Web browser to post multiple sections, one for the regular form data and one for the file contents.

An input field of type "file" within the form presents the user with a file selection control. Using this control, the user can enter the full path and name of the file to be uploaded. Most modern Web browsers also provide a "Browse" button, which allows the user to navigate to the appropriate file using a "file select" dialog box. A separate "hidden" input field may be included to set the maximum allowed size of the uploaded file. This input field must be named "MAX_FILE_SIZE" (in all capital letters) and must precede the "file" input field within the form. The input field should be of type "hidden" to prevent it from being displayed or changed, and the value is set to the maximum number of bytes allowed for the uploaded file.

Using the "MAX_FILE_SIZE" input is safer and more efficient than checking the size of the file in the form handler.

It is a good practice to display a message indicating the maximum file size on the Web form so the visitor is not surprised by an error message if that size is exceeded. A common method is to indicate the maximum size in parentheses, as in "(Maximum 5,000 bytes)", following the "file" input field.

MIME stands for Multipurpose Internet Mail Extensions. As the name implies, MIME types were originally created for including files in the body of an e-mail message. Their use has been expanded to general use for many Internet message types, including XHTML. MIME types consist of two parts, separated by a slash (/). The first part is the general classification of the file type, such as "image" or "text". The second part specifies the exact type within the general classification, as in "image/gif", "image/jpeg", "text/plain", or "text/html".

248

Retrieving the File Information

When the form is posted, information for the uploaded file is stored in the $_FILES[] autoglobal array, which was introduced in Chapter 4. An associative array element is created for each "file" input field name. The associative key of the element is the name of the input field from the form. The array element is a nested associative array containing the information about the uploaded file. Table 5-6 shows the keys of the nested associative array elements and describes the values for those keys.

Key	Value
'error'	The error code associated with the file upload; an error code of 0 indicates a successful upload
'tmp_name'	The temporary location of the file contents
'name'	The original filename
'size'	The file size (in bytes)
'type'	The file's MIME type, as specified by the client's Web browser

Table 5-6 The nested array keys of a $_FILES[] autoglobal array element

To retrieve the information from the $_FILES[] autoglobal array, use the syntax $_FILES[*filefield*][*key*], where *filefield* is replaced with the name of the "file" input element on the Web form and *key* is replaced by the appropriate key from Table 5-6. For example, assume that the Web form's <input> field was declared as follows:

```
<input type="file" name="picture_file" />
```

In the form handler, the $_FILES[] autoglobal array would contain one element, $_FILES['picture_file'], which in turn contains the following five elements:

```
$_FILES['picture_file']['error'] /* Contains the error code
    associated with the file */
$_FILES['picture_file']['tmp_name'] /* Contains the
    temporary location of the file contents */
$_FILES['picture_file']['name'] /* Contains the name of the
    original file */
$_FILES['picture_file']['size'] /* Contains the size of the
    uploaded file in bytes */
$_FILES['picture_file']['type'] /* Contains the type of the
    file */
```

The $_FILES autoglobal array is only set if file_uploads is set to "On" or 1 in the php.ini file. If you have the form set up correctly and the $_FILES autoglobal array is not getting set properly, use the phpinfo() function to verify that the file_uploads option is set to "On" or 1.

Storing the Uploaded File

As described in the previous section, the uploaded file is stored to a temporary location on the Web server. The file then needs to be moved to a more permanent location elsewhere in the directory structure.

There are some important considerations when determining the destination of the uploaded file. The first is whether uploaded files should be immediately available or if they need to be verified first. If the file needs to be verified to ensure that it is virus-free, or of the appropriate type, to list just two reasons, then the file should be stored in a "sandbox" area outside the publicly accessible Web folders. The second consideration is whether the file is a public file, which would be freely available to anyone visiting the Web site, or a private file, which would only be available to authorized visitors. A public file can be stored within the publicly accessible Web folder structure. A private file should be stored in a folder outside the publicly accessible Web folder structure, where it is only available through a download script.

Once you determine the destination, use the `move_uploaded_file()` function to move the uploaded file from its temporary location to the permanent destination. The syntax for the function is:

```
bool move_uploaded_file(filename, destination)
```

Where *filename* is the contents of `$_FILES[filefield]['tmp_name']` and *destination* is the path and filename of the location where the file will be stored. The function returns TRUE if the move succeeds, and FALSE if the move fails.

For example, to move the temporary file uploaded using the "picture_file" input field into the "uploads" subdirectory of the current directory using the file's original name, you would use the following code:

```
if (move_uploaded_file($_FILES['picture_file']['tmp_name'],
    "uploads/" . $_FILES['picture_file']['name']) ===
        FALSE)
    echo "Could not move uploaded file to \"uploads/" .
        htmlentities($_FILES['picture_file']['name']) .
        "\"<br />\n";
else {
    chmod("uploads/" . $_FILES['picture_file']['name'],
        0644);
    echo "Successfully uploaded \"uploads/" .
        htmlentities($_FILES['picture_file']['name']) .
        "\"<br />\n";
}
```

In the preceding example, notice the call to the chmod() function before the "Successfully uploaded..." message is displayed. By default, the uploaded file is owned by the user account that owns the Web server process and has only owner "read" and "write" privileges (0600). To ensure that you (and everyone else) can read the file, use chmod(*filename*, 0644); after calling the move_uploaded_file() function, replacing *filename* with the value that you used in the *destination* parameter for the move_uploaded_file() function.

To create a form to upload a file:

1. Create a new document in your text editor.

2. Type the <!DOCTYPE> declaration, <html> element, header information, and <body> element. Use the strict DTD and "File Uploader" as the content of the <title> element.

3. Add the following script section to the document body:

```php
<?php
?>
```

4. Add the following code to the script section to read the files in the "files" subdirectory. The associative array index for the $_FILES autoglobal array is the name of the file input field that will be used in the Web form ('new_file').

```php
$Dir = "files";
if (isset($_POST['upload'])) {
    if (isset($_FILES['new_file'])) {
        if (move_uploaded_file(
            $_FILES['new_file']['tmp_name'],
            $Dir . "/" . $_FILES['new_file']
            ['name']) == TRUE) {
            chmod($Dir . "/" . $_FILES['new_file']
            ['name'], 0644);
            echo "File \"" .
                htmlentities($_FILES['new_file']
                ['name']) .
                "\"successfully uploaded.
                <br />\n";
        }
        else
            echo "There was an error
                uploading \"" .
                htmlentities($_FILES['new_file']
                ['name']) .
                "\".<br />\n";
    }
}
```

5. Add the following XHTML form immediately after the closing PHP tag. Notice that the file input is named "new_file", which is the same value used earlier as the index into the $_FILES autoglobal array. Also notice the message that notifies the user of the 25,000-byte limit set in the MAX_FILE_SIZE hidden input.

```
<form action="FileUploader.php" method="POST"
enctype="multipart/form-data">
<input type="hidden" name="MAX_FILE_SIZE"
value="25000" /><br />
File to upload:<br />
<input type="file" name="new_file" /><br />
(25,000 byte limit) <br />
<input type="submit" name="upload" value="Upload the
File" />
<br />
</form>
```

6. Save the document as **FileUploader.php** in the Chapter directory for Chapter 5 and upload the file to the server.

7. Verify that the "files" directory on the Web server has read, write, and execute permissions enabled for user, group, and other.

 For most uses, granting write permission to others is not a safe choice. When making this choice, be sure you have considered the security risks. Do not grant write permissions unless it is absolutely required.

8. Open the FileUploader.php file in your Web browser by entering the following URL: *http://<yourserver>/PHP_Projects/ Chapter.05/Chapter/FileUploader.php*. Attempt to upload a file to the server. You should receive a message stating whether the upload succeeded or failed.

9. After you have successfully uploaded one or more files to the server using the FileUploader.php form, open the **ViewFiles.php** file in your Web browser by entering the following URL: *http://<yourserver>/PHP_Projects/ Chapter.05/Chapter/ViewFiles.php*. You should see the new files in the directory listing. Figure 5-7 shows the output for a new file named seahorse.jpg along with the kitten.jpg, polarbear.gif, and gorilla.gif files. Notice that the Owner ID for seahorse.jpg is different from those for the other three—seahorse.jpg was created by the user account for the PHP scripting engine, while the others were created by the account owner.

252

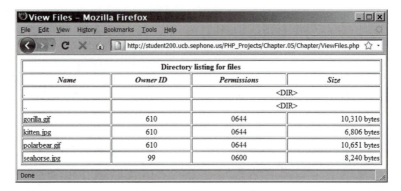

Figure 5-7 Listing of the "files" subdirectory after uploading seahorse.jpg

10. Close your Web browser window.

Downloading Files

Normally, it is not necessary to use PHP to download files from the Web server. If a file is stored in a directory that is within the public XHTML directory structure, you can provide an XHTML anchor (<a>) tag in the Web page. The user clicks the link, and the Web browser downloads the file automatically.

With files that do not reside within the public XHTML directory structure, another method is required to download the file. PHP provides the tools required to download a file from anywhere in the directory structure.

The first step is to tell the PHP script which file to download. The simplest way is with URL tokens and the $_GET[] autoglobal array. This approach allows you to embed the download in a hyperlink through an XHTML anchor (<a>) tag, similar to a standard download. Because a PHP script is downloading the file, you have the advantage of being able to include validation code within the script to ensure that the user should be allowed to retrieve the file and that the file is available before allowing the download.

The second step to downloading a file with PHP is to provide the appropriate XHTML headers to tell the client Web browser that the response contains more than just a Web page. **Headers** are information sent to the Web browser from the Web server that tell the browser about the data being sent. The types of headers to send are listed in Table 5-7.

Header	Description	Value	Example
Content-Description	Description of the message contents	A text message	`header("Content-Description: File Transfer");`
Content-Type	MIME type and subtype of the message contents	A MIME type/ subtype string	`header("Content-Type: application/force-download");`
Content-Disposition	The attributes of the attachment, especially the filename	A series of name/value pairs defining the attributes of the file	`header("Content-Disposition: attachment; filename=\"list.txt\"");`
Content-Transfer-Encoding	The method used to encode the message contents	7bit, 8bit, quoted-printable, base64, binary	`header("Content-Transfer-Encoding: base64");`
Content-Length	The length of the message contents	Number	`header("Content-Length: 5000");`

Table 5-7   Content headers for downloading a file

The most important thing to remember when sending headers from PHP is that all of the headers must be sent prior to any Web content. If even a single character of the Web page is sent prior to sending the header, the header information will be considered text within the Web page and not header information. This will prevent your file from being downloaded. The easiest way to avoid this problem is to ensure that the first characters on the first line of the PHP script are the opening PHP tag (`<?php`).

PHP uses the `header()` function to return header information to the client Web browser. The `header()` function takes a single parameter, which is a text string containing the name of the header field followed by a colon, a space, and the data to associate with the header. The headers listed in Table 5-7 are far from comprehensive, but they are the only ones you need to download a file.

For example, the following headers tell the Web browser that a file named info.doc is 5000 bytes long, is encoded using base64 encoding, and is a file being downloaded:

```
header("Content-Description: File Transfer");
header("Content-Type: application/force-download");
header("Content-Disposition: attachment;
    filename=\"info.doc\"");
header("Content-Transfer-Encoding: base64");
header("Content-Length: 5000");
```

The "Content-Type" header can be used in two ways. If you want the downloaded file to appear in the client's Web browser as if it were a normal file, use the MIME type for the file. For example, if you are downloading a JPEG image, the MIME type would be "image/jpeg". The Web browser will display the image. If you want the file to be saved to the user's hard drive instead of being opened in the Web browser, use a MIME type of "application/force-download", which instructs the Web browser to open a "save file" dialog box and write the file to disk.

The third step, once the headers have been sent, is to send the file itself. The PHP `readfile()` function reads a file from disk and sends it directly to the Web browser. The only required parameter for the `readfile()` function is a string containing the path and filename to the file being sent; on success, `readfile()` returns the number of bytes sent; on failure, `readfile()` returns FALSE.

```
readfile("/usr/uploads/info.doc");
```

You are finished when the headers have been sent and the `readfile()` function has sent the file's contents. Do not send any XHTML data, or it will become part of the downloaded file information. If, however, the headers were not sent and the `readfile()` function was not called, the PHP script can create a Web page explaining that the file could not be downloaded and why. Therefore, your code should ensure that the headers were not sent and the `readfile()` function was not called prior to sending the Web page output.

To create a PHP downloader for the files subdirectory:

1. Create a new document in your text editor.

2. Add the following script section to the document body. Be sure that there is nothing in the file before the opening PHP tag:

   ```
   <?php
   ?>
   ```

3. Add the following code to the script section to check if the requested file exists and is readable:

   ```
   $Dir = "files";
   if (isset($_GET['filename'])) {
       $FileToGet = $Dir . "/" . stripslashes
       ($_GET['filename']);
   ```

```
        if (is_readable($FileToGet)) {
        }
        else {
            $ErrorMsg = "Cannot read \"$FileToGet\"";
            $ShowErrorPage = TRUE;
        }
    }
    else {
        $ErrorMsg = "No filename specified";
        $ShowErrorPage = TRUE;
    }
    if ($ShowErrorPage) {
```

4. Add the following code in the if section of the inner
   if...else statement for the is_readable() test to download
   the file:

```
header("Content-Description: File Transfer");
header("Content-Type: application/force-download");
header("Content-Disposition: attachment;
filename=\"" . $_GET['filename'] . "\"");
header("Content-Transfer-Encoding: base64");
header("Content-Length: " . filesize($FileToGet));
readfile($FileToGet);
$ShowErrorPage = FALSE;
```

5. Add the following code immediately after the closing PHP tag
   to show the error page. Note the use of advanced escaping to
   display the Web page output.

```
<!DOCTYPE html PUBLIC "-//W3C//DTD XHTML 1.0
Strict//EN"
"http://www.w3.org/TR/xhtml1/DTD/xhtml1-strict.dtd">
<html xmlns="http://www.w3.org/1999/xhtml">
<head>
<title>File Download Error</title>
<meta http-equiv="content-type" content="text/html;
    charset=iso-8859-1" />
</head>
<body>
<p>There was an error downloading "<?php echo
htmlentities($_GET['filename']); ?>"</p>
<p><?php echo htmlentities($ErrorMsg); ?></p>
</body>
</html>
<?php
}
?>
```

6. Save the document as **FileDownloader.php** in the Chapter
   directory for Chapter 5 and upload the file to the server.

7. Reopen **ViewFiles.php**. Replace the line that reads:

```
echo "<a href=\"$FullEntryName\">" .
    htmlentities($Entry). "</a>\n";
```

with a line that reads:

```
echo "<a
    href=\"FileDownloader.php?filename=$Entry\">" .
    htmlentities($Entry). "</a>\n";
```

8. Save ViewFiles.php and upload the file to the Web server.

9. Open the ViewFiles.php file in your Web browser by entering the following URL: *http://<yourserver>/PHP_Projects/Chapter.05/Chapter/ViewFiles.php*. Click one of the highlighted filenames. Your Web browser should display a "save file" dialog box like the one shown in Figure 5-8. Save the file and verify that it downloaded correctly.

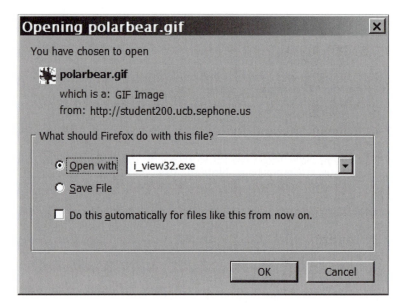

Figure 5-8   The "save file" dialog box for polarbear.gif

10. Close your Web browser window.

Short Quiz

1. What type of form input element is used to choose the file to upload?

2. What hidden form input element restricts the size of the uploaded file?

3. What is the name of the autoglobal array that contains the uploaded file information?

4. What function is used to pass headers to the client Web browser?

5. What function is used to send the contents of a file to the client Web browser?

Reading and Writing Entire Files

PHP provides functions for reading an entire file into a text string and for writing a text string as a file. Both functions are explained in this section.

Writing an Entire File

The file_put_contents() function writes a text string to a file. The syntax for this function is file_put_contents(*filename*, *string*[, *options*]). If the specified filename does not exist, it is created. However, if the specified filename does exist, any data it contains is overwritten. When you call the file_put_contents() function, you pass to it the name of the file to which you want to write data, along with a text string containing the data you want to write. For example, the following code builds a variable named $EventVolunteers that contains the names of volunteers at a charity event separated by line breaks, along with a variable named $VolunteersFile that contains the name of the file where the volunteer names will be stored. The last statement passes the $VolunteersFile and the $EventVolunteers variables to the file_put_contents() function.

```
$EventVolunteers = "Blair, Dennis\n";
$EventVolunteers .= "Hernandez, Louis\n";
$EventVolunteers .= "Miller, Erica\n";
$EventVolunteers .= "Morinaga, Scott\n";
$EventVolunteers .= "Picard, Raymond\n";
$VolunteersFile = "volunteers.txt";
file_put_contents($VolunteersFile, $EventVolunteers);
```

The file_put_contents() function returns the number of bytes that were written to the file. If no data was written to the file, the function returns a value of 0. You can use the return value to determine whether data was successfully written to the file, as follows:

```
if (file_put_contents($VolunteersFile, $EventVolunteers) > 0)
    echo "<p>Data was successfully written to the
        $VolunteersFile file.</p>\n";
else
```

```
echo "<p>No data was written to the
      $VolunteersFile
      file.</p>\n";
```

You can use an absolute or relative path with the filename you pass to the file_put_contents() function. However, even though the function will create a filename that does not exist, it will not create directories that do not exist. If you specify a nonexistent directory, you will receive an error. For this reason, you should use the is_dir() function to test whether the specified filename is a directory before you attempt to write to it.

In the next example, you will use the microtime() function to generate a unique filename. The microtime() function returns a string containing two values separated by a space. The first value is a decimal value showing the current fraction of a second, accurate to the microsecond. The second value is the current date and time in seconds. Because the current date/time value is stored in the filename, the scandir() function can sort the files in the order they were created.

In a publicly accessible application on the Internet, using the microtime() function would not be sufficient to guarantee a unique filename, although it is sufficient to use in this exercise.

To create a form that allows visitor comments on a Web site:

1. Create a new document in your text editor.

2. Type the <!DOCTYPE> declaration, <html> element, header information, and <body> element. Use the strict DTD and "Visitor Comments" as the content of the <title> element.

3. Add the following script section to the document body:

```
<?php
?>
```

4. Add the following code to the script section to store the form data entered:

```
$Dir = "comments";
if (is_dir($Dir)) {
    if (isset($_POST['save'])) {
        if (empty($_POST['name']))
            $SaveString = "Unknown Visitor\n";
        else
            $SaveString = stripslashes
                ($_POST['name']) . "\n";
        $SaveString .= stripslashes
            ($_POST['email']) . "\n";
        $SaveString .= date('r') . "\n";
        $SaveString .= stripslashes
            ($_POST['comment']);
        $CurrentTime = microtime();
        $TimeArray = explode(" ", $CurrentTime);
        $TimeStamp = (float)$TimeArray[1] +
                     (float)$TimeArray[0];
```

258

```
/* File name is " Comment.seconds.
microseconds.txt" */
$SaveFileName = "$Dir/Comment.$TimeStamp.
txt";
if (file_put_contents($SaveFileName,
$SaveString)>0)
        echo "File \"" . htmlentities
            ($SaveFileName) .
            "\" successfully saved.<br />\n";
else
        echo "There was an error writing \"" .
            htmlentities($SaveFileName) .
            "\".<br />\n";
    }
}
```

5. Add the following XHTML form immediately after the closing PHP tag:

```
<h2>Visitor Comments</h2>
<form action="VisitorComments.php" method="POST">
Your name: <input type="text" name="name" /><br />
Your email: <input type="text" name="email" /><br />
<textarea name="comment" rows="6" cols="100"></
textarea><br />
<input type="submit" name="save"
    value="Submit your comment" /><br />
</form>
```

6. Save the document as **VisitorComments.php** in the Chapter directory for Chapter 5 and upload the file to the server.

7. Create a new subdirectory named "comments". Verify that the "comments" directory on the Web server has read, write, and execute permissions enabled for user, group, and other.

8. Reopen **ViewFiles.php**, change the title to "View Comments", and immediately save the file as **ViewComments.php**.

9. Change the value of $Dir to "comments", as follows:

```
$Dir = "comments";
```

10. Convert the code that uses **FileDownloader.php** back to a standard hyperlink, as follows:

```
echo "<a href=\"$FullEntryName\">" .
    htmlentities($Entry). "</a>";
```

11. Save ViewComments.php in the Chapter directory for Chapter 5 and upload the file to the server.

12. Open the VisitorComments.php file in your Web browser by entering the following URL: *http://<yourserver>/PHP_Projects/Chapter.05/Chapter/VisitorComments.php*. Attempt

For most uses, granting write permission to others is not a safe choice. When making this choice, be sure you have considered the security risks. Do not grant write permissions unless it is absolutely required.

to submit a comment. You should receive a message stating whether the comment was saved successfully. Figure 5-9 shows an example in which the comment was successfully saved.

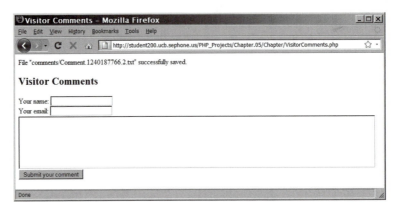

Figure 5-9 A successfully written comment using VisitorComments.php

13. After you have successfully submitted one or more comments to the server using the VisitorComments.php form, open the ViewComments.php file in your Web browser by entering the following URL: *http://<yourserver>/PHP_Projects/Chapter.05/Chapter/ViewComments.php*. You should see the new files in the directory listing. Figure 5-10 shows the output of ViewComments.php with two comments submitted.

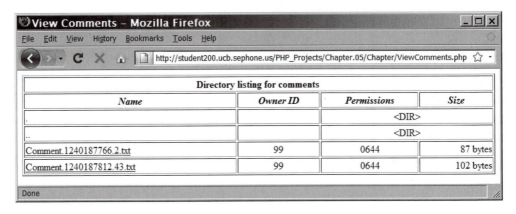

Figure 5-10 Listing of the "comments" subdirectory with two saved comments

14. Close your Web browser window.

In addition to the filename and text string arguments, you can pass a third argument to the file_put_contents() function that contains the FILE_USE_INCLUDE_PATH or FILE_APPEND constant. The

FILE_USE_INCLUDE_PATH constant instructs PHP to search for the specified filename in the path that is assigned to the include_path directive in your php.ini configuration file. The FILE_APPEND constant instructs PHP to append data to any existing contents in the specified filename instead of overwriting it.

The following example demonstrates how to use the file_put_contents() function with the FILE_APPEND constant to add the names of volunteers to the volunteers.txt file. The example consists of a single script that displays and processes a form that volunteers can use to register. Because the file_put_contents() function includes the FILE_APPEND constant, any new names that are entered in the form are appended to the volunteers.txt file. Figure 5-11 shows the form in a Web browser.

```
<h1>Coast City Charity Event Volunteers</h1>
<?php
if (isset($_POST['first_name']) && isset($_POST['last_
name'])) {
    $VolunteerFirst = addslashes($_POST['first_name']);
    $VolunteerLast = addslashes($_POST['last_name']);
    $NewVolunteer = "$VolunteerLast, $VolunteerFirst\n";
    $VolunteersFile = "volunteers.txt";
    if (file_put_contents($VolunteersFile, $NewVolunteer,
    FILE_APPEND) > 0)
        echo "<p>" . stripslashes($_POST['first_name']) .
            " " . stripslashes($_POST['last_name']) .
            " has been registered to volunteer at the
            event!</p>\n";
    else
        echo "<p>Registration error!</p>";
}
else
    echo "<p>To sign up to volunteer at the event, enter
        your first and last name and click the Register
        button.</p>";
?>
<form action="EventVolunteers.php" method="POST">
<p>First Name: <input type="text" name="first_name"
size="30" /></p>
<p>Last Name: <input type="text" name="last_name"
size="30" /></p>
<p><input type="submit" value="Register" /></p>
</form>
```

Figure 5-11   Volunteer registration form

Reading an Entire File

Table 5-8 lists the PHP functions that you can use to read the entire contents of a text file.

Function	Description
file(filename[, use_include_path])	Reads the contents of a file into an indexed array
file_get_contents(*filename*[,*options*])	Reads the contents of a file into a string
readfile(filename[,use_include_path])	Displays the contents of a file

Table 5-8   PHP functions that read the entire contents of a text file

The file_get_contents() function reads the entire contents of a file into a string. If you have a text file that contains a single block of data (that is, not a series of lines in which each represents a single piece of data), the file_get_contents() function can be useful. For example, assume that a weather service uses a text file to store daily weather forecasts. The following code examples use both the file_put_contents() function discussed in the previous section and the file_get_contents() functions. First, the file_put_contents() function is used to write the daily forecast for San Francisco to a text file named sfweather.txt:

```
$DailyForecast = "<p><strong>San Francisco daily weather
forecast</strong>: Today: Partly cloudy. Highs from
the 60s to mid 70s. West winds 5 to 15 mph. Tonight:
Increasing clouds. Lows in the mid 40s to lower 50s. West
winds 5 to 10 mph.</p>";
file_put_contents("sfweather.txt", $DailyForecast);
```

Next, the file_get_contents() function reads the contents of the sfweather.txt file into a string variable, which is then displayed with an echo statement:

```
$SFWeather = file_get_contents("sfweather.txt");
echo $SFWeather;
```

To create a Web page that displays all of the visitor comments:

1. Create a new document in your text editor.

2. Type the <!DOCTYPE> declaration, <html> element, header information, and <body> element. Use the strict DTD and "Visitor Feedback" as the content of the <title> element.

3. Add the following script section to the document body:

```
<?php
?>
```

4. Add the following code to the script section to store the form data entered:

```
$Dir = "comments";
if (is_dir($Dir)) {
    $CommentFiles = scandir($Dir);
    foreach ($CommentFiles as $FileName) {
        if (($FileName != ".") && ($FileName !=
        "..")) {
            echo "From <strong>$FileName</
            strong><br />";
            echo "<pre>\n";
            $Comment = file_get_contents
            ($Dir . "/" .
            $FileName);
            echo $Comment;
            echo "</pre>\n";
            echo "<hr />\n";
        }
    }
}
```

5. Add the following XHTML form immediately before the closing PHP tag:

```
<h2>Visitor Feedback</h2>
<hr />
```

6. Save the document as **VisitorFeedback.php** in the Chapter directory for Chapter 5 and upload the file to the server.

7. Open the VisitorFeedback.php file in your Web browser by entering the following URL: *http://<yourserver>/PHP_Projects/Chapter.05/Chapter/VisitorFeedback.php*. You should see a list of all the user comments from the "comments" subdirectory. Figure 5-12 shows an example with two comments.

8. Close your Web browser window.

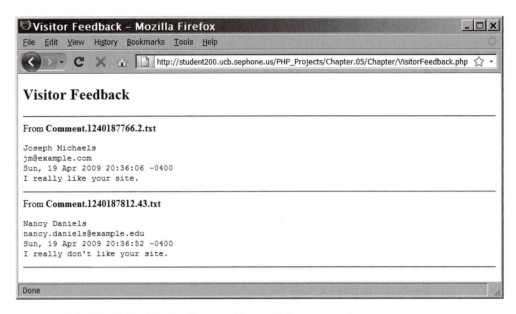

Figure 5-12 The Visitor Feedback page with two visitor comments

If you only want to display the contents of a text file, you do not need to use the file_get_contents() function to assign the contents to a variable and then display the value of the variable as a separate step. Instead, you can use the readfile() function discussed earlier to display the contents of a text file to a Web browser. For example, the following example uses the readfile() function to accomplish the same task as the file_get_contents() example you saw earlier:

```
readfile("sfweather.txt");
```

At times, text files are used to store individual lines of data, where each line represents a single unit of information. The easiest way to read the contents of a text file that stores data on individual lines is to use the file() function, which reads the entire contents of a file into an indexed array. The file() function automatically recognizes whether the lines in a text file end in \n, \r, or \n\r. Each individual line in the text file is assigned as the value of an element. You pass to the file() function the name of the text file enclosed in quotation marks. For example, the weather service that stores daily weather reports may also store average daily high, low, and mean temperatures, separated by commas, on individual lines in a single text file. The following code uses the file_put_contents() function to write the temperatures for the first week in January to a text file named sfjanaverages.txt:

```
$January = "61, 42, 48\n";
$January .= "62, 41, 49\n";
```

```
$January .= "62, 41, 49\n";
$January .= "64, 40, 51\n";
$January .= "69, 44, 55\n";
$January .= "69, 45, 52\n";
$January .= "67, 46, 54\n";
file_put_contents("sfjanaverages.txt", $January);
```

The first statement in the following code uses the file() function to read the contents of the sfjanaverages.txt file into an indexed array named $JanuaryTemps[]. The for statement then loops through each element in $JanuaryTemps[] and calls the explode() function from Chapter 3 to split each element at the comma into another array named $CurDay. The high, low, and mean averages in the $CurDay array are then displayed with echo statements. Figure 5-13 shows the output.

```
$JanuaryTemps = file("sfjanaverages.txt");
for ($i=0; $i<count($JanuaryTemps); ++$i) {
    $CurDay = explode(", ", $JanuaryTemps[$i]);
    echo "<p><strong>January " . ($i + 1) . "</strong><br
        />\n";
    echo "High: {$CurDay[0]}<br />\n";
    echo "Low: {$CurDay[1]}<br />\n";
    echo "Mean: {$CurDay[2]}</p>\n";
}
```

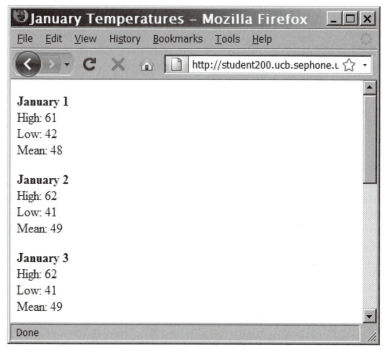

Figure 5-13 Output of individual lines in a text file

To modify the VisitorFeedback.php file so it opens the comment files with the file() function instead of the file_get_contents() function:

1. Return to the **VisitorFeedback.php** file in your text editor.

2. Replace the section of code from the opening <pre> statement to the closing </pre> statement with the following code. Notice that because the first three lines of the comment are the commenter's name and e-mail address and the date of the comment, the loop to display the comment text has a starting index of 3.

```
$Comment = file($Dir . "/" . $FileName);
echo "From: " . htmlentities($Comment[0]) . "<br />\n";
echo "Email Address: " . htmlentities($Comment[1]) .
"<br />\n";
echo "Date: " . htmlentities($Comment[2]) . "<br />\n";
$CommentLines = count($Comment);
echo "Comment:<br />\n";
for ($i = 3; $i < $CommentLines; ++$i) {
    echo htmlentities($Comment[$i]) . "<br />\n";
}
```

3. Save the VisitorFeedback.php file and upload it to the Web server.

4. Open the VisitorFeedback.php file in your Web browser by entering the following URL: *http://<yourserver>/PHP_Projects/ Chapter.05/Chapter/VisitorFeedback.php*. Figure 5-14 shows the new version of the Web page for the same two comments.

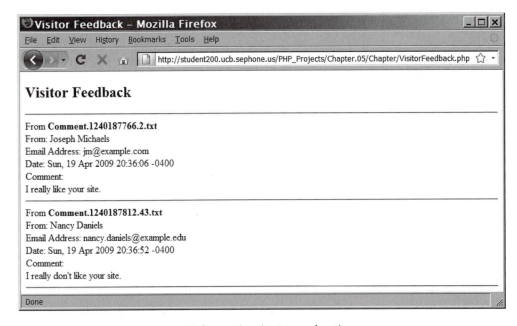

Figure 5-14 The Visitor Feedback form using the file() function

5. Close your Web browser window.

Short Quiz

1. Explain how to determine if the `file_put_contents()` function successfully wrote data to a file.

2. Explain why one should use the `is_dir()` function before using the `file_put_contents()` function to write data.

3. What function is useful for reading an entire file into a variable as a single block of text?

4. What is the difference between the `file()` and `file_get_contents()` functions?

Opening and Closing File Streams

So far, all of the functions you have seen for reading and writing files operate on an entire file at once. Sometimes, however, you may want to only read or write a small part of a file. PHP includes several functions for incrementally reading and writing files. You will learn how to use these functions later in this chapter. But before any of these functions can do their jobs, you must create a stream. A **stream** is a channel that is used for accessing a resource to which you may read and write. For example, you might use a stream to access a file. The **input stream** reads data from a resource such as a file, whereas the **output stream** writes data to a resource (again, such as a file). You have already used an output stream with the `echo` and `print` statements. Both statements send data to an output stream, which writes the data to a Web browser window. Using a file stream involves the following steps:

1. Open the file stream with the `fopen()` function.

2. Write data to or read data from the file stream.

3. Close the file stream with the `fclose()` function.

In the following sections, you will first learn how to open and close file streams, and then you will learn how to write and read data using file streams.

Opening a File Stream

When you use the `echo` or `print` statements to send data to an output stream, you only need to call each statement for the data to be sent to the stream. With external files, such as text files, you must write code that opens and closes a handle to a file. You use the fopen() function to open a handle to a file stream. The syntax for the fopen() function is $open_file = fopen(*filename*, *method*);. The $open_file variable is the handle that you can use to read data from and write data to the file. The *method* argument can be one of several values that determine what you can do with the file after you open it.

Table 5-9 lists the *method* arguments that you can use with the fopen() function. Among other things, these arguments control the position of the file pointer. Similar to the directory pointer discussed earlier, a **file pointer** is a special type of variable that refers to the currently selected line or character in a file. The file pointer is a way of keeping track of where you are in a file. Later in this chapter, you will work with functions that change the position of the file pointer.

Argument	Description
a	Opens the specified file for writing only and places the file pointer at the end of the file; attempts to create the file if it doesn't exist
a+	Opens the specified file for reading and writing and places the file pointer at the end of the file; attempts to create the file if it doesn't exist
r	Opens the specified file for reading only and places the file pointer at the beginning of the file
r+	Opens the specified file for reading and writing and places the file pointer at the beginning of the file
w	Opens the specified file for writing only and deletes any existing content in the file; attempts to create the file if it doesn't exist
w+	Opens the specified file for reading and writing and deletes any existing content in the file; attempts to create the file if it doesn't exist
x	Creates and opens the specified file for writing only; returns FALSE if the file already exists
x+	Creates and opens the specified file for reading and writing; returns FALSE if the file already exists

Table 5-9 Valid *method* argument values of the fopen() function

The following statement shows how to use the fopen() function to open a handle to a file stream:

```
$VolunteersFile = fopen("volunteers.txt", "r+");
```

Assume that the preceding statement opens a file that contains a list of people who have signed up to be a volunteer at an event. The `fopen()` function assigns the file to a handle named `$VolunteersFile`. Notice that the function uses a *method* argument of "r+", which opens the specified file for reading and writing and places the file pointer at the beginning of the file. This allows you to add new data to the beginning of the file, as illustrated in Figure 5-15.

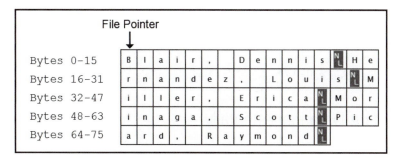

Figure 5-15 Location of the file pointer when the `fopen()` function uses a *method* argument of "r+"

If you want to open a file and place the file pointer at the end, you use a *method* argument of "a+", as shown in the following statement:

```
$VolunteersFile = fopen("volunteers.txt", "a+");
```

The preceding statement places the file pointer after the last byte of data, as illustrated in Figure 5-16.

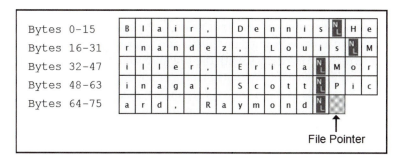

Figure 5-16 Location of the file pointer when the `fopen()` function uses a *method* argument of "a+"

By default, PHP opens a file in "text" mode, where end-of-line escape sequences in the file will be interpreted based on the operating system of the server and converted as necessary. Adding a "b" to the end of the *method* argument forces the file to be opened in "binary" mode, where no interpretation or conversion is done. Windows systems also allow for a "text conversion" mode, which converts all UNIX-style end-of-line escape sequences to the Windows style. To enable "text conversion" mode, append a "t" to the end of the *method* argument.

 When a file stream is opened for writing and the file pointer is anywhere except at the end of a file, writing to the file will overwrite any existing data in the file with the new data. Any data at that location is lost, and the logical structure of the data in the file may be corrupted. For this reason, the "r+" *method* value should be used with caution.

 For maximum compatibility, the PHP Group recommends always using binary mode and managing end-of-line escape sequences at the application level.

269

Closing a File Stream

When you finish working with a file stream, use the statement fclose($handle); to ensure that the file doesn't keep taking up space in your computer's memory and to allow other processes to read to and write from the file. Closing the file also forces the file to be "flushed." When you write to a file, the operating system often buffers the write command to a queue, saving it with other write commands. It is much faster at the file level to do multiple writes at the same time, instead of one at a time. Performing all buffered write commands is called "flushing" the write queue.

Writing Data Incrementally

The file_put_contents() function is useful if you want to quickly replace the contents of a file or append data to the end of an existing file. In addition to the file_put_contents() function, you can also use the fwrite() function to incrementally write data to a text file. The function uses the following syntax: fwrite($handle, data[, length]);. As with the file_put_contents() function, the fwrite() function returns the number of bytes that were written to the file. If no data was written to the file, the function returns a value of 0. You can use the return value to determine whether data was successfully written to the file.

The fputs() function is an alias for the fwrite() function.

Before you can use the fwrite() function, you must first open a handle to the text file with the fopen() function. Because you use the fopen() function with fwrite(), you can specify what type of operations can be performed on the file and where and how the data will be written. For example, with the file_put_contents() function, you can only replace the contents of a file or append data to the end of a file. By comparison, the *method* arguments of the fopen() function allow you to specify whether to open a file for reading or writing, whether to create a file if it doesn't exist, and whether to place the file pointer at the beginning or end of the text file.

The following code demonstrates how to use the fopen() and fclose() functions with multiple fwrite() statements to add names to the volunteers.txt file:

```
$VolunteersFile = fopen("volunteers.txt", "ab");
fwrite($VolunteersFile, "Blair, Dennis\n");
fwrite($VolunteersFile, "Hernandez, Louis\n");
fwrite($VolunteersFile, "Miller, Erica\n");
fwrite($VolunteersFile, "Morinaga, Scott\n");
fwrite($VolunteersFile, "Picard, Raymond\n");
fclose($VolunteersFile);
```

The following code contains a modified version of the single script that displays and processes a form that volunteers can use to register. This time, the script uses fopen(), fwrite(), and fclose() functions instead of the file_put_contents() function.

```
if (isset($_POST['first_name']) && isset($_POST['last_
name'])) {
        $VolunteerFirst = addslashes($_POST['first_name']);
        $VolunteerLast = addslashes($_POST['last_name']);
        $NewVolunteer = "$VolunteerLast, $VolunteerFirst\n";
        $VolunteersFile = fopen("volunteers.txt", "ab");
        if (fwrite($VolunteersFile, $NewVolunteer) > 0)
            echo "<p>" . stripslashes($_POST['first_name']) . "
                " . stripslashes($_POST['last_name']) .
                " has been registered to volunteer at the
                event!</p>\n";
        else
            echo "<p>Registration error!</p>";
        fclose($VolunteersFile);
}
else
        echo "<p>To sign up to volunteer at the event, enter
            your first and last name and click the Register
            button.</p>";
```

The length argument of the fwrite() function allows you to specify the maximum number of bytes that should be written. If the data argument you pass to the fwrite() function is greater than the value of the length argument, the data is truncated.

To modify the VisitorComments.php file so that it saves comments using the fopen(), fwrite(), and fclose() functions instead of the file_put_contents() function:

1. Return to the **VisitorComments.php** file in your text editor.

2. Replace the entire if...else statement for the file_put_contents() function with the following code:

```
$fp = fopen($SaveFileName,"wb");
if ($fp === FALSE) {
        echo "There was an error creating \"" .
        htmlentities($SaveFileName) . "\".<br />\n";
}
else {
        if (fwrite($fp, $SaveString)>0)
            echo "Successfully wrote to file \"" .
                htmlentities($SaveFileName) .
                "\".<br />\n";
        else
            echo "There was an error writing to file \""
                . htmlentities($SaveFileName) .
                "\".<br />\n";
        fclose($fp);
}
```

3. Save the VisitorComments.php file and upload it to the server.

4. Open the VisitorComments.php file in your Web browser by entering the following URL: *http://<yourserver>/PHP_Projects/Chapter.05/Chapter/VisitorComments.php*. Enter values in each of the fields and click the **Submit your comment** button. The script should function the same as it did with the file_put_contents() function.

5. Close your Web browser window.

Locking Files

When your program opens a text file via the fopen() method, there is a chance that another program will attempt to open the same file. If both programs are simply reading data from the file, there should be no problem. However, if more than one program attempts to write data to a text file at the same time, data corruption could occur. To prevent multiple users from modifying a file simultaneously, you need to use the flock() function. The basic syntax for this function is flock($handle, operation). The first argument you pass to the flock() function is the handle that represents the open file. The second argument you pass is one of the operational constants listed in Table 5-10.

Constant	Description
LOCK_EX	Opens the file with an exclusive lock for writing
LOCK_NB	Prevents the flock() function from waiting, or "blocking," until a file is unlocked
LOCK_SH	Opens the file with a shared lock for reading
LOCK_UN	Releases a file lock

Table 5-10 Operational constants of the flock() function

You use the LOCK_SH constant to create a shared lock for reading, which allows other users to read the file while you have it locked. The LOCK_EX constant creates an exclusive lock to write data to the file. An exclusive lock prevents other users from accessing the file until you are finished with it. After you finish using either lock type, you should call the flock() function with the LOCK_UN constant, which releases the lock. If you call the flock() function with either the LOCK_SH or LOCK_EX constant, and the file you want to lock is already locked by another user, your script waits until the other user releases the lock. If you don't want your script to wait until a file is unlocked, you can include the LOCK_NB constant in the operation argument. As a general rule, you should only use the LOCK_NB constant when your script needs to write an exceptionally large amount of data to a file. To use the LOCK_NB constant, separate it from the LOCK_SH or LOCK_EX constant with the | (bitwise Or) operator, as shown in the following example:

```
flock($VolunteersFile, LOCK_EX | LOCK_NB);
```

The flock() function returns a value of TRUE if it successfully locks a file and FALSE if it fails. You can use this return value to determine whether the lock was successful, as shown in the following code, which contains a modified example of the script that adds new names to the volunteers.txt file. In this example, a single name is assigned to the $NewVolunteer variable. The flock() function uses the LOCK_EX constant to lock the volunteers.txt file for writing. If the lock is successful, a nested if...else statement attempts to write the name to the file and displays a message stating whether the fwrite() function was successful. The last statement in the main if statement then uses the LOCK_UN constant with the flock() function to unlock the volunteers.txt file.

```
$VolunteersFile = fopen("volunteers.txt", "ab");
$FirstName = "Don";
$LastName = "Gosselin";
$VolunteerFirst = addslashes($FirstName);
$VolunteerLast = addslashes($LastName);
$NewVolunteer = "$VolunteerLast, $VolunteerFirst\n";
if (flock($VolunteersFile, LOCK_EX)) {
    if (fwrite($VolunteersFile, $NewVolunteer) > 0)
        echo "<p>" . stripslashes($FirstName) . " " .
            stripslashes($LastName) . " has been
            registered to volunteer at the event!</p>";
    else
        echo "<p>Registration error!</p>";
    flock($VolunteersFile, LOCK_UN);
}
else
    echo "<p>Cannot write to the file. Please try again
        later</p>";
fclose($VolunteersFile);
```

To modify the VisitorComments.php file so it uses the flock() function when writing data to a text file:

1. Return to the **VisitorComments.php** file in your text editor.

2. Modify the if statement that executes the fwrite() statement so it is contained within another if statement that executes an flock() statement to lock the file. Also, add another flock() statement that unlocks the file in place of the fclose() statement. The fclose() statement should be

It's important to understand that the PHP file locking mechanism is simply "advisory." This means that PHP does not actually shut out other programs from accessing the file, as other programming languages do. Instead, PHP only prevents other PHP scripts that use flock() from accessing a file that was locked by another PHP script. In other words, a PHP script that does not use flock() to open a file can go ahead and modify the file, even if it is exclusively locked by another PHP script. For PHP file locking to be effective, it's up to you (and your ISP) to ensure that any scripts that open a file on your server use the flock() function.

moved outside the if...else statement for the flock() function. The end of your script should appear as follows:

```
$fp = fopen($SaveFileName,"wb");
if ($fp === FALSE) {
    echo "There was an error creating \"" .
        htmlentities($SaveFileName) .
        "\".<br/>\n";
}
else {
    if (flock($fp, LOCK_EX)){
        if (fwrite($fp, $SaveString)>0)
            echo "Successfully wrote to
                file \"" .
                htmlentities(
                    $SaveFileName) .
                "\".<br />\n";
        else
            echo "There was an error
                writing to
                file \"" .
                htmlentities(
                    $SaveFileName) .
                "\".<br />\n";
        flock($fp, LOCK_UN);
    }
    else {
        echo "There was an " .
            "error locking file \"" .
            htmlentities(
                $SaveFileName) .
            " for writing\"." .
            "<br />\n";
    }
    fclose($fp);
}
}
```

3. Save the VisitorComments.php file and upload it to the Web server.

4. Open the VisitorComments.php file in your Web browser by entering the following URL: *http://<yourserver>/PHP_Projects/Chapter.05/Chapter/VisitorComments.php*. Enter values in each of the fields and click the **Submit your comment** button. The script should function the same as it did before you added the flock() statements.

5. Close your Web browser window.

Reading Data Incrementally

For large text files, reading the entire contents of the file into PHP can take up a lot of memory on your server and affect the performance of your script. Instead of reading an entire file into PHP, you can use the file pointer to iterate through a text file. As mentioned earlier, a file pointer is a special type of variable that refers to the currently selected line or character in a file. The functions listed in Table 5-11 allow you to use the file pointer to iterate through a text file.

Function	Description
fgetc($handle)	Returns a single character and moves the file pointer to the next character
fgetcsv($handle, length[,delimiter, string_enclosure])	Returns a line, parses the line for CSV fields, and then moves the file pointer to the next line
fgets($handle[, length])	Returns a line and moves the file pointer to the next line
fgetss($handle, length[,allowed_tags])	Returns a line, strips any XHTML tags the line contains, and then moves the file pointer to the next line
fread($handle, length)	Returns up to *length* characters and moves the file pointer to the next available character
stream_get_line($handle, length, delimiter)	Returns a line that ends with a specified delimiter and moves the file pointer to the next line

Table 5-11   PHP functions that iterate through a text file

You must use the fopen() and fclose() functions with the functions listed in Table 5-11. With the exception of the fgetc() and fread() functions, each time you call any of the functions listed in Table 5-11, the file pointer automatically moves to the next line in the text file. The fgetc() function does not advance the file pointer, while the fread() function advances the file pointer to the next available character. Each time you call the fgetc() function, the file pointer moves to the next character in the file.

The functions listed in Table 5-11 are often combined with the feof() function, which returns a value of TRUE when a file pointer reaches the end of a file. The feof() function accepts a single argument containing the handle for the open file. The following code demonstrates how to use the feof() function with the fgets() function, which returns a line and moves the file pointer to the next line. When reading, a line is defined as a string of characters ending with an end-of-line escape sequence or the end of the file. The code reads and parses each line in the sfjanaverages.txt text file, similar to the previous example that parsed the data by using the file() function. In the following version, a while statement uses the value returned from the feof() function as the conditional expression. The lines in the while statement then parse and display the contents of each line, and the last statement calls the fgets() function, which reads the current line and moves the file pointer to the next line.

For the fread() function, the maximum value of *length* is 8192. For the fgets() function, there is no imposed limit to the number of characters. However, prior to version 4.3, PHP would default to a *length* value of 1024 if no value was specified. If you think that most of the lines being read are longer than 8192 characters, your script will run faster when you specify the *length* value for the fgets() function than if you omit the value.

```
$JanuaryTemps = fopen("sfjanaverages.txt", "rb");
$Count = 1;
$CurAverages = fgets($JanuaryTemps);
while (!feof($JanuaryTemps)) {
    $CurDay = explode(", ", $CurAverages);
    echo "<p><strong>Day $Count</strong><br />";
    echo "High: {$CurDay[0]}<br />";
    echo "Low: {$CurDay[1]}<br />";
    echo "Mean: {$CurDay[2]}</p>";
    $CurAverages = fgets($JanuaryTemps);
    ++$Count;
}
fclose($JanuaryTemps);
```

For files other than text files, you use the fread() function instead of the fgets() function. Like the fgets() function, the fread() function reads up to *length* bytes from the file stream and advances the file pointer to the next available character. Unlike the fgets() function, the *length* parameter of the fread() function is required, and the fread() function does not stop reading characters when an end-of-line marker is found.

To modify the VisitorFeedback.php file so that it accesses the lines in the comment files with fopen(), fgets(), and fclose() functions instead of the file() function:

1. Return to the **VisitorFeedback.php** file in your text editor.

2. Replace the file() statement with the following fopen() statement and test:

```
$fp = fopen($Dir . "/" . $FileName, "rb");
if ($fp === FALSE)
    echo "There was an error reading file \"" .
        $FileName . "\".<br />\n";
else {
```

3. Replace the code that displays the contents of the file with the code that uses the `fgets()` statement:

```
echo "From <strong>$FileName</strong><br />";
$From = fgets($fp);
echo "From: " . htmlentities($From) . "<br />\n";
$Email = fgets($fp);
echo "Email Address: " . htmlentities($Email) .
    "<br />\n";
$Date = fgets($fp);
echo "Date: " . htmlentities($Date) . "<br />\n";
echo "Comment:<br />\n";
$Comment = "";
while (!feof($fp)) {
    $Comment .= fgets($fp);
}
echo htmlentities($Comment) . "<br />\n";
echo "<hr />\n"
```

4. Complete the `else` clause with the following `fclose()` statement and the closing bracket:

```
    fclose($fp);
}
```

5. Save the VisitorFeedback.php file and upload it to the server.

6. Open the VisitorFeedback.php file in your Web browser by entering the following URL: *http://<yourserver>/PHP_Projects/Chapter.05/Chapter/VisitorFeedback.php*. The script should function the same as it did before you replaced the single call to the `file()` function with multiple calls to the `fgets()` function.

7. Close your Web browser window.

Short Quiz

1. What is a file stream?

2. Explain the function of the file pointer as it relates to writing data to files.

3. Explain the term "reading data incrementally."

4. What function is used to prevent multiple users from modifying a file simultaneously?

5. What function must be called if the `fopen()` function successfully opened a file?

Managing Files and Directories

In addition to creating and accessing files, you can also use PHP to manage files and the directories that store them. In fact, you can use PHP to perform many of the same file and directory management tasks that are available on most operating systems, including copying, moving, renaming, and deleting files and directories. In this section, you will study various techniques for managing files and directories with PHP. First, you will learn how to copy and move files.

Copying and Moving Files

You use the copy() function to copy a file with PHP. The function returns a value of TRUE if it is successful or FALSE if it is not. The syntax for the copy() function is copy(source, destination). For the source and destination arguments, you can include just the name of a file to make a copy in the current directory or you can specify the entire path for each argument. The following example demonstrates how to use the copy() function to copy the sfweather.txt file to a file named sfweather01-27-2010.txt in a directory named "history." The first if statement checks whether the sfweather.txt file exists, and the first nested if statement checks whether the "history" directory exists within the current directory. If both if statements are TRUE, the copy() function attempts to copy the file.

```
if (file_exists("sfweather.txt")) {
    if(is_dir("history")) {
        if (copy("sfweather.txt",
            "history\\sfweather01-27-2010.txt"))
                echo "<p>File copied successfully.</p>\n";
        else
                echo "<p>Unable to copy the file!</p>\n";
}
else
    echo "<p>The directory does not exist!</p>\n";
}
else
    echo "<p>The file does not exist!</p>\n";
```

To use the copy() function to copy the visitor comments to a backup directory:

1. Create a new document in your text editor.

2. Type the <!DOCTYPE> declaration, <html> element, header information, and <body> element. Use the strict DTD and "Backup Comments" as the content of the <title> element.

3. Add the following script section to the document body:

```
<?php
?>
```

4. Declare the following two variables in the script section. The $Source variable contains the name of the Comments directory, "comments", and the $Destination variable contains the name of the directory "backups", where you will back up your files.

```
$Source = "comments";
$Destination = "backups";
```

5. Add the following if...else statement to the end of the script section. The if statement verifies that the "backups" directory exists and is a directory.

```
if (!is_dir($Destination))
    echo "The backup directory \"$Destination\" does
    not exist.\n";
else {
}
```

6. Within the else clause of the previous if...else statement, add the following if...else statement, which executes the copy() function:

```
if (is_dir($Source)) {
    $TotalFiles = 0;
    $FilesMoved = 0;
    $DirEntries = scandir($Source);
    foreach ($DirEntries as $Entry) {
        if (($Entry!=".") && ($Entry!="..")) {
            ++$TotalFiles;
            if (copy("$Source/$Entry",
            "$Destination/$Entry"))
                ++$FilesMoved;
            else
                echo "Could not move
                    file \"" .
                    htmlentities($Entry) .
                    "\".<br />\n";
        }
    }
    echo "<p>$FilesMoved of $TotalFiles
        comments successfully backed up.</p>\n";
}
else
    echo "<p>The source directory \"" .
        $Source . "\" does not exist!</p>\n";
```

7. Save the document as **BackupComments.php** in the Chapter directory for Chapter 5.

8. Create a new subdirectory called "backups" on the Web server. Give write permissions to the user, group, and others.

For most uses, granting write permission to others is not a safe choice. When making this choice, be sure you have considered the security risks. Do not grant write permissions unless it is absolutely required.

9. Open the BackupComments.php file in your Web browser by entering the following URL: *http://<yourserver>/PHP_Projects/Chapter.05/Chapter/BackupComments.php*. You should see the message that the comments were successfully backed up. Figure 5-17 shows the output when four files were backed up successfully. Look in your Chapter directory for Chapter 5 on the Web server and see if the "backups" directory contains copies of the comment files in your "comments" directory.

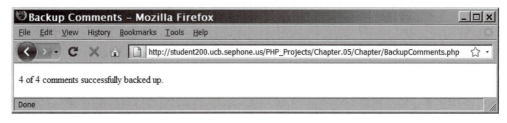

Figure 5-17 The result of successfully backing up four comment files with BackupComments.php

10. Close your Web browser window.

Renaming Files and Directories

You use the `rename()` function to rename or move a file or directory with PHP. As with the `copy()` function, the `rename()` function returns a value of TRUE if it is successful or FALSE if it is not. The syntax for the `rename()` function is `rename(old_name, new_name)`. For the `old_name` argument, you can include just the name of a file to rename the file in the current directory or you can specify the entire path to the file being renamed. For the `new_name` argument, you can include just the name of a file to rename the file named by `old_name`. If you specify a path for the `new_name` argument, and the path is different from the path for the `old_name` argument, the file is effectively moved from the old directory to the specified directory when the file is renamed. If the `new_name` argument is an existing directory, the file specified by `old_name` is moved to the new directory, but the filename remains unchanged.

The following example demonstrates how to rename and move a file. Notice that the script contains three levels of nested `if` statements to check the file and directory names, and a fourth nested `if` statement that verifies whether the `rename()` function was successful. The first `if` statement checks to see whether the original file exists, the second `if` statement determines whether the destination directory exists, and the third `if` statement confirms that a file of the same name does not exist in the target directory.

```php
$OldName = "sfweather.txt";
$NewName = "sfweather01-28-2010.txt";
$NewDirectory = "history";
if (file_exists($OldName)) {
    if(is_dir($NewDirectory)) {
        if (!file_exists($NewDirectory . "\\" . $NewName))
        {
            if (rename($OldName, $NewDirectory . "\\"
                . $NewName))
                echo "<p>File renamed
                    successfully.</p>\n";
            else
                echo "<p>Unable to rename the
                    file!</p>\n";
        }
        else
            echo "<p>The destination file already
                exists!</p>\n";
    }
    else
        echo "<p>The directory does not exist!</p>\n";
}
else
    echo "<p>The file does not exist!</p>\n";
```

Removing Files and Directories

You use the `unlink()` function to delete files and the `rmdir()` function to delete directories. You pass the name of a file to the `unlink()` function and the name of a directory to the `rmdir()` function. Both functions return a value of TRUE if successful or FALSE if not. With both functions, you can use the `file_exists()` function to determine whether a file or directory name exists before you attempt to delete it. For example, the following code uses the `file_exists()` and `unlink()` functions to delete a file:

```php
$FileName = "sfweather.txt";
if (file_exists($FileName)) {
    if(unlink($FileName))
        echo "<p>File deleted successfully.</p>\n";
    else
        echo "<p>Unable to delete the file!</p>\n";
}
else
        echo "<p>The file does not exist!</p>\n";
```

The `rmdir()` function takes a little more developmental effort because it does not work unless a directory is empty. To check whether a directory is empty, you first use the `file_exists()` function to determine whether the directory exists. Then, you use the `scandir()` function to copy the names of the files in the directory to an array. Some operating systems always list two directory entries named "." and ".." within another directory. The "." directory is a reference to the current directory, whereas the ".." directory is a reference to the directory that contains the current directory. The `rmdir()` function only works when these are the only two entries present, indicating that the directory is empty. Therefore, you need to write code that verifies that the directory you want to delete contains only the "." and ".." entries. The following example uses the `file_exists()` function to see whether the "history" directory exists, then uses the `scandir()` function and a `foreach()` loop to determine whether the directory contains any entries other than the "." and ".." entries.

```php
$DirName = "history";
if (file_exists($DirName)) {
    $DirEntries = scandir($DirName);
    $EmptyDir = TRUE;
    foreach ($DirEntries as $Dir) {
        if ($Dir != "." && $Dir != "..")
            $EmptyDir = FALSE;
    }
    if ($EmptyDir == TRUE) {
        if (rmdir($DirName))
            echo "<p>Directory deleted
                successfully.</p>\n";
        else
            echo "<p>Unable to delete the
                directory!</p>\n";
    }
    else
        echo "<p>The directory is not empty!</p>\n";
}
else
    echo "<p>The directory does not exist!</p>\n";
```

Although either method works, using the `rename()` function is quicker and uses less resources on the server than copying the file to the new location and deleting the old copy.

PHP does not contain a separate command for moving files. Instead, you can rename the file with the `rename()` function and specify a new directory in which you want to store the renamed file. Alternatively, you must copy the file with the `copy()` function, and then delete the original file with the `unlink()` function.

Short Quiz

1. During the file copy process, what function is used to delete the original file?

2. Why is it important to use the scandir() function before using the rmdir() function?

3. What two entries will exist in a directory in most operating systems, even if the directory is empty?

4. How do you move a file in PHP?

5. What is the difference between the unlink() and rmdir() functions?

Summing Up

- PHP recognizes two different file types: text and binary. Text files contain printable characters and a small set of formatting characters. Binary files are a series of bytes for which PHP attaches no special meaning.

- Different operating systems use different character sequences to identify the end of a line in a text file.

- File permissions identify the abilities that users or groups of users have for a particular file. Typical permissions include read, write, and execute.

- The chmod() function modifies the permissions of a file or directory. The fileperms() function reads the permissions of a file or directory.

- A handle is a special type of variable that PHP uses to represent a resource such as a file.

- To iterate through the entries in a directory, you open a handle to the directory with the opendir() function. You can then use the readdir() function to return the file and directory names from the open directory. You use the closedir() function to close a directory handle.

- The scandir() function returns an indexed array containing the names of files and directories in the specified directory.

- The mkdir() function creates a new directory.

- PHP includes various file and directory status functions, such as the file_exists() function, which determines whether a file or directory exists.

- PHP includes other types of functions that return additional information about files and directories, such as the filesize() function, which returns the size of a file.

- When uploading or downloading files, the server is the remote system and the client is the local machine.

- You upload a file using a Web form with an input of type "file". A hidden input named "MAX_FILE_SIZE" limits the size of the uploaded file.

- The PHP form handler retrieves the uploaded file from the $_FILES autoglobal array.

- The move_uploaded_file() function moves an uploaded file from the temporary directory to a more permanent location.

- To download a file from the XHTML directory structure, use an XHTML hyperlink. To download a file from outside the XHTML directory structure, use the header() function to identify the file and the readfile() function to send the file contents to the Web browser.

- The file_put_contents() function writes or appends a text string to a file. The file_get_contents() function reads a file into a text string. The file() function reads a file into an indexed array.

- The stream is used for accessing a resource from which you can read and to which you can write. The input stream reads data from a resource such as a file, whereas the output stream writes data to a resource (again, such as a file).

- The fopen() function opens a stream to a text file.

- A file pointer is a special type of variable that refers to the currently selected line or character in a file.

- When you finish working with a file stream, you use the fclose() function to ensure that the file doesn't keep taking up space in your computer's memory.

- The fwrite() function incrementally writes data to a text file.

- The flock() function prevents multiple users from modifying a file simultaneously.

- The `feof()` function determines if the file pointer is at the end of the file.

- PHP includes various functions, such as the `fread()` and `fgets()` functions, that allow you to use the file pointer to iteratively read a text file.

- The `copy()` function copies a file. The `rename()` function renames or moves a file or directory.

- The `unlink()` function deletes files, and the `rmdir()` function deletes directories.

- PHP does not contain a separate command for moving files. Instead, you can rename the file with the `rename()` function and specify a new directory where you want to store the renamed file. Or, you must copy the file with the `copy()` function, and then delete the original file with the `unlink()` function.

Comprehension Check

1. Which of the following escape sequences is used on Macintosh platforms? (Select all that apply.)

   a. \n

   b. \r

   c. \n\r

   d. \r\n

2. Which of the following functions sorts directory entries?

   a. scandir()

   b. readdir()

   c. opendir()

   d. sortdir()

3. Explain when you should use file and directory status functions such as `file_exists()` and `is_dir()`.

4. What is the value of the `enctype` attribute for a Web form that uploads a file?

5. What is the name of the autoglobal array that contains uploaded file information?

6. Which of the following constants can you use with the file_put_contents() function to append data to the end of a file?

   a. INCLUDE_FILE

   b. FILE_USE_INCLUDE_PATH

   c. APPEND

   d. FILE_APPEND

7. Which of the following functions reads the contents of a file into a string?

   a. file()

   b. file_get_contents()

   c. fread()

   d. readfile()

8. The file() function automatically recognizes whether the lines in a text file end in \n, \r, or \n\r. True or False?

9. Which of the following allows you to read data from a resource such as a file?

   a. an input stream

   b. an output stream

   c. a pointer

   d. a reference

10. Which of the following best describes the "w+" *method* argument?

   a. creates and opens the specified file for reading and writing; returns FALSE if the file already exists

   b. opens the specified file for reading and writing and places the file pointer at the end of the file; attempts to create the file if it doesn't exist

   c. opens the specified file for writing only and deletes any existing content in the file; attempts to create the file if it doesn't exist

   d. opens the specified file for reading and writing and deletes any existing content in the file; attempts to create the file if it doesn't exist

11. A _____ is a special type of variable that refers to the currently selected character in a file.

    a. character pointer

    b. line pointer

    c. file pointer

    d. directory pointer

12. Explain why you should call the `fclose()` function when you are finished working with a file.

13. You must open and close a file stream when you use the `file_put_contents()` function. True or False?

14. What is the correct syntax for using the `fwrite()` function to write a value of "Forestville Foods\n" to a file handle named `$SalesProspects`?

    a. `$SalesProspects = fwrite("Forestville Foods\n");`

    b. `fwrite($SalesProspects, "Forestville Foods\n");`

    c. `fwrite("Forestville Foods\n", $SalesProspects);`

    d. `fwrite("$SalesProspects, Forestville Foods\n");`

15. Explain why you should lock files before writing data to them.

16. Which of the following operational constants can you use with the `flock()` function? (Choose all that apply.)

    a. `LOCK_EX`

    b. `LOCK_NH`

    c. `LOCK_SH`

    d. `LOCK_UH`

17. Which of the following functions can you use to iterate through a text file? (Choose all that apply.)

    a. `stream_get_line()`

    b. `fgets()`

    c. `fread()`

    d. `readfile()`

18. Which of the following functions returns a value of TRUE when a file pointer reaches the end of a file?

   a. is_end()

   b. end()

   c. eof()

   d. feof()

19. Which of the following statements creates a directory named "students" at the same level as the current directory?

   a. mkdir("/students");

   b. mkdir("students");

   c. mkdir("/students/");

   d. mkdir("../students");

20. Explain the two ways in which you can move a file with PHP.

Reinforcement Exercises

 Exercise 5-1

In this project, you will create a hit counter script that keeps track of the number of hits a Web page receives. Ensure that the Projects directory has read and write permissions for everyone.

1. Create a new document in your text editor and type the <!DOCTYPE> declaration, <html> element, document head, and <body> element. Use the strict DTD and "Hit Counter" as the content of the <title> element.

2. Add the following script section to the document body:

```
<?php
?>
```

3. Add the following statement to the script section to declare a variable named $CounterFile that contains the name of the file where the hits will be stored:

```
$CounterFile = "hitcount.txt";
```

4. Add the following if statement to the end of the script section. The if statement determines whether the hitcount.txt

file already exists. If it does, the file_get_contents() function retrieves the value from the file and increments it by 1.

```
if (file_exists($CounterFile)) {
    $Hits = file_get_contents($CounterFile);
    ++$Hits;
}
```

5. Add the following else statement to the end of the script section. The else statement contains a single statement that assigns a value of 1 to the $Hits variable in the event that the hitcount.txt file has not yet been created.

```
else
    $Hits = 1;
```

6. Finally, add the following statements to the end of the script section. The echo statement displays the number of hits and the if statement updates the value in the hitcount.txt file. Remember that the file_put_contents() function opens the file if it already exists or creates the file if it doesn't exist.

```
echo "<h1>There have been $Hits hits to this page.
</h1>\n";
if (file_put_contents($CounterFile, $Hits))
        echo "<p>The counter file has been updated.
            </p>\n";
```

7. Save the document as **HitCounter.php** in the Projects directory for Chapter 5.

8. Open HitCounter.php in your Web browser by entering the following URL: *http://<yourserver>/PHP_Projects/ Chapter.05/Projects/HitCounter.php*. The first time you open the Web page, you should see a hit count of 1. Reload the Web page a few times to see if the count increases.

9. Close your Web browser window.

Exercise 5-2

In this project, you will create a Web page that allows visitors to your site to sign a guest book that is saved to a text file. Ensure that the Projects directory has read and write permissions for everyone.

1. Create a new document in your text editor and type the <!DOCTYPE> declaration, <html> element, document head, and <body> element. Use the strict DTD and "Guest Book" as the content of the <title> element.

2. Add the following text and elements to the document body:

```
<h2>Enter your name to sign our guest book</h2>
<form method="POST" action="SignGuestBook.php">
<p>First Name <input type="text" name="first_name"
/></p>
<p>Last Name <input type="text" name="last_name"
/></p>
<p><input type="submit" value="Submit" /></p>
</form>
<p><a href="ShowGuestBook.php">Show Guest Book
</a></p>
```

3. Save the document as **GuestBook.html** in the Projects directory for Chapter 5.

4. Create a new document in your text editor and type the `<!DOCTYPE>` declaration, `<html>` element, document head, and `<body>` element. Use the strict DTD and "Sign Guest Book" as the content of the `<title>` element.

5. Add the following script section to the document body:

```
<?php
?>
```

6. Add the following `if` statement to the script section to check whether the user filled in the first name and last name fields:

```
if (empty($_POST['first_name']) || empty($_
POST['last_name']))
        echo "<p>You must enter your first and last
                name. Click your browser's Back button to
                return to the Guest Book.</p>\n";
```

7. Add the following `else` clause to the end of the script section. The statements in the `else` clause use the `fwrite()` function to add visitor names to a text file named guestbook.txt.

```
else {
    $FirstName = addslashes($_POST['first_name']);
    $LastName = addslashes($_POST['last_name']);
    $GuestBook = fopen("guestbook.txt", "ab");
    if (is_writeable("guestbook.txt")) {
        if (fwrite($GuestBook, $LastName . ", " .
                    $FirstName . "\n"))
            echo "<p>Thank you for signing our
                    guest book!</p>\n";
        else
            echo "<p>Cannot add your name to the
                    guest book.</p>\n";
    }
```

```
        else
                echo "<p>Cannot write to the file.</p>\n";
        fclose($GuestBook);
    }
```

8. Save the document as **SignGuestBook.php** in the Projects directory for Chapter 5.

9. Create a document named **ShowGuestBook.php** that displays the names of visitors who have signed the guest book. Use the `readfile()` function to display the contents of the guestbook.txt file. Note that you will need to use the `<pre>` element for Web browsers to recognize the line breaks.

10. Open **GuestBook.html** in your Web browser by entering the following URL: *http://<yourserver>/PHP_Projects/ Chapter.05/Projects/GuestBook.html*. Test the form to see if you can write data to and read data from the guestbook.txt file.

11. Close your Web browser window.

Exercise 5-3

Create a document with a form that registers bowlers for a bowling tournament. Use a single text file that saves information for each bowler on a separate line. Include the bowler's name, age, and average, separated by commas. Ensure that the Projects directory has read and write permissions for everyone.

Exercise 5-4

Create a Web page to be used for storing software development bug reports in text files. Include fields such as product name and version, type of hardware, operating system, frequency of occurrence, and proposed solutions. Include links on the main page that allow you to create a new bug report and update an existing bug report. Ensure that the Projects directory has read and write permissions for everyone.

Exercise 5-5

Create a Web form for uploading pictures for a high school reunion. The form should have text input fields for the person's name and a description of the image, and a file input field for the image. To accompany each image file, create a text file that contains the name and description of the image. Create a separate Web page that displays the pictures with a caption showing the name and description fields. Ensure that the Projects directory has read and write permissions for everyone.

Discovery Projects

The Chinese Zodiac site is a comprehensive project that will be updated in the Discovery Projects in each chapter. All files for the Chinese Zodiac site will be saved in a folder named ChineseZodiac in the root Web folder on the server.

Discovery Project 5-1

Reopen **inc_site_layout.php**, which you created in Discovery Project 4-1. The file is in the Includes folder of the ChineseZodiac folder. Replace the "[Insert site layout content here]" placeholder with Web content that describes the process of developing a dynamic Web template. Be sure to differentiate between dynamic and static content and illustrate the syntax for targeting content to a dynamic content section.

Save the inc_site_layout.php file and upload it to the server. The contents of this file should appear in the dynamic content section when you click the Site Layout button or the Site Layout text hyperlink from the Chinese zodiac Web template.

Discovery Project 5-2

Create a new document in your text editor and create an All-in-One Web form that prompts the user for his or her birth year. Validate the user input to require the user to enter a number. Use a nested `if...else` statement to display the appropriate version of the message, "You were born under the sign of the [zodiac sign]", and display the zodiac image representing the posted year. Use the Chinese zodiac images that you saved in the Images folder in Discovery Project 1-4. Track the number of times each year is entered by storing a counter for each year in a file in a "statistics" subdirectory. Ensure that the PHP scripting engine has read and write permissions for the "statistics" subdirectory. Display a message at the bottom of the page showing how many times the specified year has been entered using the message "You are visitor [count] to enter [year]". Use a separate file for each year. Figure 5-18 shows a sample Web form and Figure 5-19 shows a sample output Web page.

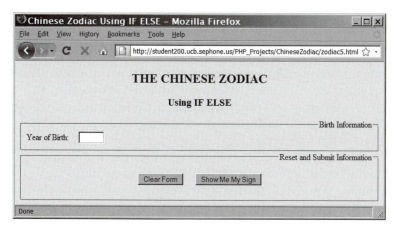

Figure 5-18 Sample Web form for the `if...else` program

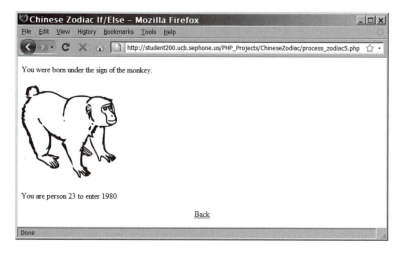

Figure 5-19 Sample output for the `if...else` statement

Save the file as **BirthYear_ifelse.php** and upload it to the ChineseZodiac folder on the server. Create the "statistics" subdirectory and ensure that the write permissions are set to allow the PHP scripting engine to write files in the directory.

Reopen the BirthYear_ifelse.php file. Modify the script to use a `switch` statement instead of the nested `if...else` statements. Save the file as **BirthYear_switch.php** and upload it to the ChineseZodiac folder on the server.

Discovery Project 5-3

Create a new document in your text editor and type the `<!DOCTYPE>` declaration, `<html>` element, document head, and `<body>` element. Use the strict DTD and "Show Source Code" as the content of the `<title>` element. This script will display the source code of a PHP script with syntax highlighting. This is accomplished by using the `file_get_contents()` function you learned in this chapter to read the script into a string, and by using a new function, `highlight_string()`. The `highlight_string()` function takes a string of PHP code and displays it with color-coded syntax highlighting in a Web browser. To use these functions, insert the following PHP code block in the body:

```php
<?php
if (isset($_GET['source_file'])) {
    $SourceFile = file_get_contents(
        stripslashes($_GET['source_file']));
    highlight_string($SourceFile);
}
else
    echo "<p>No source file name entered</p>\n";
?>
```

Save the document as **ShowSourceCode.php** in the ChineseZodiac directory and upload the document to the Web server.

Open the **inc_string_functions.php** file in your text editor and replace the "[Insert string function content here]" placeholder text with the title "String and Character Functions." Add a text navigation bar below the title with the following internal hyperlinks that link to a description of the PHP program. You can insert the text navigation bar directly in the inc_control_structures.php file or create the bar as a separate file and include it.

```
<a href="#string">String Functions</a>
<a href="#char">Character Functions</a>
```

Below the text navigation bar, create a section for each hyperlink and insert an anchor to the named section. The first section, "String Functions", is for the SimilarNames.php script you created in Discovery Project 3-4. The second section, "Character Functions", is for the EmbeddedWords.php script you created in Discovery Project 3-5. Describe the purpose of each PHP program. For example: "This script counts the number of times each letter appears in a string and compares that count to the number of times each letter appears in the names of the Chinese zodiac signs to determine if the name can be made from the characters in the string." The code for the two anchor targets is listed below.

```
<a id="string">String Functions</a>
<a id="char">Character Functions</a>
```

Below the descriptive content, insert a text hyperlink with the link text "[Test the Script]" that opens the appropriate PHP script for the section.

Add a second text hyperlink with the link text "[View the Source Code]" that displays the source code of the respective PHP program. Use the following code for the hyperlink, replacing file_name with the name of the program referenced in the "[Test the Script]" hyperlink:

```
<a href="ShowSourceCode.php?source_file=file_name">[View the
Source Code]</a>
```

Save the file and upload it to the Includes folder in the ChineseZodiac folder on the server. Open index.php by entering the following URL in your Web browser's address bar: *http://<yourserver>/ ChineseZodiac/index.php*. Click the String Functions button or menu item to display the updated inc_string_functions.php. Test the links to verify that they display properly.

 Discovery Project 5-4

Open the **inc_control_structures.php** file in your text editor and replace the "[Insert control structure content here]" placeholder text with the title "Conditional Statements and Looping Structures." Add a text navigation bar below the title with the following internal hyperlinks that link to a description of the PHP program. You can insert the text navigation bar directly in the inc_control_structures.php file or create the bar as a separate file and include it.

```
<a href="#if_else">If...Else Statement</a>
<a href="#switch">Switch Statement</a>
<a href="#while_loop">While Loop</a>
<a href="#for_loop">For Loop</a>
```

Below the text navigation bar, create a section for each hyperlink and insert an anchor to the named section. Describe the purpose of each PHP program. For example: "This all-in-one form prompts the user to enter a 4-digit birth year, which is validated for numeric input. The browser displays the user's Chinese zodiac sign and the associated zodiac image using an if...else statement." The code for the four anchor targets is listed below:

```
<a id="if_else">If...Else Statement</a>
<a id="switch">Switch Statement</a>
```

```
<a id="while_loop">While Loop</a>
<a id="for_loop">For Loop</a>
```

Below the descriptive content, insert a text hyperlink with the link text "[Test the Script]" that opens the appropriate script. For the "If... Else Statement" section, use the BirthYear_ifelse.php script created in Discovery Project 5-2. For the "Switch Statement" section, use the BirthYear_switch.php script, also created in Discovery Project 5-2. For the "While Loop" section, use the Chinese_Zodiac_while_loop. php script created in Discovery Project 2-5. For the "For Loop" section, use the Chinese_Zodiac_for_loop.php script created in Discovery Project 2-4.

Add a second text hyperlink with the link text "[View the Source Code]" that calls the ShowSourceCode.php script created in Discovery Project 5-3 to display the source code of the appropriate PHP script for this section. Use the following code for the hyperlink, replacing file_name with the name of the program referenced in the "[Test the Script]" hyperlink:

```
<a href="ShowSourceCode.php?source_file=file_name">[View the
Source Code]</a>
```

Save the file and upload it to the Includes folder in the ChineseZodiac folder on the server. Open index.php by entering the following URL in your Web browser's address bar: *http://<yourserver>/ ChineseZodiac/index.php*. Click the Control Structures button or menu item to display the updated inc_control_structures.php. Test the links to verify that they display properly.

Discovery Project 5-5

Create an All-in-One Web form with a text area box for the user to enter a Chinese proverb and write the data to a file named proverbs.txt in the ChineseZodiac directory. Be sure that the proverbs.txt file has read and write permissions for the PHP scripting engine. Use the fwrite() function to incrementally append each new proverb that is submitted using the Add Chinese Proverb button on the Web form.

Name the file **UploadProverb.php** and transfer the file to the ChineseZodiac directory on the server. Open UploadProverb.php in the Web browser and use the Web form to post a number of Chinese proverbs to the proverbs.txt file on the Web server.

Reopen **inc_footer.php** and modify the code to use the file() function to read the contents of the proverbs.txt file into an array. Count the number of items in the array using the count() function and store the result in a variable named `$ProverbCount`. Use the PHP `rand(0, $ProverbCount-1)` function to generate a random array index. Use the echo statement to display the text "A randomly displayed Chinese proverb read from a text file". Below the description, display a Chinese proverb using the random index to select the proverb from the array.

View the Chinese Zodiac Web site in the Web browser. Refresh the browser to verify that a different proverb appears each time the browser is refreshed.

Discovery Project 5-6

Create a PHP All-in-One Web form to upload images to the Images subfolder in the ChineseZodiac folder on the server. Remember that you must set the permissions on the directory to give the PHP scripting engine write access to the directory. Name the file **UploadImage.php** and save it in the ChineseZodiac folder, then upload it to the Web server.

Search the Web for at least five small dragon images. Save them in a folder and size them to approximately 100 pixels by 100 pixels. Name the images **Dragon1**, **Dragon2**, and so on with a valid image extension. Use the UploadImage.php Web form to upload the dragon images to the Web server.

In Discovery Project 6-1, you will randomly display one of the dragon images below the randomly displayed Chinese proverb.

CHAPTER 6

Manipulating Arrays

In this chapter, you will:

- ◎ Manipulate array elements
- ◎ Declare and initialize associative arrays
- ◎ Iterate through an array
- ◎ Find and extract elements and values
- ◎ Sort, combine, and compare arrays
- ◎ Understand multidimensional arrays
- ◎ Use arrays in Web forms

Earlier in this book, you learned that an array contains a set of data represented by a single variable name. You also learned that PHP includes two types of arrays: indexed and associative. You refer to the elements in an indexed array by their numeric position, whereas you refer to the elements in an associative array with an alphanumeric key. In this chapter, you will learn how to use advanced techniques on both indexed and associative arrays.

Manipulating Elements

As you use arrays in your scripts, you will undoubtedly need to add and remove elements. For example, suppose you have an online shopping cart program that uses an array to store the names of products that a customer plans to purchase. As the customer selects additional products to purchase, or decides not to purchase an item, you will need to manipulate the elements in the array of products.

In this chapter, you work on a Message Board script that allows users to post and read messages to and from a text file. (Message boards are online discussion groups in which users with similar interests exchange messages.) The Message Board script you use in this chapter is fairly simple, unlike some of the real message boards you have probably seen and used yourself. However, the Message Board script lets you practice the advanced array techniques presented in this chapter.

This simple implementation of a message board has only two pages. PostMessage.php is an All-in-One Web form for posting messages to the message board. MessageBoard.php is the page for viewing, organizing, and deleting messages. Messages are written to the messages.txt file at *PHP_Projects/Chapter.06/Chapter/MessageBoard/* on the Web server.

To create an All-in-One form for posting messages to the Message Board, which stores messages in a text file:

1. Create a new document in your text editor.

2. Type the `<!DOCTYPE>` declaration, `<html>` element, header information, and `<body>` element. Use the strict DTD and "Post Message" as the content of the `<title>` element.

3. Add the following script section to the document body:

   ```php
   <?php
   ?>
   ```

4. Add the following code to the script section to append the submitted message to the messages.txt file. The code uses the `fopen()`, `fwrite()`, and `fclose()` functions you studied in Chapter 5 to write the lines of the messages.txt file.

Remember that opening a file with the "a" *method* parameter will append to an existing file or create the file if it doesn't exist. Note the use of the strict comparison operator (===) to verify that the value is FALSE *and* the data type is Boolean. Because the message lines use the tilde (~) character to separate fields, you will need to remove any tilde characters in the message fields themselves.

```php
if (isset($_POST['submit'])) {
    $Subject = stripslashes($_POST['subject']);
    $Name = stripslashes($_POST['name']);
    $Message = stripslashes($_POST['message']);
    // Replace any '~' characters
    //       with '-' characters
    $Subject = str_replace("~", "-", $Subject);
    $Name = str_replace("~", "-", $Name);
    $Message = str_replace("~", "-", $Message);
    $MessageRecord =
        "$Subject~$Name~$Message\n";
    $MessageFile =
        fopen("MessageBoard/messages.txt",
        "ab");
    if ($MessageFile === FALSE)
        echo "There was an error saving your
            message!\n";
    else {
        fwrite($MessageFile, $MessageRecord);
        fclose($MessageFile);
        echo "Your message has been saved.\n";
    }
}
```

5. Add the following XHTML code after the PHP code block to display the Web form:

```html
<h1>Post New Message</h1>
<hr />
<form action="PostMessage.php" method="POST">
<span style="font-weight:bold">Subject:</span>
    <input type="text" name="subject" />
<span style="font-weight:bold">Name:</span>
    <input type="text" name="name" /><br />
<textarea name="message" rows="6"
    cols="80"></textarea><br />
<input type="submit" name="submit"
    value="Post Message" />
<input type="reset" name="reset"
    value="Reset Form" />
</form>
<hr />
<p>
<a href="MessageBoard.php">View Messages</a>
</p>
```

The View Messages link will not work until you create MessageBoard.php in the next exercise.

6. Save the document as **PostMessage.php** in the Chapter directory for Chapter 6 and upload the file to the server.

7. Create a subdirectory on the Web server named **MessageBoard**. Verify that the user, group, and others are given permissions to read, write, and execute for the subdirectory.

8. Open the PostMessage.php file in your Web browser by entering the following URL: *http://<yourserver>/PHP_Projects/Chapter.06/Chapter/PostMessage.php*. Figure 6-1 shows the form.

The user account for your Web server is the only account that will read and write the messages.txt file. By default, the owner of a file can read and write the file, so there is no need to use the chmod() function on the messages.txt file.

301

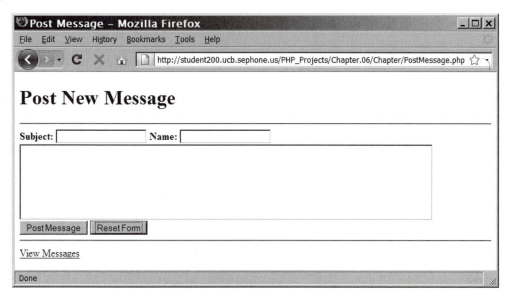

Figure 6-1 The Post New Message page of the Message Board

9. Use the form to store some messages in **messages.txt**.

To create the main page for the Message Board, which displays the messages stored in messages.txt:

1. Create a new document in your text editor.

2. Type the `<!DOCTYPE>` declaration, `<html>` element, header information, and `<body>` element. Use the strict DTD and "Message Board" as the content of the `<title>` element.

3. Add the following XHTML code and script section to the document body:

```
<h1>Message Board</h1>
<?php
?>
<p>
<a href="PostMessage.php">
    Post New Message</a>
</p>
```

4. Add the following code to the script section to read the messages.txt file and display the messages in a table. This code uses the file() function you learned in Chapter 5 to read the messages.txt file into the $MessageArray array, and the explode() function you learned in Chapter 3 to split each message string into an array of substrings based on a separator string, which in this case is a tilde (~). The array of substrings is stored in $CurrMsg.

```
if ((!file_exists("MessageBoard/messages.txt"))
        || (filesize("MessageBoard/messages.txt")
        == 0))
    echo "<p>There are no messages
            posted.</p>\n";
else {
    $MessageArray =
            file("MessageBoard/messages.txt");
    echo "<table
            style=\"background-color:lightgray\"
            border=\"1\" width=\"100%\">\n";
    $count = count($MessageArray);
    for ($i = 0; $i < $count; ++$i) {
        $CurrMsg = explode("~",
                $MessageArray[$i]);
    echo "<tr>\n";
    echo "<td width=\"5%\"
            style=\"text-align:center;
            font-weight:bold\">" .
            ($i + 1) . "</td>\n";
    echo "<td width=\"95%\"><span
            style=\"font-weight:bold\">Subject:
            </span> " .
            htmlentities($CurrMsg[0]) .
            "<br />\n";
    echo "<span
            style=\"font-weight:bold\">Name:
            </span> " .
            htmlentities($CurrMsg[1]) .
            "<br />\n";
```

```
            echo "<span
                style=\"text-decoration:underline;
                font-weight:bold\">Message
                </span><br />\n" .
                htmlentities($CurrMsg[2]) .
                "</td>\n";
            echo "</tr>\n";
    }
        echo "</table>\n";
    }
```

5. Save the document as **MessageBoard.php** in the Chapter directory for Chapter 6 and upload the file to the Web server.

6. Open the MessageBoard.php file in your Web browser by entering the following URL: *http://<yourserver>/PHP_Projects/Chapter.06/Chapter/MessageBoard.php*. Figure 6-2 shows example output for three messages.

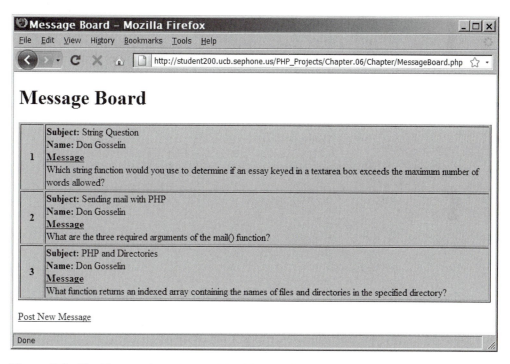

Figure 6-2   The Message Board page of the Message Board

7. Close your Web browser window.

Adding and Removing Elements from the Beginning of an Array

To add or remove elements from the beginning of an array, use the `array_shift()` and `array_unshift()` functions. The `array_shift()` function removes the first element from the beginning of an array, whereas the `array_unshift()` function adds one or more elements to the beginning of an array. You pass to the `array_shift()` function the name of the array whose first element you want to remove. You pass to the `array_unshift()` function the name of an array followed by comma-separated values for each element you want to add. For example, the following code declares and initializes an array of the top-selling vehicles in the United States for December 2008. The list needs to be updated for January 2009. The `array_shift()` function removes the first vehicle, the Chevrolet Impala, from the top of the array. The `array_unshift()` function adds the new member of the list, the Honda CR-V, to the top of the array. Figure 6-3 shows the output of the `print_r()` function. Recall from Chapter 1 that the `print_r()` function displays the indexes and values of an array. Note the use of the XHTML <pre> tags to keep the output from being displayed in a single line.

```
$TopSellers = array(
    "Chevrolet Impala",
    "Chevrolet Malibu",
    "Chevrolet Silverado",
    "Ford F-Series",
    "Toyota Camry",
    "Toyota Corolla",
    "Nissan Altima",
    "Honda Accord",
    "Honda Civic",
    "Dodge Ram");
echo "<h2>Original Array</h2>\n";
echo "<pre>\n";
print_r($TopSellers);
echo "</pre>\n";
array_shift($TopSellers);
echo "<h2>Array after Shifting</h2>\n";
echo "<pre>\n";
print_r($TopSellers);
echo "</pre>\n";
array_unshift($TopSellers, "Honda CR-V");
echo "<h2>Array after Unshifting</h2>\n";
echo "<pre>\n";
print_r($TopSellers);
echo "</pre>\n";
```

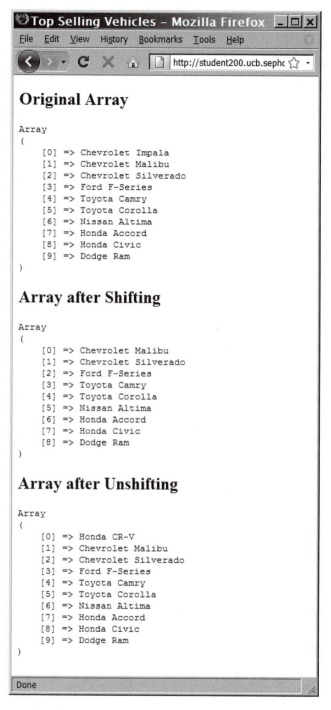

Figure 6-3 Output of an array modified with the
`array_shift()` and `array_unshift()` functions

To modify MessageBoard.php to use the `array_shift()` function to remove the first message in the Message Board script:

1. Reopen **MessageBoard.php** in your text editor.

2. Add the following code to the start of the PHP block. The code checks to see if an action was passed in the URL. If an action was passed, the messages.txt file is checked. If the messages.txt file exists and it contains messages, the contents of the messages.txt file are read into an array using the `file()` function.

```
if (isset($_GET['action'])) {
    if ((file_exists(
        "MessageBoard/messages.txt")) &&
        (filesize(
        "MessageBoard/messages.txt") != 0)) {
        $MessageArray = file(
            "MessageBoard/messages.txt");
    }
}
```

3. Add the following `switch()` statement immediately after the line that reads the contents of the messages.txt file into an array. You use a `switch()` statement instead of an `if()` statement because more cases will be added later. If the action is "Delete First", use the `array_shift()` function to remove the first element in the array.

```
switch ($_GET['action']) {
    case 'Delete First':
        array_shift($MessageArray);
        break;
} // End of the switch statement
```

4. Add the following `if()` statement after the `switch()` statement. If any messages are left in the array, the code in the block will be executed. The code will be added in the next step. If no messages are left in the array, the messages.txt file is deleted with the `unlink()` function.

```
if (count($MessageArray)>0) {
}
else
    unlink(
        "MessageBoard/messages.txt");
```

5. Insert the following code in the `if` code block of the above `if()` statement. The first statement uses the `implode()` function to convert `$MessageArray[]` into a text string, which is assigned to the `$NewMessages` variable. Recall from Chapter 3 that the `implode()` function concatenates an array of strings

into a single string. The second statement then uses the fopen() function to open a handle named $MessageStore to the messages.txt file. Notice that the fopen() function uses the "wb" *method* parameter, which opens a file for writing only and deletes all of the file's current contents. If successful, this allows the fwrite() statement to replace the entire contents of the file with the new list of messages in the $NewMessages variable.

```
$NewMessages =
    implode($MessageArray);
$MessageStore = fopen(
    "MessageBoard/messages.txt",
    "wb");
if ($MessageStore === false)
    echo "There was an error
        updating the message
        file\n";
else {
    fwrite($MessageStore,
        $NewMessages);
    fclose($MessageStore);
}
```

The script should appear as follows:

```
if (isset($_GET['action'])) {
    if ((file_exists(
        "MessageBoard/messages.txt")) &&
        (filesize(
        "MessageBoard/messages.txt") != 0)) {
        $MessageArray = file(
            "MessageBoard/messages.txt");
        switch ($_GET['action']) {
            case 'Delete First':
                array_shift($MessageArray);
                break;
        } // End of the switch statement
        if (count($MessageArray)>0) {
            $NewMessages =
                implode($MessageArray);
            $MessageStore = fopen(
                "MessageBoard/messages.txt",
                "wb");
            if ($MessageStore === false)
                echo "There was an error
                    updating the message
                    file\n";
            else {
                fwrite($MessageStore,
                    $NewMessages);
                fclose($MessageStore);
            }
        }
    }
    else
```

```
                        unlink(
                            "MessageBoard/messages.txt");
            }
    }

    if ((!file_exists("MessageBoard/messages.txt"))
            || (filesize("MessageBoard/messages.txt")
            == 0))
            echo "<p>There are no messages
                posted.</p>\n";
    else {
    . . .
```

6. Modify the paragraph element at the end of the file so it contains an anchor element that calls the MessageBoard.php file with the proper parameters to delete the first message, as follows:

```
<p>
<a href="PostMessage.php">
    Post New Message</a><br />
<a href="MessageBoard.php?action=Delete%20First">
    Delete First Message</a>
</p>
```

7. Save the MessageBoard.php file and upload the file to the server.

8. Open the MessageBoard.php file in your Web browser by entering the following URL: *http://<yourserver>/PHP_Projects/Chapter.06/Chapter/MessageBoard.php*. Click the **Delete First Message** link to test the new code. The first message in your list should be deleted.

9. Close your Web browser window.

Adding and Removing Elements from the End of an Array

The easiest way to add more elements to the end of an array is simply to use the array name and brackets syntax that you first saw in Chapter 1. For example, the first statement in the following code uses the array() construct to create the initial $HospitalDepts[] array. The second statement then adds a new value, "Pediatrics," as the fourth element of the array.

```
$HospitalDepts = array(
    "Anesthesia",
    "Molecular Biology",
    "Neurology");
$HospitalDepts[] = "Pediatrics";
```

You can also add and remove elements from the end of an array by using the `array_pop()` and `array_push()` functions. The `array_pop()` function removes the last element from the end of an array, whereas the `array_push()` function adds one or more elements to the end of an array. You pass to the `array_pop()` function the name of the array whose last element you want to remove. You pass to the `array_push()` function the name of an array followed by a comma-separated list of values for each element you want to add. In the following example, the `array_pop()` function removes the last department, "Pediatrics," from the end of the array, and the `array_push()` function adds two departments, "Psychiatry" and "Pulmonary Diseases," to the end of the array.

```
$HospitalDepts = array(
    "Anesthesia",
    "Molecular Biology",
    "Neurology",
    "Pediatrics");
array_pop($HospitalDepts);
    // Removes "Pediatrics"
array_push($HospitalDepts, "Psychiatry",
    "Pulmonary Diseases");
```

To modify MessageBoard.php to use the `array_pop()` function to remove the last message in the Message Board script:

1. Reopen **MessageBoard.php** in your text editor.

2. Add the following code as a second case to the `switch()` statement. This case uses the `array_pop()` function to remove the last element in the array.

   ```
   case 'Delete Last':
        array_pop($MessageArray);
        break;
   ```

3. Modify the paragraph element at the end of the file so it contains another anchor element that calls the MessageBoard.php file with the proper parameters to delete the last message, as follows:

   ```
   <p>
   <a href="PostMessage.php">
        Post New Message</a><br />
   <a href="MessageBoard.php?action=Delete%20First">
        Delete First Message</a><br />
   <a href="MessageBoard.php?action=Delete%20Last">
        Delete Last Message</a>
   </p>
   ```

4. Save the MessageBoard.php file and upload the file to the Web server.

5. Open the MessageBoard.php file in your Web browser by entering the following URL: *http://<yourserver>/PHP_Projects/Chapter.06/Chapter/MessageBoard.php*. Click the **Delete Last Message** link to test the new code. The last message in your list should be deleted.

6. Close your Web browser window.

Adding and Removing Elements Within an Array

So far, you have learned to add and remove elements from the beginning and end of an array. The `array_splice()` function allows you to add or remove elements located anywhere else in an array. After adding or removing array elements, the `array_splice()` function also renumbers the indexes for an array. The syntax for the function is `array_splice(array_name, start_index, number_to_delete, values_to_insert);`. The *array_name* argument indicates the name of the array you want to modify. The *start_index* argument indicates the element within the array at which elements should be added or removed. In other words, it is the index of the first element to be deleted or moved. The *number_to_delete* argument is an integer value that indicates the number of elements to remove from the array, starting with the element indicated by the *start_index* argument. The *values_to_insert* argument is a value or array of values you want to insert into the array at the index specified by the *start_index* argument. The remaining elements of the array, if any, are relocated to start at the first index after the last inserted value.

To add an element within an array, include a value of 0 as the third argument of the `array_splice()` function. For example, the `array_splice()` function in the following code adds a new element with a value of "Ophthalmology" between the "Neurology" and "Pediatrics" elements, and renumbers the elements. Because "Pediatrics" is the first element that needs to be moved, *start_index* is set to 3, the index of "Pediatrics".

```
$HospitalDepts = array(
    "Anesthesia",        // first element (0)
    "Molecular Biology", // second element (1)
    "Neurology",         // third element (2)
    "Pediatrics");       // fourth element (3)
array_splice($HospitalDepts, 3, 0,
    "Ophthalmology");
```

To add more than one element within an array, pass the `array()` construct as the fourth argument to the `array_splice()` function. Within the `array()` construct, include the new element values separated by commas, as if you were creating a new array. The following example shows how to add two new elements, "Opthalmology" and "Otolaryngology," between the "Neurology" and "Pediatrics" elements:

```
$HospitalDepts = array(
    "Anesthesia",        // first element (0)
    "Molecular Biology", // second element (1)
    "Neurology",         // third element (2)
    "Pediatrics");       // fourth element (3)
array_splice($HospitalDepts, 3, 0,
    array("Opthalmology",
        "Otolaryngology"));
```

You can also delete array elements by omitting the fourth argument from the `array_splice()` function. After the deletions, the remaining indexes are renumbered, just as when you add new elements. For example, to delete the second and third elements ("Molecular Biology" and "Neurology") from the `$HospitalDepts[]` array, you use the following `array_splice()` statement:

```
$HospitalDepts = array(
    "Anesthesia",        // first element (0)
    "Molecular Biology", // second element (1)
    "Neurology",         // third element (2)
    "Pediatrics");       // fourth element (3)
array_splice($HospitalDepts, 1, 2);
```

If you do not include the third argument (*number_to_delete*), the `array_splice()` function deletes all the elements from the second argument (*start_index*) to the end of the array.

To modify MessageBoard.php to use the `array_splice()` function to remove a specific message from the Message Board script:

1. Reopen **MessageBoard.php** in your text editor.

2. Add the following code as a third case to the `switch()` statement. This case uses the `array_splice()` function to remove the element specified by the `$_GET['message']` array element from the `$MessageArray` array.

```
case 'Delete Message':
    if (isset($_GET['message']))
        array_splice(
            $MessageArray,
            $_GET['message'],
            1);
    break;
```

3. To restrict the second column of the table to 85% of the table width, modify the code as follows:

```
echo "<td width=\"85%\"><span
    style=\"font-weight:bold\">
    Subject:</span> " .
    htmlentities($CurrMsg[0]) .
    "<br />\n";
```

4. Immediately before the line of code that defines the closing
   </tr> tag, add the following code to define a third column for
   the table:

```
echo "<td width=\"10%\"
      style=\"text-align:center\">" .
      "<a href='MessageBoard.php?" .
      "action=Delete%20Message&" .
      "message=$i'>" .
      "Delete This Message</a></td>\n";
```

The row output portion of the script should appear as follows:

```
. . .
            echo "<tr>\n";
            echo "<td width=\"5%\"
                  style=\"text-align:center;
                  font-weight:bold\">" .
                  ($i + 1) . "</td>\n";
            echo "<td width=\"85%\"><span
                  style=\"font-weight:bold\">Subject:
                  </span> " .
                  htmlentities($CurrMsg[0]) .
                  "<br />\n";
            echo "<span
                  style=\"font-weight:bold\">Name:
                  </span> " .
                  htmlentities($CurrMsg[1]) .
                  "<br />\n";
            echo "<span
                  style=\"text-decoration:underline;
                  font-weight:bold\">Message
                  </span><br />\n" .
                  htmlentities($CurrMsg[2]) .
                  "</td>\n";
            echo "<td width=\"10%\"
                  style=\"text-align:center\">" .
                  "<a href='MessageBoard.php?" .
                  "action=Delete%20Message&" .
                  "message=$i'>" .
                  "Delete This Message</a></td>\n";
            echo "</tr>\n";
. . .
```

5. Save the MessageBoard.php file and upload the file to the
   server.

6. Open the MessageBoard.php file in your Web browser by
   entering the following URL: *http://<yourserver>/PHP_
   Projects/Chapter.06/Chapter/MessageBoard.php*. Select a
   message and click the corresponding **Delete This Message**
   link. The message will be deleted from the list.

7. Close your Web browser window.

You can also use the unset() function to remove array elements and other variables. You pass to the unset() function the array name with the index number of the element you want to remove in brackets. To remove multiple elements, separate each element name with a comma. For example, the following unset() function removes the "Molecular Biology" and "Neurology" elements from the $HospitalDepts[] array:

```
unset($HospitalDepts[1], $HospitalDepts[2]);
```

One problem with the unset() function is that it does not renumber the remaining elements in the array. If you executed the print_r() function with the $HospitalDepts[] array after executing the preceding unset() function, you would see that the "Anesthesia" element has an index of 0 and "Pediatrics" still has an index of 3, as if you had not removed the "Molecular Biology" and "Neurology" elements.

To renumber an indexed array's elements, you need to use the array_values() function. You pass to this function the name of the array whose indexes you want to renumber. The array_values() function does not operate directly on an array. Instead, it returns a new array with the renumbered indexes. For this reason, you need to write a statement that assigns the array returned from the array_values() function to a new variable name or to the original array. The following statement demonstrates how to use the array_values() function to renumber the element indexes in the $HospitalDepts[] array, and then assign the renumbered array back to the $HospitalDepts[] array:

```
$HospitalDepts = array_values($HospitalDepts);
```

 The array passed to the array_values() function is passed by value, not by reference. This means that, unlike the array_splice() function, the array passed in is not changed. The return value of the array_values() function is the renumbered array. In the preceding example, the return value is written back to the same array variable that was passed to the array_values() function.

To modify the MessageBoard.php file so that it uses the unset() function instead of the array_splice() function to delete messages:

1. Return to the **MessageBoard.php** file in your text editor.

2. Modify the "Delete Message" case statement as follows to replace the array_splice() statement with the unset() and array_values() statements:

```
case 'Delete Message':
if (isset($_GET['message'])) {
    $Index = $_GET['message'];
    unset($MessageArray[$Index]);
    $MessageArray =
        array_values(
        $MessageArray);
}
break;
```

3. Save the MessageBoard.php file and upload the file to the Web server.

4. Open the MessageBoard.php file in your Web browser by entering the following URL: *http://<yourserver>/PHP_Projects/Chapter.06/Chapter/MessageBoard.php*. Select a message and click the corresponding **Delete This Message** link. The message will be deleted from the list.

5. Close your Web browser window.

Removing Duplicate Elements

You might need to ensure that an array in a script does not contain duplicate values. For example, your script may use arrays of e-mail addresses, customer names, or sales items, each of which should contain unique elements. You can use the `array_unique()` function to remove duplicate elements from an array. You pass to this function the name of the array from which you want to remove duplicate elements. As with the `array_values()` function, the `array_unique()` function does not operate directly on an array. Instead, it returns a new array with the renumbered indexes. For this reason, you need to write a statement that assigns the array returned from the `array_unique()` function to a new variable name or to the original array.

The following code shows an example of the array that contains the top-selling vehicles for 2008. The array should only contain unique values, but several of the names are duplicated. The `array_unique()` function removes the duplicate elements and then assigns the renumbered array back to the `$TopSellers[]` array. Figure 6-4 shows the output.

```php
$TopSellers = array(
    "Ford F-Series", "Chevrolet Silverado",
    "Toyota Camry", "Honda Accord",
    "Toyota Corolla", "Ford F-Series",
    "Honda Civic", "Honda CR-V", "Honda Accord",
    "Nissan Altima", "Toyota Camry",
    "Chevrolet Impala", "Dodge Ram",
    "Honda CR-V");
    echo "<p>The 2008 top selling vehicles
        are:</p>\n<p>";
    $TopSellers = array_unique($TopSellers);
    $TopSellers = array_values($TopSellers);
    for ($i = 0; $i < count($TopSellers); ++$i) {
        echo "{$TopSellers[$i]}<br />\n";
    }
    echo "</p>\n";
```

The 2008 top selling vehicles are:

Ford F-Series
Chevrolet Silverado
Toyota Camry
Honda Accord
Toyota Corolla
Honda Civic
Honda CR-V
Nissan Altima
Chevrolet Impala
Dodge Ram

Figure 6-4 Output of an array after removing duplicate values with the `array_unique()` function

The `array_unique()` function does not renumber the indexes after removing duplicate values in an array. For this reason, the preceding code includes a statement that uses the `array_values()` function to renumber the indexes in the `$TopSellers[]` array.

To modify MessageBoard.php to use the `array_unique()` function to remove duplicate messages in the Message Board script:

1. Reopen **MessageBoard.php** in your text editor.

2. Add the following code as a fourth case to the `switch()` statement. This case uses the `array_unique()` and `array_values()` functions to remove duplicate elements from the array.

```
case 'Remove Duplicates':
    $MessageArray = array_unique(
        $MessageArray);
    $MessageArray = array_values(
        $MessageArray);
    break;
```

3. Modify the paragraph element at the end of the file so it contains another anchor element that calls the MessageBoard.php file with the proper parameters to delete the duplicate messages, as follows:

```
<p>
<a href="PostMessage.php">
    Post New Message</a><br />
<a href=
    "MessageBoard.php?action=Remove%20Duplicates">
    Remove Duplicate Messages</a><br />
```

```
<a href="MessageBoard.php?action=Delete%20First">
    Delete First Message</a><br />
<a href="MessageBoard.php?action=Delete%20Last">
    Delete Last Message</a>
</p>
```

4. Save MessageBoard.php and upload the file to the Web server.

5. Open the PostMessage.php file in your Web browser by entering the following URL: *http://<yourserver>/PHP_Projects/Chapter.06/Chapter/PostMessage.php*. Add several new messages that contain identical information, and then click the **View Messages** link to display the Message Board page. You should see the duplicate messages. Click the **Remove Duplicate Messages** link to test the new code. Any duplicate versions of the same message should be deleted.

6. Close your Web browser window.

Short Quiz

1. What two functions are used to add or remove elements from the beginning of an array?

2. Briefly describe the `array_pop()` and `array_push()` functions.

3. What function is used to add a new element at any position in an array?

4. Explain the process of using the `array_splice()` function to delete an array element.

5. What function must be used in conjunction with the `array_unique()` function to renumber the indexes after the duplicates have been removed?

Declaring and Initializing Associative Arrays

As you know, PHP creates indexed arrays by default with a starting index of 0. For example, the following code uses the `array()` construct to create the indexed `$Provinces[]` array that you saw in Chapter 1:

```
$Provinces = array("Newfoundland and Labrador",
    "Prince Edward Island", "Nova Scotia",
    "New Brunswick", "Quebec", "Ontario",
    "Manitoba", "Saskatchewan", "Alberta",
    "British Columbia");
```

With associative arrays, you can use any alphanumeric keys that you want for the array elements. You specify an element's key by using the array operator (=>) in the array() construct. The syntax for declaring and initializing an associative array is as follows:

```
$array_name = array(key => value, ...);
```

For example, the following code creates an array named $ProvincialCapitals[], which contains the Canadian provinces and their capitals. The name of each province is used as the element key, and the name of each capital city is assigned as the element's value.

```
$ProvincialCapitals = array(
    "Newfoundland and Labrador" => "St. John's",
    "Prince Edward Island" => "Charlottetown",
    "Nova Scotia" => "Halifax",
    "New Brunswick" => "Fredericton",
    "Quebec" => "Quebec City",
    "Ontario" => "Toronto",
    "Manitoba" => "Winnipeg",
    "Saskatchewan" => "Regina",
    "Alberta"=>"Edmonton",
    "British Columbia" => "Victoria");
```

You can also use the following syntax to assign key values to an associative array by using array names and brackets. Note that when using this syntax, you use the standard assignment operator (=) and not the array operator (=>).

```
$ProvincialCapitals["Newfoundland and Labrador"]
    = "St. John's";
$ProvincialCapitals["Prince Edward Island"]
    = "Charlottetown";
$ProvincialCapitals["Nova Scotia"]
    = "Halifax";
...
```

The preceding syntax creates the array if it doesn't exist. If the array does exist, each assignment statement overwrites any existing elements that already use the same key or appends any new keys and values to the end of the array.

To refer to an element in an associative array, you place an element's key in single or double quotation marks inside the array brackets. The following code displays the capitals of Quebec and British Columbia:

```
echo "<p>The capital of Quebec is
    {$ProvincialCapitals['Quebec']}.</p>\n";
echo "<p>The capital of British Columbia is " .
    $ProvincialCapitals["British Columbia"] .
    ".</p>\n";
```

If you create an associative array and then add a new element without specifying a key, PHP automatically assumes that the array is indexed and assigns the new element an index of 0 or the next available integer. The following example declares and initializes an array named $TerritorialCapitals[], which contains the capitals of the Canadian territories. The first two statements assign keys to the first two elements in the array. However, because the third statement does not declare a key, the element is assigned a value of 0. Figure 6-5 shows the output of the print_r() function.

Associative arrays are best used when the array key provides additional information about the value of the array element. In the previous example, the key provided the name of the province for which the value was the name of the capital. When an array is a simple list of values, such as lines read from a text file, you should use an indexed array because there is not a key that provides additional information about the array element's value.

```
$TerritorialCapitals["Nunavut"] = "Iqaluit";
$TerritorialCapitals["Northwest Territories"]
    = "Yellowknife";
$TerritorialCapitals[] = "Whitehorse";
echo "<pre>\n";
print_r($TerritorialCapitals);
echo "</pre>\n";
```

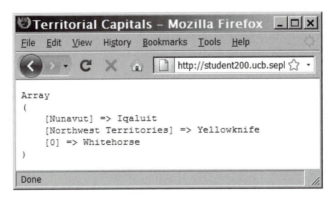

Figure 6-5   Output of an array with associative and indexed elements

The functionality of associative arrays also allows you to start the numbering of indexed arrays at any integer you want. For example, the following code uses the array() construct to declare and initialize an array named $Territories[] that contains just the names of the Canadian territories. Notice that only the first element uses the array operator (=>) to begin numbering at 1 instead of 0. The subsequent elements are automatically assigned the next available integer.

```
$Territories = array(1 => "Nunavut",
    "Northwest Territories", "Yukon Territory");
```

For the $Territories[] array created with the preceding statement, the first element is $Territories[1] ("Nunavut"), the second element is $Territories[2] ("Northwest Territories"), and the third element is $Territories[3] ("Yukon Territory"). You can also specify index values by using the array name and brackets as follows:

```
$Territories[1] = "Nunavut";
$Territories[2] = "Northwest Territories";
$Territories[3] = "Yukon Territory";
```

In many programming languages, if you declare an array and use a starting index other than 0, empty elements are created for each index between 0 and the index value you specify. In PHP, only the elements specified are created, regardless of the index. No empty elements are created. The following code shows another example of the $Territories[] array, but this time the starting index is 100. Because the second and third statements do not declare an index or key, the starting index of 100 is incremented by 1 and used as the index for the next two elements. However, as the count() function shows in Figure 6-6, the array consists of just three elements.

```
$Territories[100] = "Nunavut";
$Territories[] = "Northwest Territories";
$Territories[] = "Yukon Territory";
echo "<pre>\n";
print_r($Territories);
echo "</pre>\n";
echo '<p>The $Territories array consists of ',
    count($Territories), " elements.</p>\n";
```

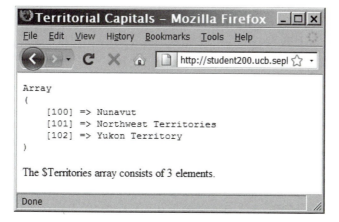

Figure 6-6 Output of an array with a starting index of 100

 Use the array_values() function to renumber an indexed array with a starting element of 0.

In the next exercise, the array returned with the file() function is converted to an associative array that uses the message subject as the key. Although the array will still be stored in the messages.txt file as an indexed array, you will use the associative version of the array later in this chapter to find and sort data in the messages.

To modify the MessageBoard.php file so that the array returned with the file() function is converted to an associative array:

1. Return to the **MessageBoard.php** file in your text editor.

2. Add the following for loop immediately after the $count declaration statement in the else clause. The for loop uses $MessageArray[], by way of $CurrMsg[], to build a new associative array named $KeyMessageArray[]. Again, the explode() function is used to split each line of $MessageArray[] into an array of message fields, which is stored in $CurrMsg[]. Notice that $KeyMessageArray[] uses the first element (index 0), the subject name, in $CurrMsg[] as the key name.

```
for ($i = 0; $i < $count; ++$i) {
    $CurrMsg = explode("~",
        $MessageArray[$i]);
    $KeyMessageArray[$CurrMsg[0]] =
        $CurrMsg[1] . "~" . $CurrMsg[2];
}
```

3. Add the following echo and print_r() statements immediately after the new for loop's closing brace. The print_r() function is only a temporary way of displaying the contents of $KeyMessageArray[] until you learn how to iterate through arrays in the next section.

```
echo "<pre>\n";
print_r($KeyMessageArray);
echo "</pre>\n";
```

4. Add a block comment around the echo statement for the opening <table> tag in the else clause.

5. Add block comments around the second for loop and echo statement for the closing </table> tag in the else clause. You will modify this for loop in the next exercise.

The else portion of your modified PHP script should appear as follows:

```php
else {
    $MessageArray =
        file("MessageBoard/messages.txt");
    /*
    echo "<table
        style=\"background-color:lightgray\"
        border=\"1\" width=\"100%\">\n";
    */
    $count = count($MessageArray);
    for ($i = 0; $i < $count; ++$i) {
        $CurrMsg = explode("~",
            $MessageArray[$i]);
        $KeyMessageArray[$CurrMsg[0]] =
            $CurrMsg[1] . "~" . $CurrMsg[2];
    }
    echo "<pre>\n";
    print_r($KeyMessageArray);
    echo "</pre>\n";
    /*
    for ($i = 0; $i < $count; ++$i) {
        $CurrMsg = explode("~",
            $MessageArray[$i]);
        echo "<tr>\n";
        echo "<td width=\"5%\"
            style=\"text-align:center;
            font-weight:bold\">" .
            ($i + 1) . "</td>\n";
        echo "<td width=\"85%\"><span
            style=\"font-weight:bold\">Subject:
            </span> " .
            htmlentities($CurrMsg[0]) .
            "<br />\n";
        echo "<span
            style=\"font-weight:bold\">Name:
            </span> " .
            htmlentities($CurrMsg[1]) .
            "<br />\n";
        echo "<span
            style=\"text-decoration:underline;
            font-weight:bold\">Message
            </span><br />\n" .
            htmlentities($CurrMsg[2]) .
            "</td>\n";
        echo "<td width=\"10%\"
            style=\"text-align:center\">" .
            "<a href='MessageBoard.php?" .
            "action=Delete%20Message&" .
            "message=$i'>" .
            "Delete This Message</a></td>\n";
        echo "</tr>\n";
    }
    echo "</table>\n";
    */
}
```

6. Save the MessageBoard.php file and upload it to the server.

7. Open the MessageBoard.php file in your Web browser by entering the following URL: *http://<yourserver>/ PHP_Projects/Chapter.06/Chapter/MessageBoard.php*. The print_r() function should output an associative version of the messages array. An example is shown in Figure 6-7.

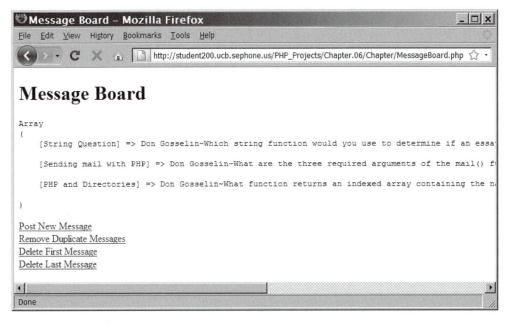

Figure 6-7   Output of the $KeyMessageArray associative array

8. Close your Web browser window.

Short Quiz

1. Describe the difference in assigning a key with an indexed array versus an associative array.

2. Explain what happens if you do not assign a key to an associative array.

3. Which operator is used to define associative array keys within the array() construct?

4. What function is used to determine the number of elements in an associative array?

5. If the statement `list[] = 'B';` immediately follows the statement `list[25] = 'A';`, what is the array index for the element whose value is 'B'?

Iterating Through an Array

In Chapter 2, you learned how to use a `foreach` statement to iterate through the elements in an array. As a refresher, the following example declares and initializes an indexed array named `$DaysOfWeek[]` and uses a `foreach` statement to iterate through it:

```
$DaysOfWeek = array("Sunday", "Monday",
      "Tuesday", "Wednesday", "Thursday",
      "Friday", "Saturday");
foreach ($DaysOfWeek as $Day) {
      echo "<p>$Day</p>\n";
}
```

Even though a `foreach` statement allows you to loop through the elements of an array, it does not change the position of the **internal array pointer**, a special type of variable that refers to the currently selected element in an array. The internal array pointer is a way of keeping track of which element you are working with in an array. Use the functions listed in Table 6-1 to iterate through an array with the internal array pointer.

Function	Description
current(*array*)	Returns the current array element
each(*array*)	Returns the key and value of the current array element and moves the internal array pointer to the next element
end(*array*)	Moves the internal array pointer to the last element
key(*array*)	Returns the key of the current array element
next(*array*)	Moves the internal array pointer to the next element
prev(*array*)	Moves the internal array pointer to the previous element
reset(*array*)	Resets the internal array pointer to the first element

Table 6-1   Array pointer iteration functions

As a simple example of how to use the iteration functions, the `next()` function in the following code moves the internal array pointer in the `$DaysOfWeek[]` array to the second array element ("Monday"), whereas the `end()` function moves the internal array pointer to the final array element ("Saturday"). The echo statements use the current() function to display the value of the element in the $DaysOfWeek[] array where the internal array pointer is located.

```
next($DaysOfWeek);
echo "<p>" . current($DaysOfWeek) . "</p>\n";
end($DaysOfWeek);
echo "<p>" . current($DaysOfWeek) . "</p>\n";
```

You might be wondering why you need iteration functions at all. Why not just use a foreach statement or other type of looping statement to iterate through an array? For indexed arrays, a looping statement is usually all you need to work with the elements in an array. However, because the keys in an associative array might not be in a predictable sequence, you can't always use a looping statement to determine which element you are currently working with in associative arrays. For example, consider the following code, in which a foreach statement is used to display the values in the $ProvincialCapitals[] array. To display an element key (which, in this case, contains the name of each province), you can use the key() function. However, the key() function only returns the key of the element at the location of the internal array pointer. Because the internal array pointer points to the first element by default, the following code displays the first element value ("Newfoundland and Labrador"), as shown in Figure 6-8:

For the Windows version of the PHP scripting engine, the key() function may not work properly within a foreach loop. Instead, you should use the advanced foreach syntax described in the next section.

```
$ProvincialCapitals = array(
    "Newfoundland and Labrador" => "St. John's",
    "Prince Edward Island" => "Charlottetown",
    "Nova Scotia" => "Halifax",
    "New Brunswick" => "Fredericton",
    "Quebec" => "Quebec City",
    "Ontario" => "Toronto",
    "Manitoba" => "Winnipeg",
    "Saskatchewan" => "Regina",
    "Alberta"=>"Edmonton",
    "British Columbia" => "Victoria");
foreach ($ProvincialCapitals as $Capital) {
    echo "The capital of " .
        key($ProvincialCapitals) .
        " is $Capital<br />\n";
}
```

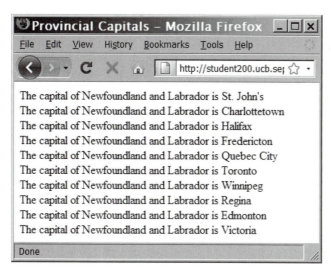

Figure 6-8 Output of an associative array without advancing the internal array pointer

One method to display the correct key for each element is to add the next() function. The following code causes the key to be displayed correctly, as shown in Figure 6-9:

```
foreach ($ProvincialCapitals as $Capital) {
    echo "The capital of " .
        key($ProvincialCapitals) .
        " is $Capital<br />\n";
    next($ProvincialCapitals);
}
```

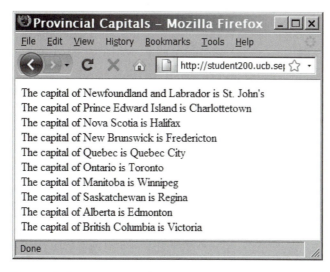

Figure 6-9 Output of an associative array while advancing the internal array pointer

If you use an iteration function to move the internal array pointer either before the first element or after the last element in an array, the only way to move the array pointer back to a valid element in the array is to use the reset() or end() functions.

325

To modify the MessageBoard.php file so it includes code that iterates through $KeyMessageArray[]:

1. Return to the **MessageBoard.php** file in your text editor.

2. Remove the echo statements for the <pre> and </pre> tags and the print_r() function. Remove the block comment around the echo statement for the <table> tag, and remove the block comments around the second for loop and the closing </table> tag from the else clause.

3. Between the two for loops, add the following statement to declare and initialize a variable named $Index. You will use the $Index variable to numerate the associative elements in $KeyMessageArray[].

   ```
   $Index = 1;
   ```

4. Modify the second for loop into the following foreach loop. Be sure to modify the portions of the code that are highlighted in bold and to add the next() statement to the end of the loop. Note that the indexes for the $CurrMsg array have changed from 1 to 0 and from 2 to 1.

```php
foreach($KeyMessageArray as $Message) {
    $CurrMsg = explode("~", $Message);
    echo "<tr>\n";
    echo "<td width=\"5%\"
        style=\"text-align:center\"><span
        style=\"font-weight:bold\">" .
        $Index . "</span></td>\n";
    echo "<td width=\"85%\"><span
        style=\"font-weight:bold\">
        Subject:</span> " .
        htmlentities(
            key($KeyMessageArray)) .
        "<br />";
    echo "<span style=\"font-weight:bold\">
        Name:</span> " .
        htmlentities($CurrMsg[0]) .
        "<br />";
    echo "<span
        style=\"text-decoration:underline;
        font-weight:bold\">
        Message</span><br />\n" .
        htmlentities($CurrMsg[1]) .
        "</td>\n";
    echo "<td width=\"10%\"
        style=\"text-align:center\">" .
        "<a href='MessageBoard.php?" .
        "action=Delete%20Message&" .
        "message=" . ($Index - 1) .
        "'>Delete This Message</a>" .
        "</td>\n";
```

```
        echo "</tr>\n";
        ++$Index;
        next($KeyMessageArray);
    }
```

5. Save the MessageBoard.php file and upload it to the server.

6. Open the MessageBoard.php file in your Web browser by entering the following URL: *http://<yourserver>/PHP_ Projects/Chapter.06/Chapter/MessageBoard.php*. The messages should display normally.

7. Close your Web browser window.

Another option for displaying the key and the element is to use the advanced foreach() syntax described in Chapter 2. You recall that the advanced syntax uses the array operator to separate the key and element values, as in the following example. The output will be the same as shown previously in Figure 6-9.

```
$ProvincialCapitals = array(
        "Newfoundland and Labrador" => "St. John's",
        "Prince Edward Island" => "Charlottetown",
        "Nova Scotia" => "Halifax",
        "New Brunswick" => "Fredericton",
        "Quebec" => "Quebec City",
        "Ontario" => "Toronto",
        "Manitoba" => "Winnipeg",
        "Saskatchewan" => "Regina",
        "Alberta"=>"Edmonton",
        "British Columbia" => "Victoria");
foreach ($ProvincialCapitals as $Province =>
        $Capital) {
        echo "The capital of $Province is
                $Capital<br />\n";
    }
```

Short Quiz

1. Describe the purpose of the internal array pointer.

2. Explain why you might need to use an internal array pointer when working with associative arrays.

3. What is the purpose of the key() function?

4. When using a foreach statement to iterate through the elements of an array, what function must be used to move to the next element in the array?

5. What two functions are used to move an internal array pointer to the beginning or end of an array?

Finding and Extracting Elements and Values

This section discusses methods for finding and extracting elements and values in an array. One of the most basic methods for finding a value in an array is to use a looping statement to iterate through the array until you find the value. For example, the for statement in the following code loops through the $HospitalDepts[] array to see if it contains "Neurology". If it does, a message displays and the break statement ends the for loop.

```
$HospitalDepts = array("Anesthesia",
    "Molecular Biology", "Neurology",
    "Pediatrics");
for ($i = 0; $i <= count($HospitalDepts); ++$i) {
    if ($HospitalDepts[$i] == "Neurology") {
        echo "<p>The hospital has a Neurology
            department.</p>\n";
        break;
    }
}
```

Rather than writing custom code like that in the preceding example, you can use functions that PHP provides for finding and extracting elements and values in an array.

Determining if a Value Exists

You can use the in_array() and array_search() functions to determine whether a value exists in an array. The in_array() function returns a Boolean value of TRUE if a given value exists in an array. The array_search() function determines whether a given value exists in an array, then returns the index or key of the first matching element if it exists or FALSE if it does not. Both functions accept two arguments: The first argument represents the value to search for (sometimes called the "needle"), and the second argument represents the name of the array in which to search (also called the "haystack"). For example, the following code uses the in_array() function to search for "Neurology" in the $HospitalDepts[] array. In this example, the in_array() function is used in an if statement's conditional expression to determine whether "Neurology" exists in the array.

```
if (in_array("Neurology", $HospitalDepts))
    echo "<p>The hospital has a Neurology
        department.</p>";
```

The following example demonstrates how to use the `array_search()` function with the `$TopSellers[]` array:

```
// This array is ordered by sales, high to low.
$TopSellers = array("Ford F-Series",
    "Chevrolet Silverado", "Toyota Camry",
    "Honda Accord", "Toyota Corolla",
    "Honda Civic", "Nissan Altima",
    "Chevrolet Impala", "Dodge Ram",
    "Honda CR-V");
$SearchVehicle = "Ford F-Series";
$Ranking = array_search($SearchVehicle,
    $TopSellers);
if ($Ranking !== FALSE) {
    ++$Ranking; // Convert the array index
        //      to the rank value
    echo "<p>The $SearchVehicle is ranked # " .
        $Ranking . " in sales for 2008.</p>\n";
}
else
    echo "<p>The $SearchVehicle is not one of
        the top ten selling vehicles for
        2008.</p>\n";
```

In the preceding code, the comparison statement in the `if` statement uses the strict not equal operator (`!==`). This operator is necessary because PHP equates a Boolean value of FALSE with 0, which is also the value that identifies the first element in an indexed array. The strict not equal operator determines whether the 0 value assigned to the `$Ranking` variable is really a Boolean value of FALSE or the index value of 0. Because "Ford F-Series" is in the first element of the array (which is identified with an index of 0), a numeric value of 0 (not a Boolean value of FALSE) is assigned to the `$Ranking` variable.

When you work with arrays, you should always ensure that your indexes or keys are unique. If you do not use unique values, multiple values will be assigned to the same array index. Because the Message Board script uses message subjects as element keys in the associative array that is displayed, you need to ensure that each subject is unique. Remember that although the MessageBoard.php script displays the message data using an associative array, the data is stored as individual lines in messages.txt that you convert to an indexed array using the `file()` function. Because the message subject is stored in an element in the array that is returned with the `file()` function, you use the `array_values()` function to check whether the subject exists as a value in the array.

To modify the Message Board script so that users can only enter unique subjects:

1. Open the **PostMessage.php** file in your text editor.

2. Add the following statements before the statement that declares and initializes the $MessageRecord variable. The first statement declares and initializes an empty array named $ExistingSubjects that you will use to determine whether a subject already exists. The if statement is very similar to the code in the MessageBoard.php file. First, the conditional expression checks whether the messages.txt file exists and if it is larger than 0 KB. If the condition evaluates to TRUE, the file() function assigns the text in messages.txt to $MessageArray[]. The for loop then explodes each element in $MessageArray[] into the $CurrMsg[] array. Finally, the subject, which is stored in $CurrMsg[0], is added to the $ExistingSubjects array.

```
$ExistingSubjects = array();
if (file_exists(
        "MessageBoard/messages.txt") &&
        filesize("MessageBoard/messages.txt")
        > 0) {
    $MessageArray = file(
        "MessageBoard/messages.txt");
    $count = count($MessageArray);
    for ($i = 0; $i < $count; ++$i) {
        $CurrMsg = explode("~",
            $MessageArray[$i]);
        $ExistingSubjects[] = $CurrMsg[0];
    }
}
```

3. Immediately after the preceding code, add the following if statement, which uses the in_array() function to determine if the entered subject is found in the $ExistingSubjects array. If the subject already exists, an error message is displayed and the $Subject variable is set to an empty string.

```
if (in_array($Subject, $ExistingSubjects)) {
    echo "<p>The subject you entered
        already exists!<br />\n";
    echo "Please enter a new subject and
        try again.<br />\n";
    echo "Your message was not saved.</p>";
    $Subject = "";
}
```

4. Add the following code shown in bold. These changes place the existing code, which saves the record to messages.txt, into an else clause for the preceding if statement. Add two new

lines to set the $Subject and $Message variables to an empty string if the message was successfully saved. The code should appear as follows, with the new code in bold:

```
else {
    $MessageRecord =
        "$Subject~$Name~$Message\n";
    $MessageFile = fopen(
        "MessageBoard/messages.txt",
        "ab");
    if ($MessageFile === false)
        echo "There was an error saving
            your message!\n";
    else {
        fwrite($MessageFile,
            $MessageRecord);
        fclose($MessageFile);
        echo "Your message has been
            saved.\n";
        $Subject = "";
        $Message = "";
    }
}
```

5. Just before the closing tag for the PHP code block, insert the following else clause to the if (isset($_POST['submit'])) statement. These lines clear out the $Subject, $Name, and $Message variables if there is no posted data.

```
else {
    $Subject = "";
    $Name = "";
    $Message = "";
}
```

The PHP code block should appear as follows:

```
<?php
if (isset($_POST['submit'])) {
    $Subject = stripslashes($_POST['subject']);
    $Name = stripslashes($_POST['name']);
    $Message = stripslashes($_POST['message']);
    // Replace any '~' characters
    //     with '-' characters
    $Subject = str_replace("~", "-", $Subject);
    $Name = str_replace("~", "-", $Name);
    $Message = str_replace("~", "-", $Message);
    $ExistingSubjects = array();
    if (file_exists(
        "MessageBoard/messages.txt") &&
        filesize("MessageBoard/messages.txt")
        > 0) {
```

331

```php
$MessageArray = file(
        "MessageBoard/messages.txt");
$count = count($MessageArray);
for ($i = 0; $i < $count; ++$i) {
        $CurrMsg = explode("~",
                $MessageArray[$i]);
        $ExistingSubjects[] = $CurrMsg[0];
    }
}
if (in_array($Subject, $ExistingSubjects)) {
        echo "<p>The subject you entered
            already exists!<br />\n";
        echo "Please enter a new subject and
            try again.<br />\n";
        echo "Your message was not saved.</p>";
        $Subject = "";
}
else {
        $MessageRecord =
            "$Subject~$Name~$Message\n";
        $MessageFile =
            fopen("MessageBoard/messages.txt",
            "ab");
        if ($MessageFile === FALSE)
            echo "There was an error saving your
                message!\n";
        else {
            fwrite($MessageFile, $MessageRecord);
            fclose($MessageFile);
            echo "Your message has been saved.\n";
            $Subject = "";
            $Message = "";
        }
    }
}
else {
    $Subject = "";
    $Name = "";
    $Message = "";
}
?>
```

6. Make the changes shown below in bold to convert the Web form into a sticky form.

```html
<span style="font-weight:bold">Subject:</span>
    <input type="text" name="subject"
    value="<?php echo $Subject; ?>" />
<span style="font-weight:bold">Name:</span>
    <input type="text" name="name"
    value="<?php echo $Name; ?>" /><br />
<textarea name="message" rows="6"
    cols="80"><?php echo $Message;
    ?></textarea><br />
```

7. Save the PostMessage.php file and upload it to the server.

8. Open the PostMessage.php file in your Web browser by entering the following URL: *http://<yourserver>/PHP_Projects/ Chapter.06/Chapter/PostMessage.php*. Add a new message. Try adding another message with exactly the same subject as the message you just entered. You should see a message in the Post Message form handler page informing you that the subject already exists. Figure 6-10 shows an attempt to post another message with the subject "String Question". Notice that the Subject field has been cleared because of the error, but the other fields have been maintained.

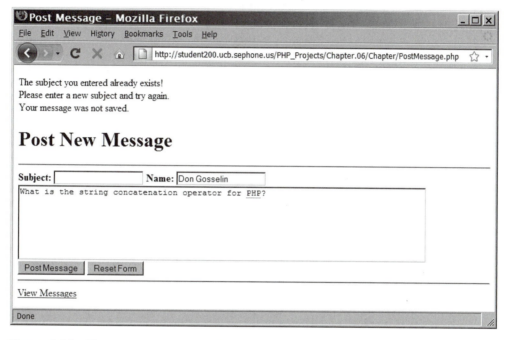

Figure 6-10   The error message for a duplicated subject when posting a new message

9. Close your Web browser window.

Determining if a Key Exists

In addition to determining whether a specific value exists in an array, you can also use the `array_key_exists()` function to determine whether a given index or key exists. You pass two arguments to the `array_key_exists()` function: The first argument represents the key to search for (the needle), and the second argument represents the name of the array in which to search (the haystack). As an example, suppose you develop an online chat room in which only members can post messages. Each visitor selects a "screen name" when he or she joins. Now suppose that the screen name is an element's key in an associative array, and the name of the member who selected the screen name is the element's value. Before assigning a member to a particular screen name in the array, you could use the array_key_exists() function to determine whether another member has already selected that screen name. The following code shows some screen names that are assigned to an array named $ScreenNames[]. Before allowing a new member to have the screen name "Fat Man," the if statement uses the array_key_exists() function to determine whether the array element already exists.

```
$ScreenNames["Dancer"] = "Daryl";
$ScreenNames["Fat Man"] = "Dennis";
$ScreenNames["Assassin"] = "Jennifer";
if (array_key_exists("Fat Man", $ScreenNames))
    echo "<p>{$ScreenNames['Fat Man']} is
        already 'Fat Man'.</p>\n";
else {
    $ScreenNames["Fat Man"] = "Don";
    echo "<p>{$ScreenNames['Fat Man']} is now
        'Fat Man'.</p>";
}
```

You can use the array_keys() function to return an indexed array that contains all the keys in an associative array, as shown in the following example. A new indexed array named $UsedScreenNames[], which contains the keys from the $ScreenNames[] array, is created with the array_keys() function. A for loop then displays the values in the $UsedScreenNames[] array.

```
$ScreenNames["Dancer"] = "Daryl";
$ScreenNames["Fat Man"] = "Dennis";
$ScreenNames["Assassin"] = "Jennifer";
$UsedScreenNames = array_keys($ScreenNames);
echo "<p>The following screen names are already
    assigned:</p>\n";
for ($i = 0; $i < count($UsedScreenNames);
    ++$i) {
    echo "<p>{$UsedScreenNames[$i]}</p>\n";
}
```

You can also pass a second argument to the array_keys() function that specifies an element value for which to search. These keys are returned only for elements that match the specified value.

Returning a Portion of an Array

You use the array_slice() function to return (copy) a portion of an array and assign it to another array. The syntax for the function is array_slice(*array_name*, *start_index*, *number_to_return*);.

The *array_name* argument indicates the name of the array from which you want to extract elements. The *start_index* argument indicates the start position within the array to begin extracting elements. The `number_to_return` argument is an integer value that indicates the number of elements to return from the array, starting with the element indicated by the `start_index` argument. The syntax for returning a portion of an array with the `array_slice()` function is very similar to the syntax for deleting a portion of an array with the `array_splice()` function. The main difference is that the `array_splice()` function removes elements, while the `array_slice()` function returns an array containing those elements.

The following example demonstrates how to use the `array_slice()` function to return the first five elements in the `$TopSellers[]` array. The elements are assigned to a new element named `$FiveTopSellers[]`. Figure 6-11 shows the output.

```
// This array is ordered by sales, high to low.
$TopSellers = array("Ford F-Series",
     "Chevrolet Silverado", "Toyota Camry",
     "Honda Accord", "Toyota Corolla",
     "Honda Civic", "Nissan Altima",
     "Chevrolet Impala", "Dodge Ram",
     "Honda CR-V");
$FiveTopSellers = array_slice($TopSellers, 0, 5);
echo "<p>The five best-selling vehicles for
     2008 are:</p>\n";
for ($i = 0; $i < count($FiveTopSellers); ++$i) {
     echo "{$FiveTopSellers[$i]}<br />\n";
}
```

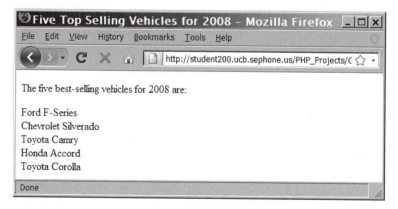

Figure 6-11 Output of an array returned with the `array_slice()` function

Short Quiz

1. Differentiate between the value returned by the `in_array()` function and the `array_search()` function.

2. What function can be used to return an indexed array of all keys in an associative array?

3. What does the `array_key_exists()` function do?

4. What function is used to return a portion of an array and assign it to another array?

Manipulating Arrays

In the preceding section, you studied techniques for working with the individual elements in an array. In this section, you will study techniques for manipulating entire arrays, including how to sort, combine, and compare arrays.

Sorting Arrays

You sort arrays using the functions listed in Table 6-2.

Function	Description
`array_multisort(array[, array, ...])`	Sorts multiple arrays or multidimensional arrays
`arsort(array[, SORT_REGULAR | SORT_NUMERIC | SORT_STRING])`	Sorts an array in descending order (largest to smallest) by value and maintains the existing keys for an associative array
`asort(array[, SORT_REGULAR | SORT_NUMERIC | SORT_STRING])`	Sorts an array in ascending order (smallest to largest) by value and maintains the existing keys for an associative array
`krsort(array[, SORT_REGULAR | SORT_NUMERIC | SORT_STRING])`	Sorts an array in descending order by key and maintains the existing keys for an associative array
`ksort(array[, SORT_REGULAR | SORT_NUMERIC | SORT_STRING])`	Sorts an array in ascending order by key and maintains the existing keys for an associative array
`natcasesort(array)`	Performs a case-sensitive natural order sort by value and maintains the existing keys for an associative array
`natsort(array)`	Performs a case-insensitive natural order sort by value and maintains the existing keys for an associative array

Table 6-2   Array sorting functions *(continues)*

(continued)

Function	Description
rsort(*array*[, SORT_REGULAR | SORT_NUMERIC | SORT_STRING])	Sorts an array in descending order by value, removes any existing keys for an associative array, and renumbers the indexes starting with 0
sort(*array*[, SORT_REGULAR | SORT_NUMERIC | SORT_STRING])	Sorts an array in ascending order by value, removes any existing keys for an associative array, and renumbers the indexes starting with 0
uaksort(*array*[, *comparison_function*])	Sorts an array in ascending order by value using a comparison function and maintains the existing keys for an associative array
uksort(*array*[, *comparison_function*])	Sorts an array in ascending order by key using a comparison function and maintains the existing keys for an associative array
usort(*array*[, *comparison_function*])	Sorts an array in ascending order by value using a comparison function, removes any existing keys for an associative array, and renumbers the indexes starting with 0

Table 6-2 Array sorting functions

The most commonly used array sorting functions are sort() and rsort() for indexed arrays, and asort(), arsort(), ksort(), and krsort() for associative arrays. These functions operate directly on an array, not on a new copy of an array, as occurs with the array_values() function. This means that you can execute each function simply by passing the name of an array to it.

The two "natural order" sort functions, natsort() and natcasesort(), use a special sorting algorithm. Rather than sorting only on the ASCII values of the corresponding characters, the algorithm treats one or more successive numeric characters as an integer value and sorts by integer value. For example, consider the following array of message filenames:

```
$MessageFiles = array(
        "message5.txt",
        "message3.txt",
        "message6.txt",
        "message1.txt",
        "message9.txt",
        "message4.txt",
        "message7.txt",
        "message2.txt",
        "message8.txt",
        "message10.txt");
```

If you used the sort() function on this array, the values would appear in the order "message1.txt", "message10.txt", "message2.txt", ..., "message9.txt". Although this ordering is correct when looking at the ASCII values, it is not the expected result. If you used the natsort() function instead, the values would appear in the order "message1.txt", "message2.txt", ..., "message9.txt", "message10.txt", because "10" is a larger numeric value than any of the other numeric values.

Keep in mind that the sort function you use depends on whether you need to sort an indexed or associative array. For example, the sort() and rsort() functions sort indexed arrays and renumber the element indexes. The following code demonstrates how to sort the indexed $FiveTopSellers array in ascending and descending order. Figure 6-12 shows the output.

```php
// This array is ordered by sales, high to low.
$TopSellers = array("Ford F-Series",
     "Chevrolet Silverado", "Toyota Camry",
     "Honda Accord", "Toyota Corolla",
     "Honda Civic", "Nissan Altima",
     "Chevrolet Impala", "Dodge Ram",
     "Honda CR-V");
$FiveTopSellers = array_slice($TopSellers, 0, 5);
echo "<p>The five best-selling vehicles for 2008
     by number of vehicles sold are:</p>\n";
for ($i = 0; $i < count($FiveTopSellers); ++$i) {
     echo "{$FiveTopSellers[$i]}<br />\n";
}
echo "</p>";
sort($FiveTopSellers);
echo "<p> The five best-selling vehicles for 2008
     in alphabetical order are:</p><p>";
for ($i = 0; $i < count($FiveTopSellers); ++$i) {
     echo "{$FiveTopSellers[$i]}<br />";
}
echo "</p>";
rsort($FiveTopSellers);
echo "<p>The five best-selling vehicles for 2008
     in reverse alphabetical order are:</p><p>";
for ($i = 0; $i < count($FiveTopSellers); ++$i) {
     echo "{$FiveTopSellers[$i]}<br />";
}
echo "</p>";
```

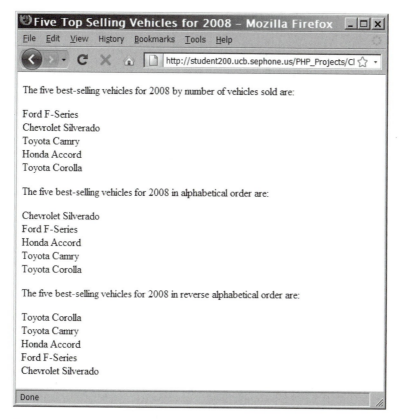

Figure 6-12 Output of an array after applying the sort() and rsort() functions

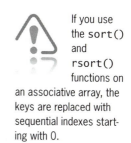

If you use the sort() and rsort() functions on an associative array, the keys are replaced with sequential indexes starting with 0.

To modify MessageBoard.php to use the sort() function to sort the messages in the Message Board script by subject in ascending order:

1. Reopen **MessageBoard.php** in your text editor.

2. Add the following code as a fifth case to the switch() statement. This case uses the sort() function to sort the array in ascending order.

```
case 'Sort Ascending':
    sort($MessageArray);
    break;
```

3. Modify the paragraph element at the end of the file so that it contains another anchor element that calls the MessageBoard.php file with the proper parameters to sort the messages in ascending order, as follows:

```
<p>
<a href="PostMessage.php">
    Post New Message</a><br />
<a href=
    "MessageBoard.php?action=Sort%20Ascending">
    Sort Subjects A-Z</a><br />
<a href=
    "MessageBoard.php?action=Remove%20Duplicates">
    Remove Duplicate Messages</a><br />
<a href="MessageBoard.php?action=Delete%20First">
    Delete First Message</a><br />
<a href="MessageBoard.php?action=Delete%20Last">
    Delete Last Message</a>
</p>
```

4. Save the MessageBoard.php file and upload it to the Web server.

5. Open the MessageBoard.php file in your Web browser by entering the following URL: *http://<yourserver>/PHP_Projects/Chapter.06/Chapter/MessageBoard.php*. Click the **Sort Subjects A-Z** link to test the new code. The message list should sort by subject in ascending order.

6. Close your Web browser window.

The following code includes a statement that uses the sort() function on the $ProvincialCapitals[] array you saw earlier. Recall that with this array, province names are used as element keys. However, the sort() function in the following code replaces the keys with indexes, as shown in Figure 6-13.

```
$ProvincialCapitals = array(
    "Newfoundland and Labrador" => "St. John's",
    "Prince Edward Island" => "Charlottetown",
    "Nova Scotia" => "Halifax",
    "New Brunswick" => "Fredericton",
    "Quebec" => "Quebec City",
    "Ontario" => "Toronto",
    "Manitoba" => "Winnipeg",
    "Saskatchewan" => "Regina",
    "Alberta" => "Edmonton",
    "British Columbia" => "Victoria");
sort($ProvincialCapitals);
echo "<pre>\n";
print_r($ProvincialCapitals);
echo "</pre>\n";
```

Figure 6-13 Output of an associative array after sorting with the `sort()` function

To sort an associative array by value and maintain the existing keys, you use the `asort()` function, as follows:

```
asort($ProvincialCapitals);
echo "<pre>\n";
print_r($ProvincialCapitals);
echo "</pre>\n";
```

The `asort()` function in the preceding code sorts the values and maintains the existing keys, as shown in Figure 6-14.

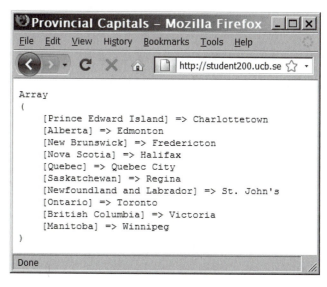

Figure 6-14 Output of an associative array after sorting with the `asort()` function

To perform a reverse sort on an associative array and maintain the existing keys, be sure to use the `arsort()` function, not the `rsort()` function. The following statement demonstrates how to perform a reverse sort on the `$ProvincialCapitals[]` array:

```
arsort($ProvincialCapitals);
```

To sort an associative array by key and maintain the existing keys, you use the `ksort()` function, as follows:

```
ksort($ProvincialCapitals);
echo "<pre>\n";
print_r($ProvincialCapitals);
echo "</pre>\n";
```

The `ksort()` function in the preceding code sorts and maintains the existing keys, as shown in Figure 6-15.

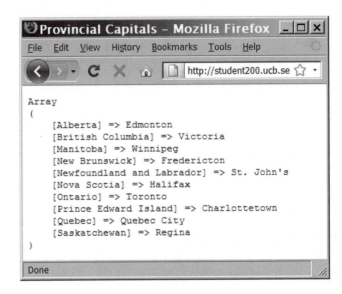

Figure 6-15 Output of an associative array after sorting with the `ksort()` function

To perform a reverse sort on an associative array by key and maintain the existing keys, use the `krsort()` function. The following statement demonstrates how to perform a reverse sort on the `$ProvincialCapitals[]` array:

```
krsort($ProvincialCapitals);
```

To modify MessageBoard.php to use the `rsort()` function to sort the messages in the Message Board script by subject in descending order:

1. Reopen **MessageBoard.php** in your text editor.

2. Add the following code as a sixth case to the `switch()` statement. This case uses the `rsort()` function to sort the array in descending order.

```
case 'Sort Descending':
    rsort($MessageArray);
    break;
```

3. Modify the paragraph element at the end of the file so that it contains another anchor element that calls the MessageBoard.php file with the proper parameters to sort the messages in descending order, as follows:

```
<p>
<a href="PostMessage.php">
    Post New Message</a><br />
<a href=
    "MessageBoard.php?action=Sort%20Ascending">
    Sort Subjects A-Z</a><br />
<a href=
    "MessageBoard.php?action=Sort%20Descending">
    Sort Subjects Z-A</a><br />
<a href=
    "MessageBoard.php?action=Remove%20Duplicates">
    Remove Duplicate Messages</a><br />
<a href="MessageBoard.php?action=Delete%20First">
    Delete First Message</a><br />
<a href="MessageBoard.php?action=Delete%20Last">
    Delete Last Message</a>
</p>
```

4. Save the MessageBoard.php file and upload it to the Web server.

5. Open the MessageBoard.php file in your Web browser by entering the following URL: *http://<yourserver>/PHP_ Projects/Chapter.06/Chapter/MessageBoard.php*. Click the **Sort Subjects Z-A** link to test the new code. The message list should sort by subject in descending order.

6. Close your Web browser window.

You can use the `shuffle()` function to randomize the order of array elements. The `shuffle()` function removes any existing keys from an associative array, and renumbers the indexes starting with 0.

Combining Arrays

If you want to combine arrays, you have two options. You can either append one array to another or merge the two arrays. To append one array to another, you use the addition (+) or additive compound assignment operator (+=). Unlike in arithmetic addition, order is important when appending one array to another array. The array on the left side of the operator is the **primary array**, or the array that PHP starts with. The array on the right side of the operator is the

secondary array, or the array being appended to the primary array. When you use either operator, PHP ignores any array elements in the secondary array where the indexes or keys already exist in the primary array. Because indexed arrays start at 0 by default, the addition operators are not an effective way of merging indexed arrays. This method works well for associative arrays, as long as none of the associative array keys of one array is found in the other array.

To help illustrate that addition operators do not work well for indexed arrays, consider the following code, which declares and initializes $Provinces[] and $Territories[] as indexed arrays. The $Territories[] array is appended to the $Provinces[] array with the addition (+) operator, and the resulting array is assigned to an array named $Canada[]. However, notice in Figure 6-16 that the $Canada[] array only contains the elements that were assigned to the $Provinces[] array. This occurs because the three indexes in the $Territories[] array (0, 1, and 2) already exist in the $Provinces[] array and are therefore ignored.

```
$Provinces = array("Newfoundland and Labrador",
    "Prince Edward Island", "Nova Scotia",
    "New Brunswick", "Quebec", "Ontario",
    "Manitoba", "Saskatchewan", "Alberta",
    "British Columbia");
$Territories = array("Nunavut",
    "Northwest Territories", "Yukon Territory");
$Canada = $Provinces + $Territories;
echo "<pre>\n";
print_r($Canada);
echo "</pre>\n";
```

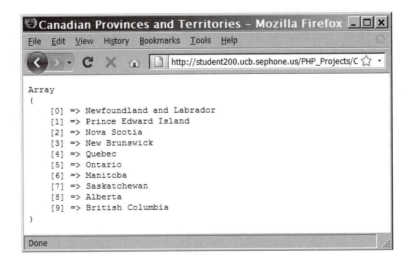

Figure 6-16   Output of two indexed arrays combined with the addition operator

In comparison, the following code declares and initializes
$ProvincialCapitals[] and $TerritorialCapitals[] as associative arrays. The $TerritorialCapitals[] array is appended to the
$ProvincialCapitals[] array with the addition (+) operator, and the
resulting array is assigned to an array named $CanadianCapitals[].
Because the keys in the $TerritorialCapitals[] array do not
exist in the $ProvincialCapitals[] array, the elements in the
$TerritorialCapitals[] array are successfully appended to the elements in the $ProvincialCapitals[] array, as shown in Figure 6-17.

```
$ProvincialCapitals = array(
    "Newfoundland and Labrador" => "St. John's",
    "Prince Edward Island" => "Charlottetown",
    "Nova Scotia" => "Halifax",
    "New Brunswick" => "Fredericton",
    "Quebec" => "Quebec City",
    "Ontario" => "Toronto",
    "Manitoba" => "Winnipeg",
    "Saskatchewan" => "Regina",
    "Alberta"=>"Edmonton",
    "British Columbia" => "Victoria");
$TerritorialCapitals = array(
    "Nunavut" => "Iqaluit",
    "Northwest Territories" => "Yellowknife",
    "Yukon Territory" => "Whitehorse");
$CanadianCapitals = $ProvincialCapitals +
    $TerritorialCapitals;
echo "<pre>\n";
print_r($CanadianCapitals);
echo "</pre>\n";
```

Figure 6-17 Output of two associative arrays combined with the addition operator

You can also combine two arrays with the compound assignment operator (+=), as follows:

```
$CanadianCapitals += $ProvincialCapitals;
$CanadianCapitals += $TerritorialCapitals;
```

Instead of appending one array to another, you can merge two or more arrays with the array_merge() function. The syntax for the function is *$new_array* = array_merge(*array1*, *array2* [, *array3*, ...]);. The array1 array is copied to the $new_array array, then the array2 array is appended to *$new_array*, then the array3 array is appended to $new_array, and so on. If you use the array_merge() function with associative arrays, the keys in the array you are appending overwrite any duplicate keys from previously merged arrays. With indexed arrays, all elements in one array are appended to another array and renumbered. The following statement demonstrates how to combine the associative $ProvincialCapitals[] and $TerritorialCapitals[] arrays:

```
$CanadianCapitals = array_merge(
    $ProvincialCapitals,
    $TerritorialCapitals);
```

The following code demonstrates how to combine the indexed $Provinces[] and $Territories[] arrays. In contrast to the examples that used the addition (+) and additive compound assignment (+=) operators, this version successfully combines both arrays, renumbers the indexes, and stores the result in the $Canada[] array, as shown in Figure 6-18.

```
$Provinces = array("Newfoundland and Labrador",
    "Prince Edward Island", "Nova Scotia",
    "New Brunswick", "Quebec", "Ontario",
    "Manitoba", "Saskatchewan", "Alberta",
    "British Columbia");
$Territories = array("Nunavut",
    "Northwest Territories", "Yukon Territory");
$Canada = array_merge($Provinces, $Territories);
echo "<pre>\n";
print_r($Canada);
echo "</pre>\n";
```

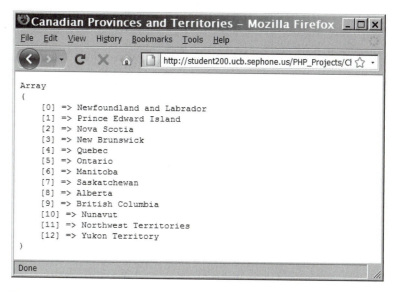

Figure 6-18 Output of two indexed arrays combined with the `array_merge()` function

In addition to appending and merging the elements in two arrays, you can create a new associative array that uses the values from one array as keys and element values from another array. To do this, you use the `array_combine()` function. For example, the following code declares a `$Territories[]` array and a `TerritorialCapitals[]` array and then combines the two arrays into a new array named `$CanadianTerritories[]`.

```
$Territories = array("Nunavut",
     "Northwest Territories",
     "Yukon Territory");
$TerritorialCapitals = array("Iqaluit",
     "Yellowknife", "Whitehorse");
$CanadianTerritories = array_combine(
     $Territories, $TerritorialCapitals);
```

To add the `array_combine()` function to the MessageBoard.php file to create a new associative array:

1. Return to the **MessageBoard.php** file in your text editor.

2. Modify the `for` loop in the `else` clause as follows. The second and third statements in the loop create two separate arrays: `$KeyArray[]` and `$ValueArray[]`. The third statement then uses the `array_combine()` function to create `$KeyMessageArray[]`.

```
        for ($i = 0; $i < $count; ++$i) {
            $CurrMsg = explode("~", $MessageArray[$i]);
            $KeyArray[] = $CurrMsg[0];
            $ValueArray[] = $CurrMsg[1]. "~" .
                $CurrMsg[2];
            $KeyMessageArray = array_combine($KeyArray,
                $ValueArray);
        }
```

3. Save the MessageBoard.php file.

4. Open the MessageBoard.php file in your Web browser by entering the following URL: *http://<yourserver>/PHP_Projects/Chapter.06/Chapter/MessageBoard.php*. The message list should look the same as it did before you added the array_combine() function.

5. Close your Web browser window.

Comparing Arrays

PHP includes several functions for comparing the contents of two or more arrays. Two of the most basic comparison functions are array_diff() and array_intersect(). The array_diff() function returns an array of elements that exist in one array but not in any other arrays to which it is compared. The syntax for the array_diff() function is $new_array = array_diff(array1, array2 [, array3, ...]);. A new array is returned containing elements that exist in $array1 but do not exist in any of the other array arguments. Keys and indexes are not renumbered in the new array. As an example, consider the following code, which declares and initializes an array named $Top10inArea[] that contains the names of the 10 largest countries in area, and another array named $Top10inPopulation[] that contains the names of the 10 largest countries in population. The array_diff() function determines which of the most populous countries are not the largest countries by comparing the values in the $Top10inPopulation[] and $Top10inArea[] arrays, and assigns the difference to the $Result[] array. The array_values() statement then renumbers the indexes in the $Result[] array. The $Result[] array contains the five countries shown in Figure 6-19; these countries are among the largest in population, but not in area.

```
$Top10inArea = array("Russia", "China",
    "Canada", "United States", "Brazil",
    "Australia", "India", "Argentina",
    "Kazakhstan", "Algeria");
$Top10inPopulation = array("China", "India",
    "United States", "Indonesia", "Brazil",
    "Pakistan", "Bangladesh", "Russia",
    "Nigeria", "Japan");
```

```
$Result = array_diff($Top10inPopulation,
    $Top10inArea);
$Result = array_values($Result);
echo "<p>The following of the most populous
    countries are not also the largest in
    area:</p>\n";
echo "<p>\n";
for ($i = 0; $i < count($Result); ++$i) {
    echo "{$Result[$i]}<br />\n";
}
echo "</p>\n";
```

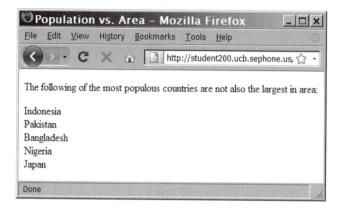

Figure 6-19 Output of an array created with the `array_diff()` function

The `array_intersect()` function returns an array of the
elements that are common to all of the arrays that are
compared. The syntax for the `array_intersect()` function is
new_array = array_intersect(*array1, array2* [, *array3, ...*]);.
As with the `array_diff()` function, keys and indexes are not renumbered in the new array, so you must use the `array_values()` function to renumber an indexed array. The following code uses the
`array_intersect()` function on the same `$Top10inArea[]` and
`$Top10inPopulation[]` arrays. The output in Figure 6-20 shows the
names of the five countries that are among the largest in both area
and population.

```
$Result = array_intersect($Top10inPopulation,
    $Top10inArea);
$Result = array_values($Result);
echo "<p>The following of the most populous
    countries are also among the largest in
    area:</p>\n";
echo "<p>\n";
for ($i = 0; $i < count($Result); ++$i) {
    echo "{$Result[$i]}<br />\n";
}
echo "</p>\n";
```

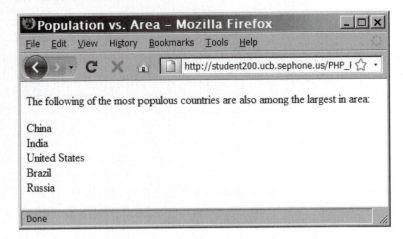

Figure 6-20   Output of an array created with the `array_intersect()` function

---

Short Quiz

1. Explain the difference between the `sort()` and `asort()` functions.

2. What is the purpose of the `ksort()` and `krsort()` functions?

3. What are the two methods of combining arrays?

4. Explain the difference between the `array_diff()` and `array_intersect()` functions.

Understanding Multidimensional Arrays

The arrays you have created so far are known as one-dimensional arrays because they consist of a single index or key. You can also create **multidimensional arrays** that consist of multiple indexes or keys. The procedures for creating multidimensional arrays are essentially the same as for indexed and associative arrays. However, to avoid confusion, you will first learn how to create indexed multidimensional arrays.

Creating Two-Dimensional Indexed Arrays

The most common type of multidimensional array is a **two-dimensional** array, which has two sets of indexes or keys. To understand how a two-dimensional array works, first consider the following one-dimensional indexed array named `$Gallons[]` that converts gallons to various other measures of volume:

```
$Gallons = array(
      128, // ounces
      16, // cups
      8, // pints
      4 // quarts
);
```

This single-dimensional array works fine if you only need to store a single set of volume conversions. However, what if you want to store additional volume conversions, such as quarts to cups? Table 6-3 lists conversion rates for each of the measures of volume in the preceding example.

	Ounces	Cups	Pints	Quarts	Gallons
Ounces	1	0.125	0.0625	0.03125	0.0078125
Cups	8	1	0.5	0.25	0.0625
Pints	16	2	1	0.5	0.125
Quarts	32	4	2	1	0.25
Gallons	128	16	8	4	1

Table 6-3   Volume conversion table

The first set of indexes (or keys) in a two-dimensional array determines the number of rows in the array, and the second set of indexes (or keys) determines the number of columns. The easiest way to create a two-dimensional array is to first create individual arrays for each of the rows the array will include. The following statements declare and initialize individual indexed arrays for each of the rows in Table 6-3:

```
$Ounces = array(1, 0.125, 0.0625, 0.03125,
      0.0078125);
$Cups = array(8, 1, 0.5, 0.25, 0.0625);
$Pints = array(16, 2, 1, 0.5, 0.125);
$Quarts = array(32, 4, 2, 1, 0.25);
$Gallons = array(128, 16, 8, 4, 1);
```

A multidimensional array in PHP is essentially "an array of arrays." To declare and initialize a multidimensional array with the preceding data, you include each of the array names as an element value in a new declaration. For example, the following statement uses each of the preceding array names to declare and initialize a two-dimensional indexed array named `$VolumeConversions[]`:

```
$VolumeConversions = array($Ounces, $Cups,
        $Pints, $Quarts, $Gallons);
```

You refer to the values in a multidimensional indexed array by including two sets of brackets following the array name with the syntax *array_name*[*index*][*index*]. The first set of brackets refers to the row, and the second set of brackets refers to the column. Table 6-4 illustrates the elements and index numbers in the `$VolumeConversions` array.

	0 (Ounces)	1 (Cups)	2 (Pints)	3 (Quarts)	4 (Gallons)
0 (Ounces)	1	0.125	0.0625	0.03125	0.0078125
1 (Cups)	8	1	0.5	0.25	0.0625
2 (Pints)	16	2	1	0.5	0.125
3 (Quarts)	32	4	2	1	0.25
4 (Gallons)	128	16	8	4	1

Table 6-4   Elements and indexes in the `$VolumeConversions[]` array

To access the conversion value from quarts to cups, you refer to the fourth row (index 3) and second column (index 1) of the `$VolumeConversions[]` array as follows: `$VolumeConversions[3][1]`. The following statement displays the conversion value from quarts to cups:

```
echo "<p>1 quart converts to " .
        $VolumeConversions[3][1] . " cups.</p>\n";
```

Use the same format to set or modify an element value in a two-dimensional indexed array. The following statement demonstrates how to set the conversion value for cups (row index 1) to quarts (column index 3):

```
$ConversionValues[1][3] = 0.25;
```

To add an indexed two-dimensional array to the MessageBoard.php file for displaying the contents of the messages.txt file:

1. Return to the **MessageBoard.php** file in your text editor.

2. Replace the first `for` loop in the `else` clause with the following `foreach` loop. This construct loops through `$MessageArray[]` and explodes each element into the `$CurrMsg[]` array. Notice that the last statement in the loop assigns the `$CurrMsg[]` array to `$KeyMessageArray[]`,

which creates a two-dimensional array. Because the $KeyMessageArray[] statement includes two array brackets at the end of the array name, each subsequent value in $CurrMsg[] is appended to $KeyMessageArray[].

```
foreach ($MessageArray as $Message) {
    $CurrMsg = explode("~", $Message);
    $KeyMessageArray[] = $CurrMsg;
}
```

3. Delete the following statement:

```
$Index = 1;
```

4. Modify the second `foreach` loop at the end of the `else` clause into the following `for` loop. The $i variable is used for looping through the elements in the first dimension of the array. However, because each "row" in the two-dimensional $KeyMessageArray[] only contains three elements (subject, name, and message), the second dimension is referred to using literal values.

```
for ($i = 0; $i < $count; ++$i) {
    echo "<tr>\n";
    echo "<td width=\"5%\"
        style=\"text-align:center\"><span
        style=\"font-weight:bold\">" .
        ($i + 1) . "</span></td>\n";
    echo "<td width=\"85%\"><span
        style=\"font-weight:bold\">
        Subject:</span> " .
        htmlentities(
            $KeyMessageArray[$i][0]) .
        "<br />";
    echo "<span style=\"font-weight:bold\">
        Name:</span> " . htmlentities(
            $KeyMessageArray[$i][1]) .
        "<br />";
    echo "<span style=\"font-weight:bold;
        text-decoration:underline\">
        Message</span><br />" .
        htmlentities(
        $KeyMessageArray[$i][2]) .
        "</td>\n";
    echo "<td width=\"10%\"
        style=\"text-align:center\"><a
        href='MessageBoard.php?" .
        "action=Delete%20Message&" .
        "message=$i'>Delete This
        Message</a></td>\n";
    echo "</tr>\n";
}
```

The if...else statement of the completed script should appear as follows:

```
if ((!file_exists("MessageBoard/messages.txt"))
    || (filesize("MessageBoard/messages.txt")
    == 0))
    echo "<p>There are no messages
        posted.</p>\n";
else {
    $MessageArray =
        file("MessageBoard/messages.txt");
    echo "<table
        style=\"background-color:lightgray\"
        border=\"1\" width=\"100%\">\n";
    $count = count($MessageArray);
    foreach ($MessageArray as $Message) {
    $CurrMsg = explode("~", $Message);
    $KeyMessageArray[] = $CurrMsg;
}
for ($i = 0; $i < $count; ++$i) {
    echo "<tr>\n";
    echo "<td width=\"5%\"
        style=\"text-align:center\"><span
        style=\"font-weight:bold\">" .
        ($i + 1) . "</span></td>\n";
    echo "<td width=\"85%\"><span
        style=\"font-weight:bold\">
        Subject:</span> " .
        htmlentities(
            $KeyMessageArray[$i][0]) .
        "<br />";
    echo "<span style=\"font-weight:bold\">
        Name:</span> " . htmlentities(
            $KeyMessageArray[$i][1]) .
        "<br />";
    echo "<span style=\"font-weight:bold;
        text-decoration:underline\">
        Message</span><br />" .
        htmlentities(
        $KeyMessageArray[$i][2]) .
        "</td>\n";
    echo "<td width=\"10%\"
        style=\"text-align:center\"><a
        href='MessageBoard.php?" .
        "action=Delete%20Message&" .
        "message=$i'>Delete This
        Message</a></td>\n";
    echo "</tr>\n";
}
    echo "</table>\n";
}
```

5. Save the MessageBoard.php file and upload it to the Web server.

6. Open the MessageBoard.php file in your Web browser by entering the following URL: *http://<yourserver>/PHP_Projects/Chapter.06/Chapter/MessageBoard.php*. The message list should look the same as it did before you added the two-dimensional array.

7. Close your Web browser window.

Creating Two-Dimensional Associative Arrays

The following statements declare the same volume conversion arrays you saw earlier, but this time as associative arrays. The primary difference in creating two-dimensional associative arrays is that you need to specify the key for each element:

```
$Ounces = array("ounces" => 1, "cups" => 0.125,
     "pints" => 0.0625, "quarts" => 0.03125,
     "gallons" => 0.0078125);
$Cups = array("ounces" => 8, "cups" => 1,
     "pints" => 0.5, "quarts" => 0.25,
     "gallons" => 0.0625);
$Pints = array("ounces" => 16, "cups" => 2,
     "pints" => 1, "quarts" => 0.5,
     "gallons" => 0.125);
$Quarts = array("ounces" => 32, "cups" => 4,
     "pints" => 2, "quarts" => 1,
     "gallons" => 0.25);
$Gallons = array("ounces" => 128, "cups" => 16,
     "pints" => 8, "quarts" => 4,
     "gallons" => 1);
```

You can access elements in the preceding arrays by specifying an element's key. For example, you can access the volume conversion from cups to pints with $Cups["pints"]. Things get a little confusing when you use the preceding array names to declare and initialize an associative version of the two-dimensional $VolumeConversions[] array. For example, the following statement is the same statement you saw earlier to declare and initialize the indexed version of the two-dimensional $VolumeConversions[] array:

```
$VolumeConversions = array($Ounces, $Cups,
     $Pints, $Quarts, $Gallons);
```

Because the preceding statement does not declare keys for the elements represented by each of the individual arrays, the first dimension in the resulting $VolumeConversions[] array is indexed and the second dimension is associative. To access the conversion value from quarts to cups, you refer to the fourth row (index 3) and second column (associative key "cups") of the $VolumeConversions[] function as follows: $VolumeConversions[3]["cups"]. Although this syntax is legal, it can be confusing. To make both dimensions associative, assign keys to each of the array names in the statement that declares and initializes the $VolumeConversions[] array, as follows:

```
$VolumeConversions = array("ounces" => $Ounces,
    "cups" => $Cups, "pints" => $Pints,
    "quarts" => $Quarts, "gallons" => $Gallons);
```

Figure 6-21 illustrates the elements and keys in the $VolumeConversions[] array.

Keys

	"Ounces"	"Cups"	"Pints"	"Quarts"	"Gallons"	← Keys
"Ounces"	1	0.125	0.0625	0.03125	0.0078125	
"Cups"	8	1	0.5	0.25	0.0625	
"Pints"	16	2	1	0.5	0.125	Elements
"Quarts"	32	4	2	1	0.25	
"Gallons"	128	16	8	4	1	

Elements

Figure 6-21   Elements and keys of the $VolumeConversions[] array

Assigning keys to each of the array names in the declaration statement for the $VolumeConversions[] array allows you to access the volume conversion value from quarts to cups by using keys for both array dimensions. The following statement displays the volume conversion value from quarts to cups.

```
echo "<p>1 quart converts to " .
    $VolumeConversions["quarts"]["cups"] .
    " cups.</p>";
```

Use the same format to modify an element value in a two-dimensional associative array. The following statement demonstrates how to modify the volume conversion value from quarts to cups:

```
$VolumeConversions["quarts"]["cups"] = 4;
```

Creating Multidimensional Arrays with a Single Statement

In the preceding two sections, you created multidimensional arrays using a series of statements. First, you created the individual arrays, and then you created the multidimensional array itself. You can also create a multidimensional array with a single statement. Instead of writing separate declaration statements, you can include the array construct for each individual array as the value for each element within the declaration statement for the multidimensional array. The following example demonstrates how to declare an indexed version of the multidimensional $VolumeConversions[] array with a single statement:

```
$VolumeConversions = array(
    array(1, 0.125, 0.0625, 0.03125,
        0.0078125), // Ounces
    array(8, 1, 0.5, 0.25, 0.0625), // Cups
    array(16, 2, 1, 0.5, 0.125), // Pints
    array(32, 4, 2, 1, 0.25), // Quarts
    array(128, 16, 8, 4, 1) // Gallons
);
```

The following example demonstrates how to declare an associative version of the multidimensional $VolumeConversions[] array with a single statement:

```
$VolumeConversions = array(
    "ounces" = array("ounces" => 1,
        "cups" => 0.125, "pints" => 0.0625,
        "quarts" => 0.03125, "gallons" =>
        0.0078125),
    "cups" = array("ounces" => 8, "cups" => 1,
        "pints" =>0.5, "quarts" => 0.25,
        "gallons" => 0.0625),
    "pints" = array("ounces" => 16, "cups" => 2,
        "pints" =>1, "quarts" => 0.5,
        "gallons" => 0.125),
    "quarts" = array("ounces" => 32, "cups" =>
        4, "pints" =>2, "quarts" => 1,
        "gallons" => 0.25),
    "gallons" = array("ounces" => 128,
        "cups" => 16, "pints" =>8, "quarts" =>
        4, "gallons" => 1)
);
```

When creating multidimensional arrays in a single statement, properly formatting your code is very important. Without proper structure and indentation, the single-statement declaration is considerably more difficult to decipher than a series of statements.

Working with Additional Dimensions

Multidimensional arrays are not limited to two dimensions. You can include as many dimensions as you need when you declare the array. However, the more dimensions you use, the more complex the array becomes. Beginning programmers rarely need to use arrays larger than two dimensions, so this book does not spend much time discussing how to create them. Nevertheless, you should understand that the concepts underlying arrays of three or more dimensions are similar to those for two-dimensional arrays. As an example, consider an array that stores quarterly sales figures by state for a company's five-person sales force. For this type of multidimensional array, you would need three indexes. The first index would consist of 50 elements, one for each state. The second index would consist of five elements, one for each salesperson. The third index would consist of four elements, one for each quarter in the year. You can think of such an array as containing 50 tables, with each table containing a row for each salesperson and a column for each quarter. Table 6-5 shows how the Alaska table might appear for the first year in an associative version of the array.

		Quarters of the year			
		Q1	Q2	Q3	Q4
Salesperson	**Sam**	874	76	98	890
	Jane	656	133	64	354
	Lisa	465	668	897	64
	Hiroshi	31	132	651	46
	Jose	654	124	126	456

Table 6-5   The Alaska table of a three-dimensional array

To create the three-dimensional array, you first declare individual arrays for each of the rows in Table 6-5. Then, you create two-dimensional arrays for each state, which consist of the individual arrays containing each salesperson's figures for that particular state. Finally, you create the three-dimensional array by assigning each of the two-dimensional state arrays as elements in the three-dimensional array. The following statements demonstrate how to build a three-dimensional array named $AnnualSales[] for the state of Alaska. The first five statements declare individual arrays for each salesperson's quarterly figures in the state. The sixth statement creates a two-dimensional array named $Alaska[] that contains the quarterly sales figures for each salesperson. The last statement creates a three-dimensional array named $AnnualSales[] by assigning the two-dimensional $Alaska[] array as an element.

```
$AlaskaForSam = array("Q1" => 874, "Q2" => 76,
    "Q3" => 98, "Q4" => 890);
$AlaskaForJane = array("Q1" => 656, "Q2" => 133,
    "Q3" => 64, "Q4" => 354);
$AlaskaForLisa = array("Q1" => 465, "Q2" => 668,
    "Q3" => 897, "Q4" => 64);
$AlaskaForHiroshi = array("Q1" => 31, "Q2" => 132,
    "Q3" => 651, "Q4" => 46);
$AlaskaForJose = array("Q1" => 654, "Q2" => 124,
    "Q3" => 126, "Q4" => 456);
$Alaska = array("Sam" => $AlaskaForSam,
    "Jane" => $AlaskaForJane, "Lisa" =>
    $AlaskaForLisa, "Hiroshi" =>
    $AlaskaForHiroshi, "Jose" =>
    $AlaskaForJose);
$AnnualSales["Alaska"] = $Alaska;
```

To access or modify a value in a three-dimensional array, you must specify all dimensions. For example, the following statement displays Hiroshi's third-quarter sales figures for Alaska:

```
echo "</p>Hiroshi's third-quarter sales figure
    for Alaska is " .
    $AnnualSales['Alaska']['Hiroshi']['Q3'] .
    ".</p>";
```

PHP differs from most other computer languages in its use of multi-dimensional arrays. Most other languages require that each row have the same number of columns. PHP is more flexible, allowing each row to have as many or as few records as needed. PHP also does not require that all rows use the same keys or indexes to refer to a specific column. Although this flexibility is very useful in the right situations, it is usually best to use a consistent number of columns with the same keys or indexes.

Short Quiz

1. What is the difference between a one-dimensional array and a multidimensional array?

2. What is the most common type of multidimensional array?

3. In a two-dimensional array, the first set of indexes can be thought of as _____, and the second set of indexes can be thought of as _____. (Fill in the blanks.)

4. What is the primary difference between creating two-dimensional associative arrays and two-dimensional indexed arrays?

5. Explain how to create a two-dimensional array in a single statement.

Using Arrays in Web Forms

One of the most useful features of PHP arrays is that you can use them with XHTML form input elements. This is convenient when you have multiple matching input fields, such as the item rows in an online order form. Several syntaxes may be used, depending on how you want the array to be created in PHP.

To have PHP store the form data in an array, you modify the name attribute of the input element to use array notation. If the indexes of the array elements are unimportant, you only need to append an opening and closing square bracket ([]) to the value of the name attribute. The data from any element with the same value for the name attribute will be appended to an array with that name.

For example, the following XHTML form code creates three input text boxes, for which the entered text will be stored as an array in $_POST['answers']:

```
<form method='post' action='ProcessForm.php'>
<p>Enter the first answer:
<input type='text' name='answers[]' /></p>
<p>Enter the second answer:
<input type='text' name='answers[]' /></p>
<p>Enter the third answer:
<input type='text' name='answers[]' /></p>
<input type='submit' name='submit'
     value='submit' />
</form>
```

When a form with input elements that use array notation for the value of the name attribute is processed within PHP, the data values for the input elements are stored in a nested array within the $_POST autoglobal array. The array is accessed by using the name specified in the name attribute without the square brackets as the associative array key for the $_POST array. For example, to access the array of answers from the previous example, you use $_POST['answers'].

Because no indexes or keys are entered in the value of the name attribute in the original form, PHP assigns an index of 0 to the first element, 1 to the second, and so forth. This is the equivalent of using the syntax answers[]='Some Text'; to assign the value of an array element within PHP.

As a nested array within the $_POST array, all of the standard PHP array notation and functions can be applied to the element of the $_POST array. Consider the following code:

```
if (is_array($_POST['answers'])) {
    $Answers = $_POST['answers'];
    if (is_array($Answers)) {
        $Index = 0;
        foreach ($Answers as $Answer) {
            ++$Index;
            echo "The answer for question " .
                " $Index is '" .
                htmlentities($Answer) .
                "'<br />\n";
        }
    }
}
```

In this example, because there are three input text fields on the original form, three lines will be displayed. The data will be displayed in the order posted, which is the order in which the input elements occur on the original Web form. Figure 6-22 shows an example output with the answers "gorilla", "kitten", and "polar bear".

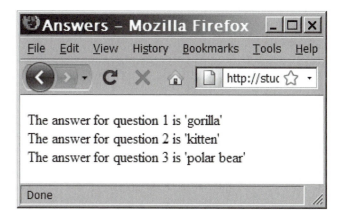

Figure 6-22   Output of an array posted from a Web form

Multidimensional array notation can also be used to process the posted form information. The following code produces the same results as the `foreach` example above, but uses multidimensional array notation, the `count()` function, and a `for` loop. The output for this example will look identical to the output of the previous example.

```
if (is_array($_POST['answers'])) {
    $Answers = $_POST['answers'];
    if (is_array($Answers)) {
        $count = count($Answers);
        for ($i = 0; $i < $count; ++$i) {
            echo "The answer for question " .
                ($i+1) . " is '" .
                htmlentities($Answers[$i]) .
                "'<br />\n";
        }
    }
}
```

If the order of the form inputs is important, you can include either an index or an associative key between the opening and closing array brackets. When using associative keys in Web forms, you do *not* use quotes around the associative array key name. The syntax `<input type='text' name='answers[Q1]' />` will work, but the syntax `<input type='text' name='answers['Q1']' />` will not.

For example, the following code will ensure that indexes 1, 2, and 3 are associated with answers 1, 2, and 3, respectively:

```
<form method='post' action='ProcessForm.php'>
<p>Enter the first answer:
<input type='text' name='answers[1]' /></p>
<p>Enter the second answer:
<input type='text' name='answers[2]' /></p>
<p>Enter the third answer:
<input type='text' name='answers[3]' /></p>
<input type='submit' name='submit'
    value='submit' />
</form>
```

The following code will associate the key 'Question 1' with the first answer, 'Question 2' with the second answer, and 'Question 3' with the third answer:

```
<form method='post' action='ProcessForm.php'>
<p>Enter the first answer:
<input type='text' name='answers[Question 1]'
    /></p>
<p>Enter the second answer:
<input type='text' name='answers[Question 2]'
    /></p>
<p>Enter the third answer:
<input type='text' name='answers[Question 3]'
    /></p>
<input type='submit' name='submit'
    value='submit' />
</form>
```

To create an All-in-One Web form quiz about the capitals of the New England states:

1. Create a new document in your text editor.

2. Type the <!DOCTYPE> declaration, <html> element, header information, and <body> element. Use the strict DTD and "New England State Capitals" as the content of the <title> element.

3. Add the following script section to the document body:

    ```
    <?php
    ?>
    ```

4. Add the following code to the script section to declare an associative array of the New England state capitals:

    ```
    $StateCapitals = array(
        "Connecticut" => "Hartford",
        "Maine" => "Augusta",
        "Massachusetts" => "Boston",
        "New Hampshire" => "Concord",
        "Rhode Island" => "Providence",
        "Vermont" => "Montpelier"
    );
    ```

5. Add the following `if...else` statement to determine if the answers have been posted:

```
if (isset($_POST['submit'])) {
}
else {
}
```

6. Add the following code to the `if` clause of the `if...else` statement to validate the answers:

```
$Answers = $_POST['answers'];
if (is_array($Answers)) {
    foreach ($Answers as
        $State => $Response) {
        $Response =
            stripslashes($Response);
        if (strlen($Response)>0) {
            if (strcasecmp(
                $StateCapitals[$State],
                $Response)==0)
                echo "<p>Correct! The
                    capital of $State is " .
                    $StateCapitals[$State] .
                    ".</p>\n";
            else
                echo "<p>Sorry, the capital
                    of $State is not '" .
                    $Response . "'.</p>\n";
        }
        else
            echo "<p>You did not enter a
                value for the capital of
                $State.</p>\n";
    }
}
echo "<p><a href='NewEnglandCapitals.php'>
    Try again?</a></p>\n";
```

7. Add the following code to the `else` clause of the `if...else` statement to display the Web form:

```
echo "<form action='NewEnglandCapitals.php'
    method='POST'>\n";
foreach ($StateCapitals as
    $State => $Response)
    echo "The capital of $State is:
        <input type='text' name='answers[" .
        $State . "]' /><br />\n";
    echo "<input type='submit'
        name='submit'
        value='Check Answers' /> ";
    echo "<input type='reset' name='reset'
        value='Reset Form' />\n";
    echo "</form>\n";
```

8. Save the document as **NewEnglandCapitals.php** in the Chapter directory for Chapter 6 and upload the file to the server.

9. Open the NewEnglandCapitals.php file in your Web browser by entering the following URL: *http://<yourserver>/PHP_Projects/Chapter.06/Chapter/NewEnglandCapitals.php*. Figure 6-23 shows the form. Enter your answers and click the **Check Answers** button to see how you did.

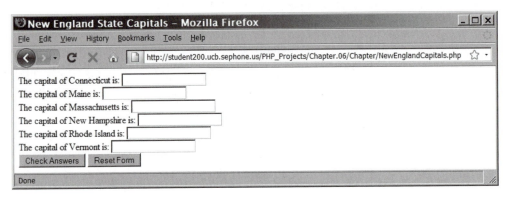

Figure 6-23 The "New England Capitals" quiz Web form

10. Close your Web browser window.

Short Quiz

1. What attribute in the Web form `<input>` tag must be changed for the value to be sent as an array element?

2. Can arrays created from Web forms be indexed arrays, associative arrays, or both? Explain.

3. Should quotation marks be used in the associative array key name for a Web form? Why or why not?

Summing Up

- The `array_shift()` function removes the first element from the beginning of an array, whereas the `array_unshift()` function adds one or more elements to the beginning of an array.

- The `array_pop()` function removes the last element from the end of an array, whereas the `array_push()` function adds one or more elements to the end of an array.

- The `array_splice()` function adds or removes array elements.

- The `unset()` function removes array elements and other variables.

- The `array_values()` function renumbers an indexed array's elements.

- The `array_unique()` function removes duplicate elements from an array.

- With associative arrays, you specify an element's key by using the array operator (=>).

- The internal array pointer refers to the currently selected element in an array.

- The `in_array()` function returns a Boolean value of TRUE if a given value exists in an array.

- The `array_search()` function determines whether a given value exists in an array and 1) returns the index or key of the first matching element if the value exists, or 2) returns FALSE if the value does not exist.

- The `array_key_exists()` function determines whether a given index or key exists.

- The `array_slice()` function returns a portion of an array and assigns it to another array.

- The most commonly used array sorting functions are `sort()` and `rsort()` for indexed arrays, and `ksort()` and `krsort()` for associative arrays.

- To append one array to another, you use the addition (+) or the compound assignment (+=) operator.

- The `array_merge()` function merges two or more arrays.

- The `array_diff()` function returns an array of elements that exist in one array but not in any other arrays to which it is compared.

- The `array_intersect()` function returns an array of elements that exist in all of the arrays that are compared.

- A multidimensional array consists of multiple indexes or keys.

- When array notation is used in the name of a Web form input, the value gets stored in a nested array within the $_POST or $_GET array.

- When using associative array notation in a Web form, you omit the quotation marks around the key name.

Comprehension Check

1. Which of the following functions removes the first element from the beginning of an array?

   a. `array_shift()`

   b. `array_unshift()`

   c. `array_push()`

   d. `array_pop()`

2. Explain the easiest way to add elements to the end of an indexed array.

3. Which of the following functions removes the last element from the end of an array? (Choose all that apply.)

   a. `array_shift()`

   b. `array_unshift()`

   c. `array_push()`

   d. `array_pop()`

4. Explain how to use the `array_splice()` function to add and remove elements to and from an array.

5. After removing elements from an array, the `unset()` function automatically renumbers the remaining elements. True or False?

6. Which of the following functions removes duplicate elements from an array?

   a. `array_duplicates()`

   b. `array_unique()`

   c. `remove_duplicates()`

   d. `unique()`

7. What is the correct syntax for declaring and initializing an associative array?

   a. `$AutoMakers = array("Ford" . "Mustang", "Chevrolet" . "Corvette");`

   b. `$AutoMakers = array("Ford" = "Mustang", "Chevrolet" = "Corvette");`

   c. `$AutoMakers = array("Ford" > "Mustang", "Chevrolet" > "Corvette");`

   d. `$AutoMakers = array("Ford" => "Mustang", "Chevrolet" => "Corvette");`

8. If an array contains a mixture of indexes and keys, what value or key is used if you do not specify one when adding a new element to the array?

9. If you declare an array in PHP and use a starting index other than 0, empty elements are created for each index between 0 and the index value you specify. True or False?

10. Which of the following functions moves an array's internal pointer to the first element?

    a. `first()`

    b. `top()`

    c. `start()`

    d. `reset()`

11. Which of the following functions returns the value of an element where an array's internal pointer is positioned?

    a. `current()`

    b. `key()`

    c. `array()`

    d. `array_values()`

12. Explain the difference between the `in_array()` and `array_search()` functions.

13. Which of the following locates a key named "Ford" in an array named `$AutoMakers[]`?

    a. `array_key_exists($AutoMakers => "Ford");`

    b. `$AutoMakers = array_key_exists("Ford");`

    c. `array_key_exists($AutoMakers, "Ford");`

    d. `array_key_exists("Ford", $AutoMakers);`

14. Explain how to use the `array_slice()` function to return a portion of an array and assign it to another array.

15. Which of the following functions performs a reverse sort on an array? (Choose all that apply.)

    a. `asort()`

    b. `usort()`

    c. `rsort()`

    d. `krsort()`

16. Which of the following operators can you use to append one array to another? (Choose all that apply.)

    a. `.`

    b. `+`

    c. `+=`

    d. `=>`

17. If you use the `array_merge()` function with indexed arrays, all elements in one array are appended to another array and renumbered. True or False?

18. Which of the following returns an array of elements that exist in all of the arrays that are compared?

    a. `usort()`

    b. `array_common()`

    c. `array_diff()`

    d. `array_intersect()`

19. Suppose you are working with an indexed two-dimensional array named `$InterestRates[][]`, where each dimension begins with an index of 0. Which of the following refers to the second element in the first dimension and the third element in the second dimension?

    a. `$InterestRates[1],[2]`

    b. `$InterestRates[1][2]`

    c. `$InterestRates[1, 2]`

    d. `$InterestRates[1].[2]`

20. Which is the correct Web form syntax for creating the auto-global element `$_POST['item']['quantity']`?

    a. `<input type="text" name="item['quantity']" />`

    b. `<input type="text" name='item["quantity"]' />`

    c. `<input type="text" name='item[quantity]' />`

    d. `<input type="text" name="item["quantity"]" />`

Reinforcement Exercises

 Exercise 6-1

Create a Song Organizer script that stores songs in a text file. Include functionality that allows users to view the song list and prevents the same song name from being entered twice. Also, include code that sorts the songs by name, deletes duplicate entries, and randomizes the song list with the **shuffle()** function.

1. Create a new document in your text editor.

2. Type the `<!DOCTYPE>` declaration, `<html>` element, header information, and `<body>` element. Use the strict DTD and "Song Organizer" as the content of the `<title>` element.

3. Add the following XHTML code and script section to the document body:

```
<h1>Song Organizer</h1>
<?php
?>
```

4. Add the following code to the script section to handle any parameters in the URL:

```
if (isset($_GET['action'])) {
    if ((file_exists("SongOrganizer/songs.txt"))
        && (filesize("SongOrganizer/songs.txt")
        != 0)) {
        $SongArray = file(
            "SongOrganizer/songs.txt");
        switch ($_GET['action']) {
        } // End of the switch statement
    }
}
```

5. Add the following code to the body of the switch statement to handle the three options (Sort Ascending, Remove Duplicates, and Shuffle):

```
case 'Remove Duplicates':
    $SongArray = array_unique(
        $SongArray);
    $SongArray = array_values(
        $SongArray);
    break;
case 'Sort Ascending':
    sort($SongArray);
    break;
case 'Shuffle':
    shuffle($SongArray);
    break;
```

6. Add the following code immediately after the switch statement to save the song list after it has been modified:

```
if (count($SongArray)>0) {
    $NewSongs = implode($SongArray);
    $SongStore = fopen(
        "SongOrganizer/songs.txt",
        "wb");
    if ($SongStore === false)
        echo "There was an error
            updating the song file\n";
    else {
        fwrite($SongStore, $NewSongs);
        fclose($SongStore);
    }
}
else
    unlink("SongOrganizer/songs.txt");
```

7. Add the following code to the end of the script section to handle any data submitted from the Web form:

```
if (isset($_POST['submit'])) {
    $SongToAdd = stripslashes(
        $_POST['SongName']) . "\n";
    $ExistingSongs = array();
    if (file_exists("SongOrganizer/songs.txt")
        && filesize("SongOrganizer/songs.txt")
        > 0) {
        $ExistingSongs = file(
            "SongOrganizer/songs.txt");
    }
}
```

8. Add the following if statement immediately after the block where the song file data was read into the $ExistingSongs array. This if statement checks to see if the song name entered is already in the song list, and displays a message if the song already exists.

```
if (in_array($SongToAdd, $ExistingSongs)) {
    echo "<p>The song you entered already
        exists!<br />\n";
    echo "Your song was not added to the
        list.</p>";
}
```

Although this form does not allow for duplicate entries, you still need to be able to remove them if necessary. There may be other methods of adding songs to the list, and the other methods may allow duplicate entries.

9. Add the following else clause to the preceding if statement. This else clause adds the new song to the song list file.

```
else {
    $SongFile = fopen(
        "SongOrganizer/songs.txt", "ab");
    if ($SongFile === false)
        echo "There was an error saving
            your message!\n";
    else {
        fwrite($SongFile, $SongToAdd);
        fclose($SongFile);
        echo "Your song has been added to
            the list.\n";
    }
}
```

10. Add the following code to the end of the script section to display the song list, or a message that there are no songs in the list if the list is empty:

```
if ((!file_exists("SongOrganizer/songs.txt"))
        || (filesize("SongOrganizer/songs.txt")
        == 0))
    echo "<p>There are no songs in the
        list.</p>\n";
else {
    $SongArray = file(
        "SongOrganizer/songs.txt");
    echo "<table border=\"1\" width=\"100%\"
        style=\"background-color:lightgray\">\n";
    foreach ($SongArray as $Song) {
        echo "<tr>\n";
        echo "<td>" . htmlentities($Song) .
            "</td>";
        echo "</tr>\n";
    }
    echo "</table>\n";
}
```

11. Add the following XHTML code immediately after the PHP script section to display hyperlinks for the three functions in the switch statement (Sort Ascending, Remove Duplicates, and Shuffle):

```
<p>
<a href="SongOrganizer.php?action=Sort%20Ascending">
    Sort Song List</a><br />
<a href="SongOrganizer.php?action=Remove%20Duplicates">
    Remove Duplicate Songs</a><br />
<a href="SongOrganizer.php?action=Shuffle">
    Randomize Song list</a><br />
</p>
```

12. Next, add the following XHTML code to create a Web form for entering new song names into the song list:

```
<form action="SongOrganizer.php" method="post">
<p>Add a New Song</p>
<p>Song Name: <input type="text" name="SongName"
    /></p>
<p><input type="submit" name="submit"
    value="Add Song to List" />
<input type="reset" name="reset"
    value="Reset Song Name" /></p>
</form>
```

13. Save the document as **SongOrganizer.php** in the Projects directory for Chapter 6 and upload the file to the server.

14. Open the SongOrganizer.php file in your Web browser by entering the following URL: *http://<yourserver>/PHP_Projects/Chapter.06/Projects/SongOrganizer.php*.

15. Close your Web browser window.

 ## Exercise 6-2

In this project, you will create a multidimensional array that contains the measurements, in inches, for several boxes that a shipping company might use to determine the volume of a box.

1. Create a new document in your text editor.

2. Type the `<!DOCTYPE>` declaration, `<html>` element, document head, and `<body>` element. Use the strict DTD and "Box Array" as the content of the `<title>` element.

3. Create a script section in the document body:

   ```
   <?php
   ?>
   ```

4. Declare and initialize an associative multidimensional array using the information shown in the following table:

	Length	Width	Depth
Small box	12	10	2.5
Medium box	30	20	4
Large box	60	40	11.5

5. Add statements to the end of the script section that display the volume (length * width * depth) of each box.

6. Save the document as **BoxArray.php** in the Projects directory for Chapter 6, and then close the document in your text editor.

7. Open the BoxArray.php file in your Web browser by entering the following URL: *http://<yourserver>/PHP_Projects/Chapter.06/Projects/BoxArray.php*.

8. Close your Web browser window.

 ## Exercise 6-3

Create a Web form that shows the mileage between European capitals. Use a two-dimensional associative array to store the mileages.

1. Create a new document in your text editor.

2. Type the `<!DOCTYPE>` declaration, `<html>` element, header information, and `<body>` element. Use the strict DTD and "European Travel" as the content of the `<title>` element.

3. Add the following script section to the document body:

```
<?php
?>
```

4. Add the following code to the script section to declare an associative array of European cities and the distances between them in kilometers, and the conversion factor for kilometers to miles:

```
$Distances = array(
    "Berlin" => array(
        "Berlin" => 0,
        "Moscow" => 1607.99,
        "Paris" => 876.96,
        "Prague" => 280.34,
        "Rome" => 1181.67
    ),
    "Moscow" => array(
        "Berlin" => 1607.99,
        "Moscow" => 0,
        "Paris" => 2484.92,
        "Prague" => 1664.04,
        "Rome" => 2374.26
    ),
    "Paris" => array(
        "Berlin" => 876.96,
        "Moscow" => 641.31,
        "Paris" => 0,
        "Prague" => 885.38,
        "Rome" => 1105.76
    ),
    "Prague" => array(
        "Berlin" => 280.34,
        "Moscow" => 1664.04,
        "Paris" => 885.38,
        "Prague" => 0,
        "Rome" => 922
    ),
    "Rome" => array(
        "Berlin" => 1181.67,
        "Moscow" => 2374.26,
        "Paris" => 1105.76,
        "Prague" => 922,
        "Rome" => 0
    )
);
$KMtoMiles = 0.62;
```

5. Add the following if statement to process the entered cities:

```php
if (isset($_POST['submit'])) {
    $StartIndex = stripslashes($_POST['Start']);
    $EndIndex = stripslashes($_POST['End']);
    if (isset(
        $Distances[$StartIndex][$EndIndex]))
        echo "<p>The distance from $StartIndex
            to $EndIndex is " .
            $Distances[$StartIndex][$EndIndex]
            . " kilometers, or " . round(
            ($KMtoMiles *
            $Distances[$StartIndex][$EndIndex]),
            2) . " miles.</p>\n";
    else
        echo "<p>The distance from $StartIndex
            to $EndIndex is not in the
            array.</p>\n";
}
```

6. Add the following XHTML code after the PHP script to display the Web form:

```html
<form action="EuropeanTravel.php" method="post">
<p>Starting City:
<select name="Start">
</select></p>
<p>Ending City:
<select name="End">
</select></p>
<p><input type="submit" name="submit"
    value="Calculate Distance" /></p>
</form>
```

7. Add the following PHP script between the opening and closing XHTML tags for the "Start" <select> element to insert the list of city names:

```php
<?php
    foreach ($Distances as
        $City => $OtherCities) {
        echo "<option value='$City'";
        if (strcmp($StartIndex,$City)==0)
            echo " selected";
        echo ">$City</option>\n";
    }
?>
```

8. Add the following PHP script between the opening and closing XHTML tags for the "End" <select> element to insert the list of city names:

```
<?php
    foreach ($Distances as
        $City => $OtherCities) {
        echo "<option value='$City'";
        if (strcmp($EndIndex,$City)==0)
            echo " selected";
        echo ">$City</option>\n";
    }
?>
```

9. Save the document as **EuropeanTravel.php** in the Projects directory for Chapter 6 and upload the file to the server.

10. Open the EuropeanTravel.php file in your Web browser by entering the following URL: *http://<yourserver>/PHP_Projects/Chapter.06/Projects/EuropeanTravel.php*.

11. Close your Web browser window.

 ## Exercise 6-4

Use the techniques you learned in this chapter to create a Guest Book script that stores visitor names and e-mail addresses in a text file. Include functionality that allows users to view the guest book and prevents the same user name from being entered twice. Also, include code that sorts the guest book by name and deletes duplicate entries.

 ## Exercise 6-5

Create an online order form as a Web form. Allow visitors to enter a quantity for at least five items for sale. Each item should have a name, description, and price. The form should have buttons to update the totals for the quantities entered and to submit the order. Save the orders to a subdirectory called **OnlineOrders** in the Projects directory for Chapter 6. Use the date and time to create a unique filename for each order.

Discovery Projects

The Chinese Zodiac site is a comprehensive project that will be updated in the Discovery Projects in each chapter. All files for the Chinese Zodiac site will be saved in a folder named ChineseZodiac in the root Web folder on the server.

 ## Discovery Project 6-1

Reopen **inc_footer.php** from the Includes folder and use the array constructs introduced in Chapter 6 to randomly display a dragon image below the randomly displayed Chinese proverbs each time the browser is refreshed. Use the small dragon images that you uploaded to the Images folder in Discovery Project 5-6.

Use the functions you learned in Chapter 5 to read the filenames from the Images folder into an array. Because you have other images in the Images folder besides your dragon images, you should filter the contents of the folder to add only files that have a filename of Dragon1, Dragon2, etc., and a valid image extension before adding them to your array. The easiest way to filter the filenames is to use a regular expression such as `'/^Dragon\d+\.(gif|jpg|png)$/'`. When the array is populated, use the `shuffle()` function to randomly reorder the array. Select the name in the first array element of the shuffled array as the random image to display.

 ## Discovery Project 6-2

Open a new document in your text editor and create an All-in-One form that prompts the user to enter the 12 zodiac signs in random order in a text box. The signs must be separated with commas. Inform the user that you will display the signs in an alphabetized list after the form has been submitted.

Use the array sort functions introduced in this chapter to alphabetize the signs and then display them in an ordered list.

Save the file as **AlphabetizeSigns.php** and upload the file to the ChineseZodiac folder on the Web server.

Reopen **inc_web_forms.php** from the Includes folder and replace the "[Insert Web forms content here]" placeholder with Web content that describes the processing of user input on a Web page. Include a description of how to create and process a Web form.

Add a section called "Alphabetizing User Input" and briefly describe the function of the AlphabetizeSigns.php script. Refer to Discovery Project 5-4 to add "[Test the Script]" and "[View the Source Code]" links below the descriptive data.

Add a text navigation bar at the top of the document with an internal link to the "Alphabetizing User Input" section.

Save the inc_web_forms.php file and upload it to the server. The contents of this file should appear in the dynamic content section when you click the Web Forms button or the Web Forms text hyperlink from the Chinese zodiac Web template.

Discovery Project 6-3

Create a PHP script with an associative array that uses image file-names as the keys and image captions as the values. Use the keys and values from the array to create a thumbnail gallery of images in which you display a small hyperlinked image to open a larger version of the image. Use the zodiac sign images that you saved in your Images folder in Chapter 1. Set a width and height for the thumbnails that are less than half of the height and width of the images. Format the display of the thumbnail gallery.

Save the file as **ZodiacGallery.php** and upload it to the ChineseZodiac folder on the Web server. Test the script.

Reopen **inc_web_forms.php** and add another text link (Image Gallery) to the text navigation bar that links to the Image Gallery descriptive text. Below the Alphabetizing Signs descriptive text, add a new section called "Image Gallery" with descriptive text and hyperlinks for "[Test the Script]" and "[View the Source Code]" for **ZodiacGallery.php**.

Discovery Project 6-4

Reopen the **BirthYear_switch.php** file created in Discovery Project 5-2, and modify the script to create a multidimensional array named $AnimalSigns[] that stores the information in the following table:

| | Animal Signs | | |
	"Start Date"	"End Date"	"President"
"Rat"	1900	2020	George Washington
"Ox"	1901	2021	Barack Obama
"Tiger"	1902	2022	Dwight Eisenhower
"Rabbit"	1903	2023	John Adams
"Dragon"	1904	2024	Abraham Lincoln
"Snake"	1905	2025	John Kennedy
"Horse"	1906	2026	Theodore Roosevelt
"Goat"	1907	2027	James Madison
"Monkey"	1908	2028	Harry Truman
"Rooster"	1909	2029	Grover Cleveland
"Dog"	1910	2030	George Walker Bush
"Pig"	1911	2031	Ronald Reagan

For example, $AnimalSigns["Monkey"] is an array that contains three elements: $AnimalSigns["Monkey"]["Start Date"] is 1908, $AnimalSigns["Monkey"]["End Date"] is 2028, and $AnimalSigns["Monkey"]["President"] is "Harry Truman."

Access the multidimensional array to display the following message in addition to the message and image displayed by the original script (text in bold will change depending on the sign being displayed): "If your Chinese zodiac sign is the **Rat**, you share a zodiac sign with President **George Washington**. Years of the **Rat** include **1900, 1912, 1924, 1936, 1948, 1960, 1972, 1984, 1996, 2008**, and **2020**."

To display the message shown above, you can use the following code. The variable $ChosenSign contains the name of the animal. The year string is stored in the $SignMessage variable.

```
$SignMessage = "If your Chinese zodiac sign is
        the $ChosenSign, you share a zodiac sign
        with President " .
        $AnimalSigns[$ChosenSign]["President"] .
        ". ";
$SignMessage .= "Years of the $ChosenSign
        include ";
for ($i = $AnimalSigns[$ChosenSign]["Start Date"];
        $i < $AnimalSigns[$ChosenSign]["End Date"];
        $i+=12)
        $SignMessage .= $i . ", ";
$SignMessage .= "and " .
        $AnimalSigns[$ChosenSign]["End Date"] . ".";
```

Save the BirthYear_switch.php script and upload the file to the ChineseZodiac folder on the Web server. Open the main page (index.php) for the Chinese Zodiac site. Click the Control Structures button or Control Structures text link and select the Switch Statement link to test the functionality of the script.

Working with Databases and MySQL

In this chapter you will:

◎ Study the basics of databases and MySQL

◎ Work with MySQL databases

◎ Define database tables

◎ Modify user privileges

◎ Work with database records

◎ Work with phpMyAdmin

A common use of Web pages is to gather information stored in a database on a Web server. Most server-side scripting languages, including PHP, allow you to create Web pages that can read and write data to and from databases. In this chapter, you will take a break from PHP to learn how to work with MySQL databases. Your goal is to learn the basics of database manipulation. Then, in Chapter 8, you will apply many of the techniques from this chapter to PHP scripts that manipulate MySQL databases.

MySQL is an open source database originally developed by MySQL AB and owned by Sun Microsystems (*http://www.mysql.com/*). Many people mistakenly believe that MySQL is part of PHP. Even though MySQL is probably the database used most often with PHP, it is just one of many databases that PHP can manipulate directly or through Open Database Connectivity (ODBC). As its name implies, MySQL uses Structured Query Language, or SQL, as its data manipulation language. MySQL is primarily used for Web applications and is extremely popular for several reasons; first and foremost, it's open source and free.

Introduction to Databases

Formally defined, a **database** is an ordered collection of information that a computer program can quickly access. You can probably think of many databases that you work with in everyday life. For example, your address book is a database. So is the card file of recipes in a kitchen. Other examples of databases include a company's employee directory and a file cabinet of client information. Essentially, any information that can be organized into ordered sets of data, and then quickly retrieved, can be considered a database. A collection of hundreds of baseball cards thrown into a shoebox is not a database because an individual card cannot be quickly or easily retrieved (except by luck). However, if the baseball card collection was organized in binders by team, and then further organized according to each player's field position or batting average, it could be considered a database because you could quickly locate a specific card.

The information stored in computer databases is actually stored in tables similar to spreadsheets. Each row in a database table is called a record. A **record** in a database is a single, complete set of related information. Each recipe in a recipe database, for instance, is a single database record. Each column in a database table is called a field. **Fields** are the individual categories of information stored in a record. Examples of fields in a recipe database might include ingredients, cooking time, cooking temperature, and so on.

To summarize, you can think of databases as consisting of tables, which consist of records, which consist of fields. Figure 7-1 shows an example of an employee directory for programmers at an application development company. The database consists of five records, one for each employee. Each record consists of six fields: `last_name`, `first_name`, `address`, `city`, `state`, and `zip`.

Rows				Fields	
last_name	first_name	address	city	state	zip
Blair	Dennis	204 Spruce Lane	Brookfield	MA	01506
Hernandez	Louis	68 Boston Post Road	Spencer	MA	01562
Miller	Erica	271 Baker Hill Road	Brookfield	MA	01515
Morinaga	Scott	17 Ashley Road	Brookfield	MA	01515
Picard	Raymond	1113 Oakham Road	Barre	MA	01531

Figure 7-1 Employee directory database

Two other types of database systems you might encounter are hierarchical databases and network databases.

The database in Figure 7-1 is an example of a flat-file database, one of the simplest types of databases. A **flat-file database** stores information in a single table, and it is usually adequate for simple collections of information. However, with large and complex collections of information, a better solution is a **relational database**, which stores information across multiple related tables. Although you will not work with a relational database in this chapter, understanding how they work is helpful because relational databases are among the most common in use today.

Understanding Table Relationships

Relational databases consist of one or more related tables. In fact, large relational databases can consist of hundreds or thousands of related tables. Regardless of the number of tables, however, you create relationships within the database by working with two tables at a time. One table in a relationship is always considered to be the primary table, and the other table is considered the related table. A **primary table** (also called a **parent table**) is the main table in a relationship that is referenced by another table. A **related table** (also called a **child table**) references a primary table in a relational database.

Tables in a relationship are connected using primary and foreign keys. A **primary key** is a field or fields that contain a unique identifier for each record in a primary table. A primary key is a type of **index**, which identifies records in a database to make retrievals and sorting faster. An index or primary key can consist of just a single field (a **simple key**), or it can be a combination of multiple fields (a **compound** or **composite key**). A **foreign key** is a field or fields in a related table that refer to the primary key in a primary table. A foreign key can also be a simple key or a compound key to match the primary key in the parent table. Primary and foreign keys link records across multiple tables in a relational database.

There are three basic types of relationships within a relational database: one-to-one, one-to-many, and many-to-many. A **one-to-one relationship** exists between two tables when a related table contains exactly one record for each record in the primary table. You create one-to-one relationships when you want to break information into multiple, logical sets. It is important to understand that information in the tables in a one-to-one relationship can usually be placed in a single table. However, you might want to break the information into multiple tables to better organize it into logical sets. Another reason for using one-to-one relationships is that you can make the information in one of the tables confidential and accessible only by certain people. For example, you might want to create a personnel table that contains basic information about employees, similar to the information in the table in Figure 7-1. Yet, you might also want to create a payroll table that contains confidential information about each employee's salary, benefits, and other types of compensation, which can be accessed only by the Human Resources and Accounting departments. Figure 7-2 shows two tables, `Employees` and `Payroll`, that have a one-to-one relationship. The primary table is the employee information table from Figure 7-1. The related table is a payroll table that contains confidential salary and compensation information. Notice that each table contains an identical number of records; one record in the primary table corresponds to one record in the related table. The relationship is achieved by adding a primary key to the `Employees` table and a foreign key to the `Payroll` table.

While primary keys must be unique, foreign keys do not have the same requirement. Duplicate foreign keys are used later in this section when one-to-many relationships are discussed.

383

Primary key

Employees table

employee_id	last_name	first_name	address	city	state	zip
101	Blair	Dennis	204 Spruce Lane	Brookfield	MA	01506
102	Hernandez	Louis	68 Boston Post Road	Spencer	MA	01562
103	Miller	Erica	271 Baker Hill Road	Brookfield	MA	01515
104	Morinaga	Scott	17 Ashley Road	Brookfield	MA	01515
105	Picard	Raymond	1113 Oakham Road	Barre	MA	01531

Foreign key

Payroll table

employee_id	start_date	pay_rate	health_coverage	year_vested	401k
101	2002	$21.25	none	na	no
102	1999	$28.00	Family Plan	2001	yes
103	1997	$24.50	Individual	na	yes
104	1994	$36.00	Family Plan	1996	yes
105	1995	$31.00	Individual	1997	yes

Figure 7-2 One-to-one relationship

A **one-to-many relationship** exists in a relational database when one record in a primary table has many related records in a related table. You create a one-to-many relationship to eliminate redundant information in a single table. Ideally, primary and foreign keys are the only pieces of information in a relational database table that should be duplicated. Breaking tables into multiple related tables to reduce redundant and duplicate information is called **normalization**. This process reduces the size of a database and decreases the opportunity for error when the same information is repeated. For example, consider the table in Figure 7-3. The table lists every programming language in which the five programmers are proficient. The repetition of programmers' names is an example of redundant information that can occur when all of the information is stored in a single table.

employee_id	last_name	first_name	language
101	Blair	Dennis	JavaScript
101	Blair	Dennis	ASP.NET
102	Hernandez	Louis	JavaScript
102	Hernandez	Louis	ASP.NET
102	Hernandez	Louis	Java
103	Miller	Erica	JavaScript
103	Miller	Erica	ASP.NET
103	Miller	Erica	Java
103	Miller	Erica	C++
104	Morinaga	Scott	JavaScript
104	Morinaga	Scott	ASP.NET
104	Morinaga	Scott	Java
105	Picard	Raymond	JavaScript
105	Picard	Raymond	ASP.NET

Figure 7-3 Table with redundant information

A one-to-many relationship provides a more efficient and less redundant method of storing this information in a database. Figure 7-4 shows the same information organized into a one-to-many relationship.

Employees table

employee_id	last_name	first_name	address	city	state	zip
101	Blair	Dennis	204 Spruce Lane	Brookfield	MA	01506
102	Hernandez	Louis	68 Boston Post Road	Spencer	MA	01562
103	Miller	Erica	271 Baker Hill Road	Brookfield	MA	01515
104	Morinaga	Scott	17 Ashley Road	Brookfield	MA	01515
105	Picard	Raymond	1113 Oakham Road	Barre	MA	01531

Languages table ("many" side)

employee_id	language
101	JavaScript
101	ASP.NET
102	JavaScript
102	ASP.NET
102	Java
103	JavaScript
103	ASP.NET
103	Java
103	C++
104	JavaScript
104	ASP.NET
104	Java
105	JavaScript
105	ASP.NET

One record in the top table is linked to many records in the bottom table

Figure 7-4 One-to-many relationship

In some databases, the table containing multiple records for one entity (for example, the programming language table in Figure 7-4) is the primary table. In these cases, the relationship is often referred to as a many-to-one relationship.

In Figure 7-4, the tables are not normalized because the language field contains duplicate values. Recall that primary and foreign keys are the only pieces of information in a relational database that should be duplicated. To further reduce repetition, you could organize the Languages table in Figure 7-4 into another one-to-many relationship. However, a better choice is to create a **many-to-many relationship**, which exists in a relational database when many records in one table are related to many records in another table.

Consider the relationship between programmers and programming languages. Each programmer can work with many programming languages, and each programming language can be used by many programmers. To create a many-to-many relationship, you must use a junction table because most relational database systems cannot work directly with many-to-many relationships. A **junction table** creates a one-to-many relationship for each of the tables in a many-to-many relationship. A junction table contains foreign keys from the two tables in a many-to-many relationship, along with any other fields that correspond to a many-to-many relationship. A junction table is often called a linking table or a cross-reference table.

In a junction table, the foreign keys may be used as a compound primary key.

Figure 7-5 contains an example of a many-to-many relationship between the Employees table and a Languages table. The Employees table contains a primary key named employee_id, and the Languages table contains a primary key named language_id. A junction table named Experience contains two foreign keys, one corresponding to the employee_id primary key in the Employees table and one corresponding to the language_id primary key in the Languages table. The Experience junction table also contains a field named years. You add records to the Experience junction table to build a list of the years that each programmer has been working with a particular programming language. Because each combination of employee_id and language_id is unique, the two columns provide a convenient compound primary key, eliminating the need for a separate primary key field.

Employees table

employee_id	last_name	first_name	address	city	state	zip
101	Blair	Dennis	204 Spruce Lane	Brookfield	MA	01506
102	Hernandez	Louis	68 Boston Post Road	Spencer	MA	01562
103	Miller	Erica	271 Baker Hill Road	Brookfield	MA	01515
104	Morinaga	Scott	17 Ashley Road	Brookfield	MA	01515
105	Picard	Raymond	1113 Oakham Road	Barre	MA	01531

One record in the `Employees` table is linked to many records in the `Experience` junction table

Languages table

language_id	language
10	JavaScript
11	ASP.NET
12	Java
13	C++

Experience junction table

employee_id	language_id	years
101	10	5
101	11	4
102	10	3
102	11	2
102	12	3
103	10	2
103	11	3
103	12	6
103	13	3
104	10	7
104	11	5
104	12	8
105	10	4
105	11	2

One record in the `Languages` table is linked to many records in the `Experience` junction table

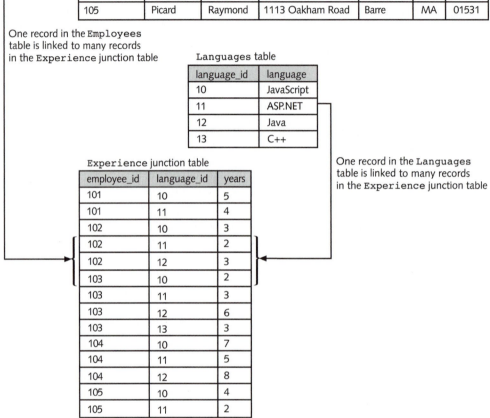

Figure 7-5 Many-to-many relationship

Working with Database Management Systems

Although a full-scale database is much more complex than the examples given so far, you now have enough information about table relationships to create and manipulate database tables. One or more applications used to access and manage a database is called a **database management system**, or **DBMS**. A DBMS is also used to define a database's **schema**, which is the structure of a database, including its tables, fields, and relationships. A DBMS runs on many different platforms, ranging from personal computers to network servers, and different DBMSs exist for different types of database formats. A DBMS that stores data in a flat-file format is called a **flat-file database management system**. A DBMS that stores data in a relational format is called a **relational database management system**, or **RDBMS**. Other types of DBMSs are hierarchical and network database management systems. In addition to the open source MySQL DBMS, some of the more popular relational DBMSs include Oracle, Sybase, and SQL Server for network servers, and Microsoft Access and Paradox for PCs.

Database management systems perform many of the same functions as other types of applications you might have encountered, such as word-processing and spreadsheet programs. For example, a DBMS creates new database files and contains interfaces that allow users to enter and manipulate data. One of the most important functions of a DBMS is the structuring and maintenance of the database file. In addition, a DBMS must ensure that data is stored correctly in a database's tables, regardless of the database format (flat-file, relational, hierarchical, or network). In relational databases, the DBMS ensures that the appropriate information is entered according to the relationship structure in the database tables. Many DBMSs also have security features that restrict user access to specific data.

Another important aspect of a DBMS is its querying capability. A **query** is a structured set of instructions and criteria for retrieving, adding, modifying, and deleting database information. Most database management systems use a **data manipulation language**, or **DML**, for creating queries. Different DBMSs support different DMLs. However, **structured query language**, or **SQL** (sometimes pronounced *sequel*), is a standard data manipulation language among many DBMSs.

Many DBMSs include tools that make it easier to build queries. MySQL includes MySQL Query Browser, a tool that allows you to work with MySQL queries in a graphical environment. You can use MySQL Query Browser to create queries by typing SQL commands into the query area at the top of the screen or by dragging tables and fields from the Schemata area to the query area.

Although working with an interface to design queries is helpful, you must still use the DBMS's data manipulation language (for example, when accessing databases with PHP). Because SQL is the underlying data manipulation language for many DBMSs, including MySQL, you will learn more about the language as you progress through this chapter.

It is important to understand that even though many DBMSs support the same database structures (flat-file, relational, hierarchical, or network), each DBMS is an individual application that creates its own proprietary file types. For example, even though Access and Paradox are both relational DBMSs, Access creates its database files in a

PostgreSQL is another open source relational DBMS that is becoming a popular alternative to MySQL. You can find more information on PostgreSQL at *http://www.postgresql.org/*.

389

Many DBMSs also use a data definition language, or DDL, for creating databases, tables, fields, and other database components.

proprietary format with an .accdb extension (.mdb for Access 2003 and earlier), whereas Paradox creates a set of database files in a different proprietary format, with the data stored in files with a .db extension. Although both Paradox and Access contain filters that allow you to import the other's file formats, the database files are not completely interchangeable between the two programs. The same is true for most DBMSs; they can import each other's file formats, but they cannot directly read each other's files.

In today's ever-evolving technology environment, an application must often access multiple databases created in different DBMSs. For example, a company might need a PHP script that simultaneously accesses a large legacy database written in Sybase and a newer database written in Oracle. Converting the large Sybase database to Oracle would be cost prohibitive. On the other hand, the company cannot continue using the older Sybase database exclusively because its needs have grown beyond the older database's capabilities. So, the company must be able to access the data in both systems.

To allow easy access to data in various database formats, Microsoft established the **Open Database Connectivity** standard (**ODBC**). ODBC allows compliant applications to access any data source for which there is an ODBC driver. ODBC uses SQL commands (known as ODBC SQL) to allow an ODBC-compliant application to access a database. Essentially, an ODBC application connects to a database for which there is an ODBC driver and then executes ODBC SQL commands. Then, the ODBC driver translates the SQL commands into a format that the database can understand. PHP includes strong support for ODBC, and includes functionality that allows you to work directly with different types of databases without going through ODBC. Some of the databases that you can access directly from PHP include Oracle, Informix, MySQL, and PostgreSQL. By eliminating the ODBC layer, your PHP scripts will be faster. Furthermore, PHP code that directly accesses a database allows you to access proprietary DBMS functions that are not supported by ODBC. Therefore, your rule of thumb should be to always use direct database access if it is available in PHP. Otherwise, use PHP's ODBC functionality to access ODBC-compliant databases.

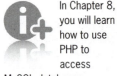

In Chapter 8, you will learn how to use PHP to access MySQL databases directly.

Querying Databases with Structured Query Language (SQL)

Programmers at IBM developed SQL in the 1970s as a way to query databases for specific criteria. Since then, SQL has been adopted by numerous DBMSs running on mainframes, minicomputers, and PCs. In 1986, the American National Standards Institute (ANSI) approved an official standard for the SQL language. In 1991, the X/Open and SQL Access Group created a standardized version of SQL known as the Common Applications Environment (CAE) SQL draft specification. Even with two major standards available, however, most DBMSs use their own version of the SQL language. MySQL corresponds primarily to the ANSI SQL standard, although it includes a few of its own extensions to the language.

SQL uses fairly easy-to-understand statements to execute database commands. SQL statements are composed of keywords that perform actions on a database. Table 7-1 lists several SQL keywords that are common to most versions of SQL.

> If you ever work directly with another DBMS, keep in mind that the SQL you learn in this chapter might not correspond directly to that DBMS's version of SQL.

391

Keyword	Description
DELETE	Deletes a row from a table
FROM	Specifies the tables from which to retrieve or delete records
INSERT	Inserts a new row into a table
INTO	Determines the table into which records should be inserted
ORDER BY	Sorts the records returned from a table
SELECT	Returns information from a table
UPDATE	Saves changes to fields in a record
WHERE	Specifies the conditions that must be met for records to be returned from a query

Table 7-1   Common SQL keywords

The simple SQL statement `SELECT * FROM Employees` returns all fields (using the asterisk wildcard) from the `Employees` table. The following code shows a more complex SQL statement that selects the `last_name` and `first_name` fields from the `Employees` table if the record's `city` field is equal to "Spencer." The results are then sorted by the `last_name` and `first_name` fields using the `ORDER BY` keyword. Notice that commas separate multiple field names.

```
SELECT last_name, first_name FROM Employees
WHERE city = "Spencer" ORDER BY last_name, first_name;
```

 You will study many of the basic SQL keywords in this chapter. For in-depth information on SQL statements supported in MySQL, refer to the MySQL Reference Manual at *http://dev.mysql.com/doc/mysql/en/index.html*.

Short Quiz

1. Explain the difference between a flat-file database and a relational database.

2. Explain the relationship between a primary key and a foreign key.

3. Describe the role of a junction (linking) table.

4. How does Open Database Connectivity (ODBC) assist in database management?

5. Define the acronym SQL and explain its role in database manipulation.

Before continuing with this chapter, be sure that you have been provided access to an account on a server with a MySQL installation, or that you have followed the instructions in Appendix B for installing and testing one of the xAMP packages.

MySQL Monitor will operate the same regardless of whether you use an SSH connection, a telnet connection, or a console window on the server. For the remainder of this chapter, the term "console window" refers to the window in which you enter commands.

Several examples in this chapter show the contents of a console window and contain both displayed text and text that you enter. To distinguish between the two types of text, the text that you enter is shown in bold, even though it won't appear in bold in the console window. Additionally, the symbol [ENTER◄┘] will indicate where you need to press the Enter key. This symbol does not actually appear on the screen.

Getting Started with MySQL

As open source software, MySQL is a logical fit with Apache and PHP, both of which are also developed as open source software. But there are other reasons for MySQL's popularity: It is also fast and reliable, and it supports other programming languages besides PHP, including C, C++, and Java. MySQL is also fairly easy to use and install and is available on a number of different platforms.

There are several ways to interface with a MySQL database server to access and manage your databases, including MySQL Monitor, phpMyAdmin, and PHP database functions. The MySQL program you will primarily use in this chapter is MySQL Monitor, which is a command-line program for manipulating MySQL databases. You execute the MySQL Monitor program with the `mysql` command, which you run through an SSH connection, a telnet connection, or in a console window on the server itself. Your instructor should provide you with the information and tools needed to create a command-line connection to the MySQL server.

In the next section, you will learn how to log in to MySQL.

Logging in to MySQL

To access or manipulate databases with MySQL programs such as MySQL Monitor (mysql) or phpMyAdmin, you need to log in to the MySQL database server. To use MySQL Monitor to log in to the server, enter the following command:

```
mysql -h host -u user -p
```

In the preceding command, the -h argument allows you to specify the host name where your MySQL database server is installed. The default value for this argument is *localhost*, so if you are working with an instance of a MySQL database server that is installed on your local computer, you do not need to specify the -h argument and host name. However, if you are working with a MySQL database server on an ISP's Web site, you need to enter your ISP's host name. The -u argument allows you to specify a user account name, and the -p switch prompts you for a password. For example, the following command logs the user name *dongosselin* into MySQL Monitor on a UNIX installation of MySQL:

```
[dongosselin] $ mysql -h php_db -u dongosselin -p[ENTER↵]
Enter password: **********[ENTER↵]
Welcome to the MySQL monitor. Commands end with ; or \g.
Your MySQL connection id is 6611 to server version: 4.1.9-nt

Type 'help;' or '\h' for help. Type '\c' to clear the buffer.

mysql>
```

You are successfully logged in when you see the mysql> prompt.

To log in to MySQL Monitor:

1. Open a new console window.

2. Log in with the following command. Be sure to replace *host* and *user* with the host name and user name provided by your ISP or instructor.

   ```
   mysql -h host -u user -p
   ```

When prompted, enter the password provided by your ISP or instructor. If you are working on a UNIX platform, your screen should look like Figure 7-6.

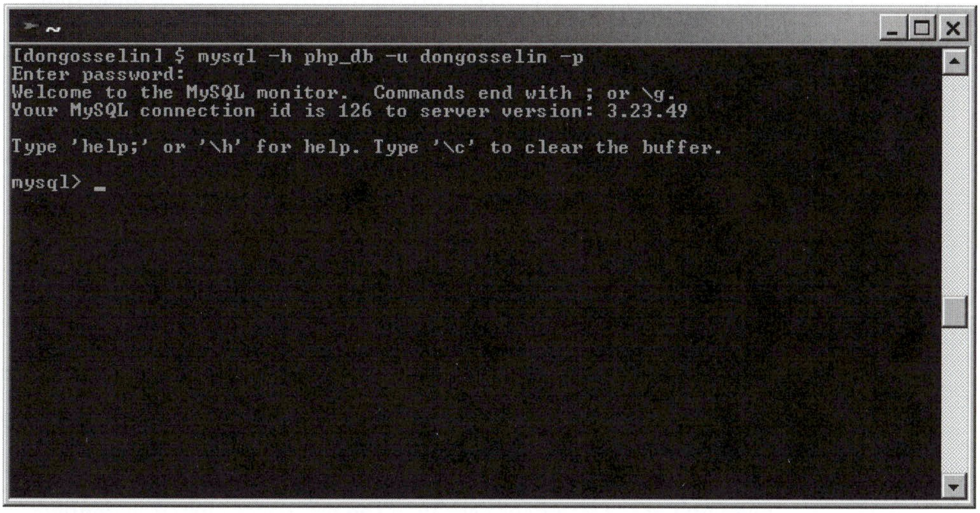

```
[dongosselin] $ mysql -h php_db -u dongosselin -p
Enter password:
Welcome to the MySQL monitor.  Commands end with ; or \g.
Your MySQL connection id is 126 to server version: 3.23.49

Type 'help;' or '\h' for help. Type '\c' to clear the buffer.

mysql> _
```

Figure 7-6 MySQL Monitor on a UNIX platform

Although the screen captures in this chapter are taken from a UNIX operating system console window, the MySQL Monitor portion of your window should appear the same regardless of which operating system you use.

When you finish working with MySQL Monitor, you can log out and exit the program by entering either the `exit` or `quit` command. You are successfully logged out when you see "Bye" and your command prompt is restored to the command line for your operating system. The following example shows how the command line appears on a Windows installation of MySQL:

```
mysql> exit[ENTER↵]
Bye

[dongosselin] $
```

To log out of MySQL Monitor:

1. Return to MySQL Monitor.

2. Type **exit** or **quit** and press **Enter**. You should see "Bye" printed to the screen and the command prompt restored to the command line for your operating system.

Working with MySQL Monitor

The `mysql>` command prompt in MySQL Monitor is where most of the action occurs when you create or manipulate databases in MySQL. If you are familiar with graphical database management systems, such as Microsoft Access, you might need some time to get used to the `mysql>` command prompt. However, keep in mind that most database management systems, including Access, use SQL to manipulate databases. MySQL just removes the graphical "front end" and allows you to enter SQL commands directly. After you become familiar with working in MySQL Monitor, you may find that you prefer manipulating databases with the `mysql>` command prompt over using a graphical DBMS because you have more precise control over your database. You may also find that a graphical front end might not always be available for the database that you need to use, so your only option is to use a command-line utility. It's also worth repeating that you must understand how to write SQL commands manually to access MySQL databases from PHP scripts, as you do in the next chapter.

When you enter a SQL command at the `mysql>` command prompt, you must terminate the command with a semicolon. For example, the following SQL statement lists all of the databases currently defined for your user name:

```
MYSQL> SHOW DATABASES;[ENTER↵]
+-------------+
| Database    |
+-------------+
| dongosselin |
| mysql       |
| test        |
+-------------+
3 rows in set (0.00 sec)
mysql>
```

If you omit the ending semicolon when you enter a SQL statement, MySQL Monitor assumes that you want to enter a multiple-line command and changes the prompt to ->, which indicates that you need to enter the next line of the command. For example, the following version of the SHOW command does not include the terminating semicolon. For this reason, the command prompt changes to -> so that you can enter more statements.

```
mysql> SHOW DATABASES[ENTER↵]
    ->
```

To finish executing the preceding statement, just type a semicolon by itself at the -> command prompt and press Enter.

The SQL keywords you enter in MySQL Monitor are not case sensitive, so you can enter any of the following statements to list the databases available to you:

```
mysql> SHOW databases;[ENTER↵]
mysql> show databases;[ENTER↵]
mysql> SHOW DATABASES;[ENTER↵]
```

Although you can use any case for SQL keywords, most programmers follow the convention of using uppercase letters for SQL keywords and using lowercase or mixed case for the names of databases, tables, and fields.

Understanding MySQL Identifiers

In MySQL, you must define identifiers (names) for databases, tables, fields, indexes, and aliases. An **alias** is an alternate name that you can use to refer to a table or field in SQL statements. In MySQL, all identifiers except aliases are limited to 64 characters in length. Aliases can be up to 255 characters. For database and table names, you can include any characters that your operating system allows in directory names and filenames, with the exception of forward slashes (/), backslashes (\), and periods (.). Fields, indexes, and aliases can consist of any characters, including forward slashes, backslashes, and periods.

You can use the up and down arrow keys on the keyboard to scroll back through previously entered commands. Once the command is selected, you can edit it. Be sure that the cursor is at the end of the command before pressing the Enter key, or anything after the insertion point will be ignored.

Identifiers in MySQL are quoted using the **backtick**, or left single quote, character ('). Any identifier may be enclosed in backticks, but certain identifiers must be enclosed in backticks. The following list shows when an identifier must be quoted.

- An identifier that includes any character except standard alphanumeric characters, underscores (_), or dollar signs ($)

- An identifier that contains one or more space characters

- An identifier that is a reserved word in MySQL

- An identifier made entirely of numeric digits

- An identifier that contains a backtick character

As shown in the preceding list, an identifier must be enclosed in backtick characters for the identifier to contain a backtick character. Additionally, the backtick character within the identifier must be escaped by preceding it with a backtick character. For example, the identifier don't must be encoded as 'don''t'.

For example, if the first name and last name fields in the Employees table include spaces, you must use backticks to refer to the fields. The following statement demonstrates how to return the first name and last name fields from the Employees table:

```
mysql> SELECT * 'first name', 'last name' FROM Employees[ENTER↵]
    -> WHERE city = "Spencer" ORDER BY 'last name', 'first
name';[ENTER↵]
```

Even though SQL keywords are not case sensitive, the case sensitivity of database and table identifiers depends on your operating system. MySQL stores each database in a directory of the same name as the database identifier. Tables are stored in the database directory in files of the same name as the table identifier. Directory names and filenames are not case sensitive on Windows platforms, but are case sensitive on UNIX/Linux systems. This means that you do not need to worry about case sensitivity in database and table names on Windows platforms, but you do need to observe letter case when referring to database and table names on UNIX/Linux systems.

Getting Help with MySQL Commands

Most of the commands you enter in MySQL Monitor are SQL commands. However, MySQL Monitor includes additional commands, such as exit and quit, which are not part of the SQL language. If you type help; or ? at the MySQL command prompt, you should see several support URLs along with the following command descriptions shown in Table 7-2:

Many other DBMSs do not allow special characters such as the space in identifiers, nor do they allow identifiers to start with a digit. To allow for portability across systems, many programmers specify identifiers using the most common naming convention, which uses a letter for the first character, followed only by letters, numbers, and the underscore (_) character.

Field and index identifiers are case insensitive on all platforms.

Command	Short Form	Description
?	\?	Synonym for "help"
clear	\c	Clear command
connect	\r	Reconnect to the server. Optional arguments are db and host.
delimiter	\d	Set query delimiter
edit	\e	Edit command with $EDITOR
ego	\G	Send command to MySQL server and display result vertically
exit	\q	Exit MySQL. Same as quit.
go	\g	Send command to MySQL server
nopager	\n	Disable pager, print to stdout
help	\h	Display this help
note	\t	Don't write into outfile
pager	\P	Set PAGER [to_pager]. Print the query results via PAGER.
print	\p	Print current command
prompt	\R	Change your MySQL prompt
quit	\q	Quit MySQL
rehash	\#	Rebuild completion hash
source	\.	Execute a SQL script file. Takes a filename as an argument.
status	\s	Get status information from the server
system	\!	Execute a system shell command
tee	\T	Set outfile [to_outfile]. Append everything into given outfile.
use	\u	Use another database. Takes database name as argument.

Table 7-2 List of common MySQL commands

Each of the preceding commands has a long and a short form. The long form of each command is not case sensitive, so you can use any case you want. (For example, QUIT and Quit are both acceptable.) However, for the sake of consistency, you should stick with the letter cases that are presented in this book for each command. The short form of each command allows you to type a backslash and a single character to execute the command. Unlike each command's long form, the short form is case sensitive. To enter the short form of the quit command, for example, you must use \q, not \Q. With both the long and short forms of each command, you can include a semicolon to terminate the line, although it is not required.

The edit, nopager, pager, and system commands are only available on UNIX/Linux systems.

To log back in to MySQL Monitor and display help for the MySQL Monitor commands:

1. Return to your console window and log back in to MySQL with the **root** account, or with the user name and password supplied by your ISP or instructor.

2. Type **help;** or **?** at the MySQL command prompt and press **Enter**. You should see a list of MySQL commands, as shown in Figure 7-7.

3. Log out by typing **\q** at the MySQL command prompt and pressing **Enter**. You should see "Bye" displayed on the screen and the command prompt restored to the command line for your operating system.

```
MySQL commands:
Note that all text commands must be first on line and end with ';'
help      (\h)    Display this help.
?         (\?)    Synonym for 'help'.
clear     (\c)    Clear command.
connect   (\r)    Reconnect to the server. Optional arguments are db and host.
edit      (\e)    Edit command with $EDITOR.
ego       (\G)    Send command to mysql server, display result vertically.
exit      (\q)    Exit mysql. Same as quit.
go        (\g)    Send command to mysql server.
nopager   (\n)    Disable pager, print to stdout.
notee     (\t)    Don't write into outfile.
pager     (\P)    Set PAGER [to_pager]. Print the query results via PAGER.
print     (\p)    Print current command.
quit      (\q)    Quit mysql.
rehash    (\#)    Rebuild completion hash.
source    (\.)    Execute a SQL script file. Takes a file name as an argument.
status    (\s)    Get status information from the server.
tee       (\T)    Set outfile [to_outfile]. Append everything into given outfile.
use       (\u)    Use another database. Takes database name as argument.

Connection id: 121   (Can be used with mysqladmin kill)

mysql>
```

Figure 7-7 MySQL command help

Short Quiz

1. What is the termination character for a SQL statement?

2. What SQL command(s) log you out of MySQL Monitor?

3. Explain how a multiline SQL statement is structured in MySQL Monitor.

4. How can you browse through previous SQL commands in MySQL Monitor?

Working with MySQL Databases

This section explains the basics of working with databases in MySQL.

Creating Databases

You use the CREATE DATABASE statement to create a new database. The following statement creates the vehicle_fleet database:

```
mysql> CREATE DATABASE vehicle_fleet;[ENTER↵]
Query OK, 1 row affected (0.00 sec)
```

If the database is created successfully, you see the "Query OK" message shown in the preceding example. If the database already exists, you see the following message:

```
mysql> CREATE DATABASE vehicle_fleet;[ENTER↵]
ERROR 1007: Can't create database 'vehicle_fleet';
database exists
```

To use a specific database, you must select it by executing the USE *database* statement, as follows:

```
mysql> USE vehicle_fleet;[ENTER↵]
Database changed
```

You see the "Database changed" message if MySQL successfully changes to the specified database. User accounts that do not have permission to work with a specified database receive an error message similar to the following:

You will study how to manage user accounts and permissions later in this chapter.

```
mysql> USE vehicle_fleet;[ENTER↵]
ERROR 1044: Access denied for user 'dongosselin'@'%' to
database 'vehicle_fleet'
```

Creating a new database does not automatically make the new database the active database. You must follow the CREATE DATABASE command with a USE *database* command to use the newly created database.

To verify that you are in the correct database, you use the MySQL built-in function DATABASE(). The DATABASE() function returns the name of the currently active database. Unlike PHP, when you call a function in MySQL, you must use the SELECT keyword before the function. This tells MySQL to execute the function and return the result. To verify that you are using the vehicle_fleet database, you would enter the following:

```
mysql> SELECT DATABASE();[ENTER↵]
```

Keep in mind that the CREATE DATABASE statement only creates a new directory for the specified database. Before you can add records to a new database, you must first define the tables and fields that will store your data. Later in this chapter, you will learn how to define tables and fields in a database.

To create a new database:

1. Return to MySQL Monitor. You should still be logged in from the preceding exercise.

2. Enter the following command to create the sitevisitors database:

   mysql> **CREATE DATABASE sitevisitors;[ENTER↵]**

3. After you see the "Query OK" message, enter the following command to select the sitevisitors database:

   mysql> **USE sitevisitors;[ENTER↵]**

4. After you see the "Database changed" message, type the following command to ensure that you selected the sitevisitors database:

   mysql> **SELECT DATABASE();[ENTER↵]**

Selecting a Database

To view the databases that are available, use the SHOW DATABASES statement shown earlier, as follows:

```
mysql> SHOW DATABASES;[ENTER↵]
+---------------+
| Database      |
+---------------+
| vehicle_fleet |
+---------------+
1 row in set (0.00 sec)
```

No database is selected when you first log in to MySQL. To work with a database, you must first select it by executing the USE *database* statement, just as you did after creating the database. For example, the following statement selects the vehicle_fleet database:

```
mysql> USE vehicle_fleet;[ENTER↵]
Database changed
```

If you forget which database is selected, you can use the SELECT DATABASE() statement to display the name of the currently selected database, as follows:

```
mysql> SELECT DATABASE();[ENTER↵]
+---------------+
| DATABASE()    |
+---------------+
| vehicle_fleet |
+---------------+
1 row in set (0.00 sec)
```

The response from the SELECT DATABASE(); command shows that you are in the vehicle_fleet database.

400

If you install a local version of MySQL, two databases are installed with it: mysql and test. The mysql database contains user accounts and other information required for your installation of the MySQL database server. The test database ensures that the database server is working properly.

To log back in to MySQL Monitor and select a database:

1. Return to your console window and log back in to MySQL with the **root** account or with the user name and password supplied by your ISP or instructor.

2. Type the following command to display the databases that are available in your MySQL installation. By default, you should only see the **mysql** and **test** databases, although your installation might include more.

    mysql> **SHOW DATABASES;[ENTER←┘]**

3. Type the following at the MySQL command prompt to select the **mysql** database:

    mysql> **USE mysql;[ENTER←┘]**

4. After you see the "Database changed" message, type the following command to ensure that you selected the **mysql** database:

    mysql> **SELECT DATABASE();[ENTER←┘]**

    Your screen should look like Figure 7-8.

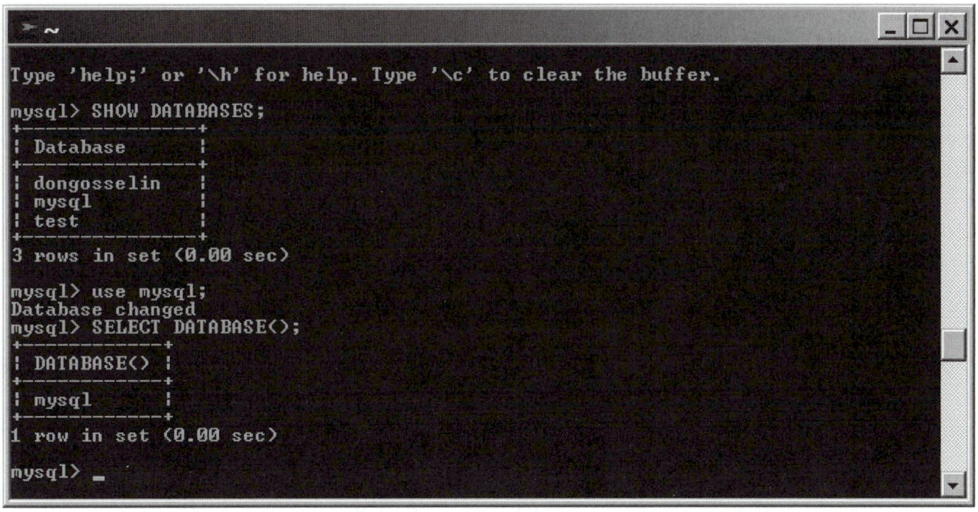

Figure 7-8 MySQL Monitor after selecting a database

Deleting Databases

To delete a database, you execute the DROP DATABASE statement, which removes all tables from the database and deletes the database itself. The syntax for the DROP DATABASE statement is as follows:

DROP DATABASE *database*;

Although the vehicle_fleet database is deleted with this command, it will be re-created for use with examples later in this chapter.

402

You must be logged in as the **root** user or have DROP privileges to delete a database. You will study privileges later in this chapter.

If you are working with an instance of MySQL that is hosted by an ISP, the **test** database might have already been deleted or you might not have sufficient privileges to delete databases.

The following statement deletes the `vehicle_fleet` database:

```
mysql> DROP DATABASE vehicle_fleet;[ENTER↵]
Query OK, 0 rows affected (0.00 sec)
```

To delete the `test` database:

1. Return to MySQL Monitor.

2. Type the following command to ensure that the `test` database exists in your MySQL installation:

   ```
   mysql> SHOW DATABASES;[ENTER↵]
   ```

3. If you see the `test` database in the list of available databases, enter the following command to delete it:

   ```
   mysql> DROP DATABASE test;[ENTER↵]
   ```

4. After you see the "Query OK" message, enter the following command again to ensure that the `test` database no longer exists:

   ```
   mysql> SHOW DATABASES;[ENTER↵]
   ```

Short Quiz

1. What statement creates a new directory for a specified database?

2. What built-in function can be used to return the name of the active database?

3. What statement must be executed to change to a specified database from the active database?

4. What statement is used to delete a database and any tables it contains?

Defining Database Tables

This section explains how to select field data types, create tables, and delete existing tables. Remember that before you can add tables to a database, you must first create the database, as described earlier in this chapter.

Specifying Field Data Types

By now, you should thoroughly understand that PHP variables consist of different data types, which are the specific categories of information that a variable can contain. Just like PHP variables, the fields in a table also store data according to type. Recall that one of the most important purposes of a variable's data type is to determine how much memory the computer allocates for the data stored in the variable. Similarly, the data types in database fields determine how much storage space the computer allocates for the data in the database. MySQL includes numerous data types that are categorized into numeric types, string types, and date/time types. Table 7-3 lists some of the common MySQL data types.

Type	Storage	Range	Special information
BOOL	1 byte	−128 to 127	0 is considered FALSE
TINYINT	1 byte	−128 to 127	
SMALLINT	2 bytes	−32,768 to 32,767	
MEDIUMINT	3 bytes	−8,388,608 to 8,388,607	
INT or INTEGER	4 bytes	−2,147,483,648 to 2,147,483,647	
BIGINT	8 bytes	−9,223,372,036,854,775,808 to 9,223,372,036,854,775,807	
FLOAT	4 bytes	−3.402823466E+38 to −1.175494351E-38, 0, and 1.175494351E-38 to 3.402823466E+38	0 to 24 bits of precision
DOUBLE or DOUBLE PRECISION	8 bytes	−1.7976931348623157E+308 to −2.2250738585072014E-308, 0, and 2.2250738585072014E-308 to 1.7976931348623157E+308	25-53 bits of precision
DATE	3 bytes	'0000-00-00', '1000-01-01' to '9999-12-31'	
TIME	3 bytes	'−838:59:59' to '838:59:59'	
CHAR(m)	Number of bytes specified by m	Fixed-length string between 0 to 255 characters	
VARCHAR(m)	Varies up to the number of bytes specified by m	Variable-length string with a maximum length between 0 to 65,535 characters	Maximum length is 255 in older versions
ENUM	Varies	One of a set of predefined strings	
SET	Varies	Zero or more of a set of predefined strings, separated by commas	

Table 7-3　Common MySQL data types

You can find a complete listing of MySQL data types in the MySQL Reference Manual at http://dev.mysql.com/doc/mysql/en/index.html.

To store text in a field, you specify a data type of CHAR(*m*) or VARCHAR(*m*). For both data types, you replace *m* with the maximum number of characters you anticipate the field will store. In general, you should use the VARCHAR(*m*) data type because the amount of storage space it occupies varies according to the number of characters in the field.

Be sure you have executed the USE statement to select a database before executing the CREATE TABLE statement, or you might create your new table in the wrong database.

You can execute the SHOW TABLES statement to display a list of the tables in the current database.

To keep your database from growing too large, you should choose the smallest data type possible for each field. For example, the SMALLINT data type stores integer values between −32,768 and 32,767 and occupies 2 bytes of storage space, regardless of how small the value is. In comparison, the BIGINT data type stores integer values between −9,223,372,036,854,775,808 and 9,223,372,036,854,775,807 and occupies 8 bytes of storage space, no matter how small the value. If you know that a value you assign to a field will always be between −32,768 and 32,767, you should use the SMALLINT data type instead of the BIGINT data type, which saves 6 bytes per record. For a single record, this is not a huge savings, but it could be for a database table with thousands or even millions of records.

Creating Tables

To create a table, you use the CREATE TABLE statement, which specifies the table and column names and the data type for each column. The syntax for the CREATE TABLE statement is as follows:

```
CREATE TABLE table_name (column_name TYPE, ...);
```

The following statement creates the vehicles table in the vehicle_fleet database. The first three columns in the table are VARCHAR data types; the license field can be a maximum of 10 characters, the make field can be a maximum of 25 characters, and the model field can be a maximum of 50 characters. The miles field is a FLOAT data type. The last field, assigned_to, is also a VARCHAR data type, with a maximum of 40 characters.

```
mysql> CREATE TABLE vehicles (license VARCHAR(10),[ENTER↵]
    -> make VARCHAR(25), model VARCHAR(50), miles FLOAT,[ENTER↵]
    -> assigned_to VARCHAR(40));[ENTER↵]
```

After you create a table, you can use the DESCRIBE statement to display how the table is structured. The following DESCRIBE statement displays the structure of the vehicles table below the command:

```
mysql> DESCRIBE vehicles;[ENTER↵]
```

Field	Type	Null	Key	Default	Extra
license	varchar(10)	YES		NULL	
make	varchar(25)	YES		NULL	
model	varchar(50)	YES		NULL	
miles	float	YES		NULL	
assigned_to	varchar(40)	YES		NULL	

```
5 rows in set (0.00 sec)
```

The result of the preceding DESCRIBE vehicles; command showed six columns, not just the two for Field and Type. The other four columns show special characteristics or restrictions on the fields that can be defined in MySQL. The values for these columns can be specified in the CREATE TABLE statement. The Null column indicates whether the field can be left empty or not. The Key field indicates which type of key, if any, is defined for the field (PRIMARY, UNIQUE, or INDEX). The Default column shows the value that will be inserted automatically in the field if no value is specified. The Extra column indicates any special features about the field, such as an auto-increment value.

Next, you will create a table named pagevisits in the sitevisitors database. The table will contain detailed information about every visit to a Web page on your site. The table will contain seven fields: page_filename, visit_date, visit_time, previous_page, request_method, remote_host, and remote_port. The visit_date field will be a DATE data type, the visit_time field will be a TIME data type, the remote_port field will be an INTEGER data type, and the rest of the fields will be VARCHAR data types. Note that the TIME data type can be used to store a specific time or a measure of time. In the pagevisits table, the visit_time field will contain the duration of each visit. For the DATE data type, dates must be entered in the format YYYY-MM-DD; for the TIME data type, times must be entered in the format HH:MM:SS.

To create the pagevisits table:

1. Return to MySQL Monitor.

2. Enter the following command to select the sitevisitors database:

   mysql> **USE sitevisitors;[ENTER↵]**

3. Enter the following command to create the pagevisits table:

   mysql> **CREATE TABLE pagevisits (page_filename VARCHAR(250), visit_date DATE,[ENTER↵]**
   -> visit_time TIME, previous_page VARCHAR(250),[ENTER↵]
   -> request_method VARCHAR(10), remote_host VARCHAR(250), remote_port INT);[ENTER↵]

4. After you see the "Query OK" message, enter the following command to view the structure of the new table. Your screen should look like Figure 7-9.

   mysql> **DESCRIBE pagevisits;[ENTER↵]**

Figure 7-9 DESCRIBE statement displaying the structure of the pagevisits table

Altering Tables

Over time, the original table definition may not be sufficient for your needs. New fields may be needed, existing fields may become obsolete, or the field modifiers may no longer be appropriate. To modify the structure of a table, you use the ALTER TABLE statement. The statement has several different syntaxes, depending on the change being made.

Adding Columns

The keyword COLUMN is required for standard SQL, but not for MySQL. When adding a single column, the parentheses around the list of column_name and column_type specifiers are optional.

To add fields to a table with the ALTER TABLE statement, use the following syntax:

```
ALTER TABLE table_name ADD [COLUMN] (column_name column_type [, column_name column_type ...]);
```

The following statement adds a new column of type INT named model_year to the vehicles table in the vehicle_fleet database:

```
mysql> ALTER TABLE vehicles ADD COLUMN (model_year INT); [ENTER↵]
```

Modifying Column Types

To change the data type of an existing field in a table with the ALTER TABLE statement, use the following syntax:

```
ALTER TABLE table_name MODIFY [COLUMN] column_name column_type;
```

406

Because the model_year field will hold only four-digit years, it can fit in a two-byte SMALLINT rather than a four-byte INT. The following statement changes the column type of the model_year field from INT to SMALLINT in the vehicles table in the vehicle_fleet database:

```
mysql> ALTER TABLE vehicles MODIFY COLUMN model_year
SMALLINT; [ENTER↵]
```

Unlike the ADD COLUMN clause, the MODIFY COLUMN clause applies to only a single field.

Renaming Columns

To change the name of an existing field in a table with the ALTER TABLE statement, use the following syntax:

```
ALTER TABLE table_name CHANGE [COLUMN] column_name
new_name column_type;
```

The following statement changes the name of the miles field to mileage in the vehicles table in the vehicle_fleet database:

```
mysql> ALTER TABLE vehicles CHANGE COLUMN miles mileage
FLOAT; [ENTER↵]
```

Like the MODIFY COLUMN clause, the CHANGE COLUMN clause applies to only a single field. The column_type must always be specified, even if it doesn't change. To change the data type of the field at the same time, you specify the new column type for column_type. As when using the MODIFY COLUMN clause, make sure that any existing data can be converted to the new data type.

Renaming Tables

To change the name of an existing table with the ALTER TABLE statement, use the following syntax:

```
ALTER TABLE table_name RENAME [TO] new_name;
```

The following statement changes the name of the vehicles table to company_cars in the vehicle_fleet database:

```
mysql> ALTER TABLE vehicles RENAME TO company_cars; [ENTER↵]
```

Removing Columns

To remove an existing field from a table with the ALTER TABLE statement, use the following syntax:

```
ALTER TABLE table_name DROP [COLUMN] column_name;
```

The following statement removes the assigned_to column from the company_cars table in the vehicle_fleet database:

```
mysql> ALTER TABLE company_cars DROP COLUMN assigned_to; [ENTER↵]
```

 Be careful when changing the data type of a column. If the data stored in the field cannot be converted to the new data type, the data will be lost. In the previous example, any data values for the model_year column that are not in the range −32,758 to 32,757 will be set to NULL.

You must be logged in as the root user or have DROP privileges to delete a table.

408

Although the company_ cars table is deleted with this command, it will be re-created for use with examples later in this chapter.

Deleting Tables

To delete a table, you execute the DROP TABLE statement, which removes all data and the table definition. The syntax for the DROP TABLE statement is as follows:

```
DROP TABLE table;
```

The following statement deletes the company_cars table from the vehicle_fleet database:

```
mysql> DROP TABLE company_cars;[ENTER↵]
```

Short Quiz

1. Explain the importance of selecting the most appropriate data type for table fields.

2. Illustrate the SQL syntax to create a table.

3. What six columns are shown in the output of the DESCRIBE table statement?

4. What SQL keywords are used with the ALTER TABLE statement to add columns, modify columns, rename columns, or remove columns for an existing table?

Modifying User Privileges

MySQL assigns **privileges** to specify which actions and operations a user can perform with a table or database. By default, only administrator accounts such as the root account have full permissions on every database object. Regular users normally cannot create or drop databases. Within a database, the database owner and the root user are the only users who can create, alter, and drop tables, unless other users are expressly granted these permissions. Users can also be restricted in their ability to insert, update, delete, and select records from tables.

For security purposes, user accounts should only be assigned the minimum necessary privileges to perform given tasks. For example, if a user should only be able to view records from a table, you should only assign the SELECT privilege to the user's account. This helps secure your database by preventing the user from unintentionally (or maliciously) changing or tampering with database records.

This section provides an overview of how to manage user privileges. Table 7-4 lists common MySQL database privileges.

Privilege	Description
ALL	Assigns all privileges to the user
ALTER	Allows the user to modify the table structure
CREATE	Allows the user to create databases, tables, and indexes
DELETE	Allows the user to delete records
DROP	Allows the user to delete databases and tables
INDEX	Allows the user to create and delete indexes
INSERT	Allows the user to add records
SELECT	Allows the user to select records
UPDATE	Allows the user to modify records
USAGE	Creates a user with no privileges

Table 7-4   Common MySQL database privileges

 For information on additional privileges, including administrator privileges, refer to the MySQL Reference Manual at *http://dev.mysql.com/doc/mysql/en/index.html*.

Granting Privileges

You use a GRANT statement to create user accounts and assign privileges. The basic syntax for the GRANT statement is as follows:

```
GRANT privilege [(column)] [, privilege [(columns)] ...]
    ON {table | * | *.* | database.*}
    TO user [IDENTIFIED BY 'password'];
```

Privileges can be granted at the following levels: column, table, database, and global. The first line in the GRANT statement syntax allows you to specify individual columns to apply privileges. The ON portion of the GRANT statement determines the level to which privileges apply at the table, database, and global levels. You can specify the name of an individual table in the current database or an asterisk, which applies privileges to all the tables in the current database. If you specify "*.*", privileges are applied at a global level to all databases in your MySQL installation. You can also indicate a specific table within another database by appending the table name to the database name with a period.

The GRANT statement creates the user account if it does not exist and assigns the specified privileges. If the user account already exists, the GRANT statement just updates the privileges. As an example, the following statement creates a new user named dongosselin and assigns SELECT, INSERT, and UPDATE privileges to the user for all tables in the currently selected database. The statement also assigns a password of 'rosebud' to the dongosselin account.

After you create a user account, you do not need to specify a password when updating privileges. However, if you specify a password other than the current password for an existing user account, the password is reset.

410

```
mysql> GRANT SELECT, INSERT, UPDATE[ENTER↵]
    -> ON *[ENTER↵]
    -> TO dongosselin IDENTIFIED BY 'rosebud';[ENTER↵]
```

The following statement assigns privileges to the user dongosselin to a table named students in the currently selected database:

```
mysql> GRANT SELECT, INSERT, UPDATE[ENTER↵]
    -> ON students[ENTER↵]
    -> TO dongosselin;[ENTER↵]
```

The following statement assigns privileges to the user dongosselin at the global level to all databases in a MySQL installation:

```
mysql> GRANT SELECT, INSERT, UPDATE[ENTER↵]
    -> ON *.*[ENTER↵]
    -> TO dongosselin;[ENTER↵]
```

The following statement assigns privileges to the user dongosselin to the company_cars table in the vehicle_fleet database:

```
mysql> GRANT SELECT, INSERT, UPDATE[ENTER↵]
    -> ON vehicle_fleet.company_cars[ENTER↵]
    -> TO dongosselin;[ENTER↵]
```

Finally, the following statement uses a wildcard (*) to assign privileges to the user dongosselin to all tables in the vehicle_fleet database:

```
mysql> GRANT SELECT, INSERT, UPDATE[ENTER↵]
    -> ON vehicle_fleet.*[ENTER↵]
    -> TO dongosselin;[ENTER↵]
```

All of the preceding examples specified the user dongosselin. MySQL does not support wildcards for the user.

To create a new user account with privileges to the sitevisitors database:

If you are working with a hosted instance of MySQL, you might not have been assigned privileges to create user accounts.

1. Return to MySQL Monitor.

2. Enter the following statement to create a new user account with CREATE, DROP, ALTER, DELETE, INDEX, INSERT, SELECT, and UPDATE privileges assigned to all the tables in the sitevisitors database. The statement also assigns a password to the account. Enter your own name (as one word) and a password you will remember.

   ```
   mysql> GRANT CREATE, DROP, ALTER, DELETE, INDEX,
   INSERT, SELECT, UPDATE[ENTER↵]
       -> ON sitevisitors.*[ENTER↵]
       -> TO yourname IDENTIFIED BY 'password';[ENTER↵]
   ```

3. Type **exit** or **quit** and press **Enter** to log out of MySQL.

4. Enter the following command to log back in to MySQL with the user account and password you just created:

```
mysql -u yourname -p
```

5. When prompted, enter the new password you assigned to the user account.

Revoking Privileges

You use the REVOKE statement to take away privileges from an existing user account for a specified table or database. The syntax for the REVOKE statement is as follows:

```
REVOKE privilege [(column)] [, privilege [(columns)]] ...
    ON {table | * | *.* | database.*}
    FROM user;
```

The following example revokes INSERT and UPDATE privileges from the dongosselin user account for the company_cars table in the vehicle_fleet database:

```
mysql> REVOKE INSERT, UPDATE[ENTER↵]
    -> ON vehicle_fleet.company_cars[ENTER↵]
    -> FROM dongosselin;[ENTER↵]
```

The REVOKE ALL PRIVILEGES statement removes all privileges from a user account for a specified table or database. The following example takes away all privileges from the dongosselin user account for the company_cars table in the vehicle_fleet database:

You must be logged in with the root account or have sufficient privileges to revoke privileges from another user account.

```
mysql> REVOKE ALL PRIVILEGES[ENTER↵]
    -> ON vehicle_fleet.company_cars[ENTER↵]
    -> FROM dongosselin;[ENTER↵]
```

In this chapter, the user account you created does not need the INDEX privilege, so you revoke it in the next exercise.

To revoke privileges:

1. Return to MySQL Monitor.

2. Type **exit** or **quit** and press **Enter** to log out of MySQL.

3. Log back in to MySQL with the root account.

4. When prompted, enter the password you assigned to the root account.

5. Enter the following command to revoke the INDEX privilege to the tables in the sitevisitors database from your user account:

```
mysql> REVOKE INDEX[ENTER↵]
    -> ON sitevisitors.*[ENTER↵]
    -> FROM yourname;[ENTER↵]
```

6. Type **exit** or **quit** and press **Enter** to log out of MySQL.

7. Log back in to MySQL with your user account.

8. Enter the following command to select the sitevisitors database:

   mysql> **use sitevisitors;**[ENTER↵]

Short Quiz

1. Explain the term "user privileges."

2. What are the four levels for which privileges may be granted?

3. What statement is used to take away privileges from an existing user account for a specified table in the database?

Working with Database Records

As described earlier, a record is a set of related field data stored as a single row in a table. A table can store an unlimited number of records, each with its own set of data. In this section, you will learn how to add records to a table and how to update and delete existing records.

Adding Records

You add individual records to a table with the INSERT statement. The basic syntax for the INSERT statement is as follows:

```
INSERT INTO table_name (column1, column2, ...)
VALUES(value1, value2, ...);
```

The values you enter into the VALUES list will be stored, in order, in the columns specified after the table name. Any values that you want left NULL can be omitted from the column list, or you can put the name in the column list and the keyword NULL in the corresponding position in the VALUES list. For example, the following statement adds a new row to the company_cars table in the vehicle_fleet database:

```
mysql> INSERT INTO company_cars (license, model_year,
make, model, mileage)[ENTER↵]
    -> VALUES('CK-2987', 2009, 'Toyota', 'Corolla',
3508.4);[ENTER↵]
```

You can also omit the column list, as follows:

```
INSERT INTO table_name VALUES(value1, value2, ...);
```

When you omit the column list, the values you enter in the VALUES list must be in the same order in which you defined the table fields, and each field in the table must have a specified value, even if the value specified is NULL. For example, the following statement adds a new row (record) to the company_cars table in the vehicle_fleet database:

```
mysql> INSERT INTO company_cars VALUES('CK-2987', 2009,[ENTER←]
    -> 'Toyota', 'Corolla', 3508.4);[ENTER←]
```

Specify NULL in any fields for which you do not have a value. For example, if you do not know the mileage of the vehicle, you can enter NULL as the last item in the VALUES list, as follows:

```
mysql> INSERT INTO company_cars VALUES('CK-2987', 2009,[ENTER←]
    -> 'Toyota', 'Corolla', NULL);[ENTER←]
```

Although it is permissible to omit the column list from the INSERT statement, it is generally considered a poor programming practice. If the structure of the table changes, values will not be assigned to the appropriate columns.

To add two records to the pagevisits table in the sitevisitors database:

1. Return to MySQL Monitor.

2. Enter the following command to add a record to the pagevisits table:

```
mysql> INSERT INTO pagevisits (page_filename, visit_
date, visit_time,[ENTER←]
    -> previous_page, request_method, remote_host,
remote_port)[ENTER←]
    -> VALUES('contact.php', '2012-03-17',
'10:32:29',[ENTER←]
    -> 'index.php', 'GET', 'cis_lab_24.example.edu',
80);[ENTER←]
```

3. After you see the "Query OK" message, add another record, as follows:

```
mysql> INSERT INTO pagevisits (page_filename, visit_
date, visit_time,[ENTER←]
    -> previous_page, request_method, remote_host,
remote_port)[ENTER←]
    -> VALUES('guest_book.php', '2012-03-17',
'10:35:18',[ENTER←]
    -> 'contact.php', 'GET', 'cis_lab_24.example.
edu', 80);[ENTER←]
```

Your screen should look like Figure 7-10.

Figure 7-10 MySQL Monitor after adding two records to the `pagevisits` table

Sometimes you need to insert more than one row of data. You can use multiple INSERT statements, but you also can insert multiple records with a single INSERT statement, using the following syntax:

```
INSERT INTO table_name (column1, column2, ...)
VALUES(value1, value2, ...), (value1, value2, ...), ...;
```

As shown above, multiple VALUE lists are separated by commas. Each value list is inserted as a separate record into the table. As with the single-record INSERT statement shown previously, the column list is optional, but should be included for good form.

In order to use the LOAD DATA statement, your account needs to be given FILE privileges, which allows the MySQL user account to access any files on the server that are available to the MySQL server account (not the user's server account).

For large data sets stored in external files, it is much more efficient to use the LOAD DATA statement to add multiple records to a database table. You use the LOAD DATA statement with the full path and name of a local text file that contains the records you want to add. The syntax for the LOAD DATA statement is as follows:

```
LOAD DATA INFILE 'file_path' INTO TABLE table_name
(column1, column2, ...);
```

Place each record in the text file on a separate line and place tabs between each field. The fields will be stored into the columns specified in the column list in the order specified. As with the INSERT statement, the column list is optional, but should always be used. If the column list is omitted, the values on each line must be in the same order in which you defined the table fields. For missing field values, do not use the keyword NULL, because it will be interpreted as the text value "NULL", not as a NULL value. Simply use consecutive tabs with nothing between them.

The following statement loads a file named company_cars.txt into the company_cars table in the vehicle_fleet database:

```
mysql> LOAD DATA INFILE 'company_cars.txt' INTO TABLE
company_cars;[ENTER↵]
```

To add new records to the pagevisits table in the sitevisitors database:

1. Return to MySQL Monitor.

2. Enter a LOAD DATA statement that inserts records from the page_visits.txt file in your Chapter directory for Chapter 7. Be certain to enter the full path for the location of your data files. Enter the following command, replacing *path_to_PHP_folders* with the full path for your PHP_Projects directory:

   ```
   mysql> LOAD DATA INFILE 'path_to_PHP_folders/
   Chapter.07/Chapter/page_visits.txt'[ENTER↵]
       -> INTO TABLE pagevisits [ENTER↵]
       -> FIELDS TERMINATED BY ',';[ENTER↵]
   ```

3. You should see a result similar to the following:

   ```
   Query OK, 12 rows affected (0.01 sec)
   Records: 12  Deleted: 0  Skipped: 0  Warnings: 0

   mysql>
   ```

Retrieving Records

You use the SELECT statement to retrieve records from a table. The basic syntax for a SELECT statement is as follows:

```
SELECT criteria FROM table_name;
```

You use the asterisk (*) wildcard with the SELECT statement to retrieve all fields from a table. You can also specify individual fields to return by separating field names with a comma. The following statement returns the model and mileage fields from the company_cars table in the vehicle_fleet database:

 The optional FIELDS TERMINATED BY clause of the LOAD DATA statement allows you to change the field separator to something other than a tab.

 If your MySQL account does not have FILE privileges, skip the following exercise.

 Use the MySQL server's directory path, not the Web URL path.

 The path names in the preceding examples are broken into multiple lines due to space limitations and would generate errors if used as shown. On UNIX/Linux and Windows platforms, you need to enter the path name on a single line or you will receive an error. Also, on Windows platforms, be sure to escape the backward slashes in your path, or use forward slashes, as shown in the preceding example.

```
mysql> SELECT model, mileage FROM company_cars;[ENTER↵]
+---------+---------+
| model   | mileage |
+---------+---------+
| Corolla |  3508.4 |
| Cobalt  | 24829.4 |
| Focus   | 24829.4 |
| Civic   | 48891.1 |
| Sentra  | 28336.7 |
| Accord  | 77484.4 |
| Camry   |   855.5 |
| Fusion  |    95.9 |
| Malibu  | 57024.2 |
| Sonata  | 62993.6 |
| Altima  | 17398.3 |
+---------+---------+
11 rows in set (0.00 sec)
```

To enter SELECT statements that return records from the pagevisits table in the sitevisitors database:

1. Return to MySQL Monitor.

2. Enter the following SELECT statement, which returns all records from the pagevisits table. Your output should look like Figure 7-11, although the lines might wrap, depending on your screen resolution.

   ```
   mysql> SELECT * FROM pagevisits;[ENTER↵]
   ```

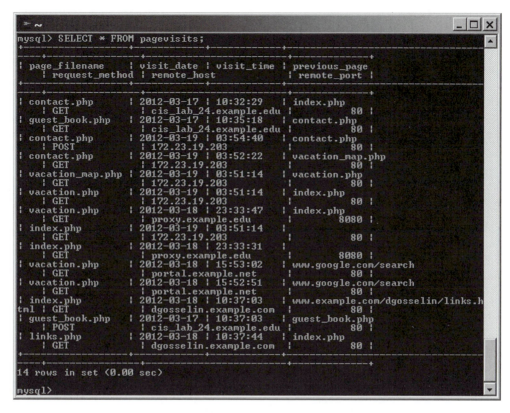

Figure 7-11   SELECT statement that returns all records from the pagevisits table

3. Enter the following SELECT statement, which returns the visit_date, previous_page, and page_filename fields from the pagevisits table. Your output should look like Figure 7-12.

```
mysql> SELECT visit_date, previous_page, page_
filename FROM pagevisits;[ENTER↵]
```

418

Figure 7-12 SELECT statement that returns the visit_date, previous_page, and page_filename fields from the pagevisits table

Using Aggregate Functions

You often need to summarize data in a set of records, rather than view the individual records. SQL offers various functions that you can include in queries to retrieve this aggregate data. Table 7-5 shows these functions.

Function	Description
AVG()	Return the average value of the argument
COUNT()	Return a count of the number of rows returned
GROUP_CONCAT()	Return a concatenated string
MAX()	Return the maximum value
MIN()	Return the minimum value
STD()	Return the population standard deviation
STDDEV_POP()	Return the population standard deviation
STDDEV_SAMP()	Return the sample standard deviation
STDDEV()	Return the population standard deviation
SUM()	Return the sum
VAR_POP()	Return the population standard variance
VAR_SAMP()	Return the sample variance
VARIANCE()	Return the population standard variance

Table 7-5 SQL aggregate functions

The GROUP_CONCAT() and VARIANCE() functions were added in Version 4.1 of MySQL. The STDDEV_POP(), STDDEV_SAMP(), VAR_POP(), and VAR_SAMP() functions were added in Version 5.0.3 of MySQL.

The COUNT() function has two unique features when compared to the other aggregate functions. First, you can use the wildcard (*) instead of a field name as the function argument. Second, the keyword DISTINCT can be used after the opening parenthesis. When the DISTINCT keyword is used, each unique value is counted as 1, no matter how many records contain that value.

There are two ways to use the aggregate functions. If only aggregate functions are used in the SELECT statement, the aggregate values include all records returned based on the WHERE clause. The following query will return 31476.991042397, the average of the mileage column for all records in the company_cars table:

```
mysql> SELECT AVG(mileage) FROM company_cars;[ENTER←]
```

To retrieve aggregate values for groups of records, you use the GROUP BY clause and include the fields that you use to group the records as part of the query. The following query will return the average mileage for each model year:

```
mysql> SELECT model_year, AVG(mileage)[ENTER←]
    -> FROM company_cars[ENTER←]
    -> GROUP BY model_year;[ENTER←]
+------------+------------------+
| model_year | AVG(mileage)     |
+------------+------------------+
|       2006 |    77484.3984375 |
|       2007 | 56302.967447917 |
|       2008 |          25998.5 |
|       2009 | 10453.350341797 |
|       2010 |  475.70000076294 |
+------------+------------------+
5 rows in set (0.00 sec)
```

To determine the number of pages visited from each remote_host:

1. Return to MySQL Monitor.

2. Enter the following SELECT statement, which returns each remote_host from the pagevisits table with the number of pages visited from that remote_host. Your output should look like Figure 7-13.

```
mysql> SELECT remote_host, COUNT(*)[ENTER←]
    -> FROM pagevisits[ENTER←]
    -> GROUP BY remote_host;[ENTER←]
```

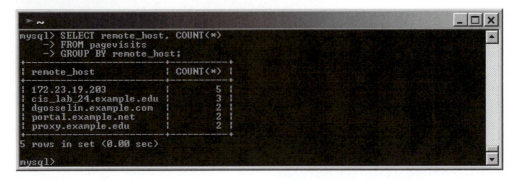

Figure 7-13 SELECT statement that returns the total number of visits from each
remote_host in the pagevisits table

3. Enter the following SELECT statement, which returns each
   remote_host from the pagevisits table with the number of
   distinct pages visited from that remote_host. Note that the
   wildcard was replaced by the name of the field that contains
   the names of the pages visited. Your output should look like
   Figure 7-14. Because three of the remote_host values had
   multiple records with the same value in the page_filename
   field, those three values had fewer distinct records than they
   had records.

   mysql> **SELECT remote_host, COUNT(DISTINCT page_
   filename)[ENTER↵]**
           -> **FROM pagevisits[ENTER↵]**
           -> **GROUP BY remote_host;[ENTER↵]**

Figure 7-14 SELECT statement that returns the number of different pages visited from
each remote_host in the pagevisits table

Sorting Query Results

You use the ORDER BY keyword with the SELECT statement to perform an alphanumeric sort of the results returned from a query. The following statement returns the make and model fields from the company_cars table in the vehicle_fleet database and sorts the results by the make field. The statement also performs a secondary sort on the model field:

```
mysql> SELECT make, model FROM company_cars ORDER BY make,
model; [ENTER←]
+-----------+---------+
| make      | model   |
+-----------+---------+
| Chevrolet | Cobalt  |
| Chevrolet | Malibu  |
| Ford      | Focus   |
| Ford      | Fusion  |
| Honda     | Accord  |
| Honda     | Civic   |
| Hyundai   | Sonata  |
| Nissan    | Altima  |
| Nissan    | Sentra  |
| Toyota    | Camry   |
| Toyota    | Corolla |
+-----------+---------+
11 rows in set (0.01 sec)
```

To perform a reverse sort, add the DESC keyword after the name of the field by which you want to perform the sort. (DESC stands for "descending.") The following statement returns the make and model fields from the company_cars table in the vehicle_fleet database and reverse sorts the results by the make field:

```
mysql> SELECT make, model FROM company_cars ORDER BY make
DESC, model; [ENTER←]
+-----------+---------+
| make      | model   |
+-----------+---------+
| Toyota    | Camry   |
| Toyota    | Corolla |
| Nissan    | Altima  |
| Nissan    | Sentra  |
| Hyundai   | Sonata  |
| Honda     | Accord  |
| Honda     | Civic   |
| Ford      | Focus   |
| Ford      | Fusion  |
| Chevrolet | Cobalt  |
| Chevrolet | Malibu  |
+-----------+---------+
11 rows in set (0.00 sec)
```

To enter several SELECT statements that sort records from the pagevisits table in the sitevisitors database:

1. Return to MySQL Monitor.

2. Enter the following SELECT statement, which returns the visit_date, previous_page, and page_filename fields from the pagevisits table, and sorts the returned records by previous_page and page_filename. Your output should look like Figure 7-15.

   ```
   mysql> SELECT visit_date, previous_page, page_
   filename[ENTER↵]
       -> FROM pagevisits ORDER BY previous_page, page_
   filename;[ENTER↵]
   ```

Figure 7-15 SELECT statement that returns the visit_date, previous_page, and page_filename fields from the pagevisits table, and sorts the returned records by previous_page and page_filename

3. Enter the following SELECT statement, which returns the visit_date, previous_page, and page_filename fields from the pagevisits table, and performs a descending sort of the returned records by visit_date. Your output should look like Figure 7-16.

   ```
   mysql> SELECT visit_date, previous_page, page_
   filename[ENTER↵]
       -> FROM pagevisits ORDER BY visit_date
   DESC;[ENTER↵]
   ```

422

Figure 7-16 SELECT statement that returns the visit_date, previous_page, and page_filename fields from the pagevisits table, and performs a descending sort of the returned records by visit_date

Filtering Query Results

The *criteria* portion of the SELECT statement determines which fields to retrieve from a table. You can also specify which records to return by using the WHERE keyword. For example, the following statement returns all records from the company_cars table in the vehicle_fleet database in which the make field is equal to "Toyota":

```
mysql> SELECT * FROM company_cars WHERE make='Toyota'; [ENTER←]
+---------+--------+---------+---------+------------+
| license | make   | model   | mileage | model_year |
+---------+--------+---------+---------+------------+
| CK-2987 | Toyota | Corolla | 3508.4  |       2009 |
| 8331-RT | Toyota | Camry   |  855.5  |       2010 |
+---------+--------+---------+---------+------------+
2 rows in set (0.00 sec)
```

SQL includes the keywords AND and OR that you can use to specify more detailed conditions about the records you want to return. For example, the following statement returns all records from the company_cars table in the vehicle_fleet database in which the model_year field is equal to 2007 and the mileage is less than 60000:

```
mysql> SELECT * FROM company_cars WHERE model_
year=2007[ENTER↵]
    -> AND mileage<60000;[ENTER↵]
+----------+-----------+--------+---------+------------+
| license  | make      | model  | mileage | model_year |
+----------+-----------+--------+---------+------------+
| AK-1234  | Honda     | Civic  | 48891.1 |       2007 |
| MN-304   | Chevrolet | Malibu | 57024.2 |       2007 |
+----------+-----------+--------+---------+------------+
2 rows in set (0.00 sec)
```

The following statement shows an example of how to use the OR keyword by returning all records from the company_cars table in the vehicle_fleet database in which the make field is equal to "Toyota" or "Honda". The statement also sorts the returned records by mileage.

```
mysql> SELECT * FROM company_cars WHERE
make='Toyota'[ENTER↵]
    -> OR make='Honda' ORDER BY mileage;[ENTER↵]
+----------+--------+---------+---------+------------+
| license  | make   | model   | mileage | model_year |
+----------+--------+---------+---------+------------+
| 8331-RT  | Toyota | Camry   |   855.5 |       2010 |
| CK-2987  | Toyota | Corolla |  3508.4 |       2009 |
| AK-1234  | Honda  | Civic   | 48891.1 |       2007 |
| C9L-2Y2  | Honda  | Accord  | 77484.4 |       2006 |
+----------+--------+---------+---------+------------+
4 rows in set (0.00 sec)
```

To enter several SELECT statements that use the WHERE keyword to filter records from the pagevisits table in the sitevisitors database:

1. Return to MySQL Monitor.

2. Enter the following SELECT statement, which returns all records from the pagevisits table in which the previous_page field is equal to "index.php". Your output should look like Figure 7-17.

```
mysql> SELECT * FROM pagevisits WHERE
previous_page='index.php';[ENTER↵]
```

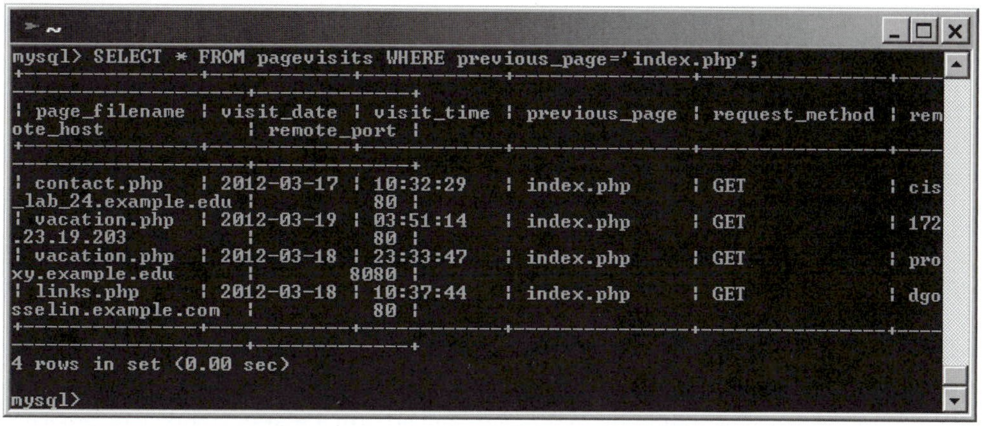

Figure 7-17 SELECT statement that returns all records from the `pagevisits` table in which the `previous_page` field is equal to "index.php"

3. Enter the following SELECT statement, which returns all records from the `pagevisits` table in which the `remote_port` field is greater than 80. Your output should look like Figure 7-18.

```
mysql> SELECT * FROM pagevisits WHERE remote_
port>80;[ENTER←]
```

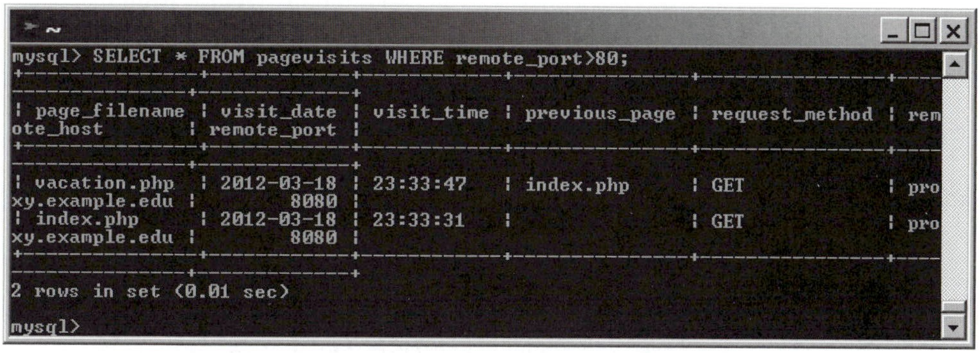

Figure 7-18 SELECT statement that returns all records from the `pagevisits` table in which the `remote_port` field is greater than 80

Updating Records

If you need to update records in a table, you use the UPDATE statement. The basic syntax for the UPDATE statement is as follows:

```
UPDATE table_name
SET column_name=value
WHERE condition;
```

The UPDATE keyword specifies the name of the table to update, and the SET keyword specifies the value to assign to the fields in the records that match the condition in the WHERE keyword. For example, the following statement modifies the mileage of the Ford Fusion to 368.2:

```
mysql> UPDATE company_cars SET mileage=368.2[ENTER↵]
    -> WHERE make='Ford'[ENTER↵]
    -> AND model='Fusion';[ENTER↵]
Query OK, 1 row affected (0.27 sec)
Rows matched: 1  Changed: 1  Warnings: 0
```

Notice that the preceding statement uses the WHERE keyword to specify that the make field should be equal to "Ford" and the model field should be equal to "Fusion". This ensures that only the correct record is updated. If the statement only specified that the make field should be equal to "Ford", the mileage field would have been updated to 368.2 for all other records in the table that included a make field with a value of "Ford".

Next, you enter several UPDATE statements to modify records from the pagevisits table in the sitevisitors database. The table contains one record that includes a value of "contact.php" in the previous_page field and another record that includes "contact.php" in the page_filename field. Assume that the page name has been changed to "contact_us.php."

To enter several UPDATE statements to modify records from the pagevisits table in the sitevisitors database:

1. Return to MySQL Monitor.

2. Enter the following UPDATE statement to modify the previous_page field in records in the pagevisits table from "contact.php" to "contact_us.php" (two rows will be changed):

   ```
   mysql> UPDATE pagevisits[ENTER↵]
       -> SET previous_page='contact_us.php'[ENTER↵]
       -> WHERE previous_page='contact.php';[ENTER↵]
   ```

3. Enter the following UPDATE statement to modify the page_filename field in records in the pagevisits table from "contact.php" to "contact_us.php" (three rows will be changed):

   ```
   mysql> UPDATE pagevisits[ENTER↵]
       -> SET page_filename='contact_us.php'[ENTER↵]
       -> WHERE page_filename='contact.php';[ENTER↵]
   ```

4. Enter the following SELECT statement to view all the records in the table. The "contact.php" values should now be "contact_us.php."

   ```
   mysql> SELECT * FROM pagevisits;[ENTER↵]
   ```

Deleting Records

To delete records from a table, you use the DELETE statement. The basic syntax for the DELETE statement is as follows:

```
DELETE FROM table_name
WHERE condition;
```

Be careful when you use the DELETE statement because it deletes all records that match the condition. Therefore, carefully construct the conditions assigned to the WHERE keyword. For example, the following statement deletes the record for the 2006 Honda Accord from the company_cars table in the vehicle_fleet database:

```
mysql> DELETE FROM company_cars WHERE model_
year=2006[ENTER←]
    -> AND make='Honda'[ENTER←]
    -> AND model='Accord';[ENTER←]
Query OK, 1 row affected (0.28 sec)
```

A bug in some versions of MySQL causes the message to show "0 rows affected" for a DELETE FROM statement without a WHERE clause, even if rows were deleted.

To delete all the records from a table, omit the WHERE clause. The following statement deletes all the records from the company_cars table:

```
mysql> DELETE FROM company_cars;[ENTER←]
Query OK, 10 rows affected (0.28 sec)
```

To delete several records from the pagevisits table in the sitevisitors database:

1. Return to MySQL Monitor.

2. Enter the following statement to delete the first record in the table:

   ```
   mysql> DELETE FROM pagevisits WHERE
   visit_date='2012-03-17'[ENTER←]
       -> AND visit_time='10:32:29';[ENTER←]
   ```

3. Enter the following statement to delete the next record in the table:

   ```
   mysql> DELETE FROM pagevisits WHERE
   visit_date='2012-03-17'[ENTER←]
       -> AND visit_time='10:35:18';[ENTER←]
   ```

4. Enter the following SELECT statement to view all the records in the table. The table should now only consist of 12 records.

   ```
   mysql> SELECT * FROM pagevisits;[ENTER←]
   ```

Short Quiz

1. When the column names are omitted from the INSERT INTO statement, what two important considerations must be followed?

2. What SQL command is used to add records from an external text file?

3. What value should be entered in a text field as a placeholder for missing values?

4. What clause can specify the delimiter in a text file that is used as a data source for a MySQL table?

5. What keyword is used to specify a reverse or descending sort order for selected records in a table?

Working with phpMyAdmin

You must learn the proper SQL syntax to store, manipulate, and retrieve data in a MySQL database from PHP, but SQL can be cumbersome for database administration and maintenance. Normally, you create the table structure in MySQL using a graphical interface and maintain the data with PHP.

Be sure that phpMyAdmin has been installed on the MySQL server before continuing with this section.

The phpMyAdmin application is an open source tool written in PHP to handle the administration of MySQL databases. The phpMyAdmin tool can perform all of the administrative tasks that you've already studied in this chapter, plus many others you haven't learned yet. The full functionality of phpMyAdmin is beyond the scope of this section, but you will learn the basics of the interface and be exposed to some common activities.

Logging in to phpMyAdmin

Your instructor should have provided you with a link to a Web page for logging in to phpMyAdmin. When you visit the Web page, you should see a page like the one shown in Figure 7-19. Enter the user name and password provided by your instructor in the appropriate fields, and then click the Login button.

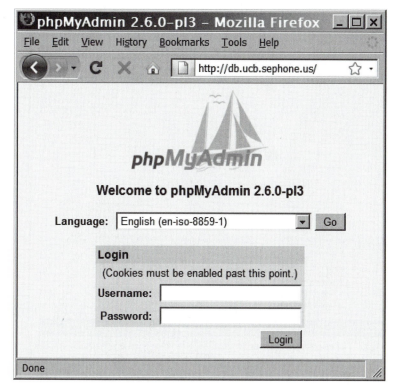

Figure 7-19 The phpMyAdmin login page

Different versions of php-MyAdmin will have a slightly different layout. Although the location on the screen may change, the features described in this section will be available somewhere on the screen.

If you enter an incorrect user name or password, you will see a page like the one shown in Figure 7-20, with an error message above the Login button. The error message will be something like "#1045 - Access denied for user *'username'*@'host' (using password: YES)", where *username* is the user name that you entered, and *host* is the name of the computer you are using. The user name and password fields are still available, so you can attempt to log in again.

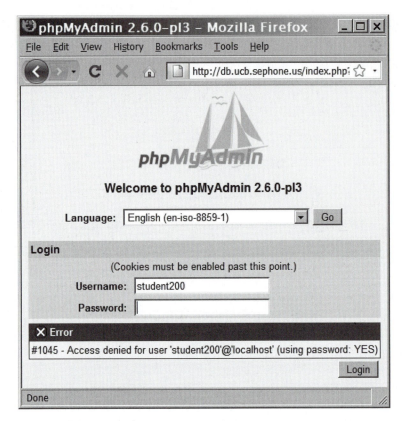

Figure 7-20 The phpMyAdmin invalid login message

Once you have successfully entered your user name and password, you should see the phpMyAdmin main screen, as shown in Figure 7-21. Whenever you need to return to the main screen, click the small house icon in the upper-left corner.

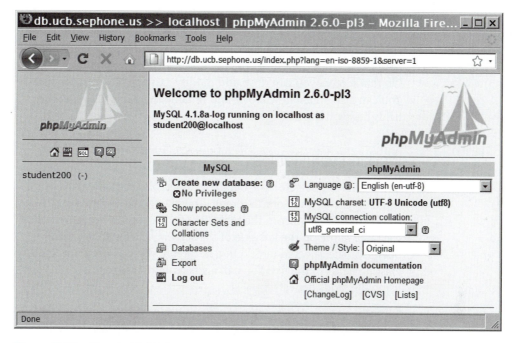

Figure 7-21   The phpMyAdmin main screen

If you have access to more than one database, the left side of the screen will display a drop-down list of databases to which you have access, with the number of tables in each database listed in parentheses after the name. When you select the database, the phpMyAdmin main screen appears. The name of the selected database and its tables will be listed on the left side of the screen below the drop-down list. Figure 7-21 shows a database (student200) with no tables defined.

Working with Databases

If you do not have access to more than one database, and you do not have privileges to create databases, you can skip this section.

The right side of the main screen has two columns, one for MySQL and one for phpMyAdmin. The first option under the MySQL column header is "Create new database". If you do not have privileges to create a new database, you cannot select this option, and the message "No Privileges" will appear beneath it, as shown in Figure 7-21. If you have privileges, a text box appears beneath the "Create new database" option with a Create button beside it. Enter the name of the new database and click the Create button. The database will be created and selected as the active database, much like entering the USE *database* command in MySQL Monitor.

431

The fourth option under the MySQL column header is "Databases". Clicking this option opens a page with four tabs across the top of the screen, and a list of the available databases beneath. Clicking a database name from the list opens the Structure page for that database. On this screen, you can drop and modify existing tables in the list. You can also create new tables and rename the database using the fields beneath the list.

Working with Tables

Once you have selected the database, any tables in that database are listed on the left side of the screen. To view the table structure, click the Properties icon from the table list of the database screen, or click the table name on the left side of the screen. The Structure page opens for the selected table. On this screen, you can drop and modify existing fields in the list. You can also create new fields and indexes using the fields beneath the list.

Click the Browse tab to open the Browse page for the selected table. This page allows you to view, edit, and delete records in the table. Click the Insert tab to open the Insert page for the selected table. This page allows you to add records to the table.

The last two tabs, Empty and Drop, are shown in red for two reasons. First, they do not take you to a separate Web page. Second, and more important, these two tabs can cause you to lose all of the data in the table. Therefore, you should only click these two tabs when you are sure that you want to delete all records from the table or remove the table from the database.

Exporting and Importing Tables

The Export tab on the Table Web page allows you to automatically generate a SQL script with all of the SQL commands to create and populate the table with all of the existing data. This is convenient when you want to move an entire table from one database to another. For example, you could do all of the exercises in this chapter in a local MySQL database. When finished, you could export all of the tables and import them in the MySQL database on the remote server for your instructor to review.

To export the table and data, click the SQL radio button in the Export list. The default "SQL options" settings do not need to be changed. Click the "Save as file" check box, ensuring that the box is checked. Click the Go button to have phpMyAdmin generate the script. The next step varies depending on the browser you are using. In Mozilla

Firefox, click the "Save file" radio button in the next dialog box and click OK. The file is automatically saved to a Downloads folder with the active database assigned as the filename and an .sql extension. Remember the name and location of your download. If you are using Internet Explorer to export the table, click the Save button in the File Download dialog box and navigate to the location where you want to save the file. The filename will be the name of the active table with an .sql extension.

To import the table and data, navigate to the Database page for the destination database. Click the SQL tab, which displays the Run SQL query screen for that database. In the lower section, click the Browse button to display the File Upload dialog box. Navigate to the file that you exported (it will have an .sql extension), and click the Open button. When you click the Go button in the lower-right corner of the screen, phpMyAdmin will load and run the script file. When completed, phpMyAdmin shows the imported script, and the table appears in the list on the left side of the screen. If the import is successful, a message appears at the top of the window: "Your SQL-query has been executed successfully". If the table could not be imported, a message appears and describes the error. Click the Structure tab to verify that the imported table now appears in the list of tables for the schema.

Because the exported file is an SQL script, you use the SQL tab to run the script that creates the table and inserts the data. The Import tab is used when importing delimited text files, much like using the LOAD DATA command in MySQL Monitor.

Short Quiz

1. What message is displayed at the database page if the user has not been assigned the privilege to create new databases?

2. The _____ tab from the table page displays the records in the selected table.

3. Describe the process of exporting the structure and contents of a table from one database and importing it into another database using the phpMyAdmin tool.

Summing Up

- A database is an ordered collection of information that a computer program can quickly access.

- A record in a database is a single, complete set of related information.

- Fields are the individual categories of information stored in a record.

- A flat-file database stores information in a single table.

- A relational database stores information across multiple related tables.

- A query is a structured set of instructions and criteria for retrieving, adding, modifying, and deleting database information.

- Structured query language, or SQL (pronounced *sequel*), is a standard data manipulation language among many database management systems.

- MySQL Monitor is a command-line program that you use to manipulate MySQL databases.

- To work with a database, you must first select it by executing the USE *database* statement.

- You use the CREATE DATABASE statement to create a new database.

- To delete a database, you execute the DROP DATABASE statement, which removes all tables from the database and deletes the database itself.

- The fields in a table also store data according to type. To keep your database from growing too large, you should choose the smallest data type possible for each field.

- To create a table, you use the CREATE TABLE statement, which specifies the table and column names and the data type for each column.

- To modify a table, you use the ALTER TABLE statement, which specifies the table being changed and the change to make.

- To delete a table, you execute the DROP TABLE statement, which removes all data and the table definition.

- You use a GRANT statement to create user accounts and assign privileges, which refer to the operations that a user can perform with a database.

- You use the REVOKE statement to take away privileges from an existing user account for a specified table or database.

- You add individual records to a table with the INSERT statement.

- To add multiple records to a database, you use the LOAD DATA statement with a local text file that contains the records you want to add.

- You use the SELECT statement to retrieve records from a table.

- You use the ORDER BY keyword with the SELECT statement to perform an alphanumeric sort of the results returned from a query. To perform a reverse sort, add the DESC keyword after the name of the field by which you want to perform the sort.

- You can specify which records to return from a database by using the WHERE keyword.

- You use the UPDATE statement to update records in a table.

- You use the DELETE statement to delete records from a table.

- The phpMyAdmin graphical tool simplifies the tasks associated with creating and maintaining databases and tables.

Comprehension Check

1. A flat-file database consists of a single table. True or False?

2. Explain how relational databases are organized.

3. What is the correct term for the individual pieces of information that are stored in a database record?

   a. element

   b. field

   c. section

   d. container

4. What is the name of one table's primary key when it is stored in another table?

   a. key symbol

   b. record link

   c. foreign key

   d. unique identifier

5. Breaking tables into multiple related tables to reduce redundant and duplicate information is called _____.

   a. normalization

   b. redundancy design

   c. splitting

   d. simplification

6. Suppose you have a relational database for a dry-cleaning company. Each customer of the company can have multiple items in a cleaning order. What type of relationship exists between the order and the items?

   a. one-to-one

   b. one-to-many

   c. many-to-one

   d. many-to-many

7. _____ has become the standard data manipulation language among many database management systems.

   a. Java

   b. SQL

   c. ASP.NET

   d. PERL

8. Files created by different database management systems are completely interchangeable. True or False?

9. What is the default value of the mysql command's -h argument?

   a. database

   b. mysqlmonitor

   c. mysqladmin

   d. localhost

10. What character must terminate SQL commands in MySQL Monitor?

    a. colon (:)

    b. semicolon (;)

    c. ampersand (&)

    d. period (.)

11. With what characters do you quote identifiers that include special characters?

    a. quotation marks (')

    b. double quotation marks (")

    c. backticks (')

    d. tildes (~)

12. SQL keywords are case sensitive in MySQL Monitor. True or False?

13. Explain case sensitivity issues for file and directory names.

14. Which of the following statements displays the available databases in your MySQL installation?

    a. `SHOW DATABASES;`

    b. `SHOW DATABASES();`

    c. `LIST FILES;`

    d. `GET LIST();`

15. What's the first thing you should do after creating a new database?

    a. Save the database.

    b. Restart MySQL Monitor.

    c. Select the database.

    d. Create a table.

16. The _____ statement changes a table named "visitors" to a table named "guests".

    a. `RENAME visitors TO guests;`

    b. `ALTER TABLE CHANGE visitors TO guests;`

    c. `ALTER TABLE visitors RENAME guests;`

    d. `RENAME TABLE visitors guests;`

17. A GRANT statement does not create new user accounts. True or False?

18. Explain how to add multiple records to a table using a single SQL statement.

19. Which of the following keywords causes the `ORDER BY` clause to perform a reverse sort of database records?

    a. DESC

    b. REVERSE

    c. DESCEND

    d. SORTR

20. Which of the following is the correct string for a filter that narrows a query result to include only records in which the `State` field is equal to Massachusetts?

    a. `WHERE State = 'Massachusetts'`

    b. `State = 'Massachusetts'`

    c. `WHERE 'State' = Massachusetts`

    d. `'State' = 'Massachusetts'`

Reinforcement Exercises

Exercise 7-1

If you do not have database creation privileges, skip steps 1 through 3. If you do not have the FILE privilege, skip this exercise.

In this project, you will create a database to contain tables of batting statistics for major league baseball teams. You will then create a table named `teamstats` in the `baseball_stats` database and add records to the new table from a file named team_stats.txt in your Projects directory for Chapter 7.

1. Log in to MySQL Monitor with your **root** account or with the user name and password supplied by your ISP or instructor.

2. Enter the following command to create a database named `baseball_stats`:

    mysql> **CREATE DATABASE baseball_stats;[ENTER↵]**

3. After you see the "Query OK" message, enter the following command to select the `baseball_stats` database:

    mysql> **USE baseball_stats;[ENTER↵]**

4. After you see the "Database changed" message, type the following command to ensure that you selected the baseball_stats database:

mysql> **SELECT DATABASE();** [ENTER↵]

5. Enter the following command to create the teamstats table. The Team field uses the VARCHAR data type. Eleven of the columns use INT data types, and the remaining two fields use FLOAT data types. Each of the statistical field names uses common baseball abbreviations, such as G for games, AB for at-bats, R for runs, and HR for home runs.

mysql> **CREATE TABLE teamstats (Team VARCHAR(50),**
FirstYear INT, [ENTER↵]
      -> **G INT, W INT, L INT, Pennants INT, WS INT,** [ENTER↵]
      -> **R INT, AB INT, H INT, HR INT, AVG FLOAT,** [ENTER↵]
      -> **RA INT, ERA FLOAT);** [ENTER↵]

6. After you see the "Query OK" message, enter the following command to display the structure of the new table:

mysql> **DESCRIBE teamstats;** [ENTER↵]

7. Enter a LOAD DATA statement that inserts records from the team_stats.txt file in your Projects directory for Chapter 7 into the teamstats table. Replace *path_to_PHP_folders* with the full path for your PHP_Projects directory for Chapter 7.

 Use the MySQL server's directory path, not the Web URL path.

mysql> **LOAD DATA INFILE 'path_to_PHP_folders/**
Chapter.07/Projects/team_stats.txt' [ENTER↵]
      -> **INTO TABLE teamstats;** [ENTER↵]

8. After you see the "Query OK" message, enter the following command to view all the records in the teamstats table:

mysql> **SELECT * FROM teamstats;** [ENTER↵]

 Exercise 7-2

In this project, you will write SQL statements that return team names, games played, and number of at-bats from the teamstats table in the baseball_stats database. You will also write SQL statements that return the teams that have the least and most all-time home runs. For these select queries, you will need to use the LIMIT keyword, which restricts the number of records returned from the database. For example, if you specify a value of 10 with the LIMIT keyword, the database returns the first 10 records that match the conditions of your query. Finally, you will write SQL statements that use the SUM() function to return the total number of games played by all teams and the AVG() function to return the common batting average for all teams.

1. Return to MySQL Monitor.

2. Enter the following SELECT statement, which returns the team, G (games played), and AB (at bats) fields from the teamstats table:

   mysql> **SELECT team, G, AB FROM teamstats;**[ENTER↵]

3. Enter the following SELECT statement, which returns the team, G (games played), and AB (at bats) fields from the teamstats table, sorted by team name:

   mysql> **SELECT team, G, AB FROM teamstats ORDER BY team;**[ENTER↵]

4. Enter the following SELECT statement, which returns the team, G (games played), and AB (at bats) fields from the teamstats table, reverse sorted by team name:

   mysql> **SELECT team, G, AB FROM teamstats ORDER BY team DESC;**[ENTER↵]

5. Enter the following SELECT statement, which returns the team and HR (home runs) fields. The statement sorts the records by the HR field and includes the LIMIT keyword, assigned a value of 1. Because the records are sorted in ascending order, the statement returns the first record, which lists the team with the least all-time home runs: the Tampa Bay Rays, with 1713.

   mysql> **SELECT team, HR FROM teamstats ORDER BY HR LIMIT 1;**[ENTER↵]

6. Enter the following SELECT statement, which also returns the team and HR (home runs) fields. The statement reverse sorts the records by the HR field and includes the LIMIT keyword, assigned a value of 1. Because the records are sorted in descending order, the statement returns the first record, which lists the team with the most all-time home runs: the New York Yankees, with 13,914.

   mysql> **SELECT team, HR FROM teamstats ORDER BY HR DESC LIMIT 1;**[ENTER↵]

7. Enter the following SELECT statement, which uses the SUM() function to return the total number of games played by summing the contents of the G fields. Because each game played was between two teams in the database, the sum will be twice the actual number of games, so you divide the result by two. You should see a value of 182,525.

   mysql> **SELECT SUM(G)/2 FROM teamstats;**[ENTER↵]

8. Enter the following SELECT statement, which uses the AVG() function to return the batting average for all teams by averaging the contents of the AVG fields. You should see a value of 0.26199999650319.

```
mysql> SELECT AVG(AVG) FROM teamstats;[ENTER↵]
```

9. Unfortunately, this is not the true all-time batting average, because each team has a different number of at-bats. Enter the following SELECT statement, which gets the weighted average per team, and divides by the total number of at-bats. You should see a value of 0.26256022536176.

```
mysql> SELECT SUM(AVG*AB)/SUM(AB) FROM
teamstats;[ENTER↵]
```

Exercise 7-3

In this project, you will add a new table for home run leaders to the baseball_stats database. Before you create the new table, you will create a text file using data from the teamstats table. You will then import the data from the text file into MySQL to create a new table named hrleaders. To create the home run leaders table, you will use the INTO OUTFILE clause with a SELECT statement. The INTO OUTFILE clause copies the returned records into a specified file. You will use the FIELDS TERMINATED BY and LINES TERMINATED BY clauses to specify how the text file should be structured. Because you will import the home run records into the new table, you separate each field with a tab and each line with a line break. If you do not have the FILE privilege, skip this exercise.

1. Return to MySQL Monitor.

2. Enter the following SQL statement, which returns the team and HR fields for the teams with the highest number of home runs. Replace *path_to_PHP_folders* with the full path for your PHP_Projects directory for Chapter 7. Notice that the statement uses the ORDER BY and DESC keywords to perform a reverse sort of the fields. The results are sent to a text file named hrleaders.txt, with each field separated by a tab and each line separated by a line break escape sequence (\n).

An error code of 13 indicates that you do not have write privileges to the destination directory.

```
mysql> SELECT team, HR FROM teamstats[ENTER↵]
    -> ORDER BY HR DESC LIMIT 10[ENTER↵]
    -> INTO OUTFILE 'path_to_PHP_folders/Chapter.07/
Projects/hrleaders.txt'[ENTER↵]
    -> FIELDS TERMINATED BY '\t'[ENTER↵]
    -> LINES TERMINATED BY '\n';[ENTER↵]
```

Use the MySQL server's directory path, not the Web URL path.

3. Enter the following command to create a table named hrleaders:

   mysql> **CREATE TABLE hrleaders (Team VARCHAR(50), HR INT);[ENTER←]**

Use the MySQL server's directory path, not the Web URL path.

4. Enter the following LOAD DATA statement to import records from the hrleaders.txt file into the hrleaders table. Replace *path_to_PHP_folders* with the full path for your PHP_Projects directory for Chapter 7.

   mysql> **LOAD DATA INFILE '*path_to_PHP_folders/* Chapter.07/Projects/hrleaders.txt'[ENTER←]**
       -> **INTO TABLE hrleaders;[ENTER←]**

5. After you see the "Query OK" message, enter the following command to view all the records in the hrleaders table:

   mysql> **SELECT * FROM hrleaders;[ENTER←]**

6. Finally, enter the following command to list the tables in the baseball_stats database. You should see the hrleaders and teamstats tables listed.

   mysql> **SHOW TABLES;[ENTER←]**

7. Exit from MySQL Monitor.

 ## Exercise 7-4

Create a demographics database with a table that contains the following fields: country, primary language, and population. Enter records for at least 10 countries. You can find demographic information for various countries in many places on the Internet, including Wikipedia (*http://www.wikipedia.org/*). Write queries that return the following:

- A list of all records sorted by country name

- The country with the highest population

- The country with the lowest population

- Countries that share a common language, such as French

 ## Exercise 7-5

Database design techniques include the ability to identify and design five normalization levels: first normal form through fifth normal form. Search the Internet or visit your local library for information on these techniques and describe how to identify and design each normalization level.

Discovery Projects

The Chinese Zodiac site is a comprehensive project that will be updated in the Discovery Projects in each chapter. All files for the Chinese Zodiac site will be saved in a folder named ChineseZodiac in the root Web folder on the server, and all database tables will be stored in the `chinese_zodiac` database.

Discovery Project 7-1

In this project, you will create a database named `chinese_zodiac` that will contain the tables for the Chinese zodiac. You will then create a table named `zodiacsigns` in the `chinese_zodiac` database and add records to the new table manually using INSERT statements. The `zodiacsigns` table will contain the defining information about each sign. At this point, the example is very simple, but it will be built upon as needed.

If you do not have database creation privileges, skip steps 1 through 3.

1. Log in to MySQL Monitor with your **root** account or with the user name and password supplied by your ISP or instructor.

2. Enter the following command to create a database named `chinese_zodiac`:

   mysql> **CREATE DATABASE chinese_zodiac;** [ENTER↵]

3. After you see the "Query OK" message, enter the following command to select the `chinese_zodiac` database:

   mysql> **USE chinese_zodiac;** [ENTER↵]

4. After you see the "Database changed" message, type the following command to ensure that you selected the `chinese_zodiac` database:

   mysql> **SELECT DATABASE();** [ENTER↵]

5. Enter the following command to create the `zodiacsigns` table. Both fields use the VARCHAR data type.

   mysql> **CREATE TABLE zodiacsigns (Sign VARCHAR(10),** [ENTER↵]
       -> President VARCHAR(75)); [ENTER↵]

6. After you see the "Query OK" message, enter the following command to display the structure of the new table:

   mysql> **DESCRIBE zodiacsigns;** [ENTER↵]

7. Use one or more INSERT statements to add records to the zodiacsigns table for each of the 12 signs of the Chinese zodiac. The values used to populate the fields come from Discovery Project 6-4.

For example, the following command will insert the appropriate values for the Rat:

```
mysql> INSERT INTO zodiacsigns (Sign, President) [ENTER←]
    -> VALUES ('Rat', 'George Washington'); [ENTER←]
```

8. After you have successfully entered information for all 12 signs, enter the following command to view all the records in the zodiacsigns table:

```
mysql> SELECT * FROM zodiacsigns; [ENTER←]
```

Discovery Project 7-2

In this project, you will create a table named zodiacfeedback in the chinese_zodiac database. This table will be used later to store user feedback about the Chinese Zodiac site.

1. Reopen MySQL Monitor.

2. Type the following command to ensure that you selected the chinese_zodiac database:

```
mysql> SELECT DATABASE(); [ENTER←]
```

3. Enter the following command to create the zodiacfeedback table. The message_date field is of type DATE and the message_time field is of type TIME. The sender and message fields are of type VARCHAR. The public_message field is of a new type called ENUM. The ENUM type requires that the field only be populated with values specified in the CREATE TABLE or ALTER TABLE statement that created the field. In this case, the public_message field can only contain the values "Y" for yes and "N" for no.

```
mysql> CREATE TABLE zodiacfeedback (message_date
DATE, [ENTER←]
    -> message_time TIME, sender VARCHAR(40), [ENTER←]
    -> message VARCHAR(250), public_message
ENUM('Y','N')); [ENTER←]
```

4. After you see the "Query OK" message, enter the following command to display the structure of the new table:

```
mysql> DESCRIBE zodiacfeedback; [ENTER←]
```

Discovery Project 7-3

Log in to MySQL Monitor. At the SQL command prompt, select the chinese_zodiac database. Enter the SQL statement to create a table named zodiacyears to store the years for each sign of the Chinese zodiac. The table should have two fields: the year and the name of the sign for that year.

Enter the SQL command to view the structure of the new table. Capture an image of the display and save the image as a file named **DP7-3.ext** (replacing the *.ext* with the appropriate extension for the image type). Upload the file to the Images folder in the ChineseZodiac directory on the server.

Discovery Project 7-4

Create a tab-delimited text file that lists the years and signs, one year per line, for the Chinese zodiac. For the years and the corresponding signs, refer to the display generated by Chinese_Zodiac_for_loop.php from Discovery Project 2-4 and Chinese_Zodiac_while_loop.php from Discovery Project 2-5. Save the text file as **zodiac_years.txt** and upload the file to the ChineseZodiac directory in the root Web folder on the server.

Enter the SQL statement to populate the zodiacyears table with the contents of the zodiac_years.txt file. Query the table and sort the results, first by sign and then by year.

Discovery Project 7-5

Create a table called randomproverb to store the proverbs from Discovery Project 5-5. The table should have a proverb_number field of type INT, a proverb field of type VARCHAR of at least 100 characters, and a display_count field to track the number of times each proverb is displayed.

Copy the proverbs.txt file (which you created in Discovery Project 5-5) from the ChineseZodiac directory to a file called proverb_load.txt and open it in your editor. Modify the file so that each line has a unique numerical index, a tab, the proverb, another tab, and a zero (for the count). Save and upload the file, then import the file into the randomproverb table using MySQL Monitor.

You will modify inc_footer.php to use this table in Discovery Project 8-5.

Manipulating MySQL Databases with PHP

In this chapter, you will:

◎ Connect to MySQL from PHP

◎ Work with MySQL databases using PHP

◎ Create, modify, and delete MySQL tables with PHP

◎ Use PHP to manipulate MySQL records

◎ Use PHP to retrieve database records

One of PHP's greatest strengths is its ability to access and manipulate databases. With its strong support for Open Database Connectivity (ODBC), you can use PHP to gain direct access to any database that is ODBC compliant, including Oracle, Informix, PostgreSQL, and MySQL. PHP also allows you to work directly with different types of databases without going through ODBC.

PHP also supports other methods of accessing data sources, including SQLite, database abstraction layer functions, and PEAR DB. SQLite and database abstraction layer functions work with file-based databases instead of server-based databases such as MySQL. The PHP Extension and Application Repository (PEAR) is a library of open source PHP code. One of the most popular PEAR code modules is PEAR DB, which simplifies access between PHP and a database server by providing a generic interface that works with various types of database systems, similar to how ODBC works. Although PEAR DB and ODBC perform similar functions, PEAR DB is designed specifically to work with PHP, whereas ODBC is a more generic protocol used by many programming languages and database management systems.

With so many database connectivity options, how do you decide which method to use for accessing databases with PHP? First, you need to select a database management system. If you are new to database development, you should probably start with an open source database such as PostgreSQL or MySQL, because they are free and fairly easy to learn. After you select a database, you need to determine whether PHP can access it directly or whether it must go through a layer such as ODBC or PEAR DB. Using ODBC or PEAR DB makes it easier for you to write PHP code that can be used with a variety of databases. However, your PHP script will be faster if it can access a database directly, without going through a PEAR DB or ODBC layer. Therefore, if you think your PHP script will need to access more than one type of database, you should use PEAR DB or ODBC. To be more precise, you should use PEAR DB over ODBC because PEAR DB is designed specifically for the PHP language. Yet, ODBC is sometimes preferable, especially when you need to access Microsoft data source products such as Access or Excel. However, if you plan to work with a single database, such as MySQL, and you are more concerned with your Web application's performance than its compatibility with multiple database systems, use PHP's direct database access if it's available for your database management system.

In this chapter, you will study how to use PHP to directly access MySQL.

Connecting to MySQL with PHP

As you work through this chapter, keep in mind that almost everything you learned about MySQL in the preceding chapter is applicable to this chapter. Although you need to learn a few new functions to access MySQL with PHP, you will execute the same SQL statements that you used with MySQL Monitor. The great benefit of using PHP or some other server-side scripting language to read from and write to a database server is that you can create a Web-based interface, which makes it much easier for visitors to interact with your database.

Before you can use PHP to read from and write to MySQL databases, you need to enable MySQL support in PHP and learn how to connect to the MySQL database server.

Determining which MySQL Package to Use

There are `mysqli_*` equivalents for each of the `mysql_*` functions used in this chapter. The code will be different because of the object-oriented nature of the `mysqli_*` functions.

In PHP versions earlier than PHP 5, support for MySQL was installed by default. However, starting with PHP 5, you must enable MySQL support in PHP by configuring your PHP installation to use the `mysqli` or `mysql` package.

The `mysqli` (MySQL Improved) package became available with PHP 5, and is designed to work with MySQL version 4.1.3 and later. If you use earlier versions of PHP or MySQL, you must use the `mysql` package. With newer versions of PHP and MySQL, you can use either `mysql` or `mysqli`. Because the `mysqli` package is the object-oriented equivalent of the `mysql` package, and object-oriented PHP is not covered until Chapter 10, this chapter concentrates on the `mysql` package.

Opening and Closing a MySQL Connection

You can use the `phpinfo()` function you learned in Chapter 1 to determine which MySQL libraries are installed on your Web server.

Before you can use PHP to access the records in a database, you must first use the `mysql_connect()` function to open a connection to a MySQL database server. Opening a connection to a database is similar to opening a handle to a text file, as you did in Chapter 5. However, instead of returning a file handle, the `mysql_connect()` function returns a link identifier as an integer if it connects successfully to the database or a Boolean `FALSE` if it doesn't. You assign the return value from the `mysql_connect()` function to a variable that you can use to access the database in your script. The basic syntax for the `mysql_connect()` function is as follows:

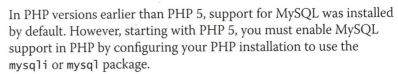

```
$connection = mysql_connect("host" [, "user", "password"])
```

In the preceding example, the *host* argument allows you to specify the host name where your MySQL database server is installed. If you are connecting to an instance of the MySQL database server that is running on the same server as the PHP scripting engine, use a value of "localhost" or "127.0.0.1" for the *host* argument. However, if you are working with a MySQL database server that is running on a different (remote) server than the PHP scripting engine, you need to enter the name or IP address of the MySQL server. The *user* and *password* arguments allow you to specify a MySQL account name and password. For example, the following command connects the user name "dongosselin" with a password of "rosebud" to a local instance of the MySQL database server. The database connection is assigned to the $DBConnect variable.

```
$DBConnect = mysql_connect("localhost", "dongosselin",
    "rosebud");
```

When your PHP script ends, any open database connections close automatically. However, you should get into the habit of explicitly closing database connections with the mysql_close() function when you finish using them. This ensures that the connection doesn't keep taking up space in your Web server's memory while the script finishes processing. You close a database connection by passing the database connection variable to the mysql_close() function. The following statement closes the $DBConnect database connection variable that was opened in the preceding statement:

```
mysql_close($DBConnect);
```

After you connect to a database with the mysql_connect() function, you can use the functions listed in Table 8-1 to return information about your installation of the MySQL server.

To change users after connecting to a database, use the mysql_change_user() function.

The mysql_get_client_info() and mysql_get_client_version() functions do not accept any arguments. These functions do not actually require a database connection, as they return information about your local client, not the MySQL server. However, you must pass the variable representing the database connection to the rest of the functions listed in Table 8-1.

Function	Description
mysql_get_client_info()	Returns the MySQL client version
mysql_get_client_version()	Returns the MySQL client version as an integer
mysql_get_host_info(*connection*)	Returns the MySQL database server connection information
mysql_get_proto_info(*connection*)	Returns the MySQL protocol version
mysql_get_server_info(*connection*)	Returns the MySQL database server version

Table 8-1   MySQL server information functions

The terms *client* and *server* require some explanation. Because the client and server are defined in relation to MySQL, the Web server where the PHP script is running is the client when communicating with the MySQL server. The mysql_get_client_info() and mysql_get_client_version() functions return information about the mysql package that PHP is using. The remainder of the functions return information about the database server and the MySQL application running on it.

To create a PHP script that connects to MySQL and uses the functions listed in Table 8-1 to display information about your installation of MySQL:

1. Create a new document in your text editor.

2. Type the `<!DOCTYPE>` declaration, `<html>` element, header information, and `<body>` element. Use the strict DTD and "MySQL Server Information" as the content of the `<title>` element.

3. Add the following heading element to the document body:

    ```
    <h1>MySQL Database Server Information</h1>
    ```

4. Add the following script section to the end of the document body:

    ```
    <?php
    ?>
    ```

5. Add the following `mysql_connect()` statement to the script section. Replace *host*, *user*, and *password* with the MySQL host name, user name, and password assigned by your instructor.

    ```
    $DBConnect = mysql_connect("host", "user", "password");
    ```

6. At the end of the script section, add the following statements, which display information about your installation of MySQL server:

    ```
    echo "<p>MySQL client version: "
        . mysql_get_client_info() . "</p>\n";
    if ($DBConnect===FALSE)
       echo "<p>Connection failed.</p>\n";
    else {
        echo "<p>MySQL connection: "
            . mysql_get_host_info($DBConnect) . "</p>\n";
        echo "<p>MySQL protocol version: "
            . mysql_get_proto_info($DBConnect) . "</p>\n";
        echo "<p>MySQL server version: "
            . mysql_get_server_info($DBConnect) . "</p>\n";
    ```

7. Finally, add the following statement to the end of the script section to close the database connection. Note that you only close the connection if the `mysql_connect` function successfully established a connection with the MySQL server:

    ```
        mysql_close($DBConnect);
    }
    ```

8. Save the document as **MySQLInfo.php** in the Chapter directory for Chapter 8, and then upload the document to the server.

9. Open the MySQLInfo.php file in your Web browser by entering the following URL: *http://<yourserver>/PHP_Projects/ Chapter.08/Chapter/MySQLInfo.php*. Your Web browser should look like Figure 8-1, although the information displayed from each function might be different for your MySQL installation.

10. Close your Web browser window.

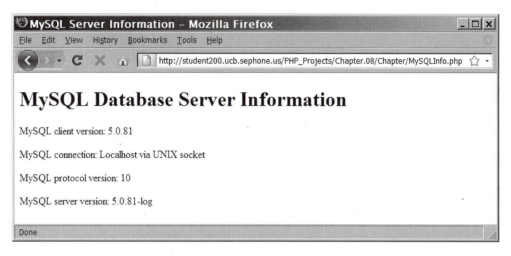

Figure 8-1 MySQLInfo.php in a Web browser

Reporting MySQL Errors

If an error prevents the connection from being created, it is useful to know why the `mysql_connect()` function failed. The `mysql_error()` function returns a text string describing the error, and the `mysql_errno()` function returns the numeric code of the error. You can use these functions when debugging your code, as they provide specific details about the cause of the error.

When debugging MySQL functions, it is often convenient to use the following abbreviated syntax to handle errors:

```
$DBConnection = (mysql_connect(...) ||
         die(mysql_error());
```

This syntax is a short way of writing code that displays the MySQL error message and exits the script if the `mysql_connect()` function fails (and returns `FALSE`). Otherwise, the return value of the `mysql_connect()` function is assigned to `$DBConnection` and the script continues processing on the next line. Because the `die()` function exits the script immediately, any further script output, such as navigation buttons or a Web form, is not displayed. For this reason, do not use the `die()` function when it will prevent the Web page from displaying properly.

To obtain error information for any other functions that access a MySQL database, such as the ones discussed in this section, you use the same two error functions. After you connect to a MySQL server, you can pass to the `mysql_errno()` and `mysql_error()` functions the variable representing the database connection. This is useful if you

If you receive a warning that PHP cannot load a dynamic library or an error message such as "Call to undefined function `mysql_connect()`", MySQL support is not correctly enabled for your PHP installation.

The `exit()` function works the same as the `die()` function, and exits the script immediately.

451

In the mysqli package, connection errors are reported using the mysqli_connect_error() and mysqli_connect_errno() functions, which do not accept any parameters. For all other database errors, the mysqli_error() and mysqli_errno() functions are used, and are called in the same manner as mysql_error() and mysql_errno().

You should never display the actual error message or error number returned by the mysql_error() and mysql_errno() functions in a production PHP script. Information returned by these functions could expose vulnerabilities of the server, providing a means of attacking it. In a production environment, these scripts should be rewritten to display a custom error message that does not reveal information about the PHP scripting engine or the MySQL database, and to write the error code and message to a log file.

have multiple connections open, and need to report on an error for a specific connection.

The mysql_error() and mysql_errno() functions only return the results of the previous mysql_*() function (excluding mysql_error() and mysql_errno() themselves). It is important to call these functions before calling another function in the mysql package; otherwise, the error information will be lost.

Suppressing Errors with the Error Control Operator

Although standard error messages generated by programming languages such as PHP are helpful to programmers, they represent a potential security risk, as mentioned earlier. Also, they may confuse less technical users, who might think they somehow caused the error. Errors can and will occur, but you should never let your users think that they did something wrong.

Functions in PHP, including those in the mysql package, normally display errors and warnings as they occur. You can suppress those messages by using the **error control operator (@)**. You can place the error control operator before any expression, although it is most commonly used with built-in PHP functions, especially functions that access external data sources such as files and databases. Using the error control operator to suppress error messages does not mean you can ignore errors. Instead, it provides a more graceful way of handling an error that does not reveal information about the underlying system. In the following example, which contains a modified version of inc_db_catalog.php, both the mysql_connect() and mysql_select_db() functions are preceded by error control operators to suppress any error messages that may occur:

```php
<?php
$DBName = "catalog";
$DBConnect = @mysql_connect("php_db", "dongosselin", "rosebud");
if ($DBConnect === FALSE)
    echo "<p>Connection error: "
                . mysql_error() . "</p>\n";
else {
    if (@mysql_select_db($DBName, $DBConnect) === FALSE) {
        echo "<p>Could not select the \"$DBName\" " .
            "database: " . mysql_error($DBConnect) .
            "</p>\n";
        mysql_close($DBConnect);
        $DBConnect = FALSE;
    }
}
?>
```

Short Quiz

1. Explain why you need to save the return value of the `mysql_connect()` function to a variable.

2. When is it valid to use the value of "localhost" as the `host` argument in the `mysql_connect()` function?

3. Explain why you should always use the `mysql_close()` function to close the database connection when you are finished accessing the database.

4. Contrast the return value of the `mysql_error()` function and the `mysql_errno()` function.

5. Describe how the error control operator is used to handle errors.

In this chapter, you will use the `mysql_error()` function to return the actual error messages from the MySQL database. This function helps you locate and correct errors in your code.

453

Using the error control operator does not disable error checking. It only suppresses the error messages from being displayed.

Working with MySQL Databases

Although you will usually use MySQL Monitor, phpMyAdmin, or similar tools to perform database structural changes, you can use PHP to perform these tasks. The `mysql` package provides the necessary functions for creating, selecting, and deleting databases.

Creating a Database

As you saw in Chapter 7, you must create a database to hold the tables that store data. In MySQL Monitor, you used the `CREATE DATABASE` statement. In PHP, you use the `mysql_create_db()` function. Its basic syntax is:

```
$result = mysql_create_db( "dbname" [, connection]);
```

You may notice that the connection value is optional. If the link connection is not specified, PHP uses the last connection opened using `mysql_connect()`. This simplifies the code if you only have one link connection open at a time. The `mysql_create_db()` function returns a Boolean `TRUE` value if successful, or `FALSE` if an error occurred.

You may not have privileges to create databases for the MySQL server to which you are connecting. If so, you may receive one of two error messages: an "insufficient privileges" message from the MySQL server or an "undefined function" message for the `mysql_create_db()` function.

The following code uses a `mysql_create_db()` statement to create a database named `catalog` from the `$DBConnect` database connection:

```
$DBName = "catalog";
$DBConnect = mysql_connect("php_db", "dongosselin", "rosebud");
if ($DBConnect === FALSE)
    echo "<p>Connection error: "
            . mysql_error() . "</p>\n";
else {
    if (mysql_create_db("$DBName", $DBConnect) === FALSE)
        echo "<p>Could not create the \"$DBName\" " .
            "database: " . mysql_error($DBConnect) .
            "</p>\n";
    else
        echo "<p>Successfully created the " .
                "\"$DBName\" database.</p>\n";
    mysql_close($DBConnect);
}
```

To create a PHP script that creates a database named `newsletter`:

1. Create a new document in your text editor.

2. Type the `<!DOCTYPE>` declaration, `<html>` element, header information, and `<body>` element. Use the strict DTD and "Creating Database" as the content of the `<title>` element.

3. Add the following script section to the end of the document body:

   ```
   <?php
   ?>
   ```

4. Add the following statements to the script section to connect to the MySQL server. Replace *host* with the MySQL server name provided by your instructor, and replace *user* and *password* with the MySQL user name and password you created in Chapter 7.

   ```
   $DBName = "newsletter";
   $DBConnect = mysql_connect("host", "user", "password");
   if ($DBConnect === FALSE)
       echo "<p>Connection error: "
               . mysql_error() . "</p>\n";
   else {
   }
   ```

5. In the `else` clause of the `if...else` statement, add the following statements to create the `newsletter` database:

```
if (mysql_create_db($DBName, $DBConnect) === FALSE)
    echo "<p>Could not create the \"$DBName\" " .
        "database: " . mysql_error($DBConnect) .
        "</p>\n";
else
    echo "<p>Successfully created the " .
        "\"$DBName\" database.</p>\n";
```

455

6. Add the following statement to the end of the else clause to close the database connection:

```
mysql_close($DBConnect);
```

7. Save the document as **CreateNewsletterDB.php** in the Chapter directory for Chapter 8, and then upload the document to the server.

8. Open CreateNewsletterDB.php in your Web browser by entering the following URL: *http://<yourserver>/PHP_Projects/Chapter.08/Chapter/CreateNewsletterDB.php*. The Web page should inform you that the newsletter database was created or provide an error message that explains why the database was not created.

If you do not have "Create Database" privileges on your MySQL server, you may see an error like the one shown in Figure 8-2.

9. Close your Web browser window.

Figure 8-2 Error message when the mysql_create_db() function is unavailable because of insufficient privileges

Selecting a Database

As you saw in Chapter 7, you must first select a database with the USE *database* statement when you log on to MySQL Monitor. You select a database or change to a different database with the mysql_select_db() function. The syntax for the function is mysql_select_db(*database [, connection]*). The function returns a Boolean value of TRUE if it successfully selects a database or FALSE if it doesn't. For example, the following code uses a mysql_select_db() statement to open the catalog database from the $DBConnect database connection, and displays a simple "Selected the "Catalog" Database" message if successful:

```php
$DBName = "catalog";
$DBConnect = mysql_connect("php_db", "dongosselin", "rosebud");
if ($DBConnect === FALSE)
    echo "<p>Connection error: "
                . mysql_error() . "</p>\n";
else {
    if (mysql_select_db($DBName, $DBConnect) === FALSE)
        echo "<p>Could not select the \"$DBName\" " .
            "database: " . mysql_error($DBConnect) . "</p>\n";
    else {
        // Use the else portion of the if statement for
        // additional statements that access or manipulate
        // the database
        echo "<p>Selected the \"$DBName\" database</p>\n";
    }
    mysql_close($DBConnect);
}
```

Usually, you have several pages that all use the same database. Also, it is a security risk to have passwords in files that are directly accessible from the Web. For these reasons, you can use an include file to connect to the MySQL server and select a database. For example, the inc_db_catalog.php file contains the following script:

```php
<?php
$DBName = "catalog";
$DBConnect = mysql_connect("php_db", "dongosselin", "rosebud");
if ($DBConnect === FALSE)
    echo "<p>Connection error: "
                . mysql_error() . "</p>\n";
else {
    if (mysql_select_db($DBName, $DBConnect) === FALSE) {
        echo "<p>Could not select the \"$DBName\" " .
            "database: " . mysql_error($DBConnect) .
            "</p>\n";
        mysql_close($DBConnect);
        $DBConnect = FALSE;
    }
}
?>
```

The primary difference between the code in an include file and the code embedded in a PHP script itself is that the code in the include file closes the connection and sets the connection variable to FALSE if the database named in $DBName could not be selected. The following PHP script uses the inc_db_catalog.php include file to produce the same output as the previous example:

```
include("inc_db_catalog.php");
if ($DBConnect !== FALSE) {
    // Use the if statement for additional statements
    // that access or manipulate the database
    echo "<p>Selected the \"$DBName\" database</p>\n";
    mysql_close($DBConnect);
}
```

The PHP script only needs to verify that $DBConnect is not FALSE before using any database functions. Also, the script only calls the mysql_close() function if $DBConnect is not FALSE, because the connection was already closed or was never successfully opened if $DBConnect is FALSE.

To create a PHP script that uses an include file to select the newsletter database:

1. Create a new document in your text editor.

2. Add the following script section:

   ```
   <?php
   ?>
   ```

3. Add the following statements to the script section to connect to the MySQL server. Replace *host* with the MySQL server name provided by your instructor, and replace *user* and *password* with the MySQL user name and password you created in Chapter 7. If you could not create the newsletter database earlier, change "newsletter" to the name of the default database provided for your user account. Note that the error control operator is used to suppress MySQL connection error messages.

   ```
   $DBName = "newsletter";
   $DBConnect = @mysql_connect("host", "user", "password");
   if ($DBConnect === FALSE)
         echo "<p>Connection error: "
                   . mysql_error() . "</p>\n";
   else {
   }
   ```

4. In the else clause of the if...else statement, add the following statements to select the newsletter database and close the connection on failure. Again, the error control operator is used to suppress error messages.

   ```
       if (@mysql_select_db($DBName, $DBConnect)
       === FALSE) {
           echo "<p>Could not select the \"$DBName\" " .
               "database: " . mysql_error($DBConnect) .
               "</p>\n";
           mysql_close($DBConnect);
           $DBConnect = FALSE;
       }
   ```

5. Save the document as **inc_db_newsletter.php**.

6. Create another new document in your text editor.

7. Type the `<!DOCTYPE>` declaration, `<html>` element, header information, and `<body>` element. Use the strict DTD and "Select Test" as the content of the `<title>` element.

8. Add the following script section to the end of the document body:

```
<?php
?>
```

9. Add the following `include()` statement to the script section:

```
include("inc_db_newsletter.php");
```

10. After the `include()` statement, add the following statements to handle a successful selection of the `newsletter` database:

```
if ($DBConnect !== FALSE) {
        echo "<p>Selected the \"$DBName\" database</p>\n";
        mysql_close($DBConnect);
}
```

11. Save the document as **SelectTest.php** in the Chapter directory for Chapter 8, and then upload inc_db_newsletter.php and SelectTest.php to the Web server.

12. Open SelectTest.php in your Web browser by entering the following URL: *http://<yourserver>/PHP_Projects/Chapter.08/ Chapter/SelectTest.php*. The Web page should inform you that the `newsletter` database was selected or should provide an error message.

13. Close your Web browser window.

Deleting a Database

As with the `mysql_create_db()` function, you may not have privileges to delete a database. If so, `$Result` will be FALSE.

To delete a database, you use the `mysql_drop_db()` function. The syntax is:

```
$Result = mysql_drop_db("dbname" [, connection]);
```

The `mysql_drop_db()` function returns TRUE if the database was successfully dropped, or FALSE if an error occurred. If a value of FALSE is returned, you use the `mysql_error()` function to display the error message.

Short Quiz

1. What PHP function is used to create a new database?

2. Name the equivalent MySQL command for the USE *database* statement used in MySQL Monitor to change to a different database.

3. You use which PHP function to delete an existing database?

For information that you want to store permanently, you should use MySQL Monitor instead of PHP to create and delete tables. Creating and deleting tables with PHP is most useful when you only need to store information temporarily for the current Web browser session.

Working with Tables

In this section, you will learn how to use PHP to work with MySQL and tables. More specifically, you will learn how to create and delete tables. As you will see, the SQL statements in this section are identical to the SQL statements you saw in Chapter 7. The only difference is that they are executed with PHP instead of MySQL Monitor.

Using `mysql_query()`

In PHP, you use the `mysql_query()` function to send SQL statements to MySQL. The `mysql_query()` function is the workhorse of PHP connectivity with MySQL; almost every SQL command you send to MySQL from PHP is executed with this function. Its basic syntax is `mysql_query(query [, connection])`. The `mysql_query()` function returns one of three values, depending on the type of query executed. For SQL statements that do not return information from the database, such as the CREATE TABLE statements, the `mysql_query()` function returns a value of TRUE if the statement executes successfully. For SQL statements that return information from the database, such as SELECT and SHOW statements, the `mysql_query()` function returns a result pointer that represents the query results. A **result pointer** is a special type of variable that refers to the currently selected row in the list of records returned by MySQL, called a **resultset**. The result pointer is a way of keeping track of where you are in a resultset. You assign the result pointer to a variable, which you can use to access the resultset in PHP. The `mysql_query()` function returns a value of FALSE for any SQL statements that fail, regardless of whether they return information from the database. As an example, the following code selects the `vehicle_fleet` database you saw in Chapter 7. The code then executes the `mysql_query()` function to select information from the `company_cars` table and assigns the result pointer to a variable named `$QueryResult`.

When mysql_query() returns a resultset, you use the mysql_num_rows() function to determine the number of records in the resultset. The mysql_num_rows() function takes a single parameter, which is the resultset variable. If the parameter is not a valid resultset, mysql_num_rows() returns FALSE.

```
$Result = @mysql_select_db("vehicle_fleet", $DBConnect);
if ($Result===FALSE)
        echo "<p>Unable to select the database.</p>"
                    . "<p>Error code " . mysql_errno($DBConnect)
                    . ": " . mysql_error($DBConnect) . "</p>";
else {
        echo "<p>Successfully opened the database.</p>";
        $SQLstring = "SELECT model_year, make, model FROM
        company_cars";
        $QueryResult = mysql_query($SQLstring, $DBConnect)
        mysql_close($DBConnect);
}
```

Creating and Deleting Tables

To create a table, you use the CREATE TABLE statement with the mysql_query() function. Be sure you have executed the mysql_select_db() function before executing the CREATE TABLE statement, or you might create your new table in the wrong database. Assuming that you have a link connection established and stored in $DBConnect and used the mysql_select_db() function to select the vehicle_fleet database, the following code creates a table named drivers in the vehicle_fleet database:

```
$SQLstring = "CREATE TABLE drivers (name VARCHAR(100), "
            . "emp_no SMALLINT, hire_date DATE, "
            . "stop_date DATE)";
$QueryResult = @mysql_query($SQLstring, $DBConnect);
if ($QueryResult===FALSE)
        echo "<p>Unable to execute the query.</p>"
                    . "<p>Error code " . mysql_errno($DBConnect)
                    . ": " . mysql_error($DBConnect) . "</p>";
else
        echo "<p>Successfully created the table.</p>";
```

If the table already exists in the selected database, the preceding code would produce the error code and message shown in Figure 8-3.

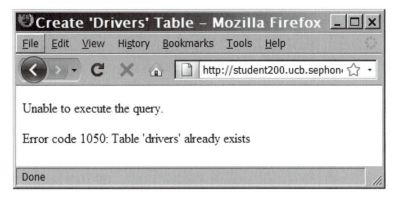

Figure 8-3 Error code and message that appear when you attempt to create a table that already exists

To prevent your code from trying to create a table that already exists, use a mysql_query() function that checks for the table using the SHOW TABLES LIKE command. If the function executes successfully and does not return 0 rows, the table already exists. You determine the number of rows in the resultset with the mysql_num_rows() function. The following code demonstrates how to check whether a table exists before attempting to create it:

```
$TableName = "drivers";
$SQLstring = "SHOW TABLES LIKE '$TableName'";
$QueryResult = @mysql_query($SQLstring, $DBConnect);
if (mysql_num_rows($QueryResult) > 0) {
    echo "<p>The $TableName table already exists!</p>";
}
else {
    $SQLstring = "CREATE TABLE drivers (name VARCHAR(100), "
                . "emp_no SMALLINT, hire_date DATE, "
                . "stop_date DATE)";
    $QueryResult = @mysql_query($SQLstring, $DBConnect);
    if ($QueryResult===FALSE)
        echo "<p>Unable to execute the query.</p>"
                . "<p>Error code " . mysql_errno
                    ($DBConnect)
                . ": " . mysql_error($DBConnect) . "</p>";
    else
        echo "<p>Successfully created the table.</p>";
}
```

One common practice in MySQL, and databases in general, is to create a numeric index that is used as a primary key identifier for each record. To identify a field as a primary key in MySQL, you include the PRIMARY KEY keywords when you first define a field with the CREATE TABLE statement. The AUTO_INCREMENT keyword is often used with a primary key to generate a unique ID for each new row in a table. For the first row inserted into a table, a field created with the

You will be introduced to the AUTO_INCREMENT keyword later in this chapter.

AUTO_INCREMENT keyword is assigned a value of 1. The value of the field for each subsequently added row is incremented by 1 from the preceding row. Another keyword that is often used with primary keys is NOT NULL, which requires a field to include a value. As an example, the following SQL statement defines a primary key named id for the company_cars table using the SMALLINT data type. The id field definition also includes the NOT NULL and AUTO_INCREMENT keywords.

```
CREATE TABLE company_cars (id SMALLINT NOT NULL AUTO_
INCREMENT PRIMARY KEY, license VARCHAR(10), model_year
SMALLINT, make VARCHAR(25), model VARCHAR(50), mileage
FLOAT);
```

To create a script that creates the subscribers table in the newsletter database the first time the script is called:

1. Create a new document in your text editor.

2. Type the <!DOCTYPE> declaration, <html> element, header information, and <body> element. Use the strict DTD and "Create 'subscribers' Table" as the content of the <title> element.

3. Add the following script section to the end of the document body:

```
<?php
?>
```

4. Add the following include() statement to the script section:

```
include("inc_db_newsletter.php");
```

5. After the include() statement, add the following statements to handle a successful selection of the newsletter database:

```
if ($DBConnect !== FALSE) {
    mysql_close($DBConnect);
}
```

6. Add the following variable declarations and mysql_query() statement immediately before the mysql_close() function. The mysql_query() statement checks the database for a table named subscribers.

```
$TableName = "subscribers";
$SQLstring = "SHOW TABLES LIKE '$TableName'";
$QueryResult = @mysql_query($SQLstring, $DBConnect);
```

7. Add the following variable declarations and mysql_query() statement immediately before the mysql_close() function. The statements in the if statement only execute if the $QueryResult contains 0 rows, which means that the table does not yet exist. Notice that the CREATE TABLE statement creates the subscriberID field as an auto-incrementing primary key.

```
      if (mysql_num_rows($QueryResult) == 0) {
          $SQLstring = "CREATE TABLE subscribers (subscriberID
              SMALLINT NOT NULL AUTO_INCREMENT PRIMARY KEY,
              name VARCHAR(80), email VARCHAR(100),
              subscribe_date DATE,
              confirmed_date DATE)";
          $QueryResult = @mysql_query($SQLstring, $DBConnect);
          if ($QueryResult === FALSE)
              echo "<p>Unable to create the subscribers
                  table.</p>"
              . "<p>Error code " . mysql_errno($DBConnect)
              . ": " . mysql_error($DBConnect) . "</p>";
          else
              echo "<p>Successfully created the "
              . "subscribers table.</p>";
      }
      else
          echo "<p>The subscribers table already
              exists.</p>";
```

8. Save the document as **CreateSubscribersTable.php** in the Chapter directory for Chapter 8, and then upload the document to the Web server.

9. Open CreateSubscribersTable.php in your Web browser by entering the following URL: *http://<yourserver>/PHP_Projects/ Chapter.08/Chapter/CreateSubscribersTable.php*. The Web page should inform you that the subscribers table was created or should provide an error message.

10. Close your Web browser window.

To delete a table, you use the DROP TABLE statement with the mysql_query() function. The following code demonstrates how to delete the drivers table using similar error handling as the code that created the table:

```
$TableName = "drivers";
$SQLstring = "SHOW TABLES LIKE '$TableName'";
$QueryResult = @mysql_query($SQLstring, $DBConnect);
if (mysql_num_rows($QueryResult) == 0)
    echo "<p>The $TableName table does not exist!</p>";
else {
    $SQLstring = "DROP TABLE $TableName";
    $QueryResult = @mysql_query($SQLstring, $DBConnect);
    if ($QueryResult === FALSE)
        echo "<p>Unable to execute the query.</p>"
            . "<p>Error code " . mysql_errno($DBConnect)
            . ": " . mysql_error($DBConnect) . "</p>";
    else
        echo "<p>Successfully deleted the table.</p>";
}
mysql_close($DBConnect);
```

464

Short Quiz

1. What function is used to send SQL statements to MySQL?

2. Describe the role of the result pointer in database querying.

3. Write a short script that demonstrates how to check whether a table exists before attempting to create it.

4. Which function returns the number of records in a resultset?

5. What MySQL statement is used with the `mysql_query()` function to delete a table?

Manipulating Records

In this section, you will learn how to use PHP to add, update, and delete database records. As you work through the rest of this chapter, you should recognize the SQL statements because you worked with them in Chapter 7. The primary difference is that, instead of manually executing SQL statements by typing them in MySQL Monitor as you did in Chapter 7, you will use PHP statements to access MySQL and execute SQL statements for you.

Adding, Deleting, and Updating Records

To add records to a table, you use the `INSERT` and `VALUES` keywords with the `mysql_query()` function. Remember that you should specify the columns that you are populating, and that the values in the `VALUES` list must be in the same order. For example, the following statements add a new row to the `company_cars` table in the `vehicle_fleet` database:

```
$SQLstring = "INSERT INTO company_cars " .
    " (license, model_year, make, model, mileage) " .
    " VALUES('CPQ-893', 2011, 'Honda', 'Insight', " .
    " 49.2)";
$QueryResult = @mysql_query($SQLstring, $DBConnect);
if ($QueryResult === FALSE)
    echo "<p>Unable to execute the query.</p>"
    . "<p>Error code " . mysql_errno($DBConnect)
    . ": " . mysql_error($DBConnect) . "</p>";
else
    echo "<p>Successfully added the record.</p>";
```

Also remember that you can specify NULL in any fields for which you do not have a value. For example, if you do not know the mileage for the Honda Insight, you can enter NULL as the last item in the VALUES list, as follows:

```
$SQLstring = "INSERT INTO company_cars " .
    " (license, model_year, make, model, mileage) " .
    " VALUES('CPQ-893', 2011, 'Honda', 'Insight', " .
    " NULL)";
```

When you add records to a table that includes an AUTO_INCREMENT field, you omit the column name and value from the lists. The following SQL statement inserts a new record into the company_cars table of the vehicle_fleet database. If it is the first record added to the table, its primary key will be assigned a value of 1.

```
INSERT INTO company_cars (license, model_year, make, model,
mileage) VALUES('AK 4321', 2012, 'Toyota', 'Prius', 23);
```

As you learned in Chapter 7, you can insert multiple value sets with a single command, using multiple value lists separated by commas.

Alternatively, you can include the column name in the list and specify NULL for the field value. The following SQL statement inserts the same new record as the previous example:

```
INSERT INTO company_cars (id, license, model_year, make, model,
mileage) VALUES(NULL, 'AK 4321', 2012, 'Toyota', 'Prius', 23);
```

To add multiple records to a database from an external file, you use the LOAD DATA statement with the name of the local text file that contains the records you want to add. The following statement loads a file named company_cars.txt into the company_cars table in the vehicle_fleet database:

```
$SQLstring = "LOAD DATA INFILE 'company_cars.txt' " .
    " INTO TABLE company_cars";
```

To update records in a table, you use the UPDATE statement with the same syntax you learned in Chapter 7. The UPDATE keyword specifies the name of the table to update and the SET keyword specifies the value to assign to the fields in the records that match the condition in the WHERE keyword. For example, the following statements modify the mileage of the 2007 Honda Civic to 50112.3 miles:

```
$SQLstring = "UPDATE company_cars SET mileage=50112.3
    WHERE license='AK-1234'";
$QueryResult = @mysql_query($SQLstring, $DBConnect);
if ($QueryResult === FALSE)
    echo "<p>Unable to execute the query.</p>"
    . "<p>Error code " . mysql_errno($DBConnect)
    . ": " . mysql_error($DBConnect) . "</p>";
else
    echo "<p>Successfully modified the record.</p>";
```

To delete records from a table, you use the DELETE statement with the mysql_query() function. Remember that the WHERE keyword determines which records to delete in the table. For example, the following statement deletes the record for the 2007 Chevrolet Malibu from the company_cars table in the vehicle_fleet database:

```
$SQLstring = "DELETE FROM company_cars WHERE make='Chevrolet'
    AND model='Malibu' AND model_year=2007";
$QueryResult = @mysql_query($SQLstring, $DBConnect);
if ($QueryResult === FALSE)
    echo "<p>Unable to execute the query.</p>"
    . "<p>Error code " . mysql_errno($DBConnect)
    . ": " . mysql_error($DBConnect) . "</p>";
else
    echo "<p>Successfully deleted the record.</p>";
```

To delete all the records in a table, omit the WHERE clause. For example, the following statement deletes all the records in the company_cars table:

```
$SQLstring = "DELETE FROM company_cars";
```

In the next exercise, you will create an All-in-One Web form that adds a new subscriber record to the subscribers table in the newsletter database. You also use the mysql_insert_id() function, which returns the ID created with AUTO_INCREMENT in the last INSERT operation. You pass to the mysql_insert_id() function the variable to which you assigned the database connection with the mysql_connect() function. The mysql_insert_id() function is useful when you need to find the primary key created for new records you add to a database table.

To create the All-in-One Web form that adds a new subscriber record to the subscribers table in the newsletter database:

1. Create a new document in your text editor.

2. Type the <!DOCTYPE> declaration, <html> element, header information, and <body> element. Use the strict DTD and "Subscribe to our Newsletter" as the content of the <title> element.

3. Add the following header and script section to the end of the document body:

```
<h1>Subscribe to our Newsletter</h1>
<?php
?>
```

4. Add the following if statement to the script section to determine whether the form has been submitted, and initialize the form if it has not been submitted:

```
if (isset($_POST['Submit'])) {
}
else {
```

```
        $ShowForm = TRUE;
        $SubscriberName = "";
        $SubscriberEmail = "";
}
```

5. In the code block for the if clause in the script section, add the
   following code to validate the submitted form data:

```
$FormErrorCount = 0;
if (isset($_POST['SubName'])) {
        $SubscriberName = stripslashes($_POST
        ['SubName']);
        $SubscriberName = trim($SubscriberName);
        if (strlen($SubscriberName) == 0) {
                echo "<p>You must include your
                        name!</p>\n";
                ++$FormErrorCount;
        }
}
else {
        echo "<p>Form submittal error (No
                'SubName' field)!</p>\n";
        ++$FormErrorCount;
}
if (isset($_POST['SubEmail'])) {
        $SubscriberEmail = stripslashes($_
        POST['SubEmail']);
        $SubscriberEmail = trim($SubscriberEmail);
        if (strlen($SubscriberEmail) == 0) {
                echo "<p>You must include your
                        email address!</p>\n";
                ++$FormErrorCount;
        }
}
else {
        echo "<p>Form submittal error (No
                'SubEmail' field)!</p>\n";
        ++$FormErrorCount;
}
```

6. Immediately after validating the submitted form data, add the
   following if...else statement to determine whether the form
   will be processed:

```
if ($FormErrorCount == 0) {
}
else
        $ShowForm = TRUE;
```

7. In the if clause of the if...else statement that determines
   whether the form will be processed, add the following variable
   assignment and include statement:

```
        $ShowForm = FALSE;
        include("inc_db_newsletter.php");
```

8. Immediately after the `include` statement, add the following `if` statement that determines if the database connection is valid:

```
if ($DBConnect !== FALSE) {
}
```

9. In the code block for the previous `if` statement, set the following variables to the values shown. Note that the `date()` function now takes the string "Y-m-d" as a parameter, which ensures that the date string is in the "YYYY-MM-DD" format that MySQL recognizes. Also note that the `id` and `confirmed_date` fields are omitted from the column list for the INSERT statement. The `id` field will be assigned automatically because it is defined with the `AUTO_INCREMENT` keyword. The `confirmed_date` field will be inserted as `NULL`.

```
$TableName = "subscribers";
$SubscriberDate = date("Y-m-d");
$SQLstring = "INSERT INTO $TableName " .
    "(name, email, subscribe_date) VALUES " .
    "('$SubscriberName', '$SubscriberEmail',
    '$SubscriberDate')";
```

10. Next, add the following code to use the `mysql_query()` function to execute the query, report any errors, and close the database connection:

```
$QueryResult = @mysql_query($SQLstring, $DBConnect);
if ($QueryResult === FALSE)
    echo "<p>Unable to insert the values into
        the subscriber table.</p>"
        . "<p>Error code " . mysql_errno($DBConnect)
        . ": " . mysql_error($DBConnect) . "</p>";
else {
    $SubscriberID = mysql_insert_id($DBConnect);
    echo "<p>" . htmlentities($SubscriberName) .
        ", you are now subscribed to our
        newsletter.<br />";
    echo "Your subscriber ID is
        $SubscriberID.<br />";
    echo "Your email address is " .
        htmlentities($SubscriberEmail)
        . ".</p>";
}
mysql_close($DBConnect);
```

 In a production environment, you would normally have separate fields for a user ID and the table's primary key.

11. Finally, add the following code immediately before the closing PHP script tag. This code uses advanced escaping to display the Web form if appropriate.

```
if ($ShowForm) {
    ?>
<form action="NewsletterSubscribe.php" method="POST">
<p><strong>Your Name: </strong>
<input type="text" name="SubName" value="<?php echo
$SubName; ?>" /></p>
<p><strong>Your Email Address: </strong>
<input type="text" name="SubEmail" value="<?php echo
$SubEmail; ?>" /></p>
<p><input type="Submit" name="Submit" value="Submit"
/></p>
</form>
    <?php
}
```

12. Save the file as **NewsletterSubscribe.php** in the Chapter directory for Chapter 8 and upload the file to the Web server.

13. Open the NewsletterSubscribe.php file in your Web browser by entering the following URL: *http://<yourserver>/PHP_ Projects/Chapter.08/Chapter/NewsletterSubscribe.php*. Enter values into the New Subscriber Registration form and click the **Submit** button. You should be assigned a new subscriber ID of 1 the first time you submit a valid name and address, a 2 the second time, and so forth. You should see a Web page similar to the one in Figure 8-4, depending on which subscriber you are.

Figure 8-4 Newsletter Subscriber Web form results

Returning Information on Affected Records

The functions `mysql_affected_rows()` and `mysql_info()` return information on the records that were affected by an INSERT, UPDATE, or DELETE query. First, you will learn how to use the `mysql_affected_rows()` function.

Using the *mysql_affected_rows()* Function

As discussed earlier, with queries that return results, such as SELECT queries, you can use the mysql_num_rows() function to find the number of records returned from the query. However, with queries that modify tables but do not return results, such as INSERT, UPDATE, and DELETE queries, you can use the mysql_affected_rows() function to determine the number of affected rows. You pass to the mysql_affected_rows() function the variable that contains the database connection returned from the mysql_connect() function—not the variable containing the result pointer from the mysql_query() function. For example, the following statements display the number of rows affected by an UPDATE query. Figure 8-5 shows the output in a Web browser.

```
$SQLstring = "UPDATE company_cars SET mileage=50112.3
     WHERE license='AK-1234'";
$QueryResult = @mysql_query($SQLstring, $DBConnect);
if ($QueryResult === FALSE)
     echo "<p>Unable to execute the query.</p>"
     . "<p>Error code " . mysql_errno($DBConnect)
     . ": " . mysql_error($DBConnect) . "</p>";
else
     echo "<p>Successfully updated "
          . mysql_affected_rows($DBConnect) . "
          record(s).</p>";
```

Figure 8-5 Output of the mysql_affected_rows() function for an UPDATE query

The following code contains another example of the mysql_affected_rows() function, this time with a DELETE query:

```
$SQLstring = "DELETE FROM company_cars WHERE license='AK-1234'";
$QueryResult = @mysql_query($SQLstring, $DBConnect);
if ($QueryResult === FALSE)
     echo "<p>Unable to execute the query.</p>"
     . "<p>Error code " . mysql_errno($DBConnect)
     . ": " . mysql_error($DBConnect) . "</p>";
```

```
else
     echo "<p>Successfully deleted "
          . mysql_affected_rows($DBConnect) . " record(s).</p>";
```

Using the *mysql_info()* Function

For queries that add or update records, or that alter a table's structure, you can use the mysql_info() function to return information about the query. This function returns the number of operations for various types of actions, depending on the type of query. For example, with INSERT queries, the mysql_info() function returns the number of records added and duplicated, along with the number of warnings. However, for LOAD DATA queries, the mysql_info() function returns the number of records added, deleted, and skipped, along with the number of warnings. As with the mysql_affected_rows() function, you pass to the mysql_info() function the variable that contains the database connection from the mysql_connect() function. The mysql_info() function returns information about the last query that was executed on the database connection. However, the mysql_info() function returns information about queries that match one of the following formats:

- INSERT INTO... (...) SELECT...

- INSERT INTO... (...) VALUES (...), (...), (...)

- LOAD DATA INFILE ...

- ALTER TABLE ...

- UPDATE ...

For any queries that do not match one of the preceding formats, the mysql_info() function returns an empty string. Notice that the format for adding records with the INSERT and VALUES keywords includes multiple value sets. The mysql_info() function only returns query information when you add multiple records with the INSERT keyword. For example, the mysql_info() function in the following example returns an empty string because the INSERT query only adds a single record:

```
$SQLstring = "INSERT INTO company_cars " .
     " (license, model_year, make, model, mileage) " .
     " VALUES('CPQ-893', 2011, 'Honda', 'Insight', " .
     " 49.2)";
$QueryResult = @mysql_query($SQLstring, $DBConnect);
if ($QueryResult === FALSE)
     echo "<p>Unable to execute the query.</p>"
     . "<p>Error code " . mysql_errno($DBConnect)
     . ": " . mysql_error($DBConnect) . "</p>";
else {
     echo "<p>Successfully added the record.</p>";
     echo "<p>" . mysql_info($DBConnect) . "</p>";
}
```

In comparison, the following statements display the query information shown in Figure 8-6 because the INSERT query adds multiple records:

```
$SQLstring = "INSERT INTO company_cars " .
        " (license, model_year, make, model, mileage) " .
        " VALUES " .
        " ('CPQ-894', 2011, 'Honda', 'Insight', 49.2), " .
        " ('CPQ-895', 2011, 'Honda', 'Insight', 17.9), " .
        " ('CPQ-896', 2011, 'Honda', 'Insight', 22.6)";
$QueryResult = @mysql_query($SQLstring, $DBConnect);
if ($QueryResult === FALSE)
        echo "<p>Unable to execute the query.</p>"
        . "<p>Error code " . mysql_errno($DBConnect)
        . ": " . mysql_error($DBConnect) . "</p>";
else {
        echo "<p>Successfully added the record.</p>";
        echo "<p>" . mysql_info($DBConnect) . "</p>";
}
```

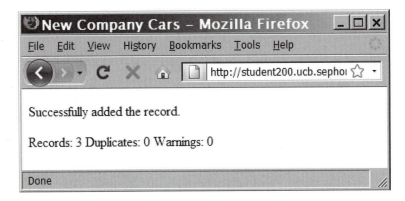

Figure 8-6   Output of the mysql_info() function for an INSERT query that adds multiple records

The mysql_info() function also returns information for LOAD DATA queries. The following statements display the output shown in Figure 8-7:

```
$SQLstring = "LOAD DATA INFILE 'company_cars.txt'
        INTO TABLE company_cars;";
$QueryResult = @mysql_query($SQLstring, $DBConnect);
if ($QueryResult === FALSE)
        echo "<p>Unable to execute the query.</p>"
        . "<p>Error code " . mysql_errno($DBConnect)
        . ": " . mysql_error($DBConnect) . "</p>";
else {
        echo "<p>Successfully added the record.</p>";
        echo "<p>" . mysql_info($DBConnect) . "</p>";
}
```

Figure 8-7 Output of the `mysql_info()` function for a LOAD DATA query

Short Quiz

1. What statement is used to add multiple records to a database from an external file?

2. Explain the purpose of the three keywords in the following SQL query:

   ```
   $SQLstring = "UPDATE company_cars SET mileage=50112.3
       WHERE license='AK-1234'";
   ```

3. What records would be deleted from the `company_cars` table using the following query?

   ```
   $SQLstring = "DELETE FROM company_cars";
   ```

4. What argument is passed to the `mysql_affected_rows()` function to determine the number of rows affected by a query?

Retrieving Records

In this section, you will learn how to use PHP to retrieve records from tables in a database.

Working with Query Results

Recall that for SQL statements that return results, such as SELECT and SHOW statements, the `mysql_query()` function returns a result pointer that represents the query results. You assign the result pointer to a variable, which you can use to access the resultset in PHP. To access the database records through the result pointer, you must use one of the functions listed in Table 8-2.

Function	Description
mysql_data_seek($Result, position)	Moves the result pointer to a specified row in the resultset
mysql_fetch_array($Result, MYSQL_ASSOC | MYSQL_NUM | MYSQL_BOTH)	Returns the fields in the current row of a resultset into an indexed array, associative array, or both, and moves the result pointer to the next row
mysql_fetch_assoc($Result)	Returns the fields in the current row of a resultset into an associative array and moves the result pointer to the next row
mysql_fetch_lengths($Result)	Returns the field lengths for the current row in a resultset into an indexed array
mysql_fetch_row($Result)	Returns the fields in the current row of a resultset into an indexed array and moves the result pointer to the next row

Table 8-2 Common PHP functions for accessing database results

First, you will learn how to use the mysql_fetch_row() function to retrieve fields into an indexed array.

Retrieving Records into an Indexed Array

In Chapter 5, you learned how to use the fgets() function, which returns a line from a text file and moves the file pointer to the next line. The mysql_fetch_row() function is very similar, in that it returns the fields in the current row of a resultset into an indexed array and moves the result pointer to the next row. You can then use the array to access the individual fields in the row. As an example, the following code displays the contents of the fields in the first row of the company_cars table in the vehicle_fleet database:

```php
$SQLstring = "SELECT * FROM company_cars";
$QueryResult = @mysql_query($SQLstring, $DBConnect);
if ($QueryResult === FALSE)
        echo "<p>Unable to execute the query.</p>"
        . "<p>Error code " . mysql_errno($DBConnect)
        . ": " . mysql_error($DBConnect) . "</p>";
else {
        $Row = mysql_fetch_row($QueryResult);
        echo "<p><strong>License</strong>: {$Row[0]}<br />";
        echo "<strong>Make</strong>: {$Row[1]}<br />";
        echo "<strong>Model</strong>: {$Row[2]}<br />";
        echo "<strong>Mileage</strong>: {$Row[3]}<br />";
        echo "<strong>Year</strong>: {$Row[4]}</p>";
}
```

The mysql_fetch_row() function in the preceding example returns the fields in the current row or a value of FALSE when it reaches the last row in the resultset. This allows you to iterate through all the rows in a resultset. The following code shows a more complete example that uses a while statement to display all of the rows in the company_cars table to an HTML table. Figure 8-8 shows how the table appears in a Web browser.

```
$SQLstring = "SELECT * FROM company_cars";
$QueryResult = @mysql_query($SQLstring, $DBConnect);
echo "<table width='100%' border='1'>\n";
echo "<tr><th>License</th><th>Make</th><th>Model</th>
    <th>Mileage</th><th>Year</th></tr>\n";
while (($Row = mysql_fetch_row($QueryResult)) !== FALSE) {
    echo "<tr><td>{$Row[0]}</td>";
    echo "<td>{$Row[1]}</td>";
    echo "<td>{$Row[2]}</td>";
    echo "<td align='right'>{$Row[3]}</td>";
    echo "<td>{$Row[4]}</td></tr>\n";
}
echo "</table>\n";
```

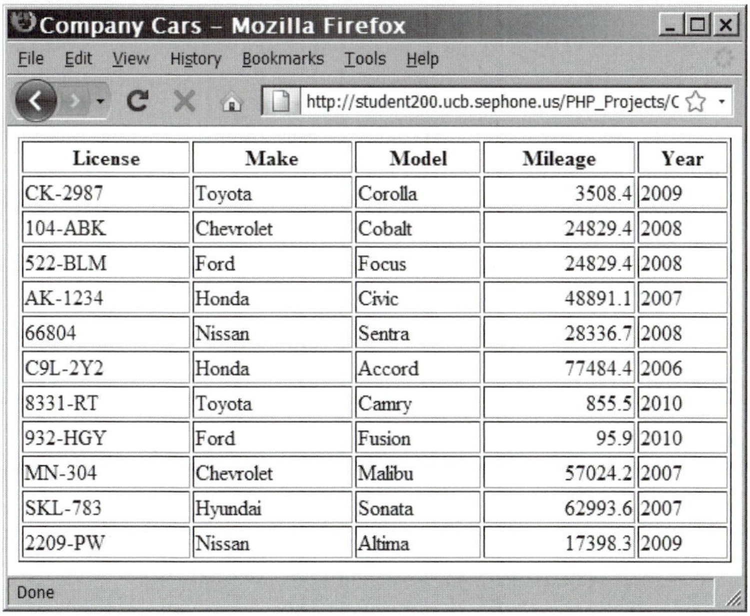

Company Cars – Mozilla Firefox

File Edit View History Bookmarks Tools Help

http://student200.ucb.sephone.us/PHP_Projects/C

License	Make	Model	Mileage	Year
CK-2987	Toyota	Corolla	3508.4	2009
104-ABK	Chevrolet	Cobalt	24829.4	2008
522-BLM	Ford	Focus	24829.4	2008
AK-1234	Honda	Civic	48891.1	2007
66804	Nissan	Sentra	28336.7	2008
C9L-2Y2	Honda	Accord	77484.4	2006
8331-RT	Toyota	Camry	855.5	2010
932-HGY	Ford	Fusion	95.9	2010
MN-304	Chevrolet	Malibu	57024.2	2007
SKL-783	Hyundai	Sonata	62993.6	2007
2209-PW	Nissan	Altima	17398.3	2009

Done

Figure 8-8 Output of the company_cars table in a Web browser

To create a script that selects and displays all of the records in the subscribers table:

1. Create a new document in your text editor.

2. Type the `<!DOCTYPE>` declaration, `<html>` element, header information, and `<body>` element. Use the strict DTD and "Newsletter Subscribers" as the content of the `<title>` element.

3. Add the following header and script section to the end of the document body:

```
<h1>Newsletter Subscribers</h1>
<?php
?>
```

4. Add the following `include()` statement to the script section:

```
include("inc_db_newsletter.php");
```

5. After the `include()` statement, add the following statements to handle a successful selection of the `newsletter` database:

```
if ($DBConnect !== FALSE) {
        mysql_close($DBConnect);
}
```

6. Add the following variable declarations and `mysql_query()` statement immediately before the `mysql_close()` function. The `mysql_query()` statement selects all existing records from the `subscribers` table.

```
$TableName = "subscribers";
$SQLstring = "SELECT * FROM $TableName";
$QueryResult = @mysql_query($SQLstring, $DBConnect);
```

7. Add the following statements immediately before the `mysql_close()` function. These statements use the `mysql_fetch_row()` function to display the results in a table:

```
echo "<table width='100%' border='1'>\n";
echo "<tr><th>Subscriber ID</th>" .
        "<th>Name</th><th>Email</th>" .
        "<th>Subscribe Date</th>" .
        "<th>Confirm Date</th></tr>\n";
while (($Row = mysql_fetch_row($QueryResult)) !== FALSE) {
        echo "<tr><td>{$Row[0]}</td>";
        echo "<td>{$Row[1]}</td>";
        echo "<td>{$Row[2]}</td>";
        echo "<td>{$Row[3]}</td>";
        echo "<td>{$Row[4]}</td></tr>\n";
};
echo "</table>\n";
```

8. Save the file as **ShowNewsletterSubscribers.php** in the Chapter directory for Chapter 8, and then upload the document to the Web server.

9. Open ShowNewsletterSubscribers.php in your Web browser by entering the following URL: *http://<yourserver>/PHP_Projects/Chapter.08/Chapter/ShowNewsletterSubscribers.php*. Your Web page should look like Figure 8-9, although you may have added or deleted more entries.

10. Close your Web browser window.

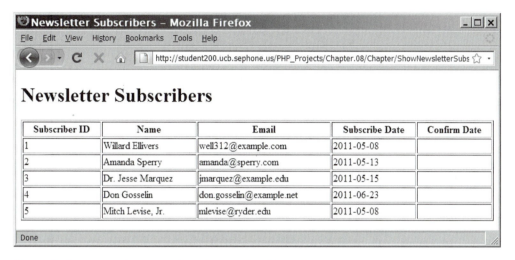

Figure 8-9 Output of the ShowNewsletterSubscribers.php script

Retrieving Records into an Associative Array

The mysql_fetch_assoc() function returns the fields in the current row of a resultset into an associative array and moves the result pointer to the next row. The primary difference between the mysql_fetch_assoc() function and the mysql_fetch_row() function is that instead of returning the fields into an indexed array, the mysql_fetch_assoc() function returns the fields into an associative array and uses each field name as the array key. For example, the following code uses the mysql_fetch_assoc() function to display the contents of the fields in the first row in the company_cars table of the vehicle_fleet database. Notice that the echo statements refer to keys instead of indexes in the $Row[] array.

```
$Row = mysql_fetch_assoc($QueryResult);
echo "<p><strong>License</strong>: {$Row['license']}<br />";
echo "<strong>Make</strong>: {$Row['make']}<br />";
echo "<strong>Model</strong>: {$Row['model']}<br />";
echo "<strong>Mileage</strong>: {$Row['mileage']}<br />";
echo "<strong>Year</strong>: {$Row['year']}</p>";
```

The following code shows an associative array version of the `while` statement that displays all of the rows in the `company_cars` table to an HTML table:

```
$SQLstring = "SELECT * FROM company_cars";
$QueryResult = @mysql_query($SQLstring, $DBConnect);
echo "<table width='100%' border='1'>\n";
echo "<tr><th>License</th><th>Make</th><th>Model</th>
    <th>Mileage</th><th>Year</th></tr>\n";
while (($Row = mysql_fetch_assoc($QueryResult)) !== FALSE) {
    echo "<tr><td>{$Row['license']}</td>";
    echo "<td>{$Row['make']}</td>";
    echo "<td>{$Row['model']}</td>";
    echo "<td align='right'>{$Row['mileage']}</td>";
    echo "<td>{$Row['year']}</td></tr>\n";
}
    echo "</table>\n";
```

To change the query statement in ShowNewsletterSubscribers.php that selects all the records in the `subscribers` table so that it uses an associative array:

1. Return to the **ShowNewsletterSubscribers.php** document in your text editor.

2. Replace the `mysql_fetch_row()` function with a `mysql_fetch_assoc()` function.

3. Modify the `echo` statements in the `while` statement so they reference the keys in the associative array instead of the index values. Your modified code should appear as follows:

    ```
    while (($Row = mysql_fetch_assoc($QueryResult))
    !== FALSE) {
        echo "<tr><td>{$Row['subscriberID']}</td>";
        echo "<td>{$Row['name']}</td>";
        echo "<td>{$Row['email']}</td>";
        echo "<td>{$Row['subscribe_date']}</td>";
        echo "<td>{$Row['confirmed_date']}</td></tr>\n";
    };
    ```

4. Save the **ShowNewsletterSubscribers.php** file and upload it to the server.

5. Open ShowNewsletterSubscribers.php in your Web browser by entering the following URL: *http://<yourserver>/PHP_Projects/ Chapter.08/Chapter/ShowNewsletterSubscribers.php*. Your Web page should look the same as it did before you modified the code to use the `mysql_fetch_assoc()` function.

6. Close your Web browser window.

Closing Query Results

When you are finished working with query results retrieved with the mysql_query() function, you should use the mysql_free_result() function to close the resultset. This ensures that the resultset doesn't keep taking up space in your Web server's memory. (As you'll recall, you need to close a database connection for the same reason.) If you do not call mysql_free_result(), the memory used by the resultset will be freed when the script completes. To close the resultset, pass to the mysql_free_result() function the variable containing the result pointer from the mysql_query() function. The following code uses the mysql_free_result() function to close the $QueryResult variable:

You can only use the mysql_free_result() function with SQL statements that return results, such as SELECT queries, and only when the SQL statement successfully returned results. If you attempt to use the mysql_free_result() function with SQL statements that do not return results, such as the CREATE DATABASE and CREATE TABLE statements, or on an empty resultset, you will receive an error.

```
$SQLstring = "SELECT * FROM company_cars";
$QueryResult = @mysql_query($SQLstring, $DBConnect);
if ($QueryResult === FALSE)
    echo "<p>Unable to execute the query.</p>"
    . "<p>Error code " . mysql_errno($DBConnect)
    . ": " . mysql_error($DBConnect) . "</p>";
else
    echo "<p>Successfully executed the query.</p>";
...
mysql_free_result($QueryResult);
mysql_close($DBConnect);
```

To add a mysql_free_result() function to the ShowNewsletterSubscribers.php script:

1. Return to the **ShowNewsletterSubscribers.php** document in your text editor.

2. Add the following statement above the mysql_close() statement:

   ```
   mysql_free_result($QueryResult);
   ```

3. Save the ShowNewsletterSubscribers.php file and upload it to the Web server. Then open the script in your Web browser by entering the following URL: *http://<yourserver>/PHP_Projects/Chapter.08/Chapter/ShowNewsletterSubscribers.php*. Your Web page should look the same as it did before you added the mysql_free_result() function.

4. Close your Web browser window.

Accessing Query Result Information

As you have learned, the functions mysql_affected_rows() and mysql_info() return information on the records that were affected by a query. You also learned that the mysql_num_rows()

function returns the number of rows in a query result. You use the mysql_num_fields() function to return the number of fields in a query result. As with the mysql_num_rows() function, the mysql_num_fields() function accepts a database connection variable as an optional argument.

The following code demonstrates how to use both functions with the query results returned from the vehicle_fleet database. If the number of rows and fields in the query result are not equal to zero, an echo statement displays the number of rows and fields. However, if the number of rows and fields in the query result are equal to zero, an echo statement displays "Your query returned no results." Figure 8-10 shows the output if the company_cars table in the vehicle_fleet database contains 11 rows and 5 fields.

```php
$SQLstring = "SELECT * FROM company_cars";
$QueryResult = @mysql_query($SQLstring, $DBConnect);
if ($QueryResult === FALSE)
        echo "<p>Unable to execute the query.</p>"
    . "<p>Error code " . mysql_errno($DBConnect)
    . ": " . mysql_error($DBConnect) . "</p>";
else
        echo "<p>Successfully executed the query.</p>";
$NumRows = mysql_num_rows($QueryResult);
$NumFields = mysql_num_fields($QueryResult);
if ($NumRows != 0 && $NumFields != 0)
        echo "<p>Your query returned " .
            mysql_num_rows($QueryResult) . " rows and "
        . mysql_num_fields($QueryResult) . " fields.</p>";
else
        echo "<p>Your query returned no results.</p>";
mysql_close($DBConnect);
```

Figure 8-10 Output of the number of rows and fields returned from a query

To add statements to the ShowNewsletterSubscribers.php script that display the number of returned rows and fields:

1. Return to the **ShowNewsletterSubscribers.php** document in your text editor.

2. Add the following statements above the `mysql_close($DBConnect);` statement:

```
$NumRows = mysql_num_rows($QueryResult);
$NumFields = mysql_num_fields($QueryResult);
echo "<p>Your query returned the above "
    . mysql_num_rows($QueryResult)
    . " rows and ". mysql_num_fields($QueryResult)
    . " fields:</p>";
```

3. Save the ShowNewsletterSubscribers.php file, upload it to the Web server, and open it in your Web browser by entering the following URL: *http://<yourserver>/PHP_Projects/Chapter.08/ Chapter/ShowNewsletterSubscribers.php*. Your Web page should look like Figure 8-11.

4. Close your Web browser window.

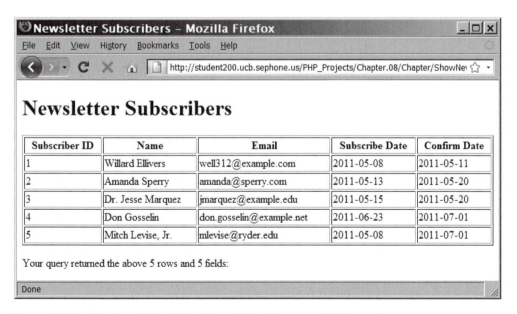

Figure 8-11 The Newsletter Subscribers table with row and field counts

Short Quiz

1. What two functions return the fields in the current row of a resultset into an indexed array and move the pointer to the next row?

2. Describe the differences between the `mysql_fetch_row()` function and the `mysql_fetch_assoc()` function.

3. Contrast the `mysql_num_rows()` function and the `mysql_num_fields()` function.

4. What function is used to close the query resultset when you are finished working with the results?

5. Explain why the `mysql_free_result()` function does not work with the CREATE DATABASE and CREATE TABLE statements.

Summing Up

- The `mysql_connect()` function opens a connection to a MySQL database server.

- The `mysql_close()` function closes a database connection.

- The `mysql_errno()` function returns the error code from the last attempted MySQL function call or zero if no error occurred.

- The `mysql_error()` function returns the error message from the last attempted MySQL function call or returns an empty string if no error occurred.

- The `die()` and `exit()` functions terminate script execution.

- The error control operator (@) suppresses error messages.

- You use the `mysql_create_db()` function to create a new database.

- The `mysql_select_db()` function selects a database.

- You use the `mysql_drop_db()` function to delete a database.

- The `mysql_query()` function sends SQL statements to MySQL.

- A result pointer is a special type of variable that refers to the currently selected row in a resultset.

- You use the CREATE TABLE statement with the mysql_query() function to create a table.

- The PRIMARY KEY clause indicates a field or fields that will be used as a referential index for the table.

- The AUTO_INCREMENT clause creates a field that is automatically updated with the next sequential value for that column.

- The NOT NULL clause creates a field that must contain data.

- You use the DROP TABLE statement with the mysql_query() function to delete a table.

- You use the LOAD DATA statement and the mysql_query() function with a local text file to add multiple records to a database.

- You use the UPDATE statement with the mysql_query() function to update records in a table.

- You use the DELETE statement with the mysql_query() function to delete records from a table.

- The mysql_info() function returns the number of operations for various types of actions, depending on the type of query.

- The mysql_fetch_row() function returns the fields in the current row of a resultset into an indexed array and moves the result pointer to the next row.

- The mysql_fetch_assoc() function returns the fields in the current row of a resultset into an associative array and moves the result pointer to the next row.

- The mysql_free_result() function closes a resultset.

- The mysql_num_rows() function returns the number of rows in a query result, and the mysql_num_fields() function returns the number of fields in a query result.

Comprehension Check

1. Which of the following functions opens a database connection?

a. open()

b. mysql_open()

c. openConnection()

d. mysql_connect()

2. Which of the following functions closes a database connection?

    a. `close()`

    b. `mysql_close()`

    c. `mysql_free()`

    d. `mysql_free_connect()`

3. To which of the following functions do you need to pass a variable representing the database connection? (Choose all that apply.)

    a. `mysql_get_client_info()`

    b. `mysql_get_host_info()`

    c. `mysql_get_proto_info()`

    d. `mysql_get_server_info()`

4. Which of the following functions terminates script execution? (Choose all that apply.)

    a. `exit()`

    b. `bye()`

    c. `die()`

    d. `quit()`

5. Describe three types of errors that can occur when accessing MySQL databases and other types of data sources with PHP.

6. The following code structure prevents MySQL error messages from being displayed if the database connection is not available. True or False?

```
$DBConnect = mysql_connect("localhost", "dongosselin",
     "rosebud");
if (!$DBConnect)
     echo "<p>The database server is not available.</p>";
else {
     echo "<p>Successfully connected to the database
          server.</p>";
     mysql_close($DBConnect);
}
```

7. Which of the following functions reports the error message from the last failed database connection attempt?

    a. `mysql_errmsg()`

    b. `mysql_error_msg()`

    c. `mysql_errno()`

    d. `mysql_error()`

8. Which of the following characters suppresses error messages in PHP?

    a. `*`

    b. `&`

    c. `#`

    d. `@`

9. What is the correct syntax for selecting a database with the `mysql_select_db()` function? (Select all that apply.)

    a. `mysql_select_db(connection)`

    b. `mysql_select_db(database)`

    c. `mysql_select_db(database, connection)`

    d. `database = mysql_select_db(connection)`

10. Write a simple code segment that demonstrates how to use a `mysql_query()` function to prevent your code from attempting to create a table that already exists.

11. Explain what a result pointer is and how to create and use one.

12. Which of the following SQL keywords creates an auto-incrementing field?

    a. `AUTO`

    b. `INCREMENT`

    c. `AUTO_INCREMENT`

    d. `AUTOINCREMENT`

13. Which of the following statements is used to create a query string in $SQLstring to delete the company_cars table?

    a. $SQLstring = "DELETE TABLE company_cars";

    b. $SQLstring = "DROP TABLE company_cars";

    c. $SQLstring = "REMOVE TABLE company_cars";

    d. $SQLstring = "CANCEL TABLE company_cars";

14. When using the INSERT and VALUE keywords to add records to a table using the mysql_query() function, what keyword is used to indicate that there is no value for a field?

15. Which of the following functions returns the number of rows affected by queries that do not return results, such as INSERT, UPDATE, and DELETE queries?

    a. mysql_affected_rows()

    b. mysql_rows()

    c. mysql_get_changed()

    d. mysql_fetch_rows()

16. The _____ function returns the number of operations for various types of actions, depending on the type of query.

    a. mysql_get_info()

    b. mysql_operations()

    c. mysql_info()

    d. mysql_num_rows()

17. Which of the following functions returns the fields in the current row of a resultset into an indexed array? (Select all that apply.)

    a. mysql_fetch_data()

    b. mysql_fetch_array()

    c. mysql_index_row()

    d. mysql_fetch_row()

18. Which of the following functions returns the fields in the current row of a resultset into an associative array?

    a. `mysql_assoc_fetch()`

    b. `mysql_fetch_keys()`

    c. `mysql_fetch_assoc()`

    d. `mysql_fetch_index()`

19. Which of the following functions closes a resultset to ensure that it doesn't keep taking up space in your Web server's memory?

    a. `mysql_free_result()`

    b. `mysql_result_close()`

    c. `mysql_free()`

    d. `mysql_close_result()`

20. Write a simple code segment that demonstrates how to use the `mysql_num_rows()` and `mysql_num_fields()` functions to determine whether a SQL query returned results.

Reinforcement Exercises

 Exercise 8-1

In this project, you will create a Web page that allows visitors to your site to sign a guest book that is saved to a database.

1. Create a new document in your text editor and type the `<!DOCTYPE>` declaration, `<html>` element, document head, and `<body>` element. Use the strict DTD and "Guest Book" as the content of the `<title>` element.

2. Add the following text and elements to the document body:

```
<h2>Enter your name to sign our guest book</h2>
<form method="POST" action="SignGuestBook.php">
<p>First Name <input type="text" name="first_name"
/></p>
<p>Last Name <input type="text" name="last_name"
/></p>
<p><input type="submit" value="Submit" /></p>
</form>
```

3. Save the document as **GuestBook.html** in the Projects directory for Chapter 8.

4. Create a new document in your text editor and type the `<!DOCTYPE>` declaration, `<html>` element, document head, and `<body>` element. Use the strict DTD and "Sign Guest Book" as the content of the `<title>` element.

5. Add the following script section to the document body:

```php
<?php
?>
```

6. Add the following statements to the script section to ensure that visitors enter their first and last names:

```php
if (empty($_POST['first_name']) || empty($_POST['last_name']))
        echo "<p>You must enter your first and last
                name! Click your browser's Back button to
                return to the Guest Book form.</p>";
```

7. Add the following statement to the script section to connect to the database. Replace *host* with the host name of your MySQL server, and *user* and *password* with the MySQL user name and password you created in Chapter 7.

```php
else {
        $DBConnect = @mysql_connect("host", "user",
        "password");
        if ($DBConnect === FALSE)
                echo "<p>Unable to connect to the database
                        server.</p>"
                        . "<p>Error code " . mysql_errno()
                        . ": " . mysql_error() . "</p>";
```

8. Add the following statements to the end of the script section to create a database named `guestbook` if it does not already exist:

```php
        else {
                $DBName = "guestbook";
                if (!@mysql_select_db($DBName, $DBConnect)) {
                        $SQLstring = "CREATE DATABASE $DBName";
                        $QueryResult = @mysql_query($SQLstring,
                        $DBConnect);
                        if ($QueryResult === FALSE)
                                echo "<p>Unable to execute the
                                        query.</p>"
                                . "<p>Error code " . mysql_
                                errno($DBConnect)
                                . ": " . mysql_error($DBConnect)
                                        . "</p>";
```

```
        else
            echo "<p>You are the first
                visitor!</p>";
    }
    mysql_select_db($DBName, $DBConnect);
```

9. Add the following statements to the end of the script section to create a table named count if it does not already exist. The table consists of a single auto-incrementing primary key field named countID.

```
$TableName = "visitors";
$SQLstring = "SHOW TABLES LIKE '$TableName'";
$QueryResult = @mysql_query($SQLstring, $DBConnect);
if (mysql_num_rows($QueryResult) == 0) {
    $SQLstring = "CREATE TABLE $TableName
    (countID SMALLINT
    NOT NULL AUTO_INCREMENT PRIMARY KEY,
    last_name VARCHAR(40), first_name VARCHAR(40))";
    $QueryResult = @mysql_query($SQLstring,
    $DBConnect);
    if ($QueryResult===FALSE)
        echo "<p>Unable to create the table.</p>"
            . "<p>Error code " . mysql_
            errno($DBConnect)
            . ": " . mysql_error($DBConnect) .
            "</p>";
```

10. Finally, add the following statements to the end of the script section. These mysql_query() statements add the visitor to the database. The last statement closes the database connection.

```
            $LastName = stripslashes($_
            POST['last_name']);
            $FirstName = stripslashes($_
            POST['first_name']);
            $SQLstring = "INSERT INTO $TableName
            VALUES(NULL, '$LastName',
            '$FirstName')";
            $QueryResult = @mysql_
            query($SQLstring, $DBConnect);
            if ($QueryResult === FALSE)
                echo "<p>Unable to execute the
                    query.</p>"
                    . "<p>Error code " . mysql_
                    errno($DBConnect)
                    . ": " . mysql_
                    error($DBConnect) . "</p>";
        else
            echo "<h1>Thank you for signing
                our guest book!</h1>";
    }
    mysql_close($DBConnect);
    }
}
```

11. Save the document as **SignGuestBook.php** in the Projects directory for Chapter 8. Upload both SignGuestBook.php and GuestBook.html to the server.

12. Open GuestBook.html in your Web browser by entering the following URL: *http://<yourserver>/PHP_Projects/ Chapter.08/Projects/GuestBook.html*. Test the form to see if you can add your name to the database.

13. Close your Web browser window.

Exercise 8-2

In this project, you will add a document to the Guest Book program you created in Reinforcement Exercise 8-1. This document displays the entries in the guest book.

1. Create a new document in your text editor and type the `<!DOCTYPE>` declaration, `<html>` element, document head, and `<body>` element. Use the strict DTD and "Guest Book Posts" as the content of the `<title>` element.

2. Add the following script section to the document body:

```
<?php
?>
```

3. Add the following statement to the script section to connect to the database. Replace *host* with the host name of your MySQL server, and *user* and *password* with the MySQL user name and password you created in Chapter 7.

```
$DBConnect = @mysql_connect("host", "user", "password");
if ($DBConnect === FALSE)
    echo "<p>Unable to connect to the database
        server.</p>"
    . "<p>Error code " . mysql_errno()
    . ": " . mysql_error() . "</p>";
```

4. Add the following statements to the end of the script section to connect to the `guestbook` database. If the database does not exist, a message reports that the guest book does not contain any entries.

```
else {
    $DBName = "guestbook";
    if (!@mysql_select_db($DBName, $DBConnect))
        echo "<p>There are no entries in the guest
            book!</p>";
```

5. Add the following statements to the end of the script section to select all the records in the `visitors` table. If no records are returned, a message reports that the guest book does not contain any entries.

```
else {
    $TableName = "visitors";
    $SQLstring = "SELECT * FROM $TableName";
    $QueryResult = @mysql_query($SQLstring,
    $DBConnect);
    if (mysql_num_rows($QueryResult) == 0)
        echo "<p>There are no entries in
            the guest book!</p>";
```

6. Add the following statements to the end of the script section to display the records returned from the `visitors` table:

```
else {
    echo "<p>The following visitors have
        signed our guest book:</p>";
    echo "<table width='100%' border='1'>";
    echo "<tr><th>First Name</th><th>Last
        Name</th></tr>";
    while (($Row = mysql_fetch_
    assoc($QueryResult)) !== FALSE) {
        echo "<tr><td>{$Row['first_
            name']}</td>";
        echo "<td>{$Row['last_name']}</
            td></tr>";
    }
```

7. Add the following statements to the end of the script section to close the database connection and the result pointer:

```
    }
    mysql_free_result($QueryResult);
    }
    mysql_close($DBConnect);
}
```

8. Save the document as **ShowGuestBook.php** in the Projects directory for Chapter 8.

9. Return to the **GuestBook.html** document in your text editor and add the following text and elements to the end of the document body:

```
<p><a href="ShowGuestBook.php">Show Guest Book</a></p>
```

10. Save the GuestBook.html file, and then open it in your Web browser by entering the following URL: *http://<yourserver>/ PHP_Projects/Chapter.08/Projects/GuestBook.html*. Click the **Show Guest Book** link to see if the script functions correctly.

11. Close your Web browser window.

 ### Exercise 8-3

Create a Web page to be used for storing software development bug reports in a MySQL database. Include fields such as product name and version, type of hardware, operating system, frequency of occurrence, and proposed solutions. Include links on the main page that allow you to create a new bug report and update an existing bug report.

 ### Exercise 8-4

Create a Web site for tracking, documenting, and managing the process of interviewing candidates for professional positions. On the main page, include a form with fields for the interviewer's name, position, and date of interview. Also include fields for entering the candidate's name, communication abilities, professional appearance, computer skills, business knowledge, and interviewer's comments. Clicking the Submit button should save the data in a MySQL database. Include a link for opening a document that displays each candidate's interview information.

 ### Exercise 8-5

Create a Web page that stores airline surveys in a MySQL database. Include fields for the date and time of the flight, flight number, and other fields you consider appropriate for identifying a particular flight. Also, include groups of radio buttons that allow the user to rate the airline on the following criteria:

- Friendliness of customer staff

- Space for luggage storage

- Comfort of seating

- Cleanliness of aircraft

- Noise level of aircraft

The radio buttons for each question should have the following options: No Opinion, Poor, Fair, Good, and Excellent. Include a View Past Survey Results button on the main survey page that displays a list of past survey results.

Discovery Projects

The Chinese Zodiac site is a comprehensive project that will be updated in the Discovery Projects in each chapter. All files for the Chinese Zodiac site will be saved in a folder named ChineseZodiac in the root Web folder on the server, and all database tables will be stored in the chinese_zodiac database.

Discovery Project 8-1

This Discovery Project will build upon Discovery Project 7-2, in which you created a zodiacfeedback table to store the date, time, sender, message content, and display status of user feedback about the Chinese Zodiac Web site.

Now you will create the user interface—a Web form that contains an appropriate title, subtitle, and instructions. Include form inputs to enter the sender's name (a text box for the sender field), message (a text area for the message field), whether the message should be publicly displayed (a check box for the public_message field), and a Submit button to transfer the data to the processing script, process_zodiac_feedback.php, which you will create in Discovery Project 8-2. Save the file as **zodiac_feedback.html** and upload the file to the ChineseZodiac directory on the server. Open the Web form in the browser to verify that all the input fields are displayed properly.

When you were introduced to Web forms in Chapter 4, you learned that the best way to validate user input was to provide sample input and/or restrict the values that could be entered in a form (like the check box used to restrict the value of the display_message field to 'Y' or 'N').

Discovery Project 8-2

In this project, you will create the **process_ zodiac_feedback.php** script to process the form information submitted with the zodiac_feedback.html Web form created in Project 8-1, and to store the information in the zodiacfeedback table in the chinese_zodiac database.

Open a blank document in the text editor and insert the following script, replacing *host* with the name of the host of the MySQL server, and *user* and *password* with your user name and password.

```php
<?php
$db_name="chinese_zodiac";
//assign the connection and selected database to a variable
$DBConnect = mysql_connect("host", "user", "password");
```

```
if ($DBConnect === FALSE)
    echo "<p>Unable to connect to the database server.</p>"
        . "<p>Error code " . mysql_errno()
        . ": " . mysql_error() . "</p>";
else {
    //select the database
    $db = mysql_select_db($db_name, $DBConnect);
    if ($db === FALSE) {
        echo "<p>Unable to connect to the database
            server.</p>"
            . "<p>Error code " . mysql_errno()
            . ": " . mysql_error() . "</p>";
        mysql_close($DBConnect);
        $DBConnect = FALSE;
    }
}
?>
```

 Because the inc_connect. php file contains information about the database server and login information, it would normally be stored in a directory outside of the Web-accessible file structure, so that it would not be directly accessible from a Web browser. To simplify this exercise, you will store the inc_connect.php file in the same directory as the other include files.

Save the file as **inc_connect.php** and upload the file to the Includes subdirectory of the ChineseZodiac directory on the Web server.

Once all fields have been validated, you will "include" the inc_connect.php file to connect to the server and select the chinese_zodiac database. Assign the table name to a variable $db_table.

Use the INSERT and VALUES keywords with the mysql_query() function to insert the values from the form into the appropriate fields in the zodiacfeedback table. Be sure to store the system date and time in the message_date and message_time fields. Include a message that thanks the user for entering a comment and reports that the comment was successfully added.

Save the form as **process_zodiac_feedback.php** and upload the file to the ChineseZodiac directory on the server. Test the script by opening zodiac_feedback.html in the browser and completing and submitting the form four times. Be sure to select 'Y' and 'N' alternately, so that some messages will be public and others will be private.

Open phpMyAdmin and use the Browse command to verify that four rows have been successfully written to the zodiacfeedback table.

 Discovery Project 8-3

Create a new PHP script in your text editor to select all rows in the zodiacfeedback table that contain a public_message value of 'Y' and save the resultset to a $QueryResult variable. Remember that you must include the inc_connect.php file.

Use the mysql_fetch_assoc() function to display the resultset in an attractive table format. Save the file as **view_zodiac_feedback.php** in the ChineseZodiac folder and upload the file to the server. Open

494

the view_zodiac_feedback.php file in the browser to verify that all public messages are displayed.

Discovery Project 8-4

Reopen **inc_web_forms.php** in the Includes subdirectory of the ChineseZodiac directory. At the bottom of the file, add two sections, one for each new link. Describe the process of the Zodiac Feedback form in the first, and describe the process of retrieving records from a database in the second. Add [Test the Script] and [View the Script] links for each. When clicked, the [Test the Script] links should open the zodiac_feedback.html and view_zodiac_feedback.php scripts. When the [View the Script] links are clicked, they should display the source code for the process_zodiac_feedback.php and view_zodiac_feedback.php scripts.

Add two new text links to the top of the file: Add Zodiac Feedback and View Zodiac Feedback, which link to the two sections you added to the bottom of the file.

Save the inc_web_forms.php file and upload it to the Includes folder in the ChineseZodiac directory on the Web server.

Open **inc_home_links_bar.php**, which you created in Discovery Project 3-3. The file is in the Includes folder in the ChineseZodiac directory on the Web server. Add a Site Feedback text link that opens zodiac_feedback.html. Save the inc_home_links_bar.php file and upload the file to the server. Display the Chinese Zodiac Web site in the browser and click the Site Feedback text link to test the site feedback process.

Discovery Project 8-5

Open **inc_footer.php**, which you created in Discovery Project 2-2 and modified in Discovery Project 5-5. Modify the file to query a random quote from the randomproverb table instead of the proverbs.txt file. Use the count() MySQL aggregate function to determine the number of proverbs in the table. Use the PHP rand() function to determine which proverb to display.

Each time you retrieve a proverb from the randomproverb table, update the display_count for that record with a MySQL query function using the index field, as follows:

```
$SQLString = "UPDATE randomproverb SET display_count ".
             " = display_count + 1 WHERE proverb = " .
             $ProverbArray;
```

Managing State Information

In this chapter, you will:

- ◎ Learn about state information
- ◎ Use hidden form fields to save state information
- ◎ Use query strings to save state information
- ◎ Use cookies to save state information
- ◎ Use sessions to save state information

Information about individual visits to a Web site is called **state information**. HTTP was originally designed to be **stateless**, which means that Web browsers stored no data about pages viewed on previous visits to a Web site. In this chapter, you will learn how to **maintain state**, or store persistent data about a Web site visit, using hidden form fields, query strings, cookies, and sessions. When you maintain state, HTTP is said to be **stateful**.

Understanding State Information

The original stateless design of the Web allowed early Web servers to process requests for Web pages quickly because they did not need to remember any unique requirements for different clients. Similarly, Web browsers needed no special information to load a particular Web page from a server. Although this stateless design was efficient, it was also limiting. Because a Web server could not remember individual user information, the browser was forced to treat every visit to a Web page as an entirely new session, even if the browser had just opened a different Web page on the same server. This design hampered interactivity and limited the amount of personal interaction a Web site could provide.

This chapter shows different methods of maintaining state information. Although the chapter focuses on establishing a user's identity and maintaining it as the user visits different pages on a Web site, this is only one example of what you can do when state information is maintained.

Web portal sites provide individual users with customizable pages made of sections, each of which displays content such as a calendar, friends list, message queue, or news headlines. Users set preferences for what each section displays. This information is stored in a database, in a record associated with the user's ID. Whenever the user returns to a previously visited page, the user's preferences are retrieved from the database and the Web page is displayed accordingly.

One of the most important reasons to maintain a visitor's identity within a Web site is for Web page access control. Consider a Web-based time tracking system, which might have links for entering, reviewing, approving, and reporting an employee's work hours. All employees need access to the links for entering and reviewing their own hours. A supervisor needs additional access to review the time sheets. A payroll clerk needs access to reports of all employees' hours, once the hours have been approved. All of these permissions can be stored in the database, linked to the user's ID. Once the visitor's identity has been established, the PHP script can limit the available pages based on permissions in the database.

Customizations do not need to be limited to an individual user's identity. A Web-based time tracking system may be shared by a number of companies. A company that has an existing Web site may already have developed a unique look for its site, with custom colors, fonts, and styles. By associating each user with a company, and storing information about that company's custom design in the database, the PHP script can display a page that matches the look of the company's own Web pages, providing a consistent user experience.

A user's browsing history can also be used to customize a Web site. Many online stores display a list of recently viewed or recently purchased merchandise when a user returns to their Web site. These individual histories and orders are stored in a database, and then retrieved when the visitor returns to the store's Web site. Some sites employ complex algorithms that analyze a user's history and then present a list of recommended items.

The four tools for maintaining state information with PHP are hidden form fields, query strings, cookies, and sessions. This chapter shows you how to use each tool to maintain state information while working with the College Internship Available Opportunities Web site, which consists of four Web pages. Figure 9-1 illustrates how visitors navigate through the Web site.

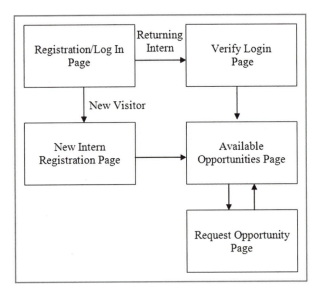

Figure 9-1 College Internship Available Opportunities Web site page flow

The first page that visitors open is the Registration/Log In page, which is in the upper-left corner of Figure 9-1. New visitors to the Web site must first get an Intern ID and enter their contact information before accessing the Available Opportunities page, which is the site's main page. Visitors are required to use a valid e-mail address as their user name. Returning visitors can enter their login information and access the Available Opportunities page directly. Figure 9-2 shows the Registration/Log In Web page.

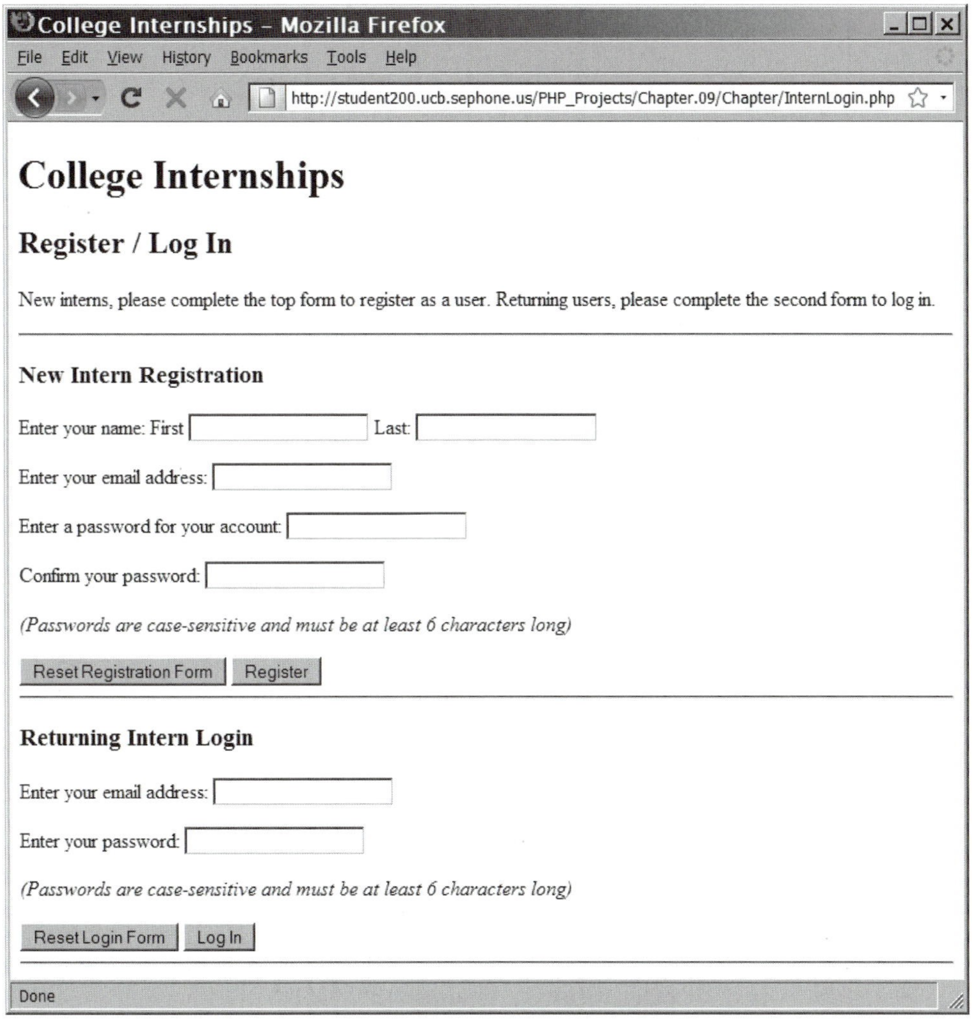

Figure 9-2 Registration/Log In Web page

After a user logs in, the Web site must keep track of information about the user the entire time the client Web browser navigates through the various pages on the site. In other words, the Web site must maintain state information about the client session.

As you work with the College Internship Available Opportunities Web site, keep in mind that the goal of this chapter is to teach you how to maintain state information with PHP. The Web site is intentionally simple to allow you to focus on using state techniques. It does not have the most efficient or elegant design possible. For example, the PHP code that makes up the Web site contains minimal validation functions to keep the code structure simple and focus on the techniques presented in this chapter. If you try to cause an error (or "break" a script), you will succeed. Most important, remember that even though the Web site requires user ID numbers and passwords, *it is not secure*. Refer to your Web server's documentation for information on how to secure your Web site.

To create a database named `internships`, along with three tables named `interns`, `opportunities`, and `assigned_opportunities`:

1. Log in to MySQL Monitor with the MySQL user name and password you created in Chapter 7.

2. Enter the following command to create a database named `internships`:

   mysql> **CREATE DATABASE internships;[ENTER↵]**

3. After you see the "Query OK" message, enter the following command to select the `internships` database:

   mysql> **USE internships;[ENTER↵]**

4. Enter the following command to create the `interns` table:

   mysql> **CREATE TABLE interns (internID SMALLINT NOT NULL AUTO_INCREMENT PRIMARY KEY, email VARCHAR(40), password_md5 VARCHAR(32), first VARCHAR(40), last VARCHAR(40));[ENTER↵]**

5. Enter the following command to create the `opportunities` table:

   mysql> **CREATE TABLE opportunities (opportunityID SMALLINT NOT NULL AUTO_INCREMENT PRIMARY KEY, company VARCHAR(40), city VARCHAR(25), start_date DATE, end_date DATE, position VARCHAR(30), description VARCHAR(250));[ENTER↵]**

6. Enter the following command to create the `assigned_opportunities` table:

   mysql> **CREATE TABLE assigned_opportunities (opportunityID SMALLINT, internID SMALLINT, date_selected DATE, date_approved DATE);[ENTER↵]**

7. Enter the following command to load the opportunities.txt file into the `opportunities` table. Be sure to include the full path to opportunities.txt.

```
mysql> LOAD DATA INFILE 'opportunities.txt' INTO
TABLE opportunities;[ENTER↵]
```

8. After you see the "Query OK" message, type **exit** or **quit** and press **Enter** to log out of MySQL Monitor.

To create the Registration/Log In page:

1. Create a new document in your text editor and type the `<!DOCTYPE>` declaration, `<html>` element, header information, and `<body>` element. Use the strict DTD and "College Internships" as the content of the `<title>` element.

2. Add the following text and elements to the document body:

```
<h1>College Internships</h1>
<h2>Register / Log In</h2>
<p>New interns, please complete the top form to
register as a user. Returning users, please complete
the second form to log in.</p>
<hr />
```

3. Add the following Web form to allow new interns to register for an intern ID:

```
<h3>New Intern Registration</h3>
<form method="post" action="RegisterIntern.php">
<p>Enter your name: First
     <input type="text" name="first" />
Last:
     <input type="text" name="last" /></p>
<p>Enter your e-mail address:
     <input type="text" name="email" /></p>
<p>Enter a password for your account:
     <input type="password" name="password" /></p>
<p>Confirm your password:
     <input type="password" name="password2" /></p>
<p><em>(Passwords are case-sensitive and
     must be at least 6 characters long)</em></p>
<input type="reset" name="reset"
     value="Reset Registration Form" />
<input type="submit" name="register"
value="Register" />
</form>
<hr />
```

4. Add a second Web form to allow returning users to log in. The VerifyLogin.php script will be created later in the chapter.

```
<h3>Returning Intern Login</h3>
<form method="post" action="VerifyLogin.php">
<p>Enter your e-mail address:
    <input type="text" name="email" /></p>
<p>Enter your password:
    <input type="password" name="password" /></p>
<p><em>(Passwords are case-sensitive and
    must be at least 6 characters long)</em></p>
<input type="reset" name="reset"
    value="Reset Login Form" />
<input type="submit" name="login" value="Log In" />
</form>
<hr />
```

502

Although this document has no PHP code sections, it is saved as a PHP file because PHP code will be added later in this chapter.

5. Save the document as **InternLogin.php** in the Chapter directory for Chapter 9 and upload the document to the server.

To create the New Intern Registration page:

1. Create a new document in your text editor and type the <!DOCTYPE> declaration, <html> element, header information, and <body> element. Use the strict DTD and "Intern Registration" as the content of the <title> element.

2. Add the following text, elements, and script section to the document body:

```
<h1>College Internship</h1>
<h2>Intern Registration</h2>
<?php
?>
```

3. Add the following code to the script section to validate the e-mail address entered. The preg_match() function is the same one used in Chapter 3.

```
$errors = 0;
$email = "";
if (empty($_POST['email'])) {
    ++$errors;
    echo "<p>You need to enter an e-mail address.</p>\n";
}
else {
    $email = stripslashes($_POST['email']);
    if (preg_match("/^[\w-]+(\.[\w-]+)*@" .
            "[\w-]+(\.[\w-]+)*(\.[a-zA-Z]{2, })$/i",
            $email) == 0) {
        ++$errors;
        echo "<p>You need to enter a valid " .
            "e-mail address.</p>\n";
        $email = "";
    }
}
```

4. Add the following code to the script section to validate the password. The code verifies that both password fields were entered, that they match, and that the password is at least 6 characters long.

```
if (empty($_POST['password'])) {
    ++$errors;
    echo "<p>You need to enter a password.</p>\n";
    $password = "";
}
else
    $password = stripslashes($_POST['password']);
if (empty($_POST['password2'])) {
    ++$errors;
    echo "<p>You need to enter a confirmation
        password.</p>\n";
    $password2 = " ";
}
else
    $password2 = stripslashes($_POST['password2']);
if ((!(empty($password))) && (!(empty($password2)))) {
    if (strlen($password) < 6) {
        ++$errors;
        echo "<p>The password is too short.</p>\n";
        $password = "";
        $password2 = "";
    }
    if ($password <> $password2) {
        ++$errors;
        echo "<p>The passwords do not match.</p>\n";
        $password = "";
        $password2 = "";
    }
}
```

5. Add the following if statement to the end of the script section to connect to the database server and open the internships database. Be sure to replace *host* with the host name of your MySQL server, and *user* and *password* with your user name and password.

```
if ($errors == 0) {
    $DBConnect = @mysql_connect("host", "user",
    "password");
    if ($DBConnect === FALSE) {
        echo "<p>Unable to connect to the database
            server. " .
            "Error code " . mysql_errno() . ": " .
            mysql_error() . "</p>\n";
        ++$errors;
    }
```

```
        else {
            $DBName = "internships";
            $result = @mysql_select_db($DBName,
            $DBConnect);
            if ($result === FALSE) {
                echo "<p>Unable to select the
                    database. " .
                    "Error code " . mysql_
                    errno($DBConnect) .
                    ": " . mysql_error($DBConnect) .
                    "</p>\n";
                ++$errors;
            }
        }
    }
```

6. Add the following statements to the end of the script section
    to verify that the e-mail address entered is not already in the
    interns table:

```
$TableName = "interns";
if ($errors == 0) {
    $SQLstring = "SELECT count(*) FROM $TableName" .
        "where email=$email";
    $QueryResult = @mysql_query($SQLstring,
        $DBConnect);
    if ($QueryResult !== FALSE) {
        $Row = mysql_fetch_row($QueryResult);
        if ($Row[0]>0) {
            echo "<p>The email address entered (" .
                htmlentities($email) .
                ") is already registered.</p>\n";
            ++$errors;
        }
    }
}
```

7. Add the following if statement to show the appropriate mes-
    sage if there were errors:

```
if ($errors > 0) {
    echo "<p>Please use your browser's BACK button
        to return" .
        " to the form and fix the errors
        indicated.</p>\n";
}
```

8. Finally, at the end of the script section, enter the following
    statements to add the new user to the interns table. Note
    that an MD5 hash of the password is stored in the database
    for security reasons. Each user's Intern ID value is the pri-
    mary key of the row in which the user's personal information
    is stored. Therefore, the mysql_insert_id() function returns

the primary key to the $InternID variable. The last statement closes the database connection.

```php
if ($errors == 0) {
    $first = stripslashes($_POST['first']);
    $last = stripslashes($_POST['last']);
    $SQLstring = "INSERT INTO $TableName " .
            " (first, last, email, password_md5) " .
            " VALUES( '$first', '$last',
            '$email', " .
            " '" . md5($password) . "')";
    $QueryResult = @mysql_query($SQLstring,
    $DBConnect);
    if ($QueryResult === FALSE) {
        echo "<p>Unable to save your registration " .
            " information. Error code " .
            mysql_errno($DBConnect) . ": " .
            mysql_error($DBConnect) . "</p>\n";
        ++$errors;
    }
    else {
        $InternID = mysql_insert_id($DBConnect);
    }
    mysql_close($DBConnect);
}
```

You learned in Chapter 8 that the primary key for a table and the public identifier (such as the "Intern ID" value) are normally separate fields.

9. Add the following text and elements immediately before the end of the script section:

```php
if ($errors == 0) {
    $InternName = $first . " " . $last;
    echo "<p>Thank you, $InternName. ";
    echo "Your new Intern ID is <strong>" .
            $InternID . "</strong>.</p>\n";
}
```

10. Save the document as **RegisterIntern.php** in the Chapter directory for Chapter 9 and upload the document to the server.

11. Open the **InternLogin.php** file in your Web browser by entering the following URL: *http://<yourserver>/PHP_ Projects/Chapter.09/Chapter/InternLogin.php*. Enter a valid e-mail address and a password of at least 6 characters in the New Intern Registration form. Be sure to enter the same password in the confirmation fields or you will receive an error. Click the **Register** button to obtain an Intern ID value. You should see the Web page shown in Figure 9-3. (The first Intern ID value should be 1.)

12. Close your Web browser window.

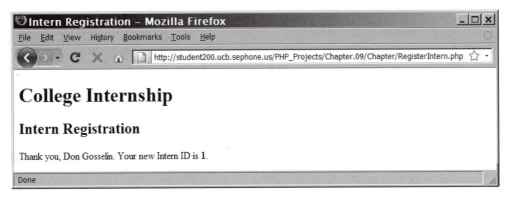

Figure 9-3 New Intern Registration Web page after successful registration

Short Quiz

1. Describe the term "state information."

2. What are the advantages of a stateless design?

3. What are the disadvantages of a stateless design?

4. What are three applications for which maintaining state information may be useful?

5. What are the four tools for maintaining state information?

Using Hidden Form Fields to Save State Information

As you should know from your study of HTML, a hidden form field is not displayed by the Web browser, so it allows you to hide information from users. You create hidden form fields with the `<input>` element. Hidden form fields temporarily store data that needs to be sent to a server along with the rest of a form, but that a user does not need to see. You create hidden form fields using the same syntax for other fields created with the `<input>` element: `<input type="hidden">`. The only attributes you can include with a hidden form field are *name* and *value*.

Hidden input elements are visible in the URL when you use the `get` method, and are visible in the source code of the Web page. Do not use a hidden input element to hold sensitive information such as passwords, because it is not secure.

When you submit a form to a PHP script, you can access the values submitted from the form by using the `$_GET[]` and `$_POST[]` autoglobals. If you then want to pass form values from one PHP script to another, you can store the values in hidden form fields, which are submitted along with other types of form fields.

Next, you will create the Verify Login and Available Opportunities pages and add a form with a hidden input on the New Intern Registration page. When the user successfully logs in using the Registration/Log In page or successfully registers as a new intern on the New Intern Registration page, the Intern ID is submitted to the Available Opportunities page.

To create the Verify Login page:

1. Create a new document in your text editor and type the `<!DOCTYPE>` declaration, `<html>` element, header information, and `<body>` element. Use the strict DTD and "Verify Intern Login" as the content of the `<title>` element.

2. Add the following text, elements, and script section to the document body:

```
<h1>College Internship</h1>
<h2>Verify Intern Login</h2>
<?php
?>
```

3. Add the following `if` statement to the script section to connect to the database server and open the `internships` database. Be sure to replace *host* with the host name of your MySQL server, and *user* and *password* with your user name and password.

```php
$errors = 0;
$DBConnect = @mysql_connect("host", "user",
"password");
if ($DBConnect === FALSE) {
    echo "<p>Unable to connect to the database
        server. " .
        "Error code " . mysql_errno() . ": " .
        mysql_error() . "</p>\n";
    ++$errors;
}
else {
    $DBName = "internships";
    $result = @mysql_select_db($DBName,
    $DBConnect);
    if ($result === FALSE) {
        echo "<p>Unable to select the database. " .
            "Error code " . mysql_
            errno($DBConnect) .
            ": " . mysql_error($DBConnect) .
            "</p>\n";
        ++$errors;
    }
}
```

4. Add the following statements to the end of the script section to verify that the e-mail address and password entered are in the `interns` table. Remember that the MD5 hash of the password is stored in the database, not the password itself.

```
$TableName = "interns";
if ($errors == 0) {
        $SQLstring = "SELECT internID, first, last FROM
        $TableName"
                . " where email='" . stripslashes($_
                POST['email']) .
                "' and password_md5='" .
                md5(stripslashes($_POST['password'])) . "'";
        $QueryResult = @mysql_query($SQLstring,
        $DBConnect);
        if (mysql_num_rows($QueryResult)==0) {
                echo "<p>The e-mail address/password " .
                        " combination entered is not valid.
                        </p>\n";
                ++$errors;
        }
        else {
                $Row = mysql_fetch_assoc($QueryResult);
                $InternID = $Row['internID'];
                $InternName = $Row['first'] . " " .
                $Row['last'];
                echo "<p>Welcome back, $InternName!</p>\n";
        }
}
```

5. Add the following `if` statement to show the appropriate message if there were errors:

```
if ($errors > 0) {
        echo "<p>Please use your browser's BACK button
                to return " .
                " to the form and fix the errors
                indicated.</p>\n";
}
```

6. Finally, add the following code to the end of the PHP script section to include the form with the hidden field if there were no errors.

```
if ($errors == 0) {
        echo "<form method='post' " .
                " action='AvailableOpportunities.php'>\n";
        echo "<input type='hidden' name='internID' " .
                " value='$InternID'>\n";
        echo "<input type='submit' name='submit' " .
                " value='View Available Opportunities'>\n";
        echo "</form>\n";
}
```

7. Save the document as **VerifyLogin.php** in the Chapter directory for Chapter 9 and upload the file to the server.

To add the form with the hidden input to the New Intern Registration page:

1. Reopen the **RegisterIntern.php** script in your text editor.

2. Add the following code to the end of the PHP script section to include the form with the hidden field if there were no errors:

```
if ($errors == 0) {
    echo "<form method='post' " .
        " action='AvailableOpportunities.php'>\n";
    echo "<input type='hidden' name='internID' " .
        " value='$InternID'>\n";
    echo "<input type='submit' name='submit' " .
        " value='View Available Opportunities'>\n";
    echo "</form>\n";
}
```

3. Save RegisterIntern.php in the Chapter directory for Chapter 9 and upload the file to the server.

To create the Available Opportunities page:

1. Create a new document in your text editor and type the <!DOCTYPE> declaration, <html> element, header information, and <body> element. Use the strict DTD and "Available Opportunities" as the content of the <title> element.

2. Add the following text, elements, and script section to the document body:

```
<h1>College Internship</h1>
<h2>Available Opportunities</h2>
<?php
?>
```

3. Add the following statement to the script section, which retrieves the Intern ID submitted in the hidden form field. If no ID was submitted, set $InternID to −1, which will not match any records. The $_REQUEST[] autoglobal array is used because it contains all of the array elements of the $_GET[], $_POST[], and $_COOKIE[] autoglobal arrays. Each of these arrays will be used later in the chapter to pass the Intern ID to this page.

```
if (isset($_REQUEST['internID']))
    $InternID = $_REQUEST['internID'];
else
    $InternID = -1;
```

In a real-world PHP application, you should use the $_GET[], $_POST[], or $_COOKIE[] autoglobal as appropriate. You should avoid using the $_REQUEST[] autoglobal because of associated security issues. (For a more complete explanation, see Appendix D, "Secure Coding with PHP".)

4. Add the following statements to the end of the script section to connect to the database server and open the `internships` database. Be sure to replace *host* with the name of your MySQL server, and *user* and *password* with your user name and password.

```
$errors = 0;
$DBConnect = @mysql_connect("host", "user",
"password");
if ($DBConnect === FALSE) {
    echo "<p>Unable to connect to the database
        server. " .
        "Error code " . mysql_errno() . ": " .
        mysql_error() . "</p>\n";
    ++$errors;
}
else {
    $DBName = "internships";
    $result = @mysql_select_db($DBName,
    $DBConnect);
    if ($result === FALSE) {
        echo "<p>Unable to select the database. " .
            "Error code " . mysql_
            errno($DBConnect) . ": " .
            mysql_error($DBConnect) . "</p>\n";
        ++$errors;
    }
}
```

5. Add the following statements to the end of the script section to retrieve the user's information from the `interns` table. Notice in this version that the SQL statement uses the Intern ID, which is stored in the `$InternID` variable, to retrieve user information from the table.

```
$TableName = "interns";
if ($errors == 0) {
    $SQLstring = "SELECT * FROM $TableName WHERE " .
            " internID='$InternID'";
    $QueryResult = @mysql_query($SQLstring, $DBConnect);
    if ($QueryResult === FALSE) {
        echo "<p>Unable to execute the query. " .
            "Error code " . mysql_
            errno($DBConnect) . ": " .
            mysql_error($DBConnect) . "</p>\n";
        ++$errors;
    }
    else {
        if (mysql_num_rows($QueryResult) == 0) {
            echo "<p>Invalid Intern ID!</p>";
            ++$errors;
        }
    }
}
```

6. Add the following statements to the end of the script section to retrieve the user's first and last names from the resultset:

```
if ($errors == 0) {
        $Row = mysql_fetch_assoc($QueryResult);
        $InternName = $Row['first'] . " " . $Row['last'];
} else
        $InternName = "";
```

7. Add the following statements to the end of the script section. The query checks the assigned_opportunities table to determine if the current intern ID has been approved for an opportunity.

```
$TableName = "assigned_opportunities";
$ApprovedOpportunities = 0;
$SQLstring = "SELECT COUNT(opportunityID) FROM
$TableName " .
        " WHERE internID='$InternID' " .
        " AND date_approved IS NOT NULL";
$QueryResult = @mysql_query($SQLstring, $DBConnect);
if (mysql_num_rows($QueryResult) > 0) {
        $Row = mysql_fetch_row($QueryResult);
        $ApprovedOpportunities = $Row[0];
        mysql_free_result($QueryResult);
}
```

8. Add the following statements to the end of the script section. The query retrieves the list of opportunity IDs from the assigned_opportunities table that has been selected for the current intern ID. The query result is stored in the $SelectedOpportunities array. The last statement frees the data retrieved by the query.

```
$SelectedOpportunities = array();
$SQLstring = "SELECT opportunityID FROM $TableName " .
        " WHERE internID='$InternID'";
$QueryResult = @mysql_query($SQLstring, $DBConnect);
if (mysql_num_rows($QueryResult) > 0) {
        while (($Row = mysql_fetch_row($QueryResult))
        !== FALSE)
                $SelectedOpportunities[] = $Row[0];
        mysql_free_result($QueryResult);
}
```

9. Add the following statements to the end of the script section. The query retrieves the list of opportunity IDs from the assigned_opportunities table that has been approved for any intern ID. An opportunity that has been approved is no longer available for selection. The query result is stored in the $AssignedOpportunities array. The last statement frees the data retrieved by the query.

```
$AssignedOpportunities = array();
$SQLstring = "SELECT opportunityID FROM $TableName " .
        " WHERE date_approved IS NOT NULL";
$QueryResult = @mysql_query($SQLstring, $DBConnect);
if (mysql_num_rows($QueryResult) > 0) {
    while (($Row = mysql_fetch_row($QueryResult))
    !== FALSE)
        $AssignedOpportunities[] = $Row[0];
    mysql_free_result($QueryResult);
}
```

10. Add the following statements to the end of the script section. The query retrieves the list of opportunities from the opportunities table. The query result is stored in the $Opportunities array. The last statement closes the database connection.

```
$TableName = "opportunities";
$Opportunities = array();
$SQLstring = "SELECT opportunityID, company, city, " .
        " start_date, end_date, position,
        description " .
        " FROM $TableName";
$QueryResult = @mysql_query($SQLstring, $DBConnect);
if (mysql_num_rows($QueryResult) > 0) {
    while (($Row = mysql_fetch_assoc($QueryResult))
    !== FALSE)
        $Opportunities[] = $Row;
        mysql_free_result($QueryResult);
}
mysql_close($DBConnect);
```

11. Add the following statements to the end of the script section. The statements dynamically build a table of the available opportunities. The table also contains links to the RequestOpportunity.php script, which you will create later in this chapter. The last paragraph element contains a link back to the Registration/Log In page.

```
echo "<table border='1' width='100%'>\n";
echo "<tr>\n";
echo "        <th style='background-color:cyan'>Company</
th>\n";
echo "        <th style='background-color:cyan'>City</th>\n";
echo "        <th style='background-color:cyan'>Start
Date</th>\n";
echo "        <th style='background-color:cyan'>End
Date</th>\n";
echo "        <th style='background-color:cyan'>Position</
th>\n";
echo "        <th style='background-color:cyan'>Description</
th>\n";
echo "        <th style='background-color:cyan'>Status</
th>\n";
```

```
echo "</tr>\n";
foreach ($Opportunities as $Opportunity) {
    if (!in_array($Opportunity['opportunityID'],
            $AssignedOpportunities)) {
        echo "<tr>\n";
        echo "    <td>" .
                htmlentities($Opportunity['company']) .
                "</td>\n";
        echo "    <td>" .
                htmlentities($Opportunity['city']) .
                "</td>\n";
        echo "    <td>" .
                htmlentities($Opportunity
                ['start_date']) .
                "</td>\n";
        echo "    <td>" .
                htmlentities($Opportunity['end_date']) .
                "</td>\n";
        echo "    <td>" .
                htmlentities($Opportunity['position']) .
                "</td>\n";
        echo "    <td>" .
                htmlentities($Opportunity
                ['description']) .
                "</td>\n";
        echo "    <td>";
        if (in_array($Opportunity['opportunityID'],
                $SelectedOpportunities))
            echo "Selected";
        else {
            if ($ApprovedOpportunities>0)
                echo "Open";
            else
                echo "<a href=
                'RequestOpportunity.php?" .
                    "internID=$InternID&" .
                    "opportunityID=" .
                    $Opportunity['opportunityID'] .
                    "'>Available</a>";
        }
        echo "</td>\n";
        echo "</tr>\n";
    }
}
echo "</table>\n";
echo "<p><a href='InternLogin.php'>Log Out</a></
p>\n";
```

Passing the Intern ID as a URL token is very insecure. Later in this chapter, you will learn better methods to maintain secure data (like the Intern ID) across Web pages.

12. Save the document as **AvailableOpportunities.php** in the Chapter directory for Chapter 9.

13. Open the **InternLogin.php** file in your Web browser by entering the following URL: *http://<yourserver>/PHP_Projects/Chapter.09/Chapter/InternLogin.php*. In the

Returning Intern Login form, enter the e-mail address and password that you registered with the New Intern Registration form and click the **Log In** button. You should see the "Welcome back" message shown in Figure 9-4.

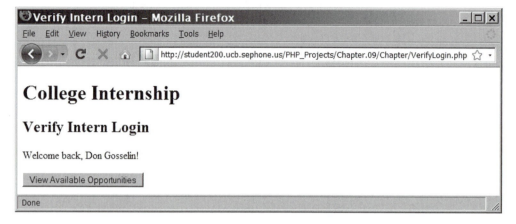

Figure 9-4 The Verify Login Web page for a successful login

14. Click the **View Available Opportunities** button to open the Available Opportunities page, which is shown in Figure 9-5.

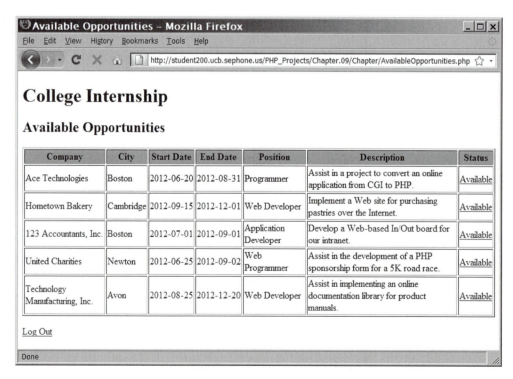

Figure 9-5 The Available Opportunities Web page with the Intern information at the top of the screen

15. Close your Web browser window.

Short Quiz

1. What two attributes are used in a hidden field to temporarily store data and send it to the server?

2. Hidden fields can be retrieved from which autoglobals?

3. Explain the risks associated with using hidden elements to submit form data using the get method.

Using Query Strings to Save State Information

One way to preserve information following a user's visit to a Web page is to append a query string to the end of a URL. As you learned in Chapter 4, a query string is a set of name/value pairs appended to a target URL. It consists of a single text string that contains one or more pieces of information. For example, the name/value pairs for a user's first and last name may consist of something like "firstName=Don" and "secondName=Gosselin". You can use a query string to pass information such as search criteria from one Web page to another; simply add a question mark (?) immediately after the URL, followed by the query string that contains the information you want to preserve in name/value pairs. In this manner, you are passing information to another Web page, similar to the way you can pass arguments to a function or method. You separate individual name/value pairs within the query string using ampersands (&). A question mark (?) and a query string are automatically appended to the URL of a server-side script for any forms that are submitted with the GET method. However, you can also append a query string to any URL on a Web page; if you do, PHP will treat the information as if it were submitted with the GET method. The following code provides an example of an <a> element that contains a query string consisting of three name/value pairs:

```
<a href="http://www.example.com/TargetPage.php?firstName=
Don&lastName=Gosselin&occupation=writer">Link Text</a>
```

You can access any query string data that is appended to a URL from PHP by using the $_GET[] autoglobal, the same as for any forms submitted with the GET method. For example, the TargetPage.php script (the target of the link) can display the values from the query string in the preceding element by using the following statements. Figure 9-6 shows the output in a Web browser.

```
echo "<p>{$_GET['firstName']} {$_GET['lastName']} is a
{$_GET['occupation']}.</p>\n";
```

Figure 9-6 Output of the contents of a query string

To modify the Verify Login page so that the Intern ID is passed as a query string instead of being stored in a hidden form field:

1. Return to the **VerifyLogin.php** document in your text editor.

2. Replace the form that contains the hidden form fields with the following text and elements. The PHP script appends a query string to the AvailableOpportunities.php URL consisting of a name/value pair of internID=$InternID.

   ```
   echo "<p><a href='AvailableOpportunities.php?" .
       "internID=$InternID'>Available " .
       " Opportunities</a></p>\n";
   ```

3. Save the VerifyLogin.php document.

4. Open the **InternLogin.php** file in your Web browser by entering the following URL: *http://<yourserver>/PHP_Projects/Chapter.09/Chapter/InternLogin.php*. In the Returning Intern Login form, enter the e-mail address and password that you registered with the New Intern Registration form and click the **Log In** button. As shown in Figure 9-7, you should see the "Welcome Back" Web page with a link instead of the Submit button.

5. Click the **Available Opportunities** link to open the Available Opportunities page. The page should open just as it did with the hidden form field.

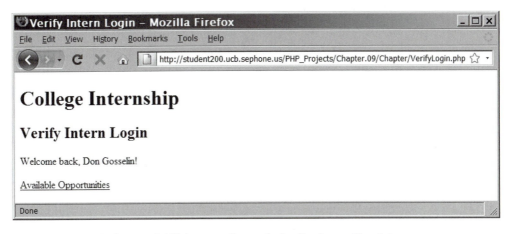

Figure 9-7 Login Successful Web page after replacing the form with a link

---

Short Quiz

1. Explain how a query string is used to pass information from one Web page to another.

2. Query strings permanently maintain state information. True or False?

3. Illustrate how the XHTML anchor (<a>) element can be used to append a query string to a hyperlink.

4. Describe how data appended to a URL can be accessed using the $_GET[] autoglobal.

Using Cookies to Save State Information

When choosing a method of saving state information, you need to consider whether you want the state information to be available after the current session of a Web page has ended—in other words, whether you want the state information to be permanent. Query strings do not permanently maintain state information because the information contained in a query string is available only when you open a Web page using that query string. After a Web page that reads a query string closes, the query string is lost. Hidden form fields maintain state information between Web pages, but the data they contain is also lost when the Web page that reads the hidden fields closes. To make it possible to store state information for more than just the current Web page, Netscape Communications added support for cookies to the Mosaic Netscape Web browser. **Cookies**, derived from the programming concept called "magic cookies," are small pieces of information about a user that are stored by a Web server in text files on the user's computer. Nearly all modern Web browsers support the use of cookies, which can be temporary or persistent. **Temporary cookies** remain available only for the current browser session. **Persistent cookies** remain available beyond the current browser session and are stored in a text file on a client computer.

Each time the Web client visits a Web server, saved cookies for the requested Web page are sent from the client to the server. The server then uses the cookies to customize the Web page for the client. Cookies were originally created for use with CGI scripts, but are now commonly used by client-side scripting languages such as JavaScript and server-side scripting languages such as PHP.

You have probably seen cookies in action if you have ever visited a Web site where you entered a user name in a prompt dialog box or in a text field, and then found that you were greeted by that user name the next time you visited the Web site. This greeting could occur with each subsequent visit to the same Web site, whether during the same browser session or during a different browser session days or weeks later. The Web page remembers your personal information by storing it locally on your computer in a cookie. Another example of a cookie is a counter that tracks the number of times an individual user has visited a Web site.

The use of cookies has a number of limitations. Individual Web browsers can limit the number of cookies each server or domain can store on a user's computer (normally between 20 and 70 cookies). In addition, Web browsers can limit the total number of cookies stored on a user's computer (at least 300). If these limits are exceeded, a Web browser may start discarding older cookies. Additionally, the maximum size for an individual cookie is limited to 4 kilobytes.

Creating Cookies

You use the setcookie() function to create cookies in PHP. The syntax is as follows:

```
setcookie(name [, value, expires, path, domain, secure])
```

You create a cookie by passing to the setcookie() function a required name argument and five optional arguments: value, expires, path, domain, and secure. You must pass each of the arguments in the order specified in the preceding syntax. To omit the value, path, and `domain` arguments, specify an empty string as the argument value. To omit the `expires` and `secure` arguments, specify 0 as the argument value.

You must call the `setcookie()` function before you send the Web browser any output, including white space, HTML elements, or output from the `echo` or `print` statements. If any output exists before you call the `setcookie()` function, you will receive an error and the function returns a value of FALSE. Also, keep in mind that users can choose whether to accept cookies that a script attempts to write to their systems. If the `setcookie()` function runs successfully, it returns a value of TRUE, even if a user rejects the cookie.

The `name` and `value` Arguments

Although the only required argument of the `setcookie()` function is the *name* attribute, a cookie is of no use if you do not specify the *value* argument because a cookie with a NULL value is indistinguishable from a nonexistent cookie. Cookies created with only the *name* and *value* arguments are temporary cookies because they are available for only the current browser session. The following code creates a cookie named `firstName` and assigns it a value of "Don":

```php
<?php
setcookie("firstName", "Don");
?>
<!DOCTYPE html PUBLIC "-//W3C//DTD XHTML 1.0 Strict//EN"
    "http://www.w3.org/TR/xhtml1/DTD/xhtml1-strict.dtd">
<html xmlns="http://www.w3.org/1999/xhtml">
<head>
<title>College Internships</title>
...
```

You can call the `setcookie()` function multiple times to create additional cookies—but again, remember that `setcookie()` statements must come before any other output on a Web page. The following example creates three cookies:

```php
setcookie("firstName", "Don");
setcookie("lastName", "Gosselin");
setcookie("occupation", "writer");
```

PHP also allows you to store cookie values in indexed or associative arrays by appending array operators ([ ]) and an index or key to the cookie name within the `setcookie()` function. The following statements create an indexed cookie array named `professional[]` that contains three cookie values:

```php
setcookie("professional[0]", "Don");
setcookie("professional[1]", "Gosselin");
setcookie("professional[2]", "writer");
```

Notice that the script section is placed above the HTML elements in the preceding example. Remember that you must call the `setcookie()` function before you send the Web browser any output, including white space, HTML elements, or output from the `echo` or `print` statements; otherwise, you will receive an error.

The following statements create an associative version of the `professional[]` cookie array:

```
setcookie("professional['firstName']", "Don");
setcookie("professional['lastName']", "Gosselin");
setcookie("professional['occupation']", "writer");
```

By default, cookies cannot include semicolons or other special characters such as commas or spaces, because cookies are transmitted between Web browsers and Web servers using HTTP, which does not allow certain nonalphanumeric characters to be transmitted in their native format. However, you can use special characters in cookies you create with PHP because the `setcookie()` function automatically encodes, or converts, special characters in a text string to their corresponding hexadecimal ASCII value, preceded by a percent sign. For example, 20 is the hexadecimal ASCII equivalent of a space character, and 25 is the hexadecimal ASCII equivalent of a percent sign (%). In URL encoded format, each space character is represented by %20, and each percent sign is represented by %25. After encoding, the contents of the string `"tip=A standard tip is 15%"` would read as follows:

`tip=A%20standard%20tip%20is%2015%25`

Encoding does not occur for standard alphanumeric characters such as A, B, and C or 1, 2, and 3, or for any of the following special characters:

```
- _ . ! ~ * ' ( )
```

It also does not encode the following characters that have special meaning in a URL:

```
; / ? : @ & = + $ ,
```

For example, the backslash (/) character is not encoded because it is used for designating a path on a file system. PHP automatically decodes special characters when you read cookie values. (You will learn how to read cookies later in this chapter.)

To modify the New Intern Registration page so that the Intern ID is stored in a temporary cookie:

1. Return to the **RegisterIntern.php** document in your text editor.

2. Cut and paste the existing PHP script section above the `<!DOCTYPE>` declaration. This is necessary because the `setcookie()` function, which you will add later in this exercise, must be called before any output statements.

3. Immediately after the opening of the PHP script section, add the following code to declare and initialize the $Body string variable:

   `$Body = "";`

The start of the opening PHP tag must be the first character on the first line of the file. If anything precedes the opening PHP tag, even white spaces or blank lines, your code will produce an error.

4. Replace each occurrence of the echo statement with the
   $Body .= assignment statement. For example, the code:

   ```
   echo "<p>You need to enter an e-mail
        address.</p>\n";
   ```

   becomes:

   ```
   $Body .= "<p>You need to enter an e-mail
        address.</p>\n";
   ```

5. Add the following setcookie() statement above the
   mysql_close() statement at the end of the script section.
   This statement creates a new cookie named internID that
   contains the newly assigned Intern ID.

   ```
   setcookie("internID", $InternID);
   ```

6. Within the <body> tags, add the following PHP script to
   display the output generated by the previous PHP script:

   ```
   <?php
   echo $Body;
   ?>
   ```

7. Save the RegisterIntern.php document and upload it to the
   Web server.

The expires Argument

For a cookie to persist beyond the current browser session, you
must use the expires argument with the setcookie() function.
You might use a cookie that expires after one week or less to store
data that needs to be maintained for a limited amount of time. For
example, a travel agency may store data in a cookie that temporarily
holds a travel reservation until it expires after one week. Or, an online
retail site may store shopping cart information in cookies that expire
after only 15 minutes. The expires argument determines how long
a cookie can remain on a client system before it is deleted. Cookies
created without an expires argument are available for only the current browser session. You assign to the expires argument a value
representing the date or time when the client system is to delete the
cookie. Use PHP's time() function to return the current time and add
to it an integer in seconds to specify the time to delete the cookie. The
following setcookie() function specifies that the firstName cookie
expires in 3600 seconds, or one hour from now:

```
setcookie("firstName", "Don", time()+3600);
```

By multiplying the number of seconds in a minute and an hour, and
then multiplying that value by the necessary number of hours or days,

When develop-
ing a PHP
script, you
may acciden-
tally create,
but not delete, persistent
cookies that your pro-
gram does not need.
Unused persistent cook-
ies can sometimes inter-
fere with the execution of
a PHP script, so you may
want to delete your
browser cookies periodi-
cally, especially while
developing a PHP script
that uses cookies. To
delete cookies in Firefox,
click Tools on the menu
bar and select Options. In
the Options dialog box,
click "Use custom set-
tings for history" in the
"Firefox will:" drop-down
box, and then click the
Show Cookies button.
Highlight the desired
cookie and click the
Remove Cookie button,
or click the Remove All
Cookies button to remove
them all. To delete cook-
ies in Microsoft Internet
Explorer, click Tools on
the menu bar and click
Internet Options. Click the
General tab of the
Internet Options dialog
box, and then click the
Delete button in the
Browsing history section.
In the next dialog box,
click the Delete cookies
button.

522

The following steps use the versions of Firefox and Internet Explorer for Windows that were available when this book was published. Different systems and versions have different procedures.

you can specify an expiration time more easily. The following example specifies that the firstName cookie expires in one week by multiplying the number of seconds in a minute (60), the number of minutes in an hour (60), the number of hours in a day (24), and then the number of days in a week (7).

```php
setcookie("firstName", "Don", time()+(60*60*24*7));
```

To create the Request Opportunity page, which creates a persistent cookie containing the date of the visitor's last selection:

1. Create a new document in your text editor and type the <!DOCTYPE> declaration, <html> element, header information, and <body> element. Use the strict DTD and "Request Opportunity" as the content of the <title> element.

2. Add the following text and elements to the document body:

```php
<h1>College Internship</h1>
<h2>Opportunity Requested</h2>
<?php
        echo $Body;
?>
```

The script section will contain a setcookie() function, so be sure to create the script section above the opening <!DOCTYPE> declaration; otherwise, you will receive an error.

3. Add a script section above the opening <!DOCTYPE> declaration:

```php
<?php
?>
```

4. Add the following statements to the script section to validate the submitted data:

```php
$Body = "";
$errors = 0;
$InternID = 0;
if (isset($_GET['internID']))
    $InternID = $_GET['internID'];
else {
    $Body .= "<p>You have not logged in or
            registered. " .
            " Please return to the " .
            " <a href='InternLogin.
            php'>Registration / " .
            " Log In page</a>.</p>";
    ++$errors;
}
if ($errors == 0) {
    if (isset($_GET['opportunityID']))
        $OpportunityID = $_GET['opportunityID'];
    else {
        $Body .= "<p>You have not selected an
                opportunity. " .
                " Please return to the " .
                " <a href='AvailableOpportunities.
                php?" .
```

```
                            "internID=$InternID'>Available " .
                            " Opportunities page</a>.</p>";
                ++$errors;
            }
        }
```

5. Add the following statements to the end of the script section to connect to the database server and open or create the internships database. Be sure to replace *host* with the name of your MySQL server, and *user* and *password* with your user name and password.

```
if ($errors == 0) {
    $DBConnect = @mysql_connect("host", "user",
    "password");
    if ($DBConnect === FALSE) {
        $Body .= "<p>Unable to connect to the
            database " .
            " server. Error code " . mysql_
            errno() . ": " .
            mysql_error() . "</p>\n";
        ++$errors;
    }
    else {
        $DBName = "internships";
        $result = @mysql_select_db($DBName,
        $DBConnect);
        if ($result === FALSE) {
            $Body .= "<p>Unable to select the
                database. " .
                "Error code " . mysql_
                errno($DBConnect) .
                ": " . mysql_error($DBConnect)
                . "</p>\n";
            ++$errors;
        }
    }
}
```

6. Add the following statements to the end of the script section to mark the opportunity as selected in the assigned_opportunities table and close the database connection. The date() function is used to return the current date and time as a formatted string. For the $DisplayDate variable, the format string "l, F j, Y, g:i A" creates a date string in a user-friendly format; the day of the week, the month name, and the day and year are followed by the time as hours and minutes AM or PM. For the $DatabaseDate variable, the format string "Y-m-d H:i:s" creates a date string in the format MySQL uses: "*yyyy-mo-dd hh:mi:ss*", where *yyyy* is a four-digit year, *mo* is a two-digit month, *dd* is a two-digit day of the month, *hh* is a two-digit number indicating

the hours since midnight, *mi* is a two-digit minute, and *ss* is a two-digit second.

```
$DisplayDate = date("l, F j, Y, g:i A");
$DatabaseDate = date("Y-m-d H:i:s");
if ($errors == 0) {
        $TableName = "assigned_opportunities";
        $SQLstring = "INSERT INTO $TableName " .
                " (opportunityID, internID, " .
                " date_selected) VALUES " .
                " ($OpportunityID, $InternID, " .
                " '$DatabaseDate')";
        $QueryResult = @mysql_query($SQLstring,
        $DBConnect) ;
        if ($QueryResult === FALSE) {
                $Body .= "<p>Unable to execute the query. " .
                        " Error code " . mysql_
                        errno($DBConnect) .
                        ": " . mysql_error($DBConnect) .
                        "</p>\n";
                ++$errors;
        }
        else {
                $Body .= "<p>Your request for opportunity
                        # " .
                        " $OpportunityID has been
                        entered " .
                        " on $DisplayDate.</p>\n";
        }
        mysql_close($DBConnect);
}
```

7. Add the following statements to the end of the script section to provide a link back to the Available Opportunities page if the Intern ID is valid, or to the Registration/Log In page if the Intern ID is not valid.

```
if ($InternID > 0)
        $Body .= "<p>Return to the <a href='" .
                "AvailableOpportunities.
                php?internID=$InternID'>" .
                "Available Opportunities</a> page.</p>\n";
else
        $Body .= "<p>Please <a href='InternLogin.
                php'>Register " .
                " or Log In</a> to use this page.</p>\n";
```

8. Add the following statements to the end of the script section to create a persistent cookie named LastRequestDate. The urlencode() function is used because of the special characters needed for the date and time. The cookie is set to expire one week from now.

```
if ($errors == 0)
    setcookie("LastRequestDate",
        urlencode($DisplayDate),
        time()+60*60*24*7);
```

9. Save the document as **RequestOpportunity.php** in the Chapter directory for Chapter 9 and upload the file to the Web server.

The `path` Argument

The `path` argument determines the availability of a cookie to other Web pages on a server. By default, a cookie is available to all Web pages in the same directory. However, if you specify a path, a cookie is available to all Web pages in the specified path and in all its subdirectories. For example, the following statement makes the cookie named `firstName` available to all Web pages located in the marketing directory or any of its subdirectories:

```
setcookie("firstName", "Don", time()+3600, "/marketing/");
```

To make a cookie available to all directories on a server, use a forward slash (/) to indicate the root directory:

```
setcookie("firstName", "Don", time()+3600, "/");
```

Many different types of Web applications use the same cookie name, such as *username* or *id*. This can cause conflicts if both Web applications are on the same Web site. Therefore, you should always place PHP applications that use cookies into their own directory and use the `path` argument to specify the directory for that application. This approach will prevent different applications from changing the same cookie, which would result in erratic behavior for the scripts.

 If you use a `/development` directory when developing cookie-based PHP applications, and place each application in its own subdirectory of the `/development` directory, you will help avoid conflicts not only between PHP applications in development, but with other PHP applications that are already installed.

The `domain` Argument

Using the `path` argument allows cookies to be shared across a server. Some Web sites, however, are very large and use a number of servers. The `domain` argument is used for sharing cookies across multiple servers in the same domain. Note that you cannot share cookies outside of a domain. For example, if the Web server `programming.gosselin.com` needs to share cookies with the Web server `writing.gosselin.com`, the `domain` argument for cookies set by `programming.gosselin.com` should be set to `.gosselin.com`. That way, cookies created by `programming.gosselin.com` are available to `writing.gosselin.com` and to all other servers in the domain `gosselin.com`.

The following code shows how to make a cookie at `programming.gosselin.com` available to all servers in the `gosselin.com` domain:

```
setcookie("firstName", "Don", time()+3600, "/",
".gosselin.com");
```

The `secure` Argument

Internet connections are not always considered safe for transmitting sensitive information. Unscrupulous people can steal personal information online, such as credit card numbers, passwords, and Social Security numbers. To protect private data transferred across the Internet, Netscape Communications developed Secure Sockets Layer, or SSL, to encrypt and transfer data across a secure connection. URLs for Web pages that support SSL usually start with `https:` instead of `http:`. The `secure` argument indicates that a cookie can only be transmitted across a secure Internet connection using HTTPS or another security protocol. To use this argument, you assign a value of 1 (for `TRUE`) or 0 (for `FALSE`) as the last argument of the `setcookie()` function. For example, to specify the `secure` attribute for a cookie, you use a statement similar to the following:

```
setcookie("firstName", "Don", time()+3600, "/",
".gosselin.com", 1);
```

Elements of the `$_COOKIE[]` autoglobal array are also automatically assigned to the `$_REQUEST[]` autoglobal array, along with all of the elements of the `$_POST[]` and `$_GET[]` autoglobal arrays.

Reading Cookies

Cookies that are available to the current Web page are automatically assigned to the `$_COOKIE[]` PHP autoglobal array. You can then access each cookie by using the cookie name as a key in the associative `$_COOKIE[]` array. (Recall that autoglobals are associative arrays.) The following statement displays the value assigned to the `firstName` cookie:

```
echo $_COOKIE['firstName'];
```

When you create a cookie with the `setcookie()` function, the cookie is not available to the current Web page until you reload it. For example, the following statement causes an error when the Web page first loads because you cannot access the `firstName`, `lastName`, and `occupation` cookies until you reload the Web page:

```
setcookie("firstName", "Don");
setcookie("lastName", "Gosselin");
setcookie("occupation", "writer");
echo "{$_COOKIE['firstName']} {$_COOKIE['lastName']} is a
{$_COOKIE['occupation']}.";
```

To ensure that a cookie is set before you attempt to use it, you can use the `isset()` function, the same as when you check whether form variables contain values.

```
setcookie("firstName", "Don");
setcookie("lastName", "Gosselin");
setcookie("occupation", "writer");
if (isset($_COOKIE['firstName'])
    && isset($_COOKIE['lastName'])
    && isset($_COOKIE['occupation']))
    echo "{$_COOKIE['firstName']} {$_COOKIE['lastName']}
        is a {$_COOKIE['occupation']}.";
```

When you store cookies in indexed or associative arrays, PHP stores the cookies as two-dimensional arrays within the `$_COOKIE[]` autoglobal. Therefore, you must use multidimensional array syntax to read each cookie value. You refer to cookie arrays by using the cookie name as the first dimension and each index or key that represents a cookie value as the second dimension. For example, the following statements create and display an indexed version of the `professional[]` cookie array:

```
setcookie("professional[0]", "Don");
setcookie("professional[1]", "Gosselin");
setcookie("professional[2]", "writer");
if (isset($_COOKIE['professional']))
    echo "{$_COOKIE['professional'][0]}
        {$_COOKIE['professional'][1]} is a
        {$_COOKIE['professional'][2]}.";
```

The following statements create and display an associative version of the `professional[]` cookie array:

```
setcookie("professional[firstName]", "Don");
setcookie("professional[lastName]", "Gosselin");
setcookie("professional[occupation]", "writer");
if (isset($_COOKIE['professional']))
    echo "{$_COOKIE['professional']['firstName']}
    {$_COOKIE['professional']['lastName']} is a
    {$_COOKIE['professional']['occupation']}.";
```

To modify the Available Opportunities page so that it reads the stored `LastRequestDate` cookie:

1. Return to the **AvailableOpportunities.php** document in your text editor.

2. Add the following statements, which read the `LastRequestDate` cookie from the `$_COOKIE[]` autoglobal array, immediately after the statement that retrieves the Intern ID from the `$_REQUEST[]` autoglobal array. You need both sets of code because the Registration/Log In page still uses a query string to log in existing users.

```
if (isset($_COOKIE['LastRequestDate']))
    $LastRequestDate = $_COOKIE['LastRequestDate'];
else
    $LastRequestDate = "";
```

3. Add the following statements above the statements that display the table of opportunities. This code displays the value of the LastRequestDate cookie if it is set.

```
if (!empty($LastRequestDate))
    echo "<p>You last requested an internship
        opportunity " .
        " on $LastRequestDate.</p>\n";
```

4. Save the AvailableOpportunities.php document and upload it to the Web server.

5. Open the **InternLogin.php** file in your Web browser by entering the following URL: *http://<yourserver>/PHP_Projects/Chapter.09/Chapter/InternLogin.php*. In the Returning Intern Login form, enter the e-mail address and password that you registered with the New Intern Registration form and click the **Log In** button. You should see the same "Welcome Back" Web page.

6. Click the **Available Opportunities** link to open the Available Opportunities page. The page should open just as it did before.

7. Click the **Available** link in the Status column of one of the opportunities to open the Request Opportunity page. You should see an acknowledgement message like the one shown in Figure 9-8.

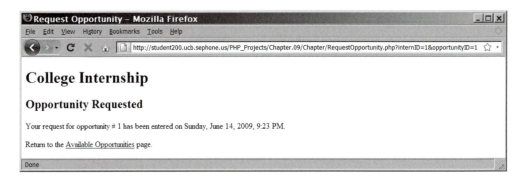

Figure 9-8 Request Opportunity Web page displaying a successful request

8. Click the **Available Opportunities** link to open the Available Opportunities page. The page should now show the opportunity as "Selected" and should display the time of your last

selection above the table. Figure 9-9 shows that Opportunity 1 was selected.

Figure 9-9   Available Opportunities Web page displaying text from a persistent cookie

9.   Close your Web browser window.

Deleting Cookies

You do not need to delete temporary cookies because they automatically cease to exist when the current browser session ends. Persistent cookies are also automatically deleted when the time assigned to the setcookie() function's expires argument elapses. To delete a persistent cookie before the time assigned to the expires argument elapses, set the value to an empty string and assign a new expiration value to a time in the past. You do this by subtracting any number of seconds from the time() function. The following statements delete the firstName, lastName, and occupation cookies by subtracting 3600 seconds (one hour) from the current time:

```
setcookie("firstName", "", time()-3600);
setcookie("lastName", "", time()-3600);
setcookie("occupation", "", time()-3600);
```

If you do not set the value to an empty string, the old value will persist until you close the Web browser.

Short Quiz

1. Detail the differences between temporary cookies and persistent cookies.

2. Describe three limitations of cookies.

3. Explain why the `setcookie()` function must be called before any output is sent to the browser.

4. Why is it important to set the expiration date of a cookie in a script when you might want to greet the user by name the next time he or she visits the Web?

5. What is the purpose of the domain argument?

Using Sessions to Save State Information

Many clients do not accept cookies due to the rampant rise of **spyware**, which is malicious software that gathers user information from a local computer for marketing and advertising purposes without the user's knowledge. Users increasingly choose to disable cookies to prevent spyware from gathering user information from stored cookies.

Cookies are a common state preservation technique used by various Web development tools in addition to PHP. However, several security issues are involved with saving state in cookies on a client computer. First, you cannot ensure the security of every client computer on which your PHP scripts will run. This means that any private information stored in cookies, including Social Security numbers and credit card information, may be accessible by hackers. Because of these risks, many clients configure their Web browsers not to accept cookies. (You can disable cookies in every current Web browser.) Unfortunately, this also disables any cookie preservation code in your PHP scripts.

The php.ini configuration file contains numerous directives that you can use to control how sessions behave in your environment.

PHP offers a more secure alternative to cookies: storing state information in sessions. The term **session** refers to a period of activity when a PHP script stores state information on a Web server. A session is similar to a temporary cookie in that it is only available for the current browser session. If you want to store state information that will be available when a client revisits your Web site in the future, you must use cookies. Sessions are a little harder to use than cookies, but because sessions store state information on a Web server rather than on the user's computer, they are much safer to use—provided you properly secure your Web server. Another benefit to using sessions is that they allow you to maintain state information even when clients disable cookies in their Web browsers.

Starting a Session

Whenever you need to work with sessions in a PHP script, you must call the session_start() function, which starts a new session or continues an existing one. When you start a new session, the session_start() function generates a unique session ID to identify the session. A **session ID** is a random alphanumeric string that looks something like 7f39d7dd020773f115d753c71290e11f. In addition to generating a session ID, the session_start() function creates a text file on the Web server that has the same name as the session ID, preceded by sess_. For example, the session ID text file for the preceding session ID would be named sess_7f39d7dd020773f115d753c71290 e11f. Any variables that are generated for a session are stored on the Web server in this text file.

Session ID text files are stored in the Web server directory specified by the session.save_path directive in your php.ini configuration file.

The session_start() function does not accept any arguments, nor does it return a value that you can use in your script. Instead, you simply call the session_start() function by itself in your PHP script, as follows:

```php
<?php
session_start();
. . .
```

Like the setcookie() function, you must call the session_start() function before you send the Web browser any output, including white space, HTML elements, or output from the echo or print statements. If any output exists before you call the session_start() function, you receive an error and the function returns a value of FALSE.

If a client's Web browser is configured to accept cookies, the session ID is assigned to a temporary cookie named PHPSESSID. However, because you cannot be certain that every client accepts cookies, you should also pass the session ID as a query string or hidden form field to any Web pages that are called as part of the current session. You pass a session ID in a name/value pair of PHPSESSID=*session ID*. You use the session_id() function to retrieve the session ID for the current session. For example, the following code starts a session and uses the session_id() function to pass the session ID as a query string to a Web page named Occupation.php:

```php
<?php
session_start();
. . .
?>
<p><a href='<?php echo "Occupation.php?PHPSESSID="
        . session_id() ?>'>Occupation</a></p>
```

532

The SID constant may or may not be defined on your system. It is enabled through a configuration setting in the php.ini file. If SID is not enabled on your system, use PHPSESSID as the name and the return value of the session_id() function as the value instead.

You can also use the constant SID, which contains a string that consists of "PHPSESSID=" and the session ID. The following example demonstrates how to use the constant SID to pass the session ID as a query string to another page:

```php
<?php
session_start();
...
?>
<p><a href='<?php echo "Occupation.php?"
        . SID ?>'>Occupation</a></p>
```

For hidden form fields, assign a value of PHPSESSID to the name attribute and use the session_id() function to assign the session ID to the value attribute of the <input> element, as follows:

```
<input type="hidden" name="PHPSESSID"
       value='<?php echo session_id() ?>' />
```

To modify the Registration/Log In page so that it uses a session that tracks the Intern ID number of the current user:

1. Return to the **InternLogin.php** document in your text editor.

2. Insert the following PHP script section above the opening <!DOCTYPE> declaration:

   ```php
   <?php
   ?>
   ```

3. Add the following session_start() statement to the beginning of the script section:

   ```php
   session_start();
   ```

4. Modify the action attribute of the two forms so they pass the session ID in a query string. The modified links should appear as follows:

   ```
   <form method="post" action="RegisterIntern.php?<?php
           echo SID; ?>">
   ...
   <form method="post" action="VerifyLogin.php?<?php
           echo SID; ?>">
   ```

5. Save the InternLogin.php document and upload it to the Web server.

Working with Session Variables

You store session state information in the $_SESSION[] autoglobal. When you call the session_start() function, PHP either initializes a new $_SESSION[] autoglobal or retrieves any variables for the current session (based on the session ID) into the $_SESSION[] autoglobal.

For example, the following code declares and initializes three variables—firstName, lastName, and occupation—in the $_SESSION[] autoglobal:

```php
<?php
session_start();
$_SESSION['firstName'] = "Don";
$_SESSION['lastName'] = "Gosselin";
$_SESSION['occupation'] = "writer";
?>
<p><a href='<?php echo "Occupation.php?"
 . session_id() ?>'>Occupation</a></p>
```

When a user clicks the Occupation link, the firstName, lastName, and occupation variables are available in the $_SESSION[] autoglobal on the Occupation.html page. If the Occupation.html page contains the following script section, it displays *Don Gosselin is a writer*:

```php
<?php
session_start();
echo "<p>" . $_SESSION['firstName'] . " " .
$_SESSION['lastName']
 . " is a " . $_SESSION['occupation'] . "</p>\n";
?>
```

As with cookies, you can use the isset() function to ensure that a session variable is set before you attempt to use it, as follows:

```php
<?php
session_start();
if (isset($_SESSION['firstName']) &&
isset($_SESSION['lastName']) &&
isset($_SESSION['occupation']))
    echo "<p>" . $_SESSION['firstName'] . " "
        . $_SESSION['lastName'] . " is a "
        . $_SESSION['occupation'] . "</p>\n";
?>
```

To modify the New Intern Registration page so that it stores the Intern ID number in the $_SESSION[] autoglobal:

1. Return to the **RegisterIntern.php** document in your text editor.

2. Add a session_start() statement to the beginning of the script section:

   ```php
   session_start();
   ```

3. Locate the statement at the end of the script section that declares the $InternID variable and modify it so the ID returned from the mysql_insert_id() function is assigned to the $_SESSION[] autoglobal, as follows:

   ```php
   $_SESSION['internID'] = mysql_insert_id($DBConnect);
   ```

4. Modify the paragraph element in the document body that displays the Intern ID so it refers to the $_SESSION['internID'] autoglobal variable instead of the $InternID variable, as follows:

```
$Body .= "Your new Intern ID is <strong>" .
        $_SESSION['internID'] . "</strong>.</p>\n";
```

5. Replace the code that uses the hidden input in a form with a link that uses the session ID, as follows:

```
$Body .= "<p><a href='AvailableOpportunities.php?" .
        SID . "'>View Available Opportunities</a></p>\n";
```

6. Save the RegisterIntern.php document and upload it to the Web server.

To modify the Verify Login page so that it stores the Intern ID number in the $_SESSION[] autoglobal:

1. Return to the **VerifyLogin.php** document in your text editor.

2. Add a PHP script section with a session_start() statement before the <!DOCTYPE> tag:

```
<?php
session_start();
?>
```

3. Locate the statement at the end of the script section that declares the $InternID variable and modify it so the ID returned from the database query is assigned to the $_SESSION[] autoglobal, as follows:

```
$_SESSION['internID'] = $Row['internID'];
```

4. Replace the code that creates a link that passes the Intern ID with a link that passes the session ID, as follows:

```
echo "<p><a href='AvailableOpportunities.php?" .
    SID . "'>Available Opportunities</a></p>\n";
```

5. Save the VerifyLogin.php document and upload it to the Web server.

To modify the Available Opportunities page so that it uses the Intern ID number from the $_SESSION[] autoglobal:

1. Return to the **AvailableOpportunities.php** document in your text editor.

2. Add a PHP script section with a session_start() statement before the <!DOCTYPE> tag:

```
<?php
session_start();
?>
```

3. Remove the following code that uses the
   $_REQUEST['internID'] element:

```
if (isset($_REQUEST['internID']))
    $InternID = $_REQUEST['internID'];
else
    $InternID = -1;
```

535

4. Modify the three queries that use $InternID so that they use
   $_SESSION['internID'] instead, as follows:

```
$SQLstring = "SELECT * FROM $TableName WHERE " .
        " internID='" . $_SESSION['internID'] . "'";
...
$SQLstring = "SELECT COUNT(opportunityID) FROM
$TableName " .
        " WHERE internID='" . $_SESSION['internID'] . "' " .
        " AND date_approved IS NOT NULL";
...
$SQLstring = "SELECT opportunityID FROM $TableName " .
        " WHERE internID='" . $_SESSION['internID'] . "'";
```

5. Modify the link to RequestOpportunity.php to use the session
   ID instead of the Intern ID, as follows:

```
echo "<a href='RequestOpportunity.php?" .
        SID . "&opportunityID=" .
        $Opportunity['opportunityID'] .
        "'>Available</a>";
```

6. Save the AvailableOpportunities.php document and upload it
   to the Web server.

To modify the RequestOpportunity.php document so that it uses the
session ID to retrieve user information:

1. Return to the **RequestOpportunity.php** document in your
   text editor.

2. Add the following statement to the beginning of the script
   section to start the session:

```
session_start();
```

3. Remove the following section that checks the
   $_GET['internID'] autoglobal:

```
if (isset($_GET['internID']))
    $InternID = $_GET['internID'];
else {
```

   and replace it with the following if statement that checks the
   $_SESSION['internID'] autoglobal:

```
if (!isset($_SESSION['internID'])) {
```

4. In both sections of code that link to the AvailableOpportunities.php page, replace the Intern ID in the link so that the session ID is passed instead, as follows:

```
$Body .= "<p>You have not selected an
          opportunity. " .
          " Please return to the " .
          " <a href='AvailableOpportunities.
          php?" .
          SID . "'>Available " .
          " Opportunities page</a>.</p>";
...
    $Body .= "<p>Return to the <a href='" .
             "AvailableOpportunities.php?" . SID .
             "'>" .
             "Available Opportunities</a> page.
             </p>\n";
```

5. Modify the insert query string so it refers to the $_SESSION['internID'] autoglobal variable instead of the $InternID variable, as follows:

```
$SQLstring = "INSERT INTO $TableName " .
             " (opportunityID, internID, " .
             " date_selected) VALUES " .
             " ($OpportunityID, " .
             $_SESSION['internID']
             . ", '$DatabaseDate')";
```

6. Locate the if statement that checks if $InternID is greater than 0, and modify it to refer to the $_SESSION['internID'] autoglobal variable instead, as follows:

```
if ($_SESSION['internID'] > 0)
```

7. Save the RequestOpportunity.php document and upload it to the Web server.

Deleting a Session

Although a session automatically ends when the current browser session ends, sometimes you need to delete a session manually. For example, you might want to give users the opportunity to end a session by clicking a Log Out button or link, or you might want a session to end if it is inactive for a specified period of time. To delete a session, you must perform the following steps:

1. Execute the session_start() function. (Remember that you must call the session_start() function whenever you need to work with sessions in a PHP script.)

2. Use the `array()` construct to reinitialize the `$_SESSION[]` autoglobal.

3. Use the `session_destroy()` function to delete the session.

For example, the following code deletes a session:

```php
<?php
session_start();
$_SESSION = array();
session_destroy();
?>
```

To modify the Registration/Log In page so that it deletes any existing sessions whenever a user opens it:

1. Return to the **InternLogin.php** document in your text editor.

2. Add the following code immediately after the `session_start()` function in the PHP script section:

   ```php
   $_SESSION = array();
   session_destroy();
   ```

3. Save the InternLogin.php document and upload it to the Web server.

4. Open the InternLogin.php file in your Web browser by entering the following URL: *http://<yourserver>/PHP_Projects/ Chapter.09/Chapter/InternLogin.php*. Enter the e-mail address and password for a registered user and click the **Log In** button. You should see the Login Successful page. Click the **Available Opportunities** link to open the Available Opportunities page. Notice the session ID appended to the URL in your browser's address box.

5. Click the **Log Out** link on the Available Opportunities page to execute the session deletion code.

6. Close your Web browser window.

Short Quiz

1. Describe two problems with cookies that do not affect sessions.

2. Explain the purpose of the temporary cookie named `PHPSESSID`.

3. How does the constant `SID` pass the session ID as a query string to another page?

4. What function is used to ensure that the session variable is set before you attempt to use it?

5. What function must be used when a visitor uses a Log Out button to end a session?

538

Summing Up

- Information about individual visits to a Web site is called state information. Maintaining state means to store persistent information about Web site visits.

- To pass form values from one PHP script to another, you can store the values in hidden form fields, which are submitted along with other types of form fields.

- One way to preserve information following a user's visit to a Web page is to append a query string to the end of a URL. To pass information from one Web page to another using a query string, add a question mark (?) immediately after a URL, followed by the query string containing the information you want to preserve in name/ value pairs.

- Cookies, also called magic cookies, are small pieces of information about a user that are stored by a Web server in text files on the user's computer. Cookies can be temporary or persistent. Temporary cookies remain available only for the current browser session. Persistent cookies remain available beyond the current browser session and are stored in a text file on a client computer.

- You use the setcookie() function to create cookies in PHP. You must call the setcookie() function before you send the Web browser any output, including white space, HTML elements, or output from the echo or print statements.

- Cookies created with only the name and value arguments of the setcookie() function are temporary cookies, because they are available for only the current browser session.

- For a cookie to persist beyond the current browser session, you must use the expires argument with the setcookie() function.

- The path argument of the setcookie() function determines the availability of a cookie to other Web pages on a server.

- The secure argument of the setcookie() function indicates that a cookie can only be transmitted across a secure Internet connection using HTTPS or another security protocol.

- To delete a persistent cookie before the time elapses in the assigned expires argument, assign a new expiration value to a time in the past and clear the value. You do this by subtracting any number of seconds from the time() function and setting the value of the cookie to the empty string.

- Sessions refer to periods of activity when a PHP script stores state information on a Web server. When you start a new session, the session_start() function generates a unique session ID to identify the session. If a client's Web browser is configured to accept cookies, the session ID is assigned to a temporary cookie named PHPSESSID.

- You must call the session_start() function before you send the Web browser any output, including white space, HTML elements, or output from the echo or print statements.

- You store session state information in the $_SESSION[] autoglobal.

- To delete a session, you execute the session_start() function, use the array() construct to reinitialize the $_SESSION[] autoglobal, and then call the session_destroy() function.

Comprehension Check

1. HTTP was originally designed to store data about individual visits to a Web site. True or False?

2. Stored information about a previous visit to a Web site is called _____ information.

   a. HTTP

   b. client-side

   c. state

   d. prior

3. Describe the different types of information about a user that a Web server might need to store.

4. Explain how to use form fields to temporarily store user information.

5. In what format are items in a query string appended to a target URL?

   a. in comma-delimited format

   b. as predefined values

   c. as name/value pairs

   d. in name, value, length format

6. Explain how query string data that is appended to a URL is retrieved in PHP.

7. What is the correct syntax for creating a temporary cookie that contains a value of "blue"?

   a. `$Color = setcookie("blue");`

   b. `setcookie("color", "blue");`

   c. `setcookie("blue", "color");`

   d. `setcookie("blue");`

8. You must manually encode and decode cookie values. True or False?

9. By default, cookies created without the `expires` argument of the `setcookie()` function are available for 24 hours. True or False?

10. Cookies created without the `expires` argument of the `setcookie()` function are called _____.

    a. transient

    b. temporary

    c. permanent

    d. persistent

11. Which of the following examples specifies that a cookie should expire in three days?

    a. `time()+48h`

    b. `time()+24h*3`

    c. `time()+60*60*24*7`

    d. `time()+60*60*24*3`

12. The availability of a cookie to other Web pages on a server is determined by the _____ argument of the setcookie() function.

    a. path

    b. directory

    c. system

    d. server

13. Which argument of the setcookie() function is used for sharing cookies outside of a domain?

    a. domain

    b. share

    c. secure

    d. You cannot share cookies outside of a domain.

14. You use the _____ to read cookies in PHP.

    a. $_COOKIE[] autoglobal

    b. $_COOKIES[] autoglobal

    c. cookie() function

    d. getcookie() function

15. How do you delete cookies before the time assigned to the setcookie() function's expires argument elapses?

    a. Assign a NULL value with the setcookie() function.

    b. Set the value to an empty string and assign a new expiration value to a time in the past.

    c. Execute the deletecookie() function.

    d. You cannot delete a cookie before the time assigned to the setcookie() function's expires argument elapses.

16. Explain the security risks involved with cookies and how sessions offer a more secure method of maintaining state.

17. Unlike the setcookie() function, you can call the session_start() function from any location on a Web page. True or False?

18. What is the name of the cookie that PHP creates for a session?

    a. SESSION

    b. PHPSESSION

    c. SESSIONID

    d. PHPSESSID

19. Explain how to pass a session ID to other PHP scripts when cookies are not available.

20. You use the _____ to access session variables in PHP.

    a. $_SESSION[] autoglobal

    b. $_SESSIONS[] autoglobal

    c. session() function

    d. getsession() function

Reinforcement Exercises

 Exercise 9-1

In this project, you will create a Cancel Selection page for the College Internship Available Opportunities Web site.

1. Create a new document in your text editor and type the <!DOCTYPE> declaration, <html> element, header information, and <body> element. Use the strict DTD and "Cancel Selection" as the content of the <title> element.

2. Add the following PHP script section before the <!DOCTYPE> tag to start a session:

```
<?php
session_start();
?>
```

3. Add the following text, elements, and script section to the document body:

```
<h1>College Internship</h1>
<h2>Cancel Selection</h2>
<?php
     echo $Body;
?>
```

4. Add the following statements to the end of the first script section, immediately after the session_start() function, to verify that the correct information was passed to this page:

```php
$Body = "";
$errors = 0;
if (!isset($_SESSION['internID'])) {
    $Body .= "<p>You have not logged in or
              registered. " .
              " Please return to the " .
              " <a href='InternLogin.
              php'>Registration / " .
              " Log In page</a>.</p>\n";
    ++$errors;
}
if ($errors == 0) {
    if (isset($_GET['opportunityID']))
        $OpportunityID = $_GET['opportunityID'];
    else {
        $Body .= "<p>You have not selected an
                  opportunity. " .
                  " Please return to the " .
                  " <a href='AvailableOpportunities.
                  php?" . SID . "'>Available " .
                  " Opportunities page</a>.</p>\n";
        ++$errors;
    }
}
```

5. Next, add the following code to connect to the database server and open the internships database. Be sure to replace *host* with the name of the MySQL server, and *user* and *password* with your user name and password.

```php
if ($errors == 0) {
    $DBConnect = @mysql_connect("host", "user",
    "password");
    if ($DBConnect === FALSE) {
        $Body .= "<p>Unable to connect to the
                  database " .
                  " server. Error code " . mysql_
                  errno() . ": " .
                  mysql_error() . "</p>\n";
        ++$errors;
    }
    else {
        $DBName = "internships";
        $result = @mysql_select_db($DBName,
        $DBConnect);
```

```
                              if ($result === FALSE) {
                                   $Body .= "<p>Unable to select the
                                        database. " .
                                        "Error code " . mysql_
                                        errno($DBConnect) .
                                        ": " . mysql_error($DBConnect)
                                        . "</p>\n";
                                   ++$errors;
                              }
                         }
                    }
```

6. Next, add the following code to delete the appropriate row from the assigned_opportunities table. Do not
   allow the selection to be deleted if it has been approved.
   (Approved selections have a date in the date_approved
   column, while selections that have not been approved have
   a NULL value in the date_approved column.) Use the
   mysql_affected_rows() function to indicate whether any
   rows were deleted.

```
if ($errors == 0) {
     $TableName = "assigned_opportunities";
     $SQLstring = "DELETE FROM $TableName" .
               " WHERE opportunityID=$OpportunityID " .
               " AND internID=" . $_
               SESSION['internID'] .
               " AND date_approved IS NULL";
     $QueryResult = @mysql_query($SQLstring,
     $DBConnect) ;
     if ($QueryResult === FALSE) {
          $Body .= "<p>Unable to execute the query. " .
               " Error code " . mysql_
               errno($DBConnect) .
               ": " . mysql_error($DBConnect) .
               "</p>\n";
          ++$errors;
     }
     else {
          $AffectedRows = mysql_affected_
          rows($DBConnect);
          if ($AffectedRows == 0)
               $Body .= "<p>You had not previously " .
                    " selected opportunity # " .
                    $OpportunityID . ".</p>\n";
          else
               $Body .= "<p>Your request for
                    opportunity # " .
                    " $OpportunityID has been " .
                    " removed.</p>\p";
     }
     mysql_close($DBConnect);
}
```

7. Add the following statements to the end of the script section to display the appropriate link for the visitor to use:

```
if ($_SESSION['internID'] > 0)
    $Body .= "<p>Return to the <a href='" .
        "AvailableOpportunities.php?" . SID . "'>" .
        "Available Opportunities</a> page.</p>\n";
else
    $Body .= "<p>Please <a href='InternLogin.
        php'>Register " .
        " or Log In</a> to use this page.</p>\n";
```

Because this Web page must inter-act with the Web pages in the Chapter directory, this file must also be uploaded to the Chapter directory, not the Projects directory.

545

8. Save the document as **CancelSelection.php** in the Chapter directory for Chapter 9.

9. Reopen the **AvailableOpportunities.php** document.

10. Find the line that displays the word "Selected" in the Status column. Replace that line with the following code that allows the intern to cancel his or her selection:

```
echo "Selected<br />" .
    "<a href='CancelSelection.php?" .
    SID . "&opportunityID=" .
    $Opportunity['opportunityID'] .
    "'>Cancel Selection</a>";
```

11. Save the AvailableOpportunities.php document. Upload it and CancelSelection.php to the Web server.

12. Open the **InternLogin.php** file in your Web browser by entering the following URL: *http://<yourserver>/PHP_Projects/Chapter.09/Chapter/InternLogin.php*. Enter the e-mail address and password for a registered user and click the **Log In** button. You should see the Login Successful page. Click the **Available Opportunities** link to open the Available Opportunities page. Locate an opportunity that you have selected, or select a new opportunity. Click the **Cancel Selection** link to open the Request Internship Web page, which is shown in Figure 9-10.

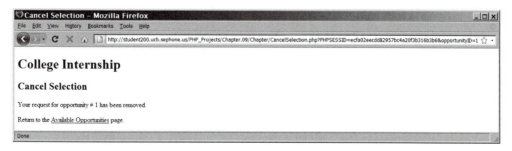

Figure 9-10 Cancel Selection Web page of the College Internship Web site

13. Click the **Available Opportunities** link to return to the Available Opportunities page. The opportunity for which you cancelled the selection should be listed as available.

14. Close your Web browser window.

 Exercise 9-2

In this project, you will create a cookies program that stores the date and time of a user's last visit.

1. Create a new document in your text editor and type the `<!DOCTYPE>` declaration, `<html>` element, header information, and `<body>` element. Use the strict DTD and "Last Visit" as the content of the `<title>` element.

2. Add the following script section above the `<!DOCTYPE>` declaration:

```
<?php
?>
```

3. Add the following `if...else` statement to the script section to assign a value to the `$LastVisit` variable. If the `$_COOKIE['lastVisit']` variable is set, the date and time of the last visit is assigned to the `$LastVisit` variable. Otherwise, the variable is assigned a value of "This is your first visit!"

```
if (isset($_COOKIE['lastVisit']))
    $LastVisit = "<p>Your last visit was on "
        . $_COOKIE['lastVisit'];
else
    $LastVisit = "<p>This is your first visit!</p>\n";
```

4. Add the following statement to the end of the script section. The statement uses the `date()` function with the `setcookie()` function to assign the date to the `$LastVisit` variable. Notice that the cookie is set to expire in one year.

```
setcookie("lastVisit", date("F j, Y, g:i a"),
    time()+60*60*24*365);
```

5. To the document body, add the following output directive, which displays the value of the `$LastVisit` variable:

```
<?php echo $LastVisit; ?>
```

6. Save the document as **LastVisit.php** in the Projects directory for Chapter 9, and then close the document in your text editor.

7. Open the LastVisit.php file in your Web browser by entering the following URL: *http://<yourserver>/PHP_Projects/ Chapter.09/Projects/LastVisit.php*. The first time you open the page, you should see "This is your first visit!" in the browser window. Reload the Web page; you should see the date and time in the browser window.

8. Close your Web browser window.

Exercise 9-3

Create a document with a "nag" counter that reminds users to register. Save the counter in a cookie and display a message reminding users to register every fifth time they visit your site. Create a form in the body of the document that includes text boxes for a user's name and e-mail address along with a Registration button. Normally, registration information would be stored in a database. For simplicity, this step will be omitted from this exercise. After a user fills in the text boxes and clicks the Registration button, delete the nag counter cookie and replace it with cookies containing the user's name and e-mail address. After registering, display the name and e-mail address cookies whenever the user revisits the site.

Exercise 9-4

You can use PHP's rand() function to generate a random integer. The rand() function accepts two arguments that specify the minimum and maximum integer to generate, respectively. For example, the statement $RandNum = rand(10, 20) generates a random integer between 10 and 20 and assigns the number to the $RandNum variable. Create a guessing game that uses sessions to store a random number between 0 and 100, along with the number of guesses the user has attempted. Each time the user guesses wrong, display the number of times the user has guessed. Include a Give Up link that displays the generated number for the current game. Also include a Start Over link that deletes the user session and uses the header("location:URL") function to navigate to the main page.

Exercise 9-5

Create a set of Web pages that registers users for a professional conference. Use a session to track users as they navigate through the Web pages. Include three separate Web pages that contain forms: the first form gathers the user's name and contact information, the second form gathers the user's company information, and the third form prompts users to select the seminars they want to attend at the conference. Include a fourth page that displays the submitted information. The fourth page should include links that allow users to edit the submitted data, along with a Submit button that saves the information to a database. A fifth page should display a confirmation that the information was successfully saved. Include code based on reading e-mail addresses that prevents the same user from registering twice.

Discovery Projects

The Chinese Zodiac site is a comprehensive project that will be updated in the Discovery Projects in each chapter. All files for the Chinese Zodiac site will be saved in a folder named ChineseZodiac in the root Web folder on the server, and all database tables will be stored in the `chinese_zodiac` database.

 Discovery Project 9-1

In this project, you will create a basic site counter to track the number of visitors to your site. Referring back to Discovery Project 8-2, connect to the server and the `chinese_zodiac` database.

In the `chinese_zodiac` database, create a new table named `visit_counter`. The table should contain two fields: `id` and `counter`. The `id` field will be an auto-incrementing primary key with an `INT` data type and the `counter` field will be an `INT` data type. Insert a new record in the table with an `id` of `NULL` and a `counter` of 0. The `id` field should be automatically set to 1.

Open a blank document in the text editor. Within PHP delimiters, include inc_connect.php and then insert the following script that sets a cookie with an expiration of one day, so that visitors are not counted each time they return to the Web page that has the counter.

```php
<?php
// include the inc_connect.php file with database
// connection data
...
/* set a cookie if this is the first visit - the expires
argument is 1 day to prevent visits from incrementing each
time the user returns to the page that contains the site
counter */
if (empty($_COOKIE["visits"])) {
    // increment the counter in the database
    mysql_query("UPDATE visit_counter " .
        " SET counter = counter + 1 " .
        " WHERE id = 1 ");
```

```
    // query the visit_counter table and assign the counter
    // value to the $visitors variable
    $queryResult = mysql_query("SELECT counter " .
        " FROM visit_counter WHERE id = 1");
    if (($row = mysql_fetch_assoc($queryResult)) !== FALSE)
        $visitors = $row['counter'];
    else
        $visitors = 1;
    // Set the cookie value
    setcookie("visits", $visitors, time()+(60*60*24));
}
else // Otherwise, assign the cookie value to the $visitor
    // variable
    $visitors = $_COOKIE["visits"];
?>
```

Save the file as **inc_site_counter.php** and upload the file to the Includes folder in the ChineseZodiac directory on the server.

Open **index.php**, which you last modified in Discovery Project 4-4, from the ChineseZodiac directory. As the first line of code, within the PHP delimiters, include the **inc_site_counter.php** script. Save the file and upload it to the ChineseZodiac directory on the server.

Open **inc_footer.php** from the Includes folder in the ChineseZodiac directory on the server. You last modified inc_footer.php in Discovery Project 8-5. At the location in the script that you would like to display your counter, add the following script:

You can use CSS or tables to format the counter to appear in any style.

```
<p>Total visitors to this site: <?php echo $visitors; ?></p>
```

Save the **inc_footer.php** file and upload it to the Includes folder in the ChineseZodiac directory on the server.

Open **index.php** in the browser. The display should read "Total visitors to this site: 1". Refresh the browser. The display should remain the same. Delete cookies in your browser and open index.php again. The display should now read "Total visitors to this site: 2".

Discovery Project 9-2

In this project, the Chinese zodiac site will have sponsors. Each sponsor needs to have a banner ad. Each time a visitor returns to the site, a different banner should appear.

For this project, you will need at least five banners that advertise products or services of interest to a visitor to the Chinese zodiac site. (These products might include fortune cookies and origami, for example.) In any graphics program, design five banners (125px by 125px), and then save them respectively as **banner1**, **banner2**, **banner3**, **banner4**, and **banner5** with a valid graphic extension. Upload these files to the Images folder in the ChineseZodiac directory on the server.

To add banner ad images to the Chinese zodiac site:

1. Open a blank document in the text editor.

2. Within PHP delimiters, insert the following code, which creates an array named $banner_array that stores the five banner images you created. Replace the *.ext* file extension with the appropriate extension for each image file type. The script then uses the count() function to store the total number of elements in the array to a variable called $banner_count.

```
$banner_array = array(
     "Images/banner1.ext",
     "Images/banner2.ext",
     "Images/banner3.ext",
     "Images/banner4.ext",
     "Images/banner5.ext");
$banner_count = count($banner_array);
```

3. Immediately after the preceding code, but within the PHP script section, add the following code that sets or updates a cookie with an expiration date of one week. If the visitor has not returned within a week, the banner ads will start fresh. To ensure that the first banner ad does not always appear when a visitor first opens the page, you will use the rand() function to select a random starting point.

```
if (empty($_COOKIE["lastbanner"])) {
     // generate a random index greater than or equal
     // to 0, and less than the number of elements in
     // the $banner_array array
     $banner_index = rand(0, $banner_count-1);
}
else {
     // assign the cookie value to the $banner_index
     // variable
     $banner_index = $_COOKIE["lastbanner"];
     // increment the banner index, and use the modulus
     // operator to ensure that the index is greater
     // than or equal to 0, and less than the number
     // of elements in the $banner_array array
     $banner_index = (++$banner_index) % $banner_count;
}
// Set or update the cookie value
setcookie("lastbanner", $banner_index,
time()+(60*60*24*7));
```

4. Save the file as **inc_banner_display.php** and upload it to the Includes folder in the ChineseZodiac directory on the server.

5. Open **index.php**, which you modified in the previous project. At the top of the document, but after the existing include() statement, write the code to include **inc_banner_display.php**.

6. Open **inc_button_nav.php** from the Includes folder. You last modified inc_button_nav.php in Discovery Project 4-2. Above the code for the navigation buttons, include the following PHP code block, which uses the `$banner_index` variable to display the corresponding image element in the array:

```php
<?php
include("Includes/inc_banner_display.php");
// statement to determine which banner image to display
$image = $banner_array[$banner_index];
?>
```

7. Immediately after the PHP code block, add the following statement that displays the appropriate image saved in the `$image` variable.

```php
<img class="btn" src="<?php echo $image; ?>"
     alt="[Banner Ad]" title="Banner Ad"
     style = "border:0" />
```

8. Save **inc_button_nav.php** and upload it to the server. Open **index.php** in the browser to verify that a banner ad appears above the button navigation. Refresh the browser. Each time the browser is refreshed, the next banner image in the array should appear. When the last banner in the array appears, the cycle should begin again with banner1.

Discovery Project 9-3

In this project, you will create a simple Web site survey with five questions that will use sessions to track the user responses.

To create the Web site survey:

1. Create a new document in the text editor and create a PHP code block at the top of the document that includes the session_start() function:

```php
<?php
session_start();
?>
```

2. Before the end of the PHP code block, insert the following array of five questions and the code to save the number of questions into the `$question_count` variable:

During the development stage, you may want to insert echo "<p>PHP Session ID is " . session_id() . "</p>\n"; in the PHP code block to display the assigned session ID.

```
$survey_questions = array(
    1 => "Was the navigation straightforward and " .
         " did all the links work?",
    2 => " Was the selection of background color, " .
         " font color, and font size appropriate?",
    3 => " Were the images appropriate and did they " .
         " complement the Web content?",
    4 => " Were the descriptions of the PHP program " .
         " complete and easy to understand?",
    5 => " Was the PHP code structured properly and " .
         " well commented?");
$question_count = count($survey_questions);
```

3. Immediately after assigning the value to $question_count, check to see if $_SESSION['CurrentQuestion'] is set using the following code. If it is set, increment it. If it is not set, set it to 0. Also, store the previous response if $_SESSION['CurrentQuestion'] is set and greater than 0 and the autoglobal element $_POST['response'] is set.

```
if (isset($_SESSION['CurrentQuestion'])) {
    if (($_SESSION['CurrentQuestion'] > 0) &&
        (isset($_POST['response']))) {
        $_SESSION['Responses'][$_
        SESSION['CurrentQuestion']]
            = $_POST['response'];
    }
    ++$_SESSION['CurrentQuestion'];
}
else
    $_SESSION['CurrentQuestion'] = 0;
```

4. After the closing PHP tag, type the <!DOCTYPE> declaration, <html> element, header information, and <body> element. Use the strict DTD and "Web Survey" as the content of the <title> element.

5. In the body of the Web page, add the following header and PHP tag:

```
<h1>Web Survey</h1>
<?php
?>
```

6. In the PHP code section, add the following code with advanced escaping to display different information based on the value of $_SESSION['CurrentQuestion']:

```
if ($_SESSION['CurrentQuestion'] == 0) {
?>
<p></p>
<?php
}
else if ($_SESSION['CurrentQuestion'] > $question_
```

```
count) {
?>
<p></p>
<?php
}
else {
}
```

7. In the if clause of the if...else statement, add a paragraph explaining the purpose of the survey, such as "Thank you for reviewing the Chinese Zodiac Web site. Your candid responses to the following five questions will help improve the effectiveness of our PHP demonstration site." This explanatory paragraph should go within the opening and closing <p> tags.

8. In the else if clause of the if...else statement, add a statement within the opening and closing <p> tags that thanks the user for completing the survey. After the opening PHP tag, add code to use the standard e-mail headers to e-mail the survey results to your e-mail address. Build the body of the message using the $_SESSION['Responses'] array. Display the survey results on the page so that the visitor can see the five questions and the selected responses.

9. In the final else clause of the if...else statement, add the following code to display the current question:

```
echo "<p>Question " . $_SESSION['CurrentQuestion'] .
    ": " . $survey_questions[$_
    SESSION['CurrentQuestion']]
    . "</p>\n";
```

10. Add the following code to insert a form with a method of post and an action of "web_survey.php" if $_SESSION['CurrentQuestion'] is less than or equal to the number of questions. Insert a hidden form field to pass the session ID from page to page. Use a nested if...else statement to display the appropriate text on the Submit button and to include radio buttons for the visitor to select an answer if a question is being displayed.

```
if ($_SESSION['CurrentQuestion'] <= $question_count)
{
    echo "<form method='post' action='web_survey.
        php'>\n";
    echo "<input type='hidden' name='PHPSESSID'
        value=' " .
        session_id() . "' />\n";
    if ($_SESSION['CurrentQuestion'] > 0) {
        echo "<p><input type='radio'
            name='response' " .
            " value='Exceeds Expectations' /> " .
            " Exceeds Expectations<br />\n";
```

```
                    echo "<input type='radio' name='response' " .
                        " value='Meets Expectations'" .
                        " checked='checked' /> " .
                        " Meets Expectations<br />\n";
                    echo "<input type='radio' name='response' " .
                        " value='Below Expectations'> " .
                        " Below Expectations</p>\n";
        }
        echo "<input type='submit' name='submit' value='";
        if ($_SESSION['CurrentQuestion'] == 0)
            echo "Start the survey";
        else if ($_SESSION['CurrentQuestion'] ==
        $question_count)
            echo "Finished";
        else
            echo "Next Question";
        echo "' />\n";
        echo "</form>\n";
    }
```

11. Save the file as **web_survey.php** and upload the file to the ChineseZodiac directory on the server.

12. Reopen **inc_state_information.php** (last modified in Discovery Project 4-1) in your text editor and add a description of the Web survey program. Include a [Test the Script] link that opens web_survey.php and a [View the Source Code] link that displays the PHP source code for the survey page. Save the file and upload it to the Includes folder in the ChineseZodiac directory on the server.

13. Open the Chinese zodiac Web site, then click the State Information button and text links to verify that the program runs properly. Click the [Test the Script] link for the Web survey to open web_survey.php. Select a response for each question. The final page should display the "thank you" message, the results of the survey, and a link back to the Chinese zodiac site if the survey was opened in a new window rather than the dynamic content section. The results should also be sent to your e-mail address.

Discovery Project 9-4

In this project, you will design the gateway portal for a Chinese zodiac social networking site that will create a login system to allow users to register, log in, create and update user profiles, display photos, and view all user profiles.

The gateway page should contain a welcome screen (with header and footer) and two sections:

1. Registered User Login [Insert placeholder text here]

2. New User Registration [Insert placeholder text here]

Insert a header, footer, and welcome content on the page and save it as **index.php** in a ZodiacProfiles subdirectory in the ChineseZodiac directory on the server.

In the browser, open index.php from the ZodiacProfiles subdirectory to verify that the gateway portal appears correctly.

Discovery Project 9-5

In this project, you will create the database tables required to store the profile information.

Referring back to Discovery Project 8-2, connect to the server and the Chinese zodiac database. Create two tables named `zodiac_profiles` and `profile_pictures` using the properties in Tables 9-1 and 9-2:

Field Name	Field Properties
profile_id	UNSIGNED INT NOT NULL AUTOINCREMENT PRIMARY KEY
first_name	VARCHAR(25) NOT NULL
last_name	VARCHAR(25) NOT NULL
user_email	VARCHAR(255) NOT NULL
user_name	VARCHAR(25) NOT NULL
user_password	VARCHAR(25) NOT NULL
user_sign	VARCHAR(25) NOT NULL
user_profile	TEXT NOT NULL

Table 9-1   The `zodiac_profiles` table

Field Name	Field Properties
profile_id	INT NOT NULL
profile_title	VARCHAR(100) NOT NULL
picture_ link	VARCHAR(200) NOT NULL

Table 9-2   The `profile_pictures` table

View the structure of the two tables in either MySQL Monitor or PHPMyAdmin, capture an image of each display, and save the images as **DP9-5a.*ext*** and **DP9-5b.ext**, respectively (replacing the .*ext* with the appropriate extension for the image type). Upload the files to an Images folder in the ZodiacProfiles subdirectory of the ChineseZodiac directory on the server.

Developing Object-Oriented PHP

In this chapter, you will:

◎ Study object-oriented programming concepts

◎ Use objects in PHP scripts

◎ Declare data members in classes

◎ Work with class member functions

The PHP programs you have written so far have mostly been self-contained—that is, most elements of the code, such as variables, statements, and functions, exist within a script section. For example, you might create a Web page for an online retailer that uses PHP to calculate the total for a sales order, including state sales tax and shipping. However, suppose the retailer sells different types of products on different Web pages, with one page selling apparel, another page selling electronics, and so on. If you want to reuse the code that calculates sales totals on multiple Web pages, you must copy all of the statements or recreate them from scratch for each Web page. Object-oriented programming takes a different approach. Essentially, object-oriented programming allows you to use and create objects, which are complex data structures built of variables and functions that work together to represent a single entity. In other words, object-oriented programming allows you to hide a complex logical construct behind a simple interface.

PHP 5 added many new object-oriented programming capabilities to the language. These capabilities rival features in other object-oriented languages, such as Java and C++. Entire books are written about object-oriented programming, but this chapter focuses on the basics to get you started in creating object-oriented PHP scripts.

Introduction to Object-Oriented Programming

The term **object-oriented programming (OOP)** refers to the concept of merging related variables and functions into a single interface. The term **object** specifically refers to programming code and data that can be treated as an individual unit or component. (Objects are often also called **components**.) For example, you might create a Loan object that calculates the number of payments required to pay off a loan. The Loan object might also store information such as the principal loan amount and the interest rate. The term **data** refers to information contained within variables or other types of storage structures. The functions associated with an object are called **methods**, and the variables associated with an object are called **properties** or **attributes**. In the Loan object example, a function that calculates the number of payments required to pay off the loan is a method. The principal loan amount and the interest rate are properties of the Loan object.

Objects can range from simple controls, such as a button, to entire programs, such as a database application. Some programs consist entirely of other objects. You'll often encounter objects that have been designed to perform a specific task. For example, in a retail sales program, you could refer to all of the code that calculates the sales total as a single object. You could then reuse that object repeatedly within the same program or in others.

C++, Java, and Visual Basic are some popular object-oriented programming languages. Programmers can use any of these languages to create objects themselves or use objects created by other programmers. Often, objects are packaged into libraries, which can be used by other programs built for the same operating system. For example, if you are creating an accounting program in Visual Basic, you can use an object named Payroll that is in a library created in C++. The Payroll object might contain one method that calculates the amount of federal and state tax to deduct, another function that calculates the FICA amount to deduct, and so on. Properties of the Payroll object might include an employee's number of tax withholding allowances, federal and state tax percentages, and the cost of insurance premiums. You do not need to know how the Payroll object was created in C++, nor do you need to recreate it in Visual Basic. You only need to know how to access the methods and properties of the Payroll object from Visual Basic.

A simple object-oriented accounting program is illustrated in Figure 10-1. In this figure, the accounting program is composed of three separate objects, or components: an AccountsReceivable object, a Payroll object, and an AccountsPayable object. It is important to understand that you do not need to rewrite these three objects for the accounting program; the program only needs to call their methods and provide the correct data to their properties.

The diagram in Figure 10-1 was created in Unified Modeling Language (UML), a language that uses symbols to represent software elements such as objects, methods, and properties. UML is useful for designing and documenting software and other types of engineering systems.

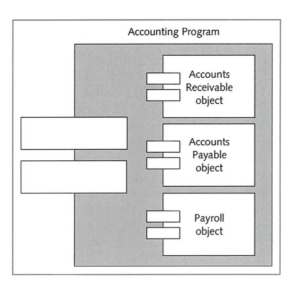

Figure 10-1 Accounting program and components

Understanding Encapsulation

Objects are **encapsulated**, which means that all code and required data are contained within the object itself. In most cases, an encapsulated object consists of a single computer file that contains all code and required data. Encapsulation places code inside what programmers like to call a "black box." When an object is encapsulated, you cannot see "inside" it—all internal workings are hidden. The code (methods and statements) and data (variables and constants) contained in an encapsulated object are accessed through an interface. An **interface** refers to the methods and properties that are required for a source program to communicate with an object. For example, the interface elements required to access a `Payroll` object might be a method named `calcNetPay()`, which calculates an employee's net pay, and properties containing the employee's name and pay rate.

When you include encapsulated objects in your programs, users can only see the methods and properties of the object that you allow them to see. By removing the ability to see inside the black box, encapsulation reduces the complexity of the code, allowing programmers who use the code to concentrate on the task of integrating it into their programs. Encapsulation also prevents other programmers from accidentally introducing a bug into a program, or from possibly even stealing the code and claiming it as their own.

You can compare a programming object and its interface to a hand-held calculator. The calculator represents an object, and you represent a program that wants to use the object. You establish an interface with the calculator object by entering numbers (the data required by the object) and then pressing calculation keys (which represent the methods of the object). You do not need to know, nor can you see, the inner workings of the calculator object. As a programmer, you are concerned only with an object's methods and properties. To continue the analogy, you are only concerned with the result you expect the calculator object to return. Figure 10-2 illustrates the idea of the calculator interface.

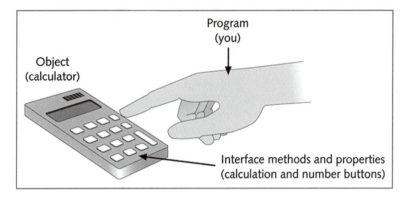

Figure 10-2 Calculator interface

Microsoft Word® is another example of an object and its interface. Word itself is actually an object made up of numerous other objects. The program window (or user interface) is one object. The items you see in the interface, such as the menu and toolbars, are used to execute methods. For example, the Bold button on the toolbar executes a bold() method. The text of your document is the data you provide to the program. You can use Word without knowing how its various methods work; you only need to know what each method does, and provide the data (text) and execute the appropriate methods when necessary. In the same way, when using objects in your payroll code, you only need to provide the necessary data (such as an employee's gross pay) and execute the appropriate method (such as the calcNetPay() method).

Object-Oriented Programming and Classes

In object-oriented programming, the code, methods, attributes, and other information that make up an object are organized into **classes**. Essentially, a class is a template, or blueprint, that serves as the basis for new objects. When you use an object in your program, you actually create an instance of the class of the object. An **instance** is an object that has been created from an existing class. An instance of an object is the equivalent of a house built from a blueprint. When you create an object from an existing class, you **instantiate** the object.

Later in this chapter, you will learn how to create, or instantiate, an object from built-in PHP classes and from custom classes that you write yourself. However, as an immediate example, consider an object named BankAccount that contains methods and properties you might use to record transactions associated with a checking or savings account. The BankAccount object is created from a BankAccount class. To use the BankAccount class, you create an instance of the class. A particular instance of an object **inherits** its methods and properties from a class—that is, it takes on the characteristics of the class on which it is based. The BankAccount object, for instance, would inherit all of the methods and properties of the BankAccount class. As another example, when you create a word-processing document, which is a type of object, it usually inherits the properties of a template on which it is based. The template is a type of class, and the document inherits characteristics of the template, such as font size, line spacing, and boilerplate text. In the same manner, programs that include instances of objects inherit the object's functionality.

Class names in traditional object-oriented programming usually begin with an uppercase letter. This convention is also followed in PHP.

In this chapter, you will create the Web site for an online order form in an online store application. The application includes information about each store and a custom inventory for each store. The primary store you will use is Gosselin's Gourmet Coffee, which sells various blends of coffee beans. The purpose of the Web site is to demonstrate code reuse with classes. As you progress through this chapter, you will develop a class named OnlineStore that handles the functionality of building a working online store. Online store classes are very popular with PHP development because of the many Web sites that allow visitors to purchase items. Rather than recreating the same functionality for each online store, you can much more easily develop the Web site by reusing an existing online store class. As you create the OnlineStore class, notice that its functionality has nothing to do with Gosselin's Gourmet Coffee or coffee beans. Instead, the code is generic enough that it can be used with any Web site that sells products, provided the pages in the site and the associated database conform to the requirements of the class.

First, you create the database and tables that store the online store information and products. The OnlineStore class requires that store information is stored in a table containing six fields: storeID, name, description, welcome, css_file, and email_address. The storeID field is the primary key and consists of a unique text field. For example, the primary key for Gosselin's Gourmet Coffee is COFFEE. The OnlineStore class also requires that product information is stored in a table containing five fields: productID, storeID, name, description, and price. The productID field is the primary key and consists of a unique text field. For example, the primary key for the first product for Gosselin's Gourmet Coffee is COFFEE001. The storeID stores the unique ID number for the store that sells the product. To keep things simple, the OnlineStore class does not store customer or payment information. Instead, the class simply uses session IDs to keep track of each user's shopping cart.

Next, you create a database named online_stores along with two tables: store_info, to contain configuration information for each store, and `inventory`, to contain product information. Your Chapter directory for Chapter 10 contains two text files, store_info.txt and inventory.txt, which contain store and product information to load into each database table.

To create the Online Stores database:

1. Log in to MySQL Monitor with the MySQL user name and password you created in Chapter 7.

2. Enter the following command to create a database named `online_stores`:

   mysql> **CREATE DATABASE online_stores;[ENTER↵]**

3. After you see the "Query OK" message, enter the following command to select the `online_stores` database:

   mysql> **USE online_stores;[ENTER↵]**

4. Enter the following command to create the `store_info` table:

   mysql> **CREATE TABLE store_info (storeID VARCHAR(10) PRIMARY KEY,[ENTER↵]**
   -> name VARCHAR(50), description VARCHAR(200), welcome TEXT,[ENTER↵]
   -> css_file VARCHAR(250), email_address VARCHAR(100));[ENTER↵]

5. After you see the "Query OK" message, enter a LOAD DATA statement that inserts records into the `store_info` table from the store_info.txt file in your Chapter directory for Chapter 10. Replace *path* with the path to your Chapter directory for Chapter 10.

   mysql> **LOAD DATA INFILE 'path/store_info.txt'[ENTER↵]**
   -> INTO TABLE store_info;[ENTER↵]

6. Enter the following command to create the `inventory` table:

   mysql> **CREATE TABLE inventory (storeID varchar(10),[ENTER↵]**
   -> productID VARCHAR(10) PRIMARY KEY,[ENTER↵]
   -> name VARCHAR(100), description VARCHAR(200), price FLOAT);[ENTER↵]

7. After you see the "Query OK" message, enter a LOAD DATA statement that inserts records into the `inventory` table from the inventory.txt file in your Chapter directory for Chapter 10. Replace *path* with the path to your Chapter directory for Chapter 10.

   mysql> **LOAD DATA INFILE 'path/inventory.txt'[ENTER↵]**
   -> INTO TABLE inventory;[ENTER↵]

8. Type **exit** or **quit** and press **Enter** to log out of MySQL Monitor.

Short Quiz

1. Discuss the benefits of object-oriented programming.

2. Explain how objects can be shared by multiple programming languages such as PHP, C++, and Visual Basic.

3. Identify three benefits of encapsulating code.

4. Define the term "instance of a class."

Using Objects in PHP Scripts

Up to this point, all of the PHP scripts you have written contained procedural statements that did not rely on objects. Many of the skills you have learned so far will help you construct object-oriented programs. However, object-oriented techniques will help you build more extensible code that is easier to reuse, modify, and enhance. In this section, you will learn how to work with database connections as objects to help you understand how to use objects in your scripts. Then, you will learn how to define your own custom classes.

Before you begin working with database connections as objects, you first need to understand a few basics of how to work with objects in PHP. You declare an object in PHP by using the new operator with a class constructor. A **class constructor** is a special function with the same name as its class; it is called automatically when an object from the class is instantiated. For example, the class constructor for the BankAccount class is BankAccount(). The syntax for instantiating an object is as follows:

```
$ObjectName = new ClassName();
```

The identifiers you use for an object name must follow the same rules as identifiers for variables: They must begin with a dollar sign, can include numbers or an underscore (but not as the first character after the dollar sign), cannot include spaces, and are case sensitive. The following statement instantiates an object named $Checking from the BankAccount class:

```
$Checking = new BankAccount();
```

564

Class constructors are primarily used to initialize properties when an object is first instantiated. For this reason, you can pass arguments to many constructor functions. For example, the BankAccount class might require you to pass the account number as a parameter, as follows:

```
$Checking = new BankAccount(01234587);
```

After you instantiate an object, you use the combination of a hyphen and a greater-than symbol (->) to access the methods and properties contained in the object. Together, these two characters are referred to as **member selection notation**. Using member selection notation is similar to using an operator in that you append one or more characters (in this case, ->) to an object, followed by the name of a method or property. With methods, you must also include a set of parentheses at the end of the method name, just as you would with functions. Like functions, methods can also accept arguments.

The following statements demonstrate how to call two methods, getBalance() and getCheckAmount(), from the $Checking object. The getBalance() method does not require any arguments, whereas the getCheckAmount() method requires an argument containing the check number.

The printf() function, which allows you to format variables in an output string, is described in Appendix C. In this example, the format specifier %.2f causes the balance to be displayed as a floating-point number (f) with two digits (specified by the 2) after the decimal point.

```
$Checking->getBalance();
$CheckNumber = 1022;
$Checking->getCheckAmount($CheckNumber);
```

To access property values in an object, you do not include parentheses at the end of the property name, as you do with functions and methods, nor do you include a dollar sign before the property name. For example, the following statements update and display the value in a property named $Balance in the $Checking object:

```
$CheckAmount = 124.75;
$Checking->Balance = $Checking->Balance + $CheckAmount;
printf("<p>Your updated checking account balance is
$%.2f.</p>", $Checking->Balance);
```

Next, you start creating the GosselinGourmetCoffee.php script, which displays the coffee products available for purchase. The first version of the script simply queries the database and displays a table with the product information. Later in this chapter, you will modify the script so it uses the OnlineStore class.

To create the GosselinGourmetCoffee.php script:

1. Create a new document in your text editor and type the <!DOCTYPE> declaration, <html> element, header information, and <body> element. Use the strict DTD and "Gosselin's Gourmet Coffee" as the content of the <title> element.

2. Add the following text and elements to the document body:

```
<h1>Gosselin's Gourmet Coffee</h1>
<h2>Description goes here</h2>
<p>Welcome message goes here</p>
<p>Inventory goes here</p>
```

At this point, the file has no PHP code sections. Normally, a file like this would be saved with an .html extension. You save it with a .php extension because you will add PHP code later in the chapter.

3. Save the document as **GosselinGourmetCoffee.php** in the Chapter directory for Chapter 10 and upload the document to the Web server.

4. Open the GosselinGourmetCoffee.php file in your Web browser by entering the following URL: *http://<yourserver>/PHP_Projects/Chapter.10/Chapter/ GosselinGourmetCoffee.php*. Your Web browser should look like Figure 10-3.

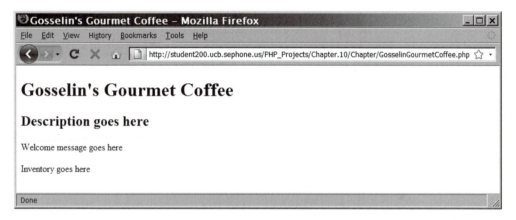

Figure 10-3   The Gosselin's Gourmet Coffee Web page

5. Close your Web browser window.

Working with Database Connections as Objects

PHP allows you to connect to and manipulate MySQL and other types of databases using either procedural statements or object-oriented techniques. Although you should not notice any performance issues when using procedural statements or object-oriented techniques to access MySQL databases, you can expect object-oriented techniques to become the preferred method as PHP continues to evolve. For this reason, you should get used to the object-oriented method of accessing MySQL databases. As mentioned in Chapter 8, the mysqli package is the object-oriented equivalent of the mysql package. The mysqli package will be used throughout this chapter.

You access MySQL database connections as objects by instantiating an object from the mysqli class. The mysqli class contains methods and properties that have the same functionality as the procedural MySQL database connection statements you have used so far. For example, the equivalent of the mysql_query() function is a method named query() in the mysqli class, and the equivalent of the mysql_affected_rows() function is a property named affected_rows in the mysqli class. Next, you will learn how to instantiate and close a MySQL database connection object.

Instantiating and Closing a MySQL Database Object

In Chapter 8, you learned how to use the mysql_connect() function to open a connection to a MySQL database server. When connecting to the MySQL database server using object-oriented techniques, you instantiate an object from the mysqli class. You pass to the mysqli class the same *host*, *user*, *password*, and *database* arguments that you pass to the mysql_connect() and mysql_select_db() functions. For example, the following statements use the mysql_connect() and mysql_select_db() functions to connect to a MySQL database server:

```
$DBConnect = mysql_connect("php_db", "dongosselin",
     "rosebud");
mysql_select_db("real_estate", $DBConnect);
```

You can use the select_db() method of the mysqli object to select a different database.

In comparison, you use the following statement to connect to the MySQL database server using a mysqli object:

```
$DBConnect = new mysqli("php_db", "dongosselin",
     "rosebud", "real_estate");
```

The preceding statement uses the mysqli() constructor function to instantiate a mysqli class object named $DBConnect.

Instead of using the mysql_close() function to explicitly close the database connection when you finish working with it, you call the close() method of the mysqli class. For example, the following statement closes the database connection represented by the $DBConnect object (remember that $DBConnect is an object of the mysqli class):

```
$DBConnect->close();
```

To add statements to the GosselinGourmetCoffee.php script that instantiate and close a database connection to the MySQL database server using a mysqli object:

1. Create a new document in your text editor with the following script section:

   ```
   <?php
   ?>
   ```

2. Add the following statements to the script section to connect to the database server using a mysqli object. The code uses

an if statement to store an error message in the $ErrorMsgs array if there was a connection error. Be sure to replace *host*, *user*, and *password* with your MySQL server name, user name, and password.

```
$ErrorMsgs = array();
$DBConnect = new mysqli("host", "user", "password",
    "online_store");
if (!$DBConnect)
    $ErrorMsgs[] = "The database server is not
                available.";
```

3. Save the document as **inc_OnlineStoreDB.php** in the Chapter directory for Chapter 10.

4. Return to the **GosselinGourmetCoffee.php** script in your text editor.

5. Add the following script section to the start of the document, before the <!DOCTYPE> tag:

```
<?php
require_once("inc_OnlineStoreDB.php");
?>
```

6. Add the following script section to the body of the document, immediately before the closing </body> tag:

```
<?php
if (count($ErrorMsgs)) {
    foreach ($ErrorMsgs as $Msg)
        echo "<p>" . $Msg . "</p>\n";
}
else
    echo "<p>Successfully connected to the
        database.<p>\n";
?>
```

7. Add the following script section to the end of the document to close the database connection:

```
<?php
$DBConnect->close();
?>
```

8. Save the GosselinGourmetCoffee.php file and then upload inc_OnlineStoreDB.php and GosselinGourmetCoffee.php to the Web server.

9. Open the GosselinGourmetCoffee.php script in your Web browser by entering the following URL: *http://<yourserver>/ PHP_Projects/Chapter.10/Chapter/GosselinGourmetCoffee. php*. You should see the message about successfully connecting to the database server (see Figure 10-4).

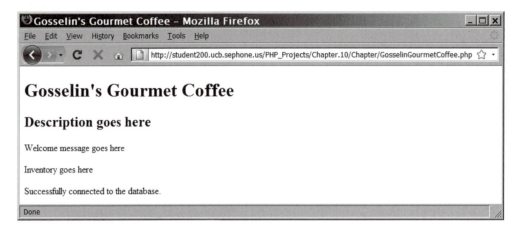

Figure 10-4   Gosselin's Gourmet Coffee Web page after connecting to the database server

10.   Close your Web browser window.

Handling MySQL Errors

When you use procedural syntax to connect to the MySQL database server, the mysql_connect() function returns a value of FALSE if the database connection attempt fails. However, when you use the mysqli() constructor function to instantiate a new database object from the mysqli class, an object is instantiated even if the database connection fails. That means the if (!$DBConnect) statement in inc_OnlineStoreDB.php would always evaluate to FALSE. To determine if the database connection attempt failed when working with the mysqli object, you need to use the connect_errno data member of the mysqli object to retrieve the error code from the last connection attempt. A value of 0 indicates no error, or a successful connection. A nonzero value indicates that the connection attempt failed, as in the following example:

```
$DBConnect = @new mysqli("php_db", "dgosselin",
"rosebud");
if ($DBConnect->connect_errno) {
    echo "<p>Unable to connect to the database server.</p>"
    . "<p>Error code " . $DBConnect->connect_errno
    . ": " . $DBConnect->connect_error . "</p>\n";
}
else {
// code that executes if the database connection attempt
// succeeded
}
```

Notice in the preceding example that the first statement, which instantiates the database connection object, uses the error control operator, @, to suppress error messages. Recall that you can place the error control operator before any expression to suppress error messages. The error control operator in the preceding example is placed before the new operator because it begins the expression that instantiates the database connection object.

It is important to note that the mysqli class members connect_errno, connect_error, errno, and error are data members, or variables, of the database connection object. In the procedural mysql package, the corresponding mysql_errno() and mysql_error() are functions.

Most of the methods of the mysqli class return values of TRUE or FALSE, depending on whether the operation was successful. Therefore, for any methods of the mysqli class that fail (as indicated by a return value of FALSE), you can use the same if...else structure as you did in Chapter 8. For example, the following statement checks the return value of the select_db() method to display an error message if a value of FALSE was returned. Notice that the object-oriented $DBConnect->errno and $DBConnect->error data members are used in place of the procedural mysql_errno() and mysql_error() functions, and that the statement which calls the select_db() method also uses the error control operator to suppress error messages.

```
$DBName = "vehicle_fleet";
$Result = @$DBConnect->select_db($DBName);
if ($Result === FALSE)
    echo "<p>Unable to select the database. " .
        "Error code " . $DBConnect->errno .
        ": " . $DBConnect->error . "</p>\n";
else {
    // Code to execute if database selected successfully.
}
```

To add MySQL error-checking functionality to the GosselinGourmetCoffee.php script:

1. Return to the **inc_OnlineStoreDB.php** script in your text editor.

2. Add the error control operator (@) before the new keyword, as follows:

   ```
   $DBConnect = @new mysqli("host", "user", "password",
       "online_stores");
   ```

3. Replace the if statement with the following if statement that checks the value of the $DBConnect object's connect_errno data member to see if it is nonzero, indicating a connection error:

```
if ($DBConnect->connect_errno)
    $ErrorMsgs[] = "Unable to connect to the
    database server." .
            " Error code " . $DBConnect->connect_errno
            . ": " . $DBConnect->connect_error;
```

4. Save the inc_OnlineStoreDB.php file.

5. Return to the **GosselinGourmetCoffee.php** script in your text editor.

6. Remove the following two lines of code that display a message if there were no errors:

```
else
    echo "<p>Successfully connected to the database
        .<p>\n";
```

7. Replace the `$DBConnect->close();` statement with the following `if` statement, which verifies that there are no connect errors before attempting to close the connection:

```
if (!$DBConnect->connect_error)
    $DBConnect->close();
```

8. Save the GosselinGourmetCoffee.php file and then upload inc_OnlineStoreDB.php and GosselinGourmetCoffee.php to the Web server.

9. Open the GosselinGourmetCoffee.php script in your Web browser by entering the following URL: *http://<yourserver>/PHP_Projects/Chapter.10/Chapter/GosselinGourmetCoffee.php*. The Web page should look the same as it did before you added the MySQL error-checking functionality, with the exception of the "Successfully connected to the database server" message, which no longer appears.

10. Close your Web browser window.

Executing SQL Statements

Recall that you send SQL statements to MySQL with procedural syntax by using the `mysql_query()` function. With a `mysqli` object, you use the `query()` method of the `mysqli` class. The `query()` method accepts a single argument representing the SQL statement you want to send to the MySQL database server. For queries that return results using procedural syntax, you use the `mysql_fetch_row()` function to return the fields in the current row of a resultset into an indexed array. You use the `mysql_fetch_assoc()` function to return the fields in the current row of a resultset into an associative array. In comparison, with a `mysqli` object, you call the `fetch_row()` and `fetch_assoc()` methods of the `mysqli` class.

The following code demonstrates how to use a `mysqli` object to execute a query that returns all the records from the `company_cars` table of the `vehicle_fleet` database. The code builds a table and uses the `fetch_row()` method to return the fields in the current row into an indexed array. The code is very similar to examples you have seen in the past few chapters. The biggest difference is that the object-oriented `query()` method, which is the equivalent of the procedural `mysql_query()` function, only returns TRUE for a successful query and FALSE for a failed query.

To retrieve the results, you call the `use_result()` method, which returns a `mysqli_result` object. You then call the `fetch_row()` and `fetch_array()` methods of the mysqli_result object, just as you called the procedural `mysql_fetch_row()` and `mysql_fetch_array()` functions. One important difference is that the object-oriented `fetch_row()` and `fetch_array()` methods return NULL if there are no more results, while the procedural `mysql_fetch_row()` and `mysql_fetch_array()` functions return FALSE.

 You must be sure to test for NULL and not FALSE when using the object-oriented methods. If you check for FALSE, your code will be stuck in an infinite loop.

```
$TableName = "company_cars";
$SQLstring = "SELECT * FROM $TableName";
$QueryResult = @$DBConnect->query($SQLstring);
if ($QueryResult === FALSE)
    echo "<p>Unable to execute the query. " .
        "Error code " . $DBConnect->errno .
        ": " . $DBConnect->error . "</p>\n";
else {
    echo "<table width='100%' border='1'>\n";
    echo "<tr><th>License</th><th>Make</th><th>Model</th>" .
        "<th>Mileage</th><th>Year</th></tr>\n";
    while (($Row = $QueryResult->fetch_row()) !== FALSE)
    {
        echo "<tr><td>{$Row[0]}</td>";
        echo "<td>{$Row[1]}</td>";
        echo "<td>{$Row[2]}</td>";
        echo "<td align='right'>{$Row[3]}</td>";
        echo "<td>{$Row[4]}</td></tr>\n";
    }
    echo "</table>\n";
}
```

To add code to the GosselinGourmetCoffee.php script that uses a `mysqli` object query to retrieve product information from the `coffee` table in the `online_store` database:

1. Return to the **GosselinGourmetCoffee.php** script in your text editor.

2. Remove the section of HTML code that displays the text "Inventory goes here".

3. Add the following `if` statement above the statement that displays the database error messages. The `if` statement verifies that there are no error messages before querying the database. The first statement within the code block for the `if` statement creates a SQL string, and the second statement uses `mysqli` class syntax to perform the query. Recall that the `storeID` value for Gosselin's Gourmet Coffee is "COFFEE".

```php
if (count($ErrorMsgs)==0) {
    $SQLstring = "SELECT * FROM inventory " .
                    "WHERE storeID='COFFEE'";
    $QueryResult = $DBConnect->query($SQLstring);
    if ($QueryResult === FALSE)
        $ErrorMsgs[] = "<p>Unable to perform the
            query. " .
            "<p>Error code " . $DBConnect->errno .
            ": " . $DBConnect->error . "</p>\n";
}
```

4. Add the following `else` clause to the `if` statement that displays the error messages. Within the `else` clause, you build a table showing the items available from the online store.

```php
else {
    echo "<table width='100%'>\n";
    echo "<tr><th>Product</th><th>Description</th>" .
        "<th>Price Each</th></tr>\n";
    while (($Row = $QueryResult->fetch_assoc()) !==
    NULL) {
        echo "<tr><td>" . htmlentities($Row['name']) .
            "</td>\n";
        echo "<td>" .
            htmlentities($Row['description']) .
            "</td>\n";
        printf("<td>$%.2f</td></tr>\n", $Row['price']);
    }
    echo "</table>";
}
```

5. Save the GosselinGourmetCoffee.php file and then upload it to the Web server.

6. Open the GosselinGourmetCoffee.php script in your Web browser by entering the following URL: *http://<yourserver>/PHP_Projects/Chapter.10/Chapter/GosselinGourmetCoffee.php*. You should see the table shown in Figure 10-5.

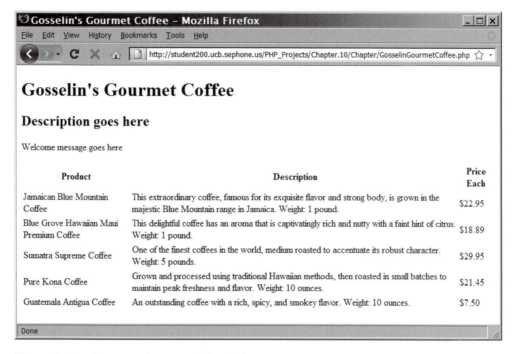

Figure 10-5 Gosselin's Gourmet Coffee Web page displaying query results

7. Close your Web browser window.

Defining Custom PHP Classes

Classes were defined earlier in this chapter as the code, methods, attributes, and other information that make up an object. In PHP, classes more specifically refer to data structures that contain variables along with functions for manipulating the variables. The term **data structure** refers to a system for organizing data. Some of the data structures you have already used include arrays, text files, and database records. The functions and variables defined in a class are called **class members**. Class variables are referred to as **data members** or **member variables**, whereas class functions are referred to as **member functions** or **function members**. To use the variables and functions in a class, you instantiate an object by declaring the object as a new instance of the class. After you instantiate an object, class data members are referred to as properties of the object and class member functions are referred to as methods of the object.

Classes are also referred to as user-defined data types or programmer-defined data types. These terms can be somewhat misleading, however, because they do not accurately reflect the fact that classes can contain member functions. In addition, classes usually contain multiple data

573

members of different data types, so calling a class a data type becomes even more confusing. One reason classes are called user-defined data types or programmer-defined data types is that you can work with a class as a single unit, or object, in the same way you work with a variable. In fact, the terms "variable" and "object" are often used interchangeably in object-oriented programming. The term "object-oriented programming" comes from the fact that you can bundle variables and functions together and use the result as a single unit (a variable or object).

This information will become clearer to you as you progress through this chapter. For now, think of the handheld calculator example. A calculator could be considered an object of a Calculation class. You access all of the Calculation class functions (such as addition and subtraction) and its data members (operands that represent the numbers you are calculating) through your calculator object. You never actually work with the Calculation class yourself, only with an object of the class (your calculator).

But why do you need to work with a collection of related variables and functions as a single object? Why not simply call each individual variable and function as necessary, without bothering with all this class business? The truth is, you are not required to work with classes; you can create much of the same functionality without classes as you can by using classes. In fact, many of the scripts that you create—and that you find in use today—do not require object-oriented techniques to be effective. Classes help make complex programs easier to manage, however, by logically grouping related functions and data and by allowing you to refer to that grouping as a single object. Another reason for using classes is to hide information that users of a class do not need to access or know about; this helps minimize the amount of information that needs to pass in and out of an object. Classes also make it much easier to reuse code or distribute your code to others for use in their programs. (You will learn how to create your own classes and include them in your scripts shortly.) Packaging related variables and functions into a class is similar to packaging them into a single include file, then using the include() statement to insert them in a PHP script. The difference is that an include file can only contain a single copy of each variable, whereas each instance of a class will contain a distinct copy of each variable.

Another reason to use classes is that instances of objects inherit their characteristics, such as class members, from the class upon which they are based. This inheritance allows you to build new classes based on existing classes without having to rewrite the code contained in the existing classes.

Creating a Class Definition

To create a class in PHP, you use the `class` keyword to write a **class definition**, which contains the data members and member functions that make up the class. The basic syntax for defining a class is as follows:

```
class ClassName {
     data member and member function definitions
}
```

The `ClassName` portion of the class definition is the name of the new class. You can use any name you want for a structure, as long as you follow the same naming conventions that you use when declaring other identifiers, such as variables and functions. Also, keep in mind that class names usually begin with an uppercase letter to distinguish them from other identifiers. Within the class's curly braces, you declare the data type and field names for each piece of information stored in the structure, the same way you declare data members and member functions that make up the class.

The following code demonstrates how to declare a class named `BankAccount`. The statement following the class definition instantiates an object of the class named `$Checking`.

```
class BankAccount {
     data member and member function definitions
}
$Checking = new BankAccount();
```

Class names in a class definition are not followed by parentheses, as function names are in a function definition.

Because the `BankAccount` class does not yet contain any data members or member functions, there isn't much you can do with the `$Checking` object. However, PHP includes a number of built-in functions that you can use to return information about the class that instantiated the object. For example, the `get_class()` function returns the name of the class that instantiated the object. You pass the name of the object to the `get_class()` function, as follows:

```
$Checking = new BankAccount();
echo 'The $Checking object is instantiated from the '
     . get_class($Checking) . " class.</p>\n";
```

See the Class/Object Functions reference in the online PHP documentation at *http:// www.php.net/docs.php* for more information on the functions you can use with classes and objects.

You can also use the `instanceof` comparison operator to determine whether an object is instantiated from a given class. The syntax for using the `instanceof` operator is *object_name* `instanceof` *class_name*. For example, the following code uses an `if` statement and the `instanceof` operator to determine whether the `$Checking` object is an instance of the `BankAccount` class:

```
$Checking = new BankAccount();
if ($Checking instanceof BankAccount)
     echo "The \$Checking object is instantiated from the
          BankAccount class.</p>\n";
```

One built-in class function that you should use whenever you declare an object is the class_exists() function, which determines whether a class exists and is available to the current script. You pass to the class_exists() function a string value containing the name of the class you want to use. The function returns a value of TRUE if the class exists and FALSE if it doesn't. For example, the following code uses the class_exists() function within an if statement's conditional expression to check for the existence of the BankAccount class. If the class exists, the $Checking object is instantiated. If the class does not exist, the else clause displays an error message.

```php
if (class_exists("BankAccount"))
        $Checking = new BankAccount();
else
        echo "<p>The BankAccount class is not available!</p>\n";
```

Storing Classes in External Files

Just as you preface the names of include files with "inc_" to easily distinguish them from regular PHP files, you can preface the name of class files with "class_", as in "class_BankAccount.php".

Although you can define a class within the same document that instantiates an object of the class, this somewhat defeats the purpose of writing code that can be easily modified and reused. If you want to reuse the class, you need to copy and paste it between scripts. Further, if you want to modify the class, you need to modify it within every script that uses it. A better solution is to define a class within a single external file that is called from each script that needs the class, using the include(), include_once(), require(), and require_once() functions that you learned in Chapter 2.

To start creating the OnlineStore class and using it in GosselinGourmetCoffee.php:

1. Create a new document in your text editor and add a PHP script section, as follows:

   ```php
   <?php
   ?>
   ```

2. Add the following class definition for the OnlineStore class to the script section:

   ```php
   class OnlineStore {
   }
   ```

3. Save the document as **class_OnlineStore.php** in the Chapter directory for Chapter 10.

4. Return to the **GosselinGourmetCoffee.php** script in your text editor.

5. Add the following statement to the PHP script section at the beginning of the file, beneath the require_once() statement for inc_OnlineStoreDB.php. This statement uses another

require_once() statement that makes the OnlineStore class available to the GosselinGourmetCoffee.php script.

```
require_once("class_OnlineStore.php");
```

6. Add the following statements beneath the statement that includes the OnlineStore class file. These statements instantiate an object of the OnlineStore class.

```
if (class_exists("OnlineStore")) {
    $Store = new OnlineStore();
}
else {
    $ErrorMsgs[] = "The OnlineStore class is not
                available!";
    $Store = NULL;
}
```

7. Add the following statements to the start of the PHP script section in the body of the document, immediately before the if statement that queries the database:

```
if ($Store !== NULL)
    echo "<p>Successfully instantiated an object of " .
        " the OnlineStore class.</p>\n";
```

8. Save the GosselinGourmetCoffee.php script and then upload both documents to the Web server.

9. Open the GosselinGourmetCoffee.php script in your Web browser by entering the following URL: *http://<yourserver>/ PHP_Projects/Chapter.10/Chapter/GosselinGourmetCoffee. php*. You should see the message shown in Figure 10-6.

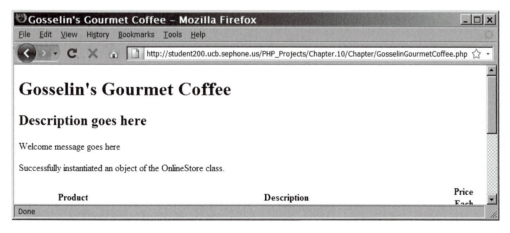

Figure 10-6   Gosselin's Gourmet Coffee Web page after instantiating an OnlineStore object

10. Close your Web browser window.

Collecting Garbage

If you have worked with other object-oriented programming languages, you might be familiar with the term **garbage collection**, which refers to cleaning up, or reclaiming, memory that is reserved by a program. When you declare a variable or instantiate a new object, you are actually reserving computer memory for the variable or object. With some programming languages, you must write code that deletes a variable or object after you finish with it. This frees the memory for use by other parts of your program or by other programs running on your computer. With PHP, you do not need to worry about reclaiming memory that is reserved for your variables or objects. Although you can manually remove a variable or object with the unset() function, there is usually no reason to do so—as with variables, PHP will automatically clean up unused memory when an object within a function goes out of scope, or at the end of the script for global objects. The one exception involves open database connections. As you learned in Chapter 8, because database connections can take up a lot of memory, you should explicitly close a database connection when you finish with it by calling the procedural mysql_close() function or the close() method of the mysqli class. This ensures that the connection doesn't keep taking up space in your computer's memory while the script finishes processing.

Short Quiz

1. Illustrate the syntax of instantiating an object.

2. What operator is used to access the methods and properties contained in an object?

3. What function of the mysqli object is used to determine if a database connection failed?

4. Illustrate the syntax used to define a PHP class.

5. Explain the term "garbage collection."

Declaring Data Members

In this section, you will learn how to declare data members within a class. Declaring and initializing data members is a little more involved than declaring and initializing standard PHP variables. To be able to declare data members, you must first understand the principle of information hiding, which you will study first.

What Is Information Hiding?

One of the fundamental principles in object-oriented programming is the concept of information hiding. Information hiding gives an encapsulated object its black box capabilities so that users of a class can see only the members of the class that you allow them to see. Essentially, the principle of **information hiding** states that class members should be hidden when other programmers (sometimes called clients) do not need to access or know about them. Information hiding helps minimize the amount of information that needs to pass in and out of an object. Information hiding also reduces the complexity of the code that clients see, allowing them to concentrate on the task of integrating an object into their programs. For example, if a client wants to add a `Payroll` object to an Accounting program, the client does not need to know the underlying details of the `Payroll` object's member functions, nor does the client need to modify any local data members that are used by those functions. The client only needs to know which of the object's member functions to call and what data (if any) needs to be passed to those member functions.

Now consider information hiding on a larger scale. Professionally developed software packages are distributed in an encapsulated format, which means that the casual user—or even an advanced programmer—cannot see the underlying details of how the software is developed. Imagine what would happen if Microsoft distributed Excel without hiding the underlying programming details. There is no need for users to see these details, because users do not need to understand how the underlying code performs the various spreadsheet calculations. Microsoft also has a critical interest in protecting proprietary information, as do you. The design and sale of software components is big business. You certainly do not want to spend a significant amount of time designing an outstanding software component, only to have unscrupulous programmers steal the code and claim it as their own. Of course, you cannot hide all of the underlying code, or other programmers will never be able to integrate your class with their applications. But you need to hide most of it.

Information hiding on any scale also prevents other programmers from accidentally introducing a bug into a program when modifying a class's internal workings. Well-intentioned programmers will often attempt to "improve" your code, no matter how well it is written. Before you distribute your classes to other programmers, your classes should be thoroughly tested and bug-free. Other programmers can thus focus on the more important task of integrating your code into their programs using the data members and member functions you designate.

To enable information hiding in your classes, you must designate access specifiers for each of your class members. You will learn about access specifiers next.

Using Access Specifiers

The first step in hiding class information is to set access specifiers for class members. **Access specifiers** control a client's access to individual data members and member functions. There are three levels of access specifiers in PHP: `public`, `private`, and `protected`. In this chapter, you will study the `public` and `private` access specifiers.

The **public access specifier** allows anyone to call the member function or to modify and retrieve the value of the data member. The **private access specifier** prevents clients from calling member functions or accessing data members, and is one of the key elements in information hiding. Private access does not restrict a class's internal access to its own members; a class's member function can modify any private data member or call any private member function. Private access restricts clients from accessing class members.

The protected access specifier is used with a more advanced object-oriented programming technique called inheritance.

Prior to PHP 5, the `var` keyword was used to declare class data members. If you use the `var` keyword to declare a data member in PHP 5, it is created with public access.

You include an access specifier at the beginning of a data member declaration statement. For example, the following statement declares a public data member named `$Balance` in the `BankAccount` class and initializes it with a value of 0:

```php
class BankAccount {
    public $Balance = 0;
}
```

It is common practice to list public class members first to clearly identify the parts of the class that can be accessed by clients.

It is considered good programming practice to always assign an initial value to a data member when you first declare it. The best way to initialize a data member is with a constructor function (discussed later in this chapter). You can also assign simple values to data members when you first declare them, although an error occurs if you attempt to use any type of expression to initialize the data member. The preceding statement is valid because it only assigns a value of 0 to the `$Balance` data member. However, the following statement is invalid because it attempts to use an expression (the addition operation) to assign a value to the `$Balance` data member:

```php
class BankAccount {
    public $Balance = 1 + 2;
}
```

Similarly, if you have a data member named `$CustomerName` in the `BankAccount` class, you can assign a simple text string to the data member as follows:

```
class BankAccount {
    public $CustomerName = "Don Gosselin";
}
```

In comparison, the following statement is invalid because it attempts to use an expression (the concatenation operation) to assign a value to the $CustomerName data member:

```
class BankAccount {
    public $CustomerName = "Don" . " " . "Gosselin";
}
```

Recall that to access a data member, you use member selection notation. Keep in mind that when you use member selection notation, you do not include a dollar sign before the data member name. For example, the following statements assign a new value to the $Balance data member and then display its value:

```
$Checking->Balance = 958.20;
printf("<p>Your checking account balance is $%.2f.</p>",
        $Checking->Balance);
```

PHP does not define a default access specifier for data members. If you attempt to declare a data member without an access specifier, an error occurs. For example, the data member declaration in the following class is invalid because it does not include an access specifier:

```
class BankAccount {
    $Balance = 0; // invalid
}
```

Next, you declare four data members, $DBConnect, $storeID, $inventory[], and $shoppingCart[], to the OnlineStore class. The $DBConnect data member stores the database connection details. The $storeID data member stores the ID of the current store. The $inventory[] array keeps track of the products in the store's inventory, and the $shoppingCart[] array keeps track of the amount of each item in a customer's shopping cart. The $inventory[] and $shoppingCart[] arrays both use the productID field from the inventory table of the online_store database as the element key. To adhere to the principles of information hiding, you must declare all of the data members as private. Later in this chapter, you will write member functions that access and manipulate the values in each array.

To add data members to the OnlineStore class:

1. Return to the **class_OnlineStore.php** script in your text editor.

2. Add the following private data member declarations to the class definition:

```
            private $DBConnect = NULL;
            private $storeID = "";
            private $inventory = array();
            private $shoppingCart = array();
```

3. Save the class_OnlineStore.php script.

Serializing Objects

In Chapter 9, you learned about PHP's various state preservation techniques, including how to use sessions. In addition to keeping track of current Web site visitors, session variables can store information that can be shared among multiple scripts that are called as part of the same session. But how do you share objects within the same session? You could assign the value of an object's data members to session variables, but you would need to instantiate a new object and reassign the session variable values to the data members each time you call a new script. However, this approach would be difficult if you have an object with dozens of data members. A better choice is to serialize the object between script calls within the same session. **Serialization** refers to the process of converting an object into a string that you can store for reuse. Serialization stores both data members and member functions into strings, which can be stored in text files and databases or passed to another script. To serialize an object, you pass an object name to the serialize() function. The following statement serializes the $Checking object and assigns the returned string to a variable named $SavedAccount:

```
$SavedAccount = serialize($Checking);
```

Serialization is also used to store the data in large arrays.

To convert serialized data back into an object, you use the unserialize() function. The following statement converts the serialized data in the $SavedAccount variable back into the $Checking object:

```
$Checking = unserialize($SavedAccount);
```

To use serialized objects between scripts, you assign a serialized object to a session variable. For example, the following statements serialize the $Checking object and assign the returned string to a variable named SavedAccount in the $_SESSION autoglobal:

Later in this chapter, you will learn how to use two special serialization methods, __sleep() and __wakeup(), in your classes.

```
session_start();
$_SESSION('SavedAccount') = serialize($Checking);
```

Converting a serialized value in a session variable is very similar to converting a serialized value in a standard variable. The following statement converts the serialized data in the SavedAccount session variable back into the $Checking object:

```
$Checking = unserialize($_SESSION('SavedAccount'));
```

To modify the GosselinGourmetCoffee.php script so it uses sessions to store serialized OnlineStore objects:

1. Return to the **GosselinGourmetCoffee.php** script in your text editor.

2. Add a session_start() statement to the first script section at the start of the file:

```php
<?php
session_start();
require_once("inc_OnlineStoreDB.php");
require_once("class_OnlineStore.php");
...
```

3. At the end of the first script section, replace the if...else statement that instantiates the $Store object with the following version, which calls the unserialize() function if the currentStore variable exists in the $_SESSION autoglobal:

```php
if (class_exists("OnlineStore")) {
    if (isset($_SESSION['currentStore']))
        $Store = unserialize($_SESSION['currentStore']);
    else
        $Store = new OnlineStore();
}
else {
    $ErrorMsgs[] = "The OnlineStore class is not
                    available!";
    $Store = NULL;
}
```

4. Add the following statement to the end of the else clause at the end of the second script section, just after the echo "</table>"; statement. This statement will serialize the $Store object into a variable named currentStore in the $_SESSION autoglobal:

```php
$_SESSION['currentStore'] = serialize($Store);
```

5. Save the GosselinGourmetCoffee.php script.

Short Quiz

1. Describe the concept of information hiding.

2. List the three levels of access specifiers in PHP.

3. Differentiate between a public access specifier and a private access specifier.

4. Explain why objects should be serialized.

5. Describe the steps used to pass a serialized object between scripts.

Working with Member Functions

Because member functions perform most of the work in a class, you will now learn about the various techniques associated with them. Member functions are usually declared as public, but they can also be declared as private. Public member functions can be called by anyone, whereas private member functions can be called only by other member functions in the same class.

You might wonder about the usefulness of a private member function, which cannot be accessed by a client of the program. Suppose your program needs some sort of utility function that clients have no need to access. For example, the BankAccount class might need to calculate interest by calling a function named calcInterest(). To use your program, the client does not need to access the calcInterest() function. By making the calcInterest() function private, you protect your program and add another level of information hiding. A general rule of thumb is to create public member functions for any functions that clients need to access and to create private member functions for any functions that clients do not need to access.

You declare a member function within the body of a class definition and include an access specifier before the function keyword. Other than including an access specifier, there is little difference between standard functions and member functions. Unlike data members, you are not required to define a member function with an access specifier. If you do exclude the access specifier, the member function's default access is public. However, it's good programming practice to include an access specifier with any member function definition to clearly identify the accessibility of the function. The following statement demonstrates how to declare a member function named withdrawal() in the BankAccount class:

```php
class BankAccount {
    public $Balance = 958.20;
    public function withdrawal($Amount) {
        $this->Balance -= $Amount;
    }
}
if (class_exists("BankAccount"))
    $Checking = new BankAccount();
```

```
else
     exit("<p>The BankAccount class is not available!</p>");
printf("<p>Your checking account balance is $%.2f.</p>",
     $Checking->Balance);
$Cash = 200;
$Checking->withdrawal(200);
printf("<p>After withdrawing $%.2f, your checking account
     balance is $%.2f.</p>", $Cash, $Checking->Balance);
```

The following version of the withdrawal() function raises an error because the statement within the function attempts to subtract a value from the undefined local variable named $Balance:

```
public function withdrawal($Amount) {
     $Balance -= $Amount;
}
```

Using the $this Reference

Within a class function, it is often necessary to refer to members of the object. Outside of the class, you refer to the members of the object using the name of the object, the member selection notation (->), and the name of the member function or variable. Within the class function definition, you cannot use the object name (no objects of the class are instantiated until after the class is defined). PHP provides a special reference, $this, to refer to the current object of the class. The $this reference uses member selection notation to access class members in the same way you use an instantiated object to refer to a data member. If you do not use the $this reference to refer to a data member from within a member function, PHP treats the data member as a variable that is local to the scope of the function.

Initializing with Constructor Functions

When you first instantiate an object from a class, you will often want to assign initial values to data members or perform other types of initialization tasks, such as calling a function member that might calculate and assign values to data members. Although you can assign simple values to data members when you declare them, a better choice is to use a constructor function. A **constructor function** is a special function that is called automatically when an object from a class is instantiated. You define and declare constructor functions the same way you define other functions, although you do not include a return type because constructor functions do not return values. Each class definition can contain its own constructor function, named either __construct() (with two leading underscore characters) or the same name as the class. PHP first searches for the __construct()

function within a class definition. You do not need to specify an access specifier with a constructor function, although if you do, you can only specify public access. The following code demonstrates how to use the __construct() function to initialize the data members in the BankAccount class (note the use of the $this reference):

```
class BankAccount {
    private $AccountNumber;
    private $CustomerName;
    private $Balance;
    function __construct() {
        $this->AccountNumber = 0;
        $this->Balance = 0;
        $this->CustomerName = "";
    }
}
```

The following code demonstrates how to create a constructor function using the same name as its class:

The __con-struct() function takes precedence over a function with the same name as the class.

```
class BankAccount {
    private $AccountNumber;
    private $CustomerName;
    private $Balance;
    function BankAccount() {
        $this->AccountNumber = 0;
        $this->Balance = 0;
        $this->CustomerName = "";
    }
}
```

For classes that use a database connection, constructor functions are commonly used in PHP to handle the database connection tasks.

To add a __construct() function to the OnlineStore class:

1. Return to the **class_OnlineStore.php** script in your text editor.

2. Add the following __construct() function definition to the end of the class declaration:

   ```
   function __construct() {
   }
   ```

3. Add the following statements to the __construct() function to instantiate a database object. Notice that the first statement uses the $this reference to refer to the $DBConnect data member that you declared earlier. The assignment statement copies the local $DBConnect variable, created in inc_OnlineStoreDB.php, to the object data member of the same name.

   ```
   include("inc_OnlineStoreDB.php");
   $this->DBConnect = $DBConnect;
   ```

4. Save the class_OnlineStore.php script.

5. Return to the **GosselinGourmetCoffee.php** script.

6. Delete the following line that requires inc_OnlineStoreDB.php. You no longer need the line because the OnlineStore class handles the database connection details.

```
require_once("inc_OnlineStoreDB.php");
```

7. Save the GosselinGourmetCoffee.php script.

Cleaning Up with Destructor Functions

Just as a default constructor function is called when a class object is first instantiated, a destructor function is called when the object is destroyed. A **destructor function** cleans up any resources allocated to an object after the object is destroyed. A destructor function is commonly called in two ways: when a script ends or when you manually delete an object with the unset() function. You generally do not need to use a destructor function, although many programmers use one to close previously opened file handles and database connections. To add a destructor function to a PHP class, create a function named __destruct() (with two leading underscore characters). The following code contains a destructor function that closes the database connection opened with the constructor function:

```
function __construct() {
    $DBConnect = new mysqli("php_db", "dongosselin",
        "rosebud", "real_estate")
}
function __destruct() {
    $DBConnect->close();
}
```

To add a __destruct() function to the OnlineStore class that closes the database object you instantiated with the __construct() function:

1. Return to the **class_OnlineStore.php** script in your text editor.

2. Add the following __destruct() function definition to the end of the class declaration:

```
function __destruct() {
}
```

3. Add the following statement to the __destruct() function to close the database object. Again, notice that the statement uses the $this reference to refer to the $DBConnect data member.

```
if (!$this->DBConnect->connect_error)
    $this->DBConnect->close();
```

4. Save the class_OnlineStore.php script.

5. Return to the **GosselinGourmetCoffee.php** script.

6. Delete the final PHP script section. You no longer need it because the OnlineStore class handles the database connection details.

```php
<?php
if (!$DBConnect->connect_error)
    $DBConnect->close();
?>
```

7. Save the GosselinGourmetCoffee.php script.

Writing Accessor and Mutator Functions

Even if you make all data members in a class private, you can still allow your program's clients to retrieve or modify the value of data members via accessor and mutator functions. **Accessor functions** are public member functions that a client can call to retrieve the value of a data member. Similarly, **mutator functions** are public member functions that a client can call to modify the value of a data member. Because accessor functions often begin with the word "set" and mutator functions often begin with "get," they are also called set or get functions, respectively. Set functions modify data member values; get functions retrieve data member values. To allow a client to pass a value to your program that will be assigned to a private data member, you include parameters in a set function's definition. You can then write code in the body of the set function that validates the data passed from the client, prior to assigning values to private data members. For example, if you write a class named Payroll that includes a private data member containing the current state income-tax rate, you could write a public accessor function named getStateTaxRate() that allows clients to retrieve the variable's value. Similarly, you could write a public mutator function named setStateTaxRate() that performs various types of validation on the data passed from the client (such as making sure the value is not null or not greater than 100%) prior to assigning a value to the private state tax rate data member.

Another term for accessor is **observer**, and another term for mutator is **transformer**.

Another use of the accessor and mutator functions is to hide any internal data conversion from the client. Your data member can only store a single value, such as length or amount. To store this value, you must use a particular measurement unit, such as feet or U.S. dollars. To store a value represented in different units, such as centimeters or Japanese yen, the client would normally have to do the conversion before setting the value or after getting it. With accessor and mutator functions, you simply provide alternate set and get member functions that hide the conversion from the client. For example, consider a Temperature class with a private data member temp, two public accessor functions named getTempF() and getTempC(), and two public mutator functions, setTempF() and setTempC(). Because the client can never see temp, the client cannot tell if the temperature is stored within the Temperature class in degrees Fahrenheit or degrees Celsius. It doesn't matter to the client, though, because the client can set or get the value using either unit.

The following code demonstrates how to use set and get member functions with the $Balance data member in the BankAccount class. The setBalance() function is declared with an access specifier of public and accepts a single parameter containing the value to assign to the $Balance data member. The getBalance() function is also declared as public and contains a single statement that returns the value assigned to the $Balance data member. Statements at the end of the example call the functions to set and get the $Balance data member.

```php
class BankAccount {
    private $Balance = 0;
    public function setBalance($NewValue) {
        $this->Balance = $NewValue;
    }
    public function getBalance() {
        return $this->Balance;
    }
}
if (class_exists("BankAccount"))
    $Checking = new BankAccount();
else
    exit("<p>The BankAccount class is not available!</p>");
$Checking->setBalance(100);
echo "<p>Your checking account balance is "
    . $Checking->getBalance() . "</p>\n";
```

Next, you add two mutator functions and two accessor functions to the OnlineStore class: setStoreID(), getStoreInformation(), getProductList(), and addItem(). The setStoreID() function assigns a value to the $storeID data member. The getStoreInformation() function queries the database and returns an array with the store information. The getProductList() function queries the database and displays a table with the product information. The addItem() function allows users to add items in the table to their shopping carts.

To add the four functions to the OnlineStore class:

1. Return to the **class_OnlineStore.php** script in your text editor.

2. Add the following setStoreID() function to the end of the class definition. The function stores the store ID and populates the $inventory[] array from the inventory table based on the store ID. At the same time, the $shoppingCart[] array is initialized. Notice that the data is only initialized if the new $storeID value is different from the current $storeID data member value, and that the new $storeID value is only kept if it matches a store ID in the inventory table.

```php
public function setStoreID($storeID) {
    if ($this->storeID != $storeID) {
        $this->storeID = $storeID;
        $SQLString = "SELECT * FROM inventory " .
            " where storeID = '" .
            $this->storeID . "'";
        $QueryResult = @$this->DBConnect->
        query($SQLString);
        if ($QueryResult === FALSE) {
            $this->storeID = "";
        }
        else {
            $this->inventory = array();
            $this->shoppingCart = array();
            while (($Row = $QueryResult->fetch_
            assoc())
                    !== NULL) {
                $this->inventory[$Row['productID']]
                    = array();
                $this->inventory[$Row['productID']]
                ['name']
                    = $Row['name'];
                $this->inventory[$Row['productID']]
                ['description']
                    = $Row['description'];
                $this->inventory[$Row['productID']]
                ['price']
                    = $Row['price'];
                $this->
                shoppingCart[$Row['productID']]
                = 0;
            }
        }
    }
}
```

3. Add the following getStoreInformation() function to the end of the class definition. If the $storeID data member is empty or there is a database error, the function returns FALSE.

```php
public function getStoreInformation() {
    $retval = FALSE;
    if ($this->storeID != "") {
        $SQLString = "SELECT * FROM store_info " .
                " where storeID = '" .
                $this->storeID . "'";
        $QueryResult = @$this->DBConnect->
        query($SQLString);
        if ($QueryResult !== FALSE) {
            $retval = $QueryResult->fetch_assoc();
        }
    }
    return($retval);
}
```

4. Add the following `getProductList()` function to the end of the class definition. This code is similar to the statements you added earlier to the GosselinGourmetCoffee.php script, except that this version adds an Add Item link to each row in the table that executes the `addItem()` function to add a product to the shopping cart. The statements that build the Add Item link append the session ID variable to the link to keep track of the current session if cookies are disabled on the user's Web browser. The link is also appended with the product ID of the current product and the type of operation, which other Web pages that utilize the class will use to determine which member function to call. This function will return TRUE for success or FALSE for failure.

```php
public function getProductList() {
    $retval = FALSE;
    $subtotal = 0;
    if (count($this->inventory) > 0) {
        echo "<table width='100%'>\n";
        echo "<tr><th>Product</
            th><th>Description</th>" .
            "<th>Price Each</th><th># in Cart</th>" .
            "<th>Total Price</th><th> </
            th></tr>\n";
        foreach ($this->inventory as $ID => $Info) {
            echo "<tr><td>" .
                htmlentities($Info['name'])
                . "</td>\n";
            echo "<td>" .
                htmlentities($Info['description']) .
                "</td>\n";
            printf("<td class='currency'>$%.2f
                </td>\n", $Info['price']);
            echo "<td class='currency'>" .
                $this->shoppingCart[$ID] .
                "</td>\n";
            printf("<td class='currency'>$%.2f
                </td>\n", $Info['price'] *
                $this->shoppingCart[$ID]);
```

```
               echo "<td><a href='" .
                    $_SERVER['SCRIPT_NAME'] .
                    "?PHPSESSID=" . session_id() .
                    "&ItemToAdd=$ID'>Add " .
                    " Item</a></td>\n";
               $subtotal += ($Info['price'] *
                    $this->shoppingCart[$ID]);
          }
          echo "<tr><td colspan='4'>Subtotal</td>\n";
          printf("<td class='currency'>$%.2f</td>\n",
               $subtotal);
          echo "<td> </td></tr>\n";
          echo "</table>";
          $retval = TRUE;
     }
     return($retval);
}
```

5. Add the following addItem() function to the end of the class definition. The first statement retrieves the product ID that was appended to the Add Item link in the getProductList() function you added in the last step. The second statement adds 1 to the count of that item in the $shoppingCart[] array.

```
public function addItem() {
     $ProdID = $_GET['ItemToAdd'];
     if (array_key_exists($ProdID, $this->
     shoppingCart))
          $this->shoppingCart[$ProdID] += 1;
}
```

6. Save the class_OnlineStore.php script.

To modify the GosselinGourmetCoffee.php script so that it calls the member functions you just added to the OnlineStore class:

1. Return to the **GosselinGourmetCoffee.php** script in your text editor.

2. Add the following variable declarations to the first script section, immediately after the require_once() call:

```
$storeID = "COFFEE";
$storeInfo = array();
```

3. Modify the nested if statement that creates the new OnlineStore object as follows:

```
if (class_exists("OnlineStore")) {
     if (isset($_SESSION['currentStore']))
          $Store = unserialize($_
          SESSION['currentStore']);
     else {
          $Store = new OnlineStore();
     }
```

```
        $Store->setStoreID($storeID);
        $storeInfo = $Store->getStoreInformation();
    }
    else {
        $ErrorMsgs[] = "The OnlineStore class is not
                available!";
        $Store = NULL;
    }
```

 Be sure to add curly braces around the statements in the nested if statement.

4. Modify the `<title>` tag as follows to display the store name:

    ```
    <title><?php echo $storeInfo['name']; ?></title>
    ```

5. Add the following `<link>` tag immediately after the `<title>` tag to include the style sheet for this store:

    ```
    <link rel="stylesheet" type="text/css" href="<?php echo
            $storeInfo['css_file']; ?>" />
    ```

6. Modify the first three statements in the body of the document as follows to display the store information:

    ```
    <h1><?php echo htmlentities($storeInfo['name']); ?></h1>
    <h2><?php echo htmlentities($storeInfo['description']);
    ?></h2>
    <p><?php echo htmlentities($storeInfo['welcome']); ?></p>
    ```

7. Replace the entire PHP script section below the previous three lines with the following PHP script section that shows the inventory in a table and sets the session variable:

    ```
    <?php
        $Store->getProductList();
        $_SESSION['currentStore'] = serialize($Store);
    ?>
    ```

8. Save the GosselinGourmetCoffee.php script and then upload it to the Web server.

9. Open the GosselinGourmetCoffee.php script in your Web browser by entering the following URL: *http://<yourserver>/ PHP_Projects/Chapter.10/Chapter/GosselinGourmetCoffee. php.* Your Web browser should look similar to Figure 10-7. Do not click any of the links or reload the Web page. If you do, you will receive error messages because you still need to add several other functions to the OnlineStore class.

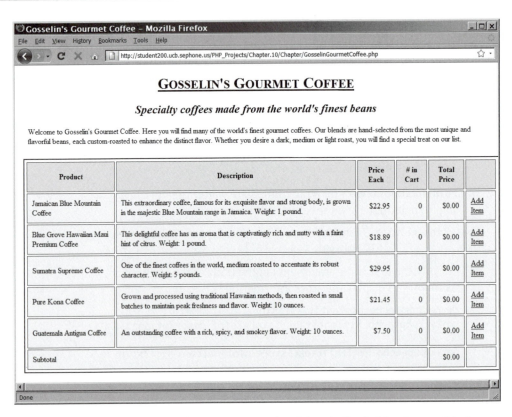

Figure 10-7   Web page after adding accessors and mutators to the `OnlineStore` object

10.   Close your Web browser window.

Serialization Functions

When you serialize an object with the `serialize()` function, PHP looks in the object's class for a special function named `__sleep()` (with two leading underscores), which you can use to perform many of the same tasks as a destructor function. However, because a destructor function is always called when a script that instantiates an object of a class ends, you do not need to duplicate any functionality between a destructor function and the `__sleep()` function. The primary reason for including a `__sleep()` function in a class is to specify which data members of the class to serialize. If you do not include a `__sleep()` function in your class, the `serialize()` function serializes all of its data members.

You don't necessarily have to serialize every data member in a class, particularly for large objects that contain numerous data members. If you do include a `__sleep()` function in your class, the function must return an array of the data members to serialize or you will receive an error. For example, the following code demonstrates how to use a __sleep() function to serialize only the $Balance data member in the BankAccount class. Notice how the name 'Balance', not the $Balance data member, is passed to the array constructor: It does not include the $this reference or a dollar sign. Instead, you simply pass the name of the data member, without the leading dollar sign, surrounded by either single or double quotation marks.

```
function __sleep() {
    $SerialVars = array('Balance');
    return $SerialVars;
}
```

Although the destructor function is always called, a constructor function is only called when you instantiate a new class object. This means that when you use the unserialize() function to restore a serialized class object, the constructor function does not execute. However, when the unserialize() function executes, PHP looks in the object's class for a special function named __wakeup() (with two leading underscore characters), which you can use to perform many of the same tasks as a constructor function. You use the __wakeup() function to perform any initialization the class requires when the object is restored. A typical use of the __wakeup() function is to initialize data members that were not saved with the serialization process, if there are any. Another use of the __wakeup() function is to restore any database or file connections that were lost during object serialization.

To add a __wakeup() function to the OnlineStore class that restores the connection to the online_store database when an object is restored with the unserialize() function:

1. Return to the **class_OnlineStore.php** script in your text editor.

2. Add the following __wakeup() function definition to the end of the class declaration:

   ```
   function __wakeup() {
   }
   ```

3. Add the following statements to the __wakeup() function to restore the database connection:

   ```
   include("inc_OnlineStoreDB.php");
   $this->DBConnect = $DBConnect;
   ```

4. Save the class_OnlineStore.php script and upload it to the Web server.

To modify the GosselinGourmetCoffee.php script so it will add an item to the cart when the visitor clicks the Add Item link:

1. Return to the **GosselinGourmetCoffee.php** script in your text editor.

2. Add the following if statement after the call to the getStoreInformation() member function in the first script section. The if statement checks for the $_GET['ItemToAdd'] variable. If it is set, the addItem() method of the $Store object executes. (You will add more operations in the Reinforcement Exercises section later in this chapter.)

   ```
   if (isset($_GET['ItemToAdd']))
       $Store->addItem();
   ```

   The complete if clause should look like the following code:

   ```
   if (class_exists("OnlineStore")) {
       if (isset($_SESSION['currentStore']))
           $Store = unserialize($_
           SESSION['currentStore']);
       else {
           $Store = new OnlineStore();
       }
       $Store->setStoreID($storeID);
       $storeInfo = $Store->getStoreInformation();
       if (isset($_GET['ItemToAdd']))
           $Store->addItem();
   }
   ```

3. Save the GosselinGourmetCoffee.php script and upload it to the Web server.

4. Open the GosselinGourmetCoffee.php script in your Web browser by entering the following URL: *http://<yourserver>/ PHP_Projects/Chapter.10/Chapter/GosselinGourmetCoffee. php*. Click the Add Item links for the various coffees. Your Web browser should look similar to Figure 10-8, with updated item amounts, prices, and subtotal values.

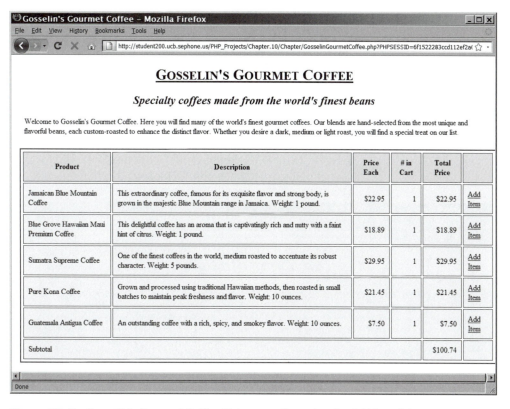

Figure 10-8 Gosselin's Gourmet Coffee Web page after using the Add Item links

5. Close your Web browser window.

In studying the various class techniques presented in this chapter, you might have forgotten that the goal of object-oriented programs is code reuse. Now that you have developed the OnlineStore class, you will see how easy it is to reuse the code on other Web pages by creating the OldTymeAntiques.php and ElectronicsBoutique.php scripts.

To create the OldTymeAntiques.php and ElectronicsBoutique.php scripts:

1. Return to the **GosselinGourmetCoffee.php** script in your text editor and immediately save it as **OldTymeAntiques.php**.

2. Change the assignment of the $storeID variable as follows:

   ```
   $storeID = "ANTIQUE";
   ```

3. Save the OldTymeAntiques.php script and then immediately save it as **ElectronicsBoutique.php.**

4. Change the assignment of the $storeID variable as follows:

   ```
   $storeID = "ELECBOUT";
   ```

5. Save the ElectronicsBoutique.php script and close it in your text editor.

6. Open the OldTymeAntiques.php script in your Web browser by entering the following URL: *http://<yourserver>/PHP_Projects/Chapter.10/Chapter/OldTymeAntiques.php*. Notice how the entire appearance of the page has changed, as well as the items available for sale. Figure 10-9 shows the Old Tyme Antiques Web page. Click the Add Item links for the different items. Everything should work just like it did for the GosselinGourmetCoffee.php Web page.

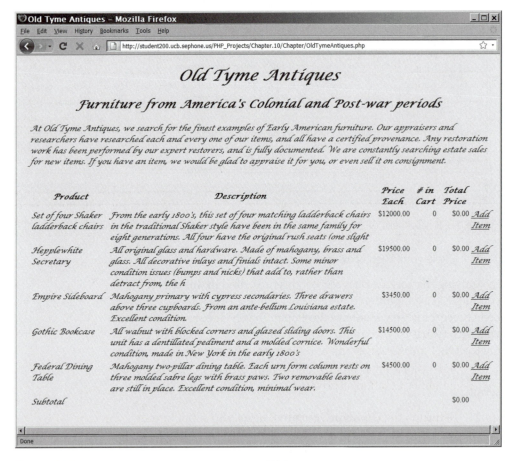

Figure 10-9 The Old Tyme Antiques online store Web page

7. Open the ElectronicsBoutique.php script in your Web browser by entering the following URL: *http://<yourserver>/PHP_Projects/Chapter.10/Chapter/ElectronicsBoutique.php*. Notice how the appearance of the page and the items available for sale have changed again.

Figure 10-10 shows the Electronics Boutique Web page. Click the Add Item links for the different items. Everything should work normally for this site.

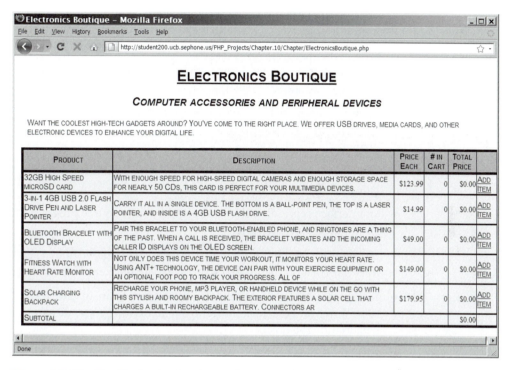

Figure 10-10   The Electronics Boutique online store Web page

8. Close your Web browser window.

Short Quiz

1. Describe a situation in which you might want to declare a member function as private.

2. Explain the purpose of the $this reference.

3. What two names may be assigned to a constructor function?

4. Describe the purpose of a destructor function.

5. Describe the purpose of accessors and mutators.

Summing Up

- The term "object-oriented programming" (OOP) refers to the creation of reusable software objects that can be easily incorporated into multiple programs. The term "object" specifically refers to programming code and data that can be treated as an individual unit or component. (Objects are often called components.)

- The term "data" refers to information contained within variables or other types of storage structures.

- The functions associated with an object are called methods, and the variables associated with an object are called properties or attributes.

- Objects are encapsulated, which means that all code and required data are contained within the object itself.

- An interface represents elements required for a source program to communicate with an object.

- In object-oriented programming, the code, methods, attributes, and other information that make up an object are organized into classes.

- An instance is an object that has been created from an existing class. When you create an object from an existing class, you are instantiating the object.

- A particular instance of an object inherits its methods and properties from a class—that is, it takes on the characteristics of the class on which it is based.

- A constructor is a special function with the same name as its class; it is called automatically when an object from the class is instantiated.

- The term "data structure" refers to a system for organizing data.

- The functions and variables defined in a class are called class members. Class variables are referred to as data members or member variables, whereas class functions are referred to as member functions or function members.

- A class definition contains the data members and member functions that make up the class.

- PHP provides the following functions that allow you to use external files in your PHP scripts: include(), require(), include_once(), and require_once().

- The principle of information hiding states that class members should be hidden when other programmers do not need to access or know about them.

- Access specifiers control a client's access to individual data members and member functions.

- Serialization refers to the process of converting an object into a string that you can store for reuse.

- A constructor function is a special function that is called automatically when an object from a class is instantiated.

- A destructor function cleans up any resources allocated to an object after the object is destroyed.

- Accessor functions are public member functions that a client can call to retrieve the value of a data member.

- Mutator functions are public member functions that a client can call to modify the value of a data member.

- When you serialize an object with the serialize() function, PHP looks in the object's class for a special function named __sleep(), which you can use to perform many of the same tasks as a destructor function.

- When the unserialize() function executes, PHP looks in the object's class for a special function named __wakeup(), which you can use to perform many of the same tasks as a constructor function.

Comprehension Check

1. Reusable software objects are often referred to as
    _____.

    a. methods

    b. components

    c. widgets

    d. functions

2. Explain the benefits of object-oriented programming.

3. The functions associated with an object are called
    _____.

    a. properties

    b. fields

    c. methods

    d. attributes

4. The term "black box" refers to _____.

    a. a property

    b. debugging

    c. encapsulation

    d. an interface

5. A(n) _____ is an object that has been created from an existing class.

    a. pattern

    b. structure

    c. replica

    d. instance

6. An object inherits its characteristics from a class. True or False?

7. A function that is used as the basis for an object is called a(n) _____.

    a. method

    b. class

    c. class constructor

    d. object variable

8. Which of the following operators is used in member selection notation?

    a. >

    b. ->

    c. =>

    d. .

9. What is the correct syntax to connect to the MySQL database server using a `mysqli` object?

    a. `$Variable = mysqli_connect("host", "user", "password", "database_name");`

    b. `$Variable = new mysqli_connect("host", "user", "password", "database_name");`

c. `$Variable = mysqli("host", "user", "password", "database_name");`

d. `$Variable = new mysqli("host", "user", "password", "database_name");`

10. Explain how to handle a MySQL connection error using a `mysqli` object.

11. The terms "variable" and "object" are often used interchangeably in object-oriented programming. True or False?

12. Class names usually begin with a(n) _____ to distinguish them from other identifiers.

    a. number

    b. exclamation mark (!)

    c. ampersand (&)

    d. uppercase letter

13. Which of the following functions returns the name of the class upon which an object is based?

    a. `class_of()`

    b. `instanceof()`

    c. `class_name()`

    d. `get_class()`

14. What extension should you use for external PHP scripts, and why?

15. Explain the principle of information hiding.

16. Which of the following access specifiers prevents clients from calling member functions or accessing data members?

    a. `internal`

    b. `public`

    c. `private`

    d. `privileged`

604

17. Which of the following is a valid name for a constructor function?

    a. `construct()`

    b. `__construct()`

    c. `constructor()`

    d. `__constructor()`

18. When is a destructor called? (Choose all that apply.)

    a. when a script ends

    b. when the constructor function ends

    c. when you delete a class object with the `unset()` function

    d. when you call the `serialize()` function

19. Explain the use of accessor and mutator functions. How are accessor functions often named? How are mutator functions often named?

20. When serializing objects, how do you specify which data members to serialize?

Reinforcement Exercises

 Exercise 10-1

In this project, you will add two member functions, `removeItem()` and `emptyCart()`, to the `OnlineStore` class. These functions allow you to remove individual items or all items from the shopping cart.

To add the `removeItem()` and `emptyCart()` member functions to the `OnlineStore` class:

1. In your text editor, open the **class_OnlineStore.php** script from your Chapter directory for Chapter 10.

2. Add the following `removeItem()` function definition to the end of the class definition. The statements use the `$_GET['ItemToRemove']` variable to identify the item. If the item is found and the value in the `$shoppingCart[]` array data member for that item is greater than 0, subtract 1 from the `$shoppingCart[]` array element.

```
private function removeItem() {
    $ProdID = $_GET['ItemToRemove'];
    if (array_key_exists($ProdID, $this->
    shoppingCart))
        if ($this->shoppingCart[$ProdID]>0)
            $this->shoppingCart[$ProdID] -= 1;
}
```

3. Add the following emptyCart() function definition to the end of the class declaration. The statements empty the cart by setting the value of all of the elements of the $shoppingCart[] array data member to 0.

```
private function emptyCart() {
    foreach ($this->shoppingCart as $key => $value)
        $this->shoppingCart[$key] = 0;
}
```

4. Add the following processUserInput() function definition to the end of the class declaration. The statements call the appropriate member function based on elements found in the $_GET[] array.

```
public function processUserInput() {
    if (!empty($_GET['ItemToAdd']))
        $this->addItem();
    if (!empty($_GET['ItemToRemove']))
        $this->removeItem();
    if (!empty($_GET['EmptyCart']))
        $this->emptyCart();
}
```

5. Modify the declaration of the addItem() function to change it from public to private, as follows:

private function addItem() {

6. Next, you need to modify the getProductList() member function so that it displays links that call the removeItem() and emptyCart() functions. First, find and remove the following statement from the foreach loop:

```
echo "<td><a href='" .
    $_SERVER['SCRIPT_NAME'] .
    "?PHPSESSID=" . session_id() .
    "&ItemToAdd=$ID'>Add " .
    " Item</a></td>\n";
```

7. Replace the echo statement removed above with the following pair of echo statements:

```
echo "<td><a href='" .
     $_SERVER['SCRIPT_NAME'] .
     "?PHPSESSID=" . session_id() .
     "&ItemToAdd=$ID'>Add " .
     " Item</a><br />\n";
echo "<a href='" . $_SERVER['SCRIPT_
NAME'] .
     "?PHPSESSID=" . session_id() .
     "&ItemToRemove=$ID'>Remove " .
     " Item</a></td>\n";
```

8. Modify the echo statement immediately before the echo statement that displays the closing `</table>` tag (the one with the ` ` element within `<td>` tags) to read as follows:

```
echo "<td><a href='" .
     $_SERVER['SCRIPT_NAME'] .
     "?PHPSESSID=" . session_id() .
     "&EmptyCart=TRUE'>Empty " .
     " Cart</a></td></tr>\n";
```

9. Save the class_OnlineStore.php script.

10. Open the **GosselinGourmetCoffee.php** file. Remove the following statement:

```
if (isset($_GET['ItemToAdd']))
     $Store->addItem();
```

11. Replace the statement you just deleted with the following statement:

```
$Store->processUserInput();
```

12. Save and close the GosselinGourmetCoffee.php file.

13. Repeat Steps 10 through 12 for both the **OldTymeAntiques.php** file and the **ElectronicsBoutique.php** file.

14. Upload all four files (class_OnlineStore.php, GosselinGourmetCoffee.php, OldTymeAntiques.php, and ElectronicsBoutique.php) to the Web server.

15. Open the GosselinGourmetCoffee.php script in your Web browser by entering the following URL: *http://<yourserver>/ PHP_Projects/Chapter.10/Chapter/GosselinGourmetCoffee. php*. Click the Remove Item link for various products to verify that you cannot remove an item that hasn't been entered. Click the Add Item link to add items, and then click the Remove Item link for those items to verify that the count is reduced. Finally, click the Empty Cart link to verify that the count for all of the items goes to 0. Figure 10-11 shows the

Gosselin's Gourmet Coffee Web page after adding the remove item and empty cart functionality.

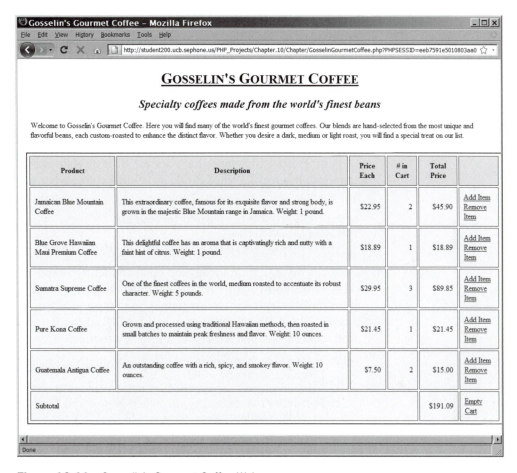

Figure 10-11   Gosselin's Gourmet Coffee Web page

16.   Close your Web browser window.

 Exercise 10-2

In this project, you will add a `checkout()` function to the `OnlineStore` class that allows customers to check out by saving order information to a database table. For the sake of simplicity, the `checkout()` function does not record customer information, although it does use the session ID to uniquely identify each order.

To add a `checkout()` function to the `OnlineStore` class:

1. Log in to MySQL Monitor with the MySQL user name and password you created in Chapter 7.

2. Enter the following command to select the `online_stores` database:

```
mysql> USE online_stores;[ENTER↵]
```

3. Enter the following command to create a table named `orders`, which will contain each shopping cart order. The table consists of three columns: `orderID`, `productID`, and `quantity`. Remember from Chapter 9 that a session ID is 32 characters, and that a product ID was defined as 10 characters earlier in this chapter in the `inventory` table.

```
mysql> CREATE TABLE orders (productID
VARCHAR(10),[ENTER↵]
     -> orderID VARCHAR(32), quantity INT);[ENTER↵]
```

4. Leave the MySQL Monitor session open and return to the **class_OnlineStore.php** script in your text editor. Add the following `checkout()` function definition to the end of the class definition. The `foreach` loop builds a SQL string for each product in the shopping cart and inserts it into the database.

```php
public function checkout() {
    $ProductsOrdered = 0;
    foreach($this->shoppingCart as $productID =>
    $quantity) {
        if ($quantity > 0) {
            ++$ProductsOrdered;
            $SQLstring = "INSERT INTO orders " .
                " (orderID, productID, quantity) " .
                " VALUES('" . session_id() . "', " .
                "'$productID', $quantity)";
            $QueryResult =
                $this->DBConnect->
                query($SQLstring);
        }
    }
    echo "<p><strong>Your order has been " .
        "recorded.</strong></p>\n";
}
```

If this were a checkout form for a real online store, code would need to be added to ensure that only one order was placed for a single session value. For simplicity, that step is omitted in this example.

5. In the `getProductList()` member function, immediately after the `echo` statement for the closing `</table>` tag, insert the following `echo` statement:

```php
echo "<p><a href=' 'Checkout.php?PHPSESSID=" .
    session_id() . "&CheckOut=$storeID'>Checkout</
    a></p>\n";
```

6. Save the class_OnlineStore.php script.

 Exercise 10-3

In this project, you will create a script named Checkout.php that calls the checkout() function you created in Exercise 10-2.

To create the Checkout.php script:

1. Create a new document in your text editor and type the <!DOCTYPE> declaration, <html> element, header informa- tion, and <body> element. Use the strict DTD and leave the <title> element empty for now.

2. Add the following PHP script section to the start of the docu- ment, above the <!DOCTYPE> tag:

```php
<?php
session_start();
require_once("class_OnlineStore.php");
$storeID = $_GET['CheckOut'];
$storeInfo = array();
if (class_exists("OnlineStore")) {
    if (isset($_SESSION['currentStore']))
        $Store = unserialize($_
        SESSION['currentStore']);
    else {
        $Store = new OnlineStore();
    }
    $Store->setStoreID($storeID);
    $storeInfo = $Store->getStoreInformation();
}
else {
    $ErrorMsgs[] = "The OnlineStore class is not
                    available!";
    $Store = NULL;
}
?>
```

3. Modify the <title> tag as follows to display the store name:

```
<title><?php echo $storeInfo['name']; ?> Checkout</
title>
```

4. Add the following <link> tag immediately after the <title> tag to include the style sheet for this store:

```
<link rel="stylesheet" type="text/css" href="<?php
echo
        $storeInfo['css_file']; ?>" />
```

5. Add the following statements in the body of the document to display the store information:

```
<h1><?php echo htmlentities($storeInfo['name']);
?></h1>
<h2>Checkout</h2>
```

6. Add the following PHP script section to the end of the document body. The statement in the script section calls the checkout() method.

```
<?php
$Store->checkout();
?>
```

7. Save the document as **Checkout.php** in the Chapter directory for Chapter 10 and then upload both Checkout.php and class_OnlineStore.php to the Web server.

8. Open the **GosselinGourmetCoffee.php** script in your Web browser by entering the following URL: *http://<yourserver>/PHP_Projects/Chapter.10/Chapter/GosselinGourmetCoffee.php*. Use the shopping category links to add several products to your shopping cart, and then click the Checkout link on the Your Shopping Cart page. You should see the message confirming your order.

9. Close your Web browser window.

10. Return to MySQL Monitor in your console window and enter the following command. The products you entered should appear in the database table.

    mysql> **SELECT * FROM orders;[ENTER⏎]**

11. Type **exit** or **quit** and press **Enter** to log out of MySQL Monitor.

 Exercise 10-4

Create a Movies class that determines the cost of a ticket to a cinema, based on the moviegoer's age. Assume that the cost of a full-price ticket is $10. Assign the age to a private data member. Use a public member function to determine the ticket price, based on the following schedule:

Age	Price
Under 5	Free
5 to 17	Half price
18 to 55	Full price
Over 55	$2 off

Exercise 10-5

Write a class-based All-in-One Web form that calculates the correct amount of change to return when performing a cash transaction. The script should have an include file that defines a class named Change. Allow the user (a cashier) to enter the cost of a transaction and the exact amount of money that the customer hands over to pay for the transaction. Use set and get functions to store and retrieve both amounts to and from private data members. Then use member functions to determine the largest amount of each denomination to return to the customer. Assume that the largest denomination a customer will use is a $100 bill. Therefore, you need to calculate the correct amount of change to return, the number of $50, $20, $10, $5, and $1 bills to return, and the number of quarters, dimes, nickels, and pennies to return. For example, if the price of a transaction is $5.65 and the customer hands the cashier $10, the cashier should return $4.35 to the customer as four $1 bills, a quarter, and a dime. Include code that requires the user to enter a numeric value for the two cash transaction fields.

Discovery Projects

The Chinese Zodiac site is a comprehensive project that you have updated in the Discovery Projects in each chapter. All files for the Chinese Zodiac site are saved in a folder named ChineseZodiac in the root Web folder on the server, and all database tables are stored in the chinese_zodiac database.

Discovery Project 10-1

In this project, you will create an event_calendar table in MySQL to store an event calendar, and an EventCalendar class for manipulating the event_calendar table. In later projects, you will create Web pages to add and delete events, and to display the calendar. For the sake of simplicity, the ability to add and remove events will not be restricted, and the events will consist of only a date, a title, and a description.

To create the EventCalendar class and the MySQL event_calendar table:

1. Log in to MySQL Monitor with the MySQL user name and password you created in Chapter 7.

2. Enter the following command to select the chinese_zodiac database:

    ```
    mysql> USE chinese_zodiac;[ENTER←]
    ```

3. Enter the following command to create a table named event_calendar, which will contain each calendar event. The table consists of four columns: EventID, EventDate, Title, and Description. The EventID field is an auto-incrementing primary key. The EventDate field is of type DATE, and Title and Description are both VARCHAR fields.

    ```
    mysql> CREATE TABLE event_calendar (EventID
    INT[ENTER←]
        -> AUTO_INCREMENT PRIMARY KEY, EventDate
    DATE,[ENTER←]
        -> Title VARCHAR(50), Description
    VARCHAR(250));[ENTER←]
    ```

4. Type **exit** or **quit** and press **Enter** to log out of MySQL Monitor.

5. Create a new document in your text editor and add a PHP script section, as follows:

    ```
    <?php
    ?>
    ```

6. Add the following code to connect to the chinese_zodiac database on the MySQL server. Replace *host*, *user*, and *password* with the name of the MySQL server and the user name and password you created in Chapter 7.

    ```
    $ErrorMsgs = array();
    $DBConnect = @new mysqli("host", "user", "password",
        "chinese_zodiac");
    if ($DBConnect->connect_error)
        $ErrorMsgs[] = "The database server is not
        available. " .
                        "Connect Error is " . $mysqli->
                        connect_errno .
                        " " . $mysqli->connect_error . ".";
    ```

7. Save the document as **inc_ChineseZodiacDB.php** in the Includes subfolder of the ChineseZodiac folder.

8. Create a new document in your text editor and add a PHP script section, as follows:

    ```
    <?php
    ?>
    ```

9. Add the following class definition for the `EventCalendar` class to the script section:

```
class EventCalendar {
}
```

10. Add the following statement to the start of the class definition to declare the private data member `$DBConnect`:

```
private $DBConnect = NULL;
```

11. Add the following `__construct()` function to the end of the class definition:

```
function __construct() {
    include("Includes/inc_ChineseZodiacDB.php");
    $this->DBConnect = $DBConnect;
}
```

12. Add the following `__destruct()` function to the end of the class definition:

```
function __destruct() {
    if (!$this->DBConnect->connect_error)
        $this->DBConnect->close();
}
```

13. Add the following `__wakeup()` function to the end of the class definition:

```
function __wakeup() {
    include("Includes/inc_ChineseZodiacDB.php");
    $this->DBConnect = $DBConnect;
}
```

14. Save the document as **class_EventCalendar.php** in the ChineseZodiac folder.

 ## Discovery Project 10-2

In this project, you will create a Web page to add events to the Chinese zodiac event calendar. You will also add a member function to the `EventCalendar` class that will add the new event to the `event_calendar` table in the database.

To create the Web page to add events to the calendar using the `EventCalendar` class:

1. Reopen the **class_EventCalendar.php** file in the text editor.

2. Add the following `addEvent()` function to the end of the class definition. Notice that, although the `$Date` and `$Title`

parameters cannot be empty, the $Description parameter can be empty.

```php
public function addEvent($Date, $Title,
$Description) {
    if ((!empty($Date)) && (!empty($Title))) {
        $SQLstring = "INSERT INTO event_calendar" .
            " (EventDate, Title, Description) " .
            " VALUES('$Date', '$Title', '" .
            $Description . "')";
        $QueryResult =
            $this->DBConnect->query($SQLstring);
        if ($QueryResult === FALSE)
            echo "<p>Unable to save the event. " .
                "Error code " . $this->
                DBConnect->errno .
                ": " . $this->DBConnect->error
                . "</p>\n";
        else
            echo "<p>The event was successfully
                saved.</p>\n";
    }
    else
        echo "<p>You must provide a date and title
            for the event.</p>\n";
}
```

3. Save class_EventCalendar.php and close it in the text editor.

4. Create a new document in your text editor and type the <!DOCTYPE> declaration, <html> element, header information, and <body> element. Use the strict DTD and "Add Calendar Event" as the content of the <title> element.

5. Add the following PHP script section to the beginning of the document, above the <!DOCTYPE> declaration, to create or retrieve an EventCalendar object:

```php
<?php
session_start();
require_once("class_EventCalendar.php");
if (class_exists("EventCalendar")) {
    if (isset($_SESSION['currentCalendar']))
        $Calendar = unserialize($_
        SESSION['currentCalendar']);
    else {
        $Calendar = new EventCalendar ();
    }
}
else {
    $Calendar = NULL;
}
?>
```

6. Add the following statements and PHP code section to the body of the document:

```php
<h1>Add Calendar Event</h1>
<?php
    if (isset($_POST['EventDate']) &&
            isset($_POST['EventTitle']) &&
            isset($_POST['EventDesc'])) {
        if ($Calendar === NULL)
            echo "<p>There was an error " .
                creating the EventCalendar" .
                object.</p>\n";
        else
            $Calendar->addEvent(
                stripslashes($_POST['EventDate']),
                stripslashes($_POST['EventTitle']),
                stripslashes($_POST['EventDesc']));
            $_SESSION('currentCalendar') =
            serialize($Calendar);
    }
?>
```

7. Add the following Web form to the end of the document body to allow user input of the event information:

```html
<form action="AddCalendarEvent.php?PHPSESSID=<?php
echo
    session_id(); ?>" method="POST">
    <p>Date (yyyy-mm-dd): <input type="text"
        name="EventDate" /> (required)</p>
    <p>Title: <input type="text"
        name="EventTitle" /> (required)</p>
    <p>Title: <input type="text"
        name="EventDesc" /> (optional)</p>
    <p><input type="submit" name="submit"
        value="Save Event" /></p>
</form>
```

8. Add the following link to the end of the document body to allow users to visit the events calendar:

```html
<a href="EventCalendar.php?PHPSESSID=<?php echo
    session_id(); ?>">View the event calendar</a>
```

9. Save the document as **AddCalendarEvent.php** in the ChineseZodiac folder and upload the document to the Web server.

 Discovery Project 10-3

In this project, you will create a Web page to display the Chinese zodiac event calendar in a monthly calendar format. For each day with events, you will display the event title as a hyperlink to an "Event

Details" page, which you will create in Discovery Project 10-4. You will also add a member function to the EventCalendar class that will display the events from the event_calendar table in the database for a specified month.

To create the Web page to display a monthly event calendar using the EventCalendar class:

1. Reopen the **class_EventCalendar.php** file in the text editor.

2. Add the following getMonthlyCalendar() function to the end of the class definition, which has parameters for the desired month and year. Notice that if the $Year or $Month parameters are empty, the current year or month is retrieved using the date() function.

```php
public function getMonthlyCalendar($Year, $Month) {
    if (empty($Year))
        $Year = date('Y'); // Four digit year
    if (empty($Month))
        $Month = date('n'); // Month number, no
                            // leading 0
    $FirstDay = mktime(0,0,0,$Month,1,$Year);
    $FirstDOW = date('w',$FirstDay); // Day of week
    $LeapYearFlag = date('L',$FirstDay); // 1=Leap
                            // Year, 0=Not
    $MonthName = date('F',$FirstDay); // Month name
    if ($Month == 2)
        $LastDay = 28 + $LeapYearFlag;
    else if (($Month == 4) || ($Month == 6) ||
            ($Month == 9) || ($Month == 11))
        $LastDay = 30;
    else
        $LastDay = 31;
    echo "<table>\n";
    // Create the calendar heading
    echo "<tr><td><a href='" . $_SERVER['SCRIPT_NAME'] .
        "?PHPSESSID=" . session_id() . "&Year=" .
        ($Year - 1) .
        "&Month=$Month'>Previous Year</a></td>\n";
    if ($Month==1)
        echo "<td><a href='" . $_SERVER['SCRIPT_
            NAME'] .
            "?PHPSESSID=" . session_id() . "&Year=" .
            ($Year - 1) . "&Month=12'>Previous " .
            "Month</a></td>\n";
    else
        echo "<td><a href='" . $_SERVER['SCRIPT_
            NAME'] .
            "?PHPSESSID=" . session_id() .
            "&Year=$Year" .
            "&Month=" . ($Month - 1) . "'>Previous " .
            "Month</a></td>\n";
```

```
echo "<td colspan='3'>$MonthName $Year</td>\n";
if ($Month==12)
    echo "<td><a href='" . $_SERVER['SCRIPT_
        NAME'] .
        "?PHPSESSID=" . session_id() . "&Year=" .
        ($Year + 1) . "&Month=1'>Next " .
        "Month</a></td>\n";
else
    echo "<td><a href='" . $_SERVER['SCRIPT_
        NAME'] .
        "?PHPSESSID=" . session_id() .
        "&Year=$Year" .
        "&Month=" . ($Month + 1) . "'>Next " .
        "Month</a></td>\n";
echo "<td><a href='" . $_SERVER['SCRIPT_NAME'] .
        "?PHPSESSID=" . session_id() .
        "&Year=" . ($Year - 1) .
        "&Month=$Month'>Previous Year</a></
        td></tr>\n";
echo "<tr>";
// insert empty cells for days from Sunday to
// the first day
for ($i = 0; $i < $FirstDOW; ++$i)
    echo "<td> </td>";
for ($i = 1; $i <= $LastDay; ++$i) {
    if ((($FirstDOW + $i) % 7) == 1)
        echo "<tr>";
    echo "<td valign='top'>$i";
    $SQLstring = "SELECT EventID, Title " .
            " FROM event_calendar " .
            " WHERE EventDate='$Year-$Month-
            $i'";
    $QueryResult = @$this->DBConnect->
            query($SQLstring);
    if ($QueryResult !== FALSE) {
        if ($QueryResult->num_rows > 0) {
            while (($Row = $QueryResult->
            fetch_assoc()) !== NULL)
            echo "<br /><a
                href='EventDetails.php?"
                . "PHPSESSID=" .
                session_id() .
                "&EventID=" .
                $Row['EventID'] .
                "'>" .
                htmlentities($Row['Title'])
                . "</a>";
            }
        }
        echo "</td>";
        if ((($FirstDOW + $i) % 7) == 0)
            echo "</tr>";
}
```

```
// insert empty cells for
// days after the last day
if ((($i + $j + $FirstDOW) % 7) != 0) {
    for ($j = 0; (($i + $j + $FirstDOW) % 7)
        != 0; ++$j)
        echo "<td> </td>";
    echo "</tr>";
}
}
}
```

3. Save class_EventCalendar.php and close it in the text editor.

4. Create a new document in your text editor and type the <!DOCTYPE> declaration, <html> element, header information, and <body> element. Use the strict DTD and "Event Calendar" as the content of the <title> element.

5. Add the following PHP script section to the beginning of the document, above the <!DOCTYPE> declaration, to create or retrieve an EventCalendar object:

```php
<?php
session_start();
require_once("class_EventCalendar.php");
if (class_exists("EventCalendar")) {
    if (isset($_SESSION['currentCalendar']))
        $Calendar = unserialize($_
        SESSION['currentCalendar']);
    else {
        $Calendar = new EventCalendar ();
    }
}
else {
    $Calendar = NULL;
}
?>
```

6. Add the following statements and PHP code section to the body of the document:

```php
<h1>Event Calendar </h1>
<?php
    if ($Calendar === NULL)
        echo "<p>There was an error creating the " .
            " EventCalendar object.</p>\n";
    else
        $Calendar->getMonthlyCalendar(
        $_GET['Year'],
            $_GET['Month']);
?>
```

7. Add the following link to the end of the document body to allow users to add events to the calendar:

```
<a href="AddCalendarEvent.php?PHPSESSID=<?php echo
    session_id(); ?>">Add an event to the
    calendar</a>
```

8. Save the document as **EventCalendar.php** in the ChineseZodiac folder.

9. Upload EventCalendar.php and class_EventCalendar.php to the Web server.

10. Open EventCalendar.php in your Web browser by entering the following URL: *http://<yourserver>/ChineseZodiac/EventCalendar.php*. You will see an empty calendar for the current month and year. Use the link at the bottom of the page to add some events to the calendar, then use the link at the bottom of the page to return to the event calendar. Use the links in the calendar header to browse through the calendar and find the events you entered. Remember that the links for the events will not work until you complete Discovery Project 10-4.

Discovery Project 10-4

Create an **EventDetails.php** file to display the title and description of the event based on the event ID passed to the script. Add a member function called `getEventDetails()` that accepts the event ID as a parameter and retrieves and displays the event information. Use sessions to serialize and unserialize the `EventCalendar` object.

Discovery Project 10-5

Create a **RemoveCalendarEvent.php** file to remove an event from the calendar based on the event ID passed to the script. Add a member function called `removeCalendarEvent()` that accepts the event ID as a parameter and deletes the event information from the database. Use sessions to serialize and unserialize the `EventCalendar` object. Modify the `getMonthlyCalendar()` member function to add a link after each event's title that will call the RemoveCalendarEvent.php file with the event ID as a parameter.

Working with XHTML

As explained in Chapter 1, PHP is an embedded scripting language. A PHP script is embedded, or contained within, an XHTML page. Because of this restriction, familiarity with XHTML is required for using PHP. This appendix provides a brief overview of XHTML and shows you how to install some development tools to assist you with building XHTML and PHP files.

Installing an Editor

For many users of this book, the instructor and the school will provide a complete and integrated development environment. However, if such tools are not provided, you will need a text editor for creating your PHP files. You may also need an FTP or SCP client so that you can upload the PHP files to a Web server.

In this section, you will learn how to install Portable Apps Suite and Notepad++ for Windows. Portable Apps Suite is a tool that allows you to run programs that are installed on a flash drive. Notepad++ is a text editor with an integrated FTP client.

Installing Portable Apps Suite

Because USB flash drives have become larger and faster, you can install applications directly onto the flash drive. By attaching the flash drive to any compatible system, you can access your programs even if they are not installed on that machine. This makes it easier to develop

Web pages at home and on school computers using the same development tools.

There are USB flash drive "portable application" solutions for most operating systems. For Macintosh systems, the FSuite CD provides a collection of portable applications. Linux users have Portable Apps for Linux, and even a version of Linux that boots from a USB drive. Portable Apps Suite is the Windows solution. Through the integrated Portable Apps menu, installed applications can be launched.

To install Portable Apps Suite for Windows:

1. Insert the USB flash drive into an available port.

2. Open your Web browser and enter *http://www.portableapps. com* in the location bar to go to the Portable Apps home page.

3. Click Suite on the navigation bar of the Portable Apps Web page to open the Suite home page. From the Suite home page, click the Download button, select the version you want to install (Platform, Suite Lite, or Standard) and start the download. Save the downloaded file to the USB drive.

4. When the download is complete, open Windows Explorer, navigate to the USB drive, and double-click the PortableApps. com_*type*_Setup_*version*_*language*.exe file on your flash drive, where *type* is "Platform," "Suite_Light," or "Suite," *version* is the current version number, and *language* is a two-letter language abbreviation (such as "en" for English).

5. Install the Portable Apps program in the root directory of your flash drive.

6. After the installation is complete, view the contents of the flash drive and double-click the StartPortableApps.exe file. The Portable Apps menu displays a list of installed programs, as shown in Figure A-1. Also, a Portable Apps icon appears in the system tray on the taskbar.

The full process of downloading and installing Portable Apps Suite may take up to 20 minutes, depending on the version you selected and the download speed.

Figure A-1   The Portable Apps menu

Installing Notepad++

A graphical HTML editor can simplify the task of creating Web pages. However, graphical HTML editors automatically add many unfamiliar elements and attributes to documents that can confuse you and distract from the learning process. Therefore, this book shows you how to create Web pages using a simple text editor.

If your instructor has not required a specific text editor to complete your assignments, many options are available. Programs such as TextPad, TextWrangler, jEdit, NEdit, and Notepad++ all provide PHP syntax highlighting, which assists you by color-coding XHTML and PHP keywords, comments, and operators. Many text editors, including the ones listed above, also provide PHP parsers to check the syntax of a PHP script and highlight any errors.

Notepad++ is available to install as part of Portable Apps Suite for Windows. You can install it in your Portable Apps Suite, where it will appear as a menu item. Additionally, Notepad++ has an integrated FTP client, which simplifies uploading files to a Web server.

To download and install Notepad++ for the Portable Apps Suite:

1. Return to the PortableApps.com Web site and select the Applications menu link.

2. In the Development section, click the Notepad++ Portable link.

3. Download the Notepad++ program directly to the root directory of your flash drive.

4. Close your browser and return to the Portable Apps menu. If the menu is closed, you can display it by clicking the Portable Apps icon in the system tray on the taskbar.

5. From the Portable Apps menu, click the Options button and select Install New Application. Navigate to the NotepadPlusPlusPortable_*xxx*.paf.exe file, where *xxx* is the version of Notepad++ on your flash drive. Click Open to install Notepad++.

6. When the installation is complete, redisplay the Portable Apps menu by clicking the Portable Apps Menu icon on the taskbar. Notepad++ Portable appears in the menu list.

7. Click the Notepad++ Portable option in the Portable Apps menu to open Notepad ++.

8. You will learn to configure Notepad++ as you begin to create Web pages using XHTML and PHP. For now, click the Close button on the title bar to close Notepad++.

9. To close the Portable Apps program, click the Portable Apps Menu icon on the taskbar to open the menu. Click the X button in the lower-right corner to close the menu, which will remove the icon from the system tray on the taskbar. (It is important to close the Portable Apps program correctly to ensure that your server profiles are available the next time you launch the program.) You can also right-click the Portable Apps Menu icon and select Exit to close the application.

10. The next time you insert your flash drive in the USB port, select "Start PortableApps.com using the program provided on this device" and click OK.

11. When the Portable Apps menu appears, select Notepad++ from the menu.

Several popular features of Notepad++ are described in the following list. Take some time to explore all the features so you can take full advantage of Notepad++. Figure A-2 shows Notepad++ with a PHP script loaded.

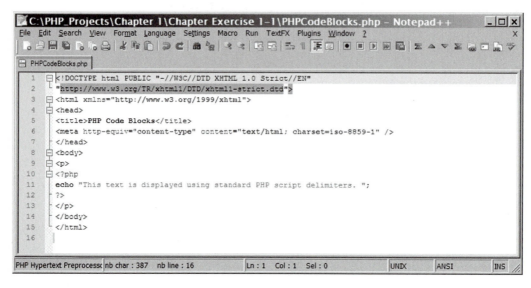

Figure A-2   The Notepad++ editor

The syntax highlighting is not applied until the document is saved.

- Syntax highlighting is a useful debugging technique as you learn to write PHP code because it displays elements, attributes, and values in the source code in a different color. Syntax highlighting is applied using the default style, but you can configure your own syntax highlighting for XHTML, CSS, and PHP using the Style Configurator option in the Settings menu.

- The toolbar has two Save icons—one that saves the current document and one that saves all open documents.

- Options in the Run menu display the current document in either the Internet Explorer or Mozilla Firefox browser. (Firefox is the default installation with Portable Apps Suite.)

- Select Plugins | FTP SynchronizeA | Show FTP Folders to display an FTP pane to the right of the Notepad++ window. Click the Open Settings Dialog icon to open a dialog box that lets you create a server profile. After you create a profile, you can click the Connect icon in the FTP pane to connect to your remote server account and upload files directly to your server from Notepad++.

- For a Web page to appear in the browser, it must reside in the folder structure within the base Web directory (www or public_html). To upload the current file to a folder on the server, click the folder and select "Upload current file to folder" from the FTP toolbar. To upload a file from your flash drive, right-click the folder, select "Upload other file here. . .", and navigate to the destination of the file you want to upload.

If you are using another text editor, use the help system or documentation to explore its features. Many features in Notepad++ are available in other editors, and other editors may offer different features, such as automatically closing XHTML tags. The more familiar you are with the text editor, the easier it will be for you to build PHP scripts.

Once you have a basic understanding of Notepad++ or the text editor you will use, you are ready to explore the XHTML specification and learn how to format XHTML pages using Cascading Styles Sheets (CSS).

The Basics of XHTML

In 2001, the World Wide Web Consortium (W3C) released a formal recommendation for XHTML 1.0. This XHTML specification requires a stricter coding standard than the earlier HTML 4.0 standard to accommodate multiple browsers and to maintain compatibility with other media devices, such as PDAs and mobile phones. One goal of XHTML is to separate information from presentation. To accomplish this goal, the W3C decided that some common HTML elements and attributes used for display and formatting would not be supported in XHTML. Instead, the W3C recommends that you use CSS to format the document for browser display.

 The W3C does not actually release a version of a particular technology. Instead, it issues a formal recommendation for a technology, which essentially means that the technology is (or will be) a recognized industry standard.

DOCTYPE Declaration

All XHTML documents require a DOCTYPE declaration, which associates a Document Type Definition (DTD) with the document so the parser can compare the XHTML file against the rules defined by the DTD. You can use three types of DTDs with XHTML documents: strict, transitional, and frameset. To understand the differences among the DTDs, you need to understand the concept of deprecated HTML elements. Elements and attributes are said to be **deprecated** if they will not be supported by future XHTML versions or are not currently supported by various handheld devices. Common HTML elements that are deprecated in the XHTML 1.0 specification include <applet>, <basefont>, <center>, <dir>, <isindex>, <menu>, <s> or <strike>, and <u>. Deprecated attributes include alink, align, border, background, color, face, height, language, link, name, size, text, vlink, and width. For an extensive list of deprecated elements and attributes, read the XHTML specification at the W3C Web site (*http://www.w3.org/*).

One of the most significant deprecated attributes is the `name` attribute, which is widely used in the HTML 4.0 specification. It was typically used in the `<applet>`, `<frame>`, `<iframe>`, and `<img>` element tags, and in the pseudo `<a>` element. A common practice in HTML was to name a section in a document using `<a name = "top">...</a>`. The attribute value `"top"` could then be referenced as the destination of a text hyperlink, as in `<a href = "#top">Go to Top</a>`. In XHTML, the `name` attribute has been replaced by the `id` attribute. Because not all browsers have support for the `id` attribute, it is a good idea to enter both a `name` and `id` attribute with the same value to ensure backward compatibility.

The three DTDs are distinguished in part by the degree to which they allow or do not allow deprecated HTML elements:

- Strict—The strict DTD definition restricts the use of deprecated tags. Because the markup validated by the strict definition leaves no room for interpretation, CSS must be used to format the content for browser display. A DOCTYPE definition for the strict document type is as follows:

```
<!DOCTYPE html PUBLIC "-//W3C//DTD XHTML 1.0 Strict//EN"
    "http://www.w3.org/TR/xhtml1/DTD/xhtml1-strict.dtd">
```

- Transitional—The transitional DTD definition allows the use of deprecated tags during a conversion period when newer versions of XHTML are released and older versions become outdated. Because deprecated formatting tags are allowed, the transitional definition does not require the use of CSS, although it is recommended.

```
<!DOCTYPE html PUBLIC "-//W3C//DTD XHTML 1.0
    Transitional//EN"
"http://www.w3.org/TR/xhtml1/DTD/xhtml1-transitional.dtd">
```

- Frames—The frames DTD definition must be used when you want to insert the `<frameset>` and `<frame>` elements on your page. Because frames have been deprecated and do not meet accessibility standards, you should limit or (better yet) eliminate the use of framesets in Web documents. In HTML code, framesets have been replaced by a `<table>` or CSS layout. In PHP, the concept of dividing the browser window into separate sections, each displaying an individual XHTML page, has been replaced by a Web template that uses include statements to populate dynamic content sections.

```
<!DOCTYPE html PUBLIC "-//W3C//DTD XHTML 1.0 Frameset//EN"
    "http://www.w3.org/TR/xhtml1/DTD/xhtml1-frameset.dtd">
```

 For all activities and projects in this book, you will code your pages to meet the specifications defined for the strict DTD.

Structure of an XHTML Document

The DOCTYPE declaration must be the first line of code in your Web page. Next, you should include the four paired tags that structure an XHTML document: `<html>`, `<head>`, `<title>`, and `<body>`. The following template meets the strict DTD specifications:

```
<!DOCTYPE html PUBLIC "-//W3C//DTD XHTML 1.0 Strict//EN"
    "http://www.w3.org/TR/xhtml1/DTD/xhtml1-strict.dtd">
<html xmlns="http://www.w3.org/1999/xhtml" xml:lang="en"
    lang="en">
    <head>
        <meta http-equiv="Content-Type"
            content="text/html; charset=iso-8859-1" />
        <title>XHTML 1.0 Strict Template</title>
    </head>
    <body>
        <p>[Placeholder for XHTML content]</p>
    </body>
</html>
```

In the `<head>` section, you must include a `<meta>` element to provide information about the Web page's character encoding. If you do not indicate a character encoding scheme, the Web browser will guess at which character scheme to use, which may affect how the Web page appears in the browser. You should assign a value of `"text/html;charset=iso-8859-1"` to the `<meta>` element's content attribute to specify the iso8859-1 character set, which represents English and many western European languages. The following statement shows how to construct the content-type `<meta>` elements:

```
<meta http-equiv="Content-Type" content="text/html;
    charset=iso-8859-1" />
```

All XHTML documents must use `<html>` as the root element. The XML namespace attribute xmlns is required in the `<html>` element and must be assigned a URI (Uniform Resource Identifier) of `"http://www.w3.org/1999/xhtml"`.

You may want to save this XHTML template as **xhtml_template.html** and modify it whenever you need to structure a new XHTML document. Simply add the new content to the template file and save the modified Web document with an extension of .html or .php.

Well-formed XHTML Documents

Although XHTML uses the same syntax as HTML, it requires that your code be well formed. A well-formed document must follow a predefined syntax or structure. XHTML is a Web standard maintained by the W3C that ensures your code meets the specifications defined for the DTD you selected. In order for an XHTML document to be well formed:

- All markup tags must be lowercase.

- All elements must have both an opening and closing tag or be a single self-closing tag.

- All tags must be properly nested.

- All attributes must be assigned a value (enclosed in single or double quotation marks).

Lowercase Markup Tags

Unlike earlier versions of HTML, where the standard was to key markup tags in uppercase characters to distinguish them from content, XHTML requires that you key all tags in lowercase characters, as shown in the following code:

`<title>XHTML 1.0 Strict Template</title>`

Required Opening and Closing Tags

> In XHTML, you cannot close an empty element with a matching closing tag. The syntax `<img src = "geek. png" alt = "picture of a geek god">` `</img>` is invalid.

In HTML, tags that did not mark up content, such as `<br>`, `<hr>`, and `<img>`, were called **empty elements** and did not require a closing tag. In XHTML, you must insert a forward slash character (/) before the closing right angle bracket of an empty element, essentially opening and closing the tag within the left and right angle brackets. These are often called **self-closing tags**. The W3C recommends that you insert a space before the forward slash character, as shown in the following code:

`<img src = "geek.png" alt = "picture of geek god" />`

In HTML, even though the paragraph `<p>` selector marked up a section of text, it did not require an ending `</p>` tag to mark the end of the paragraph. A blank line would be inserted with or without the closing `</p>` tag. In XHTML, the ending paragraph tag is required.

Properly Nested Tags

Nesting refers to how elements are placed inside other elements. When you apply multiple tags to mark up the same content, you must open and close the markup tags in a specific order. In HTML, you could enter `<strong><em>Bold and Italicized Content</strong></em>` to bold and italicize the marked-up text. HTML was not concerned with the order in which elements were opened and closed. In XHTML, when you nest tags, the first tag opened must be the last tag closed, as shown in the following code. The `<strong>` and `</strong>` tags are shown in bold to identify them as the outer tags. The `<em>` and `</em>` tags are the inner tags.

`<strong><em>Bold and Italicized Content</em></strong>`

Attributes and Values

When you added an attribute and value to a tag in HTML, placing the value in quotation marks was optional unless the value contained spaces, as in `<table width = 750>`. In XHTML, all attribute values must be surrounded by matching single (') or double (") quotation marks, such as `<table width = "750">`. In HTML, you were also allowed to use a "minimized" version of the attribute/value pair. For example, it was common to shorten the attribute/value pair `checked = "checked"` to the word `checked`. When specifying that a particular radio button was already selected, you could use `<input type = "radio" name = "gender" value = "male" checked>`. In XHTML, all attributes must be specified with the "maximized" version using the attribute/value pair. The following code shows the XHTML syntax to set the `"gender"` radio button and select the value of `"male"`:

```
<input type = "radio" name = "gender" value = "male"
    checked = "checked" />
```

HTML used a number of other minimized attributes, such as `selected`, `multiple`, and `noresize`, that must be specified using the maximized version in XHTML. For a complete list of minimized attributes, visit the W3C Web site at *http://www.w3c.org*.

Validating an XHTML Document

After you save your XHTML document, you should validate it against the style rules defined by the strict, transitional, or frameset definitions.

In a browser, enter *http://validator.w3.org/* in the location bar to access W3C's Markup Validation Service. You can validate files by URI, File Upload, or Direct Input. If the document meets the standards specified by the DOCTYPE (in this instance, the XHTML 1.0 Strict), your results document will appear as shown in Figure A-3.

	This document was successfully checked as XHTML 1.0 Strict!
Result:	Passed
File :	[ ] Browse... *Use the file selection box above if you wish to re-validate the uploaded file CarDonations.html*
Encoding :	utf-8 (detect automatically) ▼
Doctype :	XHTML 1.0 Strict (detect automatically) ▼
Root Element:	html
Root Namespace:	http://www.w3.org/1999/xhtml

Figure A-3   Validating a well-formed XHTML document

If the structure of the XHTML document does not meet the standards of the XHTML 1.0 strict DTD, the Validation Output in the results document will explain the errors. An example is shown in Figure A-4.

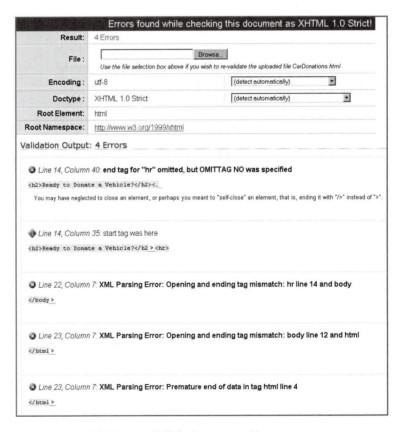

Figure A-4   Validating an XHTML document with errors

In this instance, the end tag for the <hr> selector was omitted on line 14 of the XHTML document.

`<h2>Ready to Donate a Vehicle?</h2><hr>`

Once the code has been modified to insert the forward slash character before the closing right angle bracket in the <hr /> selector, you can save the document, upload it to the server, return to the W3C Markup Validator, and click the Revalidate button to recheck the modified document.

In the preceding example, the Validator identified four errors, although there was only one error in the XHTML document (the omission of the forward slash character in the <hr> tag). Once the initial error is corrected, the document will be checked and approved as XHTML 1.0 Strict. It is a good idea to locate and correct the errors sequentially because correcting the first error will often also correct the remaining errors.

If you are using Firefox and have installed the Web Developer Tool Bar (*https://addons.mozilla. org/en-US/firefox/ addon/60*), you can select Tools | Web Developer | Tools | Validate HTML to validate the currently displayed browser page.

631

Using Cascading Style Sheets

When coding an XHTML document to meet the standards of the "Strict 1.0," the W3C recommends that you separate the data from the display using Cascading Style Sheets. The term **cascading** refers to the ability of Web pages to use CSS information from more than one source. When a Web page has access to multiple CSS sources, the styles "cascade" or "fall together." In CSS-based design, the XHTML content of the Web page is typed in the body of the XHTML document and formatted by rules defined in a CSS style. To change colors, sizes, and layout, you simply modify a style definition in the CSS.

Just like XHTML, CSS have their own type of language and syntax, which is defined by the W3C, the same organization that defines XHTML standards. To review the guide of current W3C CSS specifications, go to the CSS home page at *http://www.w3.org/Style/CSS/*.

Formatting the Document Display

A **style** is a collection of design rules (declarations) that defines how the XHTML content will be displayed in a browser. Styles may be used to define the display of fonts, text, colors, backgrounds, lists, boxes, and layers. You can define a style for an XHTML tag in three ways:

- Inline
- Internal (also referred to as Embedded or Global)
- External (also referred to as Linked)

The Inline Style

To apply an inline style to an XHTML tag, such as the <body>, <h1>, <p>, or <hr /> tag, you define the style using the style attribute of the XHTML tag. To define a style, you append CSS attributes and values as the value of the style attribute.

```
<h1 style="text-align: center;">Content</h1>
```

Each CSS attribute is separated from its value by a colon (:). You can include multiple style declarations in an inline style by separating each declaration with a semicolon (;). The following code illustrates the syntax to apply multiple style declarations to an <h1> XHTML tag:

```
<h1 style="text-align: center; color: green; font-weight:
bold">Content</h1>
```

To apply an inline style to XHTML content that is not marked up by an XHTML tag, use opening and closing <span> tags around the content, and use the style attribute of the <span> tag to define the CSS attributes and values. For example, to display the word "awesome" in bold in the sentence "CSS is an **awesome** formatting tool!" to distinguish the word from the rest of the text, you would use the following XHTML syntax:

```
<p>CSS is an <span style = "font-weight:
    bold;">awesome</span> formatting tool.</p>
```

Internal Style

You can use an internal style sheet to create styles that apply to an entire Web page. You create an internal style sheet within opening and closing <style> tags in the <head> section of the XHTML document, usually below the ending </title> tag. Any style definitions are applied to all instances of the element contained in the body of the XHTML document. Note the term *selector* in the following code; CSS uses this term to refer to an XHTML tag, such as h1 or p. Note that CSS does not enclose the tag name in angle brackets (< and >).

```
   ...
    </title>
    <style>
        selector
        {
        attribute: value;
        attribute: value;
        }
    </style>
</head>
```

If you type each style definition on a separate line with proper indenting, it is easier to read the code, and syntax errors are easier to locate and correct. You can, however, type the entire style definition on a single line:

```
selector { attribute: value; attribute: value; }
```

You can also group selectors so they share the same style declarations by separating each selector with a comma, as shown in the following code:

```
    ...
    </title>
    <style>
         h1, h4, p
         {
         text-decoration: underline;
         font-style: italic;
         }
    </style>
</title>
```

If you need to apply the same style to an entire section of your document (such as a sidebar), you can enclose the section in an opening and closing div (for "division") tag. An id attribute must be inserted in the div tag to uniquely identify the division. When defining a style for the id attribute, you place the (#) flag character before the unique id you assign to the div tag.

For example, if you wanted to *apply* the sidebar style to a section of a document, you would use the following syntax:

```
<div id = "sidebar">
    ...
</div>
```

To *define* the styles for the sidebar division, you would include the following CSS code within the opening and closing <style> tags:

```
#sidebar { background-color: lightblue; }
```

If you want to define a style that can be applied to multiple selectors, you should define a class. Classes are used to style elements that occur many times in a document (such as the <p> element). When defining a style for the class attribute, you place the (.) flag character before the name you assign to the class attribute in the paragraph tag.

To *define* a class called title, you would place the following CSS code within the opening and closing <style> tags:

```
.title { font-variant: small-caps; color: navy; }
```

To *apply* the title style class to a <p> tag within the body of the XHTML document, you would use the following syntax:

```
<p class = "title">
```

You can apply the class = "title" attribute/value pair to any other XHTML tags whose content needs to be formatted in small caps with navy text.

External or Linked Style Sheet

An **external style sheet**, sometimes called a **linked style sheet**, is used to define a style definition for like tags (such as all <h1> elements) in multiple pages in one or more Web sites. You create an external style sheet as a separate text document that contains only text—no XHTML tags. The external style sheet is saved with an extension of .css to identify it as a Cascading Style Sheet.

You can also use CSS comments with internal styles, within the <style> and </style> tags. Outside these tags, you still need to use the HTML comment tag <!-- ... -->.

You should add comments to style definitions to help you document and maintain the style sheet over time. The comments should include information to remind yourself or others of what the code is doing. A comment in CSS begins with a forward slash followed by an asterisk (/*) and ends with an asterisk followed by a forward slash (*/).

```
/* A CSS comment */
```

The following example includes a comment that explains how the h1 style definition formats the <h1> tag in the XHTML document:

```
/* formats the h1 selector with a font that is teal, Arial
or Arial Rounded MT Bold (if not available, the default
sans-serif font), and uppercase */
h1
    {
    color: teal;
    font-family: Arial,'Arial Rounded MT Bold',sans-serif;
    text-transform: uppercase;
    }
```

If a value in your style definition contains a space, you must enclose the value in either single or double quotation marks, as shown above with 'Arial Rounded MT Bold'.

You can attach this .css document to every page in your Web site to which you want to apply a style definition. You do this by linking the XHTML document to the external style sheet. This link information is usually inserted below the ending </title> tag and above the <style> section in your XHTML document. However, the link information can be placed anywhere in the <head> section, except between the beginning and ending tags of any element in the <head> section, such as the <title> or <style> tags. The syntax to link the XHTML document to the external style sheet is shown in the following code:

```
<link href = "filename.css" rel = "stylesheet"
    type = "text/css" />
```

You would replace *filename.css* with the path and filename of the external style sheet; the value of the rel attribute is always "stylesheet", and the value of the type attribute is always "text/css".

If your Web page does not appear in the browser with the styles that you declared in your external style sheet, check for an error in the following:

- Placement of the link statement in the XHTML document

- Syntax of the link element

- Reference to the external style sheet (filename case, extension, and location)

- Syntax of the CSS styles

- Commenting style in the external style sheet

Style Specificity

Sometimes, you may want one of the tags in your Web page to be formatted with a different style from the one you defined in your external style sheet. You can override the external style sheet with an internal style sheet or an inline style. Table A-1 illustrates the order of specificity for CSS styles.

Style	Application	Specificity
Inline	Applies styles to individual selectors in the body of the XHTML document	Overrides styles declared in internal or external style sheets
Internal	Applies styles to all like selectors in a Web page	Overrides styles declared in the external style sheet
External	Applies styles to all like selectors in the Web site	

Table A-1   CSS style specificity

Validating CSS Styles

Enter *http://jigsaw.w3.org/css-validator* in the location bar of your Web browser to validate your CSS styles at the W3C CSS Validation Service. If the Web page validates correctly, you will receive a message that the document validates as CSS level 2.1. If there are errors in the CSS styles, you will be given a results document that identifies the source of the errors. Once the errors have been corrected, you can revalidate the CSS styles.

Many resources on the Internet provide examples and tutorials that explain the syntax, attributes, and values of XHTML and CSS.

If you are using Firefox and you have installed the Web Developer Tool Bar (*https://addons.mozilla.org/en-US/firefox/addon/60*), you can select Tools | Web Developer | Tools | Validate CSS to validate the CSS that is applied to the displayed browser document.

Configuring a Personal Web Server

Understanding how to install and configure the software required for creating and delivering PHP scripts is considered a critical skill for Web developers. Even if you have access to a remote server running Apache, PHP, and MySQL, you may prefer to develop and test your PHP scripts on a local server before uploading them to the production environment.

PHP can be executed on a variety of platforms, including Windows, Linux, and Mac OS. You can download and install a local Web server running the Apache Web server, the MySQL database management system, and the PHP scripting engine with open source packages, referred to as xAMP. The x will change depending on the operating system. The A, M, and P refer to Apache, MySQL, and PHP, respectively. You can install WAMP on a Windows computer, LAMP on a Linux computer, and MAMP on a Macintosh computer. These integrated packages make installing and configuring a Web server a less technical process than installing each of the applications individually.

Many Linux distributions come with LAMP already installed and configured.

Installing xAMP

All of the xAMP packages are designed for easy installation on the destination system, although the details vary. The following instructions explain how to install WAMP on a Windows computer. You would follow a similar process to install LAMP on a Linux machine or MAMP on a Macintosh platform.

Before beginning the installation process, ensure that you have the appropriate privileges or that you are logged in as the system superuser.

To install WAMP on a Windows computer:

1. In the location bar of your browser, enter *http://www.wampserver.com/en/download.php*, click the download link, and select Download WampServer. Click the Save button to save the executable file on any storage device. It should only take a few minutes to download the WampServer application. When the installation program has finished downloading, a Download Complete message appears and an icon representing an install program is displayed on your storage device.

2. Double-click the install program icon to begin the installation process. Click the Run button. If you have a previous version of WAMP installed on your machine, you may be prompted to delete the older version before continuing.

3. You are welcomed by the standard setup screen, which recommends that you close all other applications before continuing. Click Next.

4. Read the terms of the license agreement. If you accept the terms, click the "I accept the agreement" radio button. Click Next.

5. By default, WAMP will be installed in C:\wamp\. Selecting the default install location will make Web pages easily accessible to the Web browser. Click Next.

6. The Select Additional Tasks option appears. You can click the Create a Quick Launch icon to add an icon to the system tray on your desktop each time Windows is launched, and you can click the Create a Desktop icon to add a program shortcut on the desktop, which you could use to restart the server if you manually exit the WampServer. Click Next.

7. Click the Install button to begin the installation. The files will be installed in the C:\wamp\ folder. Click OK.

8. If Firefox is installed on the Windows computer on which you are installing the WampServer, you will be asked if you want to use Firefox as your default browser with this application. Click Yes, because Firefox comes with some useful tools for Web design.

9. To complete your e-mail configuration, you can leave the Simple Mail Transfer Protocol (SMTP) at the default location of "localhost," enter your e-mail address at the e-mail prompt, and click Next.

10. You have completed the setup, and WampServer should be successfully installed on your local computer. By default, the "Launch the WampServer now" option is selected. You can leave this option selected so you can walk through a short overview of the WampServer tools that are available to help you manage Apache, MySQL, and PHP.

Testing the *x*AMP Installation

After installing your *x*AMP server, you should test your configuration to ensure that everything was installed correctly. Again, depending on the platform, the actual steps will vary by system. The following steps are for the Windows operating system, but they are illustrative of the steps you would use on any system.

To test the local WAMP server:

1. Navigate to the C:\wamp\ directory. You will see a number of files and folders that WampServer requires to run the application.

2. Double-click the www folder (the root Web folder on your local machine). By default, the Web folder contains one PHP file named index.php. Only files that are stored inside the www folder or folders under it can be displayed in your Web browser.

3. To display index.php in the browser, open Firefox and enter *http://localhost/index.php* in the location bar.

4. The index page displays your server configurations that specify what versions of Apache, MySQL, and PHP you are running. The `phpinfo()` link in the Tools menu provides a link to detailed information about your PHP installation. In Chapter 1 of this book, you used the `phpinfo()` function to display the server configurations on the remote server. The phpMyAdmin option links to an open source tool written in PHP to handle the administration of MySQL databases (discussed in Chapter 7). The SQLLitemanager option links to a database manager that is an extension of Firefox.

 If you installed the WampServer files to a location other than the default option (C:\wamp\), use the actual location in place of C:\wamp\ in the following steps.

 Notice that you can also open the WampServer menu and click the www directory option to open the C:\wamp\www\ folder.

 You can use either localhost or 127.0.0.1 (the localhost IP address) to refer to your local computer. You can simply enter "localhost" or "127.0.0.1" because most modern Web browsers prepend the hypertext transfer protocol (http://) to the URL. If index.php is in the root Web folder, it is selected as the default page to display in the browser.

 You can also access "localhost" in your browser by selecting localhost from the WampServer menu.

You may have noticed that when you selected the "Launch WampServer now" option during installation, a small gauge-shaped icon appeared in the system tray on your taskbar. When you move your cursor over the WampServer icon, a Tooltip displays "WAMPSERVER – server offline." (The difference between "offline" and "online" will be explained later.) For now, click the WampServer icon and select Stop All Services from the Quick Admin section of the menu. The WampServer application closes and the icon is removed from the system tray.

Working with the WampServer Menu

After you install the WampServer, you can launch the application as you would any other Windows application. Click the Start button on the taskbar and select Programs | WampServer | Start WampServer. The WampServer icon appears in the system tray on the taskbar.

With the application running, you can click the WampServer icon to display available menu options. If you click Apache or MySQL under the Powered by Anaska heading, you can verify that the service is running. If you select Apache from the WampServer menu and select Service from the submenu, you will see that the Stop Service option is active, but the Start/Resume Service option is grayed out (inactive). You can use the Stop Service option to stop the Web server while leaving other services available. Once the service is stopped, the Stop Service option is grayed out (inactive), but the Start/Resume Service option is active. You can then use the Start/Resume Service option to restart the Web server.

When you finish using the WampServer, you can click the WampServer icon and select Stop All Services or right-click the icon and select Exit.

The same Stop Service and Start/Resume Service options are available for all of the WampServer services.

It is a good idea to exit the WampServer when you are not developing Web pages because it uses computer resources and memory.

Accessing WampServer Online

Typically, the local installation of WampServer is for development purposes and the files are uploaded to a production server after they have been tested. You probably do not want Web pages saved on your local server to be globally accessible on the Web. For this reason, the default option for accessibility is set to Put Offline.

To allow files saved in the root Web folder of your local computer to be accessed outside your LAN:

1. On your LAN gateway, enable port 80 for http in firewalls.

2. On your LAN gateway, forward port 80 for http to the Internet Protocol (IP) address of the computer that has WAMP installed.

3. From the WampServer menu, click Put Online.

4. Access your Web files by substituting "localhost" with your Web IP address, which you can find at the Where is My IP Web site (*whereismyip.com*) or by checking your gateway's configuration.

You take security risks by allowing Internet users to access your local Web, PHP, and MySQL servers. Use this option with caution.

Installing the Directory Structure for Student Files

As discussed in the preface, all of the files created and used for the exercises, Reinforcement Exercises, and Discovery Projects in this book conform to a standard directory layout. A .zip archive file that contains the layout and all the files needed to complete the exercises is available at the Cengage Web site (*www.cengage.com*). To install the directories and files, simply unzip the archive file in the Web folder on your local server (C:\wamp\www\ is the default for WAMP).

Formatting Strings

Using the printf() and sprintf() Functions

PHP includes the printf() and sprintf() functions, which format text strings for output. The printf() function outputs a text string directly, similar to the print and echo statements, whereas the sprintf() function formats a string and returns the formatted value so that you can assign it to a variable.

Both functions accept as a first argument a **format control string**, which contains instructions for formatting text strings. You surround the format control string with single or double quotation marks, the same as you do for other types of strings. Each function also accepts additional arguments containing the data to be formatted by the format control string. Within the format control string, you include a conversion specification for each of the data elements you want to format, along with any other text that you want to appear in the formatted string. A **conversion specification** begins with a percent symbol (%) and specifies the formatting you want to apply to a data element. You must include a conversion specification for each argument that is passed to the printf() or sprintf() function after the format control string. For example, the following code contains a printf() function with two conversion specifications in the format control string: one for the $FirstName variable and one for the $SecondName variable:

```
$FirstName = "Gosselin";
$SecondName = "Gauselin";
printf("<p>The name %s is also spelled %s.</p>\n",
    $FirstName, $SecondName);
```

Notice that each conversion specification consists of a percent symbol followed by the letter s. The letter following the percent symbol in a conversion specification is a **type specifier**, which determines the display format of each data argument that is passed to the printf() or sprintf() function. A type specifier of s simply displays the data argument as a standard string. The preceding example is equivalent to the following code, which uses an echo statement.

```
$FirstName = "Gosselin";
$SecondName = "Gauselin";
echo "<p>The name $FirstName is also spelled $SecondName
    </p>\n";
```

If you are only using a simple %s conversion specification, it will be easier to use the standard PHP syntax instead. For more complex formatting, the printf() and sprintf() functions provide options that are not available in the standard PHP syntax. These options are explained next.

Specifying Types

Table C-1 lists the type specifiers you can use with the printf() and sprintf() functions.

Type Specifier	Description
b	Displays the argument as a binary integer
c	Displays the ASCII character for the index specified by the argument
d	Displays the argument as a decimal integer
u	Displays the argument as an unsigned decimal integer
f	Displays the argument as a floating-point number
o	Displays the argument as an octal integer
s	Displays the argument as a string
x	Displays the argument as a lowercase hexadecimal integer
X	Displays the argument as an uppercase hexadecimal integer

Table C-1   PHP type specifiers

The following code demonstrates how to use each of the type specifiers listed in Table C-1. Figure C-1 shows the output.

```
$Value = 163;
print("<p>\n ");
printf("Binary integer: %b<br />\n ", $Value);
printf("ASCII character: %c<br />\n ", $Value);
printf("Decimal integer: %d<br />\n ", $Value);
printf("Unsigned decimal integer: %u<br />\n ", $Value);
printf("Floating-point number: %f<br />\n ", $Value);
printf("Octal integer: %o<br />\n ", $Value);
printf("String: %s<br />\n ", $Value);
printf("Lowercase hexadecimal integer: %x<br />\n ", $Value);
printf("Uppercase hexadecimal integer: %X<br />\n ", $Value);
print("</p>\n");
```

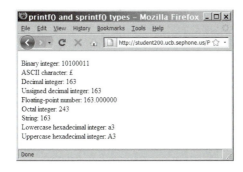

Figure C-1 Using the `printf()` and `sprintf()` types

Determining Decimal Number Precision

A common use of the string formatting functions is to format numbers to be displayed with a specified number of decimal places. For example, it's often necessary to format numbers as currency, with two decimal places. However, a variable that contains the currency value you want to display might be an integer that does not contain decimal places, or it might be a floating-point number that has more than two decimal places. By default, the f type specifier formats numbers with six decimal places. To specify a different number of decimal places, add a period and an integer representing the desired number of decimal places between the percent symbol and the f type specifier in a conversion specification. In the following code, a value of 99.5 is assigned to the $RetailPrice variable. When the value in the $RetailPrice variable is multiplied by 5% to add sales tax, the resulting value is 104.475, which is assigned to the $PriceWithTax variable. The value is then formatted to two decimal places with the printf() statement. Figure C-2 shows the output.

```
$RetailPrice = 99.5;
$PriceWithTax = $RetailPrice * 1.05;
printf("<p>The retail price is $%.2f.</p>\n",
     $RetailPrice);
printf("<p>The price with 5%% sales tax is $%.2f.</p>\n",
     $PriceWithTax);
```

You can only use a period and number of decimals in a conversion specification that uses the f type specifier.

Figure C-2 Using the `printf()` statement to format a number to two decimal places

Specifying Padding

In addition to specifying the number of decimal places that appear to the right of a decimal point, you can specify the number of characters used to output the data argument. For example, you might have a variable that counts the number of visitors to your Web site. Instead of just displaying the number of visitors, you might want to format it to display the number of visitors out of a million by padding the beginning of the number with zeroes. To pad the beginning of a string with zeroes, include a 0 and an integer representing the number of characters the number should have between the percent symbol and type specifier in a conversion specification. For example, the conversion specification in the following `sprintf()` statement specifies that the number should consist of seven characters. Because the string representation of the `$Visitors` variable only contains four characters, the beginning of the number is padded with three extra zeroes, as shown in Figure C-3.

Use two percent signs (%%) to include a percent symbol as a character in a format control string.

```
$DisplayValue = sprintf("%07d", 5767);
echo "<p>You are visitor number " .
     $DisplayValue . ".</p>\n";
```

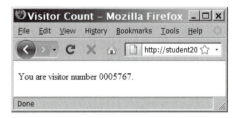

Figure C-3 Padding a value with leading zeroes

You can also specify that a string should be padded with spaces instead of a 0. Simply use a space instead of the 0 or exclude the 0 in a conversion specification. However, most Web browsers automatically replace multiple spaces on a Web page with a single space, unless you use the `<pre>` element. If you want to pad a number with any character other than a 0 or a space, you must precede it with a single quotation mark (`'`). For example, the following code pads a string with asterisks (*) instead of spaces or zeroes. Figure C-4 shows the output.

```
$Payment = 1410.23;
printf("<p>Pay the amount of \$%'*9.2f.</p>\n", $Payment);
```

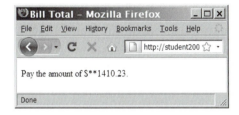

Figure C-4   Padding with asterisks

Formatting Numbers

You can use the `number_format()` function to add commas that separate thousand values and determine the number of decimal places to display. Even if you use the `printf()` or `sprintf()` function, you need to use the `number_format()` function to add commas to separate thousands in a number. However, you should understand that the `number_format()` function also converts numeric variables to strings. For this reason, you must use the `s` type specifier in a conversion specification to refer to a numeric variable that has been converted to a string with the `number_format()` function. For example, the following code uses the `number_format()` function to add comma separators and two decimal places to the `$Payment` variable. Because the `number_format()` function converts the `$Payment` variable to a string, the `printf()` statement uses the `s` type specifier in the conversion specification. Figure C-5 shows the output.

```
$Payment = 1410;
$Payment = number_format($Payment, 2);
printf("<p>Pay the amount of $%s.</p>\n", $Payment);
```

into a
the numbe
characters in
a string, not
the number of digits in an
integer. This includes the
decimal point and deci-
mal places. For example,
the number 345.10 con-
sists of six characters. If
you pad the formatting
string with zeroes and
specify that the format-
ting string should contain
eight characters, the
number will be formatted
as 00345.10.

If you add a plus sign (+) immediately following the percent symbol in a conversion specification, positive numbers are formatted with a plus sign before them and negative numbers are formatted with a minus sign (–) before them. Otherwise, only negative numbers will have a sign preceding the value.

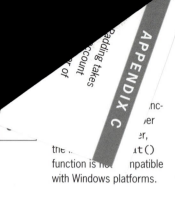

Pay the amount of $1,410.00.

the ... `t()`
function is not npatible
with Windows platforms.

Figure C-5 Using the `printf()` and
`number_format()` functions together

Formatting Alignment

By default, strings are formatted with right alignment. However, if
you add a hyphen (-) immediately following the percent symbol in
a conversion specification, a string is formatted with left alignment.
For example, each of the `printf()` statements in the following code
contains two conversion specifications: one for the description of a
travel expense and one for the amount of a travel expense. The first
conversion specification for the travel expense descriptions contains
a hyphen (-) immediately following the percent symbol, which aligns
the descriptions to the left. However, the second conversion specification for the amounts does not contain hyphens, so these descriptions are right-aligned by default.

```php
<p><strong>Expense Report</strong></p>
<pre>
<?php
$Travel = number_format(465.43, 2);
$Accommodations = number_format(276.2, 2);
$Meals = number_format(97.34, 2);
print("Description          Amount\n");
print("************************************\n");
printf("%-15s %20s\n", "Travel", $Travel);
printf("%-15s %20s\n", "Accommodations",
    $Accommodations);
printf("%-15s %20s\n", "Meals", $Meals);
?>
</pre>
```

In the preceding example, notice that the PHP script section is con-
tained within an XHTML <pre> element. This element is necessary
to instruct the Web browser to print the multiple spaces in the script.

Putting It All Together

Combining all of the elements described in the previous sections, the following code shows the general syntax for a conversion specification:

```
% [+][pad][-][length][.decimal]type
```

In the preceding line of code, [+] is the optional plus sign. It indicates that numeric fields should always display a plus or minus sign before the value. Recall that the default setting is only to display the sign if the value is negative. This option is only used for numeric *type* values.

[*pad*] is the optional pad character to insert if the length of the argument value is less than the length specified in [*length*]. For zeroes or spaces, the character '0' or ' ' is sufficient. All other characters must be preceded by a single quotation mark ('). If [*pad*] is omitted, the value is padded with spaces. This option is only used if [*length*] is specified.

[-] is the optional hyphen that indicates the field should be left-aligned. The default setting is right alignment. This option is only used if [*length*] is specified and the length of the string is less than the value of *length*.

[*length*] is the optional minimum number of characters to be used when displaying the value. If a string is shorter than the number of characters specified by *length*, pad characters will be added until the string is the specified *length*. Pad characters are added to the beginning of the string by default, but you can pad at the end of the string by specifying [-]. Strings that are longer than the *length* value will be displayed in full, not truncated.

[.*decimal*] is the optional number of digits to display after the decimal point for numeric values. This number is included in the number of characters specified by [*length*]. You must put the decimal point before the *decimal* value to indicate that you are specifying the number of decimal places. For string values, [.*decimal*] specifies the maximum string length. Any strings longer than *decimal* will be truncated to be *decimal* characters long.

type is the required type specifier that indicates the data type of the data argument. The valid type specifiers are shown in Table C-1 earlier in this appendix.

Secure Coding with PHP

Understanding PHP Security Issues

Viruses, worms, data theft by hackers, and other security threats are facts of life when it comes to Web-based applications. If you put an application into a production environment without considering security issues, you are asking for trouble. To combat security violations, you need to consider both Web server security issues and secure coding issues. Web server security involves the use of technologies such as firewalls, which employ both software and hardware to prevent access to private networks connected to the Internet. One important technology is the Secure Sockets Layer (SSL) protocol, which encrypts data and transfers it across a secure connection. Although Web server security is critical, the topic is better addressed in books on Apache, Internet Information Services, and other types of Web servers. Be sure to research security issues for your Web server and operating system before activating a production Web site.

To provide even stronger software security, many technology companies, including Microsoft and Oracle, require their developers and other technical staff to adhere to secure coding practices and principles. **Secure coding**, or **defensive coding**, refers to writing code that minimizes intentional or accidental security problems. Secure coding has become a major goal for many information technology companies, due to the exorbitant cost of fixing security flaws in commercial software. According to one study, it is 100 times more expensive to fix security flaws in released software than to apply secure coding techniques during the development phase. The National Institute of Standards & Technology estimates that $60 billion a year is spent identifying and correcting software errors. In addition, politicians have become interested in regulating software security. Tom Ridge, former Secretary of the U.S. Department of Homeland Security, said, "A few lines of code can wreak more havoc than a bomb." Government scrutiny gives information technology companies strong incentive to voluntarily improve the security of software products before state and federal governments pass legislation that requires such security.

Basically, all code is insecure unless proven otherwise. There is no magic formula for writing secure code, although you can use various techniques to minimize security threats in your programs. This appendix reviews some of the secure coding techniques you have already studied in this book.

Even if you follow the recommendations in this appendix, your code may not be absolutely secure. This appendix does not list every security issue with PHP, databases, and Web development. As a Web programmer, you should continually familiarize yourself with new threats as they appear and modify your code to avoid the threats whenever possible.

 For more information on PHP security, visit the PHP Security Consortium (PHPSC) Web site at *http://phpsec. org/*. PHPSC is an international group of PHP experts dedicated to promoting secure programming practices within the PHP community.

Using Secure Programming Techniques

This section includes a number of recommendations for making your code more secure, including tips for securing Web forms, verifying user identities, and securing data stored in files on the Web server.

Validating Submitted Form Data

In Chapter 4, you learned how to validate data that is submitted to your scripts. Web developers often use JavaScript with forms to validate or process form data before the data is submitted to a server-side script. For example, customers may use an online order form to order merchandise from your Web site. After customers click the form's Submit button, you can use JavaScript to ensure that customers have entered important information, such as their name, shipping address, and so on. The problem with using JavaScript to validate form data is that you cannot always ensure that the data was submitted to your PHP script from the Web page containing the JavaScript validation code. Hackers know how to bypass JavaScript validation code in an XHTML form by appending a query string directly to the URL of the PHP script that processes the form. Therefore, you should always include PHP code to validate any submitted data. If your PHP script lacks such code, you cannot be sure that all of the necessary data was submitted (such as a shipping address for an online order), nor can you tell if a hacker is attempting to submit malicious data that might harm your script or your Web site. Also recall that the POST method sends form data as a transmission separate from the URL specified by the action attribute. This is one reason to use POST rather than GET as the method for submitting form data. However, you do not guarantee the safety of your site by having users submit form data from a Web page using the POST method. Anyone who thoroughly understands HTTP headers can construct a separate transmission that contains the form data required by your script.

To ensure that your script receives the proper data, use the isset() and empty() functions to determine if form variables contain values. The isset() function determines whether a variable has been declared and initialized (or "set"), whereas the empty() function determines whether a variable is empty. You pass to both functions the name of the variable you want to check. If a submitted form value must be numeric data, you should use an is_numeric() function to test the variable. This ensures that hackers cannot break your code by sending alphabetic values to scripts that expect numeric values.

Avoiding the $_REQUEST[] Autoglobal Array

The $_REQUEST[] autoglobal array aggregates the elements of the $_GET[], $_POST[], and $_COOKIE[] autoglobal arrays into a single array. Many programmers use the $_REQUEST[] array for the convenience of not having to determine whether a Web form was submitted using the GET or POST method. However, because the $_COOKIE[] array is added to the $_REQUEST[] array last, any $_COOKIE[] array elements with the same associative array key as an element in the $_GET[] or $_POST[] arrays will be overwritten with the values from the $_COOKIES[] array. This provides hackers with a way to inject potentially dangerous data into your system.

Using Sessions to Validate User Identities

Always use sessions to validate user identities, especially at commercial sites that include shopping cart mechanisms. Because sessions store state information on a Web server, they are much safer to use—provided you properly secure your Web server. The randomly generated alphanumeric string that composes a session ID is extremely difficult to guess, so hackers probably cannot use this value to impersonate a user. If a hacker does obtain another user's session ID, he can use it to steal sensitive data, such as credit card information.

Even with sessions, however, there is a chance that a hacker can obtain a user's session ID. For a detailed discussion of session security issues, refer to the PHP Security Consortium's Security Guide at *http://phpsec.org/projects/guide/.*

You can also use sessions with Web forms to ensure that the form data was submitted from your server and not from a remote site.

Storing Code in External Files

Chapter 10 discusses how to store classes in external files. However, external files are not limited to classes; you can use them to store any type of code. Storing code in external files helps to secure your scripts by hiding the code from hackers. This also helps to protect your code from other programmers who might steal your scripts and claim them as their own.

In general, you should use the include() and include_once() functions for XHTML code that will not prevent a script from running if the external file is not available. For PHP code that is required for your script to execute, you should use the require() or require_once() functions, which halt the processing of the Web page if the external file is not available.

Choosing a Location for External Files

Your Web server has specific directories from which users are allowed to retrieve files. The easiest way to ensure that a site visitor cannot access a file is to store it outside those directories. As discussed in Chapter 2, the include() family of functions can read files stored outside of the Web structure. Files that contain secure information or details about the underlying server should always be stored outside the Web directory structure. This is also a good idea for include files that do not contain sensitive information, because the practice prevents a visitor from accessing the file directly.

Because Web site visitors cannot directly access externally placed files, it is a good idea to store many other types of files outside the Web structure as well, including log files, data files, and user-submitted files.

For example, you could create a PHP_Includes directory at the same level as your public_html or www directory. Within that directory, you could include a PHP file named inc_db_info.php that assigns the host name, user name, password, and database for a MySQL database to variables named $db_host, $db_user, $db_password, and $db_database. Then, you could add the following line of code to the beginning of any PHP script that needs to access the database:

```
require_once("../PHP_Includes/inc_db_info.php"):
```

After including the inc_db_info.php file, you will need to modify your code to use the predefined variables rather than strings. The following code would be used to open a database connection using the `mysql` package:

```
$DBConnect = @mysql_connect($db_host,
                            $db_user,
                            $db_password);
if ($DBConnect === FALSE)
    echo "<p>Connection error: "
            . mysql_error() . "</p>\n";
else {
    if (@mysql_select_db($db_database, $DBConnect)
            === FALSE)
        echo "<p>Could not select the \"" .
            $db_database . "\" database: " .
            mysql_error($DBConnect) .
            "</p>\n";
    ...
}
```

The following code would be used to open a database connection using the `mysql i` package:

The user account associated with the Web server needs to have read permissions on the include files for the `include()` family of functions to work.

```
$DBConnect = @new mysqli($db_host,
                         $db_user,
                         $db_password,
                         $db_database);
```

Because the file that contains the database information is not accessible from a Web browser, the information is more secure than if it was stored in the public_html or www folder, or if the information was coded directly into each script that uses the MySQL database.

Choosing an External File Extension

You can use any file extension for include files, although many programmers use an extension of .inc for XHTML files and other types of information that do not need to be processed by the Web server. Although you can use the .inc extension for external files containing PHP scripts, you should avoid doing so unless your Web server is configured to process .inc files as PHP scripts. If it isn't, anyone can view the contents of the file simply by entering the full URL in a Web browser. This creates a potential security risk, especially if the external file contains proprietary code or sensitive information such as passwords. Because most Web servers process the contents of a PHP script and only return XHTML to the client, your safest bet is to use an extension of .php for external files that contain PHP code.

Accessing Databases through a Proxy User

In Chapter 7, you learned that you should create an account that requires a password for each user who needs to access your database. For most Web sites, it's impossible to predict how many visitors might need to use a Web application to access a database. Therefore, instead of creating a separate database account for each visitor, you only need to create a single account that a PHP script uses to access the database for a user by proxy. A **proxy** performs a request for another person. In general, you should create a separate account for each Web application that needs to access a database. You then use PHP code, as in the following example, to access the database for the user by proxy:

```
$DBConnect = @new mysqli("host", "proxy_user", "password");
  if ($DBConnect->connect_errno())
    echo "<p>Unable to connect to the database server.</p>"
      . "<p>Error code " . $DBConnect->connect_errno()
      . ": " . $DBConnect->connect_error() . "</p>";
  else
...
```

Changing Settings in php.ini

Configuration settings for PHP are stored in the php.ini file on the Web server. The default settings attempt to balance security requirements against convenience. To secure your Web site, check the following settings. If you are running your own Web server, you might be able to edit the php.ini file directly. Otherwise, you might need to contact the system administrator for your Web server and ask to have the settings modified.

Handling Magic Quotes

Because the data that a user submits to a PHP script might contain single or double quotes, you should also use escape sequences for any user data your script receives, especially before you write it to a text file, database, or other data source. Older versions of PHP include a feature called **magic quotes**, which automatically adds a backslash (\) to any single quote ('), double quote ("), or NULL character contained in data that a user submits to a PHP script.

 Magic quotes and their associated functions and directives are deprecated as of PHP 5.3.0 and are removed as of PHP 6.

By default, the `magic_quotes_gpc` directive is the only magic quote directive enabled in your php.ini configuration file when you install PHP. Magic quotes are unpopular with programmers because it's easy to forget that they are enabled. A better approach is to disable magic quotes in your php.ini configuration file and instead manually escape text strings with the `addslashes()` function. This function accepts a single argument representing the text string you want to escape and returns a string containing the escaped string. If you want to display an escaped text string that contains escape characters, you can use the `stripslashes()` function to remove the slashes that were added with the `addslashes()` function.

If a script you are writing might be run on multiple Web servers and you cannot be sure whether magic quotes will be enabled, you can use the get_magic_quotes_gpc() function to determine whether magic quotes have been applied to data from the Web form already. The following example from the php.net Web site shows how to use the get_magic_quotes_gpc() function:

```
if (!get_magic_quotes_gpc()) {
    $lastname = addslashes($_POST['lastname']);
}
else {
    $lastname = $_POST['lastname'];
}
```

Disabling the `register_globals` Directive

Before PHP version 4.2.0, client, server, and environment information was automatically available as global variables that you could access directly in your scripts. For example, instead of using $_SERVER["SERVER_SOFTWARE"] to obtain information about your server software, you could simply use $SERVER_SOFTWARE. Similarly, a field named "email" in a submitted form could be accessed with $email instead of $_GET["email"]. However, making such information automatically available exposes security issues that an unscrupulous hacker can exploit. You can still use the old global variables by finding the register_globals directive in your php.ini configuration file and changing its value to "on." However, for your code to be secure, the PHP Group strongly recommends that you leave the register_globals directive turned off and instead use autoglobal arrays, such as $_GET and $_POST, to access client, server, and environment information in your scripts.

Reporting Errors

The php.ini configuration file contains two directives, display_errors and display_startup_errors, that determine whether error messages are displayed in a Web browser. The display_errors directive displays script error messages, whereas the display_startup_errors directive displays errors that occur when PHP starts. By default, the display_errors directive is assigned a value of "On" and the display_startup_errors directive is assigned a value of "Off." Although displaying error messages is useful when you develop PHP scripts, the PHP Group strongly recommends that you turn off the feature for scripts that run in production environments and save any errors in a log file instead. Hackers can use any displayed error messages to identify potential weaknesses in your Web site. The PHP Group also recommends that you only turn on the display_startup_errors directive when debugging a script.

Error Handling and Debugging

Regardless of their experience, knowledge, and ability, all programmers introduce errors into their programs. Thus, they must devote part of their programming education to mastering the art of debugging. As you learned at the beginning of this book, debugging is the act of tracing and resolving errors in a program. Debugging is an essential skill for any programmer, regardless of the programming language.

Determining the Error Type

Three basic types of errors can occur in a program: syntax errors, run-time errors, and logic errors.

Syntax Errors

Syntax errors, or **parse errors**, occur when the PHP scripting engine fails to recognize code. Syntax errors can be caused by incorrect use of PHP code, misspelled words, or references to objects, methods, and variables that do not exist. For example, if a programmer omits a method's closing parenthesis, the scripting engine generates a syntax error. As another example, the statement `ehco` `"<p>Hello World!</p>";` causes a syntax error because `echo` is misspelled. Similarly, the following statements cause a syntax error because the `$Hello` variable is incorrectly typed with a lowercase 'h'. (Remember that identifiers in PHP are case sensitive.)

Syntax errors in compiled languages, such as C++, are also called compile-time errors because they are usually discovered when a program is compiled. Because PHP is an interpreted language, syntax errors are not discovered until a program executes.

```
$Hello = "<p>Hello World!</p>\n";
echo $hello;
```

Run-Time Errors

A **run-time error** occurs when the PHP scripting engine encounters code it cannot execute while the rest of the program is executing. Run-time errors differ from syntax errors in that they do not necessarily represent PHP language errors. For example, consider the statement customFunction();, which calls a custom PHP function named customFunction(). This statement does not generate a syntax error because it is legal (and usually necessary) to create and then call custom functions in a PHP program. However, if your program includes the call statement but does not include code that creates the function in the first place, your program generates a run-time error. The error occurs when the scripting engine attempts to call the function but cannot find it.

The following code shows another example of a run-time error. In this example, an echo statement attempts to display the contents of a variable named $MessageVar, which is set by calling the user-defined function GetMessageString(). Because the function is not declared anywhere in the document, a run-time error occurs.

```
<?php
$MessageVar = GetMessageString();
echo $MessageVar;
?>
```

When investigating a run-time error, keep in mind that the culprit might actually be a syntax error. Because syntax errors do not occur until the scripting engine attempts to execute the code, they often manifest as run-time errors. For example, suppose your code includes a function that contains a statement with a syntax error. This syntax error will not be caught until the function executes at run time.

Logic Errors

A **logic error** is a flaw in a program's design that prevents the program from running as you anticipate. In this context, "logic" refers to the execution of program statements and procedures in the correct order to produce the desired results.

One common logic error is the creation of an infinite loop, in which a loop statement never ends because its conditional expression is never updated or is never FALSE. For example, the following code creates an infinite loop because the third argument in the for statement's parentheses never changes the value of the $Count variable:

```
for ($Count = 10; $Count >= 0; $Count) {
    if ($Count == 0)
        echo "<p>We have liftoff!</p>\n";
    else
        echo "<p>Liftoff in $Count seconds.</p>\n";
}
```

Because the $Count variable is never updated in the preceding example, it continues to have a value of 10 through each iteration of the loop, and "Liftoff in 10 seconds" is repeatedly displayed in a browser window. To correct this logic error, you add a decrement operator to the third argument in the for statement's constructor, as follows:

```
for ($Count = 10; $Count >= 0; --$Count) {
    if ($Count == 0)
        echo "<p>We have liftoff!</p>\n";
    else
        echo "<p>Liftoff in $Count seconds.</p>\n";
}
```

Handling and Reporting Errors

The first line of defense in locating PHP program bugs are the error messages you receive when the PHP scripting engine encounters an error. PHP generates four basic types of errors: parse errors, fatal errors, notices, and warnings. Parse errors are syntax errors, whereas the other three types are run-time errors.

Parse error messages occur when a PHP script contains a syntax error that prevents your script from running. For example, the following code raises a parse error because the for() statement is missing its opening brace ({). Figure E-1 shows the resulting parse error message in a Web browser.

```
<?php
for ($Count = 10; $Count >= 0; --$Count)
    if ($Count == 0)
        echo "<p>We have liftoff!</p>\n";
    else
        echo "<p>Liftoff in $Count seconds.</p>\n";
}
?>
```

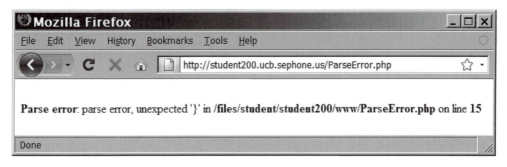

Figure E-1 A parse error message

Two important pieces of information are displayed with a parse error: the line number in the document where the error occurred and a description of the error. Note that the line number in an error message is counted from the start of the document, not just from the start of a script section.

Keep in mind that error messages only indicate the general location of an error in a program, not the exact nature of an error. You cannot assume that the line specified by an error message is the actual problem. The parse error message in Figure E-1 indicates that the error occurred on line 15, because the PHP scripting engine searches to the end of the script for the for() statement's opening brace. However, the real problem is that the opening brace should be the first character following the closing parenthesis in the for() statement's conditional expression.

Fatal error messages are raised when a script contains a run-time error that prevents it from executing. A typical fatal error message occurs when a script attempts to call a function that does not exist.

Warning and notice messages may be suppressed in your PHP configuration. The next section explains how to enable them to help you debug your code.

Warning messages are raised for run-time errors that do not prevent a script from executing. For example, a warning message occurs when you attempt to divide a number by 0, or if you pass the wrong number of arguments to a function.

Notice messages are raised for potential run-time errors that do not prevent a script from executing. Notices are less severe than warnings and are typically raised when a script attempts to use an undeclared variable.

Configuring the Way PHP Displays Errors

The php.ini configuration file contains various directives that control how the PHP scripting engine handles errors. PHP also includes various functions that you can use to control error handling at run time.

Displaying Errors in the Web Browser

The php.ini configuration file contains two directives, `print_errors` and `print_startup_errors`, which determine whether error messages are displayed in a Web browser. The `print_errors` directive displays script error messages, whereas the `print_startup_errors` directive displays errors that occur when PHP first starts. By default, the `print_errors` directive is assigned a value of "On," and the `print_startup_errors` directive is assigned a value of "Off." Although displaying error messages is useful when you develop PHP scripts, the PHP Group strongly recommends that you turn this feature off for scripts that run in production environments, and instead save any errors in a log file. Hackers can use any displayed error messages to identify potential weaknesses in your Web site, so the PHP Group also recommends that you only turn on the `print_startup_errors` directive when debugging a script.

One piece of information that is available to hackers is shown in Figure E-1. The error message shows the location of the file in the server's directory structure and exposes the underlying directory structure to visitors.

Setting the Error Reporting Level

The `error_reporting` directive in the php.ini configuration file determines which types of error messages PHP should generate. Setting the error reporting level can be useful in helping you debug your scripts. However, keep in mind that changing the error messages generated by PHP does not prevent errors from occurring; it only prevents the error messages from being displayed in the Web browser or written to a log file.

By default, the `error_reporting` directive is assigned a value of E_ALL, which displays all errors, warnings, and notices in the Web browser. You can also assign the directive the error levels listed in Table E-1. Note that each error level can be set using either the constant or integer listed in the table.

Constant	Integer	Description
	0	Turns off all error reporting
E_ERROR	1	Reports fatal run-time errors
E_WARNING	2	Reports run-time warnings
E_PARSE	4	Reports syntax errors
E_NOTICE	8	Reports run-time notices
E_CORE_ERROR	16	Reports fatal errors that occur when PHP first starts
E_COMPILE_WARNING	32	Reports warnings generated by the Zend Scripting Engine
E_COMPILE_ERROR	64	Reports errors generated by the Zend Scripting Engine
E_USER_ERROR	256	Reports user-generated error messages
E_USER_WARNING	512	Reports user-generated warnings
E_USER_NOTICE	1024	Reports user-generated notices
E_ALL	2047	Reports errors, warnings, and notices, with the exception of E_STRICT notices
E_STRICT	2048	Reports strict notices, which are code recommendations that ensure compatibility with PHP 5

Table E-1   Error reporting levels

To generate a combination of error levels, separate the levels assigned to the error_reporting directive with the bitwise Or operator (|). For example, the following statement specifies that PHP will only report fatal and parse errors:

```
error_reporting = E_ERROR | E_PARSE
```

The bitwise Xor operator (^) can be used in place of the &~.

To specify that the E_ALL error should exclude certain types of messages, separate the levels with bitwise And (&) and Not operators (~). The following statement specifies that PHP should report all errors except run-time notices:

```
error_reporting = E_ALL &~ E_NOTICE
```

Instead of modifying the values assigned to the error_reporting directive in the php.ini configuration file, you can use the error_reporting() function to specify the messages to report in a particular script. Use the same bitwise operators to separate reporting levels that you pass to the error_reporting() function. The following statement uses the error_reporting() function so that PHP only reports fatal and parse errors:

```
error_reporting(E_ERROR | E_PARSE);
```

The following statement uses the error_reporting() function to specify that PHP should report all errors except run-time notices:

```
error_reporting(E_ALL &~ E_NOTICE);
```

To disable error messages for a particular script, place the `error_reporting()` function at the beginning of a script section and pass to it a value of 0, as follows:

```
error_reporting(0);
```

Logging Errors to a File

Remember that for security reasons, you should disable the display of error messages for any scripts that run in a production environment. Unless you work for a large company with separate development and production systems, you will probably use the same server to execute scripts in development and to execute scripts in production. In this situation, it's not feasible to use your php.ini configuration file to enable and disable the `print_errors` and `print_startup_errors` directives each time you want to work on a script. A better choice is to log all errors to a text file.

PHP logs errors to a text file according to the error reporting level assigned to the `error_reporting` directive in the php.ini configuration file, or the level that you set for an individual script with the `error_reporting()` function. The php.ini configuration file includes several parameters for handling error logging, including the `log_errors` and `error_log` directives. The `log_errors` directive determines whether PHP logs errors to a file; it is assigned a default value of "Off." The `error_log` directive identifies the text file where PHP will log errors. You can assign either a path and filename or `syslog` to the `error_log` directive. On UNIX and Linux systems, a value of `syslog` specifies that PHP should use the `syslog` protocol to forward the message to the system log file. On Windows systems, a value of `syslog` forwards messages to the Event Log service.

Using Basic Debugging Techniques

Although error messages are valuable because they point out problems with your scripts, they cannot always help you identify the source of a problem. This section discusses basic debugging techniques that can help you locate problems in your PHP scripts.

Tracing Errors with `echo` Statements

When you cannot locate a bug in your program by using error messages or examining your code, or if you suspect a logic error (which would not generate an error message), you must trace your code. **Tracing** is the examination of individual statements in an executing

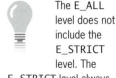

The E_ALL level does not include the E_STRICT level. The E_STRICT level always needs to be explicitly included.

661

If you place echo statements in a program to trace a problem, place them at a different level of indentation than other statements to distinguish them from the actual program.

For arrays, you can use the print_r() function or the var_dump() function in place of the echo statement.

program. The echo statement provides one of the most useful ways to trace PHP code. You place an echo statement at different points in your program and use it to display the contents of a variable or the value returned from a function. An echo statement is especially useful when you want to trace a bug in your program by analyzing a list of values. Using this technique, you can monitor values as they change during program execution. To trace the problem, you can place an echo statement at the point in the program where you think the error might be located.

If your program has multiple functions and functions calling functions, it is often useful to insert echo statements that display Entering function() and Leaving function() at the beginning and end of each function, respectively. For functions that take input parameters, it may help to display the values of the parameters in the Entering function() string. For functions that return a value, it may be helpful to display the return value, as in Leaving function(), returning X. This will allow you to see when each function is called, what values are passed, when each function returns, and what values are returned.

When the main script or a function contains a long series of statements, and you know that one of the statements is failing, you might be able to find the culprit by adding an echo statement that displays a simple sequence count between each statement, as in the following code segment:

```
...
CustomFunctionA();
echo "<p>Step 5</p>\n";
CustomFunctionB();
echo "<p>Step 6</p>\n";
CustomFunctionC();
...
```

If the Web browser displays "Step 5" but does not display "Step 6", then you know that CustomFunctionB() is causing the script to fail.

Using Comments to Locate Bugs

Another method of locating bugs in a PHP program is to transform lines that might be causing problems into comments. In other words, you can "comment out" problematic lines. This technique helps you isolate the statement that is causing the error. In some cases, you can comment out individual lines that might be causing an error, or you can comment out all lines except the ones that you know work. When you first receive an error message, start by commenting out only the statement specified by the line number in the error message.

Save the script, and then open it again in your Web browser to see if you receive another error. If you receive additional error messages, comment out those statements as well. After you eliminate the error messages, examine the statements you've commented out to find the cause of the bug.

Often, you will see the error immediately and not need to comment out code or use any other tracing technique. However, after you stare at the same code for a long time, simple spelling errors are not always easy to spot. Commenting out lines that you know are causing trouble is a good technique for isolating and correcting even the simplest bugs.

Do not comment out statements that span multiple lines or statements on a line that contains an opening or closing brace. This introduces further parsing errors into your code.

Analyzing Logic

The cause of an error in a particular statement is often the result of an error in a preceding line of code.

At times, errors in PHP code stem from logic problems that are difficult to spot using tracing techniques. When you suspect that your code contains logic errors, you must analyze each statement for errors. For example, the following code contains a logic flaw that prevents it from functioning correctly:

```
if (!isset($_POST['firstName']))
    echo "<p>You must enter your first name!</p>\n";
    exit();
echo "<p>Welcome to my Web site, " .
        $_POST['firstName'] . "!</p>\n";
```

If you were to execute the preceding code, you would never see the last echo statement, even if a value were assigned to the $_POST['firstName'] variable. If you examine the if statement more closely, you will see that it ends after it executes the echo statement. The exit() statement following the variable declaration is not part of the if structure, because the if statement does not include a set of braces to enclose the lines it executes when the conditional evaluation returns true. For this reason, the exit() statement always executes, even when the user correctly assigns a value to the $_POST['firstName'] variable. For the code to execute properly, the if statement must include braces as follows:

```
if (!isset($_POST['firstName'])) {
    echo "<p>You must enter your first name!</p>\n";
    exit();
}
echo "<p>Welcome to my Web site, " .
    $_POST['firstName'] . "!</p>\n";
```

The following for statement shows another example of an easily overlooked logic error:

```
for ($Count = 1; $Count < 6; ++$Count);
    echo "$Count<br />\n";
```

The preceding code should display the numbers 1 through 5 on the screen. However, the line `for ($Count = 1; $Count < 6; ++$Count);` contains an ending semicolon, which marks the end of the `for` loop. The loop executes five times and changes the value of `count` to 6, but does nothing else because there are no statements before its ending semicolon. The line `echo "$Count<br />\n";` is a separate statement that executes only once, displaying the number 6 on the screen. The code is syntactically correct, but does not function as you anticipated. As you can see from these examples, it is easy to overlook very minor logic errors in your code.

Formatting Code

It is much easier to review your code and analyze your logic by ensuring that your code is properly formatted. By indenting your code properly and using standard formatting for nested code blocks, you can often locate a missing closing brace or a scope issue.

Commenting Code

Sometimes it is difficult to tell what a particular section of code is supposed to do. By commenting those sections with a description of the intended function, you can avoid trying to figure out what the code is supposed to do and concentrate on verifying that the code will accomplish what you intended. Comments also assist in marking **context switches**, in which your script stops doing one task and starts another.

Examining Your Code

When you use an editor like Notepad++, the editor automatically color-codes your source code based on the file extension. This helps you track down many types of syntax errors. For example, if the code after a block comment is the same color as the block comment, you probably did not include the closing `*/` for the block comment. Another common error is accidentally mixing opening and closing quotation marks, such as using a single quotation mark at the beginning of a string and a double quotation mark at the end of the string. When this error occurs, the text will appear in the color used to highlight strings until another single quotation mark occurs.

Examining the Script Output

The purpose of a PHP script is to generate XHTML code that is interpreted and displayed by a Web browser. When debugging, it is usually better to see the actual XHTML code generated by the PHP script rather than the Web browser's formatted display. Often you can see problems in the source code that you cannot see in the browser window itself, such as empty <p> tags, missing attributes or values, and fields with incorrect values. Most Web browsers allow you to view the underlying XHTML code for a Web page.

For example, assume you were attempting to use the $_SERVER['SCRIPT_NAME'] autoglobal as the value of the action attribute of a <form> tag, but typed $_SERVER['SCIPT_NAME'] instead. By looking at the source code, you could see that the value of the action attribute of the <form> tag was empty. This would indicate the source of the error.

Combining Debugging Techniques

As you can see from the preceding examples, no single technique will find all errors. It is often more efficient to track down a bug by combining debugging techniques. For example, consider the following code, which should display the Canadian territories and capitals:

```
$TerritorialCapitals = array(
    array("Territory" => "Nunavut",
            "Capital" => "Iqaluit"),
    array("Territory" =>
            "Northwest Territories",
            "Capital" => "Yellowknife"),
    array("Territory" =>
            "Yukon Territory",
            "capital" => "Whitehorse"));
$TerritoryCount=count($TerritorialCapitals);
for ($i=1;$i<=$TerritoryCount;++$i) {
    echo "<p>" . $TerritorialCapitals[$i]["Capital"] .
            " is the capital of " .
            $TerritorialCapitals[$i]["Territory"] .
            "</p>";
}
```

As Figure E-2 shows, this code has some problems. The first territory, Nunavut, is not displayed anywhere on the list. Whitehorse is not displayed as the capital of the Yukon Territory, and one line displays neither a capital nor a territory. Several techniques can help to isolate the cause of these problems.

To view the source code for a Web page in Mozilla Firefox 3, you select View from the menu bar and then select Page Source. In Apple Safari 4, you select View from the menu bar and then select View Source. In Microsoft Internet Explorer 7, you click the Page button and then select View Source from the pop-up menu. Most Windows browsers also allow you to view the source code by right-clicking the page and selecting View Source from the pop-up menu.

In Chapter 3, you learned how to use the \n escape sequence to insert a line break at the end of the string. This approach is useful when you look at the script output in your Web browser. Without using \n escape sequences to format the XHTML source code, the code will appear on a single line, which makes it difficult to follow.

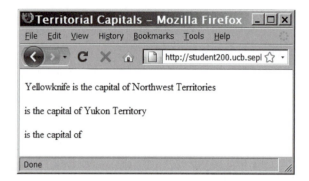

Figure E-2   Web page for a PHP script that is not working correctly

First, examine the code. It is already properly formatted, so you can tell that the structure of the code blocks and the array declaration are correct.

Next, examine the script output shown in Figure E-3. As you can see, the entire body of the Web page source code is on a single line, which makes it difficult to read through the XHTML code. To help with debugging, place a \n after the closing </p> tag.

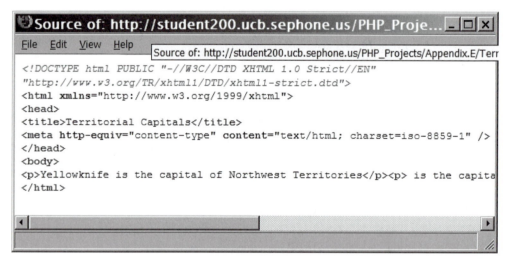

Figure E-3   Unformatted output of a PHP script that is not working correctly

Next, you can use echo statements to verify that variables are being set correctly. Add the following code immediately after the $TerritorialCapitals[] array declaration to verify the contents. The print_r() function will display the contents of the array, and using the <pre> tag will ensure that the array is displayed correctly on the Web page.

```
// DEBUG: Verifying $TerritorialCapitals
echo "<pre>\n";
echo "\$TerritorialCapitals => ";
print_r($TerritorialCapitals);
echo "</pre>\n";
// DEBUG: End verifying $TerritorialCapitals
```

There are three lines of output in Figure E-2, so the $TerritoryCount variable is probably set correctly. However, you can add the following line of code after the declaration of $TerritoryCount to verify the value:

```
// DEBUG: Verifying $TerritoryCount
echo "<p>\$TerritoryCount = " .
    $TerritoryCount . "</p>\n";
```

As with $TerritoryCount, it appears that the for loop is working correctly because there are three lines of output in Figure E-2. However, you can add the following line of code to the beginning of the for loop code block to verify the value of $i:

```
// DEBUG: Verifying $i
echo "<p>In for loop: \$i = " .
    $i . "</p>\n";
```

Notice that all of the code added for debugging purposes is commented, and that each comment has the text "DEBUG:" before the description, which makes it easier to find and remove all of the debugging code once the script is working correctly. Also notice that the debugging code for the $TerritorialCapitals[] array consists of multiple statements. As a result, a comment marks both the beginning and end of the debugging code, which helps ensure that all of the debugging code is removed.

As a final step, you can add the following code to the beginning of the script to enable all possible error and warning messages. The PHP scripting engine is very good at locating syntax and run-time errors, so you should use it whenever possible. Sometimes, the PHP scripting engine can even help locate logic errors.

```
// DEBUG: Show all warnings
error_reporting(E_ALL | E_STRICT);
```

When you finish, your code should look like the following:

```
// DEBUG: Show all warnings
error_reporting(E_ALL | E_STRICT);
$TerritorialCapitals = array(
    array("Territory" => "Nunavut",
            "Capital" => "Iqaluit"),
    array("Territory" =>
            "Northwest Territories",
            "Capital" => "Yellowknife"),
```

```
        array("Territory" =>
                "Yukon Territory",
                "capital" => "Whitehorse"));
// DEBUG: Verifying $TerritorialCapitals
echo "<pre>\n";
echo "\$TerritorialCapitals => ";
print_r($TerritorialCapitals);
echo "</pre>\n";
// DEBUG: End verifying $TerritorialCapitals
$TerritoryCount=count($TerritorialCapitals);
// DEBUG: Verifying $TerritoryCount
echo "<p>\$TerritoryCount = " .
        $TerritoryCount . "</p>\n";
for ($i=1;$i<=$TerritoryCount;++$i) {
        // DEBUG: Verifying $i
        echo "<p>In for loop: \$i = " .
        $i . "</p>\n";
        echo "<p>" . $TerritorialCapitals[$i]["Capital"] .
                " is the capital of " .
                $TerritorialCapitals[$i]["Territory"] .
                "</p>\n";
}
```

When you run the script this time, much more information is available to you. First, examine the XHTML source code, as shown in
Figure E-4. Although the debugging has created extra code, you
should be able to find the lines that display the names of the territories and capitals. Review those lines to see what data is actually missing. This is important because Web browsers often do not display data
that is embedded in malformed tags. Without looking at the source
code, you cannot tell if the data is actually missing or just hidden.

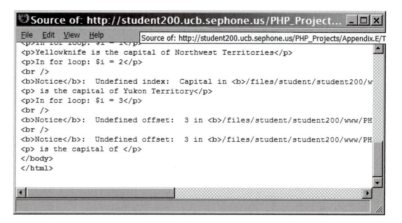

Figure E-4 Source code for a PHP script with debugging statements

Now that you've confirmed that the data is actually missing, you can review the debugging information available on the

page itself, as shown in Figure E-5. At the top of the page, the $TerritorialCapitals[] array is populated as expected. The next message indicates that the $TerritoryCount variable is set to 3.

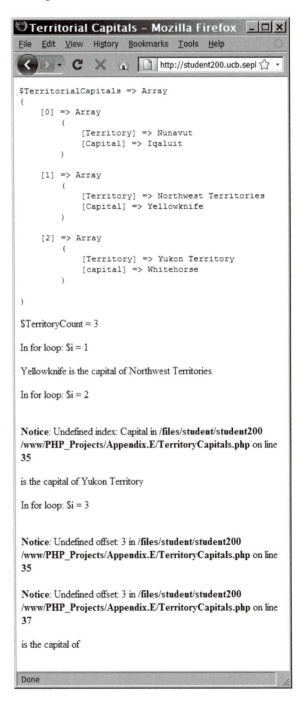

```
$TerritorialCapitals => Array
    (
        [0] => Array
            (
                [Territory] => Nunavut
                [Capital] => Iqaluit
            )

        [1] => Array
            (
                [Territory] => Northwest Territories
                [Capital] => Yellowknife
            )

        [2] => Array
            (
                [Territory] => Yukon Territory
                [capital] => Whitehorse
            )

    )
```

$TerritoryCount = 3

In for loop: $i = 1

Yellowknife is the capital of Northwest Territories

In for loop: $i = 2

Notice: Undefined index: Capital in /files/student/student200 /www/**PHP_Projects/Appendix.E/TerritoryCapitals.php** on line **35**

is the capital of Yukon Territory

In for loop: $i = 3

Notice: Undefined offset: 3 in /files/student/student200 /www/**PHP_Projects/Appendix.E/TerritoryCapitals.php** on line **35**

Notice: Undefined offset: 3 in /files/student/student200 /www/**PHP_Projects/Appendix.E/TerritoryCapitals.php** on line **37**

is the capital of

Figure E-5 Web page for a PHP script with debugging statements

In the next line, you can see that $i is set to 1 and that Yellowknife is displayed as the capital of the Northwest Territories. The array output at the beginning of the page shows that the array index for the element with "Northwest Territories" and "Yellowknife" is indeed 1. The array index for "Nunavut" and "Iqaluit" is 0. So, to display Nunavut, you need to adjust the starting value of $i to 0.

Next, you see that $i gets incremented to 2, which is expected. After that, the PHP scripting engine displays a notice that the index Capital is undefined. By looking at the array output, you can see that for $TerritorialCapitals[2], the index of the nested array element is "capital" with a lowercase 'c'. Change this to an uppercase 'C'.

After displaying the line with the missing capital, you see that $i is set to 3, followed by two warning messages about an undefined offset of 3. Look at the lines identified by the message, and note that these two lines display the values of the $TerritorialCapitals[] array. Again, look back to the array output, and note that the last array element is 2, not 3. To fix this, you need to change the comparison in the for loop from $i<=$TerritoryCount to $i<$TerritoryCount.

After making the three changes to the code and removing all of the debugging statements, run the script again. You will see the expected results, as shown in Figure E-6. By using a combination of debugging techniques, you found and fixed all of the errors much faster and more easily than if you had applied a single technique.

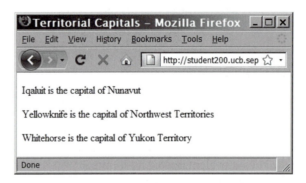

Figure E-6 Output from a PHP script with the errors fixed

Connecting to SQL Server and Oracle Databases

Working with Different Databases

In Chapter 8, you learned how to use the mysql package in PHP to interact with a MySQL database. PHP also provides packages to connect with most other databases, including dBase, Informix, PostgreSQL, SQLite, and Sybase. The two most popular database management systems (DBMSs) are Microsoft SQL Server and Oracle. Each DBMS operates differently, and the packages used to access those systems are different as well. Some of the key differences are highlighted in the following sections.

Working with SQL Server

The mssql package provides the functions to connect to and work with a Microsoft SQL Server database. Many of the functions are similar to packages you have already used to communicate with a MySQL database. Table F-1 lists all of the mysql_* functions covered in Chapter 8, along with the equivalent mssql_* functions, where available. The final column highlights the differences, if any, between the MySQL function and the SQL Server function.

MySQL function from the mysql package	Equivalent SQL Server function from the mssql package	Special notes and differences
mysql_affected_rows()	mssql_rows_affected()	Same
mysql_change_user()	N/A	No equivalent
mysql_close()	mssql_close()	Same
mysql_connect()	mssql_connect()	Same
mysql_create_db()	N/A	No equivalent
mysql_drop_db()	N/A	No equivalent
mysql_data_seek()	mssql_data_seek()	Same
mysql_errno()	N/A	No equivalent
mysql_error()	mssql_get_last_message()	Function takes no parameters
mysql_fetch_array()	mssql_fetch_array()	Same
mysql_fetch_assoc()	mssql_fetch_assoc()	Same
mysql_fetch_lengths()	N/A	No equivalent
mysql_fetch_row()	mssql_fetch_row()	Same
mysql_free_result()	mssql_free_result()	Same
mysql_get_client_info()	N/A	No equivalent
mysql_get_client_version()	N/A	No equivalent
mysql_get_host_info()	N/A	No equivalent
mysql_get_proto_info()	N/A	No equivalent
mysql_query()	mssql_query()	Same
mysql_get_server_info()	N/A	No equivalent
mysql_info()	mssql_rows_affected()	Query result is required, not an optional connection
mysql_insert_id()	N/A	No equivalent
mysql_num_fields()	mssql_num_fields()	Same
mysql_num_rows()	mssql_num_rows()	Same
mysql_select_db()	mssql_select_db()	Same

Table F-1   mssql package equivalents of mysql package functions

T-SQL, which is short for Transact-SQL, is the SQL Server version of SQL.

For mysql package functions that do not have equivalents in the mssql package, you can usually achieve the same or similar results through a direct database query using the mssql_query() function. You only have to know the appropriate T-SQL syntax.

As you can tell from the functions in Table F-1, the mssql package is very similar to the mysql package you learned about in Chapter 8.

The following example shows how to query the `company_cars` table in the `vehicle_fleet` database if the database were in SQL Server instead of MySQL. All of the functions are the same as the ones used in Chapter 8, except that the prefix is `mssql_` instead of `mysql_`, and the `mysql_error()` function is replaced with the `mssql_get_last_message()` function. You would replace *host*, *user*, and *password* with the host name, user name, and password needed for the SQL server on your system.

```php
$DBName = "vehicle_fleet";
$DBConnect = @mssql_connect(host,
        user, password);
if ($DBConnect === FALSE)
    echo "<p>Connection error: " .
        mssql_get_last_message() . "</p>\n";
else {
    if (@mssql_select_db($DBName, $DBConnect)
            === FALSE) {
        echo "<p>Could not select the \"" .
            $DBName . "\" database: " .
            mssql_get_last_message() .
            "</p>\n";
        mssql_close($DBConnect);
        $DBConnect = FALSE;
    }
}
if ($DBConnect !== FALSE) {
    $SQLstring = "SELECT * FROM company_cars";
    $QueryResult = @mssql_query($SQLstring, $DBConnect);
    if ($QueryResult === FALSE)
        echo "<p>Unable to execute the query.</p>\n" .
            "<p>Error: " . mssql_get_last_message() .
            "</p>\n";
    else {
        $numRows = mssql_num_rows($result);
        echo "<h1>" . $numRows . " Car" .
            ($numRows == 1 ? "" : "s") .
            " Found</h1>\n";
        if ($numRows>0) {
            echo "<table>\n";
            echo " <tr><th>License</th>";
            echo "<th>Make</th>";
            echo "<th>Model</th>";
            echo "<th>Mileage</th>";
            echo "<th>Year</th></tr>\n";
            while ($Row =
                mssql_fetch_row($QueryResult)) {
                echo " <tr><td>{$Row[0]}</td>";
                echo "<td>{$Row[1]}</td>";
                echo "<td>{$Row[2]}</td>";
                echo "<td>{$Row[3]}</td>";
                echo "<td>{$Row[4]}</td></tr>\n";
            }
```

```
                        echo "</table>\n";
                        mssql_free_result($QueryResult);
                }
        }
        mssql_close($DBConnect);
        $DBConnect = FALSE;
}
```

One common problem when retrieving data from an SQL Server database in PHP is Unicode. **Unicode** is a standard for encoding text characters on a computer, similar to ASCII. Unicode contains many more characters than ASCII, and often uses more than one byte per character. PHP and MySQL do not support Unicode, but SQL Server does.

To support Unicode, SQL Server has three data types not found in MySQL. The NCHAR type is the Unicode equivalent of the CHAR type, the NTEXT type is the Unicode equivalent of the TEXT type, and the NVARCHAR type is the Unicode equivalent of the VARCHAR type. Fields defined as NCHAR, NTEXT, and NVARCHAR in SQL Server cannot be used directly in PHP. Fortunately, SQL Server provides the T-SQL CONVERT() function.

For example, assume that the country column of an addresses table is defined as an NVARCHAR(50). If it were a regular VARCHAR(50), you could use the following code for the query string:

```
$query = "SELECT country FROM addresses";
```

However, because it is an NVARCHAR(50), you would use the following code for the query string:

```
$query = "SELECT CONVERT(VARCHAR(50),country) AS country
FROM addresses";
```

Working with Oracle

PHP provides the OCI8 package for accessing an Oracle database. As with the mssql package, there are differences between the functions in the OCI8 package and the mysql package. Table F-2 shows the OCI8 equivalents of the mysql_* functions covered in Chapter 8.

MySQL function from the mysql package	Equivalent Oracle function from the OCI8 package	Special notes and differences
mysql_affected_rows()	oci_num_rows()	Same
mysql_change_user()	N/A	No equivalent
mysql_close()	oci_close()	Connection is required
mysql_connect()	oci_connect()	Host name comes after user name and password
mysql_create_db()	N/A	No equivalent
mysql_drop_db()	N/A	No equivalent
mysql_data_seek()	N/A	No equivalent
mysql_errno()	oci_error()	Returns the error code and message in an associative array
mysql_error()	oci_error()	Returns the error code and message in an associative array
mysql_fetch_array()	oci_fetch_array()	Same
mysql_fetch_assoc()	oci_fetch_assoc()	Same
mysql_fetch_lengths()	N/A	No equivalent
mysql_fetch_row()	oci_fetch_row()	Same
mysql_free_result()	oci_cancel()	Same
mysql_get_client_info()	N/A	No equivalent
mysql_get_client_version()	N/A	No equivalent
mysql_get_host_info()	N/A	No equivalent
mysql_get_proto_info()	N/A	No equivalent
mysql_query()	oci_parse() and oci_execute()	See below
mysql_get_server_info()	oci_server_version()	Same
mysql_info()	oci_num_rows()	Query result is required, not an optional connection
mysql_insert_id()	N/A	No equivalent
mysql_num_fields()	oci_num_fields()	Same
mysql_num_rows()	oci_num_rows()	Same
mysql_select_db()	N/A	No equivalent

Table F-2   OCI8 package equivalents of mysql package functions

The OCI8 package divides query execution into two parts to simplify **data binding**, which is a more efficient, though more complex, way of sending data to and retrieving data from the database.

One of the most important differences between the mysql package and the OCI8 package is that OCI8 uses two functions, oci_parse() and oci_execute(), in place of the single mysql_query() function. The oci_parse() function prepares the query in the Oracle database and returns a handler to the statement. The statement handler is then passed to the oci_execute() function, where it is validated and executed. If successful, the oci_execute() function returns TRUE and the resultset can be retrieved using the parsed query, as shown later in this section.

Another important difference when working with Oracle is that it does not normally allow the database (or *schema*, in Oracle terminology) to be changed. To access a table in another schema, you precede the table name with the schema name and a period. In Oracle syntax, you would enter the following code to select all of the records in the company_cars table of the vehicle_fleet schema:

```
SELECT * FROM vehicle_fleet.company_cars;
```

The following example shows how you would query the company_cars table in the vehicle_fleet schema if the schema were in Oracle. Because the OCI8 package is significantly different from either the mssql or mysql package, portions of the code are different. However, notice that the same steps are performed, and in the same sequence. The only difference is in *how* the steps are performed. Again, you would replace *host*, *user*, and *password* with the host name, user name, and password needed for the Oracle server on your system.

```
$DBName = "vehicle_fleet";
// The host is last for Oracle
$DBConnect = @oci_connect(user,
        password, host);
if ($DBConnect === FALSE)
    echo "<p>Connection error: " .
        oci_error() . "</p>\n";
else {
    // Precede the table name with
    // the schema (database) name
    $SQLstring = "SELECT * FROM $DBName.company_cars";
    $Query = @oci_parse($SQLstring, $DBConnect);
    if ($Query === FALSE)
        echo "<p>Unable to parse the query.</p>\n" .
            "<p>Error: " . mssql_get_last_message() .
            "</p>\n";
    else {
        if (@oci_execute($Query) === FALSE)
            echo "<p>Unable to execute the query.</p>\n" .
                "<p>Error: " . oci_get_last_message() .
                "</p>\n";
```

```
        else {
            $numRows = oci_num_rows($Query);
            echo "<h1>" . $numRows . " Car" .
                ($numRows == 1 ? "" : "s") .
                " Found</h1>\n";
            if ($numRows>0) {
                echo "<table>\n";
                echo " <tr><th>License</th>";
                echo "<th>Make</th>";
                echo "<th>Model</th>";
                echo "<th>Mileage</th>";
                echo "<th>Year</th></tr>\n";
                while ($Row =
                    oci_fetch_row($Query)) {
                    echo " <tr><td>{$Row[0]}</td>";
                    echo "<td>{$Row[1]}</td>";
                    echo "<td>{$Row[2]}</td>";
                    echo "<td>{$Row[3]}</td>";
                    echo "<td>{$Row[4]}</td></tr>\n";
                }
                echo "</table>\n";
                oci_free_statement($Query);
            }
        }
    }
    oci_close($DBConnect);
    $DBConnect = FALSE;
}
```

As with SQL Server, the functions listed as having no OCI8 equivalent can still be performed by a query to the database. The version of SQL used in Oracle is called PL/SQL, or Procedural Language/SQL.

Index